Leading
Constitutional
Decisions

Eighteenth Edition
Leading Constitutional Decisions

Robert F. Cushman

with Susan P. Koniak

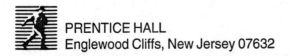

PRENTICE HALL
Englewood Cliffs, New Jersey 07632

Library of Congress Cataloging-in-Publication Data

Cushman, Robert Fairchild
    Leading constitutional decisions / Robert F. Cushman with Susan P.
Koniak. -- 18th ed.
        p.   cm.
    Includes index.
    ISBN 0-13-529439-8
    1. United States--Constitutional law--Cases.   I. Koniak, Susan P.
II. Title.
KF4549.C83   1992
342.73'002643--dc20
[347.30202643]   91-19388
                                                                  CIP

Acquisition Editor: Karen Horton
Editor-in-Chief: Charlyce Jones-Owens
Production Editor: Linda Zuk, WordCrafters Editorial Services, Inc.
Cover Designer:
Prepress Buyer: Debbie Kesar
Manufacturing Buyer: Mary Ann Gloriande
Supplements Editor: Sharon Chambliss

©1992 by Prentice-Hall, Inc.
A Division of Simon & Schuster
Englewood Cliffs, New Jersey 07632

Printed in the United States of America

10 9 8 7 6 5 4 3 2 1

ISBN 0-13-529439-8

Prentice-Hall International (UK) Limited, *London*
Prentice-Hall of Australia Pty. Limited, *Sydney*
Prentice-Hall Canada Inc., *Toronto*
Prentice-Hall Hispanoamericana, S.A., *Mexico*
Prentice-Hall of India Private Limited, *New Delhi*
Prentice-Hall of Japan, Inc., *Tokyo*
Simon & Schuster Asia Pte. Ltd., *Singapore*
Editora Prentice-Hall do Brasil, Ltda., *Rio de Janeiro*

Contents

Chapter Three
THE NATIONALIZATION OF THE BILL OF RIGHTS   158

Chapter Four
FIRST AMENDMENT RIGHTS   231

Preface

No one can understand how our American national government works, or how it came to be the kind of government it is, without being familiar with the way in which the Supreme Court of the United States does its work, and with some of the decisions that are milestones in the growth of our American constitutional system.

The Supreme Court does not work in a vacuum. Its decisions upon important constitutional questions can be fully understood only when viewed against the background of history, politics, and economics out of which they grew. The introductory notes attempt to reconstruct this background, to suggest the significance of the cases in our constitutional development, and, to a limited extent, to indicate the relationship of the decisions printed to other—and perhaps equally important—ones that could not be included.

In editing the cases and writing the notes the guiding assumptions have, in general, been these: (1) The job of the Supreme Court is to provide reasoned opinions so that lower courts and administrators can apply its rulings intelligently to similar problems; (2) The extent to which the Court supplies such guidance and the skill with which it develops its present reasoning from what has gone before are measures of how well it is doing its job; and (3) Students should be encouraged to evaluate this aspect of the Court's work.

While the introductory notes have been edited to include recent developments in the case law and political scene, the emphasis in this edition, as in earlier ones, is on the evolution of the ideas used to explain our Constitution rather than on stating "the law" of any particular moment. And so that students will have ammunition with which to engage in intellectual battle, some important dissents have been included and a fuller exploration of a few problems has been favored over a more superficial treatment of many.

This edition has been updated to include cases through the 1989-1990 term of the Supreme Court. New cases include Morrison v. Olson (special prosecutor); DeShaney v. Winnebago Soc. Serv. (government's obligation to protect individuals); Bowers v. Hardwick (sodomy); United States v. Eichman (flag burning); Edwards v. Aguillard (creation science); and Richmond v. Croson (affirmative action). In addition, to provide a more complete background of the legal development of the race problem, the classic case of Dred Scott v. Sandford has been included.

While every effort has been made to have the final version of the cases conform to one of the printed versions of the reports, case citations and page references, statute citation and footnotes have been omitted without ellipses. Footnotes appear with increasing frequency in the more recent cases as the justices often elect to put their most cogent and intelligible arguments there rather than in the text of the opinion itself.

Special thanks are extended to Mead Data Central, Inc., for permitting access to LEXIS. The last-minute checking to ensure the accuracy of the opinions and their citations owes its effectiveness largely to LEXIS. My deepest gratitude goes also to Professor Nancy Kassop of the State University of New York at New Paltz, an acknowledged authority on presidential power, for her help with the note to Morrison v. Olson.

Leading
Constitutional
Decisions

The Separation of Powers

A. The Judicial Branch

MARBURY v. MADISON

1 Cranch 137; 2 L. Ed. 60 (1803)

Although the election in the autumn of 1800 brought to the Federalists a defeat from which they never recovered, President Adams and his Federalist associates did not retire from office until March 1801. The Federalists had been for some time considering plans to reform the federal courts by remodeling the Judiciary Act of 1789, and now in the eleventh hour they boldly set themselves to the task with renewed energy in order, undoubtedly, to insure a fortress for Federalist principles which would not easily be broken down. Accordingly they passed the Judiciary Act of February 13, 1801, which relieved the Supreme Court justices of circuit court duty, reduced the size of the Supreme Court from six to five, and created six new circuit courts with 16 new judgeships. Two weeks later Congress passed an act providing that the President might appoint for the District of Columbia for five-year terms as many justices of the peace as he thought necessary. President Adams proceeded during the last 16 days of his administration to fill these newly created vacancies (58 in all) with loyal Federalists; and the task of signing their commissions occupied him until well into the night before the inauguration of Jefferson on March 4, 1801. Among the judicial appointments made by Adams in the closing weeks of his administration was that of John Marshall, a staunch Federalist, to be Chief Justice of the United States.

The federal courts had already incurred the bitter animosity of the Jeffersonians, largely because of the vigor with which they had enforced the obnoxious Alien and Sedition Acts of 1798; and the Republicans were enraged beyond measure at what they deemed the effrontery of the Federalists in enacting the Judiciary Act of 1801. The judiciary was caustically referred to by Randolph as a "hospital for decayed politicians," while Jefferson wrote to a friend, "The Federalists have retired into the judiciary as a stronghold . . . and from that battery all the works of republicanism are to be beaten down and erased." One of the first efforts of the Republican administration was to repeal the Judiciary Act of 1801, and after a long and acrimonious debate this was accomplished, March 8, 1802. The repealing act restored the Supreme Court justices to circuit court duty, restored the size of the Supreme Court to six, and abolished the new circuit judgeships which had been created. The Federalists in Congress bitterly assailed the repealing statute as unconstitutional. Marshall himself apparently adhered to that view, and probably would have held the law void if it had come before him immediately in his judicial capacity. In order to prevent this, however, the repealing act had so altered the sessions of the Supreme Court that it did not convene again for 14 months, by which time acquiescence in the act by the judges affected made a decision of unconstitutionality impracticable.

However, when the Court convened in February 1803, the case of Marbury v. Madison was on the docket. Marbury was one of those whom President Adams had appointed to a five-year justiceship of the peace in the District of Columbia. His commission, signed and sealed on March 3, was among four that had not been delivered when Jefferson had taken office on March 4. It was, in fact, Marshall, then serving as Secretary of State as well as Chief Justice, who had sealed but had not delivered Marbury's commission. Jefferson immediately ordered his new Secretary of State, James Madison, to withhold the commission; and Marbury filed suit asking the Supreme Court in the exercise of its original jurisdiction to issue a writ of mandamus to compel Madison to give him his commission. The right to issue such a writ had been conferred upon the Court by a provision of the Judiciary Act of 1789, and jurisdiction thereunder had been exercised by the Court twice before Marshall's accession to the bench. When the case came on for argument, it assumed very largely the aspect of a quarrel between the President and the judiciary. Marbury's own interest in it was small, since Jefferson made it fairly clear that he had no intention of giving Marbury his commission even if the Court ordered him to do so. The Republicans seem to have expected that the Court would issue the mandamus asked for, and there were open threats that Marshall and his colleagues would be impeached if that occurred.

Marshall's decision that the Constitution forbade the Court to issue the writ of mandamus asked for by Marbury might have placated the Republicans had he not in their judgment gratuitously gone beyond the necessities of the case. While holding that the Court could not take jurisdiction and decide the case, inasmuch as the statute authorizing it was unconstitutional, he nonetheless pointed out that Marbury was entitled to his commission; that a writ of mandamus was the proper remedy; and that the executive was properly subject to mandamus if the case were started in the proper court. In addition he scolded the administration for not delivering the commission. In the storm of criticism thereby engendered, the judicial review aspect of the case seems largely to have escaped attack; and when, six months later, a circuit court held unconstitutional another act of Congress abolishing fees granted by an earlier law to justices of the peace in the District of Columbia, it evoked no criticism of any kind. The case, not in any official report, is noted by Charles Warren, *The Supreme Court in United States History,* Vol. I, 255.

No more vehement argument has ever raged in the field of constitutional law and theory than that over the genesis of the power of judicial review. Did the framers of the Constitution intend to grant the power as part of the checks and balances system in the first three articles? Or did Chief Justice Marshall "usurp" this power for the judiciary in his decision in Marbury v. Madison? Scholars still disagree, and the real intention of the framers will probably never be known. But a number of things are certain. It is certain that this was the first case in which the Supreme Court openly and clearly held unconstitutional an act of Congress. It is equally certain that the idea of judicial review did not originate with Marshall. Most of the arguments which he used in his famous opinion had been presented again and again in the debates in

Congress on the Repeal Act of 1802, and the basic theory had been advanced by Hamilton in Number 78 of *The Federalist*. Moreover, the lower federal courts, without exciting opposition, had held invalid the act of Congress making them, in effect, claims commissioners for pension claims (a fact pointed out by Marshall in his opinion); and a number of earlier state cases have been considered as embodying the principle; see Bayard v. Singleton (1787). That Marshall cited no precedents to bolster his interpretation of judicial power is not particularly surprising. As a jurist he relied heavily on deductive reasoning, and in neither Gibbons v. Ogden (1824) nor McCulloch v. Maryland (1819), two of his most famous opinions, did he cite a single case as precedent.

There is evidence that public opinion tended to look upon the power of judicial review as one of the normal incidents of judicial power. The Court considered the constitutionality of the carriage tax in Hylton v. United States (1796); and its refusal to declare it unconstitutional, as well as the refusal of the lower federal courts to hold unconstitutional the Alien and Sedition Acts and the United States Bank Charter, was bitterly condemned by the Republicans, who seemed to feel that the courts were neglecting their duty in not sustaining the Constitution against legislative usurpation of power. That Congress itself recognized the power is perhaps evidenced by their alteration of the term of the Supreme Court to prevent the Repeal Act of 1802 from coming to the Court for review for more than a year after its enactment.

The power of the Supreme Court to declare acts of Congress unconstitutional has so long been an integral part of our constitutional system, and Marshall's reasoning in the case of Marbury v. Madison so impressive, that it is easy to lose sight of the fact that a most cogent argument may be made against the establishment of the power, and that had the Supreme Court never enjoyed it the results would probably not have been calamitous. Jefferson, Marshall's most bitter personal and political adversary, never admitted the paramount authority of the Supreme Court to determine the validity of an act of Congress, but held that each of the three departments of the national government, being equal and separate, was equally empowered "to decide on the validity of an act according to its own judgement and uncontrolled by the opinions of any other department."

This view was shared by many other thoughtful men of the day. In the exercise of its power of judicial review the Court will not pass upon what it terms "political questions," questions the final determination of which has been confided by the Constitution to the discretion of the political departments, that is, the legislative or the executive. According to the view of Jefferson and his followers, all questions involving the constitutionality of acts of Congress which might come before the Court would be "political questions." The statute might conflict with the Constitution, but that fact would not of itself endow the Court with any power to invalidate it. Rather it would be the duty of the Court to enforce the statute without questioning its validity.

Of the statutes of Congress held void by the Supreme Court, only a few have involved problems of any vital or lasting importance. As Justice Holmes declared, "the United States would not come to an end if we lost our power to declare an act of Congress void." In fact, the power to declare an act of Congress invalid is a power very much less important to the maintenance of our system of government than the power to pass upon the validity of state legislation. This latter authority may well be regarded as vital to the preservation of our federal system by providing a necessary method of policing the inevitable power struggle between the national government and the governments of the several states.

The case of Marbury v. Madison has a certain strategic significance which should not be left out of account. The next case in which an act of Congress was invalidated by the

Supreme Court was the famous Dred Scott case, decided in 1857. By that time nearly 70 years had elapsed from the time of the formation of our constitutional system, and the Court was composed of men holding nationalistic views far less strong than those of Marshall and his associates. Moreover, Marbury v. Madison involved the use of judicial power to protect the Court itself against interference by the legislature, a use reasonably easy to justify in view of the separation of powers; while the Dred Scott case involved the use of congressional power in quite another field. Had the power of judicial review not been exercised and the doctrine established in the case of Marbury v. Madison, one may well conjecture whether our constitutional development would have been the same.

The Supreme Court has always had its critics, and following particularly unpopular decisions invalidating acts of Congress the attacks have been exceedingly bitter. Such decisions as the Dred Scott case, the Income Tax Cases, and a whole series of cases prior to 1937 which invalidated social legislation, stirred up opposition which reduced the prestige of the Court and which endured until either a constitutional amendment or the Court itself changed the effect of the ruling. Recognizing the wide latitude left to the judges in interpreting the Constitution, and the manifest political and economic character of many of their decisions, a number of critics have attacked the power of judicial review as an undemocratic instrument of government in an increasingly democratic society, and from time to time some of the justices on the Court itself have appeared to share this view. It was in response to such critics that Justice Roberts, speaking for six members of the Court in United States v. Butler (1936), felt called upon to explain what is viewed as the traditional role of the Court in exercising its power of judicial review:

"When an act of Congress is appropriately challenged in the courts as not conforming to the constitutional mandate the judicial branch of the Government has only one duty—to lay the article of the Constitution which is invoked beside the statute which is challenged and to decide whether the latter squares with the former. All the court does, or can do, is to announce its considered judgment upon the question. The only power it has, if such it may be called, is the power of judgment. This court neither approves nor condemns any legislative policy. Its delicate and difficult office is to ascertain and declare whether the legislation is in accordance with, or in contravention of, the provisions of the Constitution; and, having done that, its duty ends."

Against the background of this conflict it is interesting to note that at no time in our history has the power of judicial review been seriously endangered. Despite attacks on the Court's decisions, on its personnel, and even on the procedures by which review is exercised, no major political party has ever urged the complete abolition of the power of review itself. The resounding defeat in Congress of the so-called "Court Packing Plan," suggested by President Franklin D. Roosevelt at the height of his popularity, indicates that popular dissatisfaction with the use of the power of judicial review does not necessarily imply a feeling that the Court should be dominated by the political branches of the government.

Undaunted by the experiences of the Roosevelt era Attorney General Edwin Meese 3rd, speaking for the administration of Ronald Reagan, in 1985 launched an all out campaign to effect dramatic changes in constitutional law and underlying doctrine. He announced that in his opinion the only valid interpretation of the Constitution was one which reflected the values of the original framers and established a policy that no person would be nominated for a federal judgeship who did not subscribe to this point of view.

While the "intent of the framers" is one of the earliest techniques of constitutional interpretation, it tends to produce extremely conservative results by today's standards and has largely given way to techniques which more closely reflect the current needs of a modern society. Moreover, assuming it was the intent of the framers to have the document interpreted by the courts at all, it may fairly be argued that they did not intend it to be interpreted with the rigidity of a statute. As Justice Marshall emphasized in McCulloch v. Maryland (1819), "we must never forget that it is a constitution we are expounding." Also, it is worth noting that even in the opinion below, Marshall does not rely on the intent of the framers for support. Pushed far enough, an interpretation based exclusively on "original intent" would virtually emasculate the due process clauses of the Fifth and Fourteenth Amendments and could conceivably result in abandoning judicial review entirely.

The response of the Court was unprecedented. Two justices publicly attacked the government's position, one of them naming Meese by name, and even (then) Justice Rehnquist, the Court's most conservative member, urged him to take a more moderate tone.

Mr. Chief Justice **Marshall** delivered the opinion of the Court, saying in part:

In the order in which the court has viewed this subject, the following questions have been considered and decided.

1st. Has the applicant a right to the commission he demands? [The Court finds that he has.]

2d. If he has a right, and that right has been violated, do the laws of his country afford him a remedy? [The Court finds that they do.]

3d. If they do afford him a remedy, is it a mandamus issuing from this court? . . .

This, then, is a plain case for a mandamus, either to deliver the commission, or a copy of it from the record; and it only remains to be inquired,

Whether it can issue from this court.

The act to establish the judicial courts of the United States authorizes the Supreme Court "to issue writs of mandamus in cases warranted by the principles and usages of law, to any courts appointed, or persons holding office, under the authority of the United States."

The Secretary of State, being a person holding an office under the authority of the United States, is precisely within the letter of the description, and if this court is not authorized to issue a writ of mandamus to such an officer, it must be because the law is unconstitutional, and therefore absolutely incapable of conferring the authority, and assigning the duties which its words purport to confer and assign.

The constitution vests the whole judicial power of the United States in one Supreme Court, and such inferior courts as congress shall, from time to time, ordain and establish. . . .

In the distribution of this power it is declared that "the Supreme Court shall have original jurisdiction in all cases affecting ambassadors, other public ministers and consuls, and those in which a state shall be a party. In all other cases, the Supreme Court shall have appellate jurisdiction." . . .

If it had been intended to leave it in the discretion of the legislature to apportion the judicial power between the supreme and inferior courts according to the will of that body, it would certainly have been useless to have proceeded further than to have defined the judicial power, and the tribunals in which it should be vested. The subsequent part of the section is mere surplusage, is entirely without meaning, . . . the distribution of jurisdiction, made in the constitution, is form without substance. . . .

It cannot be presumed that any clause in the constitution is intended to be without effect; and, therefore, such a construction is inadmissible, unless the words require it. . . .

To enable this court, then, to issue a mandamus, it must be shown to be an exercise of appellate jurisdiction, or to be necessary to enable them to exercise appellate jurisdiction. . . .

It is the essential criterion of appellate jurisdiction, that it revises and corrects the proceedings in a cause already instituted, and does not create that cause. Although, therefore, a mandamus may be directed to courts, yet to issue such a writ to an officer for the delivery of a paper, is in effect the same as to sustain an original action for that paper, and, therefore, seems not to belong to appellate, but to original jurisdiction. Neither is it necessary in such a case as this, to enable the court to exercise its appellate jurisdiction.

The authority, therefore, given to the Supreme Court, by the act establishing the judicial courts of the United States, to issue writs of mandamus to public officers, appears not to be warranted by the constitution; and it becomes necessary to inquire whether a jurisdiction so conferred can be exercised.

The question, whether an act, repugnant to the constitution, can become the law of the land, is a question deeply interesting to the United States; but, happily, not of an intricacy proportioned to its interest. It seems only necessary to recognize certain principles, supposed to have been long and well established, to decide it.

That the people have an original right to establish, for their future government, such principles, as, in their opinion, shall most conduce to their own happiness is the basis on which the whole American fabric has been erected. The exercise of this original right is a very great exertion; nor can it, nor ought it, to be frequently repeated. The principles, therefore, so established, are deemed fundamental. And as the authority from which they proceed is supreme, and can seldom act, they are designed to be permanent.

This original and supreme will organizes the government, and assigns to different departments their respective powers. It may either stop here, or establish certain limits not to be transcended by those departments.

The government of the United States is of the latter description. The powers of the legislature are defined and limited; and that those limits may not be mistaken, or forgotten, the constitution is written. To what purpose are powers limited, and to what purpose is that limitation committed to writing, if these limits may, at any time, be passed by those intended to be restrained? The distinction between a government with limited and unlimited powers is abolished, if those limits do not confine the persons on whom they are imposed, and if acts prohibited and acts allowed, are of equal obligation. It is a proposition too plain to be contested, that the constitution controls any legislative act repugnant to it; or, that the legislature may alter the constitution by an ordinary act.

Between these alternatives there is no middle ground. The constitution is either a superior paramount law, unchangeable by ordinary means, or it is on a level with ordinary legislative acts, and, like other acts, is alterable when the legislature shall please to alter it.

If the former part of the alternative be true, then a legislative act contrary to the constitution is not law: if the latter part be true, then written constitutions are absurd attempts, on the part of the people, to limit a power in its own nature illimitable.

Certainly all those who have framed written constitutions contemplate them as forming the fundamental and paramount law of the nation, and, consequently, the theory of every such government must be, that an act of the Legislature, repugnant to the constitution, is void.

This theory is essentially attached to a written constitution, and, is consequently, to be considered, by this court, as one of the fundamental principles of our society. It is not therefore to be lost sight of in the further consideration of this subject.

If an act of the Legislature, repugnant to the constitution, is void, does it, notwithstanding its invalidity, bind the courts, and oblige them to give it effect? Or, in other words, though it be not law, does it constitute a rule as operative as if it was a law? This would be to overthrow in fact what was established in theory; and would seem, at first view, an absurdity too gross to be insisted on. It shall, however, receive a more attentive consideration.

It is emphatically the province and duty of the judicial department to say what the law is. Those who apply the rule to particular cases, must of necessity expound and interpret that rule. If two laws conflict with each other, the courts must decide on the operation of each.

So if a law be in opposition to the constitution; if both the law and the constitution apply to a particular case, so that the court must either decide that case conformably to the law, disregarding the constitution; or conformably to the constitution, disregarding the law; the court must determine which of these conflicting rules governs the case. This is of the very essence of judicial duty.

If, then, the courts are to regard the constitution, and the constitution is superior to any ordinary act of the Legislature, the constitution, and not such ordinary act, must govern the case to which they both apply.

Those then, who controvert the principle that the constitution is to be considered, in court, as a paramount law, are reduced to the necessity of maintaining that courts must close their eyes on the constitution, and see only the law.

This doctrine would subvert the very foundation of all written constitutions. It would declare that an act which, according to the principles and theory of our government, is entirely void, is yet, in practice, completely obligatory. It would declare that if the legislature shall do what is expressly forbidden, such act, notwithstanding the express prohibition, is in reality effectual. It would be giving to the legislature a practical and real omnipotence, with the same breath which professes to restrict their powers within narrow limits. It is prescribing limits, and declaring that those limits may be passed at pleasure.

That it thus reduces to nothing what we have deemed the greatest improvement on political institutions, a written constitution, would of itself be sufficient, in America, where written constitutions have been viewed with so much reverence, for rejecting the construction. But the peculiar expressions of the constitution of the United States furnish additional arguments in favor of its rejection.

The judicial power of the United States is extended to all cases arising under the constitution.

Could it be the intention of those who gave this power, to say that in using it the constitution should not be looked into? That a case arising under the constitution should be decided without examining the instrument under which it arises?

This is too extravagant to be maintained.

In some cases, then, the constitution must be looked into by the judges. And if they can open it at all, what part of it are they forbidden to read or to obey?

There are many other parts of the constitution which serve to illustrate this subject.

It is declared that "no tax or duty shall be laid on articles exported from any State." Suppose a duty on the export of cotton, of tobacco, or of flour; and a suit instituted to recover it. Ought judgment to be rendered in such a case? Ought the judges to close their eyes on the constitution, and only see the law?

The constitution declares "that no bill of attainder or ex post facto law shall be passed."

If, however, such a bill should be passed, and a person should be prosecuted under it; must the court condemn to death those victims whom the constitution endeavors to preserve?

"No person," says the constitution, "shall be convicted of treason unless on the testimony of two witnesses to the same overt act, or on confession in open court."

Here the language of the constitution is addressed especially to the courts. It prescribes, directly for them, a rule of evidence not to be departed from. If the legislature should change that rule, and declare one witness, or a confession out of court, sufficient for conviction, must the constitutional principle yield to the legislative act?

From these, and many other selections which might be made, it is apparent, that the framers of the constitution contemplated that instrument as a rule for the government of courts, as well as of the legislature.

Why otherwise does it direct the judges to take an oath to support it? This oath certainly applies in an especial manner, to their conduct in their official character. How immoral to impose it on them, if they were to be used as the instruments, and the knowing instruments, for violating what they swear to support!

The oath of office, too, imposed by the legislature, is completely demonstrative of the legislative opinion on this subject. It is in these words: "I do solemnly swear that I will administer justice without respect to persons, and do equal right to the poor and to the rich; and that I will faithfully and impartially discharge all the duties incumbent on me as ————, according to the best of my abilities and understanding agreeably to the constitution and laws of the United States."

Why does a judge swear to discharge his duties agreeably to the constitution of the United States, if that constitution forms no rule for his government? if it is closed upon him, and cannot be inspected by him?

If such be the real state of things, this is worse than solemn mockery. To prescribe, or to take this oath, becomes equally a crime.

It is also not entirely unworthy of observation, that in declaring what shall be the supreme law of the land, the constitution itself is first mentioned; and not the laws of the United States generally, but those only which shall be made in pursuance of the constitution, have that rank.

Thus, the particular phraseology of the constitution of the United States confirms and strengthens the principle, supposed to be essential to all written constitutions, that a law repugnant to the constitution is void; and that courts, as well as other departments, are bound by that instrument.

The rule must be discharged.

BAKER v. CARR

369 U. S. 186; 7 L. Ed. 2d 663; 82 S. Ct. 691 (1962)

  Second only to the power of judicial review itself is the power to decide which constitutional issues will come before the Supreme Court and which will not. There are always persons standing in the wings ready to challenge every governmental action on constitutional grounds, and the Court has articulated rules to determine who may bring such challenges and who may not. How these rules are interpreted and applied determines in large measure both the course of constitutional development and the role which the Court itself will play in the constitutional system.

  In his opinion in Marbury v. Madison (1803) Marshall grounded his constitutional argument for judicial review upon the language of Article III, which extends to the Supreme Court (and inferior courts) judicial power to be exercised in "all cases, in law and equity, arising under this Constitution. . . ." In short, the reason why the Court occasionally declares an act of Congress unconstitutional is that, according to Marshall, it has to do so in deciding the "cases and controversies" coming before it in the exercise of its "judicial powers." Thus Marshall permanently tied judicial review to "cases and controversies." This has meant, over the years, that only when one of the parties in an actual "case" relies for his rights upon a statute will the Court undertake to decide whether or not that statute violates the Constitution; furthermore, it will do so only when such a decision is essential to the disposal of the case. Since Article III also extends judicial power to "such inferior courts as the Congress may from time to time ordain and establish," these lower courts also exercise the power of judicial review. Under the statutes, however, such lower court decisions striking down laws as unconstitutional are subject to review by the Supreme Court, and almost invariably they are so reviewed. The Supreme Court has the last word.

  But what is a "case" or "controversy" within the meaning of Article III? An essential requirement is that there be actual litigants with conflicting interests of such a nature that they are subject to judicial determination. Following the admission to citizenship of the Cherokee Indians, Congress had by law altered the original distribution of tribal property. Since this had the effect of reducing the amount of lands and funds to which certain Indians were entitled, its constitutionality was seriously questioned. To settle the matter Congress passed an act specifically providing that David Muskrat and others might bring suits in the court of claims, with a right of appeal to the Supreme Court, to test the constitutionality of the redistribution statutes. The courts involved were ordered to give preference to these suits; the Attorney General was ordered to defend them; and if Muskrat et al. won, the government was to pay their attorney's fees. In Muskrat v. United States (1911) the Supreme Court held there was no case or controversy involved and refused jurisdiction. The United States, the Court pointed out, was not claiming Muskrat's land and had no interest adverse to his. "The whole purpose of the law is to determine the constitutional validity of this class of legislation, in a suit not arising between parties concerning a property right necessarily involved in the decision in question, but in a proceeding against the government in its sovereign capacity, and concerning which the only judgment required is to settle the doubtful character of the legislation in question. . . . In a legal sense the judgment could not be executed, and amounts in fact to no more than an expression of opinion upon the validity of the acts in question."

  Another important corollary of its refusal to exercise nonjudicial powers is the doctrine of "political questions." Very early in the exercise of its power of judicial review the Court pointed out that certain powers are vested in the legislative or executive departments of the government to be exercised in a purely discretionary manner, and that whether they have been constitutionally exercised or not is a "political question" which the Court will not undertake to decide. One of the early and very striking instances of this type of question was that which was raised in the famous case of Luther v. Borden.

This case arose out of the following facts: the original constitution of Rhode Island, which was merely the colonial charter with a few minor adaptations, provided for a very restricted suffrage based upon the possession of property; and the right to vote continued to be thus limited long after universal male suffrage had been rather generally adopted throughout the country. Many efforts were made to have the constitution amended so as to put the franchise upon a more democratic basis, but all such attempts were defeated by the relatively small group of legal voters. In 1841 the popular feeling regarding the situation ran even higher than before; mass meetings were held throughout the state, and without any semblance of constitutional sanction the citizens were directed to choose, by universal male suffrage, delegates to a constitutional convention. The convention thus formed duly met and drafted a new state constitution, which established adult male suffrage and made many other changes. A popular referendum was conducted in which all the adult male citizens of the state were permitted to vote, and the new constitution was approved by a majority of the votes cast. The leader of the whole movement was a young lawyer, Thomas W. Dorr, who was elected governor under the new constitution and immediately attempted to put the new government into operation.

The regular charter government, of course, did not recognize the validity of any of these acts. It called out the state militia, declared martial law, and finally appealed to President Tyler to send federal troops to aid in putting down the insurrection. The President took steps to comply with this request and the "Dorr Rebellion" collapsed. Dorr himself was captured, tried for treason, and finally sentenced to life imprisonment. He was later pardoned. He naturally had managed to arouse a good deal of sympathy for his cause outside the state, particularly among the Democrats, and it was felt that it would be desirable to present to the Supreme Court of the United States the question of the legality of the new constitution and the acts done under it. This was tried first by Dorr himself by attempting to sue out a writ of habeas corpus in the Supreme Court, but that tribunal dismissed the petition for want of jurisdiction; see Ex parte Dorr (1845). Under the assumption that the same issue could be raised collaterally, the civil controversy between Luther and Borden, relatively unimportant in itself, was pushed through to the Supreme Court.

Luther had been a supporter of the Dorr movement; and in an effort to arrest him, Borden and others who were enrolled as members of the militia under the charter government broke into Luther's house. This act they justified upon the ground that martial law had been declared and that they were acting under the orders of their superior officers. Luther, however, sued Borden for trespass, claiming that the act of the legislature establishing martial law was void inasmuch as the Dorr government, elected by the people of the state, was the lawful government. The Supreme Court held that the question of which government is the established one in a state is a political question, which the Constitution gives Congress the exclusive right to decide, and the courts would not entertain this question even where Congress had not acted, as was the case here due to the brief tenure of the Dorr government. (It should be noted that in January, 1842, the charter government had called a constitutional convention and drafted a new constitution, which was ratified by the people in due form and went into effect in 1843. Thus the Dorr movement did not entirely fail in its purposes.)

There are, of course, numerous other questions which have been held by the courts to be "political" in character. Such is the question whether there is a sufficient emergency to justify the President, acting under the authority of an act of Congress, in calling out the militia to repel invasion or to put down insurrection; see Martin v. Mott (1827). Such, also, are many of the questions which arise for determination in the course of conducting foreign relations; as, for instance, the recognition of a foreign government, the acquisition of territory, the determination of boundaries, the existence or termination of a treaty, and the like. The early case of Foster v. Neilson (1829), raising the question as to the title to certain territory which was the subject of international dispute, emphasized the unwillingness of the Court to attempt to settle this type of question. The question whether or not a state of the Union has a republican form of government within the meaning of that clause of the Constitution guaranteeing such form of government was squarely raised in 1912 in the case of Pacific States Telephone & Telegraph Co. v. Oregon. In 1902 Oregon had amended its state constitution to establish the initiative and referendum. In 1906 a law was proposed by popular initiative and duly enacted by the people which imposed certain taxes on corporations. The plaintiff corporation resisted the payment of the tax on the ground that the incorporation of the initiative and referendum into the constitutional system of the state destroyed the republican character of its government and thus robbed it of lawful authority. The argument was that republican government means representative government and that representative government is destroyed by the system of direct legislation. The Supreme Court refused to pass on the question whether Oregon had a republican form of government or not and pointed out that that question was political in character and had been determined by Congress in admitting senators and representatives of the state to their seats in Congress.

In Coleman v. Miller (1939) the Court held that most of the questions relating to the procedure of federal amendments are "political" in nature. The Court was there asked to rule that the Child Labor Amendment could no longer be validly ratified because it had been before the states for ratification for too long a time, and that a state which had once rejected a proposed amendment could not later ratify it. On each point the Court held that the final decision rested with Congress, not with the Court. But in Powell v. McCormack (1969) the Court rejected the contention of the House of Representatives that the question of Adam Clayton Powell Jr.'s right to his House seat was a political one because the Constitution made each house "the judge of the . . . qualifications of its own members." This power, the Court held, was limited to judging the existence of those qualifications for representatives explicitly stated in the Constitution—and only those. Powell, it was conceded, met these formal qualifications.

By far the most important political question in terms of its political impact on our system of government involved the apportionment of legislators, state and federal, among the election districts set within the states. One of the anomalous by-products of our system of representative government is the fact that voters are not equally represented in the legislature. This is true because the districts from which representatives are elected vary in population, with the result that the influence of one voter in electing his representative may be much greater than the influence of another voter in another district. Also the boundaries of legislative districts are drawn by state legislatures; and astute politicians, by the skillful juggling of these district lines, have achieved wonderful feats of inflating or deflating party voting strength by what is called the "gerrymander." Quite as important, however, has been the effect of what is known as the "silent gerrymander," the underrepresentation of cities and overrepresentation of rural areas achieved simply by a failure over the years to redraw district lines to keep pace with the movement of the population from the farm to the city.

Both the state and federal legislatures had long felt the oppressive effect of the "silent gerrymander" in Illinois. The Illinois constitution of 1870 provided that the state should be divided into 51 state senatorial districts, from each of which one state senator and three state representatives should be chosen. The legislature, after each census, was to redraw the lines of these districts to meet changes in population. By the turn of the century it was obvious that more than half the population of the state would shortly be concentrated in the metropolitan area of Chicago. Legislators from the down-state rural districts, enjoying a comfortable legislative majority, felt no inclination to yield their political control by reapportioning the state to give the growing metropolis the proportion of the 51 districts to which its population clearly entitled it.

Nor were they any more willing to grant the Chicago metropolitan area its fair share of seats in Congress than in the state legislature itself. At the time the present case arose, it had not reapportioned congressional seats since 1901. Finally, with one congressional district in Chicago having a population of 914,053, while another in southern Illinois had a population of 112,116, the Supreme Court was asked in Colegrove v. Green (1946) to enjoin the use of these districts in the impending election. The Court, voting four to three, denied the injunction. Speaking for himself and Justices Reed and Burton, Justice Frankfurter held this to be a political question which the Court could not decide. Since the "times, manner and places" clause of Art. I, Sec. 4, gave Congress power to secure fair representation it was up to Congress or the states to cure the inequities. "Whether Congress faithfully discharges its duty or not, the subject has been committed to the exclusive control of the Congress. An aspect of government from which the judiciary, in view of what is involved, has been excluded by the clear intention of the Constitution cannot be entered by the federal courts because Congress may have been in default in exacting from States obedience to its mandate." This opinion was widely construed as the ruling of the case, although Justice Rutledge concurred on different grounds.

The first break in the Court's attitude came in 1960 in the case of Gomillion v. Lightfoot. There the Court, without passing upon the truth of the alleged discrimination, unanimously rejected the idea that legislative apportionment could never be the subject for judicial review. The issue raised was unique. An Alabama statute of 1957 had redefined the boundaries of the city of Tuskeegee, within which is the well-known Tuskeegee Institute. The city, which had been square in shape, was transformed "into a strangely irregular twenty-eight sided figure," with the intention and result of removing from the city "all save four or five of its 400 black voters while not removing a single white voter or resident." The blacks thus excluded could not, as a result, vote in municipal elections. The lower federal courts, relying in part upon Colegrove v. Green, had dismissed the complaint attacking the validity of the statute. In an opinion by Justice Frankfurter, eight justices agreed that the plaintiffs had a right to have a court decide whether the weird apportionment denied them the right to vote, in violation of the Fifteenth Amendment. Justice Whittaker, denying that the right to vote was involved "inasmuch as no one has the right to vote in . . . an area in which he does not reside," argued that the discrimination violated both the equal protection and due process clauses of the Fourteenth Amendment.

Mr. Justice **Brennan** delivered the opinion of the Court, saying in part:

This civil action was brought . . . to redress the alleged deprivation of federal constitutional rights. The complaint, alleging that by means of a 1901 statute of Tennessee apportioning the members of the General Assembly among the State's 95 counties, "these plaintiffs and others similarly situated, are denied the equal protection of the laws accorded them by the Fourteenth Amendment to the Constitution of the United States by virtue of the debasement of their votes," was dismissed by a three-judge court. . . . We hold that the dismissal was error, and remand the cause to the District Court for trial and further proceedings consistent with this opinion.

The General Assembly of Tennessee consists of the Senate with 33 members and the House of Representatives with 99 members. The Tennessee Constitution provides in Art. II as follows: . . . [The text of sections 3–6 follows.]

Thus, Tennessee's standard for allocating legislative representation among her counties is the total number of qualified voters resident in the respective counties, subject only to minor qualifications. . . . In 1901 the General Assembly abandoned separate enumeration in favor of reliance upon the Federal Census and passed the Apportionment Act here in controversy. In the more than 60 years since that action, all proposals in both Houses of the General Assembly for reapportionment have failed to pass.

Between 1901 and 1961, Tennessee has experienced substantial growth and redistribution of her population. In 1901 the population was 2,020,616, of whom 487,380 were eligible to vote. The 1960 Federal Census reports the State's population at 3,567,089, of whom 2,092,891 are eligible to vote. The relative standings of the counties in terms of qualified voters have changed significantly. It is primarily the continued application of the 1901 Apportionment Act to this shifted and enlarged voting population which gives rise to the present controversy.

Indeed, the complaint alleges that the 1901 statute, even as of the time of its passage, "made no apportionment of Representatives and Senators in accordance with the constitutional formula . . . , but instead arbitrarily and capriciously apportioned representatives in the Senate and House without reference . . . to any logical or reasonable formula whatever." It is further alleged that "because of the population changes since 1900, and the failure of the Legislature to reapportion itself since 1901," the 1901 statute became "unconstitutional and obsolete." Appellants also argue that, because of the composition of the legislature effected by the 1901 Apportionment Act, redress in the form of a state constitutional amendment to change the entire mechanism for reapportioning, or any other change short of that, is difficult or impossible. The complaint concludes that "these plaintiffs and others similarly situated, are denied the equal protection of the laws accorded them by the Fourteenth Amendment to the Constitution of the United States by virtue of the debasement of their votes." They seek a declaration that the 1901 statute is unconstitutional and an injunction restraining the appellees from acting to conduct any further elections under it. They also pray that unless and until the General Assembly enacts a valid reapportionment, the District Court should either decree a reapportionment by mathematical application of the Tennessee constitutional formulae to the most recent Federal Census figures, or direct the appellees to conduct legislative elections, primary and general, at large. They also pray for such other and further relief as may be appropriate.

I. The District Court's Opinion and Order of Dismissal.

[Here summarized.]

In light of the District Court's treatment of the case, we hold today only (a) that the court possessed jurisdiction of the subject matter; (b) that a justiciable cause of action is stated upon which appellants would be entitled to appropriate relief; and (c) because appellees raise the issue before this Court, that the appellants have standing to challenge the Tennessee apportionment statutes. Beyond noting that we have no cause at this stage to doubt the District Court will be able to fashion relief if violations of constitutional rights are found, it is improper now to consider what remedy would be most appropriate if appellants prevail at the trial.

II. Jurisdiction of the Subject Matter.

The District Court was uncertain whether our cases withholding federal judicial relief rested upon a lack of federal jurisdiction or upon the inappropriateness of the subject matter for judicial consideration—what we have designated "nonjusticiability." The distinction between the two grounds is significant. In the instance of nonjusticiability, consideration of the cause is not wholly and immediately foreclosed; rather, the Court's inquiry necessarily proceeds to the point of deciding whether the duty asserted can be judicially identified and its breach judicially determined, and whether protection for the right asserted can be judicially molded. In the instance of lack of jurisdiction the cause either does not "arise under" the Federal Constitution, laws or treaties (or fall within one of the other enumerated categories of Art. III § 2), or is not a "case or controversy" within the meaning of that section; or the cause is not one described by any jurisdictional statute. Our conclusion that this cause presents no nonjusticiable "political question" settles the only possible doubt that it is a case or controversy. Under the present heading of "Jurisdiction of the Subject Matter" we hold only that the matter set forth in the complaint does arise under the Constitution. . . .

Article III § 2, of the Federal Constitution provides that "The judicial Power shall extend to all Cases, in Law and Equity, arising under this Constitution, the Laws of the United States, and Treaties made, or which shall be made, under their Authority. . . ," It is clear that the cause of action is one which "arises under" the Federal Constitution. The complaint alleges that the 1901 statute effects an apportionment that deprives the appellants of the equal protection of the laws in violation of the Fourteenth Amendment. Dismissal of the complaint upon the ground of lack of jurisdiction of the subject matter would, therefore, be justified only if that claim were "so attenuated and unsubstantial as to be absolutely devoid of merit." . . . Since the District Court obviously and correctly did not deem the asserted federal constitutional claim unsubstantial and frivolous, it should not have dismissed the complaint for want of jurisdiction of the subject matter. And of course no further consideration of the merits of the claim is relevant to a determination of the court's jurisdiction of the subject matter. . . ,

An unbroken line of our precedents sustains the federal courts' jurisdiction of the subject matter of federal constitutional claims of this nature. The first cases involved the redistricting of States for the purpose of electing Representatives to the Federal Congress. When the Ohio Supreme Court sustained Ohio legislation against an attack for repugnancy to Art. I § 4, of the Federal Constitution, we affirmed on the merits and expressly refused to dismiss for want of jurisdiction "in view . . . of the subject-matter of the controversy and the Federal characteristics which inhere in it. . . ." Ohio ex rel. Davis v. Hildebrant [1916]. When the Minnesota Supreme Court affirmed the dismissal of a suit to enjoin the Secretary of State of Minnesota from acting under Minnesota redistricting legislation, we reviewed the constitutional merits of the legislation and reversed the State Supreme Court. Smiley v. Holm [1932]. . . .

The appellees refer to Colegrove v. Green [1946], as authority that the District Court lacked jurisdiction of the subject matter. Appellees misconceive the holding of that case. The holding was precisely contrary to their reading of it. Seven members of the Court participated in the decision. Unlike many other cases in this field which have assumed without discussion that there was jurisdiction, all three opinions filed in Colegrove discussed the question. Two of the opinions expressing the views of four of the Justices, a majority, flatly held that there was jurisdiction of the subject matter. Mr. Justice Black joined by Mr. Justice Douglas and Mr. Justice Murphy stated: "It is my judgment that the District Court had jurisdiction. . . ." Mr. Justice Rutledge, writing separately, expressed agreement with this conclusion. . . .

We hold that the District Court has jurisdiction of the subject matter of the federal constitutional claim asserted in the complaint.

III. Standing.

A federal court cannot "pronounce any statute, either of a State or of the United States, void, because irreconcilable with the Constitution, except as it is called upon to adjudge the legal rights of litigants in actual controversies." . . . Have the appellants alleged such a personal stake in the outcome of the controversy as to assure that concrete adverseness which sharpens the presentation of issues upon which the court so largely depends for illumination of difficult constitutional questions? This is the gist of the question of standing. It is, of course, a question of federal law. . . .

We hold that the appellants do have standing to maintain this suit. Our decisions plainly support this conclusion. Many of the cases have assumed rather than articulated the premise in deciding the merits of similar claims. And Colegrove v. Green squarely held that voters who allege facts showing disadvantage to themselves as individuals have standing to sue. . . .

These appellants seek relief in order to protect or vindicate an interest of their own, and of those similarly situated. Their constitutional claim is, in substance, that the 1901 statute constitutes arbitrary and capricious state action, offensive to the Fourteenth Amend‹ ment in its irrational disregard of the standard of apportionment prescribed by the State's Constitution or of any standard, effecting a gross disproportion of representation to voting population. The injury which appellants assert is that this classification disfavors the voters in the counties in which they reside, placing them in a position of constitutionally unjus‐ tifiable inequality vis‐à‐vis voters in irrationally favored counties. A citizen's right to a vote free of arbitrary impairment by state action has been judicially recognized as a right secured by the Constitution, when such impairment resulted from dilution by a false tally, cf. United States v. Classic [1941], or by a refusal to count votes from arbitrarily selected precincts, . . . or by a stuffing of the ballot box, cf. Ex parte Siebold [1880]. . . .

It would not be necessary to decide whether appellants' allegations of impairment of their votes by the 1901 apportionment will, ultimately, entitle them to any relief, in order to hold that they have standing to seek it. If such impairment does produce a legally cognizable injury, they are among those who have sustained it. They are asserting "a plain, direct and adequate interest in maintaining the effectiveness of their votes," . . . not merely a claim of "the right, possessed by every citizen, to require that the Government be administered according to law. . . ." Fairchild v. Hughes [1922]. . . , They are entitled to a hearing and to the District Court's decision on their claims. "The very essence of civil liberty certainly consists in the right of every individual to claim the protection of the laws, whenever he receives an injury." Marbury v. Madison.

IV. Justiciability.

In holding that the subject matter of this suit was not justiciable, the District Court relied on Colegrove v. Green, and subsequent per curiam cases. The court stated: "From a review of these decisions there can be no doubt that the federal rule . . . is that the federal courts . . . will not intervene in cases of this type to compel legislative reapportionment." We understand the District Court to have read the cited cases as compelling the conclusion that since the appellants sought to have a legislative apportionment held unconstitutional, their suit presented a "political question" and was therefore nonjusticiable. We hold that this challenge to an apportionment presents no nonjusticiable "political question." The cited cases do not hold the contrary.

Of course the mere fact that the suit seeks protection of a political right does not mean it presents a political question. Such an objection "is little more than a play upon words." . . . Rather, it is argued that apportionment cases, whatever the actual wording of the complaint, can involve no federal constitutional right except one resting on the guaranty of a republican form of government, and that complaints based on that clause have been held to present political questions which are nonjusticiable.

We hold that the claim pleaded here neither rests upon nor implicates the Guaranty Clause and that its justiciability is therefore not foreclosed by our decisions of cases involving that clause. The District Court misinterpreted Colegrove v. Green and other decisions of this Court on which it relied. Appellants' claim that they are being denied equal protection is justiciable, and if "discrimination is sufficiently shown, the right to relief under the equal protection clause is not diminished by the fact that the discrimination relates to political rights." . . . To show why we reject the argument based on the Guaranty Clause, we must examine the authorities under it. But because there appears to be some uncertainty as to why those cases did present political questions, and specifically as to whether this apportionment case is like those cases, we deem it necessary first to consider the contours of the "political question" doctrine.

Our discussion, even at the price of extending this opinion, requires review of a number of political question cases, in order to expose the attributes of the doctrine—attributes which, in various settings, diverge, combine, appear, and disappear in seeming disorderliness. Since that review is undertaken solely to demonstrate that neither singly nor collectively do these cases support a conclusion that this apportionment case is nonjusticiable, we of course do not explore their implications in other contexts. That review reveals that in the Guaranty Clause cases and in the other "political question" cases, it is the relationship between the judiciary and the coordinate branches of the Federal Government, and not the federal judiciary's relationship to the States, which gives rise to the "political question."

We have said that "In determining whether a question falls within [the political question] category, the appropriateness under our system of government of attributing finality to the action of the political departments and also the lack of satisfactory criteria for a judicial determination are dominant considerations." Coleman v. Miller [1939]. The nonjusticiability of a political question is primarily a function of the separation of powers. Much confusion results from the capacity of the "political question" label to obscure the need for case-by-case inquiry. Deciding whether a matter has in any measure been committed by the Constitution to another branch of government, or whether the action of that branch exceeds whatever authority has been committed, is itself a delicate exercise in constitutional interpretation, and is a responsibility of this Court as ultimate interpreter of the Constitution. To demonstrate this requires no less than to analyze representative cases and to infer from them the analytical threads that make up the political question doctrine. We shall then show that none of those threads catches this case. . . .

[Here follows a long summary of cases involving the political question doctrine as they have arisen in the fields of (1) foreign relations, (2) dates of duration of hostilities, (3) validity of enactments, (4) status of Indian tribes, and (5) republican form of government.]

We come, finally, to the ultimate inquiry whether our precedents as to what constitutes a nonjusticiable "political question" bring the case before us under the umbrella of that doctrine. A natural beginning is to note whether any of the common characteristics which we have been able to identify and label descriptively are present. We find none: The question here is the consistency of state action with the Federal Constitution. We have no question decided, or to be decided, by a political branch of government coequal with this Court. Nor do we risk embarrassment of our government abroad, or grave disturbance at home if we take issue with Tennessee as to the constitutionality of her action here challenged. Nor need the appellants, in order to succeed in this action, ask the Court to enter upon policy determinations for which judicially manageable standards are lacking. Judicial standards under the Equal Protection Clause are well developed and familiar, and it has been open to courts since the enactment of the Fourteenth Amendment to determine, if on the particular facts they must, that a discrimination reflects *no* policy, but simply arbitrary and capricious action. . .

We conclude that the complaint's allegations of a denial of equal protection present a justiciable constitutional cause of action upon which appellants are entitled to a trial and a decision. The right asserted is within the reach of judicial protection under the Fourteenth Amendment.

The judgment of the District Court is reversed and the cause is remanded for further proceedings consistent with this opinion.

Reversed and remanded.

Mr. Justice **Whittaker** did not participate in the decision of this case.

Mr. Justice **Douglas**, concurring, said in part:

While I join the opinion of the Court and, like the Court, do not reach the merits, a word of explanation is necessary. I put to one side the problems of "political" questions involving the distribution of power between this Court, the Congress, and the Chief Executive. We have here a phase of the recurring problem of the relation of the federal courts to state agencies. More particularly, the question is the extent to which a State may weight one person's vote more heavily than it does another's. . . .

I agree with my Brother Clark that if the allegations in the complaint can be sustained a case for relief is established. We are told that a single vote in Moore County, Tennessee, is worth 19 votes in Hamilton County, that one vote in Stewart or in Chester County is worth nearly eight times a single vote in Shelby or Knox County. The opportunity to prove that an "invidious discrimination" exists should therefore be given the appellants. . . .

With the exceptions of Colegrove v. Green, MacDougall v. Green [1948], South v. Peters [1950], and the decisions they spawned, the Court has never thought that protection of voting rights was beyond judicial cognizance. Today's treatment of those cases removes the only impediment to judicial cognizance of the claims stated in the present complaint. . . .

Mr. Justice **Clark**, concurring, said in part:

One emerging from the rash of opinions with their accompanying clashing of views may well find himself suffering a mental blindness. The Court holds that the appellants have alleged a cause of action. However, it refuses to award relief here—although the facts are undisputed—and fails to give the District Court any guidance whatever. One dissenting opinion, bursting with words that go through so much and conclude with so little, contemns the majority action as "a massive repudiation of the experience of our whole past." Another describes the complaint as merely asserting conclusory allegations that Tennessee's apportionment is "incorrect," "arbitrary," "obsolete," and "unconstitutional." I believe it can be shown that this case is distinguishable from earlier cases dealing with the distribution of political power by a State, that a patent violation of the Equal Protection Clause of the United States Constitution has been shown, and that an appropriate remedy may be formulated.

I. . . .

. . . The widely heralded case of Colegrove v. Green was one not only in which the Court was bobtailed but in which there was no majority opinion. Indeed, even the "political question" point in Mr. Justice Frankfurter's opinion was no more than an alternative ground. Moreover, the appellants did not present an equal protection argument. While it has served as a Mother Hubbard to most of the subsequent cases, I feel it was in that respect ill-cast and for all of these reasons put it to one side. . . .

II

The controlling facts cannot be disputed. . . .

. . . The frequency and magnitude of the inequalities in the present districting admit of no policy whatever. . . . It leaves but one conclusion, namely that Tennessee's apportionment is a crazy quilt without rational basis. . .

[Examples are given of the inequalities in apportionment in Tennessee.]

The truth is that—although this case has been here for two years and has had over six hours' argument (three times the ordinary case) and has been most carefully considered over and over again by us in Conference and individually—no one, not even the State nor the dissenters, has come up with any rational basis for Tennessee's apportionment statute.

. . . Like the District Court, I conclude that appellants have met the burden of showing "Tennessee is guilty of a clear violation of the state constitution and of the [federal] rights of the plaintiffs. . . ."

III.

Although I find the Tennessee apportionment statute offends the Equal Protection Clause, I would not consider intervention by this Court into so delicate a field if there were any other relief available to the people of Tennessee. But the majority of the people of Tennessee have no "practical opportunities for exerting their political weight at the polls" to correct the existing "invidious discrimination." Tennessee has no initiative and referendum. I have searched diligently for other "practical opportunities" present under the law. I find none other than through the federal courts. .

IV. . . .

As John Rutledge (later Chief Justice) said 175 years ago in the course of the Constitutional Convention, a chief function of the Court is to secure the national rights. Its decision today supports the proposition for which our forebears fought and many died, namely, that to be fully conformable to the principle of right, the form of government must be representative. That is the keystone upon which our government was founded and lacking which no republic can survive. It is well for this Court to practice self-restraint and discipline in constitutional adjudication,but never in its history have those principles received sanction where the national rights of so many have been so clearly infringed for so long a time. National respect for the courts is more enhanced through the forthright enforcement of those rights rather than by rendering them nugatory through the interposition of subterfuges. In my view the ultimate decision today is in the greatest tradition of this Court.

Mr. Justice **Stewart** wrote a brief concurring opinion.

Mr. Justice **Frankfurter,** whom Mr. Justice **Harlan** joins, dissenting, said in part:

The Court today reverses a uniform course of decision established by a dozen cases, including one by which the very claim now sustained was unanimously rejected only five years ago. The impressive body of rulings thus cast aside reflected the equally uniform course of our political history regarding the relationship between population and legislative representation—a wholly different matter from denial of the franchise to individuals because of race, color, religion or sex. Such a massive repudiation of the experience of our whole past in asserting destructively novel judicial power demands a detailed analysis of the role of this Court in our constitutional scheme. Disregard of inherent limits in the effective exercise of the Court's "judicial Power" not only presages the futility of judicial intervention in the essentially political conflict of forces by which the relation between population and representation has time out of mind been and now is determined. It may well impair the Court's position as the ultimate organ of "the supreme Law of the Land" in that vast range of legal problems, often strongly entangled in popular feeling, on which this Court must pronounce. The Court's authority—possessed of neither the purse nor the sword—ultimately rests on sustained public confidence in its moral sanction. Such feeling must be nourished by the Court's complete detachment, in fact and in appearance, from political entanglements and by abstention from injecting itself into the clash of political forces in political settlements. . . .

. . . The Framers carefully and with deliberate forethought refused so to enthrone the judiciary. In this situation, as in others of like nature, appeal for relief does not belong here. Appeal must be to an informed, civically militant electorate. In a democratic society like ours, relief must come through an aroused popular conscience that sears the conscience of the people's representatives. In any event there is nothing judicially more unseemly nor more self-defeating than for this Court to make in terrorem pronouncements, to indulge in merely empty rhetoric, sounding a word of promise to the ear, sure to be disappointing to the hope. . . .

[Mr. Justice Frankfurter continued in a long and heavily documented opinion to support the position he had taken in Colegrove v. Green.]

Mr. Justice **Harlan** wrote a dissenting opinion in which Mr. Justice **Frankfurter** joined.

VALLEY FORGE CHRISTIAN COLLEGE v. AMERICANS UNITED

454 U. S. 464; 70 L. Ed. 2d 700; 102 S. Ct. 752 (1982)

Another critical component of a case or controversy is that the parties have "standing" to sue; that they allege the kind of personal injury that entitles them to judicial relief. In 1923 Mrs. Frothingham, a wealthy Massachusetts resident, challenged the constitutionality of a federal statute which provided financial aid to states struggling to reduce maternal and infant mortality and protect the health of mothers and infants. She argued that such invalid expenditures increased her taxes, thus taking her money "without due process of law." Faced with the awesome prospect that any taxpayer could challenge the validity of any federal "statute whose administration requires the outlay of public money," the Court seemed relieved to hold that such a suit could not be maintained. In Frothingham v. Mellon (1923) it held that the share of the taxes that any individual taxpayer contributed to the funds of the United States was "comparatively minute and indeterminable": hence, the injury done to the taxpayer was too slight to entitle her to sue to enjoin them.

The importance of these seemingly technical legal questions regarding standing cannot be overemphasized, for it is in the decision of these issues that the Court establishes the role it will play in the governmental process. For example, it is not hard to imagine that the Court could reasonably have found that Mrs. Frothingham had suffered sufficient injury to warrant relief, thus opening up to judicial review all the things the government does with its money. And by deciding in Baker v. Carr (1962) that a person was "injured" by malapportionment and thus had standing to sue, the Court extended to the judiciary control over this long-standing and seemingly insoluble problem. The extent to which the Court should play an "activist" role, moving aggressively into new areas to solve difficult social problems, or exercise "judicial self-restraint" and stay out of them, is a matter on which members of the Court over the years have been sharply and often bitterly divided. It is an area, too, in which the political branches attempt to exert influence upon the Court, and in Senate hearings on the confirmation of Justice O'Connor she was sharply questioned on her attitude about the role of the Court.

Despite the frailty of the Frothingham reasoning as applied, say, to taxpayers like AT&T and General Motors, the case stood as a general bar to federal taxpayer suits until, in 1968, the Court held in Flast v. Cohen that a taxpayer could challenge the use of federal money to support religious schools. The Court distinguished the precision of the prohibition against aiding religion implicit in the First Amendment from the more general limits of the due process clause involved in the Frothingham case. In deciding Flast the Court also noted that not only was aid to religion forbidden, but since the aid involved was financial and Flast was suing as a taxpayer there was a connection, or "nexus," between the status of the challenger and the government action being challenged.

In the years following Flast v. Cohen (1968) the Court dealt with the problem of standing largely in terms of a person's right to complain about the actions of government agencies that affected him or her adversely. The essential test under Article III was whether the individual had alleged sufficient injury to provide a case or controversy, and in a series of cases the Court found injury in such widely varied allegations as: (1) The Comptroller of the Currency was permitting injurious business competition by letting banks sell data processing services (Data Processing Service v. Camp, 1970); (2) the Secretary of Agriculture had changed the agricultural subsidy rules to make a tenant farmer more dependent on his landlord (Barlow v. Collins, 1970); and (3) the ICC was raising railroad rates, thus discouraging the use of recyclable materials and damaging the environment (United States v. SCRAP, 1973). All of these cases rested on a provision of the Administrative Procedure Act authorizing judicial review where a person is "adversely affected or aggrieved by agency action," and in each case the petitioners alleged personal injury.

Only in Sierra Club v. Morton (1972) did the Court fail to find injury. There the well-known nature club had sought to enjoin the building of a ski resort in Mineral King Valley and Sequoia National Park, but unlike those involved in the SCRAP case, it had failed to claim that it or any of its members used the park and would suffer actual injury as a result of injury to the environment. It is interesting to note that the decisive allegations of injury in SCRAP were no more than that SCRAP members "suffered economic, recreational and aesthetic harm directly as a result of the adverse environmental impact of the railroad freight structure" which would "discourage the use of 'recyclable' materials, and promote the use of new raw materials that compete with scrap, thereby adversely affecting the environment."

In distinguishing the SCRAP case from Sierra, decided the year before, the Court made clear that the only test was the threat of actual personal injury. "Unlike the specific and geographically limited federal action of which the petitioner complained in Sierra Club, the challenged agency action in this case is applicable to substantially all the Nation's railroads, and thus allegedly has an adverse environmental impact on all the natural resources of the country. Rather than a limited group of persons who used a picturesque valley in California, all persons who utilize the scenic resources of the country, and indeed all who breathe its air, could claim harm similar to that alleged by the environmental groups here. But we have already made it clear that standing is not to be denied simply because many people suffer the same injury. . . . To deny standing to persons who are in fact injured simply because many others are also injured, would mean that the most injurious and widespread Government actions could be questioned by nobody. We cannot accept that conclusion."

While it is essential to "standing" that a person allege personal injury, the "personalness" of the injury must itself meet certain tests. In Schlesinger v. Reservists to Stop the War (1974) members of the group brought a class action on behalf of themselves and all others who wanted to stop the war in Vietnam by the process of persuading Congress to take action. They pointed out that Article I, § 6, cl. 2, provides that no person "holding office under the United States, shall be a member of either house" of Congress and challenged the membership of congressmen in the military reserves on the ground that they were personally injured by such membership both as citizens and as taxpayers. Such membership in the military, they argued, denied them representatives who could approach the Vietnam War question impartially.

The Court rejected their right to sue as citizens on the ground that they had failed to allege actual injury, since the failure of congressmen to observe the Incompatibility Clause "would adversely affect only the generalized interest of all citizens in constitutional governance, and that is an abstract injury. . . . To permit a complainant who has no concrete injury to require a court to rule on important constitutional issues in the abstract would create the potential for abuse of the judicial process, distort the role of the Judiciary in its relationship to the Executive and the Legislature and open the Judiciary to an arguable charge of providing " 'government by injunction.' " The Court distinguished the Data Processing and SCRAP cases, noting that they provide "the setting for a focused consideration of a concrete injury," while in the present case "it can be only a matter of speculation whether the claimed violation has caused concrete injury to the particular complainant." Nor could they sue as taxpayers, since the Incompatibility Clause was not a limit on the spending power and thus failed part of the "logical nexus" test of Flast v. Cohen.

In United States v. Richardson, decided the same day as Schlesinger, the Court rejected a taxpayer suit brought to compel Congress to make public the expenditures of the Central Intelligence Agency. This agency had by statute been exempted from the constitutional requirement of Article I, Sec. 9, Cl. 8 that "no money shall be drawn from the treasury, but in consequence of appropriations made by law; and a regular statement and account of the receipts and expenditures of all public money shall be published from time to time." The taxpayer's claim failed the test of Flast v. Cohen since "there is no 'logical nexus' between the asserted status of taxpayer and the claimed failure of the Congress to require the Executive to supply a more detailed report of the expenditures of that agency." Justice Douglas, in dissent, pointed out that the purpose of the clause was to let a taxpayer see how his money was being spent.

Justice **Rehnquist** delivered the opinion of the Court, saying in part:

I.

Article IV, § 3, Cl. 2, of the Constitution vests Congress with the "Power to dispose of and make all needful Rules and Regulations respecting the . . . Property belonging to the United States." Shortly after the termination of hostilities in the Second World War, Congress enacted the Federal Property and Administrative Services Act of 1949. The Act was designed, in part, to provide "an economical and efficient system for . . . the disposal of surplus property." In furtherance of this policy, federal agencies are directed to maintain adequate inventories of the property under their control and to identify excess property for transfer to other agencies able to use it. Property that has outlived its usefulness to the federal government is declared "surplus" and may be transferred to private or other public entities.

The Act authorizes the Secretary of Health, Education, and Welfare (now the Secretary of Education) to assume responsibility for disposing of surplus real property "for school, classroom, or other educational use." Subject to the disapproval of the Administrator of General Services, the Secretary may sell or lease the property to nonprofit, tax exempt educational institutions for consideration that takes into account "any benefit which has accrued or may accrue to the United States" from the transferee's use of the property. By regulation, the Secretary has provided for the computation of a "public benefit allowance," which discounts the transfer price of the property "on the basis of benefits to the United States from the use of such property for educational purposes."

The property which spawned this litigation was acquired by the Department of the Army in 1942, as part of a larger tract of approximately 181 acres of land northwest of Philadelphia. The Army built on that land the Valley Forge General Hospital, and for 30 years thereafter, that hospital provided medical care for members of the Armed Forces. In April 1973, as part of a plan to reduce the number of military installations in the United States, the Secretary of Defense proposed to close the hospital, and the General Services Administration declared it to be "surplus property."

The Department of Health, Education, and Welfare (HEW) eventually assumed responsibility for disposing of portions of the property, and in August 1976, it conveyed a 77-acre tract to petitioner, the Valley Forge Christian College. The appraised value of the property at the time of conveyance was $577,500. This appraised value was discounted, however, by the Secretary's computation of a 100 percent public benefit allowance, which permitted petitioner to acquire the property without making any financial payment for it. The deed from HEW conveyed the land in fee simple with certain conditions subsequent, which required petitioner to use the property for 30 years solely for the educational purposes described in petitioner's application. In that description, petitioner stated its intention to conduct "a program of education . . . meeting the accrediting standards of the State of Pennsylvania, The American Association of Bible Colleges, the Division of Education of the General Council of the Assemblies of God and the Veterans Administration."

Petitioner is a nonprofit educational institution operating under the supervision of a religious order known as the Assemblies of God. By its own description, petitioner's purpose is "to offer systematic training on the collegiate level to men and women for Christian service as either ministers or laymen." . . .

In September 1976, respondents Americans United for Separation of Church and State, Inc. (Americans United), and four of its employees, learned of the conveyance through a news release. Two months later, they brought suit in the United States District Court for the District of Columbia, later transferred to the Eastern District of Pennsylvania to challenge the conveyance on the ground that it violated the Establishment Clause of the First Amendment. In its amended complaint, Americans United described itself as a nonprofit organization composed of 90,000 "taxpayer members." The complaint asserted that each member "would be deprived of the fair and constitutional use of his (her) tax dollar for constitutional purposes in violation of his (her) rights under the First Amendment of the United States Constitution." Respondents sought a declaration that the conveyance was null and void, and an order compelling petitioner to transfer the property back to the United States. . . .

II.

Article III of the Constitution limits the "judicial power" of the United States to the resolution of "cases" and "controversies." The constitutional power of federal courts cannot be defined, and indeed has no substance, without reference to the necessity "to adjudge the legal rights of litigants in actual controversies." . . . The requirements of Art. III are not satisfied merely because a party requests a court of the United States to declare its legal rights, and has couched that request for forms of relief historically associated with courts of law in terms that have a familiar ring to those trained in the legal process. The judicial power of the United States defined by Art. III is not an unconditioned authority to determine the constitutionality of legislative or executive acts. The power to declare the rights of individuals and to measure the authority of governments, this Court said 90 years ago, "is legitimate only in the last resort, and as a necessity in the determination of real, earnest and vital controversy." Chicago & Grand Trunk R. Co. v. Wellman (1892). Otherwise, the power "is not judicial . . . in the sense in which judicial power is granted by the Constitution to the courts of the United States." . . .

As an incident to the elaboration of this bedrock requirement, this Court has always required that a litigant have "standing" to challenge the action sought to be adjudicated in the lawsuit. The term "standing" subsumes a blend of constitutional requirements and prudential considerations . . . and it has not always been clear in the opinions of this Court whether particular features of the "standing" requirement have been required by Art. III ex proprio vigore, or whether they are requirements that the Court itself has erected and which were not compelled by the language of the Constitution. . . .

A recent line of decisions, however, has resolved that ambiguity, at least to the following extent: at an irreducible minimum, Art. III requires the party who invokes the court's authority to "show that he personally has suffered some actual or threatened injury as a result of the putatively illegal conduct of the defendant," Gladstone, Realtors v. Village of Bellwood (1979), and that the injury "fairly can be traced to the challenged action" and "is likely to be redressed by a favorable decision," Simon v. Eastern Kentucky Welfare Rights Org. (1976). In this manner does Art. III limit the federal judicial power "to those disputes which confine federal courts to a role consistent with a system of separated powers and which are traditionally thought to be capable of resolution through the judicial process." Flast v. Cohen [1968].

The requirement of "actual injury redressable by the court," Simon, serves several of the "implicit policies embodied in Art. III," Flast. It tends to assure that the legal questions presented to the court will be resolved, not in the rarified atmosphere of a debating society, but in a concrete factual context conducive to a realistic appreciation of the consequences of judicial action. . . .

The Art. III aspect of standing also reflects a due regard for the autonomy of those persons likely to be most directly affected by a judicial order. The federal courts have abjured appeals to their authority which would convert the judicial process into "no more than a vehicle for the vindication of the value interests of concerned bystanders." United States v. SCRAP (1973). Were the federal courts merely publicly funded forums for the ventilation of public grievances or the refinement of jurisprudential understanding, the concept of "standing" would be quite unnecessary. But the "cases and controversies" language of Art. III forecloses the conversion of courts of the United States into judicial versions of college debating forums. . . . The exercise of judicial power, which can so profoundly affect the lives, liberty, and property of those to whom it extends, is therefore restricted to litigants who can show "injury in fact" resulting from the action which they seek to have the Court adjudicate.

The exercise of the judicial power also affects relationships between the coequal arms of the National Government. The effect is, of course, most vivid when a federal court declares unconstitutional an act of the Legislative or Executive branch. While the exercise of that "ultimate and supreme function" . . . is a formidable means of vindicating individual rights, when employed unwisely or unnecessarily it is also the ultimate threat to the continued effectiveness of the federal courts in performing that role. While the propriety of such action by a federal court has been recognized since Marbury v. Madison (1803), it has been recognized as a tool of last resort on the part of the federal judiciary throughout its nearly 200 years of existence. . . . Proper regard for the complex nature of our constitutional structure requires neither that the Judicial Branch shrink from a confrontation with the other two coequal branches of the Federal government, nor that it hospitably accept for adjudication claims of constitutional violation by other branches of government where the claimant has not suffered cognizable injury. Thus, this Court has "refrain[ed] from passing upon the constitutionality of an act [of the representative branches] unless obliged to do so in the proper performance of our judicial function, when the question is raised by a party whose interests entitle him to raise it." Blair v. United States (1919). The importance of this precondition should not be underestimated as a means of "defin[ing] the role assigned to the judiciary in a tripartite allocation of power." Flast v. Cohen.

Beyond the constitutional requirements, the federal judiciary has also adhered to a set of prudential principles that bear on the question of standing. Thus, this Court has held that "the plaintiff generally must assert his own legal rights and interests, and cannot rest his claim to relief on the legal rights or interests of third parties." . . . In addition, even when the plaintiff has alleged redressable injury sufficient to meet the requirements of Art. III, the Court has refrained from adjudicating "abstract questions of wide public significance" which amount to "generalized grievances," pervasively shared and most appropriately addressed in the representative branches. Finally, the Court has required that the plaintiff's complaint fall within "the zone of interests to be protected or regulated by the statute or constitutional guarantee in question." [Data Processing Service] v. Camp (1970). . . .

We need not mince words when we say that the concept of "Article III standing" has not been defined with complete consistency in all of the various cases decided by this Court which have discussed it, nor when we say that this very fact is probably proof that the concept cannot be reduced to a one-sentence or one-paragraph definition. But of one thing we may be sure: Those who do not possess Art. III standing may not litigate as suitors in the courts of the United States.* Article III, which is every bit as important in its circumscription of the judicial power of the United States as in its granting of that power, is not merely a troublesome hurdle to be overcome if possible so as to reach the "merits" of a lawsuit which a party desires to have adjudicated; it is a part of the basic charter promulgated by the Framers of the Constitution at Philadelphia in 1787, a charter which created a general government, provided for the interaction between that government and the governments of the several States, and was later amended so as to either enhance or limit its authority with respect to both States and individuals.

III.

The injury alleged by respondents in their amended complaint is the "depriv[ation] of the fair and constitutional use of [their] tax dollar." As a result, our discussion must begin with Frothingham v. Mellon (1923). . . .

[The Court here summarizes both Frothingham v. Mellon and Doremus v. Board of Education (1952), showing that both turned on the failure to show direct pecuniary injury.]

The Court again visited the problem of taxpayer standing in Flast v. Cohen (1968). The taxpayer plaintiffs in Flast sought to enjoin the expenditure of federal funds under the Elementary and Secondary Education Act of 1965, which they alleged were being used to support religious schools in violation of the Establishment Clause. The Court developed a two-part test to determine whether the plaintiffs had standing to sue. First, because a taxpayer alleges injury only by virtue of his liability for taxes, the Court held that "a taxpayer will be a proper party to allege the unconstitutionality only of exercises of congressional power under the taxing and spending clause of Art. I, § 8, of the Constitution." Second, the Court required the taxpayer to "show that the challenged enactment exceeds specific constitutional limitations upon the exercise of the taxing and spending power and not simply that the enactment is generally beyond the powers delegated to Congress by Art. I, § 8."

The plaintiffs in Flast satisfied this test because "[t]heir constitutional challenge [was] made to an exercise by Congress of its power under Art. I, § 8, to spend for the general welfare," and because the Establishment Clause, on which plaintiffs' complaint rested, "operates as a specific constitutional limitation upon the exercise by Congress of the taxing and spending power conferred by Art. I, § 8." The Court distinguished Frothingham v. Mellon on the ground that Mrs. Frothingham had relied, not on a specific limitation on the power to tax and spend, but on a more general claim based on the Due Process Clause. Thus, the Court reaffirmed that the "case or controversy" aspect of standing is unsatisfied "where

---

*Justice Brennan's dissent takes us to task for "tend[ing] merely to obfuscate, rather than inform, our understanding of the meaning of rights under the law." Were this court constituted to operate a national classroom on "the meaning of rights" for the benefit of interested litigants, this criticism would carry weight. The teaching of Art. III, however, is that constitutional adjudication is available only on terms prescribed by the Constitution, among which is the requirement of a plaintiff with standing to sue. The dissent asserts that this requirement "overrides no other provision of the Constitution." . . . Art. III obligates a federal court to act only when it is assured of the power to do so, that is, when it is called upon to resolve an actual case or controversy. Then, and only then, may it turn its attention to other constitutional provisions and presume to provide a forum for the adjudication of rights. . . . .

a taxpayer seeks to employ a federal court as a forum in which to air his generalized grievances about the conduct of government or the allocation of power in the Federal System.''

Unlike the plaintiffs in Flast, respondents fail the first prong of the test for taxpayer standing. Their claim is deficient in two respects. First, the source of their complaint is not a congressional action, but a decision by HEW to transfer a parcel of federal property. Flast limited taxpayer standing to challenges directed ''only [at] exercises of congressional power.'' See Schlesinger v. Reservists Committee to Stop the War [1974] (denying standing because the taxpayer plaintiffs ''did not challenge an enactment under Art. I, § 8, but rather the action of the Executive Branch'').

Second, and perhaps redundantly, the property transfer about which respondents complain was not an exercise of authority conferred by the Taxing and Spending Clause of Art. I, § 8. The authorizing legislation, the Federal Property and Administrative Services Act of 1949, was an evident exercise of Congress' power under the Property Clause, Art. IV, § 3, cl. 2. Respondents do not dispute this conclusion, and it is decisive of any claim of taxpayer standing under the Flast precedent.* . . .

IV. . . .

The complaint in this case shares a common deficiency with those in Schlesinger and [United States v.] Richardson. Although they claim that the Constitution has been violated, they claim nothing else. They fail to identify any personal injury suffered by the plaintiffs *as a consequence* of the alleged constitutional error, other than the psychological consequence presumably produced by observation of conduct with which one disagrees. That is not an injury sufficient to confer standing under Art. III, even though the disagreement is phrased in constitutional terms. It is evident that respondents are firmly committed to the constitutional principle of separation of church and State, but standing is not measured by the intensity of the litigant's interest or the fervor of his advocacy. ''[T]hat concrete adverseness which sharpens the presentation of issues,'' Baker v. Carr, is the anticipated consequence of proceedings commenced by one who has been injured in fact; it is not a permissible substitute for the showing of injury itself.

In reaching this conclusion, we do not retreat from our earlier holdings that standing may be predicated on noneconomic injury. See, e.g., United States v. SCRAP; [Data Processing Service] v. Camp. We simply cannot see that respondents have alleged an *injury of any* kind, economic or otherwise, sufficient to confer standing. Respondents complain of a transfer of property located in Chester County, Pa. The named plaintiffs reside in Maryland and Virginia; their organizational headquarters are located in Washington, D.C. They learned of the transfer through a news release. Their claim that the Government has violated the Estab-

---

*Although not necessary to our decision, we note that any connection between the challenged property transfer and respondents' tax burden is at best speculative and at worst nonexistent. . . . In fact, respondents' only objection is that the Government did not receive adequate consideration for the transfer, because petitioner's use of the property will not confer a public benefit. Assuming, arguendo, that this proposition is true, an assumption by no means clear, there is no basis for believing that a transfer to a different purchaser would have added to Government receipts. As the Government argues, ''the ultimate purchaser would, in all likelihood, have been another non-profit institution or local school district rather than a purchaser for cash.'' . . .

lishment Clause does not provide a special license to roam the country in search of governmental wrongdoing and to reveal their discoveries in federal court. The federal courts were simply not constituted as ombudsmen of the general welfare.

V. . . .

. . . Respondents' claim of standing implicitly rests on the presumption that violations of the Establishment Clause typically will not cause injury sufficient to confer standing under the "traditional" view of Art. III. But "[t]he assumption that if respondents have no standing to sue, no one would have standing, is not a reason to find standing." Schlesinger v. Reservists Committee to Stop the War. This view would convert standing into a requirement that must be observed only when satisfied. Moreover, we are unwilling to assume that injured parties are nonexistent simply because they have not joined respondents in their suit. . . .

Were we to accept respondents' claim of standing in this case, there would be no principled basis for confining our exception to litigants relying on the Establishment Clause. Ultimately, that exception derives from the idea that the judicial power requires nothing more for its invocation than important issues and able litigants. The existence of injured parties who might not wish to bring suit becomes irrelevant. Because we are unwilling to countenance such a departure from the limits on judicial power contained in Art. III, the judgment of the Court of Appeals is reversed.

It is so ordered.

Justice **Brennan,** with whom Justice **Marshall** and Justice **Blackmun** join, dissenting, said in part:

A plaintiff's standing is a jurisdictional matter for Art. III courts, and thus a "threshold question" to be resolved before turning attention to more "substantive" issues. . . . But in consequence there is an impulse to decide difficult questions of substantive law obliquely in the course of opinions purporting to do nothing more than determine what the Court labels "standing"; this accounts for the phenomenon of opinions, such as the one today, that tend merely to obfuscate, rather than inform, our understanding of the meaning of rights under the law. The serious by-product of that practice is that the Court disregards its constitutional responsibility when, by failing to acknowledge the protections afforded by the Constitution, it uses "standing to slam the courthouse door against plaintiffs who are entitled to full consideration of their claims on the merits." . . .

I. . . .

. . . The Court makes a fundamental mistake when it determines that a plaintiff has failed to satisfy the two-pronged "injury-in-fact" test, or indeed any other test of "standing," without first determining whether the Constitution or a statute defines injury, and creates a cause of action for redress of that injury, in precisely the circumstance presented to the Court. . . .

The "case and controversy" limitation of Art. III overrides no other provision of the Constitution.* To construe that Article to deny standing " 'to the class for whose sake [a] constitutional protection is given,' " . . . simply turns the Constitution on its head. . . .

II. . . .

B.

In 1947, nine Justices of this Court recognized that the Establishment Clause does impose a very definite restriction on the power to tax. The Court held in Everson v. Board of Education that the " 'establishment of religion' clause of the First Amendment means at least this:"

"No tax in any amount, large or small, can be levied to support any religious activities or institutions, whatever they may be called, or whatever form they may adopt, to teach or practice religion."

The members of the Court could not have been more explicit. "One of our basic rights is to be free of taxation to support a transgression of the constitutional command that the authorities 'shall make no law respecting an establishment of religion, or prohibiting the free exercise thereof.' " (Jackson, J., dissenting). "[A]part from efforts to inject religious training or exercises and sectarian issues into the public schools, the only serious threat to maintaining that complete and permanent separation of religion and civil power which the First Amendment commands is through the use of the taxing power to support religion, religious establishments, or establishments having a religious foundation whatever their form or special religious function. . . . [M]oney taken by taxation from one is not to be used or given to support another's religious training or belief, or indeed one's own." (Rutledge, J., dissenting). . . .

[Justice Brennan here reviews the history of the adoption of the establishment clause.]

It is clear in the light of this history, that one of the primary purposes of the Establishment Clause was to prevent the use of tax monies for religious purposes. *The taxpayer was the direct and intended beneficiary of the prohibition on financial aid to religion.* This basic understanding of the meaning of the Establishment Clause explains why the Court in Everson, while rejecting appellant's claim on the merits, perceived the issue presented there as it did. The appellant sued "in his capacity as a district taxpayer," challenging the actions of the Board of Education in passing a resolution providing reimbursement to parents for the cost of transporting their children to parochial schools, and seeking to have that resolution "set aside." Appellant's Establishment Clause claim was precisely that the "statute . . . forced inhabitants to pay taxes to help support and maintain" church schools. It seems obvious that all the Justices who participated in Everson would have agreed with Justice Jackson's succinct statement of the question presented: "Is it constitutional to tax this com-

---

*When the Constitution makes it clear that a particular person is to be protected from a particular form of government action, then that person has a "right" to be free of that action; when that right is infringed, then there is injury, and a personal stake, within the meaning of Article III.

plainant to pay the cost of carrying pupils to Church schools of one specified denomination?'' (Jackson, J., dissenting). Given this view of the issues, could it fairly be doubted that this taxpayer alleged injury in precisely the form that the Establishment Clause sought to make actionable?

C.

In Flast v. Cohen (1968), federal taxpayers sought to challenge the Department of Health, Education, and Welfare's administration of the Elementary and Secondary Education Act of 1965: specifically the Department's practice of allowing funds distributed under that Act to be used to finance instruction in religious schools. Appellants urged that the use of federal funds for such a purpose violated the Establishment and Free Exercise Clauses of the First Amendment, and sought a declaration that this use of federal funds was not authorized by the Act, or that to the extent the use was authorized, the Act was ''unconstitutional and void.'' ... The Frothingham rule stood as a seemingly absolute barrier to the maintenance of the claim. The Court held, however, the Frothingham barrier could be overcome by any claim that met both requirements of a two part ''nexus'' test.

The Justices who participated in Flast were not unaware of the Court's continued recognition of a federally cognizable ''case or controversy'' when a *local* taxpayer seeks to challenge as unconstitutional the use of a *municipality's* funds—the propriety of which had, of course, gone unquestioned in Everson. The Court was aware as well of the rule stated in Doremus v. Board of Education (1952) that the interest of a taxpayer, even one raising an Establishment Clause claim, was limited to the actions of a government involving the expenditure of funds. But in reaching its holding, it is also quite clear that the Court was responding, not only to Everson's continued acceptance of municipal taxpayer actions but also to Everson's exposition of the history and meaning of the Establishment Clause. See Flast.

It is at once apparent that the test of standing formulated by the Court in Flast sought to reconcile the developing doctrine of taxpayer ''standing'' with the Court's historical understanding that the Establishment Clause was intended to prohibit the Federal Government from using tax funds for the advancement of religion, and thus the constitutional imperative of taxpayer standing in certain cases brought pursuant to the Establishment Clause. The two-pronged ''nexus'' test offered by the Court, despite its general language, is best understood as ''a determinant of standing of plaintiffs alleging only injury as taxpayers who challenge alleged violations of the Establishment and Free Exercise Clauses of the First Amendment,'' and not as a general statement of standing principles. ... The test explains what forms of governmental action may be attacked by someone alleging only taxpayer status, and, without ruling out the possibility that history might reveal another similarly founded provision, explains why an Establishment Clause claim is treated differently from any other assertion that the Federal Government has exceeded the bounds of the law in allocating its largesse. Thus, consistent with Doremus, Flast required, as the first prong of its test, that the taxpayer demonstrate a logical connection between his taxpayer status and the type of legislation attacked. Appellants' challenge to a program of grants to educational institutions clearly satisfied this first requirement. As the second prong, consistent with the prohibition of taxpayer claims of the kind advanced in Frothingham, appellants were required to show a connection between their status and the precise nature of the infringement alleged. They had no difficulty meeting this requirement: the Court agreed that the Establishment Clause jealously protects taxpayers from diversion of their funds to the support of religion through the offices of the Federal Government. . . .

It may be that Congress can tax for *almost* any reason, or for no reason at all. There is, so far as I have been able to discern, but one constitutionally imposed limit on that authority. Congress cannot use tax money to support a church, or to encourage religion. That is "*the* forbidden exaction." Everson v. Board of Education (Rutledge, J., dissenting) (emphasis added). In absolute terms the history of the Establishment Clause of the First Amendment makes this clear. History also makes it clear that the federal taxpayer is a singularly "proper and appropriate party to invoke a federal court's jurisdiction" to challenge a federal bestowal of largesse as a violation of the Establishment Clause. Each, and indeed every, federal taxpayer suffers precisely the injury that the Establishment Clause guards against when the Federal Government directs that funds be taken from the pocketbooks of the citizenry and placed into the coffers of the ministry.

A taxpayer cannot be asked to raise his objection to such use of his funds at the time he pays his tax. Apart from the unlikely circumstance in which the Government announced in advance that a particular levy would be used for religious subsidies, taxpayers could hardly assert that they were being injured until the Government actually lent its support to a religious venture. . . . Surely, then, a taxpayer must have standing at the time that he learns of the Government's alleged Establishment Clause violation to seek equitable relief in order to halt the continuing and intolerable burden on his pocketbook, his conscience, and his constitutional rights.

III.

Blind to history, the Court attempts to distinguish this case from Flast by wrenching snippets of language from our opinions, and by perfunctorily applying that language under color of the first prong of Flast's two-part nexus test. The tortuous distinctions thus produced are specious, at best: at worst, they are pernicious to our constitutional heritage.

First, the Court finds this case different from Flast because here the "source of [plaintiff's] complaint is not a *congressional* action, but a decision by HEW to transfer a parcel of federal property." This attempt at distinction cannot withstand scrutiny. Flast involved a challenge to the actions of the Commissioner of Education, and other officials of HEW, in disbursing funds under the Elementary and Secondary Education Act of 1965 to "religious and sectarian" schools. . . . In the present case, respondents challenge HEW's grant of property pursuant to the Federal Property and Administrative Services Act of 1949, seeking to enjoin HEW "from making a grant of this and other property to the [defendant] so long as such a grant will violate the Establishment Clause." . . .

More fundamentally, no clear division can be drawn in this context between actions of the Legislative Branch and those of the Executive Branch. To be sure, the First Amendment is phrased as a restriction on Congress' legislative authority; this is only natural since the Constitution assigns the authority to legislate and appropriate only to the Congress. But it is difficult to conceive of an expenditure for which the last governmental actor, either implementing directly the legislative will, or acting within the scope of legislatively delegated authority, is not an Executive Branch official. The First Amendment binds the Government as a whole, regardless of which branch is at work in a particular instance.

The Court's second purported distinction between this case and Flast is equally un- availing. The majority finds it "decisive" that the Federal Property and Administrative Services Act of 1949 "was an evident exercise of Congress' power under the Property Clause, Art. IV, § 3, cl. 2," while the Government action in Flast was taken under Art. I, § 8. The Court relies on United States v. Richardson (1974) and Schlesinger v. Reservists Com- mittee to Stop the War (1974) to support the distinction between the two Clauses, noting that those cases involved alleged deviations from the requirements of Art. I, § 9, cl. 7 and Art. I, § 6, cl. 2, respectively. The standing defect in each case was *not*, however, the failure to allege a violation of the Spending Clause; rather, the taxpayers in those cases had not com- plained of the distribution of Government largesse, and thus failed to meet the essential requirement of taxpayer standing recognized in Doremus.

It can make no constitutional difference in the case before us whether the donation to the petitioner here was in the form of a cash grant to build a facility, see Tilton v. Richardson (1971), or in the nature of a gift of property including a facility already built. That this is a meaningless distinction is illustrated by Tilton. In that case, taxpayers were afforded standing to object to the fact that the Government had not received adequate assurance that if the property that it financed for use as an educational facility was later converted to religious uses, it would receive full value for the property, as the Constitution requires. The complaint here is precisely that, although the property at issue is actually being used for a sectarian purpose, the Government has not received, nor demanded, full value payment. Whether undertaken pursuant to the Property Clause or the Spending Clause, the breach of the Establishment Clause, and the relationship of the taxpayer to that breach, is precisely the same. . .

Justice **Stevens,** dissenting, said in part:

In Parts I, II, and III of his dissenting opinion, Justice Brennan demonstrates that respondent taxpayers have standing to mount an Establishment Clause challenge against the Federal Government's transfer of property worth $1,300,000 to the Assemblies of God. For the Court to hold that plaintiffs' standing depends on whether the Government's transfer was an exercise of its power to spend money, on the one hand, or its power to dispose of tangible property, on the other, is to trivialize the standing doctrine.

One cannot read the Court's opinion and the concurring opinions of Justice Stewart and Justice Fortas in Flast v. Cohen without forming the firm conclusion that the plaintiffs' invocation of the Establishment Clause was of decisive importance in resolving the standing issue in that case. Justice Fortas made this point directly: . . .

"Perhaps the vital interest of a citizen in the establishment issue, without reference to his taxpayer's status, would be acceptable as a basis for this challenge. We need not decide this. But certainly, I believe, we must recognize that our principle of judicial scrutiny of legislative acts which raise important constitutional questions requires that the issue here presented—the separation of state and church—which the Founding Fathers regarded as fundamental to our constitutional system— should be subjected to judicial testing. This is not a question which we, if we are to be faithful to our trust, should consign to limbo, unacknowledged, unresolved, and undecided. . . ."

Today the Court holds, in effect, that the Judiciary has no greater role in enforcing the Establishment Clause than in enforcing other "norm[s] of conduct which the Federal Government is bound to honor" such as the Accounts Clause . . . and the Incompatibility Clause. . . . Ironically, however, its decision rests on the premise that the difference between a disposition of funds pursuant to the Spending Clause and a disposition of realty pursuant to the Property Clause is of fundamental jurisprudential significance. With all due respect, I am persuaded that the essential holding of Flast v. Cohen attaches special importance to the Establishment Clause and does not permit the drawing of a tenuous distinction between the Spending Clause and the Property Clause.

For this reason, and for the reasons stated in Parts I, II, and III of Justice Brennan's opinion, I would affirm the judgment of the Court of Appeals.

EX PARTE McCARDLE

7 Wallace 506; 19 L. Ed. 264 (1869)

A court, in order to be a court and behave like one, must possess two kinds of authority. The first is jurisdiction, which is the power of the court to bring parties before it for the purpose of deciding the kinds of disputes in which those parties are involved. What the court can do about a dispute properly before it depends upon its possession of judicial power. Both jurisdiction and judicial power are provided for the federal courts in Article III of the Constitution.

Article III provides that "the judicial power shall extend to all cases . . ." and then proceeds to enumerate two classes of cases to which federal jurisdiction extends. One class of cases comes to the courts because of their subject matter. These are cases in which so-called "federal questions" are raised, i.e., questions of the interpretation of the Constitution, laws or treaties of the United States. A second category is based on the nature of the parties to the suit and includes generally cases where the state courts might not be impartial. Here are the cases between states and between citizens of different states.

Since lower federal courts are invested with judicial power by Article III, does the phrase "judicial power *shall extend*" mean that any federal court, as soon as it is created by Congress, is fully invested with both kinds of jurisdiction? The answer is no, despite the urging of Federalists who favored a strong independent judiciary. The wording of the Judiciary Act of 1789 creating the courts and the circumstances surrounding its passage both indicate a legislative acceptance of the idea that Congress has complete control over the jurisdiction of the lower federal courts; ten years later, in Turner v. Bank of North America (1799), the Supreme Court approved that interpretation. Congress had specifically denied the courts a portion of the jurisdiction based upon diversity of citizenship; and the bank argued that since diversity jurisdiction was given by Article III, Congress had no power to take it away. The Court upheld the congressional limitation and refused to take jurisdiction. Congress has made free use of its power to grant, withhold, or distribute the jurisdiction of the lower federal courts as it has thought wise. Some of the jurisdiction mentioned in Article III, such as diversity jurisdiction in cases involving small sums, has never been conferred on the federal courts at all. It was not until 1875 that the lower federal courts were given jurisdiction over cases involving federal questions.

The Constitution, in providing for the Supreme Court, distinguishes between its *original* jurisdiction to decide cases which start in the Supreme Court and its *appellate* jurisdiction to decide cases which come to it on appeal, or by other procedure, from some other court. Article III provides that "in all cases affecting ambassadors, other public ministers, and consuls, and those in which a State shall be a party, the Supreme Court shall have original jurisdiction. In all the other cases before mentioned, the Supreme Court shall have appellate jurisdiction, both as to law and fact, with such exceptions, and under such regulations as the Congress shall make." The Supreme Court held in Marbury v. Madison (1803) that Congress cannot validly enlarge the original jurisdiction of the Court. That portion of the Judiciary Act of 1789 which purported to enlarge the original jurisdiction of the Court to include the power to issue writs of mandamus was held unconstitutional.

But to what extent and by what means may Congress control the appellate jurisdiction of the Supreme Court? The present case was one of a series of attempts by the Southern states to get from the Supreme Court a clear decision on the validity of the military reconstruction program set up by Congress after the Civil War. The behavior of the Court must to some extent be judged in the light of the bitterness which this conflict engendered. McCardle, a Southern newspaper editor, was arrested for sedition and tried and convicted by a federal military commission. When his petition to the circuit court for a writ of habeas corpus was denied, he appealed directly to the Supreme Court under a statute designed, ironically, to provide quick access to the Supreme Court for blacks and federal officers in the South. The Court unanimously agreed that the statute gave it jurisdiction in McCardle's case; and in view of its denunciation of military commissions in Ex parte Milligan three years before (1866), there was a widespread expectation that the Court would hold the Reconstruction Acts unconstitutional because of their establishment of military government throughout much of the South.

To prevent possible judicial sabotage of its reconstruction program, the House had already passed a bill providing that the Court could invalidate acts of Congress only by a two-thirds vote, but the Senate had not concurred. Then, with argument in the McCardle case already concluded, Congress undertook to block a decision of the Court by repealing the law by which jurisdiction to hear McCardle's appeal had been conferred.

Despite impeachment proceedings against him, the President vetoed the act; but it was repassed over his veto. The Court, which had waited to see whether the repealing statute would pass, put off until the following term the question of the effect of this repeal on its jurisdiction in the McCardle case. Justices Grier and Field bitterly excoriated their brethren for what they regarded as a shameful and cowardly delay in deciding the case.

Four years later the Court again faced a confrontation with Congress over an attempt to withdraw jurisdiction and this time it did not back down. Klein, a former supporter of the Confederacy, had been granted a pardon by President Johnson. Johnson granted pardons and reinstatements of their confiscated property to persons such as Klein on condition they took an oath to support the United States. Title to confiscated property had always remained with the owners, but to get it or its value back from the Treasury they had to sue in the Court of Claims. Although the Supreme Court had previously upheld the binding nature of such conditional pardons, Congress, liking neither the pardons nor the return of the property to former rebels, by statute ordered the Court of Claims (or the Supreme Court on appeal) to consider the acceptance of the pardon by the individual as conclusive evidence of disloyalty and ordered the suits dismissed for lack of jurisdiction.

The Supreme Court in United States v. Klein (1872) held the act invalid. It conceded that Congress had complete control over the organization and jurisdiction of the Court of Claims and could confer or withhold the right of appeal from its decisions, adding "and if this act did nothing more, it would be our duty to give it effect. . . .

"But the language of the proviso shows plainly that it does not intend to withhold appellate jurisdiction except as a means to an end. Its great and controlling purpose is to deny to pardons granted by the President the effect which this court had adjudged them to have. . . .

"It seems to us that this is not an exercise of the acknowledged power of Congress to make exceptions and prescribe regulations to the appellate power.

"The court is required to ascertain the existence of certain facts and thereupon to declare that its jurisdiction on appeal has ceased. . . . What is this but to prescribe a rule for the decision of a cause in a particular way? . . .

"Congress has already provided that the Supreme Court shall have jurisdiction of the judgments of the court of claims on appeal. Can it prescribe a rule in conformity with which the court must deny to itself the jurisdiction thus conferred, because and only because its decision, in accordance with settled law, must be adverse to the government and favorable to the suitor? This question seems to us to answer itself."

The Court noted that "to the Executive alone is intrusted the power of pardon; and it is granted without limit." Clearly it included the right to remove the guilt which had justified the confiscation, and Congress, by using the pardon to prove guilt, was denying the pardon its legal effect. Without any allusion whatever to Ex parte McCardle the Court simply concluded that the provision had been "inserted in the appropriation bill through inadvertence" and declined to enforce it.

In 1982 over 30 bills were introduced in Congress that would strip the Supreme Court and lower federal courts of jurisdiction in certain constitutional cases or the power to grant certain remedies in those cases. The issues involved included abortion, prayer in the public schools and busing as a means to desegregate schools. These bills were defeated, in large measure because of the lobbying efforts against them by organized groups concerned with the substantive issues involved, e.g., freedom of choice abortion rights. In 1983 a new crop of bills to limit the jurisdiction of the federal courts surfaced. In an effort to avoid the attention of the organized issue groups and enhance the chance that these new bills would be passed, they were drafted in procedural terms. The 1983 bills make no mention of abortion, busing or prayer in schools; instead, they speak of curtailing "federal-question" jurisdiction, revising judicial appropriation procedures, overseeing the conduct of federal judges and overturning the "incorporation doctrine"—the constitutional rule by which courts apply the Bill of Rights to the states. The language of these bills may be stripped of all the emotionally-charged words contained in the 1982 bills, but to date none of them has been successful. In September 1985 the Senate rejected by a vote of sixty-two to thirty-six a bill introduced by Senator Jesse Helms of North Carolina to withdraw court jurisdiction over school prayer cases. In a related but quite different approach, the anti-abortion forces got into the 1984 Republican national platform a provision pledging the appointment of judges committed to their position.

In the last analysis, if Congress finds itself in conflict with the Supreme Court on constitutional issues, it may always seek to employ the direct and orderly process of constitutional amendment to accomplish its ends. It has done this in three cases. Chisolm v. Georgia (1793) was nullified by the Eleventh Amendment; the Dred Scott case (1857), ruling on the nature and source of citizenship, was nullified by the first section of the Fourteenth Amendment; while the Sixteenth Amendment reversed at least part of the Court's ruling in the Income Tax Cases (1895). Such changes are not easy to accomplish, however, and most efforts to alter or nullify controversial Court decisions have been unsuccessful. Moreover, as the history of both the Fourteenth Amendment and the Income Tax Amendment makes clear, the meaning of an amendment is subject to the interpretation of the Supreme Court just as was the original constitutional provision.

Mr. Chief Justice **Chase** delivered the opinion of the Court, saying in part:

The first question necessarily is that of jurisdiction; for, if the Act of March, 1868, takes away the jurisdiction defined by the Act of February, 1867, it is useless, if not improper, to enter into any discussion of other questions.

It is quite true, as was argued by the counsel for the petitioner, that the appellate jurisdiction of this court is not derived from Acts of Congress. It is, strictly speaking, conferred by the Constitution. But it is conferred "with such exceptions and under such regulations as Congress shall make."

It is unnecessary to consider whether, if Congress had made no exceptions and no regulations, this court might not have exercised general appellate jurisdiction under rules prescribed by itself. From among the earliest Acts of the first Congress, at its first session, was the Act of September 24th, 1789, to establish the judicial courts of the United States. That Act provided for the organization of this court, and prescribed regulations for the exercise of its jurisdiction.

The source of that jurisdiction, and the limitations of it by the Constitution and by statute, have been on several occasions subjects of consideration here. In the case of Durousseau v. U. S. [1810]; Wiscart v. Dauchy [1796], particularly, the whole matter was carefully examined, and the court held, that while "the appellate powers of this court are not given by the Judicial Act, but are given by the Constitution;" they are, nevertheless, "limited and regulated by that Act, and by such other Acts as have been passed on the subject." The court said, further, that the Judicial Act was an exercise of the power given by the Constitution to Congress "of making exceptions to the appellate jurisdiction of the Supreme Court."

"They have described affirmatively," said the court, "its jurisdiction, and this affirmative description has been understood to imply a negation of the exercise of such appellate power as is not comprehended within it."

The principle that the affirmation of appellate jurisdiction implies the negation of all such jurisdiction not affirmed having been thus established, it was an almost necessary consequence that Acts of Congress, providing for the exercise of jurisdiction, should come to be spoken of as Acts granting jurisdiction, and not as Acts making exceptions to the constitutional grant of it.

The exception to appellate jurisdiction in the case before us, however, is not an inference from the affirmation of other appellate jurisdiction. It is made in terms. The provision of the Act of 1867, affirming the appellate jurisdiction of this court in cases of habeas corpus, is expressly repealed. It is hardly possible to imagine a plainer instance of positive exception.

We are not at liberty to inquire into the motives of the Legislature. We can only examine into its power under the Constitution; and the power to make exceptions to the appellate jurisdiction of this court is given by express words.

What, then, is the effect of the repealing Act upon the case before us? We cannot doubt as to this. Without jurisdiction the court cannot proceed at all in any cause. Jurisdiction is power to declare the law, and when it ceases to exist, the only function remaining to the court is that of announcing the fact and dismissing the cause. And this is not less clear upon authority than upon principle.

Several cases were cited by the counsel for the petitioner in support of the position that jurisdiction of this case is not affected by the repealing Act. But none of them, in our judgment, afford any support to it. . . .

On the other hand, the general rule, supported by the best elementary writers, is, that ''when an Act of the Legislature is repealed, it must be considered, except as to transactions past and closed, as if it never existed.'' And the effect of repealing Acts upon suits under Acts repealed, has been determined by the adjudications of this court. The subject was fully considered in Norris v. Crocker [1852], and more recently in [Insurance Company] v. Ritchie [1867]. In both of these cases it was held that no judgment could be rendered in a suit after the repeal of the Act under which it was brought and prosecuted.

It is quite clear, therefore, that this court cannot proceed to pronounce judgment in this case, for it has no longer jurisdiction of the appeal; and judicial duty is not less fitly performed by declining ungranted jurisdiction than in exercising firmly that which the Constitution and the laws confer.

Counsel seem to have supposed, if effect be given to the repealing Act in question, that the whole appellate power of the court, in cases of habeas corpus, is denied. But this is in error. The Act of 1868 does not except from that jurisdiction any cases but appeals from circuit courts under the Act of 1867. It does not affect the jurisdiction which was previously exercised. . . .

The appeal of the petitioner in this case must be dismissed for want of jurisdiction.

B. The Legislative Branch

BARENBLATT v. UNITED STATES

360 U. S. 109; 3 L. Ed. 2d 1115; 79 S. Ct. 1081 (1959)

The legislative power of Congress is the power to pass laws, and the actual process of lawmaking is not subject to judicial control. The extent to which Congress can, by making laws, enlarge or diminish the powers of the judiciary and executive is discussed in connection with those branches. But may Congress, as a means of performing its own delegated functions, use the powers usually thought of as belonging to another branch? The power to subpoena witnesses and punish them for contempt by fine and imprisonment if they do not appear and testify is a vital and inherent judicial power. No court is really a court without it. Can a house of Congress borrow this judicial power as a means of performing its own delegated functions without violating the doctrine of the separation of powers?

This question was effectively dealt with in McGrain v. Daugherty (1927). Early in the

Harding administration scandals were uncovered in the federal government, with the result that the Senate created a special committee to investigate the Department of Justice and the activities and inactivities of Mr. Daugherty, which were believed to amount to misconduct in office and the prevention of proper law enforcement. In the course of the investigation the committee subpoenaed Mally S. Daugherty, brother of the Attorney General, to appear before it and testify. This he refused to do. The Senate then issued a warrant ordering the sergeant-at-arms to arrest Mally Daugherty and bring him before the Senate to testify.

The Court upheld the Senate action. Its opinion mentioned that in 1792 the House of Representatives had appointed a select committee to inquire into the ill-fated St. Clair expedition against the Indians; and it then reviewed the legislative practice, congressional enactments, and court decisions bearing on the power of Congress to conduct inquires and to punish for contempt. The Court concluded "that the power of inquiry—with process to enforce it—is an essential and appropriate auxiliary to the legislative function." However, it is a power which may validly be used only "in aid of the legislative function." Daugherty had alleged, and the lower court had agreed, that the committee was not seeking information to help it in legislation, but was in reality putting the Attorney General on trial. The Supreme Court disagreed. It said, "the only legitimate object the Senate could have in ordering the investigation was to aid it in legislating; and we think the subject-matter was such that the presumption should be indulged that this was the object. An express avowal of the object would have been better; but . . . was not indispensable."

The power to investigate and compel the attendance of witnesses may also be used by Congress to facilitate its exercise of nonlegislative congressional powers. In the case of Barry v. United States ex rel. Cunningham (1929) the Court upheld the power of a Senate committee investigating senatorial campaign expenditures in Pennsylvania to punish for contempt a witness who refused to answer relevant questions. There can be no doubt of the similar right of a committee of the House of Representatives to punish recalcitrant witnesses in a hearing on the question of bringing impeachment charges against an officer of the government.

There are two ways in which either house of Congress may exercise its power to punish a stubborn witness for contempt. First, it may pass a resolution holding him in contempt and punishing him summarily. He may be fined, or he may be sent at once to prison. In Anderson v. Dunn (1821) the Supreme Court held that such imprisonment could not, however, extend beyond the adjournment of Congress. While Congress still enjoys this power of direct and summary punishment for contempt, experience early proved it unsatisfactory in a number of ways. Accordingly, in 1857 Congress provided a second method for dealing with the problem. It passed a statute making it a crime for a person to refuse to testify or answer questions before either house of Congress or any congressional committee when subpoenaed to do so. The maximum penalty is a fine of $1000 or a year in prison. The statute is summarized in the opinion in the present case. The procedure under this statute is as follows: if a witness refuses to testify before a congressional investigating committee, the committee reports this refusal to the House (or Senate) and that body, usually as a matter of routine, passes a resolution declaring the witness to be in contempt of the House or Senate. This resolution is then sent to the United States Attorney in the District of Columbia, who presents the matter to a grand jury for indictment under the statute. If thus indicted, the witness is tried in the federal district court, and at his trial presents any legal or constitutional defenses he thinks he has. Punishment is, of course, imposed by the court.

The opinion of the Court in McGrain v. Daugherty (1927) had very reasonably given Congress and its committees a sense of security from judicial interference with the legislative power to compel testimony. The Court had generously declared that if there were a possible legislative purpose which could be served by a congressional demand for evidence and facts, the Court would presume that that was the purpose of the investigation whether it was or not. What more latitude could Congress and its committees wish? But the McGrain case had not given congressional committees carte blanche. There were two reservations: the investigation must be in aid of a valid congressional duty or power, and the questions asked of witnesses must be relevant to the purpose of the inquiry.

From the time of their origin, congressional committees that were set up to investigate subversive or "un-American" activities were in a number of respects sui generis. They were given by Congress roving commissions to find out what they could about persons, organizations, or movements which were believed to be subversive or unorthodox, and to suggest ways and means of defeating these undermining influences. Very early in the game these committees convinced themselves that their most useful function was the public "exposure" of persons of dubious loyalty. This had been explicitly stated by Congressman Martin Dies when his resolution calling for the creation of the House Committee on Un-American Activities was being debated in the House. He said, "I am not in a position to say whether we can legislate effectively in reference to this matter, but I do know that exposure in a democracy of subversive activities is the most effective weapon that we have in our possession." During the Second World War and the subsequent cold war, House and Senate committees investigating subversion were dominated by this zeal to "expose" persons or groups whose loyalty was open to question, in the well-grounded belief that an aroused public opinion would inflict its own nonlegal punishments or reprisals. The "exposure" of disloyalty or crime came to be generally accepted as the controlling purpose of such legislative investigating committees. The idea that committee investigations were justifiable only if they aided Congress in considering legislation or in carrying out specific non-legislative congressional powers was almost wholly forgotten.

When, in 1967, the Supreme Court in Watkins v. United States held void a conviction for contempt of HUAC, it understandably came as a profound and unwelcome shock to those who regarded our congressional committees on subversive activities as the most useful defenders of our national security and as enjoying unrestricted authority in their investigations. Apparently striking at the very core of the committee, the Court made clear that "there is no congressional power to expose for the sake of exposure," and "investigations conducted solely for the personal aggrandizement of the investigators or to 'punish' those investigated are indefensible." Moreover, questions asked of a witness had to be pertinent to the matter under inquiry, and the vagueness of the term "unAmerican" and the "excessively broad charter" of HUAC, coupled with the failure of the committee itself to define the "question under inquiry," made it impossible for the witness to judge whether or not the committee had the right to insist that he answer. "Fundamental fairness," said the Court, "demands that no witness be compelled to make such a determination with so little guidance."

The decision in the Barenblatt case, printed below, came as a shock to those who had welcomed the Watkins decision and as a relief to its critics. Not only did the Court not strike dead the HUAC, but it seemed to back away from Chief Justice Warren's statement in Watkins that the Committee could not "expose for the sake of exposure." But the impression that Barenblatt had in effect overruled Watkins proved to be unwarranted, and in subsequent cases the Supreme Court both sustained and struck down convictions for contempt of congressional committees. In Braden v. United States and Wilkinson v. United States the Court in 1961 upheld by five-to-four votes the contempt convictions of the defendants who refused to testify before the HUAC. Although the Committee's investigation was apparently sparked by the opposition these men had expressed to the work of the Committee, the Court held that this did not alter the validity of what, on the basis of Barenblatt, was an otherwise valid investigation. In Deutch v. United States (1961), on the other hand, the Court held that questions regarding Communist activity at Cornell University were not pertinent to an investigation of Communism in the Albany, New York, labor movement. In the 1970's Congress abolished its committees on "un-American activities" but in 1981 the Senate established within its judiciary committee a subcommittee on "security and terrorism."

The decision of the cases just discussed turned on whether the legislative committee was authorized to investigate a particular activity, and if it was, whether the question asked of the witness was pertinent to such investigation. In 1962 the Court added a new dimension to this last problem. In Russell v. United States, it held that a prosecution for contempt was void unless the indictment by which the charge was brought stated explicitly the purpose of the investigation. The indictment in question had listed as a separate count each question the witness had refused to answer, but had stated merely that they were pertinent without stating what the subject of the inquiry was. This, said the Court, not only made it impossible to make an independent judgment of pertinency on appeal but did not indicate to the defendant with sufficient clarity the exact crime for which he was being tried.

For twenty-five years the Supreme Court has been asked to hold that there was a constitutional "right to silence" flowing from the First Amendment which would justify a person in refusing to testify before a legislative committee. The Court has never conceded such a right, but in 1963 in Gibson v. Florida Investigation Committee it upheld for the first time against a legislative committee the closely related claim of "associational privacy." The Florida committee, in the course of investigating Communist infiltration of the civil rights movement, subpoenaed the membership lists of the Miami chapter of the NAACP. The Court sustained the chapter's refusal to produce them. Conceding the right of the state to inform itself, the Court held that absent any tie-in, or "nexus," between the NAACP and subversion, there was no showing of "an overriding and compelling state interest" sufficient to override the right of association. A similar result was reached in De Gregory v. Attorney General (1966), where the New Hampshire attorney general sought to inquire into De Gregory's Communist activities of a decade earlier. Since the record was "devoid of any evidence that there is any communist movement in New Hampshire," there was no such " 'overriding and compelling state interest' . . . that would warrant intrusion into the realm of political and associational privacy. . . ." Justices Harlan, Stewart, and Clark dissented on the ground that the purpose of the inquiry was to find out if there were such a "movement."

In the summer of 1987 the nation was treated to a first-hand view of a congressional investigating committee at work. Two, and sometimes three, major television networks cancelled their regular programs while the nation watched a joint House and Senate committee question witnesses in an effort to find out: (1) whether the sale of arms to Iran was in fact an "arms for hostages" deal; (2) whether the extra money made on the arms sale went to aid the Nicaraguan contras; and (3) what the President of the United States had known about these things and how much he had approved or authorized. Two key witnesses, Admiral John Poindexter, the President's national security advisor, and his aide, Lt. Col. Oliver North, testified under a limited grant of immunity from prosecution. Both had pleaded the Fifth Amendment on the ground that an independent counsel appointed by Congress was investigating their roles in the affair with the possibility they might face criminal charges. In late July, confronted with much conflicting testimony and questions about the veracity of some witnesses, the committee adjourned to write its report.

Mr. Justice **Harlan** delivered the opinion of the Court, saying in part:

Once more the Court is required to resolve the conflicting constitutional claims of congressional power and of an individual's right to resist its exercise. The congressional power in question concerns the internal process of Congress in moving within its legislative domain; it involves the utilization of its committees to secure "testimony needed to enable it efficiently to exercise a legislative function belonging to it under the Constitution." Mc-Grain v. Daugherty [1927]. The power of inquiry has been employed by Congress throughout our history, over the whole range of the national interests concerning which Congress might legislate or decide upon due investigation not to legislate; it has similarly been utilized in determining what to appropriate from the national purse, or whether to appropriate. The scope of the power of inquiry, in short, is as penetrating and far-reaching as the potential power to enact and appropriate under the Constitution.

Broad as it is, the power is not, however, without limitations. Since Congress may only investigate into those areas in which it may potentially legislate or appropriate, it cannot inquire into matters which are within the exclusive province of one of the other branches of the Government. Lacking the judicial power given to the Judiciary, it cannot inquire into matters that are exclusively the concern of the Judiciary. Neither can it supplant the Executive in what exclusively belongs to the Executive. And the Congress, in common with all branches of the Government, must exercise its powers subject to the limitations placed by the Constitution on governmental action, more particularly in the context of this case the relevant limitations of the Bill of Rights.

The congressional power of inquiry, its range and scope, and an individual's duty in relation to it, must be viewed in proper perspective. . . . The power and the right of resistance to it are to be judged in the concrete, not on the basis of abstractions. In the present case congressional efforts to learn the extent of a nationwide, indeed world wide, problem have brought one of its investigating committees into the field of education. Of course, broadly viewed, inquiries cannot be made into the teaching that is pursued in any of our educational institutions. When academic teaching-freedom and its corollary learning-freedom, so essential to the well-being of the Nation, are claimed, this Court will always be on the alert against intrusion by Congress into this constitutionally protected domain. But this does not mean that the Congress is precluded from interrogating a witness merely because he is a teacher. An educational institution is not a constitutional sanctuary from inquiry into matters that may otherwise be within the constitutional legislative domain merely for the reason that inquiry is made of someone within its walls.

In the setting of this framework of constitutional history, practice and legal precedents, we turn to the particularities of this case.

We here review petitioner's conviction for contempt of Congress, arising from his refusal to answer certain questions put to him by a Subcommittee of the House Committee on Un-American Activities during the course of an inquiry concerning alleged Communist infiltration into the field of education. . . .

Petitioner's various contentions resolve themselves into three propositions: First, the compelling of testimony by the Subcommittee was neither legislatively authorized nor constitutionally permissible because of the vagueness of Rule XI of the House of Representatives, Eighty-third Congress, the charter of authority of the parent Committee. Second, petitioner was not adequately apprised of the pertinency of the Subcommittee's questions to the subject matter of the inquiry. Third, the questions petitioner refused to answer infringed rights protected by the First Amendment.

Subcommittee's Authority to Compel Testimony

At the outset it should be noted that Rule XI authorized this Subcommittee to compel testimony within the framework of the investigative authority conferred on the Un-American Activities Committee. Petitioner contends that Watkins v. United States [1957] nevertheless held the grant of this power in all circumstances ineffective because of the vagueness of Rule XI in delineating the Committee jurisdiction to which its exercise was to be appurtenant. This view of Watkins was accepted by two of the dissenting judges below.

The Watkins Case cannot properly be read as standing for such a proposition. A principal contention in Watkins was that the refusals to answer were justified because the requirement of 2 USC § 192 that the questions asked be "pertinent to the question under inquiry" had not been satisfied. This Court reversed the conviction solely on that ground, holding that Watkins had not been adequately apprised of the subject matter of the Subcommittee's investigation or the pertinency thereto of the questions he refused to answer. In so deciding the Court drew upon Rule XI only as one of the facets in the total mise en scène in its search for the "question under inquiry" in that particular investigation. The Court, in other words, was not dealing with Rule XI at large, and indeed in effect stated that no such issue was before it. That the vagueness of Rule XI was not alone determinative is also shown by the Court's further statement that aside from the Rule "the remarks of the chairman or members of the Committee, or even the nature of the proceedings themselves, might sometimes make the topic [under inquiry] clear." In short, while Watkins was critical of Rule XI, it did not involve the broad and inflexible holding petitioner now attributes to it.

Petitioner also contends, independently of Watkins, that the vagueness of Rule XI deprived the Subcommittee of the right to compel testimony in this investigation into Communist activity. We cannot agree with this contention, which in its furthest reach would mean that the House Un-American Activities Committee under its existing authority has no right to compel testimony in any circumstances. Granting the vagueness of the Rule, we may not read it in isolation from its long history in the House of Representatives. Just as legislation is often given meaning by the gloss of legislative reports, administrative interpretation, and long usage, so the proper meaning of an authorization to a congressional committee is not to be derived alone from its abstract terms unrelated to the definite content furnished them by the course of congressional actions. The Rule comes to us with a "persuasive gloss of legislative history," which shows beyond doubt that in pursuance of its legislative concerns in the domain of "national security" the House has clothed the Un-American Activities Committee with pervasive authority to investigate Communist activities in this country. . . .

[The Court here summarizes the history of the Committee, showing the wide range of areas in which it had pursued its search for Communists.]

In the context of these unremitting pursuits, the House has steadily continued the life of the Committee at the commencement of each new Congress; it has never narrowed the powers of the Committee, whose authority has remained throughout identical with that contained in Rule XI; and it has continuingly supported the Committee's activities with substantial appropriations. Beyond this, the Committee was raised to the level of a standing committee of the House in 1945, it having been but a special committee prior to that time.

In light of this long and illuminating history it can hardly be seriously argued that the investigation of Communist activities generally, and the attendant use of compulsory process, was beyond the purview of the Committee's intended authority under Rule XI.

We are urged, however, to construe Rule XI so as at least to exclude the field of education from the Committee's compulsory authority. . . .

[The Court finds Congress was aware of and did not disapprove previous investigations in this field.]

In this framework of the Committee's history we must conclude that its legislative authority to conduct the inquiry presently under consideration is unassailable, and that independently of whatever bearing the broad scope of Rule XI may have on the issue of "pertinency" in a given investigation into Communist activities, as in Watkins, the Rule cannot be said to be constitutionally infirm on the score of vagueness. The constitutional permissibility of that authority otherwise is a matter to be discussed later.

Pertinency Claim

Undeniably a conviction for contempt under 2 USC § 192 cannot stand unless the questions asked are pertinent to the subject matter of the investigation. Watkins v. United States. But the factors which led us to rest decision on this ground in Watkins were very different from those involved here.

In Watkins the petitioner had made specific objection to the Subcommittee's questions on the ground of pertinency; the question under inquiry had not been disclosed in any illuminating manner; and the questions asked the petitioner were not only amorphous on their face, but in some instances clearly foreign to the alleged subject matter of the investigation— "Communism in labor."

In contrast, petitioner in the case before us raised no objections on the ground of pertinency at the time any of the questions were put to him. . . .

We need not, however, rest decision on petitioner's failure to object on this score, for here "pertinency" was made to appear "with undisputable clarity." First of all, it goes without saying that the scope of the Committee's authority was for the House, not a witness, to determine, subject to the ultimate reviewing responsibility of this Court. What we deal with here is whether petitioner was sufficiently apprised of "the topic under inquiry" thus authorized "and the connective reasoning whereby the precise questions asked relate[d] to it." In light of his prepared memorandum of constitutional objections there can be no doubt that this petitioner was well aware of the Subcommittee's authority and purpose to question him as it did. In addition the other sources of this information which we recognized in Watkins leave no room for a "pertinency" objection on this record. The subject matter of the inquiry had been identified at the commencement of the investigation as Communist infiltration into the field of education. Just prior to petitioner's appearance before the Subcommittee, the scope of the day's hearings had been announced as "in the main communism in education and the experiences and background in the party by Francis X. T. Crowley. It will deal with activities in Michigan, Boston, and in some small degree, New York." Petitioner had heard the Subcommittee interrogate the witness Crowley along the same lines as he, petitioner, was evidently to be questioned, and had listened to Crowley's testimony identifying him as a former member of an alleged Communist student organization at the University of Michigan while they both were in attendance there. Further, petitioner had stood mute in the face of the Chairman's statement as to why he had been called as a witness by the Subcommittee. And, lastly, unlike Watkins, petitioner refused to answer questions as to his own Communist Party affiliations, whose pertinency of course was clear beyond doubt.

Petitioner's contentions on this aspect of the case cannot be sustained.

Constitutional Contentions

Our function, at this point, is purely one of constitutional adjudication in the particular case and upon the particular record before us, not to pass judgment upon the general wisdom or efficacy of the activities of this Committee in a vexing and complicated field.

The precise constitutional issue confronting us is whether the Subcommittee's inquiry into petitioner's past or present membership in the Communist Party transgressed the provisions of the First Amendment, which of course reach and limit congressional investigations. Watkins.

The Court's past cases establish sure guides to decision. Undeniably, the First Amendment in some circumstances protects an individual from being compelled to disclose his associational relationships. However, the protections of the First Amendment, unlike a proper claim of the privilege against self-incrimination under the Fifth Amendment, do not afford a witness the right to resist inquiry in all circumstances. Where First Amendment rights are asserted to bar governmental interrogation resolution of the issue always involves a balancing by the courts of the competing private and public interests at stake in the particular circumstances shown. These principles were recognized in the Watkins Case. . . .

The first question is whether this investigation was related to a valid legislative purpose, for Congress may not constitutionally require an individual to disclose his political relationships or other private affairs except in relation to such a purpose. See Watkins v. United States.

That Congress has wide power to legislate in the field of Communist activity in this Country, and to conduct appropriate investigations in aid thereof, is hardly debatable. The existence of such power has never been questioned by this Court, and it is sufficient to say, without particularization, that Congress has enacted or considered in this field a wide range of legislative measures, not a few of which have stemmed from recommendations of the very Committee whose actions have been drawn in question here. In the last analysis this power rests on the right of self-preservation, "the ultimate value of any society," Dennis v. United States [1951]. Justification for its exercise in turn rests on the long and widely accepted view that the tenets of the Communist Party include the ultimate overthrow of the Government of the United States by force and violence, a view which has been given formal expression by the Congress. . . .

. . . To suggest that because the Communist Party may also sponsor peaceable political reforms the constitutional issues before us should now be judged as if that Party were just an ordinary political party from the standpoint of national security, is to ask this Court to blind itself to world affairs which have determined the whole course of our national policy since the close of World War II, . . . and to the vast burdens which these conditions have entailed for the entire Nation.

We think that investigatory power in this domain is not to be denied Congress solely because the field of education is involved. Nothing in the prevailing opinions in Sweezy v. New Hampshire [1957] stands for a contrary view. The vice existing there was that the questioning of Sweezy, who had not been shown ever to have been connected with the Communist Party, as to the contents of a lecture he had given at the University of New Hampshire, and as to his connections with the Progressive Party, then on the ballot as a normal political party in some 26 States, was too far removed from the premises on which the constitutionality of the State's investigation had to depend to withstand attack under the Fourteenth Amendment. This is a very different thing from inquiring into the extent to which the Communist Party has succeeded in infiltrating into our universities, or elsewhere, persons and groups committed to furthering the objective of overthrow. Indeed we do not understand petitioner here to suggest that Congress in no circumstances may inquire into Communist activity in the field of education. Rather, his position is in effect that this particular investigation was aimed not at the revolutionary aspects but at the theoretical classroom discussion of communism.

In our opinion this position rests on a too constricted view of the nature of the investigatory process, and is not supported by a fair assessment of the record before us. An investigation of advocacy of or preparation for overthrow certainly embraces the right to identify a witness as a member of the Communist Party, and to inquire into the various manifestations of the Party's tenets. The strict requirements of a prosecution under the Smith Act, see Dennis v. United States [1951] and Yates v. United States [1957], are not the measure of the permissible scope of a congressional investigation into "overthrow," for of necessity the investigatory process must proceed step by step. Nor can it fairly be concluded that this investigation was directed at controlling what is being taught at our universities rather than at overthrow. The statement of the Subcommittee Chairman at the opening of the investigation evinces no such intention, and so far as this record reveals nothing thereafter transpired which would justify our holding that the thrust of the investigation later changed. The record discloses considerable testimony concerning the foreign domination and revolutionary purposes and efforts of the Communist Party. That there was also testimony on the abstract philosophical level does not detract from the dominant theme of this investigation—Communist infiltration furthering the alleged ultimate purpose of overthrow. And certainly the conclusion would not be justified that the questioning of petitioner would have exceeded permissible bounds had he not shut off the Subcommittee at the threshold.

Nor can we accept the further contention that this investigation should not be deemed to have been in furtherance of a legislative purpose because the true objective of the Committee and of the Congress was purely "exposure." So long as Congress acts in pursuance of its constitutional power, the Judiciary lacks authority to intervene on the basis of the motives which spurred the exercise of that power. "It is, of course, true," as was said in McCray v. United States [1904], "that if there be no authority in the judiciary to restrain a lawful exercise of power by another department of the government, where a wrong motive or purpose has impelled to the exertion of the power, that abuses of a power conferred may be temporarily effectual. The remedy for this, however, lies, not in the abuse by the judicial authority of its functions, but in the people, upon whom, after all, under our institutions, reliance must be placed for the correction of abuses committed in the exercise of a lawful power." These principles of course apply as well to committee investigations into the need for legislation as to the enactments which such investigations may produce. Thus, in stating in the Watkins Case that "there is no congressional power to expose for the sake of exposure," we at the same time declined to inquire into the "motives of committee members," and recognized that their "motives alone would not vitiate an investigation which had been instituted by a House of Congress if that assembly's legislative purpose is being served." Having scrutinized this record we cannot say that the unanimous panel of the Court of Appeals which first considered this case was wrong in concluding that "the primary purposes of the inquiry were in aid of legislative processes." Certainly this is not a case like Kilbourn v. Thompson [1881], where "the House of Representatives not only exceeded the limit of its own authority, but assumed a power which could only be properly exercised by another branch of the government, because it was in its nature clearly judicial." The constitutional legislative power of Congress in this instance is beyond question.

Finally, the record is barren of other factors which in themselves might sometimes lead to the conclusion that the individual interests at stake were not subordinate to those of the state. There is no indication in this record that the Subcommittee was attempting to pillory witnesses. Nor did petitioner's appearance as a witness follow from indiscriminate dragnet procedures, lacking in probable cause for belief that he possessed information which might be helpful to the Subcommittee. And the relevancy of the questions put to him by the Subcommittee is not open to doubt.

We conclude that the balance between the individual and the governmental interests here at stake must be struck in favor of the latter, and that therefore the provisions of the First Amendment have not been offended.

We hold that petitioner's conviction for contempt of Congress discloses no infirmity and that the judgment of the Court of Appeals must be

Affirmed.

Mr. Justice **Black,** with whom Chief Justice **Warren** and Mr. Justice **Douglas** concurred, dissented on grounds that (1) the term "un-American" was so vague as to make the Committee's mandate void for vagueness under the due process clause; (2) the Court's "balancing test" is not the way to determine the scope of freedom of speech, and if it were, the Court should have balanced the interest of society in "being able to join organizations, advocate causes and make political 'mistakes' "against the government's limited interest in making laws in the area of free speech—an interest which cannot reasonably be equated with "self-preservation"; (3) the chief aim of the HUAC is to "try witnesses and punish them because they are or have been Communists," which constitutes a bill of attainder.

Mr. Justice **Brennan** dissented, saying in part:

I would reverse this conviction. It is sufficient that I state my complete agreement with my Brother Black that no purpose for the investigation of Barenblatt is revealed by the record except exposure purely for the sake of exposure. This is not a purpose to which Barenblatt's rights under the First Amendment can validly be subordinated. An investigation in which the processes of law-making and law-evaluating are submerged entirely in exposure of individual behavior—in adjudication, of a sort, through the exposure process—is outside the constitutional pale of congressional inquiry. Watkins v. United States.

IMMIGRATION AND NATURALIZATION SERVICE v. CHADHA

462 U. S. 919; 77 L. Ed. 2d 317; 103 S. Ct. 2764 (1983)

Despite the fact that the Constitution makes Congress the country's lawmaker, it is the President who is popularly viewed as the country's legislative leader. It is he who promises what the country's policies will be if he is elected President; it is he who gets the blame if he can't produce or a policy turns out to be a failure. It is he who speaks to the nation on the state of the union and his administration is the source of most of the proposals which ultimately become law. As an integrated policy source he has a tremendous competitive edge over a two-house and internally fragmented Congress. His threat to veto a bill is usually enough to get it changed, if not to defeat it entirely. It is he who presents the national budget—a volume exceeding in size the telephone directory of most major cities and indicating what national programs should receive financial support and how much. Lastly, it is his office that interprets and enforces on a day-to-day basis the laws that are enacted, thus giving them their final coloration.

The efforts of Congress to articulate the nation's policies are hopelessly encumbered by the sheer size of the task and an early response of Congress was to delegate some of the job to the executive. The Supreme Court finally condoned this delegation, noting that it was not the true "legislative power of the United States" that was being delegated, but "quasi-legislative" power. "If Congress shall lay down by legislative action an intelligible principle to which the person or body authorized to [make such rules] is directed to conform, such legislative action is not a forbidden delegation of legislative power"; see J. W. Hampton, Jr., & Co. v. United States (1928). In this way, through their votes and lobbying efforts, the people would have a say in what the policies would be, while their actual effectuation would be placed in the hands of technically trained career civil servants.

In theory, the Court was to police the delegations, watching to see that Congress had provided guidance clear enough that a court, viewing the administrative rules resulting from the delegation, could see that they were within the legislative policy. But in the years since the dramatic striking down of the National Industrial Recovery Act in Schechter Poultry Corp. v. United States (1935), Congress' policies have been allowed to get vaguer and vaguer and the policing function has been virtually abandoned. With a civil service of over two million persons dispensing annually billions of dollars, comprehensive surveillance has become impossible and the question of "who's in charge here?" has gradually given way to a realization that no one is or can be in charge. The Administration is just too big.

Despite this, Congress tries periodically to wrest control over certain personnel and functions from the President and earliest among these efforts was the creation of the so-called "independent regulatory commissions." These were set up to police various aspects of the economy, setting rates to be charged and insuring the fairness of business practices. They were deliberately created outside the traditional departmental structure, given authority that included both legislative and judicial, and in some cases their members were made exempt from the removal power of the president. Without any very clear explanation of how these agencies fit into the separation-of-powers picture, the Court in Humphrey's Executor v. United States (1935) upheld their creation and their independence of the President and they became known as the "headless fourth branch of government." These commissions, while enjoying independence from day-to-day supervision, are dependent upon the President for both their appointments and operating budgets. If they actively oppose the policies of the President their effectiveness can be seriously frustrated.

Another innovation by Congress was to delegate its authority to the President but retain a veto power over the result. One of the most complex and persistent problems resulting from the enormous growth of government has been that of structural organization. How, with some two million people on your staff, do you organize them so they are subject to some kind of control by the policy-making levels of the government? Since the creation of administrative agencies and the assignment of powers to them is a legislative task, Congress was under increasing pressure to undertake a comprehensive reorganization. For years presidents had been pressing for action, but each agency lived in dread of being abolished, people who did business with the agencies feared loss of influence should changes be made, and a general fear of increased presidential power resulting from increased efficiency held the matter at a standstill. Finally President Hoover, with a solid reputation as an administrator, persuaded Congress to delegate to him the authority to restructure the government and Congress agreed, reserving to itself the power to nullify any changes of which it disapproved by a vote of both houses of Congress.

The bill was signed in the closing hours of the Hoover administration and it was not until 1939, following the report of the Commission on Administrative Management, that President Franklin Roosevelt got through the first of a series of reorganization acts. While the independent commissions, and some favored agencies like the Comptroller General and the Corp of Army Engineers were not to be touched, five measures finally became law without being blocked by the veto power reserved by Congress. The "legislative veto" was peculiarly adapted to the problems of administrative reorganization with whose complexities and political ramifications Congress was ill-equipped to deal and it reappeared in the Reorganization Act of 1949 under which President Truman put into effect many of the recommendations made by the Hoover Commission for dealing with the potpourri of agencies resulting from the war. The extension of the legislative veto into other areas of legislative policy has become increasingly popular and instead of requiring a veto by both houses, Congress in some cases required a veto by only one.

The result of the legislative veto is not only to turn the law-making process end for end but to bring the Congress into an active role in administering the laws—a role for which it is ill suited and which the framers pretty clearly did not intend it to play. Under normal circumstance Congress passes a general law and leaves it to the administrative branch, under the direction of the President whose job it is to see the laws faithfully executed, to interpret and apply it to particular individuals. Administrative or judicial hearings, or sometimes both, assure that the law is properly applied. The background of the Chadha case illustrates how the turn-about took place in the field of alien deportation.

In 1924 Congress by law required the Secretary of Labor to deport any alien who was in the United States unlawfully. No discretion was given the Secretary and it was clearly the policy of Congress that no illegal alien was to remain in the country. However, an alien with political influence could get a congressman to introduce a "private bill" exempting him or her from the order. A committee of Congress, sitting as a quasi-judicial body, would decide whether the alien was deserving of exemption and if he was the bill was reported for a vote of the house involved. If it passed both houses and was signed by the President the alien could stay.

Thousands of applications for suspension were received each year and the enormous burden of this task finally prompted Congress in 1940 to authorize the Attorney General to exercise his discretion and suspend deportation in deserving cases. But Congress, unwilling to release administrative control completely, provided that the Attorney General's decision to suspend could be set aside by a vote of both houses of Congress. In 1948 this was changed to provide that both houses had to *approve* the Attorney General's suspension; but this proved as onerous as the private bill technique and in 1952 Congress provided that either house, acting alone, could veto the Attorney General's suspension. Chadha was an East Indian whose student visa had expired. Following full hearing before an immigration judge at which he demonstrated "extreme hardship" the Attorney General recommended to Congress that his deportation be suspended. A year and a half later, and one day before the congressional veto power would have expired, the resolution opposing permanent residence was brought to the House floor and voted on, debate apparently consisting of the subcommittee chairman's decision that of 340 cases, Chadha and five others "did not meet these statutory requirements, particularly as it relates to hardship."

The assertion in Justice White's dissent that nearly 200 statutes would be held invalid by the Chadha decision, even if overstated, far exceeds the total number of statutes heretofore held invalid by the Court and gives some idea of the extent to which Congress has been exchanging with the President the roles prescribed for it by the Constitution. In Alaska Airlines v. Brock (1987) the Court reaffirmed the Chadha decision and, as it had done in Chadha, held the legislative veto provision unconstitutional but severable from the rest of the statute.

Chief Justice **Burger** delivered the opinion of the Court, saying in part:

III.

A.

We turn now to the question whether action of one House of Congress under § 244(c)(2) violates strictures of the Constitution. We begin, of course, with the presumption that the challenged statute is valid. Its wisdom is not the concern of the courts; if a challenged action does not violate the Constitution it must be sustained. . . .

By the same token, the fact that a given law or procedure is efficient, convenient, and useful in facilitating functions of government, standing alone, will not save it if it is contrary to the Constitution. Convenience and efficiency are not the primary objectives—or the hallmarks—of democratic government and our inquiry is sharpened rather than blunted by the fact that Congressional veto provisions are appearing with increasing frequency in statutes which delegate authority to executive and independent agencies: "Since 1932, when the first veto provision was enacted into law, 295 congressional veto-type procedures have been inserted in 196 different statutes as follows: from 1932 to 1939, five statutes were affected; from 1940-49, nineteen statutes; between 1950-59, thirty-four statutes; and from 1960-69, forty-nine. From the year 1970 through 1975, at least one hundred sixty-three such provisions were included in eighty-nine laws." . . .

Justice White undertakes to make a case for the proposition that the one-House veto is useful "political invention," and we need not challenge that assertion. We can even concede this utilitarian argument although the long range political wisdom of this "invention" is arguable. It has been vigorously debated and it is instructive to compare the views of the protagonists. . . . But policy arguments supporting even useful "political inventions" are subject to the demands of the Constitution which defines powers and, with respect to this subject, sets out just how those powers are to be exercised.

Explicit and unambiguous provisions of the Constitution prescribe and define the respective functions of the Congress and of the Executive in the legislative process. Since the precise terms of those familiar provisions are critical to the resolution of this case, we set them out verbatim.

[The Court here prints Article I, § 1, Article I, § 7, cl.2 and Article I, § 7, cl. 3, with selected emphasis.]

These provisions of Art. I are integral parts of the constitutional design for the separation of powers. We have recently noted that "[t]he principle of separation of powers was not simply an abstract generalization in the minds of the Framers: it was woven into the documents that they drafted in Philadelphia in the summer of 1787." Buckley v. Valeo [1976]. Just as we relied on the textual provision of Art. II, § 2, cl. 2, to vindicate the principle of separation of powers in Buckley, we find that the purposes underlying the Presentment Clauses, Art. I, § 7, cls. 2, 3 and the bicameral requirement of Art. I, § 1 and § 7, cl. 2, guide our resolution of the important question presented in this case. The very structure of the articles delegating and separating powers under Arts. I, II, and III exemplify the concept of separation of powers and we now turn to Art. I.

B.

The Presentment Clauses

The records of the Constitutional Convention reveal that the requirement that all legislation be presented to the President before becoming law was uniformly accepted by the Framers. Presentment to the President and the Presidential veto were considered so imperative that the draftsmen took special pains to assure that these requirements could not be circumvented. During the final debate on Art. I, § 7, cl. 2, James Madison expressed concern that it might easily be evaded by the simple expedient of calling a proposed law a "resolution" or "vote" rather than a "bill." ... As a consequence, Art. I, § 7, cl. 3 was added.

The decision to provide the President with a limited and qualified power to nullify proposed legislation by veto was based on the profound conviction of the Framers that the powers conferred on Congress were the powers to be most carefully circumscribed. It is beyond doubt that lawmaking was a power to be shared by both Houses and the President. In The Federalist No. 73, Hamilton focused on the President's role in making laws: "If even no propensity had ever discovered itself in the legislative body to invade the rights of the Executive, the rules of just reasoning and theoretic propriety would of themselves teach us that the one ought not to be left to the mercy of the other, but ought to possess a constitutional and effectual power of self-defence." ...

The President's role in the lawmaking process also reflects the Framers' careful efforts to check whatever propensity a particular Congress might have to enact oppressive, improvident, or ill-considered measures. The President's veto role in the legislative process was described later during public debates on ratification: "It establishes a salutary check upon the legislative body, calculated to guard the community against the effects of faction, precipitancy, or of any impulse unfriendly to the public good which may happen to influence a majority of that body.... The primary inducement to conferring the power in question upon the Executive is to enable him to defend himself; the secondary one is to increase the chances in favor of the community against the passing of bad laws through haste, inadvertence, or design." The Federalist No. 73. (Hamilton).... The Court also has observed that the Presentment Clauses serve the important purpose of assuring that a "national" perspective is grafted on the legislative process: "The President is a representative of the people just as the members of the Senate and of the House are, and it may be, at some times, on some subjects, that the President elected by all the people is rather more representative of them all than are the members of either body of the Legislature whose constituencies are local and not countrywide. ... ." Myers v. United States.

C.

Bicameralism

The bicameral requirement of Art. I, §§ 1,7 was of scarcely less concern to the Framers than was the Presidential veto and indeed the two concepts are interdependent. By providing that no law could take effect without the concurrence of the prescribed majority of the Members of both Houses, the Framers reemphasized their belief, already remarked upon in connection with the Presentment Clauses, that legislation should not be enacted unless it has been carefully and fully considered by the Nation's elected officials. In the Constitutional Convention debates on the need for a bicameral legislature, James Wilson, later to become a Justice of this Court, commented: "Despotism comes on mankind in different shapes. Sometimes in an Executive, sometimes in a military, one. Is there danger of a Legislative despotism? Theory & practice both proclaim it. If the Legislative authority be not restrained, there can be neither liberty nor stability; and it can only be restrained by dividing it within itself, into distinct and independent branches. In a single house there is no check, but the inadequate one, of the virtue & good sense of those who compose it." . . .

Hamilton argued that a Congress comprised of a single House was antithetical to the very purposes of the Constitution. Were the Nation to adopt a Constitution providing for only one legislative organ, he warned: "we shall finally accumulate, in a single body, all the most important prerogatives of sovereignty, and thus entail upon our posterity one of the most execrable forms of government that human infatuation ever contrived. Thus we should create in reality that very tyranny which the adversaries of the new Constitution either are, or affect to be, solicitous to avert." The Federalist No. 22.

This view was rooted in a general skepticism regarding the fallibility of human nature later commented on by Joseph Story: "Public bodies, like private persons, are occasionally under the dominion of strong passions and excitements; impatient, irritable, and impetuous. . . . If [a legislature] feels no check but its own will, it rarely has the firmness to insist upon holding a question long enough under its own view, to see and mark it in all its bearings and relations to society." . . . These observations are consistent with what many of the Framers expressed, none more cogently than Hamilton in pointing up the need to divide and disperse power in order to protect liberty: "In republican government, the legislative authority necessarily predominates. The remedy for this inconveniency is to divide the legislature into different branches; and to render them, by different modes of election and different principles of action, as little connected with each other as the nature of their common functions and their common dependence on the society will admit." The Federalist No. 51. . . .

We see therefore that the Framers were acutely conscious that the bicameral requirement and the Presentment Clauses would serve essential constitutional functions. The President's participation in the legislative process was to protect the Executive Branch from Congress and to protect the whole people from improvident laws. The division of the Congress into two distinctive bodies assures that the legislative power would be exercised only after opportunity for full study and debate in separate settings. The President's unilateral veto power, in turn, was limited by the power of two thirds of both Houses of Congress to overrule a veto thereby precluding final arbitrary action of one person. . . . It emerges clearly that the prescription for legislative action in Art. I, §§ 1, 7 represents the Framers' decision that the legislative power of the Federal government be exercised in accord with a single, finely wrought and exhaustively considered procedure.

IV.

The Constitution sought to divide the delegated powers of the new federal government into three defined categories, Legislative, Executive and Judicial, to assure, as nearly as possible, that each Branch of government would confine itself to its assigned responsibility. The hydraulic pressure inherent within each of the separate Branches to exceed the outer limits of its power, even to accomplish desirable objectives, must be resisted.

Although not "hermetically" sealed from one another, . . . the powers delegated to the three Branches are functionally identifiable. When any Branch acts, it is presumptively exercising the power the Constitution has delegated to it. . . . When the Executive acts, it presumptively acts in an executive or administrative capacity as defined in Art. II. And when, as here, one House of Congress purports to act, it is presumptively acting within its assigned sphere.

Beginning with this presumption, we must nevertheless establish that the challenged action under § 244(c)(2) is of the kind to which the procedural requirements of Art. I, § 7 apply. Not every action taken by either House is subject to the bicameralism and presentment requirements of Art. I. Whether actions taken by either House are, in law and fact, an exercise of legislative power depends not on their form but upon "whether they contain matter which is properly to be regarded as legislative in its character and effect."

Examination of the action taken here by one House pursuant to § 244(c)(2) reveals that it was essentially legislative in purpose and effect. In purporting to exercise power defined in Art. I. § 8, cl. 4 to "establish an uniform Rule of Naturalization," the House took action that had the purpose and effect of altering the legal rights, duties and relations of persons, including the Attorney General, Executive Branch officials and Chadha, all outside the legislative branch. Section 244(c)(2) purports to authorize one House of Congress to require the Attorney General to deport an individual alien whose deportation otherwise would be cancelled under § 244. The one-House veto operated in this case to overrule the Attorney General and mandate Chadha's deportation; absent the House action, Chadha would remain in the United States. Congress has *acted* and its action has altered Chadha's status.

The legislative character of the one-House veto in this case is confirmed by the character of the Congressional action it supplants. Neither the House of Representatives nor the Senate contends that, absent the veto provision in § 244(c)(2), either of them, or both of them acting together, could effectively require the Attorney General to deport an alien once the Attorney General, in the exercise of legislatively delegated authority,* had determined the alien should remain in the United States. Without the challenged provision in § 244(c)(2), this could have been achieved, if at all, only by legislation requiring deportation. Similarly, a veto by one House of Congress under § 244(c)(2) cannot be justified as an attempt at amending the standards set out in § 244(a)(1), or as a repeal of § 244 as applied

---

*Congress protests that affirming the Court of Appeals in this case will sanction "lawmaking by the Attorney General. . . . Why is the Attorney General exempt from submitting his proposed changes in the law to the full bicameral process?" To be sure, some administrative agency action—rule making, for example—may resemble "lawmaking." . . . This Court has referred to agency activity as being "quasi-legislative" in character. Humphrey's Executor v. United States (1935). Clearly, however, "[i]n the framework of our Constitution, the President's power to see that the laws are faithfully executed refutes the idea that he is to be a lawmaker." Youngstown Sheet & Tube Co. v. Sawyer (1952). When the Attorney General performs his duties pursuant to § 244 he does not exercise "legislative" power. . . . It is clear, therefore, that the Attorney General acts in his presumptively Art. II capacity when he administers the Immigration and Nationality Act. Executive action under legislatively delegated authority that might resemble "legislative" action in some respects is not subject to the approval of both Houses of Congress and the President for the reason that the Constitution does not so require. That kind of Executive action is always subject to check by the terms of the legislation that authorized it; and if that authority is exceeded it is open to judicial review as well as the power of Congress to modify or revoke the authority entirely. A one-House veto is clearly legislative in both character and effect and is not so checked; the need for the check provided by Art. I, ss§ 1, 7 is therefore clear. Congress' authority to delegate portions of its power to administrative agencies provides no support for the argument that Congress can constitutionally control administration of the laws by way of a Congressional veto.

to Chadha. Amendment and repeal of statutes, no less than enactment, must conform with Art. I.

The nature of the decision implemented by the one-House veto in this case further manifests its legislative character. After long experience with the clumsy, time consuming private bill procedure, Congress made a deliberate choice to delegate to the Executive Branch, and specifically to the Attorney General, the authority to allow deportable aliens to remain in this country in certain specified circumstances. It is not disputed that this choice to delegate authority is precisely the kind of decision that can be implemented only in accordance with the procedures set out in Art. I. Disagreement with the Attorney General's decision on Chadha's deportation—that is, Congress' decision to deport Chadha—no less than Congress' original choice to delegate to the Attorney General the authority to make that decision, involves determinations of policy that Congress can implement in only one way; bicameral passage followed by presentment to the President. Congress must abide by its delegation of authority until that delegation is legislatively altered or revoked. . . .

. . . The bicameral requirement, the Presentment Clauses, the President's veto, and Congress' power to override a veto were intended to erect enduring checks on each Branch and to protect the people from the improvident exercise of power by mandating certain prescribed steps. To preserve those checks, and maintain the separation of powers, the carefully defined limits on the power of each Branch must not be eroded. To accomplish what has been attempted by one House of Congress in this case requires action in conformity with the express procedures of the Constitution's prescription for legislative actions: passage by a majority of both Houses and presentment to the President.

The veto authorized by § 244(c)(2) doubtless has been in many respects a convenient shortcut; the "sharing" with the Executive by Congress of its authority over aliens in this manner is, on its face, an appealing compromise. In purely practical terms, it is obviously easier for action to be taken by one House without submission to the President; but it is crystal clear from the records of the Convention, contemporaneous writings and debates, that the Framers ranked other values higher than efficiency. The records of the Convention and debates in the States preceding ratification underscore the common desire to define and limit the exercise of the newly created federal powers affecting the states and the people. There is an unmistakable expression of a determination that legislation by the national Congress be a step-by-step, deliberate and deliberative process.

Justice **Powell,** concurring in the judgment, said in part:

The Court's decision, based on the Presentment Clauses, Art. I, § 7, cl. 2 and 3, apparently will invalidate every use of the legislative veto. The breadth of this holding gives one pause. Congress has included the veto in literally hundreds of statutes, dating back to the 1930s. Congress clearly views this procedure as essential to controlling the delegation of power to administrative agencies.* One reasonably may disagree with Congress'

---

*As Justice White's dissenting opinion explains, the legislative veto has been included in a wide variety of statutes, ranging from bills for executive reorganization to the War Powers Resolution. Whether the veto complies with the Presentment Clauses may well turn on the particular context in which it is exercised, and I would be hesitant to conclude that every veto is unconstitutional on the basis of the unusual example presented by this litigation.

assessment of the veto's utility, but the respect due its judgment as a coordinate branch of Government cautions that our holding should be no more extensive than necessary to decide this case. In my view, the case may be decided on a narrower ground. When Congress finds that a particular person does not satisfy the statutory criteria for permanent residence in this country it has assumed a judicial function in violation of the principle of separation of powers. Accordingly, I concur in the judgment. . . .

I.

A. . . .

One abuse that was prevalent during the Confederation was the exercise of judicial power by the state legislatures. The Framers were well acquainted with the danger of subjecting the determination of the rights of one person to the "tyranny of shifting majorities." Jefferson observed that members of the General Assembly in his native Virginia had not been prevented from assuming judicial power, and " '[t]hey have accordingly *in many* instances *decided rights* which should have been left to *judiciary controversy.*' " . . .

It was to prevent the recurrence of such abuses that the Framers vested the executive, legislative, and judicial powers in separate branches. Their concern that a legislature should not be able unilaterally to impose a substantial deprivation on one person was expressed not only in this general allocation of power, but also in more specific provisions, such as the Bill of Attainder Clause. . . . This Clause, and the separation of powers doctrine generally, reflect the Framers' concern that trial by a legislature lacks the safeguards necessary to prevent the abuse of power. . . .

On its face, the House's action appears clearly adjudicatory. The House did not enact a general rule; rather it made its own determination that six specific persons did not comply with certain statutory criteria. It thus undertook the type of decision that traditionally has been left to other branches. Even if the House did not make a de novo determination, but simply reviewed the Immigration and Naturalization Services's findings, it still assumed a function ordinarily entrusted to the federal courts. . . .

The impropriety of the House's assumption of this function is confirmed by the fact that its action raises the very danger the Framers sought to avoid—the exercise of unchecked power. In deciding whether Chadha deserves to be deported, Congress is not subject to any internal constraints that prevent it from arbitrarily depriving him of the right to remain in this country. Unlike the judiciary or an administrative agency, Congress is not bound by established substantive rules. Nor is it subject to the procedural safeguards, such as the right to counsel and a hearing before an impartial tribunal, that are present when a court or an agency adjudicates individual rights. The only effective constraint on Congress' power is political, but Congress is most accountable politically when it prescribes rules of general applicability. When it decides rights of specific persons, those rights are subject to "the tyranny of a shifting majority."

Justice **White,** dissenting, said in part:

Today the Court not only invalidates § 244(c)(2) of the Immigration and Nationality Act, but also sounds the death knell for nearly 200 other statutory provisions in which Congress has reserved a "legislative veto." For this reason, the Court's decision is of surpassing importance. And it is for this reason that the Court would have been well-advised to decide the case, if possible, on the narrower grounds of separation of powers, leaving for full consideration the constitutionality of other congressional review statutes operating on such varied matters as war powers and agency rulemaking, some of which concern the independent regulatory agencies.

The prominence of the legislative veto mechanism in our contemporary political system and its importance to Congress can hardly be overstated. It has become a central means by which Congress secures the accountability of executive and independent agencies. Without the legislative veto, Congress is faced with a Hobson's choice: either to refrain from delegating the necessary authority, leaving itself with a hopeless task of writing laws with the requisite specificity to cover endless special circumstance across the entire policy landscape, or in the alternative, to abdicate its lawmaking function to the executive branch and independent agencies. To choose the former leaves major national problems unresolved; to opt for the latter risks unaccountable policymaking by those not elected to fill that role. Accordingly, over the past five decades, the legislative veto has been placed in nearly 200 statutes. The device is known in every field of governmental concern: reorganization, budgets, foreign affairs, war powers, and regulation of trade, safety, energy, the environment and the economy. . . .

II. . . .

If the legislative veto were as plainly unconstitutional as the Court strives to suggest, its broad ruling today would be more comprehensible. But, the constitutionality of the legislative veto is anything but clear cut. The issue divides scholars, courts, attorneys general, and the two other branches of the National Government. If the veto devices so flagrantly disregarded the requirements of Article I as the Court today suggests, I find it incomprehensible that Congress, whose members are bound by oath to uphold the Constitution, would have placed these mechanisms in nearly 200 separate laws over a period of 50 years. . . .

. . . The power to exercise a legislative veto is not the power to write new law without bicameral approval or presidential consideration. The veto must be authorized by statute and may only negate what an Executive department or independent agency has proposed. On its face, the legislative veto no more allows one House of Congress to make law than does the presidential veto confer such power upon the President. . . .

Justice **Rehnquist,** with whom Justice **White** joined, wrote a short dissenting opinion.

MORRISON v. OLSON

487 U. S. 654; 101 L. Ed. 2d 569; 108 S. Ct. 2597 (1988)

Probably the simplest and most effective control that can be exercised over government policy is to remove those who are carrying out the policy. Normally, the threat of such removal is enough to induce compliance. In a variety of ways Congress has tried to effect a form of the removal power. In 1867, in order to assure sympathetic enforcement of its reconstruction policies following the Civil War, Congress passed the Tenure of Office Act. Among other things it provided that all officers, including Secretary of War Stanton, should hold office until their successors should be confirmed by the Senate. The Act was passed over President Johnson's veto and was in effect until its repeal in 1887. It was posthumously held invalid, along with a later act providing a similar guarantee for first, second and third class postmasters, in Myers v. United States. Chief Justice Taft, who had served a term as President, wrote a 70-page opinion rejecting the right of the Senate to participate in the removal process.

Congress, however, has another ace up its sleeve. Under its authority to create an executive office, it has frequently listed qualifications which the officer must possess, and such qualifications limit the President's appointing power since they can be readily enforced through the Senate's power to refuse confirmation.

In an effort to use this technique as a form of removal power, Congress has occasionally gone further and has added qualifications to an existing office for the purpose of ousting an incumbent. In 1938 it provided by a rider to an appropriation act that no salary should be paid any reclamation commissioner who had not had ten years' experience as an engineer. The rider was aimed at a particular reclamation commissioner on the West Coast who had incurred the displeasure of certain Senators, and whose sole training as a newspaperman barred him from drawing further salary under the new law. The officer, however, continued in office without pay, and the following year Congress repealed the rider and reimbursed him.

Eventually, Congress went too far. In 1943 it provided by law that no salary should be paid to three named individuals, whom the House Committee on Un-American Activities had charged with subversion, until they were reappointed by the President and confirmed by the Senate. Although the Court refused to consider the question of the removal power of Congress, in United States v. Lovett (1946) it held the statute void as a bill of attainder. In 1931 the Senate attempted to withdraw the confirmation it had given to the appointment of a member of the Federal Power Commission—after he had assumed office. In United States v. Smith (1932) the Court, in an unusual decision, avoided any constitutional issue by holding that such a move was forbidden by the rules of the Senate.

The statute creating the office of Comptroller General provides that he shall be appointed by the President with the consent of the Senate, but that he may be removed only by impeachment or by the joint address of both houses of Congress. Under President Reagan, the nation's budget deficit reached record proportions. Congress passed the Gramm-Rudman-Hollings act as the belt-tightening first step to a new, more cost-conscious, responsible Congress. Congress, in passing the annual budget, would meet certain spending goals. If it failed, it would be forced into austerity by the Comptroller-General who would institute "automatic, across the board cuts" whenever the sum total of congressional appropriations exceeded Congress' goals. Gramm-Rudman-Hollings was Congress tying itself to the mast to avoid the sirens. In Bowsher v. Synar (1986) the Supreme Court made explicit that "Congress cannot reserve for itself the power of removal of an officer charged with the execution of the laws except by impeachment. To permit the execution of the laws to be vested in an officer answerable only to Congress would, in practical terms, reserve in Congress control over the execution of the laws." It found that the budget cutting function of the Comptroller General was executive in nature and could "see no escape from the conclusions that, because Congress had retained removal authority over the Comptroller General, he may not be entrusted with executive powers. . . . By placing the responsibility for execution of the Balanced Budget and Emergency Deficit Control Act in the hands of an officer who is subject to removal only by itself, Congress in effect has retained control over the execution of the Act and has intruded into the executive function. The Constitution does not permit such intrusion."

The present case involves the validity of the provision by Congress for "special prosecutors" to investigate alleged misdeeds by administration officials. As the inquiry into the Watergate scandal began to suggest that President Nixon might be implicated, the President fired special prosecutor Archibald Cox for refusing to drop the investigation. See the note to United States v. Nixon. It was popularly assumed that the firing was done by the President to conceal his personal involvement in the conspiracy, and it was under the threat of impeachment that the President agreed to appoint a new special prosecutor.

While the government had used special prosecutors on an ad hoc basis in the past, the dramatic spectacle of the administration using its power over the office to conceal its own misdeeds brought a widespread demand for an investigative office less subject to pressure from those it was investigating. The result was the passage of the Ethics in Government Act of 1978 which made permanent provision for the appointment of special prosecutors (independent counsels, as they were renamed in the 1982 revision of the Act).

To reduce the possible misuse of the office as in the Watergate situation and to provide the special prosecutor with a greater measure of independence, a number of provisions were included in the law. First, a Special Division of the District of Columbia Circuit Court of Appeals was created, its members chosen by the Chief Justice of the United States from among sitting federal judges, and it was this court that selected the special prosecutors and spelled out their jurisdictions. Thus, while the special prosecutor was *in* the executive branch, he or she was appointed, not by the executive, but by the judiciary. Removal was to be by the Attorney General "only for good cause," and termination was to be by the special counsel or by the Special Division at the completion of the task.

Second, the Attorney General, if he were persuaded that there was evidence warranting investigating an alleged violation of law, was required to conduct a preliminary investigation. Only if he were persuaded that "there are no reasonable grounds to believe further investigation is warranted" was he not required to request of the court the appointment of a special prosecutor.

Third, once a special prosecutor had been appointed, the Justice Department was required to suspend all further investigations of its own regarding the matter.

It was not long before the independent counsel provisions of the 1978 law produced strong reactions from both supporters and critics. The proponents, citing the Watergate investigation and the "Saturday Night Massacre," rested their argument on political grounds. How could the Justice Department and the President himself be expected vigorously and impartially to investigate and prosecute alleged wrongdoing of their own administration's executive branch officials?

Critics, on the other hand, faced with these arguments, relied on constitutional arguments. They viewed the "independence" from presidential control which was the purpose of the act as one of its most objectionable features. They argued that criminal prosecution was an exclusive and "core executive function" that cannot be shared with the judicial branch to which the law delegated the appointment of the special prosecutors, and that such delegation constituted a violation of the separation of powers doctrine. Second, opponents of the law charged that the appointment provisions of the law violated the appointments clause of Article II. Special prosecutors, they claimed, were "principal" officers of the United States and must be appointed by the president with the advice and consent of the Senate—not "inferior" officers whose appointment Congress may vest in "the President alone, the courts or department heads."

Following the law's enactment in 1978 four special prosecutors were appointed to investigate various officials of the Carter and Reagan administrations. Two of President Carter's aides, Chief of Staff Hamilton Jordan and national campaign manager Tim Kraft, were the subject of special prosecutor investigation and, with the advent of the Republican administration, Reagan's first Secretary of Labor Raymond Donovan was investigated. In none of these cases did the prosecutor recommend criminal prosecution. After special prosecutor Leon Silverman declined to prosecute Donovan on federal charges of ties to organized crime because of "insufficient credible evidence" (in Silverman's own words, the witnesses against Donovan were "inherently incredible"), Donovan was subsequently prosecuted and acquitted in New York state on similar criminal charges.

At the time that the present case reached the Supreme Court a dramatic second round of investigations, stemming in part from testimony at the Iran-Contra hearings, was in various stages of progress. Five such investigations were going on simultaneously and all those being investigated were upper echelon administrators in the Reagan administration—the only group specified by the law as eligible for such attention. Among these were the investigations of (1) former White House Deputy Chief of Staff and Assistant to the President Michael Deaver, by special prosecutor Whitney North Seymour, Jr.; (2) former White House aide Lyn Nofziger by special prosecutor James McKay; and (3) several former executive branch officials alleged to have masterminded the Iran-Contra affair, including Lt. Colonel Oliver North and former National Security Adviser John Poindexter and three others, by special prosecutor Lawrence Walsh. By the time the present case reached the Court, Deaver and Nofziger had been the first officials to be convicted of federal ethics law violations by special prosecutors under the 1978 law. North and Poindexter were later tried and convicted of conspiring to defraud the government.

Perhaps the least well-known to the public was the investigation by special prosecutor Alexia Morrison of Theodore B. Olson, Assistant Attorney General for the Office of Legal Counsel (the President's lawyer), on charges of lying to Congress during a controversy over the Environmental Protection Agency. This was the case the Supreme Court chose for review.

Chief Justice **Rehnquist** delivered the opinion of the Court, saying in part:

This case presents us with a challenge to the independent counsel provisions of the Ethics in Government Act of 1978. We hold today that these provisions of the Act do not violate the Appointments Clause of the Constitution, Art. II, § 2, cl. 2, or the limitations of

Article III, nor do they impermissibly interfere with the President's authority under Article II in violation of the constitutional principle of separation of powers. . . .

III.

The Appointments Clause of Article II reads as follows: "[The President] shall nominate, and by and with the Advice and Consent of the Senate, shall appoint Ambassadors, other public Ministers and Consuls, Judges of the supreme Court, and all other Officers of the United States, whose Appointments are not herein otherwise provided for, and which shall be established by Law: but the Congress may by Law vest the Appointment of such inferior Officers, as they think proper, in the President alone, in the Courts of Law, or in the Heads of Departments." The parties do not dispute that "[t]he Constitution for purposes of appointment . . . divides all its officers into two classes." . . . As we stated in Buckley v. Valeo (1976): "Principal officers are selected by the President with the advice and consent of the Senate. Inferior officers Congress may allow to be appointed by the President alone, by the heads of departments, or by the Judiciary." The initial question is, accordingly, whether appellant is an "inferior" or a "principal" officer. If she is the latter, as the Court of Appeals concluded, then the Act is in violation of the Appointments Clause.

The line between "inferior" and "principal" officers is one that is far from clear, and the Framers provided little guidance into where it should be drawn. . . . We need not attempt here to decide exactly where the line falls between the two types of officers, because in our view appellant clearly falls on the "inferior officer" side of that line. Several factors lead to this conclusion.

First, appellant is subject to removal by a higher Executive Branch official. Although appellant may not be "subordinate" to the Attorney General (and the President) insofar as she possesses a degree of independent discretion to exercise the powers delegated to her under the Act, the fact that she can be removed by the Attorney General indicates that she is to some degree "inferior" in rank and authority. Second, appellant is empowered by the Act to perform only certain, limited duties. An independent counsel's role is restricted primarily to investigation and, if appropriate, prosecution for certain federal crimes. Admittedly, the Act delegates to appellant "full power and independent authority to exercise all investigative and prosecutorial functions and powers of the Department of Justice," but this grant of authority does not include any authority to formulate policy for the Government or the Executive Branch, nor does it give appellant any administrative duties outside of those necessary to operate her office. The Act specifically provides that in policy matters appellant is to comply to the extent possible with the policies of the Department.

Third, appellant's office is limited in jurisdiction. Not only is the Act itself restricted in applicability to certain federal officials suspected of certain serious federal crimes, but an independent counsel can only act within the scope of the jurisdiction that has been granted by the Special Division pursuant to a request by the Attorney General. Finally, appellant's office is limited in tenure. There is concededly no time limit on the appointment of a particular counsel. Nonetheless, the office of independent counsel is "temporary" in the sense that an independent counsel is appointed essentially to accomplish a single task, and when that task is over the office is terminated, either by the counsel herself or by action of the Special Division. Unlike other prosecutors, appellant has no ongoing responsibilities that extend beyond the accomplishment of the mission that she was appointed for and authorized by the Special Division to undertake. In our view, these factors relating to the "ideas of tenure, duration . . . and duties" of the independent counsel . . . are sufficient to establish that appellant is an "inferior" officer in the constitutional sense. . . .

This does not, however, end our inquiry under the Appointments Clause. Appellees argue that even if appellant is an "inferior" officer, the Clause does not empower Congress to place the power to appoint such an officer outside the Executive Branch. They contend that the Clause does not contemplate congressional authorization of "interbranch appointments," in which an officer of one branch is appointed by officers of another branch. The relevant language of the Appointments Clause is worth repeating. It reads: " . . . but the Congress may by Law vest the Appointment of such inferior Officers, as they think proper, in the President alone, in the courts of Law, or in the Heads of Departments." On its face, the language of this "excepting clause" admits of no limitation on innerbranch appointments. Indeed, the inclusion of "as they think proper" seems clearly to give Congress significant discretion to determine whether it is "proper" to vest the appointment of, for example, executive officials in the "courts of Law." We recognized as much in one of our few decisions in this area, Ex parte Siebold, where we stated: "It is no doubt usual and proper to vest the appointment of inferior officers in that department of the government, executive or judicial, or in that particular executive department to which the duties of such officers appertain. But there is no absolute requirement to this effect in the Constitution; and, if there were, it would be difficult in many cases to determine to which department an office properly belonged. . . .

"But as the Constitution stands, the selection of the appointing power, as between the functionaries named, is a matter resting in the discretion of Congress. And, looking at the subject in a practical light, it is perhaps better that it should rest there, than that the country should be harassed by the endless controversies to which a more specific direction on this subject might have given rise." Our only decision to suggest otherwise, Ex parte Hennen (1839), from which the first sentence in the above quotation from Siebold was derived, was discussed in Siebold and distinguished as "not intended to define the constitutional power of Congress in this regard, but rather to express the law or rule by which it should be governed." Outside of these two cases, there is very little, if any, express discussion of the propriety of interbranch appointments in our decisions, and we see no reason now to depart from the holding of Siebold that such appointments are not proscribed by the excepting clause.

We also note that the history of the Clause provides no support for appellees' position. Throughout most of the process of drafting the Constitution, the Convention concentrated on the problem of who should have the authority to appoint judges. At the suggestion of James Madison, the Convention adopted a proposal that the Senate should have this authority and several attempts to transfer the appointment power to the President were rejected.

The August 6, 1787, draft of the Constitution reported by the Committee of Detail retained Senate appointment of Supreme Court Judges, provided also for Senate appointment of ambassadors, and vested in the President the authority to "appoint officers in all cases not otherwise provided for by this Constitution." This scheme was maintained until September 4, when the Committee of Eleven reported its suggestions to the Convention. This Committee suggested that the Constitution be amended to state that the President "shall nominate and by and with the advice and consent of the Senate shall appoint ambassadors, and other public Ministers, Judges of the Supreme Court, and all other Officers of the [United States], whose appointments are not otherwise herein provided for." After the addition of "Consuls" to the list, the Committee's proposal was adopted and was subsequently reported to the Convention by the Committee of Style. It was at this point, on September 15, that Gouverneur Morris moved to add the Excepting Clause to Art. II, § 2. The one comment made on this motion was by Madison, who felt that the Clause did not go far enough in that it did not allow Congress to vest appointment powers in "Superior Officers below Heads of Departments." The first vote on Morris' motion ended in a tie. It was then put forward a second time, with the urging that "some such provision [was] too necessary, to be omitted." This time the proposal was adopted. As this discussion shows, there was little or no debate on the question of whether the Clause empowers Congress to provide for interbranch appointments, and there is nothing to suggest that the Framers intended to prevent Congress from having that power.

We do not mean to say that Congress' power to provide for interbranch appointments of "inferior officers" is unlimited. In addition to separation of powers concerns, which would arise if such provisions for appointment had the potential to impair the constitutional functions assigned to one of the branches, Siebold itself suggested that Congress' decision to vest the appointment power in the courts would be improper if there was some "incongruity" between the functions normally performed by the courts and the performance of their duty to appoint. . . . In this case, however, we do not think it impermissible for Congress to vest the power to appoint independent counsel in a specially created federal court. We thus disagree with the Court of Appeals' conclusion that there is an inherent incongruity about a court having the power to appoint prosecutorial officers.† We have recognized that courts may appoint private attorneys to act as prosecutor for judicial contempt judgments. . . . In Go-Bart Importing Co. v. United States (1931), we approved court appointment of United States commissioners, who exercised certain limited prosecutorial powers. In Siebold, as well, we indicated that judicial appointment of federal marshals, who are "executive officer[s]," would not be inappropriate. . . . Congress of course was concerned when it created the office of independent counsel with the conflicts of interest that could arise in situations when the Executive Branch is called upon to investigate its own high-ranking officers. If it were to remove the appointing authority from the Executive Branch, the most logical place to put it was in the Judicial Branch. In the light of the Act's provision making the judges of the Special Division ineligible to participate in any matters relating to an independent counsel they have appointed, we do not think that

---

†Indeed, in light of judicial experience with prosecutors in criminal cases, it could be said that courts are especially well qualified to appoint prosecutors. This is not a case in which judges are given power to appoint an officer in an area in which they have no special knowledge or expertise, as in, for example, a statute authorizing the courts to appoint officials in the Department of Agriculture or the Federal Energy Regulatory Commission.

appointment of the independent counsel by the court runs afoul of the constitutional limitation on ''incongruous'' interbranch appointments.

IV.

Appellees next contend that the powers vested in the Special Division by the Act conflict with Article III of the Constitution. We have long recognized that by the express provision of Article III, the judicial power of the United States is limited to ''Cases'' and ''Controversies.'' See Muskrat v. United States (1911). As a general rule, we have broadly stated that ''executive or administrative duties of a nonjudicial nature may not be imposed on judges holding office under Art. III of the Constitution.'' Buckley, (citing United States v. Ferreira (1852); Hayburn's Case (1792)). The purpose of this limitation is to help ensure the independence of the Judicial Branch and to prevent the judiciary from encroaching into areas reserved for the other branches. . . . With this in mind, we address in turn the various duties given to the Special Division by the Act.

Most importantly, the Act vests in the Special Division the power to choose who will serve as independent counsel and the power to define his or her jurisdiction. Clearly, once it is accepted that the Appointments Clause gives Congress the power to vest the appointment of officials such as the independent counsel in the ''courts of Law,'' there can be no Article III objection to the Special Division's exercise of that power, as the power itself derives from the Appointments Clause, a source of authority for judicial action that is independent of Article III.† Appellees contend, however, that the Division's Appointments Clause powers do not encompass the power to define the independent counsel's jurisdiction. We disagree. In our view, Congress' power under the Clause to vest the ''Appointment'' of inferior officers in the courts may, in certain circumstances, allow Congress to give the courts some discretion in defining the nature and scope of the appointed official's authority. Particularly when, as here, Congress creates a temporary ''office'' the nature and duties of which will by necessity vary with the factual circumstances giving rise to the need for an appointment in the first place, it may vest the power to define the scope of the office in the court as an incident to the appointment of the officer pursuant to the Appointments Clause. This said, we do not think that Congress may give the Division *unlimited* discretion to determine the independent counsel's jurisdiction. In order for the Division's definition of the counsel's jurisdiction to be truly ''incidental'' to its power to appoint, the jurisdiction that the court decides upon must be demonstrably related to the factual circumstances that gave rise to the Attorney General's investigation and request for the appointment of the independent counsel in the particular case.

The Act also vests in the Special Division various powers and duties in relation to the independent counsel that, because they do not involve appointing the counsel or defining his

---

†We do not think that judicial exercise of the power to appoint, per se, is in any way inconsistent as a functional matter with the courts' exercise of their Article III powers. We note that courts have long participated in the appointment of court officials such as United States commissioners or magistrates . . . without disruption of normal judicial functions. And certainly the court in Ex parte Hennen (1839) deemed it entirely appropriate that a court should have the authority to appoint its own clerk.

or her jurisdiction, cannot be said to derive from the Division's Appointments Clause authority. These duties include granting extensions for the Attorney General's preliminary investigation; receiving the report of the Attorney General at the conclusion of his preliminary investigation; referring matters to the counsel upon request; receiving reports from the counsel regarding expenses incurred; receiving a report from the Attorney General following the removal of an independent counsel; granting attorney's fees upon request to individuals who were investigated but not indicted by an independent counsel; receiving a final report from the counsel; deciding whether to release the counsel's final report to Congress or the public and determining whether any protective orders should be issued; and terminating an independent counsel when his or her task is completed.

Leaving aside for the moment the Division's power to terminate an independent counsel, we do not think that Article III absolutely prevents Congress from vesting these other miscellaneous powers in the Special Division pursuant to the Act. . . .

We are more doubtful about the Special Division's power to terminate the office of the independent counsel. . . . As appellees suggest, the power to terminate, especially when exercised by the Division on its own motion, is "administrative" to the extent that it requires the Special Division to monitor the progress of proceedings of the independent counsel and come to a decision as to whether the counsel's job is "completed." It also is not a power that could be considered typically "judicial," as it has few analogues among the court's more traditional powers. Nonetheless, we do not, as did the Court of Appeals, view this provision as a significant judicial encroachment upon executive power or upon the prosecutorial discretion of the independent counsel.

We think that the Court of Appeals overstated the matter when it described the power to terminate as a "broadsword and . . . rapier" that enables the court to "control the pace and depth of the independent counsel's activities." The provision has not been tested in practice, and we do not mean to say that an adventurous special court could not reasonably construe the provision as did the Court of Appeals; but it is the duty of federal courts to construe a statute in order to save it from constitutional infirmities, . . . and to that end we think a narrow construction is appropriate here. The termination provisions of the Act do not give the Special Division anything approaching the power to *remove* the counsel while an investigation or court proceeding is still underway—this power is vested solely in the Attorney General. As we see it, "termination" may occur only when the duties of the counsel are truly "completed" or "so substantially completed" that there remains no need for any continuing action by the independent counsel. It is basically a device for removing from the public payroll an independent counsel who has served his or her purpose, but is unwilling to acknowledge the fact. So construed, the Special Division's power to terminate does not pose a sufficient threat of judicial intrusion into matters that are more properly within the Executive's authority to require that the Act be invalidated as inconsistent with Article III.

Nor do we believe, as appellees contend, that the Special Division's exercise of the various powers specifically granted to it under the Act poses any threat to the "impartial and independent federal adjudication of claims within the judicial power of the United States." . . . We reach this conclusion for two reasons. First, the Act as it currently stands gives the Special Division itself no power to review any of the actions of the independent counsel or any of the actions of the Attorney General with regard to the counsel. Accordingly, there is no risk of partisan or biased adjudication of claims regarding the independent counsel by that court. Second, the Act prevents members of the Special Division from participating in "*any* judicial proceeding concerning a matter which involves such independent counsel while such independent counsel is serving in that office or which involves the exercise of such independent counsel's official duties, regardless of whether such independent counsel is still serving in that office." ... We think both the special court and its judges are sufficiently isolated by these statutory provisions from the review of the activities of the independent counsel so as to avoid any taint of the independence of the judiciary such as would render the Act invalid under Article III.

We emphasize, nevertheless, that the Special Division has *no* authority to take any action or undertake any duties that are not specifically authorized by the Act. The gradual expansion of the authority of the Special Division might in another context be a bureaucratic success story, but it would be one that would have serious constitutional ramifications. The record in other cases involving independent counsels indicate [sic] that the Special Division has at times given advisory opinions or issued orders that are not directly authorized by the Act. Two examples of this were cited by the Court of Appeals, which noted that the Special Division issued "orders" that ostensibly exempted the independent counsel from conflict of interest laws. In another case, the Division reportedly ordered that a counsel postpone an investigation into certain allegations until the completion of related state criminal proceedings. The propriety of the Special Division's actions in these instances is not before us as such, but we nonetheless think it appropriate to point out not only that there is no authorization for such actions in the Act itself, but that the division's exercise of unauthorized powers risks the transgression of the constitutional limitations of Article III that we have just discussed.

V.

We now turn to consider whether the Act is invalid under the constitutional principle of separation of powers. Two related issues must be addressed: The first is whether the provision of the Act restricting the Attorney General's power to remove the independent counsel to only those instances in which he can show "good cause," taken by itself, impermissibly interferes with the President's exercise of his constitutionally appointed functions. The second is whether, taken as a whole, the Act violates the separation of powers by reducing the President's ability to control the prosecutorial powers wielded by the independent counsel.

A.

Two Terms ago we had occasion to consider whether it was consistent with the separation of powers for Congress to pass a statute that authorized a Government official who is removable only by Congress to participate in what we found to be "executive powers." Bowsher v. Synar (1986). We held in Bowsher that "Congress cannot reserve for itself the power of removal of an officer charged with the execution of the laws except by impeachment." A primary antecedent for this ruling was our 1926 decision in Myers v. United States.

Myers had considered the propriety of a federal statute by which certain postmasters of the United States could be removed by the President only "by and with the advice and consent of the Senate." There too, Congress' attempt to involve itself in the removal of an executive official was found to be sufficient grounds to render the statute invalid. As we observed in Bowsher, the essence of the decision in Myers was the judgment that the Constitution prevents Congress from "draw[ing] to itself . . . the power to remove or the right to participate in the exercise of that power. To do this would be to go beyond the words and implications of the [Appointments Clause] and to infringe the constitutional principle of the separation of governmental powers."

Unlike both Bowsher and Myers, this case does not involve an attempt by Congress itself to gain a role in the removal of executive officials other than its established powers of impeachment and conviction. The Act instead puts the removal power squarely in the hands of the Executive Branch; an independent counsel may be removed from office, "only by the personal action of the Attorney General, and only for good cause." There is no requirement of congressional approval of the Attorney General's removal decision, though the decision is subject to judicial review. In our view, the removal provisions of the Act make this case more analogous to Humphrey's Executor v. United States (1935) and Wiener v. United States (1958) than to Myers or Bowsher.

In Humphrey's Executor, the issue was whether a statute restricting the President's power to remove the commissioners of the Federal Trade Commission only for "inefficiency, neglect of duty, or malfeasance in office" was consistent with the Constitution. We stated that whether Congress can "condition the [President's power of removal] by fixing a definite term and precluding a removal except for cause, will depend upon the character of the office." Contrary to the implication of some dicta in Myers, the President's power to remove Government officials simply was not "all-inclusive in respect of civil officers with the exception of the judiciary provided for by the Constitution." At least in regard to "quasi-legislative" and "quasi-judicial" agencies such as the FTC, "[t]he authority of Congress, in creating [such] agencies, to require them to act in discharge of their duties independently of executive control . . . includes, as an appropriate incident, power to fix the period during which they shall continue in office, and to forbid their removal except for cause in the meantime." In Humphrey's Executor, we found it "plain" that the Constitution did not give the President "illimitable power of removal" over the officers of independent agencies. Were the President to have the power to remove FTC commissioners at will, the "coercive influence" of the removal power would "threate[n] the independence of [the] commission."

Similarly, in Wiener we considered whether the President had unfettered discretion to remove a member of the War Claims Commission, which had been established by Congress in the War Claims Act of 1948. The Commission's function was to receive and adjudicate certain claims for compensation from those who had suffered personal injury or property damage at the hands of the enemy during World War II. Commissioners were appointed by the President, with the advice and consent of the Senate, but the statute made no provision for the removal of officers, perhaps because the Commission itself was to have a limited existence. As in Humphrey's Executor, however, the Commissioners were entrusted by Congress with adjudicatory powers that were to be exercised free from executive control. In this context, "Congress did not wish to have hang over the Commission the Damocles' sword of removal by the President for no reason other than that he preferred to have on that Commission men of his own choosing." Accordingly, we rejected the President's attempt to remove a Commissioner "merely because he wanted his own appointees on [the] Commission," stating that "no such power is given to the President directly by the Constitution, and none is impliedly conferred upon him by statute."

Appellees contend that Humphrey's Executor and Wiener are distinguishable from this case because they did not involve officials who performed a "core executive function." They argue that our decision in Humphrey's Executor rests on a distinction between "purely executive" officials and officials who exercise "quasi-legislative" and "quasi-judicial" powers. In their view, when a "purely executive" official is involved, the governing precedent is Myers, not Humphrey's Executor. And, under Myers, the President must have absolute discretion to discharge "purely" executive officials at will.

We undoubtedly did rely on the terms "quasi-legislative" and "quasi-judicial" to distinguish the officials involved in Humphrey's Executor and Wiener from those in Myers, but our present considered view is that the determination of whether the Constitution allows Congress to impose a "good cause"-type restriction on the President's power to remove an official cannot be made to turn on whether or not that official is classified as "purely executive."† The analysis contained in our removal cases is designed not to define rigid categories of those officials who may or may not be removed at will by the President, but to ensure that Congress does not interfere with the President's exercise of the "executive power" and his constitutionally appointed duty to "take care that the laws be faithfully executed" under Article II. Myers was undoubtedly correct in its holding, and in its broader suggestion that there are some "purely executive" officials who must be removable by the President at will if he is to be able to accomplish his constitutional role. But as the Court noted in Wiener:

"The assumption was short-lived that the Myers case recognized the President's inherent constitutional power to remove officials no matter what the relation of the executive to the discharge of their duties and no matter what restrictions Congress may have imposed regarding the nature of their tenure." At the other end of the spectrum from Myers, the characterization of the agencies in Humphrey's Executor and Wiener as "quasi-legislative" or "quasi-judicial" in large part reflected our judgment that it was not essential to the President's proper execution of his Article II powers that these agencies be headed up by individuals who were removable at will. We do not mean to suggest that an analysis of the functions served by the officials at issue is irrelevant. But the real question is whether the removal restrictions are of such a nature that they impede the President's ability to perform his constitutional duty, and the functions of the officials in question must be analyzed in that light.

Considering for the moment the "good cause" removal provision in isolation from the other parts of the Act at issue in this case, we cannot say that the imposition of a "good

---

†Indeed, this Court has never held that the Constitution prevents Congress from imposing limitations on the President's power to remove all executive officials simply because they wield "executive" power. Myers itself expressly distinguished cases in which Congress had chosen to vest the appointment of "inferior" executive officials in the head of a department. In such a situation, we saw no specific constitutional impediment to congressionally imposed restrictions on the President's removal powers. See also United States v. Perkins (1886) (" 'The constitutional authority in Congress to thus vest the appointment [of inferior officers in the heads of departments] implies authority to limit, restrict, and regulate the removal by such laws as Congress may enact in relation to the officers so appointed' ") (quoting the Court of Claims' decision in the case).

cause'' standard for removal by itself unduly trammels on executive authority. There is no real dispute that the functions performed by the independent counsel are ''executive'' in the sense that they are law enforcement functions that typically have been undertaken by officials within the Executive Branch. As we noted above, however, the independent counsel is an inferior officer under the Appointments Clause, with limited jurisdiction and tenure and lacking policymaking or significant administrative authority. Although the counsel exercises no small amount of discretion and judgment in deciding how to carry out his or her duties under the Act, we simply do not see how the President's need to control the exercise of that discretion is so central to the functioning of the Executive Branch as to require as a matter of constitutional law that the counsel be terminable at will by the President.

Nor do we think that the ''good cause'' removal provision at issue here impermissibly burdens the President's power to control or supervise the independent counsel, as an executive official, in the execution of his or her duties under the Act. This is not a case in which the power to remove an executive official has been completely stripped from the President, thus providing no means for the President to ensure the ''faithful execution'' of the laws. Rather, because the independent counsel may be terminated for ''good cause,'' the Executive, through the Attorney General, retains ample authority to assure that the counsel is competently performing his or her statutory responsibilities in a manner that comports with the provisions of the Act. Although we need not decide in this case exactly what is encompassed within the term ''good cause'' under the Act, the legislative history of the removal provision also makes clear that the Attorney General may remove an independent counsel for ''misconduct.'' Here, as with the provision of the Act conferring the appointment authority of the independent counsel on the special court, the congressional determination to limit the removal power of the Attorney General was essential, in the view of Congress, to establish the necessary independence of the office. We do not think that this limitation as it presently stands sufficiently deprives the President of control over the independent counsel to interfere impermissibly with his constitutional obligation to ensure the faithful execution of the laws.†

B.

The final question to be addressed is whether the Act, taken as a whole, violates the principle of separation of powers by unduly interfering with the role of the Executive Branch. Time and again we have reaffirmed the importance in our constitutional scheme of the separation of governmental powers into the three coordinate branches. . . . As we stated in Buckley v. Valeo (1976), the system of separated powers and checks and balances established in the Constitution was regarded by the Framers as ''a self-executing safeguard against the encroachment or aggrandizement of one branch at the expense of the other.'' We have not hesitated to invalidate provisions of law which violate this principle. On the other hand, we have never held that the Constitution requires that the three Branches of Govern-

---

†We see no constitutional problem in the fact that the Act provides for judicial review of the removal decision. The purpose of such review is to ensure that an independent counsel is removed only in accordance with the will of Congress as expressed in the Act. The possibility of judicial review does not inject the Judicial Branch into the removal decision, nor does it, by itself, put any additional burden on the President's exercise of executive authority. . . .

ment "operate with absolute independence." . . . In the often-quoted words of Justice Jackson: "While the Constitution diffuses power the better to secure liberty, it also contemplates that practice will integrate the dispersed powers into a workable government. It enjoins upon its branches separateness but interdependence, autonomy but reciprocity." Youngstown Sheet & Tube Co. v. Sawyer (1952) (concurring opinion).

We observe first that this case does not involve an attempt by Congress to increase its own powers at the expense of the Executive Branch. . . . Unlike some of our previous cases, most recently Bowsher v. Synar, this case simply does not pose a "dange[r] of congressional usurpation of Executive Branch functions." Indeed, with the exception of the power of impeachment—which applies to all officers of the United States—Congress retained for itself no powers of control or supervision over an independent counsel. The Act does empower certain Members of Congress to request the Attorney General to apply for the appointment of an independent counsel, but the Attorney General has no duty to comply with the request, although he must respond within a certain time limit. Other than that, Congress' role under the Act is limited to receiving reports or other information and oversight of the independent counsel's activities, functions that we have recognized generally as being incidental to the legislative function of Congress. See McGrain v. Daugherty (1927).

Similarly, we do not think that the Act works any *judicial* usurpation of properly executive functions. As should be apparent from our discussion of the Appointments Clause above, the power to appoint inferior officers such as independent counsel is not in itself an "executive" function in the constitutional sense, at least when Congress has exercised its power to vest the appointment of an inferior office in the "courts of Law." We note nonetheless that under the Act the Special Division has no power to appoint an independent counsel sua sponte; it may only do so upon the specific request of the Attorney General, and the courts are specifically prevented from reviewing the Attorney General's decision not to seek appointment. In addition, once the court has appointed a counsel and defined his or her jurisdiction, it has no power to supervise or control the activities of the counsel. As we pointed out in our discussion of the Special Division in relation to Article III, the various powers delegated by the statute to the Division are not supervisory or administrative, nor are they functions that the Constitution requires be performed by officials within the Executive Branch. The Act does give a federal court the power to review the Attorney General's decision to remove an independent counsel, but in our view this is a function that is well within the traditional power of the judiciary.

Finally, we do not think that the Act "impermissibly undermine[s]" the powers of the Executive Branch or "disrupts the proper balance between the coordinate branches [by] prevent[ing] the Executive Branch from accomplishing its constitutionally assigned functions." . . . It is undeniable that the Act reduces the amount of control or supervision that the Attorney General and, through him, the President exercises over the investigation and prosecution of a certain class of alleged criminal activity. The Attorney General is not allowed to appoint the individual of his choice; he does not determine the counsel's jurisdiction; and his power to remove a counsel is limited. Nonetheless, the Act does give the Attorney General several means of supervising or controlling the prosecutorial powers that may be wielded by an independent counsel. Most importantly, the Attorney General retains the power to remove the counsel for "good cause," a power that we have already concluded provides the Executive with substantial ability to ensure that the laws are "faithfully executed'' by an independent counsel. No independent counsel may be appointed without a specific request by the Attorney General, and the Attorney General's decision not to request appointment if he finds ''no reasonable grounds to believe that further investigation is warranted'' is committed to his unreviewable discretion. The Act thus gives the Executive a degree of control over the power to initiate an investigation by the independent counsel. In addition, the jurisdiction of the independent counsel is defined with reference to the facts submitted by the Attorney General, and once a counsel is appointed, the Act requires that the counsel abide by Justice Department policy unless it is not ''possible'' to do so. Notwithstanding the fact that the counsel is to some degree ''independent'' and free from Executive supervision to a greater extent than other federal prosecutors, in our view these features of the Act give the Executive Branch sufficient control over the independent counsel to ensure that the President is able to perform his constitutionally assigned duties. . . .

Justice **Kennedy** took no part in the consideration or decision of this case.

Justice **Scalia** dissenting, said in part:

I.

The present case began when the Legislative and Executive Branches became ''embroiled in a dispute concerning the scope of the congressional investigatory power,'' which—as is often the case with such interbranch conflicts—became quite acrimonious. In the course of oversight hearings into the administration of the Superfund by the Environmental Protection Agency (EPA), two subcommittees of the House of Representatives requested and then subpoenaed numerous internal EPA documents. The President responded by personally directing the EPA Administrator not to turn over certain of the documents, and by having the Attorney General notify the congressional subcommittees of this assertion of executive privilege. In his decision to assert executive privilege, the President was counseled by appellee Olson, who was then Assistant Attorney General of the Department of Justice for the Office of Legal Counsel, a post that has traditionally had responsibility for providing legal advice to the President (subject to approval of the Attorney General). The House's response was to pass a resolution citing the EPA Administrator, who had possession of the documents, for contempt. Contempt of Congress is a criminal offense. The United States Attorney, however, a member of the Executive Branch, initially took no steps to prosecute the contempt citation. Instead, the Executive Branch sought the immediate assistance of the Third Branch by filing a civil action asking the District Court to declare that the EPA Administrator had acted lawfully in withholding the documents under a claim of executive privilege. The District Court declined (in my view correctly) to get involved in the controversy, and urged the other two Branches to try ''[c]ompromise and cooperation, rather than confrontation.'' After further haggling, the two Branches eventually reached an agreement giving the House Subcommittees limited access to the contested documents.

Congress did not, however, leave things there. Certain Members of the House remained angered by the confrontation, particularly by the role played by the Department of Justice. Specifically, the Committee remained disturbed by the possibility that the Department had persuaded the President to assert executive privilege despite reservations by the

EPA; that the Department had "deliberately and unnecessarily precipitated a constitutional confrontation with Congress"; that the Department had not properly reviewed and selected the documents as to which executive privilege was asserted; that the Department had directed the United States Attorney not to present the contempt certification involving the EPA Administrator to a grand jury for prosecution; that the Department had made the decision to sue the House of Representatives; and that the Department had not adequately advised and represented the President, the EPA and the EPA Administrator. Accordingly, staff counsel of the House Judiciary Committee were commissioned (apparently without the knowledge of many of the Committee's Members) to investigate the Justice Department's role in the controversy. That investigation lasted $2\frac{1}{2}$ years, and produced a 3,000-page report issued by the Committee over the vigorous dissent of all but one of its minority-party members. That report, which among other charges questioned the truthfulness of certain statements made by Assistant Attorney General Olson during testimony in front of the Committee during the early stages of its investigation, was sent to the Attorney General along with a formal request that he appoint an independent counsel to investigate Mr. Olson and others.

As a general matter, the Act before us here requires the Attorney General to apply for the appointment of an independent counsel within 90 days after receiving a request to do so, unless he determines within that period that "there are no reasonable grounds to believe that further investigation or prosecution is warranted." As a practical matter, it would be surprising if the Attorney General had any choice (assuming this statute is constitutional) but to seek appointment of an independent counsel to pursue the charges against the principal object of the congressional request, Mr. Olson. Merely the political consequences (to him and the President) of seeming to break the law by refusing to do so would have been substantial. How could it not be, the public would ask, that a 3,000-page indictment drawn by our representatives over $2\frac{1}{2}$ years does not even establish "reasonable grounds to believe" that further investigation or prosecution is warranted with respect to at least the principal alleged culprit? But the Act establishes more than just practical compulsion. Although the Court's opinion asserts that the Attorney General had "no duty to comply with the [congressional] request," that is not entirely accurate. He *had* a duty to comply unless he could conclude that there were "*no reasonable grounds to believe*," not that prosecution was warranted, but merely that "*further investigation*" was warranted, (emphasis added), after a 90-day investigation in which he was prohibited from using such routine investigative techniques as grand juries, plea bargaining, grants of immunity or even subpoenas. The Court also makes much of the fact that "the courts are specifically prevented from reviewing the Attorney General's decision not to seek appointment." Yes, but *Congress* is not prevented from reviewing it. The context of this statute is acrid with the smell of threatened impeachment. Where, as here, a request for appointment of an independent counsel has come from the Judiciary Committee of either House of Congress, the Attorney General must, if he decides not to seek appointment, explain to that Committee why.

Thus, by the application of this statute in the present case, Congress has effectively compelled a criminal investigation of a high-level appointee of the President in connection with his actions arising out of a bitter power dispute between the President and the Legislative Branch. Mr. Olson may or may not be guilty of a crime; we do not know. But we do know that the investigation of him has been commenced, not necessarily because the President or his authorized subordinates believe it is in the interest of the United States, in the sense that it warrants the diversion of resources from other efforts, and is worth the cost in money and in possible damage to other governmental interests; and not even, leaving aside those normally considered factors, because the President or his authorized subordinates necessarily believe that an investigation is likely to unearth a violation worth prosecuting; but only because the Attorney General cannot affirm, as Congress demands, that there are *no reasonable grounds to believe* that further investigation is warranted. The decisions regarding the scope of that further investigation, its duration, and, finally, whether or not prosecution should ensue, are likewise beyond the control of the President and his subordinates.

II.

If to describe this case is not to decide it, the concept of a government of separate and coordinate powers no longer has meaning. The Court devotes most of its attention to such relatively technical details as the Appointments Clause and the removal power, addressing briefly and only at the end of its opinion the separation of powers. As my prologue suggests, I think that has it backwards. Our opinions are full of the recognition that it is the principle of separation of powers, and the inseparable corollary that each department's "defense must . . . be made commensurate to the danger of attack, . . ." which gives comprehensible content to the Appointments Clause, and determines the appropriate scope of the removal power. Thus, while I will subsequently discuss why our appointments and removal jurisprudence does not support today's holding, I begin with a consideration of the fountainhead of that jurisprudence, the separation and equilibration of powers. . . .

. . . Article II, § 1, cl. 1, of the Constitution provides:

"The executive Power shall be vested in a President of the United States."

As I described at the outset of this opinion, this does not mean *some of* the executive power, but *all of* the executive power. It seems to me, therefore, that the decision of the Court of Appeals invalidating the present statute must be upheld on fundamental separation-of-powers principles if the following two questions are answered affirmatively: (1) Is the conduct of a criminal prosecution (and of an investigation to decide whether to prosecute) the exercise of purely executive power? (2) Does the statute deprive the President of the United States of exclusive control over the exercise of that power? Surprising to say, the Court appears to concede an affirmative answer to both questions, but seeks to avoid the inevitable conclusion that since the statute vests some purely executive power in a person who is not the President of the United States it is void.

The Court concedes that "[t]here is no real dispute that the functions performed by the independent counsel are 'executive'." . . . She is vested with the "full power and independent authority to exercise all *investigative and prosecutorial* functions and powers of the Department of Justice [and] the Attorney General." (emphasis added). Governmental investigation and prosecution of crimes is a quintessentially executive function. See . . . Buckley v. Valeo (1976); United States v. Nixon (1974).

As for the second question, whether the statute before us deprives the President of exclusive control over that quintessentially executive activity: The Court does not, and could not possibly, assert that it does not. That is indeed the whole object of the statute. Instead, the Court points out that the President, through his Attorney General, has at least *some* control. That concession is alone enough to invalidate the statute, but I cannot refrain from pointing out that the Court greatly exaggerates the extent of that "some" Presidential control. "Most importan[t]" among these controls, the Court asserts, is the Attorney General's "power to remove the counsel for 'good cause.' " This is somewhat like referring to shackles as an effective means of locomotion. As we recognized in Humphrey's Executor v. United States (1935)—indeed, what Humphrey's Executor was all about—limiting removal power to "good cause" is an impediment to, not an effective grant of, Presidential control. We said that limitation was necessary with respect to members of the Federal Trade Commission, which we found to be "an agency of the legislative and judicial departments," and "wholly disconnected from the executive department," because "it is quite evident that one who holds his office only during the pleasure of another, cannot be depended upon to maintain an attitude of independence against the latter's will." What we in Humphrey's Executor found to be a means of eliminating Presidential control, the Court today considers the "most importan[t]" means of assuring Presidential control. Congress, of course, operated under no such illusion when it enacted this statute, describing the "good cause" limitation as "protecting the independent counsel's ability to act independently of the President's direct control" since it permits removal only for "misconduct." . . .

V.

The purpose of the separation and equilibration of powers in general, and of the unitary Executive in particular, was not merely to assure effective government but to preserve individual freedom. Those who hold or have held offices covered by the Ethics in Government Act are entitled to that protection as much as the rest of us, and I conclude my discussion by considering the effect of the Act upon the fairness of the process they receive. Only someone who has worked in the field of law enforcement can fully appreciate the vast power and the immense discretion that are placed in the hands of a prosecutor with respect to the objects of his investigation. Justice Robert Jackson, when he was Attorney General under President Franklin Roosevelt, described it in a memorable speech to United States Attorneys, as follows:

"There is a most important reason why the prosecutor should have, as nearly as possible, a detached and impartial view of all groups in his community. Law enforcement is not automatic. It isn't blind. One of the greatest difficulties of the position of prosecutor is that he must pick his cases, because no prosecutor can even investigate all of the cases in which he receives complaints. If the Department of Justice were to make even a pretense of reaching every probable violation of federal law, ten times its present staff will be inadequate. We know that no local police force can strictly enforce the traffic laws, or it would arrest half the driving population on any given morning. What every prosecutor is practically required to do is to select the cases for prosecution and to select those in which the offense is the most flagrant, the public harm the greatest, and the proof the most certain.

"If the prosecutor is obliged to choose his case, it follows that he can choose his defendants. Therein is the most dangerous power of the prosecutor: that he will pick people that he thinks he should get, rather than cases that need to be prosecuted. With the law books filled with a great assortment of crimes, a prosecutor stands a fair chance of finding at least a technical violation of some act on the part of almost anyone. In such a case, it is not a question of discovering the commission of a crime and then looking for the man who has committed it, it is a question of picking the man and then searching the law books, or putting investigators to work, to pin some offense on him. It is in this realm—in which the prosecutor picks some person whom he dislikes or desires to embarrass, or selects some group of unpopular persons and then looks for an offense, that the greatest danger of abuse of prosecuting power lies. It is here that law enforcement becomes personal, and the real crime becomes that of being unpopular with the predominant or governing group, being attached to the wrong political views, or being personally obnoxious to or in the way of the prosecutor himself.''

Under our system of government, the primary check against prosecutorial abuse is a political one. The prosecutors who exercise this awesome discretion are selected and can be removed by a President, whom the people have trusted enough to elect. Moreover, when crimes are not investigated and prosecuted fairly, nonselectively, with a reasonable sense of proportion, the President pays the cost in political damage to his administration. If federal prosecutors ''pick people that [they] thin[k] [they] should get, rather than cases that need to be prosecuted,'' if they amass many more resources against a particular prominent individual, or against a particular class of political protesters, or against members of a particular political party, than the gravity of the alleged offenses or the record of successful prosecutions seems to warrant, the unfairness will come home to roost in the Oval Office. I leave it to the reader to recall the examples of this in recent years. That result, of course, was precisely what the Founders had in mind when they provided that all executive powers would be exercised by a *single* Chief Executive. As Hamilton put it, ''[t]he ingredients which constitute safety in the republican sense are a due dependence on the people, and a due responsibility.'' . . . The President is directly dependent on the people, and since there is only *one* President, *he* is responsible. The people know whom to blame, whereas ''one of the weightiest objections to a plurality in the executive . . . is that it tends to conceal faults and destroy responsibility.''

That is the system of justice the rest of us are entitled to, but what of that select class consisting of present or former high-level Executive-Branch officials? If an allegation is made against them of any violation of any federal criminal law (except Class B or C misdemeanors or infractions) the Attorney General must give it his attention. That in itself is not objectionable. But if, after a 90-day investigation without the benefit of normal investigatory tools, the Attorney General is unable to say that there are ''no reasonable grounds to believe'' that further investigation is warranted, a process is set in motion that is *not* in the full control of persons ''dependent on the people,'' and whose flaws cannot be blamed on the President. An independent counsel is selected, and the scope of his or her authority prescribed, by a panel of judges. What if they are politically partisan, as judges have been known to be, and select a prosecutor antagonistic to the administration, or even to the particular individual who has been selected for this special treatment? There is no remedy for that, not even a political one. Judges, after all, have life tenure, and appointing a surefire enthusiastic prosecutor could hardly be considered an impeachable offense. So if there is anything wrong with the selection, there is effectively no one to blame. The independent counsel thus selected proceeds to assemble a staff. As I observed earlier, in the nature of things this has to be done by finding lawyers who are willing to lay aside their current careers for an indeterminate amount of time, to take on a job that has no prospect of permanence and little prospect for promotion. One thing is certain, however: it involves investigating and perhaps prosecuting a particular individual. Can one imagine a less equitable manner of fulfilling the Executive responsibility to investigate and prosecute? What would be the reaction if, in an area not covered by this statute, the Justice Department posted a public notice inviting applicants to assist in an investigation and possible prosecution of a certain prominent person? Does this not invite what Justice Jackson described as "picking the man and then searching the law books, or putting investigators to work, to pin some offense on him"? To be sure, the investigation must relate to the area of criminal offense specified by the life-tenured judges. But that has often been (and nothing prevents it from being) very broad—and should the independent counsel or his or her staff come up with something beyond that scope, nothing prevents him or her from asking the judges to expand his or her authority or, if that does not work, referring it to the Attorney General, whereupon the whole process would recommence and, if there [were] "reasonable basis to believe" that further investigation was warranted, that new offense would be referred to the Special Division, which would in all likelihood assign it to the same independent counsel. It seems to me not conducive to fairness. But even if it were entirely evident that unfairness was in fact the result—the judges hostile to the administration, the independent counsel an old foe of the President, the staff refugees from the recently defeated administration—*there would be no one accountable to the public to whom the blame could be assigned.*

I do not mean to suggest that anything of this sort (other than the inevitable self-selection of the prosecutory staff) occurred in the present case. I know and have the highest regard for the judges on the Special Division, and the independent counsel herself is a woman of accomplishment, impartiality and integrity. But the fairness of a process must be adjudged on the basis of what it permits to happen, not what it produced in a particular case. It is true, of course, that a similar list of horribles could be attributed to an ordinary Justice Department prosecution—a vindictive prosecutor, an antagonistic staff, etc. But the difference is the difference that the Founders envisioned when they established a single Chief Executive accountable to the people: the blame can be assigned to someone who can be punished.

C. The Executive Branch

EX PARTE MILLIGAN

4 Wallace 2; 18 L. Ed. 281 (1866)

The Constitution gives Congress the power to declare war and to raise and support armies but the war power which has developed from these simple grants staggers the imagination by its scope and variety. This is because, as Chief Justice Hughes put it in Home Building & Loan Ass'n. v. Blaisdell (1934), "the war power of the Federal Government . . . is a power to wage war successfully." In short, what is necessary to win the war Congress may do, and the Supreme Court has shown no inclination to hold void new and drastic war measures. In World War II the war power was invoked to fix price ceilings, to ration food and fuel, to commandeer factories, and to direct the production, distribution, and consumption of commodities. Our entire economy was mobilized for the war effort. A number of specific war powers exercised by Congress have been challenged in the courts, but in every case unsuccessfully.

The power of Congress to draft men into the armed services was attacked during World War I, although the draft had been resorted to sporadically and inefficiently during the Civil War. In 1917 Congress passed the Selective Draft Act, which made all male citizens between the ages of 21 and 30 subject to national military service. Public officers, ministers of religion, and theological students were exempt from the draft, while conscientious objectors who were affiliated with a "well recognized" pacifist religious sect were permitted to engage in noncombatant duty. In Selective Draft Law Cases (Arver v. United States, 1918) the Supreme Court unanimously held the act valid. The power to compel men to serve in the armed forces is reasonably implied from the power to raise and support armies, for a grant of power with no compulsion behind it is no power at all. The exemption of ministers and theological students is not an "establishment of religion" forbidden by the First Amendment; nor does compulsory military service constitute "involuntary servitude" forbidden by the Thirteenth Amendment.

In the Selective Training and Service Act of 1940, Congress changed the exemption rule, making it unnecessary to belong to a pacifist sect if a person's conscientious objection were based on "religious training and belief." The meaning of this phrase was spelled out in more detail in the Selective Service Act of 1948 (renamed in 1951 the Universal Military Training and Service Act): "Religious training and belief," according to the act, was to be defined as "an individual's belief in a relation to a Supreme Being involving duties superior to those arising from any human relation, but [not including] essentially political, sociological, or philosophical views or a merely personal moral code." In United States v. Seeger (1965), the Supreme Court held that this belief in a Supreme Being was not confined to a belief in God, in the traditional sense, but included any "sincere and meaningful belief which occupies in the life of its possessor a place parallel to that filled by the God of those admittedly qualifying for the exemption. . . ."

In 1967, following continued bitter and sometimes violent demonstrations against the draft, General Lewis B. Hershey, then head of the Selective Service System, recommended to the country's draft boards that persons engaged in illegal demonstrations be reclassified if necessary and inducted promptly into the armed service. In 1968 over 500 students who returned their draft cards as a protest against the Vietnam War had their student deferment cancelled and were inducted into the army. The Supreme Court, in Gutknecht v. United States (1970), held that the Selective Service System was not authorized by law to use "immediate induction as a disciplinary or vindictive measure."

Congress, following the Seeger decision, amended the draft act to make explicit that only religiously motivated CO's could be exempted from service, and in United States v. Sisson (297 Fed. Supp. 902, 1969), district judge Charles E. Wyzanski, Jr., of Boston upset the conviction of a nonreligious objector to the Vietnam War both on the ground that the act amounted to an establishment of religion, and that the government's interest in fighting in Vietnam was insufficient to outweigh Sisson's individual rights. The Supreme Court held that Sisson had in effect been ordered acquitted and refused to review the case.

Among the techniques devised for protesting both the war and the draft was the public burning of a person's draft card, and following a wave of such draft-card burning episodes an outraged Congress had in 1965 made it a crime to "knowingly destroy" a draft card. The following year a Boston University philosophy student publicly burned his draft card as part of a "demonstration against the [Vietnam] war and against the draft." In United States v. O'Brien (1968) the Supreme Court denied that the First Amendment had been violated and sustained his conviction under the act. ". . . We think it clear that a government regulation is sufficiently justified if it is within the constitutional power of the government; if it furthers an important or substantial governmental interest; if the governmental interest is unrelated to the suppression of free expression; and if the incidental restriction on alleged First Amendment freedom is no greater than is essential to the furtherance of that interest." Judged by these standards, "the many functions performed by the Selective Service certificates establish beyond doubt that Congress has a legitimate and substantial interest in preventing their wanton and un-restrained destruction."

In 1973 Congress amended the Military Selective Service Act to forbid actual conscrip-tion but authorized the President in his discretion to register those eligible for compulsory military service. President Carter, in 1980, ordered all male persons between the ages of 18 and 26 to register for the draft. Failure to so register was a criminal offense. In Rostker v. Goldberg (1981) this was challenged on the ground that only men had to register, but was held valid. While roughly 8.4 of the 9 million eligibles registered, an estimated 674,000 refused to do so and the government, faced with the impossibility of prosecuting that many violators, resorted to two techniques. One of these, a purely administrative action, involved instigating prosecution (after pleading with them to register) against those who publicly announced that they were not registered or were not going to register, or whose identity as nonregistrants was reported by others to the Department of Justice. In Wayte v. United States (1985) the Supreme Court, while conceding that the thirteen chosen for prosecution had all been "vocal" nonregistrants, rejected the charge that their First Amendment rights of protest had been infringed. Relying on O'Brien, it noted that "when, as here, ' "speech" and "nonspeech" elements are combined in the same course of conduct, a sufficiently important governmental interest in regulating the nonspeech element can justify incidental limitations on First Amendment freedoms.' " Moreover, "the passive enforcement policy also meets the final requirement of the O'Brien test, for it placed no more limitation on speech than was necessary to ensure registration for the national defense." The Court also rejected the view that a person could gain immunity from prosecution under the statute simply by reporting his refusal to abide by it.

A second technique devised for obtaining compliance with the draft law was a congres-sional statute of 1983 withholding financial aid to college students who were not registered for the draft. In Selective Service v. Minnesota Pub. Int. Res. Gp. (1984) the Court found that the statute was not a bill of attainder since it did not inflict punishment. Any eligible student could obtain the financial aid simply by registering. Nor was there a problem of compulsory self-in-crimination as a result of having to date a late registration, since none of those involved in the suit had sought to register and hence had had no occasion either to assert a Fifth Amendment privilege or to press a claim of immunity.

It is apparent from the challenges to the draft laws, mentioned above, that one of the evils of war seems frequently to be a certain incompatibility between the demands of military necessity and a punctilious regard for the civil rights of the individual. Certainly in war emer-gencies the citizen finds his liberty curtailed and his rights abridged in ways that in times of peace would seem intolerable. There is plenty of evidence that President Lincoln, largely supported by public opinion, definitely proceeded during the Civil War upon the theory that questions of constitutional power were to be dealt with in the light of the great objective of preserving the Union. No President has ever invaded private constitutional rights more flagrantly, or from worthier motives, than he. This may be illustrated by the famous case of Ex parte Merryman (1861). Merryman was a Southern agitator residing in Maryland who persisted during the early days of the war in conduct and utterances which in the judgment of the military authorities hindered the success of the Northern cause. He was thereupon arrested and locked up in the military prison at Fort McHenry. Merryman promptly petitioned Chief Justice Taney for a writ of habeas corpus. Taney issued the writ, directed to the general in command of the fort. The general did not honor the writ, replying that he was authorized by the President to suspend the writ of habeas corpus, but would seek further instructions; and he declined to obey the writ further. Taney thereupon issued a writ of contempt against the general and sent the United States marshal to serve it. The marshal reported that he had not been allowed to enter the outer gate of the fort, although he had sent in his card, and that he had not been able to serve the writ. Taney, while protesting that the marshal had a perfect right to summon a posse comitatus and storm the fort, excused him from that duty. Rather, he contented himself with writing a full account of the entire case which he addressed to President Lincoln and which concluded with the observation that it now remained for the President, acting in fulfillment of his solemn oath of office, to enforce the laws, execute the judgment of the court, and release the prisoner. Lincoln made no answer whatever to this document, but Merryman was later released from military confinement and turned over to the civil authorities.

The Supreme Court did not decide any case directly challenging presidential power while the war was in progress, although in 1864 an attempt was made to bring before that tribunal on a writ of habeas corpus the validity of the arrest of the notorious agitator, Vallandigham. The Court held that it was without jurisdiction and dismissed the case; see Ex parte Vallandigham (1864). It is interesting to speculate what the results might have been had the Supreme Court locked horns with the President in such a case; if, for example, the Milligan case had come up for decision during the early part of the war instead of in 1866.

The facts in the Milligan case were as follows: Milligan, a civilian, was arrested by order of General Hovey, who commanded the military district of Indiana; was tried in October, 1864, by a military commission which had been established under presidential authority; was found guilty of initiating insurrection and of various treasonable and disloyal practices; and was sentenced to be hanged on May 19, 1865. This sentence was approved by President Johnson. On May 10, 1865, Milligan sued out a writ of habeas corpus to the United States circuit court in Indiana, alleging the unconstitutional character of the proceedings under which he had been convicted and claiming the right of trial by jury as guaranteed by the Constitution. Thus, for the first time, the Supreme Court faced the question of the right of the President to suspend the writ of habeas corpus and to substitute trial by military authority for trial in the ordinary civil courts in districts outside the actual field of military operations.

The Supreme Court itself found difficulty in agreeing upon the important questions presented. They all held that a military commission set up by the President under such circumstances and without special authority from Congress was unlawful and without any power whatsoever. Five of the judges took the view that neither Congress nor the President had the power to set up military tribunals except in the actual theater of war where the civil courts were no longer functioning. Four judges, while denying such power to the President, held that it could be exercised by Congress. The Court decided, however, that Milligan had been unlawfully convicted and he was released.

The subsequent story of the case is not without interest. Milligan's sentence had been commuted to life imprisonment by the President in June, 1865, and he had been imprisoned by General Hovey in the Ohio penitentiary until his final release on April 10, 1866, as a result of the decision of the Supreme Court. On March 13, 1868, he brought an action of damages against General Hovey for unlawful imprisonment. The case was tried in the federal circuit court and the jury rendered a verdict for Milligan, but awarded only nominal damages inasmuch as the two-year statute of limitations allowed him to recover damages only for his imprisonment between March 13 and April 10, 1866.

The fact that the decision in the Milligan case set up a powerful judicial protection against military and executive invasion of individual constitutional rights was not sufficient to distract contemporary attention from the vital political consequences of the rule regarding congressional power which was laid down. Congress was in the midst of the important work of reconstruction. The radical leaders of the Republican party were committed to a policy of reconstruction which should keep the Southern states under the control of federal military forces until conditions seemed to warrant the adoption of a less drastic policy. But the doctrine of the Milligan case, by condemning military government in peaceful sections where the civil courts were open, was obviously incompatible with any such form of military reconstruction. It looked as though the Court were trying to prevent the carrying out of the congressional policy, and the decision was received with an outburst of anger by the congressional leaders. There was some talk of impeaching the judges; Congress went forward with its plans for military government in the South in contemptuous disregard for the decision, and utterances from prominent men were not lacking to the effect that the Court would come off the loser in any combat over the validity of the reconstruction plan adopted. It is an interesting fact that the constitutionality of these reconstruction acts was never passed upon by the Supreme Court. See the cases of Mississippi v. Johnson (1867) and Ex parte McCardle (1869).

Mr. Justice **Davis** delivered the opinion of the Court, saying in part:

The importance of the main question presented by this record cannot be overstated, for it involves the very framework of the government and the fundamental principles of American liberty.

During the late wicked Rebellion, the temper of the times did not allow that calmness in deliberation and discussion so necessary to a correct conclusion of a purely judicial question. Then, considerations of safety were mingled with the exercise of power, and feelings and interests prevailed which are happily terminated. Now that the public safety is assured, this question, as well as all others, can be discussed and decided without passion or the admixture of any element not required to form a legal judgment. We approach the investigation of this case fully sensible of the magnitude of the inquiry and the necessity of full and cautious deliberation. . . .

The controlling question in the case is this: Upon the facts stated in Milligan's petition, and the exhibits filed, had the Military Commission mentioned in it jurisdiction, legally, to try and sentence him? Milligan, not a resident of one of the rebellious states, or a prisoner of war, but a citizen of Indiana for twenty years past, and never in the military or naval service, is, while at his home, arrested by the military power of the United States, imprisoned and, on certain criminal charges preferred against him, tried, convicted, and sentenced to be hanged by a military commission, organized under the direction of the military commander of the military district of Indiana. Had this tribunal the legal power and authority to try and punish this man?

No graver question was ever considered by this court, nor one which more nearly concerns the rights of the whole people; for it is the birthright of every American citizen when charged with crime, to be tried and punished according to law. The power of punishment is alone through the means which the laws have provided for that purpose, and if they are ineffectual, there is an immunity from punishment, no matter how great an offender the individual may be, or how much his crimes may have shocked the sense of justice of the country, or endangered its safety. By the protection of the law human rights are secured; withdraw that protection, and they are at the mercy of wicked rulers, or the clamor of an excited people. If there was law to justify this military trial, it is not our province to interfere; if there was not, it is our duty to declare the nullity of the whole proceedings. The decision of this question does not depend on argument or judicial precedents, numerous and highly illustrative as they are. These precedents inform us of the extent of the struggle to preserve liberty and to relieve those in civil life from military trials. The founders of our government were familiar with the history of that struggle; and secured in a written Constitution every right which the people had wrested from power during a contest of ages. By that Constitution and the laws authorized by it, this question must be determined. The provisions of that instrument on the administration of criminal justice are too plain and direct to leave room for misconstruction or doubt of their true meaning. Those applicable to this case are found in that clause of the original Constitution which says "that the trial of all crimes, except in case of impeachment, shall be by jury;" and in the fourth, fifth, and sixth articles of the amendments. . . ,

Time has proven the discernment of our ancestors; for even these provisions, expressed in such plain English words, that it would seem the ingenuity of man could not evade them, are now, after the lapse of more than seventy years, sought to be avoided. Those great and good men foresaw that troublous times would arise, when rulers and people would become restive under restraint, and seek by sharp and decisive measures to accomplish ends deemed just and proper; and that the principles of constitutional liberty would be in peril, unless established by irrepealable law. The history of the world had taught them that what was done in the past might be attempted in the future. The Constitution of the United States is a law for rulers and people, equally in war and in peace, and covers with the shield of its protection all classes of men, at all times, and under all circumstances. No doctrine, involving more pernicious consequences, was ever invented by the wit of man than that any of its provisions can be suspended during any of the great exigencies of government. Such a doctrine leads directly to anarchy or despotism, but the theory of necessity on which it is based is false; for the government, within the Constitution, has all the powers granted to it which are necessary to preserve its existence, as has been happily proved by the result of the great effort to throw off its just authority.

Have any of the rights guaranteed by the Constitution been violated in the case of Milligan? and if so, what are they?

Every trial involves the exercise of judicial power; and from what source did the Military Commission that tried him derive their authority? Certainly no part of the judicial power of the country was conferred on them; because the Constitution expressly vests it "in one Supreme Court and such inferior courts as the Congress may from time to time ordain and establish," and it is not pretended that the commission was a court ordained and established by Congress. They cannot justify on the mandate of the President; because he is controlled by law, and has his appropriate sphere of duty, which is to execute, not to make, the laws; and there is "no unwritten criminal code to which resort can be had as a source of jurisdiction."

But it is said that the jurisdiction is complete under the "laws and usages of war."

It can serve no useful purpose to inquire what those laws and usages are, whence they originated, where found, and on whom they operate; they can never be applied to citizens in states which have upheld the authority of the government, and where the courts are open and their process unobstructed. This court has judicial knowledge that in Indiana the Federal authority was always unopposed, and its courts always open to hear criminal accusations and redress grievances; and no usage of war could sanction a military trial there for any offense whatever of a citizen in civil life, in nowise connected with the military service. Congress could grant no such power; and to the honor of our national legislature be it said, it has never been provoked by the state of the country even to attempt its exercise. One of the plainest constitutional provisions was, therefore, infringed when Milligan was tried by a court not ordained and established by Congress, and not composed of judges appointed during good behavior.

Why was he not delivered to the circuit court of Indiana to be proceeded against according to law? No reason of necessity could be urged against it; because Congress had declared penalties against the offenses charged, provided for their punishment, and directed that court to hear and determine them. And soon after this military tribunal was ended, the circuit court met, peacefully transacted its business, and adjourned. It needed no bayonets to protect it, and required no military aid to execute its judgments. It was held in a state, eminently distinguished for patriotism, by judges commissioned during the Rebellion, who were provided with juries, upright, intelligent, and selected by a marshal appointed by the President. The government had no right to conclude that Milligan, if guilty, would not receive in that court merited punishment; for its records disclose that it was constantly engaged in the trial of similar offenses, and was never interrupted in its administration of criminal justice. If it was dangerous, in the distracted condition of affairs, to leave Milligan unrestrained of his liberty, because he "conspired against the government, afforded aid and comfort to rebels, and incited the people to insurrection," the law said arrest him, confine him closely, render him powerless to do further mischief; and then present his case to the grand jury of the district, with proofs of his guilt and, if indicted, try him according to the course of the common law. If this had been done, the Constitution would have been vindicated, the law of 1863 enforced, and the securities for personal liberty preserved and defended.

Another guarantee of freedom was broken when Milligan was denied a trial by jury. The great minds of the country have differed on the correct interpretation to be given to various provisions of the Federal Constitution; and judicial decision has been often invoked to settle their true meaning; but until recently no one ever doubted that the right of trial by jury was fortified in the organic law against the power of attack. It is now assailed; but if ideas can be expressed in words, and language has any meaning, this right—one of the most valuable in a free country—is preserved to every one accused of crime who is not attached to the Army, or Navy, or Militia in actual service. The sixth Amendment affirms that "in all criminal prosecutions the accused shall enjoy the right to a speedy and public trial by an impartial jury," language broad enough to embrace all persons and cases; but the fifth, recognizing the necessity of an indictment, or presentment, before any one can be held to answer for high crimes, "excepts cases arising in the land or naval forces, or in the militia, when in actual service, in time of war or public danger;" and the framers of the Constitution, doubtless, meant to limit the right to trial by jury, in the Sixth Amendment, to those persons who were subject to indictment or presentment in the Fifth.

The discipline necessary to the efficiency of the army and navy required other and swifter modes of trial than are furnished by the common law courts; and, in pursuance of the power conferred by the Constitution, Congress has declared the kinds of trial and the manner in which they shall be conducted, for offenses committed while the party is in the military or naval service. Every one connected with these branches of public service is amenable to the jurisdiction which Congress has created for their government, and, while thus serving, surrenders his right to be tried by the civil courts. All other persons, citizens of states where the courts are open, if charged with crime, are guaranteed the inestimable privilege of trial by jury. . . .

It is claimed that martial law covers with its broad mantle the proceedings of this military commission. The proposition is this: That in a time of war the commander of an armed force (if in his opinion the exigencies of the country demand it, and of which he is to judge) has the power, within the lines of his military district, to suspend all civil rights and their remedies, and subject citizens as well as soldiers to the rule of his will; and in the exercise of his lawful authority cannot be restrained, except by his superior officer or the President of the United States.

If this position is sound to the extent claimed, then when war exists, foreign or domestic, and the country is subdivided into military departments for mere convenience, the commander of one of them can, if he chooses, within the limits, on the plea of necessity, with the approval of the Executive, substitute military force for and to the exclusion of the laws, and punish all persons, as he thinks right and proper, without fixed or certain rules.

The statement of this proposition shows its importance; for, if true, republican government is a failure, and there is an end of liberty regulated by law. Martial law, established on such a basis, destroys every guarantee of the Constitution, and effectually renders the "military independent of and superior to the civil power"— the attempt to do which by the King of Great Britain was deemed by our fathers such an offense, that they assigned it to the world as one of the causes which impelled them to declare their independence. Civil liberty and this kind of martial law cannot endure together; the antagonism is irreconcilable and, in the conflict, one or the other must perish.

This nation, as experience has proved, cannot always remain at peace, and has no right to expect that it will always have wise and humane rulers, sincerely attached to the principles of the Constitution. Wicked men, ambitious of power, with hatred of liberty and contempt of law, may fill the place once occupied by Washington and Lincoln; and if this right is conceded, and the calamities of war again befall us, the dangers to human liberty are frightful to contemplate. If our fathers had failed to provide for just such a contingency, they would have been false to the trust reposed in them. They knew—the history of the world told them—the nation they were founding, be its existence short or long, would be involved in war; how often or how long continued, human foresight could not tell; and that unlimited power, wherever lodged at such a time, was especially hazardous to freemen. For this, and other equally weighty reasons, they secured the inheritance they had fought to maintain, by incorporating in a written Constitution the safeguards which time had proved were essential to its preservation. Not one of these safeguards can the President or Congress or the Judiciary disturb, except the one concerning the writ of habeas corpus.

It is essential to the safety of every government that, in a great crisis, like the one we have just passed through, there should be a power somewhere of suspending the writ of habeas corpus. In every war, there are men of previously good character, wicked enough to counsel their fellow citizens to resist the measures deemed necessary by a good government to sustain its just authority and overthrow its enemies; and their influence may lead to dangerous combinations. In the emergency of the times, an immediate public investigation according to law may not be possible; and yet, the peril to the country may be too imminent to suffer such persons to go at large. Unquestionably, there is then an exigency which demands that the government, if it should see fit, in the exercise of a proper discretion, to make arrests, should not be required to produce the person arrested in answer to a writ of habeas corpus. The Constitution goes no further. It does not say after a writ of habeas corpus is denied a citizen, that he shall be tried otherwise than by the course of common law. If it had intended this result, it was easy by the use of direct words to have accomplished it. The illustrious men who framed that instrument were guarding the foundations of civil liberty against the abuses of unlimited power; they were full of wisdom, and the lessons of history informed them that a trial by an established court, assisted by an impartial jury, was the only sure way of protecting the citizen against oppression and wrong. Knowing this, they limited the suspension to one great right, and left the rest to remain forever inviolable. But it is insisted that the safety of the country in time of war demands that this broad claim for martial law shall be sustained. If this were true, it could be well said that a country, preserved at the sacrifice of all the cardinal principles of liberty, is not worth the cost of preservation. Happily, it is not so.

It will be borne in mind that this is not a question of the power to proclaim martial law, when war exists in a community and the courts and civil authorities are overthrown. Nor is it a question what rule a military commander, at the head of his army, can impose on States in rebellion to cripple their resources and quell the insurrection. The jurisdiction claimed is much more extensive. The necessities of the service, during the late Rebellion, required that the loyal states should be placed within the limits of certain military districts and commanders appointed in them; and, it is urged, that this, in a military sense, constituted them the theatre of military operations; and, as in this case, Indiana had been and was again threatened with invasion by the enemy, the occasion was furnished to establish martial law. The conclusion does not follow from the premises. If armies were collected in Indiana, they were to be employed in another locality, where the laws were obstructed and the national authority disputed. On her soil there was no hostile foot; if once invaded, that invasion was at an end, and with it all pretext for martial law. Martial law cannot arise from a threatened invasion. The necessity must be actual and present; the invasion real, such as effectually closes the courts and deposes the civil administration.

It is difficult to see how the safety of the country required martial law in Indiana. If any of her citizens were plotting treason, the power of arrest could secure them, until the government was prepared for their trial, when the courts were open and ready to try them. It was as easy to protect witnesses before a civil as a military tribunal; and as there could be no wish to convict, except on sufficient legal evidence, surely an ordained and established court were better able to judge of this than a military tribunal composed of gentlemen not trained to the profession of the law.

It follows, from what has been said on this subject, that there are occasions when martial rule can be properly applied. If, in foreign invasion or civil war, the courts are actually closed, and it is impossible to administer criminal justice according to law, then, on the theatre of active military operations, where war really prevails, there is a necessity to furnish a substitute for the civil authority, thus overthrown, to preserve the safety of the army and society; and as no power is left but the military, it is allowed to govern by martial rule until the laws can have their free course. As necessity creates the rule, so it limits its duration; for, if this government is continued after the courts are reinstated, it is a gross usurpation of power. Martial rule can never exist where the courts are open, and in the proper and unobstructed exercise of their jurisdiction. It is also confined to the locality of actual war. Because, during the late Rebellion it could have been enforced in Virginia, where the national authority was overturned and the courts driven out, it does not follow that it should obtain in Indiana, where that authority was never disputed, and justice was always administered. And so in the case of a foreign invasion, martial rule may become a necessity in one state, when, in another, it would be ''mere lawless violence.'' . . .

The two remaining questions in this case must be answered in the affirmative. The suspension of the privilege of the writ of habeas corpus does not suspend the writ itself. The writ issues as a matter of course; and on the return made to it the court decides whether the party applying is denied the right of proceeding any further with it.

If the military trial of Milligan was contrary to law, then he was entitled, on the facts stated in his petition, to be discharged from custody by the terms of the act of Congress of March 3d, 1863. The provisions of this law having been considered in a previous part of this opinion, we will not restate the views there presented. Milligan avers he was a citizen of Indiana, not in the military or naval service, and was detained in close confinement, by order of the President, from the 5th day of October, 1864, until the 2d day of January, 1865, when the circuit court for the district of Indiana, with a grand jury, convened in session at Indianapolis; and afterwards, on the 27th day of the same month, adjourned without finding an indictment or presentment against him. If these averments were true (and their truth is conceded for the purposes of this case), the court was required to liberate him on taking certain oaths prescribed by the law, and entering into recognizance for his good behavior.

But it is insisted that Milligan was a prisoner of war, and, therefore, excluded from the privileges of the statute. It is not easy to see how he can be treated as a prisoner of war, when he lived in Indiana for the past twenty years, was arrested there, and had not been, during the late troubles, a resident of any of the states in rebellion. If in Indiana he conspired with bad men to assist the enemy, he is punishable for it in the courts of Indiana; but, when tried for the offense, he cannot plead the rights of war; for he was not engaged in legal acts of hostility against the government, and only such persons, when captured, are prisoners of war. If he cannot enjoy the immunities attaching to the character of a prisoner of war, how can he be subject to their pains and penalties? . . .

Mr. Chief Justice **Chase,** for himself and Mr. Justice **Wayne,** Mr. Justice **Swayne,** and Mr. Justice **Miller,** delivered an opinion in which he differed from the Court in several important points, but concurred in the judgment in the case.

YOUNGSTOWN SHEET & TUBE COMPANY v. SAWYER

343 U. S. 579; 96 L. Ed. 1153; 72 S. Ct. 863 (1952)

The President exercises the bulk of his policy-making powers under delegations of authority made to him by Congress. But there are important areas in which he enjoys powers granted not by Congress but by the Constitution itself. The conduct of foreign affairs has traditionally been the concern of the executive branch of government, and the Constitution of the United States recognizes this fact. The President appoints our foreign ambassadors, ministers, and consuls. He alone receives ambassadors and other public ministers from abroad and thereby "recognizes" the governments by which such officers are sent. It is he who, usually through his Secretary of State, negotiates treaties. But Congress has some power with respect to foreign affairs. Treaties or other agreements which call for the expenditure of money will be ineffective unless Congress appropriates that money by statute. The Senate must consent to the appointments of our diplomatic representatives, and two-thirds of the Senate must give its approval to a treaty. This latter requirement has tended to limit the use of the treaty power to fairly formal and important international agreements, among which have been military alliances, the making of peace, and adherence to international organizations.

A substantial proportion of our international agreements take the form of executive agreements concluded between the President and the executive of a foreign nation. Some of these, particularly in the field of foreign trade, are specifically authorized by Congress. Others are made solely on the authority of the President as chief executive. While the Constitution provides that treaties shall be the law of the land, and executive agreements made with congressional consent would also have the authority of law, there has long been some doubt about the binding nature of an agreement made by the executive alone.

In 1937, in United States v. Belmont, the Court laid this doubt to rest. In 1918 the Soviet government nationalized the Petrograd Metal Works and confiscated its property and assets, wherever situated. Some of these assets were on deposit in Belmont's bank in New York. In 1933 the President, by receiving the Soviet ambassador, recognized the Soviet government as the legitimate government of Russia. A final settlement of the claims and counter-claims between the two countries was concluded in the Litvinov Assignments, and the claim to all money due the Soviet government from American nationals was assigned to the United States, including the deposits in Belmont's bank. The assignments were made by an exchange of diplomatic correspondence between the Soviet government and the United States and were not submitted to the Senate in the form of a treaty. The Supreme Court upheld the assignments despite the argument that they were against the public policy both of New York and the United States and therefore void. "The recognition, establishment of diplomatic relations, the assignment, and agreements with respect thereto, were all parts of one transaction, resulting in an international compact between the two governments. That the negotiations, acceptance of the assignments and agreements and understandings in respect thereto were within the competence of the President may not be doubted. Government power over internal affairs is distributed between the national government and the several states. Governmental power over external affairs is not distributed, but is vested exclusively in the national government. And in respect of what was done here, the Executive had authority to speak as the sole organ of that government. The assignment and the agreements in connection therewith did not, as in the case of treaties, as that term is used in the treaty-making clause of the Constitution (Article II, Sec. 2), require the advice and consent of the Senate."

Another area in which the President receives direct constitutional powers is found in Article II which makes the President the Commander in Chief of the Army and Navy. This is clearly not a power merely to command the disposition of the armed forces. But if it is more than that, how much more? A democratic distrust of executive power cannot alter the fact that in times of war a near-dictatorship may be necessary to preserve the nation. In such times Congress has wisely delegated vast areas of authority to the President. But where Congress has not done so, and the President has felt that the emergency justified it, he has often acted on his own authority. The fact that Congress usually gives belated approval to such executive acts hardly obscures the fact that the crucial policy decisions are made by the executive.

The Constitution gives Congress the power to declare war; but may the President on his own authority decide that a state of war exists, and on the strength of this decision take action affecting the lives and property of American citizens? Following the firing upon Fort Sumter in 1861, President Lincoln declared the existence of a state of insurrection and called out the militia. Authority to do this had been given him by Congress, and the Court had held in Martin v. Mott (1827) that vesting of this discretion in the President was valid. But a week after Sumter the President, acting wholly on his own authority, declared a naval blockade of the Confederate ports. Pursuant to this proclamation four blockade runners were captured and condemned. The Court sustained this action in the Prize Cases (1863), pointing out that "if a war be made by invasion of a foreign nation, the President is not only authorized but bound to resist force, by force. He does not initiate the war, but is bound to accept the challenge without waiting for any special legislative authority. And whether the hostile party be a foreign invader, or States organized in rebellion, it is none the less a war. . . ." The proclamation of a blockade was held "itself, official and conclusive evidence to the court that a state of war existed which demanded and authorized a recourse to such a measure, under the circumstances peculiar to the case."

Even the most drastic and dictatorial exercises of power by the President acting under his authority as Commander in Chief have usually not resulted in clarifying or determining the actual constitutional scope of pure executive power. This is because Congress in nearly all such cases has hastened to shore up the President's authority by legislative ratification of what he has done. Thus when Congress came into session on July 4, 1861, it underwrote the President's blockade of Southern ports by passing an act "approving, legalizing and making valid all the acts, proclamations, and orders of the President, &c., as if they had been issued and done under the previous express authority and direction of the Congress. . . ." In 1944, following the issue of the executive order creating military districts from which persons of Japanese ancestry were excluded (see Korematsu v. United States, 1944), Congress made it a crime to "enter, remain in, leave, or commit any act in any military area . . . prescribed [by executive order] . . . contrary to the order of the Secretary of War or any such military commander. . . ."

On November 4, 1979, Iranian radicals, demanding the return of the deposed Shah, took hostage 53 members of the American embassy in Tehran. President Carter refused to return the Shah, ordered frozen all Iranian assets in the United States, and nullified all claims against such assets including some still in the process of litigation. Fourteen months later the hostages were released in exchange for the return of the assets to Iran. In Dames & Moore v. Regan (1981) the Court upheld the presidential seizure. It distinguished the Youngstown case, noting that "from the history of acquiescence in executive claims settlement—we conclude that the President was authorized to suspend pending claims. . . ." The constitutional grants of power over foreign affairs and as Commander in Chief have always been interpreted as being independent grants to the President to make important policy decisions in these two fields, and whatever power Congress has in these areas can be delegated to the President virtually without limit. In contrast to this his duty to "take care that the laws be faithfully executed" seems a requirement that he carry out the laws of Congress. In the case of In re Neagle (1890) the Court interpreted this clause, too, as a grant of policy-making authority. The laws are not merely the laws of Congress, but include independent acts of the President himself. There is, moreover, a peace of the United States, and the President, as chief executive, is protector of that peace with power to prevent violations.

The case arose out of an extraordinary set of circumstances. A long and bitter legal battle involving title to more than a million dollars had culminated in the United States circuit court in California at a time when Justice Field of the United States Supreme Court was sitting as circuit justice. The disappointed contestant was represented by her husband, a lawyer named Terry, who had once been chief justice of the California supreme court. At the close of the case Mrs. Terry accused Justice Field of selling justice, and the United States marshal was ordered to quiet her. A fight ensued and Terry and his wife went to prison for six months for contempt of court. Upon their release they threatened to kill Justice Field if he ever came back to California. Since the law at that time required Supreme Court justices to ride circuit, the matter was laid before the Attorney General; and when Field again returned to California, Neagle, a deputy marshal, was detailed to serve as a bodyguard. Terry, following up his threat, tried to make a murderous attack upon the Justice in a railroad restaurant where the Justice had stopped while traveling on circuit duty. He was about to draw his knife when Neagle shot and killed him. Neagle was promptly arrested by the local authorities and held for murder. He was released from the custody of the state court upon a writ of habeas corpus by the federal circuit court on the ground that he was held in custody for "an act done in pursuance of a law of the United States" within the meaning of the federal statute providing for the issuance of the writ in such cases.

The most significant feature of the case is that the "law of the United States" in pursuance of which Neagle acted was not an act of Congress, but merely an executive order issued by authority of the President. In sustaining Neagle's release the Court holds that the President in the exercise of the duty imposed upon him to see that the laws are faithfully executed may, without special statutory authority, appoint an officer to protect the life of a federal judge. It was on the President's power to "take care that the laws be faithfully executed" that Chief Justice Vinson relied in his dissent in the Steel Seizure Case, printed below.

This case climaxed a long dispute between the steel companies and the steel workers. On December 18, 1951, the United Steel Workers of America, CIO, gave notice that it would strike on December 31. The Federal Mediation and Conciliation Service failed to effect a settlement. The Federal Wage Stabilization Board, to which President Truman referred the dispute on December 22, also failed. The President did not invoke the provisions of the Taft-Hartley Act, which would have set up a "period of waiting" before a strike. On April 4, 1952, the union announced that it would call a nationwide strike on April 9. A few hours before the strike was to begin the President directed Secretary of Commerce Sawyer to seize and operate most of the country's steel mills. The Secretary issued the appropriate orders. The President reported the seizure to Congress on April 9, and again on April 21, but Congress took no action. The steel companies complied under protest with the seizure order, but sought a temporary injunction to restrain the government's action. On April 30, the district court of the District of Columbia issued a preliminary injunction, which was stayed on the same day by the court of appeals.

On May 3, the Supreme Court, by-passing the court of appeals, brought the case to its docket by certiorari. It heard argument on May 12, and decided the case on June 2. These dates indicate the celerity with which the Supreme Court can act when the national interest requires speed.

The difficulty and complexity of the case is shown by the fact that the Court divided six to three, and that seven justices wrote separate opinions, totaling 128 pages. The Court did not face here the naked question of the President's power to seize the steel plants in the absence of any congressional enactments or expressions of policy. Congress had provided limited powers of seizure in the Selective Service Act of 1948 and in the Defense Production Act of 1950. Furthermore, in its debates on the Taft-Hartley Act of 1947 Congress had considered an amendment authorizing seizure of plants by the President in case of a strike, and had rejected it. In fact, over a period of years, Congress had made it clear that the seizure of private property in time of emergency was a problem to be controlled by congressional policy. For a variety of reasons, the majority of the Court found that this legislative occupation of the field made untenable the President's claim of authority to seize the plants as an exercise of inherent executive power or as Commander in Chief. Congress had set up various procedures for the President to follow in such cases, and he had not followed them.

Mr. Justice **Black** delivered the opinion of the Court, saying in part:

We are asked to decide whether the President was acting within his constitutional power when he issued an order directing the Secretary of Commerce to take possession of and operate most of the Nation's steel mills. The mill owners argue that the President's order amounts to lawmaking, a legislative function which the Constitution has expressly confided to the Congress and not to the President. The Government's position is that the order was made on findings of the President that his action was necessary to avert a national catastrophe which would inevitably result from a stoppage of steel production, and that in meeting this grave emergency the President was acting within the aggregate of his constitutional powers as the Nation's Chief Executive and the Commander in Chief of the Armed Forces of the United States. . . .

The President's power, if any, to issue the order must stem either from an act of Congress or from the Constitution itself. There is no statute that expressly authorizes the President to take possession of property as he did here. Nor is there any act of Congress to which our attention has been directed from which such a power can fairly be implied. Indeed, we do not understand the Government to rely on statutory authorization for this seizure. There are two statutes which do authorize the President to take both personal and real property under certain conditions. [The Selective Service Act of 1948 and the Defense Production Act of 1950.] However, the Government admits that these conditions were not met and that the President's order was not rooted in either of the statutes. The Government refers to the seizure provisions of one of these statutes (§ 201 (b) of the Defense Production Act) as "much too cumbersome, involved, and time-consuming for the crisis which was at hand."

Moreover, the use of the seizure technique to solve labor disputes in order to prevent work stoppages was not only unauthorized by any congressional enactment; prior to this controversy, Congress had refused to adopt that method of settling labor disputes. When the Taft-Hartley Act was under consideration in 1947, Congress rejected an amendment which would have authorized such governmental seizures in cases of emergency. Apparently it was thought that the technique of seizure, like that of compulsory arbitration, would interfere with the process of collective bargaining. Consequently, the plan Congress adopted in that Act did not provide for seizure under any circumstances. Instead, the plan sought to bring about settlements by use of the customary devices of mediation, conciliation, investigation by boards of inquiry, and public reports. In some instances temporary injunctions were authorized to provide cooling-off periods. All this failing, unions were left free to strike after a secret vote by employees as to whether they wished to accept their employers' final settlement offer.

It is clear that if the President had authority to issue the order he did, it must be found in some provisions of the Constitution. And it is not claimed that express constitutional language grants this power to the President. The contention is that presidential power should be implied from the aggregate of his powers under the Constitution. Particular reliance is placed on provisions in Article II which say that "The executive Power shall be vested in a President . . ." ; that "he shall take Care that the Laws be faithfully executed;" and that he "shall be Commander in Chief of the Army and Navy of the United States."

The order cannot properly be sustained as an exercise of the President's military power as Commander in Chief of the Armed Forces. The Government attempts to do so by citing a number of cases upholding broad powers in military commanders engaged in day-to-day fighting in a theater of war. Such cases need not concern us here. Even though "theater of war" be an expanding concept, we cannot with faithfulness to our constitutional system hold that the Commander in Chief of the Armed Forces has the ultimate power as such to take possession of private property in order to keep labor disputes from stopping production. This is a job for the Nation's lawmakers, not for its military authorities.

Nor can the seizure order be sustained because of the several constitutional provisions that grant executive power to the President. In the framework of our Constitution the President's power to see that the laws are faithfully executed refutes the idea that he is to be a lawmaker. The Constitution limits his functions in the lawmaking process to the recommending of laws he thinks wise and the vetoing of laws he thinks bad. And the Constitution is neither silent nor equivocal about who shall make laws which the President is to execute. The first section of the first article says that "All legislative Powers herein granted shall be vested in a Congress of the United States." . . .

The President's order does not direct that a congressional policy be executed in a manner prescribed by Congress—it directs that a presidential policy be executed in a manner prescribed by the President. The preamble of the order itself, like that of many statutes, sets out reasons why the President believes certain policies should be adopted, proclaims these policies as rules of conduct to be followed, and again, like a statute, authorizes a government official to promulgate additional rules and regulations consistent with the policy proclaimed and needed to carry that policy into execution. The power of Congress to adopt such public policies as those proclaimed by the order is beyond question. It can authorize the taking of private property for public use. It can make laws regulating the relationships between employers and employees, prescribing rules designed to settle labor disputes, and fixing wages and working conditions in certain fields of our economy. The Constitution did not subject this lawmaking power of Congress to presidential or military supervision or control.

It is said that other Presidents without congressional authority have taken possession of private business enterprises in order to settle labor disputes. But even if this be true, Congress has not thereby lost its exclusive constitutional authority to make laws necessary and proper to carry out the powers vested by the Constitution ''in the Government of the United States, or any Department or Officer thereof.''

The Founders of this Nation entrusted the lawmaking power to the Congress alone in both good and bad times. It would do no good to recall the historical events, the fears of power and the hopes for freedom that lay behind their choice. Such a review would but confirm our holding that this seizure order cannot stand.

The judgment of the District Court is Affirmed.

Mr. Justice **Frankfurter,** concurring with the judgment and opinion of the Court, said in part:

Apart from his vast share of responsibility for the conduct of our foreign relations, the embracing function of the President is that ''he shall take Care that the Laws be faithfully executed. . . .'' Art. II, § 3. The nature of that authority has for me been comprehensively indicated by Mr. Justice Holmes. ''The duty of the President to see that the laws be executed is a duty that does not go beyond the laws or require him to achieve more than Congress sees fit to leave within his power.'' Myers v. United States [1926]. The powers of the President are not as particularized as are those of Congress. But unenumerated powers do not mean undefined powers. The separation of powers built into our Constitution gives essential content to undefined provisions in the frame of our government. . . .

A scheme of government like ours no doubt at times feels the lack of power to act with complete, all-embracing, swiftly moving authority. No doubt a government with distributed authority, subject to be challenged in the courts of law, at least long enough to consider and adjudicate the challenge, labors under restrictions from which other governments are free. It has not been our tradition to envy such governments. In any event our government was designed to have such restrictions. The price was deemed not too high in view of the safeguards which these restrictions afford. . . .

Mr. Justice **Douglas,** concurring with the judgment and opinion of the Court, said in part:

There can be no doubt that the emergency which caused the President to seize these steel plants was one that bore heavily on the country. But the emergency did not create power; it merely marked an occasion when power should be exercised. And the fact that it was necessary that measures be taken to keep steel in production does not mean that the President, rather than the Congress, had the constitutional authority to act. The Congress, as well as the President, is trustee of the national welfare. The President can act more quickly than the Congress. The President with the armed services at his disposal can move with force as well as with speed. All executive power—from the reign of ancient kings to the rule of modern dictators—has the outward appearance of efficiency.

Legislative power, by contrast, is slower to exercise. There must be delay while the ponderous machinery of committees, hearings, and debates is put into motion. That takes time; and while the Congress slowly moves into action, the emergency may take its toll in wages, consumer goods, war production, the standard of living of the people, and perhaps even lives. Legislative action may indeed often be cumbersome, time-consuming, and apparently inefficient. But as Mr. Justice Brandeis stated in his dissent in Myers v. United States:

"The doctrine of the separation of powers was adopted by the Convention of 1787, not to promote efficiency but to preclude the exercise of arbitrary power. The purpose was, not to avoid friction, but, by means of the inevitable friction incident to the distribution of the governmental powers among three departments, to save the people from autocracy."

We therefore cannot decide this case by determining which branch of government can deal most expeditiously with the present crisis. The answer must depend on the allocation of powers under the Constitution. That in turn requires an analysis of the conditions giving rise to the seizure and of the seizure itself. . . .

The great office of President is not a weak and powerless one. The President represents the people and is their spokesman in domestic and foreign affairs. The office is respected more than any other in the land. It gives a position of leadership that is unique. The power to formulate policies and mould opinion inheres in the Presidency and conditions our national life. The impact of the man and the philosophy he represents may at times be thwarted by the Congress. Stalemates may occur when emergencies mount and the Nation suffers for lack of harmonious, reciprocal action between the White House and Capitol Hill. That is a risk inherent in our system of separation of powers. The tragedy of such stalemates might be avoided by allowing the President the use of some legislative authority. The Framers with memories of the tyrannies produced by a blending of executive and legislative power rejected that political arrangement. Some future generation may, however, deem it so urgent that the President have legislative authority that the Constitution will be amended. We could not sanction the seizure and condemnations of the steel plants in this case without reading Article 2 as giving the President not only the power to execute the laws but to make some. Such a step would most assuredly alter the pattern of the Constitution.

We pay a price for our system of checks and balances, for the distribution of power among the three branches of government. It is a price that today may seem exorbitant to many. Today a kindly President uses the seizure power to effect a wage increase and to keep the steel furnaces in production. Yet tomorrow another President might use the same power to prevent a wage increase, to curb trade-unionists, to regiment labor as oppressively as industry thinks it has been regimented by this seizure.

Mr. Justice **Jackson,** concurring in the judgment and opinion of the Court, said in part:

That seems to be the logic of an argument tendered at our bar—that the President having, on his own responsibility, sent American troops abroad derives from that act "affirmative power" to seize the means of producing a supply of steel for them. . . .

I cannot foresee all that it might entail if the Court should indorse this argument. Nothing in our Constitution is plainer than that declaration of a war is entrusted only to Congress. Of course, a state of war may in fact exist without a formal declaration. But no doctrine that the Court could promulgate would seem to me more sinister and alarming than that a President whose conduct of foreign affairs is so largely uncontrolled, and often even is unknown, can vastly enlarge his mastery over the internal affairs of the country by his own commitment of the Nation's armed forces to some foreign venture. . . .

The Solicitor General lastly grounds support of the seizure upon nebulous, inherent powers never expressly granted but said to have accrued to the office from the customs and claims of preceding administrations. The plea is for a resulting power to deal with a crisis or an emergency according to the necessities of the case, the unarticulated assumption being that necessity knows no law. . . .

The appeal, however, that we declare the existence of inherent powers ex necessitate to meet an emergency asks us to do what many think would be wise, although it is something the forefathers omitted. They knew what emergencies were, knew the pressures they engender for authoritative action, knew, too, how they afford a ready pretext for usurpation. We may also suspect that they suspected that emergency powers would tend to kindle emergencies. . . .

In the practical working of our Government we already have evolved a technique within the framework of the Constitution by which normal executive powers may be considerably expanded to meet an emergency. Congress may and has granted extraordinary authorities which lie dormant in normal times but may be called into play by the Executive in war or upon proclamation of a national emergency. In 1939, upon congressional request, the Attorney General listed ninety-nine such separate statutory grants by Congress of emergency or war-time executive powers. They were invoked from time to time as need appeared. Under this procedure we retain Government by law—special, temporary law, perhaps, but law nonetheless. The public may know the extent and limitations of the powers that can be asserted, and persons affected may be informed from the statute of their rights and duties.

In view of the ease, expedition and safety with which Congress can grant and has granted large emergency powers, certainly ample to embrace this crisis, I am quite unimpressed with the argument that we should affirm possession of them without statute. Such power either has no beginning or it has no end. If it exists, it need submit to no legal restraint. I am not alarmed that it would plunge us straightway into dictatorship, but it is at least a step in that wrong direction. . . .

But I have no illusion that any decision by this Court can keep power in the hands of Congress if it is not wise and timely in meeting its problems. A crisis that challenges the President equally, or perhaps primarily, challenges Congress. If not good law, there was worldly wisdom in the maxim attributed to Napoleon that "The tools belong to the man who can use them." We may say that power to legislate for emergencies belongs in the hands of Congress, but only Congress itself can prevent power from slipping through its fingers.

The essence of our free Government is "leave to live by no man's leave, underneath the law"—to be governed by those impersonal forces which we call law. Our Government is fashioned to fulfill this concept so far as humanly possible. The Executive, except for recommendation and veto, has no legislative power. The executive action we have here originates in the individual will of the President and represents an exercise of authority without law. No one, perhaps not even the President, knows the limits of the power he may seek to exert in this instance and the parties affected cannot learn the limit of their rights. We do not know today what powers over labor or property would be claimed to flow from Government possession if we should legalize it, what rights to compensation would be claimed or recognized, or on what contingency it would end. With all its defects, delays and inconveniences, men have discovered no technique for long preserving free government except that the Executive be under the law, and that the law be made by parliamentary deliberations.

Such institutions may be destined to pass away. But it is the duty of the Court to be last, not first, to give them up.

Mr. Justice **Burton,** concurring in the opinion and judgment of the Court, said in part:

. . . In the case before us, Congress authorized a procedure which the President declined to follow. Instead, he followed another procedure which he hoped might eliminate the need for the first. Upon its failure, he issued an executive order to seize the steel properties in the face of the reserved right of Congress to adopt or reject that course as a matter of legislative policy.

This brings us to a further crucial question. Does the President, in such a situation, have inherent constitutional power to seize private property which makes congressional action in relation thereto unnecessary? We find no such power available to him under the present circumstances. The present situation is not comparable to that of an imminent invasion or threatened attack. We do not face the issue of what might be the President's constitutional power to meet such catastrophic situations. Nor is it claimed that the current seizure is in the nature of a military command addressed by the President, as Commander-in-Chief, to a mobilized nation waging, or imminently threatened with, total war.

The controlling fact here is that Congress, within its constitutionally delegated power, has prescribed for the President specific procedures, exclusive of seizure, for his use in meeting the present type of emergency. Congress has reserved to itself the right to determine where and when to authorize the seizure of property in meeting such an emergency. Under these circumstances, the President's order of April 8 invaded the jurisdiction of Congress. It violated the essence of the principle of the separation of governmental powers. Accordingly, the injunction against its effectiveness should be sustained.

Mr. Justice **Clark,** concurring in the judgment of the Court, said in part:

. . . In my view . . . the Constitution does grant to the President extensive authority in times of grave and imperative national emergency. In fact, to my thinking, such a grant may well be necessary to the very existence of the Constitution itself. As Lincoln aptly said, ''[is] it possible to lose the nation and yet preserve the Constitution?'' In describing this authority I care not whether one calls it ''residual,'' ''inherent,'' ''moral,'' ''implied,'' ''aggregate,'' ''emergency,'' or otherwise. . .

I conclude that where Congress has laid down specific procedures to deal with the type of crisis confronting the President, he must follow those procedures in meeting the crisis; but that in the absence of such action by Congress, the President's independent power to act depends upon the gravity of the situation confronting the nation. I cannot sustain the seizure in question because here . . . Congress had prescribed methods to be followed by the President in meeting the emergency at hand. . . .

. . . The Government made no effort to comply with the procedures established by the Selective Service Act of 1948, a statute which expressly authorizes seizures when producers fail to supply necessary defense matèriel. . . .

Mr. Chief Justice **Vinson,** with whom Justices **Reed** and **Minton** joined, dissented, saying in part:

Focusing now on the situation confronting the President on the night of April 8, 1952, we cannot but conclude that the President was performing his duty under the Constitution "to take Care that the Laws be faithfully executed"—a duty described by President Benjamin Harrison as "the central idea of the office."

The President reported to Congress the morning after the seizure that he acted because a work stoppage in steel production would immediately imperil the safety of the Nation by preventing execution of the legislative programs for procurement of military equipment. And, while a shutdown could be averted by granting the price concessions requested by plaintiffs, granting such concessions would disrupt the price stabilization program also enacted by Congress. Rather than fail to execute either legislative program, the President acted to execute both.

Much of the argument in this case has been directed at straw men. We do not now have before us the case of a President acting solely on the basis of his own notions of the public welfare. Nor is there any question of unlimited executive power in this case. The President himself closed the door to any such claim when he sent his Message to Congress stating his purpose to abide by any action of Congress, whether approving or disapproving his seizure action. Here, the President immediately made sure that Congress was fully informed of the temporary action he had taken only to preserve the legislative programs from destruction until Congress could act.

The absence of a specific statute authorizing seizure of the steel mills as a mode of executing the laws— both the military procurement program and the anti-inflation program—has not until today been thought to prevent the President from executing the laws. Unlike an administrative commission confined to the enforcement of the statute under which it was created, or the head of a department when administering a particular statute, the President is a constitutional officer charged with taking care that a "mass of legislation" be executed. Flexibility as to mode of execution to meet critical situations is a matter of practical necessity. . . .

As the District Judge stated, this is no time for "timorous" judicial action. But neither is this a time for timorous executive action. Faced with the duty of executing the defense programs which Congress had enacted and the disastrous effects that any stoppage in steel production would have on those programs, the President acted to preserve those programs by seizing the steel mills. There is no question that the possession was other than temporary in character and subject to congressional direction—either approving, disapproving or regulating the manner in which the mills were to be administered and returned to the owners. The President immediately informed Congress of his action and clearly stated his intention to abide by the legislative will. No basis for claims of arbitrary action, unlimited powers or dictatorial usurpation of congressional power appears from the facts of this case. On the contrary, judicial, legislative and executive precedents throughout our history demonstrate that in this case the President acted in full conformity with his duties under the Constitution. Accordingly, we would reverse the order of the District Court.

UNITED STATES v. NIXON

418 U. S. 683; 41 L. Ed. 2d 1039; 94 S. Ct. 3090 (1974)

In setting up a government based on the separation of powers, the framers deliberately devised a form in which authority was divided and policies would necessarily be made as a result of compromise rather than by a single person or body. Given what they viewed as a choice between "liberty" and "tyranny," they opted for liberty, but the decision to sacrifice speed and efficiency for debate and compromise was perhaps easier to make then than it would be now. The image of George III and the teachings of Montesquieu were fresh in their minds, government played a minimal role in people's lives, and the slowness of communications made quick decisions less important than they are today.

Since the turn of the century, and especially in the last forty years, all this has changed dramatically. The role of government has grown until it is the dominant force in people's lives, the world has shrunk until the most distant part is only a few hours away, the specter of George III has been relegated to the pages of history, and effective policy-making power has been steadily shifted to the President. With the new pace of the world and our intimate involvement in the affairs of other countries, the frustration and delays imposed by the separation of powers seem barely tolerable. Although given virtually dictatorial powers, presidents like Lincoln and Franklin Roosevelt had not betrayed the public trust and that kind of presidency seemed essential to the effectiveness of the United States in that area of world politics upon which our national safety depended. Demands for more government and more efficiency were inexorable and few people saw in them a threat to essential democratic values. The choice made by the framers seemed scarcely relevant.

Against this background it is easy to view Watergate as a turn in destiny—a Gilbert and Sullivan operetta played to awaken us to our danger. For it is hard to imagine a more improbable plot in which to set a crucial test of presidential power. Any competent writer of fiction could do better. On June 17, 1972, seven men were caught breaking into the Democratic National Committee headquarters in the Watergate, a luxury apartment-office complex a few blocks from the White House. (The reasons for the break-in are still obscure.) Instead of immediately admitting White House involvement in the affair with an apology for the enthusiasm of his followers (a course which he could almost certainly have survived politically), the President and his staff undertook the bizarre and dramatically ill-fated "Watergate cover-up." The outcome was the resignation, on August 9, 1974, of the President of the United States.

The burglary itself was the culmination of some three years of White House-directed investigation and harassment of political enemies, sparked in part by leaks to the press of the secret bombing of Cambodia and the "Pentagon Papers," and in part by a growing fear that President Nixon might not be reelected in 1972. A successful entry into the Democratic National Committee headquarters the month before had netted nothing of value, and this entry was apparently for the purpose of placing additional electronic bugging equipment.

Five of the "Watergate Seven" pleaded guilty to the burglary and the other two, both members of the Committee to Reelect the President, were convicted. While the upshot of the trial was to suggest that Watergate was merely the work of a few enthusiastic but misguided underlings whose intense loyalty to the President had led them into illegal activities, something about the trial itself belied this conclusion. At its close the presiding judge, John J. Sirica, stated that in his opinion the entire truth had not come out, and on the day of the sentencing he read in court a letter from James W. McCord, Jr., one of those convicted, stating that others involved in the break-in had not been prosecuted, that there had been perjury during the trial, and that pressure had been brought on him and others to plead guilty and keep silent.

A shocked Senate investigating committee heard McCord's story; then called John W. Dean III, a former counsel to the President. Dean testified for a week, explaining how the White House staff, and ultimately the President, had congratulated him on successfully limiting the case to the few who had been tried and discussed with him the question of executive clemency and hush money for some of them. He said the President had known of the White House involvement almost from the beginning and had been actively involved in permitting the cover-up to continue. Implicated by Dean's testimony were former Attorney General John Mitchell and top presidential aides H. R. Haldeman and John Ehrlichman. White House denials raised the question: Who was telling the truth?

The present constitutional issue appeared with the startling disclosure that presidential conversations for the previous two years had been recorded on tape including, apparently, those crucial conversations with John Dean. Since it seemed the credibility issue could thus be easily resolved, an immediate demand was made for the tapes; but the President, citing the separation of powers and the absolute right of the President to keep his conversations confidential, refused to release them either to the Senate committee or to Archibald Cox, the special prosecutor heading the government's investigation of the matter.

There the issue was joined. Judge Sirica, after hearing argument in August of 1973, ordered the President to turn the tapes over to Cox. (He declined to enforce the Senate committee's subpoena for want of jurisdiction.) He conceded that executive privilege did exist, but denied "that it is the Executive that finally determines whether its privilege is properly invoked. . . . Judicial control over the evidence in a case cannot be abdicated to the caprice of executive officers." Nor was he persuaded by the argument based on the separation of powers. Whatever the merits of Mississippi v. Johnson (1867), it would be unrealistic to argue since Youngstown Sheet and Tube Co. v. Sawyer (1952) that compulsory court process cannot touch the White House. "In all candor," he added, "the court fails to perceive any reason for suspending the power of courts to get evidence and rule on questions of privilege in criminal matters simply because it is the President of the United States who holds the evidence." He ordered the tapes turned over to him for in-camera inspection with the understanding that unprivileged portions would be made available to the grand jury. After an abortive effort to get the two parties to compromise, the court of appeals sustained Judge Sirica's order; Nixon v. Sirica, 487 Fed. 2d 700 (1973).

Despite a widespread assumption that the President would seek from the Supreme Court that "definitive decision" by which he had announced he would abide, he instead decided to avoid a "constitutional crisis" by declining to appeal the decision and ordered Cox, as "an employee of the executive branch," not to pursue the matter further. Declining to follow the court's order, he proposed instead to provide White House "summaries" of the tapes. Cox rejected the offer, and on October 20, in what has become known as the "Saturday Night Massacre," the President accepted the resignation of Attorney General Elliot Richardson when he refused to fire Cox, then fired Deputy Attorney General Ruckelshaus when *he* refused to fire Cox, and finally persuaded Solicitor General Robert H. Bork to fire Cox and his staff of ninety investigators.

Three days later, bowing to a "fire storm" of public protest and the start of formal impeachment proceedings in the House of Representatives, the President agreed to turn over the tapes themselves. By the end of the week Leon Jaworski, a former head of the American Bar Association, had been chosen as the new special prosecutor and was assured even more independence than Cox had enjoyed. (To assure the independence of prosecutors chosen to investigate malfeasance in the executive branch, Congress in 1978 passed the Ethics in Government Act discussed in the note to Morrison v. Olson).

Although two of the nine tapes ordered released turned out to be missing, and one had an unexplained eighteen-minute gap in it, enough was produced to clinch the indictments of seven more conspirators, including Mitchell, Haldeman, and Ehrlichman, on charges of conspiring to obstruct justice. On Jaworski's advice that a sitting president could not be indicted, President Nixon was named merely as an "unindicted co-conspirator." On order of Judge Sirica the grand jury evidence, including the tapes Jaworski had received, was turned over to the House Judiciary Committee for use in its impeachment investigation.

But the constitutional confrontation was not over. The House committee subpoenaed forty-two more conversations and Jaworski sixty-four, but the President refused to yield and instead made public some 1200 pages of White House-edited transcripts—among them some which had already been released under court order. The public response to this brutally candid glimpse of the workings of the Nixon presidency was one of horrified shock, and demands for his impeachment became overwhelming. If he would release this kind of material, the argument ran, what was he concealing?

In a last-ditch stand the President not only elected to carry Jaworski's subpoena to the Supreme Court, but to protest his being named an unindicted co-conspirator (a point later dismissed by the Court). Over the objection of the President, the Court agreed to by-pass the court of appeals and hear argument in the closing days of its term. The President, in a series of procedural maneuvers, argued that no case or controversy existed, since the dispute between the President and Jaworski was entirely within the executive branch and the President could decide what evidence he wanted to present in prosecuting a case. The Court, in the case below, rejected this argument on the ground that Jaworski had been given freedom to ask for just such information, that the President had promised him complete freedom to pursue in court any interference by the executive, and this was, in fact, "the kind of controversy courts traditionally resolve."

It is important to note that President Nixon did not claim executive privilege from the tapes on the ground that they contained material involving either military or diplomatic matters. He claimed, rather, that all personal presidential conversations with his aides were privileged because without the assurance of such confidentiality the President could not get the uninhibited advice he needed and the presidency would thus be weakened. It was, in effect, a claim that the sanctity of the presidency was the highest constitutional value, and it was this claim that the Court rejected in the present case.

The President's last constitutional crisis came in the wake of the Court's decision. In 1832, following the Supreme Court's decision in Worcester v. Georgia, President Andrew Jackson is reputed to have said, "John Marshall has made his decision, now let him enforce it." The realization that the court has no enforcement machinery at its command must make such a response a tempting one, and President Nixon, who alone knew what the tapes contained, reputedly agonized a whole day over the question whether or not to defy the Supreme Court. But wiser counsel prevailed and he agreed to comply with the Court's order.

Within a week of the Court's decision, while arguing whether to wait for the contents of the tapes, the House Judiciary Committee voted three articles of impeachment against the President. And President Nixon, even as he began complying with the Court order to release the tapes, elected to release transcripts of three of them which showed that he had known about the Watergate break-in from the beginning. With his concession that he had from the outset lied not only to his supporters in Congress, but even to his own lawyer, those on the judiciary committee who had argued that the President should not be impeached changed their minds. Next morning three members of the congressional leadership visited the President to tell him he could count on no more than ten votes in the House against impeachment and no more than fifteen votes in the Senate against removal. That night, in a television broadcast to the nation, President Nixon resigned his office, effective the following noon.

Mr. Chief Justice **Burger** delivered the opinion of the Court, saying in part:

IV. The Claim of Privilege

A.

Having determined that the requirements of Rule 17(c) were satisfied, we turn to the claim that the subpoena should be quashed because it demands "confidential conversations between a President and his close advisors that it would be inconsistent with the public interest to produce." The first contention is a broad claim that the separation of powers doctrine precludes judicial review of a President's claim of privilege. The second contention is that if he does not prevail on the claim of absolute privilege, the court should hold as a matter of constitutional law that the privilege prevails over the subpoena duces tecum.

In the performance of assigned constitutional duties each branch of the Government must initially interpret the Constitution, and the interpretation of its powers by any branch is due great respect from the others. The President's counsel, as we have noted, reads the Constitution as providing an absolute privilege of confidentiality for all Presidential communications. Many decisions of this Court, however, have unequivocally reaffirmed the holding of Marbury v. Madison (1803) that "[i]t is emphatically the province and duty of the judicial department to say what the law is."

No holding of the Court has defined the scope of judicial power specifically relating to the enforcement of a subpoena for confidential Presidential communications for use in a criminal prosecution, but other exercises of power by the Executive Branch and the Legislative Branch have been found invalid as in conflict with the Constitution. Powell v. McCormack (1969); Youngstown Sheet & Tube Co. v. Sawyer (1952). In a series of cases, the Court interpreted the explicit immunity conferred by express provisions of the Constitution on Members of the House and Senate by the Speech or Debate Clause, U. S. Const. Art. I, § 6. Doe v. McMillan (1973); Gravel v. United States (1972). . . . Since this Court has consistently exercised the power to construe and delineate claims arising under express powers, it must follow that the Court has authority to interpret claims with respect to powers alleged to derive from enumerated powers.

Our system of government "requires that federal courts on occasion interpret the Constitution in a manner at variance with the construction given the document by another branch." Powell v. McCormack. And in Baker v. Carr [1962], the Court stated: "Deciding whether a matter has in any measure been committed by the Constitution to another branch of government, or whether the action of that branch exceeds whatever authority has been committed, is itself a delicate exercise in constitutional interpretation, and is a responsibility of this Court as ultimate interpreter of the Constitution.'' Notwithstanding the deference each branch must accord the others, the "judicial Power of the United States" vested in the federal courts by Art. III, § 1, of the Constitution can no more be shared with the Executive Branch than the Chief Executive, for example, can share with the Judiciary the veto power, or the Congress share with the Judiciary the power to override a Presidential veto. Any other conclusion would be contrary to the basic concept of separation of powers and the checks and balances that flow from the scheme of a tripartite government. . . . We therefore reaffirm that it is the province and duty of this Court ''to say what the law is'' with respect to the claim of privilege presented in this case. Marbury v. Madison.

B.

In support of his claim of absolute privilege, the President's counsel urges two grounds, one of which is common to all governments and one of which is peculiar to our system of separation of powers. The first ground is the valid need for protection of communications between high Government officials and those who advise and assist them in the performance of their manifold duties; the importance of this confidentiality is too plain to require further discussion. Human experience teaches that those who expect public dissemination of their remarks may well temper candor with a concern for appearances and for their own interests to the detriment of the decisionmaking process.* Whatever the nature of the privilege of confidentiality of Presidential communications in the exercise of Art. II powers, the privilege can be said to derive from the supremacy of each branch within its own assigned area of constitutional duties. Certain powers and privileges flow from the nature of enumerated powers;† the protection of the confidentiality of Presidential communications has similar constitutional underpinnings.

The second ground asserted by the President's counsel in support of the claim of absolute privilege rests on the doctrine of separation of powers. Here it is argued that the independence of the Executive Branch within its own sphere, Humphrey's Executor v. United States (1935); Kilbourn v. Thompson (1881), insulates a President from a judicial

---

*There is nothing novel about governmental confidentiality. The meetings of the Constitutional Convention in 1787 were conducted in complete privacy. 1 M. Farrand, The Records of the Federal Convention of 1787, pp. xi-xxv (1911). Moreover, all records of those meetings were sealed for more than 30 years after the Convention. Most of the Framers acknowledged that without secrecy no constitution of the kind that was developed could have been written. C. Warren, The Making of the Constitution 134-139 (1937).

†The Special Prosecutor argues that there is no provision in the Constitution for a Presidential privilege as to the President's communications corresponding to the privilege of Members of Congress under the Speech or Debate Clause. But the silence of the Constitution on this score is not dispositive. "The rule of constitutional interpretation announced in McCulloch v. Maryland [1819] that that which was reasonably appropriate and relevant to the exercise of a granted power was to be considered as accompanying the grant, has been so universally applied that it suffices merely to state it." Marshall v. Gordon (1917).

subpoena in an ongoing criminal prosecution, and thereby protects confidential Presidential communications.

However, neither the doctrine of separation of powers, nor the need for confidentiality of high-level communications, without more, can sustain an absolute, unqualified Presidential privilege of immunity from judicial process under all circumstances. The President's need for complete candor and objectivity from advisers calls for great deference from the courts. However, when the privilege depends solely on the broad, undifferentiated claim of public interest in the confidentiality of such conversations, a confrontation with other values arises. Absent a claim of need to protect military, diplomatic, or sensitive national security secrets, we find it difficult to accept the argument that even the very important interest in confidentiality of Presidential communications is significantly diminished by production of such material for in camera inspection with all the protection that a district court will be obliged to provide.

The impediment that an absolute, unqualified privilege would place in the way of the primary constitutional duty of the Judicial Branch to do justice in criminal prosecutions would plainly conflict with the function of the courts under Art. III. In designing the structure of our Government and dividing and allocating the sovereign power among three co-equal branches, the Framers of the Constitution sought to provide a comprehensive system, but the separate powers were not intended to operate with absolute independence. "While the Constitution diffuses power the better to secure liberty, it also contemplates that practice will integrate the dispersed powers into a workable government. It enjoins upon its branches separateness but interdependence, autonomy but reciprocity." Youngstown Sheet & Tube Co. v. Sawyer. (Jackson, J., concurring). To read the Art. II powers of the President as providing an absolute privilege as against a subpoena essential to enforcement of criminal statutes on no more than a generalized claim of the public interest in confidentiality of nonmilitary and nondiplomatic discussions would upset the constitutional balance of "a workable government" and gravely impair the role of the courts under Art. III.

C.

Since we conclude that the legitimate needs of the judicial process may outweigh Presidential privilege, it is necessary to resolve those competing interests in a manner that preserves the essential functions of each branch. The right and indeed the duty to resolve that question does not free the judiciary from according high respect to the representations made on behalf of the President. United States v. Burr, 25 F. Cas. 187 (No. 14,694) (1807).

The expectation of a President to the confidentiality of his conversations and correspondence, like the claim of confidentiality of judicial deliberations, for example, has all the values to which we accord deference for the privacy of all citizens and added to those values the necessity for protection of the public interest in candid, objective, and even blunt or harsh opinions in Presidential decision making. A President and those who assist him must be free to explore alternatives in the process of shaping policies and making decisions and to do so in a way many would be unwilling to express except privately. These are the considerations justifying a presumptive privilege for Presidential communications. The privilege is fundamental to the operation of government and inextricably rooted in the separation of powers under the Constitution. In Nixon v. Sirica, 487 F. 2d 700 (1973), the Court of Appeals held that such Presidential communications are "presumptively privileged," and this position is accepted by both parties in the present litigation. We agree with Mr. Chief Justice Marshall's observation, therefore, that "[i]n no case of this kind would a court be required to proceed against the President as against an ordinary individual." United States v. Burr.

But this presumptive privilege must be considered in light of our historic commitment to the rule of law. This is nowhere more profoundly manifest than in our view that "the twofold aim [of criminal justice] is that guilt shall not escape or innocence suffer." Berger v. United States [1935]. We have elected to employ an adversary system of criminal justice in which the parties contest all issues before a court of law. The need to develop all relevant facts in the adversary system is both fundamental and comprehensive. The ends of criminal justice would be defeated if judgments were to be founded on a partial or speculative presentation of the facts. The very integrity of the judicial system and public confidence in the system depend on full disclosure of all the facts, within the framework of the rules of evidence. To ensure that justice is done, it is imperative to the function of courts that compulsory process be available for the production of evidence needed either by the prosecution or by the defense. . . .

In this case the President challenges a subpoena served on him as a third party requiring the production of materials for use in a criminal prosecution; he does so on the claim that he has a privilege against disclosure of confidential communications. He does not place his claim of privilege on the ground they are military or diplomatic secrets. As to these areas of Art. II duties the courts have traditionally shown the utmost deference to Presidential responsibilities. In [Chicago] & S. Air Lines v. Waterman S. S. Corp. (1948), dealing with Presidential authority involving foreign policy considerations, the court said: "The President, both as Commander-in-Chief and as the Nation's organ for foreign affairs, has available intelligence services whose reports are not and ought not to be published to the world. It would be intolerable that courts, without the relevant information, should review and perhaps nullify actions of the Executive taken on information properly held secret." In United States v. Reynolds (1953), dealing with a claimant's demand for evidence in a damage case against the Government the Court said: "It may be possible to satisfy the court, from all the circumstances of the case, that there is a reasonable danger that compulsion of the evidence will expose military matters which, in the interest of national security, should not be divulged. When this is the case, the occasion for the privilege is appropriate, and the court should not jeopardize the security which the privilege is meant to protect by insisting upon an examination of the evidence, even by the judge alone, in chambers." No case of the Court, however, has extended this high degree of deference to a President's generalized interest in confidentiality. Nowhere in the Constitution, as we have noted earlier, is there any explicit reference to a privilege of confidentiality, yet to the extent this interest relates to the effective discharge of a President's powers, it is constitutionally based.

The right to the production of all evidence at a criminal trial similarly has constitutional dimensions. The Sixth Amendment explicitly confers upon every defendant in a criminal trial the right "to be confronted with the witnesses against him" and "to have compulsory process for obtaining witnesses in his favor." Moreover, the Fifth Amendment also guarantees that no person shall be deprived of liberty without due process of law. It is the manifest duty of the courts to vindicate those guarantees, and to accomplish that it is essential that all relevant and admissible evidence be produced.

In this case we must weigh the importance of the general privilege of confidentiality of Presidential communications in performance of his responsibilities against the inroads of such a privilege on the fair administration of criminal justice.* The interest in preserving confidentiality is weighty indeed and entitled to great respect. However, we cannot conclude that advisers will be moved to temper the candor of their remarks by the infrequent occasions of disclosure because of the possibility that such conversations will be called for in the context of a criminal prosecution.

On the other hand, the allowance of the privilege to withhold evidence that is demonstrably relevant in a criminal trial would cut deeply into the guarantee of due process of law and gravely impair the basic function of the courts. . . . Without access to specific facts a criminal prosecution may be totally frustrated. The President's broad interest in confidentiality of communications will not be vitiated by disclosure of a limited number of conversations preliminarily shown to have some bearing on the pending criminal cases.

We conclude that when the ground for asserting privilege as to subpoenaed materials sought for use in a criminal trial is based only on the generalized interest in confidentiality, it cannot prevail over the fundamental demands of due process of law in the fair administration of criminal justice. The generalized assertion of privilege must yield to the demonstrated, specific need for evidence in a pending criminal trial. . . .

Mr. Justice **Rehnquist** took no part in the consideration or decision of these cases.

---

*We are not here concerned with the balance between the President's generalized interest in confidentiality and the need for relevant evidence in civil litigation, nor with that between the confidentiality interest and congressional demands for information, nor with the President's interest in preserving state secrets. We address only the conflict between the President's assertion of a generalized privilege of confidentiality and the constitutional need for relevant evidence in criminal trials.

2

The Division of Powers between State and Federal Governments

A. The Theory of Federalism

McCULLOCH v. MARYLAND

4 Wheaton 316; 4 L. Ed. 579 (1819)

Perhaps the most difficult problem faced by the government of a large nation is the reconciliation of local and national interests. To be strong, a country must have a strong central government. To be strong it must also have the support of its people, and this support will come only if the people are allowed to solve at the local level those problems which they regard as local in nature. The American Revolution stemmed from the failure of George III to allow his American colonies sufficient local autonomy, and the framers of the new Constitution knew that they must find a wiser adjustment of these competing interests and loyalties if the country were to endure as a political unit. The solution they worked out was to delegate in Article I, Sec. 8, certain enumerated powers to the national government. The Tenth Amendment declared that those powers not so delegated were left to the states, or to the people, to be later assigned by constitutional amendments.

One of the axioms of American constitutional law is that Congress has only powers that are delegated to it by the Constitution, or are reasonably implied from those so delegated. The origin and history of this theory of national power is as follows: when Randolph proposed the Virginia Plan in the Constitutional Convention of 1787, it contained the only sound principle by which the powers of nation and state could be divided. It stated: " . . . the national legislature ought to be empowered . . . to legislate in all cases to which the separate states are incompetent, or in which the harmony of the United States may be interrupted by the exercise of individual legislation." This stated a principle rather than a method of allocating powers, and as a principle it was received with approval by the Convention. After two months of debate the Convention created a committee of detail to formulate the text of a constitution and gave it various instructions. The instruction with regard to national powers was that: "The national legislature ought to possess the legislative rights vested in Congress by the Confederation; and, moreover, to legislate in all cases for the general interests of the Union, and also in those to which the states are separately incompetent, or in which the harmony of the United States may be interrupted by individual legislation." Acting upon this instruction the committee of detail reported back to the Convention the specific enumeration of the powers of Congress found in Article I, Sec. 8. The committee, adhering, as did the entire Convention, to the principle of delegated powers, thus gave to the new Congress all of the powers then believed to be described in the article of instruction; and by providing for amendments in Article V, it created the means by which those powers could be increased or altered when it seemed desirable to do so.

In spite of this very conclusive evidence to the contrary, it has sometimes been urged that the framers intended that Congress should have the power to deal with any truly national problem whether that power is delegated to it or not. James Wilson, a member of the Convention of 1787 and later a justice of the Supreme Court, is quoted, not too convincingly, as sponsoring this theory. It remained for President Theodore Roosevelt to publicize the doctrine in his forceful discussions of what he called the New Nationalism. He pointed out the awkward consequences of the fact that business combinations had grown to such proportions that they were beyond the legislative reach of any state or states, and yet could not be effectively controlled by Congress since the power of Congress was limited to the interstate commerce aspects of big business. In one of his better phrases he referred to the "twilight zone" in our constitutional system, a zone lying safely between state and federal authority, to which "malefactors of great wealth" might repair and be safe from punishment and restraint. He urged that "when-ever the states cannot act, because the need to be met is not one merely of a single locality, then the national government, representing all the people, should have complete power to act."

The Supreme Court rejected this doctrine out of hand in Kansas v. Colorado (1907), a case in which the United States tried to intervene in a dispute over the control of river water on the ground that the problem of reclaiming arid land was "national," since it was beyond the geographical jurisdiction of any one state. The Court emphasized that ours is a government of "enumerated powers" and pointed out that the Tenth Amendment had been adopted because of a "widespread fear that the national government might, under the pressure of a supposed general welfare, attempt to exercise powers which had not been granted."

Although the Court has never questioned the doctrine that the national government is one of delegated powers, as early as 1819 in McCulloch v. Maryland, printed below, it made clear that the fact that they were delegated did not mean they must be given a narrow or rigid interpretation. When Congress in 1791 chartered the First Bank of the United States, it was only after a most full and bitter argument as to whether it had the power to do so. Hamilton, who had proposed the creation of the bank, had written an elaborate opinion defending it as an exercise of a power reasonably implied from those expressly delegated to Congress. Jefferson and his friends had stoutly maintained that congressional powers must be strictly construed and that the granting of the charter was an act of unwarrantable usurpation. Nevertheless the charter of the First Bank was never attacked in the courts as being unconstitutional, and the institution continued to exist until its charter expired in 1811.

The financial conditions ensuing after the War of 1812 made the reestablishment of the bank desirable, and the Second Bank of the United States was accordingly chartered in 1816. Almost immediately it incurred the bitter odium of large sections of the country, especially of the West and South. The bank was largely under the control of the Federalists, who were accused of using it as a political machine and of wielding its great influence for political purposes; its stock was largely held by British capitalists and other foreign investors; and it was accused of being responsible for a period of financial depression which brought ruin to thousands. It is true that the bank had begun operations under corrupt and inefficient management and had encouraged a high degree of inflation of credits. This had resulted in heavy losses to investors; in the state of Maryland the Baltimore branch collapsed with a loss to Maryland investors alone of a sum variously estimated from $1,700,000 to $3,000,000. Wiser counsel prevailed shortly, however, and the bank faced about and embarked upon a financial course as conservative as it had hitherto been headlong. It refused to accept the bank notes of the imprudent state banks and insisted upon the liquidation of its credits. One after another these overinflated state banks failed, and hundreds of speculators were ruined. Money was almost unobtainable.

While most of this financial disaster was the inevitable result of the orgies of inflation and speculation in which the frontier communities in particular had been indulging, the Bank of the United States was popularly regarded as the cause of the disaster, as the ruthless "money trust" which was ruining the prosperity of the country. A popular demand for legislative control of the bank was set up, and eight states passed either laws or constitutional amendments restricting the activities of the bank or imposing heavy burdens upon it. The law involved in this case, passed by the legislature of Maryland, which was particularly hostile to the bank because of its earlier debacle, is typical of this legislative onslaught.

The Maryland statute forbade all banks not chartered by the state itself to issue bank notes save upon special stamped paper obtainable upon the payment of a very heavy tax. This requirement could be commuted by the payment of an annual tax to the state of $15,000. A penalty of $500 forfeiture was inflicted for each offense, an amount which in the case of the now large and prosperous Baltimore branch of the Bank of the United States would have come possibly to millions of dollars. McCulloch, the cashier of the branch in Baltimore, issued notes without complying with the state law, and this action was brought on behalf of the state of Maryland to recover the penalties.

The case was argued for nine days before the Supreme Court by the greatest lawyers of the day; William Pinkney, Daniel Webster, and William Wirt defended the bank, while Luther Martin, Joseph Hopkinson, and Walter Jones represented the state of Maryland. The opinion of Marshall in the case is commonly regarded as his greatest state paper.

The announcement of the decision was the signal for a veritable storm of abuse directed against the Supreme Court. Judge Roane of the Virginia court of appeals published a series of newspaper attacks upon the decision so bitter that Marshall was led to write a reply in his defense. The Virginia legislature passed a resolution urging that the Supreme Court be shorn of its power to pass upon cases to which states were parties. Ohio, which had previously passed a law taxing each branch of the Bank of the United States within its limits $50,000 a year, defied the Supreme Court and proceeded to collect the tax in spite of its decision, a position from which it was later obliged to withdraw; see Osborn v. The Bank of the United States (1824). The attack upon the Court in this case was directed in large part against the failure of that tribunal to invalidate an act of Congress (incorporating the bank) and not against the exercise of the judicial veto. The decision was particularly odious to the strict constructionists because it not only sustained the doctrine of the implied powers of Congress but also recognized the binding effect of an implied limitation upon the states preventing them from interfering with the functioning of federal agencies.

The doctrine of implied powers in Congress was not new in this case. Not only had it been ably expounded by Hamilton, as mentioned above, but in the case of United States v. Fisher (1805), which had been decided 14 years before, Marshall himself had given expression to the doctrine; but as that case did not relate to any such important political issue as did the bank case, the decision at that time had evoked no comment.

While it is clear from Kansas v. Colorado that Congress has no authority in the absence of a delegation of power, are there limits to the way in which Congress can exercise those powers that are clearly delegated? From time to time, and in connection with various powers of Congress, the Court has held that there are. In Ashton v. Cameron County Water Dist. (1936) Congress was held unable to extend the bankruptcy power to a state agency, since to do so would be to "pass laws inconsistent with the idea of sovereignty," and in Hammer v. Dagenhart (1918) the Court held for the first time that the powers reserved to the states by the Tenth Amendment acted as a limit on the use of congressional power. There the Court struck down the use of the commerce power to control child labor. The philosophy underlying this decision is that the powers of Congress cannot be used to achieve ends which have not been delegated to Congress, and hence, according to the Tenth Amendment, are reserved to the states.

Perhaps the most lucid explanation of this doctrine, dubbed "dual federalism" by Professor E. S. Corwin, is that made by Justice Roberts in the case of United States v. Butler (1936): "From the accepted doctrine that the United States is a government of delegated powers, it follows that those not expressly granted, or reasonably to be implied from such as are conferred, are reserved to the states or to the people. To forestall any suggestion to the contrary, the Tenth Amendment was adopted. The same proposition, otherwise stated, is that powers not granted are prohibited. None to regulate agricultural production is given, and therefore legislation by Congress for that purpose is forbidden.

"It is an established principle that the attainment of a prohibited end may not be accomplished under the pretext of the exertion of powers which are granted."

The doctrine of dual federalism, in the form that appears here, was destined to be short-lived. In the Social Security Act Cases in 1937 the Court sustained an almost identical use of the tax power, and in United States v. Darby in 1941 the Court consciously abandoned it, noting that the Tenth Amendment "states but a truism that all is retained which has not been surrendered."

Mr. Chief Justice **Marshall** delivered the opinion of the Court, saying in part:

In the case now to be determined, the defendant, a sovereign State, denies the obligation of a law enacted

by the legislature of the Union; and the plaintiff, on his part, contests the validity of an Act which has been passed by the legislature of that State. The Constitution of our country, in its most interesting and vital parts, is to be considered; the conflicting powers of the government of the Union and of its members, as marked in that Constitution, are to be discussed; and an opinion given, which may essentially influence the great operations of the government. No tribunal can approach such a question without a deep sense of its importance, and of the awful responsibility involved in its decision. But it must be decided peacefully, or remain a source of hostile legislation, perhaps of hostility of a still more serious nature; and if it is to be so decided, by this tribunal alone can the decision be made. On the Supreme Court of the United States has the Constitution of our country devolved this important duty.

The first question made in the cause is, has Congress power to incorporate a bank? . . .

In discussing this question, the counsel for the State of Maryland have deemed it of some importance, in the construction of the Constitution, to consider that instrument not as emanating from the people, but as the act of sovereign and independent states. The powers of the general government, it has been said, are delegated by the states, who alone are truly sovereign; and must be exercised in subordination to the states, who alone possess supreme dominion.

It would be difficult to sustain this proposition. The convention which framed the Constitution was, indeed, elected by the state legislatures. But the instrument, when it came from their hands, was a mere proposal, without obligation, or pretensions to it. It was reported to the then existing Congress of the United States, with a request that it might "be submitted to a convention of delegates, chosen in each state, by the people thereof, under the recommendation of its legislature, for their assent and ratification." This mode of proceeding was adopted; and by the convention, by Congress, and by the state legislatures, the instrument was submitted to the people. They acted upon it, in the only manner in which they can act safely, effectively, and wisely, on such a subject, by assembling in convention. It is true, they assembled in their several states; and where else should they have assembled? No political dreamer was ever wild enough to think of breaking down the lines which separate the states, and of compounding the American people into one common mass. Of consequence, when they act, they act in their states. But the measures they adopt do not, on that account, cease to be the measures of the people themselves, or become the measures of the state governments.

From these conventions the Constitution derives its whole authority. The government proceeds directly from the people; is "ordained and established" in the name of the people; and is declared to be ordained, "in order to form a more perfect union, establish justice, insure domestic tranquility, and secure the blessings of liberty to themselves and to their posterity." The assent of the states, in their sovereign capacity, is implied in calling a convention, and thus submitting that instrument to the people. But the people were at perfect liberty to accept or reject it; and their act was final. It required not the affirmance, and could not be negatived, by the state governments. The Constitution, when thus adopted, was of complete obligation, and bound the state sovereignties.

It has been said, that the people had already surrendered all their powers to the state sovereignties, and had nothing more to give. But, surely, the question whether they may resume and modify the powers granted to government, does not remain to be settled in this country. Much more might the legitimacy of the general government be doubted, had it been created by the states. The powers delegated to the state sovereignties were to be exercised by themselves, not by a distinct and independent sovereignty, created by themselves. To the formation of a league, such as was the Confederation, the state sovereignties were certainly competent. But when, "in order to form a more perfect union," it was deemed necessary to change this alliance into an effective government, possessing great and sovereign powers, and acting directly on the people, the necessity of referring it to the people, and of deriving its powers directly from them, was felt and acknowledged by all.

The government of the Union, then (whatever may be the influence of this fact on the case), is emphatically and truly a government of the people. In form and in substance it emanates from them, its powers are granted by them, and are to be exercised directly on them, and for their benefit.

This government is acknowledged by all to be one of enumerated powers. The principle, that it can exercise only the powers granted to it, would seem too apparent to have required to be enforced by all those arguments which its enlightened friends, while it was depending before the people, found it necessary to urge. That principle is now universally admitted. But the question respecting the extent of the powers actually granted, is perpetually arising, and will probably continue to arise, as long as our system shall exist.

In discussing these questions, the conflicting powers of the general and State governments must be brought into view, and the supremacy of their respective laws, when they are in opposition, must be settled.

If any one proposition could command the universal assent of mankind, we might expect it would be this: that the government of the Union, though limited in its powers, is supreme within its sphere of action. This would seem to result necessarily from its nature. It is the government of all; its powers are delegated by all; it represents all, and acts for all. Though any one State may be willing to control its operations, no State is willing to allow others to control them. The nation, on those subjects on which it can act, must necessarily bind its component parts. But this question is not left to mere reason: the people have, in express terms, decided it, by saying, "this Constitution, and the laws of the United States, which shall be made in pursuance thereof," "shall be the supreme law of the land," and by requiring that the members of the State legislatures, and the officers of the executive and judicial departments of the States, shall take the oath of fidelity to it.

The government of the United States, then, though limited in its powers, is supreme; and its laws, when made in pursuance of the Constitution, form the supreme law of the land, "anything in the Constitution or laws of any State to the contrary notwithstanding."

Among the enumerated powers, we do not find that of establishing a bank or creating a corporation. But there is no phrase in the instrument which, like the Articles of Confederation, excludes incidental or implied powers; and which requires that everything granted shall be expressly and minutely described. Even the Tenth Amendment, which was framed for the purpose of quieting the excessive jealousies which had been excited, omits the word "expressly," and declares only that the powers "not delegated to the United States, nor prohibited to the States, are reserved to the States or to the people"; thus leaving the question, whether the particular power which may become the subject of contest, has been delegated to the one government, or prohibited to the other, to depend on a fair construction of the whole instrument. The men who drew and adopted this amendment, had experienced the embarrassments resulting from the insertion of this word in the Articles of Confederation, and probably omitted it to avoid those embarrassments. A constitution, to contain an accurate detail of all the subdivisions of which its great powers will admit, and of all the means by which they may be carried into execution, would partake of the prolixity of a legal code, and could scarcely be embraced by the human mind. It would probably never be understood by the public. Its nature, therefore, requires, that only its great outlines should be marked, its important objects designated, and the minor ingredients which compose those objects be deduced from the nature of the objects themselves. That this idea was entertained by the framers of the American Constitution, is not only to be inferred from the nature of the instrument, but from the language. Why else were some of the limitations, found in the ninth section of the first article, introduced? It is also, in some degree, warranted by their having omitted to use any restrictive term which might prevent its receiving a fair and just interpretation. In considering this question, then, we must never forget, that it is a constitution we are expounding.

Although, among the enumerated powers of government, we do not find the word "bank," or "incorporation," we find the great powers to lay and collect taxes; to borrow money; to regulate commerce; to declare and conduct a war; and to raise and support armies and navies. The sword and the purse, all the external relations, and no inconsiderable portion of the industry of the nation, are entrusted to its government. It can never be pretended that these vast powers draw after them others of inferior importance, merely because they are inferior. Such an idea can never be advanced. But it may, with great reason, be contended, that a government, entrusted with such ample powers, on the due execution of which the happiness and prosperity of the nation so vitally depends, must also be entrusted with ample means for their execution. The power being given, it is the interest of the nation to facilitate its execution. It can never be their interest, anu cannot be presumed to have been their intention, to clog and embarrass its execution by withholding the most appropriate means. Throughout this vast republic, from the St. Croix to the Gulf of Mexico, from the Atlantic to the Pacific, revenue is to be collected and expended, armies are to be marched and supported. The exigencies of the nation may require, that the treasure raised in the North should be transported to the South, that raised in the East conveyed to the West, or that this order should be reversed. Is that construction of the Constitution to be preferred which would render these operations difficult, hazardous, and expensive? Can we adopt that construction (unless the words imperiously require it) which would impute to the framers of that instrument, when granting these powers for the public good, the intention of impeding their exercise by withholding a choice of means? If, indeed, such be the mandate of the Constitution, we have only to obey; but that instrument does not profess to enumerate the means by which the powers it confers may be executed; nor does it prohibit the creation of a corporation, if the existence of such a being be essential to the beneficial exercise of those powers. It is, then, the subject of fair inquiry, how far such means may be employed. It is not denied, that the powers given to the government imply the ordinary means of execution. That, for example, of raising revenue, and applying it to national purposes, is admitted to imply the power of conveying money from place to place, as the exigencies of the nation may require, and of employing the usual means of conveyance. But it is denied that the government has its choice of means; or, that it may employ the most convenient means, if, to employ them, it be necessary to erect a corporation.

. . . The power of creating a corporation, though appertaining to sovereignty, is not, like the power of making war, or levying taxes, or of regulating commerce, a great substantive and independent power, which cannot be implied as incidental to other powers, or used as a means of executing them. It is never the end for which other powers are exercised, but a means by which other objects are accomplished. No contributions are made to charity for the sake of an incorporation, but a corporation is created to administer the charity; no seminary of learning is instituted in order to be incorporated, but the corporate character is conferred to subserve the purposes of education. No city was ever built with the sole object of being incorporated, but is incorporated as affording the best means of being well governed. The power of creating a corporation is never used for its own sake, but for the purpose of effecting something else. No sufficient reason is, therefore, perceived, why it may not pass as incidental to those powers which are expressly given, if it be a direct mode of executing them.

But the Constitution of the United States has not left the right of Congress to employ the necessary means, for the execution of the powers conferred on the government, to general reasoning. To its enumeration of powers is added that of making ''all laws which shall be necessary and proper, for carrying into execution the foregoing powers, and all other powers vested by this Constitution, in the government of the United States, or in any department thereof.''

The counsel for the State of Maryland have urged various arguments, to prove that this clause, though in terms a grant of power, is not so in effect; but is really restrictive of the general right, which might otherwise be implied, of selecting means for executing the enumerated powers.

In support of this proposition, they have found it necessary to contend, that this clause was inserted for the purpose of conferring on Congress the power of making laws. That, without it, doubts might be entertained, whether Congress could exercise its powers in the form of legislation.

But could this be the object for which it was inserted? . . . That a legislature, endowed with legislative powers, can legislate, is a proposition too self-evident to have been questioned.

But the argument on which most reliance is placed, is drawn from the peculiar language of this clause. Congress is not empowered by it to make all laws, which may have relation to the powers conferred on the government, but such only as may be ''necessary and proper'' for carrying them into execution. The word ''necessary'' is considered as controlling the whole sentence, and as limiting the right to pass laws for the execution of the granted powers, to such as are indispensable, and without which the power would be nugatory. That it excludes the choice of means, and leaves to Congress, in each case, that only which is most direct and simple.

Is it true, that this is the sense in which the word ''necessary'' is always used? Does it always import an absolute physical necessity, so strong, that one thing, to which another may be termed necessary, cannot exist without that other? We think it does not. If reference be had to its use, in the common affairs of the world, or in approved authors, we find that it frequently imports no more than that one thing is convenient, or useful, or essential to another. To employ the means necessary to an end, is generally understood as employing any means calculated to produce the end, and not as being confined to those single means, without which the end would be entirely unattainable. Such is the character of human language that no word conveys to the mind, in all situations, one single definite idea; and nothing is more common than to use words in a figurative sense. Almost all compositions contain words, which, taken in their rigorous sense, would convey a meaning different from that which is obviously intended. It is essential to just construction, that many words which import something excessive, should be understood in a more mitigated sense—in that sense which common usage justifies. The word ''necessary'' is of this description. It has not a fixed character peculiar to itself. It admits of all degrees of comparison; and is often connected with other words, which increase or diminish the impression the mind receives of the urgency it imports. A thing may be necessary, very necessary, absolutely or indispensably necessary. To no mind would the same idea be conveyed, by these several phrases. . . . This word, then, like others, is used in various senses; and, in its construction, the subject, the context, the intention of the person using them, are all to be taken into view.

Let this be done in the case under consideration. The subject is the execution of those great powers on which the welfare of a nation essentially depends. It must have been the intention of those who gave these powers, to insure, as far as human prudence could insure, their beneficial execution. This could not be done by confiding the choice of means to such narrow limits as not to leave it in the power of Congress to adopt any which might be appropriate, and which were conducive to the end. This provision is made in a constitution intended to endure for ages to come, and, consequently, to be adapted to the various crises of human affairs. To have prescribed the means by which government should, in all future time, execute its powers, would have been to change, entirely, the character of the instrument, and give it the properties of a legal code. It would have been an unwise attempt to provide, by immutable rules, for exigencies which, if foreseen at all, must have been seen dimly, and which can be best provided for as they occur. To have declared that the best means shall not be used, but those alone without which the power given would be nugatory, would have been to deprive the legislature of the capacity to avail itself of experience, to exercise its reason, and to accommodate its legislation to circumstances. . . .

But the argument which most conclusively demonstrates the error of the construction contended for by the counsel for the State of Maryland, is founded on the intention of the convention, as manifested in the whole clause. To waste time and argument in proving that, without it, Congress might carry its powers into execution, would be not much less idle than to hold a lighted taper to the sun. As little can it be required to prove, that in the absence of this clause, Congress would have some choice of means. That it might employ those which, in its judgment, would most advantageously effect the object to be accomplished. That any means adapted to the end, any means which tended directly to the execution of the constitutional powers of the government, were in themselves constitutional. This clause, as construed by the State of Maryland, would abridge and almost annihilate this useful and necessary right of the legislature to select its means. That this could not be intended, is, we should think, had it not been already controverted, too apparent for controversy. We think so for the following reasons:

1st. The clause is placed among the powers of Congress, not among the limitations on those powers.

2d. Its terms purport to enlarge, not to diminish the powers vested in the government. It purports to be an additional power, not a restriction on those already granted. No reason has been or can be assigned, for thus concealing an intention to narrow the discretion of the national legislature, under words which purport to enlarge it. The framers of the Constitution wished its adoption, and well knew that it would be endangered by its strength, not by its weakness. Had they been capable of using language which would convey to the eye one idea, and after deep reflection, impress on the mind another, they would rather have disguised the grant of power, than its limitation. If then, their intention had been, by this clause, to restrain the free use of means which might otherwise have been implied, that intention would have been inserted in another place, and would have been expressed in terms resembling these: "In carrying into execution the foregoing powers, and all others," etc., "no laws shall be passed but such as are necessary and proper." Had the intention been to make this clause restrictive, it would unquestionably have been so in form as well as in effect.

The result of the most careful and attentive consideration bestowed upon this clause is, that if it does not enlarge, it cannot be construed to restrain the powers of Congress, or to impair the right of the legislature to exercise its best judgment in the selection of measures, to carry into execution the constitutional powers of the government. If no other motive for its insertion can be suggested, a sufficient one is found in the desire to remove all doubts respecting the right to legislate on that vast mass of incidental powers which must be involved in the Constitution, if that instrument be not a splendid bauble.

We admit, as all must admit, that the powers of the government are limited, and that its limits are not to be transcended. But we think the sound construction of the Constitution must allow to the national legislature that discretion, with respect to the means by which the powers it confers are to be carried into execution, which will enable that body to perform the high duties assigned to it, in the manner most beneficial to the people. Let the end be legitimate, let it be within the scope of the Constitution, and all means which are appropriate, which are plainly adapted to that end, which are not prohibited, but consist with the letter and spirit of the Constitution, are constitutional. . . .

If a corporation may be employed indiscriminately with other means to carry into execution the powers of the government, no particular reason can be assigned for excluding the use of a bank, if required for its fiscal operations. To use one, must be within the discretion of Congress, if it be an appropriate mode of executing the powers of government. That it is a convenient, a useful, and essential instrument in the prosecution of its fiscal operations, is not now a subject of controversy. All those who have been concerned in the administration of our finances, have concurred in representing its importance and necessity; and so strongly have they been felt, that statesmen of the first class, whose previous opinions against it had been confirmed by every circumstance which can fix the human judgment, have yielded those opinions to the exigencies of the nation. . . .

But, were its necessity less apparent, none can deny its being an appropriate measure; and if it is, the degree of its necessity, as has been very justly observed, is to be discussed in another place. Should Congress, in the execution of its powers, adopt measures which are prohibited by the constitution; or should Congress, under the pretext of executing its powers, pass laws for tne accomplishment of objects not entrusted to the government, it would become the painful duty of this tribunal, should a case requiring such a decision come before it, to say that such an act was not the law of the land. But where the law is not prohibited, and is really calculated to effect any of the objects entrusted to the government, to undertake here to inquire into the degree of its necessity, would be to pass the line which circumscribes the judicial department, and to tread on legislative ground. This court disclaims all pretensions to such a power. . . .

After the most deliberate consideration, it is the unanimous and decided opinion of this court, that the Act to incorporate the Bank of the United States is a law made in pursuance of the Constitution, and is a part of the supreme law of the land. . . .

It being the opinion of the court that the act incorporating the bank is constitutional; and that the power of establishing a branch in the State of Maryland might be properly exercised by the bank itself, we proceed to inquire:

2. Whether the State of Maryland may, without violating the Constitution, tax that branch?

That the power of taxation is one of vital importance; that it is retained by the States; that it is not abridged by the grant of a similar power to the government of the Union; that it is to be concurrently exercised by the two governments: are truths which have never been denied. But, such is the paramount character of the Constitution, that its capacity to withdraw any subject from the action of even this power, is admitted. The States are expressly forbidden to lay any duties on imports or exports, except what may be absolutely necessary for executing their inspection laws. If the obligation of this prohibition must be conceded—if it may restrain a State from the exercise of its taxing power on imports and exports; the same paramount character would seem to restrain, as it certainly may restrain, a State from such other exercise of this power, as is in its nature incompatible with, and repugnant to, the constitutional laws of the Union. A law, absolutely repugnant to another, as entirely repeals that other as if express terms of repeal were used.

On this ground the counsel for the bank place its claim to be exempted from the power of a State to tax its operations. There is no express provision for the case, but the claim has been sustained on a principle which so entirely pervades the Constitution, is so intermixed with the materials which compose it, so interwoven with its web, so blended with its texture, as to be incapable of being separated from it, without rending it into shreds.

This great principle is, that the Constitution and the laws made in pursuance thereof are supreme; that they control the Constitution and laws of the respective States, and cannot be controlled by them. From this, which may be almost termed an axiom, other propositions are deduced as corollaries, on the truth or error of which, and on their application to this case, the cause has been supposed to depend. These are, 1st. That a power to create implies a power to preserve. 2d. That a power to destroy, if wielded by a different hand, is hostile to, and incompatible with, these powers to create and preserve. 3d. That where this repugnancy exists, that authority which is supreme must control, not yield to that over which it is supreme. . . .

The power of Congress to create, and of course to continue, the bank, was the subject of the preceding part of this opinion; and is no longer to be considered as questionable.

That the power of taxing it by the States may be exercised so as to destroy it, is too obvious to be denied. But taxation is said to be an absolute power, which acknowledges no other limits than those expressly prescribed in the Constitution, and like sovereign power of every other description, is trusted to the discretion of those who use it. . . .

The argument on the part of the State of Maryland, is, not that the States may directly resist a law of Congress, but that they may exercise their acknowledged powers upon it, and that the Constitution leaves them this right in the confidence that they will not abuse it. . . .

That the power to tax involves the power to destroy; that the power to destroy may defeat and render useless the power to create; that there is a plain repugnance, in conferring on one government a power to control the constitutional measures of another, which other, with respect to those very measures, is declared to be supreme over that which exerts the control, are propositions not to be denied. But all inconsistencies are to be reconciled by the magic of the word "confidence." Taxation, it is said, does not necessarily and unavoidably destroy. To carry it to the excess of destruction would be an abuse, to presume which, would banish that confidence which is essential to all government.

But is this a case of confidence? Would the people of any one State trust those of another with a power to control the most insignificant operations of their State government? We know they would not. Why, then, should we suppose that the people of any one State should be willing to trust those of another with a power to control the operations of a government to which they have confided their most important and most valuable interests? In the legislature of the Union alone, are all represented. The legislature of the Union alone, therefore, can be trusted by the people with the power of controlling measures which concern all, in the confidence that it will not be abused. This, then, is not a case of confidence, and we must consider it as it really is.

If we apply the principle for which the State of Maryland contends, to the Constitution generally, we shall find it capable of changing totally the character of that instrument. We shall find it capable of arresting all the measures of the government, and of prostrating it at the foot of the States. The American people have declared their Constitution, and the laws made in pursuance thereof, to be supreme; but this principle would transfer the supremacy, in fact, to the States.

If the States may tax one instrument, employed by the government in the execution of its powers, they may tax any and every other instrument. They may tax the mail; they may tax the mint; they may tax patent rights; they may tax the papers of the custom-house; they may tax judicial process; they may tax all the means employed by the government, to an excess which would defeat all the ends of government. This was not intended by the American people. They did not design to make their government dependent on the States. . . .

It has also been insisted, that, as the power of taxation in the general and State governments is acknowledged to be concurrent, every argument which would sustain the right of the general government to tax banks chartered by the States, will equally sustain the right of the States to tax banks chartered by the general government.

But the two cases are not on the same reason. The people of all the States have created the general government, and have conferred upon it the general power of taxation. The people of all the States, and the States themselves, are represented in Congress, and, by their representatives, exercise this power. When they tax the chartered institutions of the States, they tax their constituents; and these taxes must be uniform. But when a State taxes the operations of the government of the United States, it acts upon institutions created, not by their own constituents, but by people over whom they claim no control. It acts upon the measures of a government created by others as well as themselves, for the benefit of others in common with themselves. The difference is that which always exists, and always must exist, between the action of the whole on a part, and the action of a part on the whole—between the laws of a government declared to be supreme, and those of a government which, when in opposition to those laws, is not supreme.

But if the full application of this argument could be admitted, it might bring into question the right of Congress to tax the State banks, and could not prove the right of the States to tax the Bank of the United States.

The court has bestowed on this subject its most deliberate consideration. The result is a conviction that the States have no power, by taxation or otherwise, to retard, impede, burden or in any manner control, the operations of the constitutional laws enacted by Congress to carry into execution the powers vested in the general government. This is, we think, the unavoidable consequence of that supremacy which the Constitution has declared.

We are unanimously of opinion, that the law passed by the legislature of Maryland, imposing a tax on the Bank of the United States, is unconstitutional and void.

This opinion does not deprive the States of any resources which they originally possessed. It does not extend to a tax paid by the real property of the bank, in common with the other real property within the State, nor to a tax imposed on the interest which the citizens of Maryland may hold in this institution, in common with other property of the same description throughout the State. But this is a tax on the operations of the bank, and is, consequently, a tax on the operation of an instrument employed by the government of the Union to carry its powers into execution. Such a tax must be unconstitutional. . . .

NATIONAL LEAGUE OF CITIES v. USERY

426 U. S. 833; 49 L. Ed. 2d 245 ; 96 S. Ct. 2465 (1976)

The traditional concept of federalism, that Congress is delegated certain powers and those that are left over are reserved to the states, has never commanded universal approval and has brought to the Court a number of thorny issues, each, in its own way, involving the question whether a state had a "sovereignty" that exempted it from the use of delegated federal authority.

Early among these was the problem of the status of newly created states. The power which Congress possesses to admit new states into the Union is a purely discretionary power. No territory has any right to claim statehood, but must wait until it seems wise to Congress to confer that status. It is not surprising, therefore, that Congress should assume that in the exercise of an unquestioned power to grant or withhold the privilege of admission it might exact such conditions from the incoming state as it saw fit. Congress, in fact, proceeded upon this theory, and as early as 1802 it compelled Ohio, as the price of admission into the Union, to agree not to tax for a period of five years lands within the state which were sold to persons by the United States government. This imposing of conditions of various kinds upon the incoming states became a settled policy of Congress, and the stipulations agreed to covered a considerable range of topics. They related to the disposition of public lands, many of them being much more detailed than the Ohio provision: to the use of navigable waters; to the protection of the rights of citizens of the United States; to slavery; to civil and religious liberty; to the right to vote.

In 1910 Arizona was authorized by a congressional enabling act to draw up a state constitution preparatory to entering the Union. The constitution framed contained provisions for the popular recall of judges. While Congress somewhat reluctantly passed a resolution admitting Arizona into the Union, President Taft, being bitterly opposed to the recall of judges, vetoed the resolution. A new resolution was then passed providing that Arizona be admitted on condition that the objectionable provision be stricken out of the constitution. This was done and Arizona became a member of the Union. The state thereupon promptly restored the recall of judges by amending the new state constitution, and has retained the provision ever since.

While it is clear that Congress can impose conditions upon the new states by simply refusing admission if it refuses to comply, it is a rather curious fact that the question of the binding nature of these restrictions was not brought before the Supreme Court until 1911 in the case of Coyle v. Smith. As a result of a complex political compromise, Oklahoma was admitted as a state with an irrevocable agreement that it would not move its capital from the city of Guthrie until 1913. In 1910, a bill initiated by the people providing that the state capital should forthwith be moved to Oklahoma City was approved by the voters of Oklahoma. This was, of course, in plain violation of the "irrevocable" agreement which the state had made, and a proceeding was instituted to test the validity of the law. In sustaining the right of the state to move its capital at its discretion regardless of its agreement, the Supreme Court enunciated the important doctrine of the political equality of the states.

In Coyle v. Smith (1911) the Court noted that "the definition of 'a state' is found in the powers possessed by the original states which adopted the Constitution," and that Article IV of the Constitution only granted Congress power to admit "new states into *this* Union." " 'This Union,' " the Court added, "was and is a union of states, equal in power, dignity, and authority, each competent to exert that residuum of sovereignty not delegated to the United States by the Constitution itself." Since any of the original thirteen states could have relocated its capital city at will, so could Oklahoma.

A distinction, however, should be noted between those conditions imposed upon incoming states which relate to political or governmental authority and which would therefore place the state upon an unequal footing in the Union, and those conditions in the nature of business agreements or contracts which relate to property. Thus, for example, the agreement of a new state to conditions in its Enabling Act that lands given to it by the United States in trust for certain purposes has been held enforceable like any other trust agreement. See Ervien v. United States (1919) in which New Mexico, which was given lands for school purposes, was held properly enjoined from using them for advertising the resources of the state.

It may be said that the vital question of whether one of the states of the Union may constitutionally secede was effectively and permanently answered upon the battlefields of the Civil War. Four years after the war had ended, however, the Supreme Court found itself under the necessity of deciding, in the case of Texas v. White (1869), whether the Southern states had at any time during the period of attempted secession been actually out of the Union. Was secession, in point of law, constitutionally possible? The facts in this case were as follows:

In 1850 the United States gave the state of Texas $10,000,000 in five percent bonds in settlement of certain boundary claims. Half were held in Washington; half were delivered to the state, and made payable to the state or bearer and redeemable after December 31, 1864. A Texas law was passed providing that the bonds should not be available in the hands of any holder until after their endorsement by the governor. Texas joined the Confederacy at the outbreak of the war, and in 1862 the state legislature repealed the act requiring the endorsement of the bonds by the governor and created a military board to provide for the expenses of the war, empowering the board to use any bonds in the state treasury for this purpose up to $1,000,000. In 1865 this board made a contract with White and others for the transfer of some of the bonds for military supplies. None of the bonds was endorsed by the governor of the state. Immediately upon the close of the war, but while the state was still "unreconstructed" or unrestored to its former normal status as a member of the Union, suit was brought by the governor of the state to get the bonds back and to enjoin White and the other defendants from receiving payment for them from the federal government. The suit was brought by Texas in the Supreme Court of the United States as an original action, and at the very threshold of the case arose the question whether Texas, after her efforts at secession, was still a "state" within the meaning of Article III of the Constitution extending the original jurisdiction of the Supreme Court to those cases "in which a State shall be party." Texas at this time was still unrepresented in Congress and the radical Republicans like Stevens claimed that she was out of the Union.

The Court held that secession was constitutionally impossible and that Texas had never ceased to be a state in the Union. Chief Justice Chase said the Articles of Confederation created what was solemnly declared to be a "perpetual Union"; that the Constitution was ordained "to form a more perfect Union"; and he concluded that: "The Constitution, in all of its provisions, looks to an indestructible union, composed of indestructible states." The fact that Texas, by her own efforts at secession, had temporarily given up the rights and privileges of membership in the Union did not alter the fact that she could not sever the constitutional ties which bound her to that Union. The Court accordingly took jurisdiction in the case and decided that Texas was entitled to recover the bonds.

In cases of spectacular importance the Supreme Court faced the issue of who holds title to the land beneath the sea within the so-called "three-mile" limit. The discovery of oil off the coasts of California, Louisiana, and Texas gave this underwater land tremendous value; and the three states, assuming the land was theirs, leased to various oil companies the right to drill for offshore oil. The United States, asserting that it was "the owner in fee simple, or possessed of paramount rights in and powers over" this land, brought suit to enjoin the states from trespassing upon it. The Supreme Court, in United States v. California (1947), invoked the "equal footing" rule announced in Coyle v. Smith to sustain the United States, at least in its claim to "paramount rights." The original 13 states, the Court found, had not "separately acquired ownership to the three-mile belt or the soil under it" so as to require the extension of similar rights to California.

The Court decided the claims of Louisiana (United States v. Louisiana, 1950) on the basis of the California decision. But United States v. Texas (1950) presented a slightly different problem. Texas had been an independent nation prior to its admission to the Union and had had undoubted title to its offshore lands. The Court applied the Coyle argument in reverse: "The 'equal footing' clause, we hold, works the same way in the converse situation presented by this case. It negatives any implied, special limitation of any of the paramount powers of the United States in favor of a State. . . . When Texas came into the Union, she ceased to be an independent nation. She then became a sister State on an 'equal footing' with all the other States. That act concededly entailed a relinquishment of some of her sovereignty. . . . We hold that as an incident to the transfer of that sovereignty any claim that Texas may have had to the marginal sea was relinquished to the United States."

The "tidelands oil" question became an issue in the 1952 presidential campaign, and the victorious Republican Congress redeemed its campaign pledge to cede to the three states the lands which they claimed. Since the acts ceded title to the land extending to the original boundaries of the states, the Gulf states claimed three leagues (nine nautical miles) of marginal sea. Congress' right to make this cession was upheld in Alabama v. Texas in 1954, but in 1960 the Court held that only Texas and Florida were entitled to three leagues. The fact that this apparently leaves these states sticking out some six miles beyond the boundaries of the United States raises potential problems in international law which the Court declined to answer. "It is sufficient for present purposes to note that there is no question of Congress' power to fix state land and water boundaries as a domestic matter. Such a boundary, fully effective as between Nation and State, undoubtedly circumscribes the extent of navigable *inland* waters and underlying lands owned by the State under the [equal footing] rule." See United States v. Louisiana (1960).

With the judicial turnabout of 1937 went the long-standing doctrine of "dual federalism" (see the note to McCulloch v. Maryland) under which the reserved powers of the states were held to check the delegated powers of Congress. But while important powers have accrued to Congress from the increased use of interstate commerce facilities, Congress has not ordinarily sought to use this new authority to injure the states or subvert their authority. Congress, after all, represents the people of the states as well as the people of the nation. Most uses of this growing federal power have resulted from the inability of the states to cope with problems which have spread beyond their jurisdiction or which exceed their financial resources.

While the doctrine of dual federalism dealt with above involved the right of a state to exercise the police power reserved to it under the Tenth Amendment, there was another area in which the states asserted their independence from the national government and that was in the area of intergovernmental tax immunity. What was at stake here was not the state's power to control public policy, but rather its right to a continued existence, unimpeded by the "power to destroy" implicit in the federal tax power.

Chief Justice Marshall had suggested in McCulloch v. Maryland (1819) that while the states could not tax the federal government, there was no similar bar to the federal government taxing the states. In Collector v. Day (1871), however, the Court held void the application of a federal income tax statute to the income of a state judge. The judge, the Court held, was the embodiment of the state's judicial system, and to permit the national government to tax him would be to permit it to cripple or destroy an instrumentality of the state. The immunity of the state from such a destructive attack, it found, lay in the implicit assumption in the Constitution of the continued existence of the states and their indispensibility to the very existence of the national government. "Without them, the general government itself would disappear from the family of nations."

The result of the decision was the proliferation over the years of the things that were considered instrumentalities. All employees, property, earnings from oil leases, and the income from bonds issued by either government were immune from taxation by the other. Even patents and copyrights were considered federal instrumentalities and royalties earned under them were free from state taxation.

In one area the Court refused to extend immunity. When a state engaged in what was commonly thought of as a private business, as South Carolina did when it went into the liquor business, it had to pay federal taxes on the business like everyone else. The state could not deprive the federal government of its sources of revenue by taking over businesses on which that revenue depended. See South Carolina v. United States (1905).

The Court eventually came to the realization that the true beneficiaries of all this immunity were not the governments involved but a select group of favored individuals, and in the 1930s began retracting the doctrine. Finally, in Graves v. New York ex rel. O'Keefe (1939), it held that government employees were not the embodiment of an essential instrumentality and a tax upon their income was not a tax on the government for which they worked. Collector v. Day was overruled.

The withdrawal of constitutional immunity tipped the scales in favor of the federal government which could, of course, always protect its own instrumentalities under the supremacy clause. While the Court continued to pay lip-service to the immunity doctrine, when the shrinking was complete there were few who doubted that, should Congress elect to tax the income from municipal bonds (the only important tangible vestige of the immunity left) the Court would find the tax constitutional. Clearly, the theories on which the immunity rested had long been abandoned by the Court.

Oddly enough, only the tax power had ever been held limited by the sovereign immunity of the states. In University of Illinois v. United States (1933) the Court had upheld a tax on the importation of scientific equipment by the state on the ground that in taxing imports Congress was really exercising the *commerce* power and not the *tax* power. And in United States v. California (1936) it held valid the federal regulation of a railroad owned by a state. While it might have done this on the ground that the railroad was not an essential government activity, the Court made clear that it was "unimportant to say whether the state conducted its railroad in its 'sovereign' or in its 'private' capacity. . . . The sovereign power of the state is necessarily diminished to the extent of grants of power to the federal government in the Constitution. . . . California, by engaging in interstate commerce by rail, has subjected itself to the commerce power . . . ."

As recently as 1968, in Maryland v. Wirtz, the Court reaffirmed United States v. California and held valid the extension of the federal minimum wage laws to the employees of state schools and hospitals on the ground that they were major users of interstate goods. In 1975, in Fry v. United States, the Court upheld on the same ground the application of the wage freeze to state employees under the Economic Stabilization Act of 1970.

It is against this background of the undisturbed 30-year accretion of federal power that one must view the Usery case, printed below. In 1974 Congress amended the Fair Labor Standards Act to extend its protection to all public employees, federal, state, or local, who are "engaged in commerce, or in the production of goods for commerce, or employees handling, selling, or otherwise working on goods or materials that have been moved in or produced for commerce." Since the effect was to impose federal minimum wage and maximum hours regulations upon all government agencies, a number of states and cities and their representative organizations challenged the validity of the amendments.

Mr. Justice **Rehnquist** delivered the opinion of the Court, saying in part:

II

It is established beyond peradventure that the Commerce Clause of Art. I of the Constitution is a grant of plenary authority to Congress. That authority is, in the words of Mr. Chief Justice Marshall in Gibbons v. Ogden (1824), "the power to regulate; that is, to prescribe the rule by which commerce is to be governed."

When considering the validity of asserted applications of this power to wholly private activity, the Court has made it clear that "[e]ven activity that is purely intrastate in character may be regulated by Congress, where the activity, combined with like conduct by others similarly situated, affects commerce among the States or with foreign nations." Fry v. United States (1975). . . .

Appellants in no way challenge these decisions establishing the breadth of authority granted Congress under the commerce power. Their contention, on the contrary, is that when Congress seeks to regulate directly the activities of States as public employers, it transgresses an affirmative limitation on the exercise of its power akin to other commerce power affirmative limitations contained in the Constitution. Congressional enactments which may be fully within the grant of legislative authority contained in the Commerce Clause may nonetheless be invalid because found to offend against the right to trial by jury. . . .

This Court has never doubted that there are limits upon the power of Congress to override state sovereignty, even when exercising its otherwise plenary powers to tax or to regulate commerce which are conferred by Art. I of the Constitution. In [Maryland v. Wirtz (1968)], for example, the Court took care to assure the appellants that it had "ample power to prevent . . . 'the utter destruction of the State as a sovereign political entity,' " which they feared. . . . In Fry, the Court recognized that an express declaration of this limitation is found in the Tenth Amendment: "While the Tenth Amendment has been characterized as a 'truism,' stating merely that 'all is retained which has not been surrendered,' United States v. Darby (1941), it is not without significance. The Amendment expressly declares the constitutional policy that Congress may not exercise power in a fashion that impairs the States' integrity or their ability to function effectively in a federal system." . . .

In Metcalf & Eddy v. Mitchell (1926), the Court likewise observed that "neithei government may destroy the other nor curtail in any substantial manner the exercise of its powers."

Appellee Secretary argues that the cases in which this Court has upheld sweeping exercises of authority by Congress, even though those exercises pre-empted state regulation of the private sector, have already curtailed the sovereignty of the States quite as much as the 1974 amendments to the Fair Labor Standards Act. We do not agree. It is one thing to recognize the authority of Congress to enact laws regulating individual business necessarily subject to the dual sovereignty of the government of the Nation and of the State in which they reside. It is quite another to uphold a similar exercise of congressional authority directed, not to private citizens, but to the States as States. We have repeatedly recognized that there are attributes of sovereignty attaching to every state government which may not be impaired by Congress, not because Congress may lack an affirmative grant of legislative authority to reach the matter, but because the Constitution prohibits it from exercising the authority in that manner. In Coyle v. Oklahoma [Smith] (1911), the Court gave this example of such an attribute:

"The power to locate its own seat of government and to determine when and how it shall be changed from one place to another, and to appropriate its own public funds for that purpose, are essentially and peculiarly state powers. That one of the original thirteen States could now be shorn of such powers by an act of Congress would not be for a moment entertained."

One undoubted attribute of state sovereignty is the States' power to determine the wages which shall be paid to those whom they employ in order to carry out their governmental functions, what hours those persons will work, and what compensation will be provided where these employees may be called upon to work overtime. The question we must resolve here, then, is whether these determinations are " 'functions essential to separate and independent existence,' " so that Congress may not abrogate the States' otherwise plenary authority to make them.

In their complaint appellants advanced estimates of substantial costs which will be imposed upon them by the 1974 amendments. . . .

Judged solely in terms of increased costs in dollars, these allegations show a significant impact on the functioning of the governmental bodies involved. The Metropolitan Government of Nashville and Davidson County, Tenn., for example, asserted that the Act will increase its costs of providing essential police and fire protection, without any increase in service or in current salary levels, by $938,000 per year. . . .

Increased costs are not, of course, the only adverse effects which compliance with the Act will visit upon state and local governments, and in turn upon the citizens who depend upon those governments. In its complaint in intervention, for example, California asserted that it could not comply with the overtime costs (approximately $750,000 per year) which the Act required to be paid to California Highway Patrol cadets during their academy training program. California reported that it had thus been forced to reduce its academy training program from 2,080 hours to only 960 hours, a compromise undoubtedly of substantial importance to those whose safety and welfare may depend upon the preparedness of the California Highway Patrol. . . .

Quite apart from the substantial costs imposed upon the States and their political subdivisions, the Act displaces state policies regarding the manner in which they will structure delivery of those governmental services which their citizens require. The Act, speaking directly to the States qua States, requires that they shall pay all but an extremely limited minority of their employees the minimum wage rates currently chosen by Congress. It may well be that as a matter of economic policy it would be desirable that States, just as private employers, comply with these minimum wage requirements. But it cannot be gainsaid that the federal requirement directly supplants the considered policy choices of the States' elected officials and administrators as to how they wish to structure pay scales in state employment. The State might wish to employ persons with little or no training, or those who wish to work on a casual basis, or those who for some other reason do not possess minimum employment requirements, and pay them less than the federally prescribed minimum wage. It may wish to offer part-time or summer employment to teenagers at a figure less than the minimum wage, and if unable to do so may decline to offer such employment at all. But the Act would forbid such choices by the States. . . .

. . . If Congress may withdraw from the States the authority to make those fundamental employment decisions upon which their systems for performance of these functions must rest, we think there would be little left of the States' " 'separate and independent existence.' " Coyle. Thus, even if appellants may have overestimated the effect which the Act will have upon their current levels and patterns of governmental activity, the dispositive factor is that Congress has attempted to exercise its Commerce Clause authority to prescribe minimum wages and maximum hours to be paid by the States in their capacities as sovereign governments. In so doing, Congress has sought to wield its power in a fashion that would impair the States' "ability to function effectively in a federal system." Fry. This exercise of congressional authority does not comport with the federal system of government embodied in the Constitution. We hold that insofar as the challenged amendments operate to directly displace the States' freedom to structure integral operations in areas of traditional governmental functions, they are not within the authority granted Congress by Art. I, § 8, cl. 3.

III.

One final matter requires our attention. Appellee has vigorously urged that we cannot, consistently with the Court's decisions in Maryland v. Wirtz (1968), and Fry, rule against him here. It is important to examine this contention so that it will be clear what we hold today, and what we do not. . . .

We think our holding today quite consistent with Fry. The enactment at issue there was occasioned by an extremely serious problem which endangered the well-being of all the component parts of our federal system and which only collective action by the National Government might forestall. The means selected were carefully drafted so as not to interfere with States' freedom beyond a very limited, specific period of time. . . . The limits imposed upon the commerce power when Congress seeks to apply it to the States are not so inflexible as to preclude temporary enactments tailored to combat a national emergency. . . .

With respect to the Court's decision in Wirtz, we reach a different conclusion. . . . There are undoubtedly factual distinctions between the two situations, but in view of the conclusions expressed earlier in this opinion we do not believe the reasoning in Wirtz may any longer be regarded as authoritative.

Wirtz relied heavily on the Court's decision in United States v. California (1936). The opinion quotes the following language from that case: " '[We] look to the activities in which the states have traditionally engaged as marking the boundary of the restriction upon the federal taxing power. But there is no such limitation upon the plenary power to regulate commerce. The state can no more deny the power if its exercise has been authorized by Congress than can an individual.' "

But we have reaffirmed today that the States as States stand on a quite different footing from an individual or a corporation when challenging the exercise of Congress' power to regulate commerce. We think the dicta* from United States v. California, simply wrong.† Congress may not exercise that power so as to force directly upon the States its choices as to how essential decisions regarding the conduct of integral governmental functions are to be made. . . .

While there are obvious differences between the schools and hospitals involved in Wirtz, and the fire and police departments affected here, each provides an integral portion of those governmental services which the States and their political subdivisions have traditionally afforded their citizens. We are therefore persuaded that Wirtz must be overruled. . . .

Mr. Justice **Blackmun,** concurring, said in part:

I may misinterpret the Court's opinion, but it seems to me that it adopts a balancing approach, and does not outlaw federal power in areas such as environmental protection, where the federal interest is demonstrably greater and where state facility compliance with imposed federal standards would be essential. With this understanding on my part of the Court's opinion, I join it.

Mr. Justice **Brennan,** with whom Mr. Justice **White** and Mr. Justice **Marshall** join, dissenting, said in part:

My Brethren do not successfully obscure today's patent usurpation of the role reserved for the political process by their purported discovery in the Constitution of a restraint derived from sovereignty of the States on Congress' exercise of the commerce power. Mr. Chief Justice Marshall recognized that limitations "prescribed in the constitution," Gibbons v. Ogden [1824], restrain Congress' exercise of the power. . . . Thus laws within the commerce

---

*The holding of United States v. California, as opposed to the language quoted in the texts, is quite consistent with our holding today. There California's activity to which the congressional command was directed was not in an area that the States have regarded as integral parts of their governmental activities. It was, on the contrary, the operation of a railroad engaged in "common carriage by rail in interstate commerce. . . ."

†Mr. Justice Brennan's dissent leaves no doubt from its discussion that in its view Congress may under its commerce power deal with the States as States just as they might deal with private individuals. We venture to say that it is this conclusion, rather than the one we reach, which is in the words of the dissent a "startling restructuring of our federal system. . . ."

power may not infringe individual liberties protected by the First Amendment . . . or the Sixth Amendment. . . . But there is no restraint based on state sovereignty requiring or permitting judicial enforcement anywhere expressed in the Constitution; our decisions over the last century and a half have explicitly rejected the existence of any such restraint on the commerce power.

We said in United States v. California (1936), for example: "The sovereign power of the states is necessarily diminished to the extent of the grants of power to the federal government in the Constitution. . . . [T]he power of the state is subordinate to the constitutional exercise of the granted federal power." . . . "[It] is not a controversy between equals" when the Federal government "is asserting its sovereign power to regulate commerce. . . . [T]he interests of the nation are more important than those of any State." Sanitary District v. United States (1925). . . .

My Brethren thus have today manufactured an abstraction without substance, founded neither in the words of the Constitution nor on precedent. An abstraction having such profoundly pernicious consequences is not made less so by characterizing the 1974 amendments as legislation directed against the "States qua States." Of course, regulations that this Court can say are not regulations of "commerce" cannot stand, . . . and in this sense "[t]he Court has ample power to prevent . . . 'the utter destruction of the State as a sovereign political entity.' " Maryland v. Wirtz (1968). But my Brethren make no claim that the 1974 amendments are not regulations of "commerce"; rather they overrule Wirtz in disagreement with historic principles that United States v. California reaffirmed: "[W]hile the commerce power has limits, valid general regulations of commerce do not cease to be regulations of commerce because a State is involved. If a state is engaging in economic activities that are validly regulated by the Federal Government when engaged in by private persons, the State too may be forced to conform its activities to federal regulation." Wirtz. . . .

The reliance of my Brethren upon the Tenth Amendment as "an express declaration of [a state sovereignty] limitation," not only suggests that they overrule governing decisions of this Court that address this question but must astound scholars of the Constitution. For not only early decisions, Gibbons v. Ogden, McCulloch v. Maryland, and Martin v. Hunter's Lessee, (1816), hold that nothing in the Tenth Amendment constitutes a limitation on congressional exercise of powers delegated by the Constitution to Congress. . . . Rather, as the Tenth Amendment's significance was more recently summarized:

"The amendment states but a truism that all is retained which has not been surrendered. *There is nothing in the history of its adoption to suggest that it was more than declaratory of the relationship between the national and state governments as it had been established by the Constitution before the amendment* or that its purpose was other than to allay fears that the new national government might seek to exercise powers not granted, and that the states might not be able to exercise fully their reserved powers. . . ." . . . United States v. Darby (emphasis added). . . .

[The Court here discusses the rejection in Case v. Bowles (1946) of the idea that the war power was limited by state sovereignty. Among the cases relied on there was United States v. California.]

Even more significant for our purposes is the Court's citation of United States v. California, a case concerned with Congress' power to regulate commerce, as supporting the rejection of the State's contention that state sovereignty is a limitation on Congress' war power. California directly presented the question whether any state sovereignty restraint precluded application of the Federal Safety Appliance Act to a state-owned and -operated railroad. The State argued "that as the state is operating the railroad without profit, for the purpose of facilitating the commerce of the port, and is using the net proceeds of operation for harbor improvement, . . . it is engaged in performing a public function in its sovereign capacity and for that reason cannot constitutionally be subjected to the provisions of the federal Act." Mr. Justice Stone rejected the contention in an opinion for a unanimous Court. His rationale is a complete refutation of today's holding: "That in operating its railroad [the State] is acting within a power reserved to the states cannot be doubted. . . . The only question we need consider is whether the exercise of that power, in whatever capacity, must be in subordination to the power to regulate interstate commerce, which has been granted specifically to the national government. The sovereign power of the states is necessarily diminished to the extent of the grants of power to the federal government in the Constitution. . . .

"The analogy of the constitutional immunity of state instrumentalities from federal taxation, on which [California] relies, is not illuminating. That immunity is implied from the nature of our federal system and the relationship within it of state and national governments, and is equally a restriction on taxation by either of the instrumentalities of the other. Its nature requires that it be so construed as to allow to each government reasonable scope for its taxing power . . . which would be unduly curtailed if either by extending its activities could withdraw from the taxing power of the other subjects of taxation traditionally within it. . . . Hence, we look to the activities in which the states have traditionally engaged as marking the boundary of the restriction upon the federal taxing power. *But there is no such limitation upon the plenary power to regulate commerce. The state can no more deny the power if its exercise has been authorized by Congress than can an individual.''* (emphasis added).

Today's repudiation of this unbroken line of precedents that firmly reject my Brethren's ill-conceived abstraction can only be regarded as a transparent cover for invalidating a congressional judgment with which they disagree. The only analysis even remotely resembling that adopted today is found in a line of opinions dealing with the Commerce Clause and the Tenth Amendment that ultimately provoked a constitutional crisis for the Court in the 1930's. E.g. Carter v. Carter Coal Co. (1936); United States v. Butler (1936); Hammer v. Dagenhart (1918). . . . It may have been the eventual abandonment of the overly restrictive construction of the commerce power that spelled defeat for the Court-packing plan, and preserved the integrity of this institution, see, e.g., United States v. Darby (1941); Mulford v. Smith (1939); NLRB v. Jones & Laughlin Steel Corp. (1937), but my Brethren today are transparently trying to cut back on that recognition of the scope of the commerce power. My Brethren's approach to this case is not far different from the dissenting opinions in the cases that averted the crisis. . . .

. . . I cannot recall another instance in the Court's history when the reasoning of so many decisions covering so long a span of time has been discarded in such a roughshod manner. That this is done without any justification not already often advanced and consistently rejected, clearly renders today's decision an ipse dixit reflecting nothing but displeasure with a congressional judgment.

My Brethren's treatment of Fry v. United States (1975), further illustrates the paucity of legal reasoning or principle justifying today's result. Although the Economic Stabilization Act "displace[d] the States' freedom"—the reason given for invalidating the 1974 amendments—the result in Fry is not disturbed since the interference was temporary and only a national program enforced by the Federal Government could have alleviated the country's economic crisis. Thus, although my Brethren by fiat strike down the 1974 amendments without analysis of countervailing national considerations, Fry by contrary logic remains undisturbed because, on balance, countervailing national considerations override the inter-ference with the State's freedom. Moreover, it is sophistry to say the Economic Stabilization Act "displaced no state choices," but that the 1974 amendments do. Obviously the Stabiliza-tion Act—no less than every exercise of a national power delegated to Congress by the Constitution—displaced the State's freedom. It is absurd to suggest that there is a constitu-tionally significant distinction between curbs against increasing wages and curbs against paying wages lower than the federal minimum. . . .

A sense of the enormous impact of States' political power is gained by brief reference to the federal budget. The largest estimate by any of the appellants of the cost impact of the 1974 amendments—$1 billion—pales in comparison with the financial assistance the States receive from the Federal Government. In fiscal 1977 the President's proposed budget recom-mends $60.5 billion in federal assistance to the States, exclusive of loans. . . . Appellants complain of the impact of the amended FLSA on police and fire departments, but the 1977 budget contemplates outlays for law enforcement assistance of $716 million. Concern is also expressed about the diminished ability to hire students in the summer if States must pay them a minimum wage, but the Federal Government's "summer youth program" provides $400 million for 670,000 jobs. Given this demonstrated ability to obtain funds from the Federal Government for needed state services, there is little doubt that the States' influence in the political process is adequate to safeguard their sovereignty.

Mr. Justice **Stevens,** dissenting, said in part:

I agree that it is unwise for the federal Government to exercise its power in the ways described in the Court's opinion. For the proposition that regulation of the minimum price of a commodity—even labor—will increase the quantity consumed is not one that I can readily understand. That concern, however, applies with even greater force to the private sector of the economy where the exclusion of the marginally employable does the greatest harm and, in all events, merely reflects my views on a policy issue which has been firmly resolved by the branches of government having power to decide such questions.

GARCIA v. SAN ANTONIO METRO

469 U. S. 528; 83 L. Ed. 2d 1016; 105 S. Ct. 1005 (1985)

Justice **Blackmun** delivered the opinion of the Court, saying in part:

We revisit in these cases an issue raised in National League of Cities v. Usery (1976). In that litigation, this Court, by a sharply divided vote, ruled that the Commerce Clause does not empower Congress to enforce the minimum-wage and overtime provisions of the Fair

Labor Standards Act (FLSA) against the States "in areas of traditional governmental functions." Although National League of Cities supplied some examples of "traditional governmental functions," it did not offer a general explanation of how a "traditional" function is to be distinguished from a "nontraditional" one. Since then, federal and state courts have struggled with the task, thus imposed, of identifying a traditional function for purposes of state immunity under the Commerce Clause.

In the present cases, a Federal District Court concluded that municipal ownership and operation of a mass-transit system is a traditional governmental function and thus, under National League of Cities, is exempt from the obligations imposed by the FLSA. Faced with the identical question, three Federal Courts of Appeals and one state appellate court have reached the opposite conclusion.

Our examination of this "function" standard applied in these and other cases over the last eight years now persuades us that the attempt to draw the boundaries of state regulatory immunity in terms of "traditional governmental function" is not only unworkable but is inconsistent with established principles of federalism and, indeed, with those very federalism principles on which National League of Cities purported to rest. That case, accordingly, is overruled. . . .

II.

Appellees have not argued that SAMTA [San Antonio Metropolitan Transit Authority] is immune from regulations under the FLSA on the ground that it is a local transit system engaged in intrastate commercial activity. In a practical sense, SAMTA's operation might well be characterized as "local." Nonetheless, it long has been settled that Congress' authority under the Commerce clause extends to intrastate economic activities that affect interstate commerce. . . . Heart of Atlanta Motel, Inc. v. United States (1964); . . . United States v. Darby (1941). . . . Were SAMTA a privately owned and operated enterprise, it could not credibly argue that Congress exceeded the bounds of its Commerce Clause powers in prescribing minimum wages and overtime rates for SAMTA's employees. Any constitutional exemption from the requirements of the FLSA therefore must rest on SAMTA's status as a governmental entity rather than on the "local" nature of its operations.

The prerequisites for governmental immunity under National League of Cities were summarized by this Court in Hodel [v. Virginia Surface Mining & Recl. Assn. (1981)]. Under that summary, four conditions must be satisfied before a state activity may be deemed immune from a particular federal regulation under the Commerce Clause. First, it is said that the federal statute at issue must regulate "the 'States as States.' " Second, the statute must "address matters that are indisputably 'attribute[s] of state sovereignty.' " Third, state compliance with the federal obligation must "directly impair [the States'] ability 'to structure integral operations in areas of traditional governmental functions.' " Finally, the relation of state and federal interests must not be such that "the nature of the federal interest . . . justifies state submission."

The controversy in the present cases has focused on the third Hodel requirement— that the challenged federal statute trench on "traditional governmental functions." The

District Court voiced a common concern: "Despite the abundance of adjectives, identifying which particular state functions are immune remains difficult." Just how troublesome the task has been is revealed by the results reached in other federal cases. Thus, [lower federal] courts have held that regulating ambulance services . . . ; licensing automobile drivers . . . ; operating a municipal airport . . . ; performing solid waste disposal . . . ; and operating a highway authority . . . , are functions protected under National League of Cities. At the same time, courts have held that issuance of industrial development bonds . . . ; regulation of intrastate natural gas sales . . . ; regulation of traffic on public roads . . . ; regulation of air transportation . . . ; operation of a telephone system . . . ; leasing and sale of natural gas . . . ; operation of a mental health facility . . . ; and provision of in-house domestic services for the aged and handicapped . . . , are *not* entitled to immunity. We find it difficult, if not impossible, to identify an organizing principle that places each of the cases in the first group on one side of a line and each of the cases in the second group on the other side. The constitutional distinction between licensing drivers and regulating traffic, for example, or between operating a highway authority and operating a mental health facility, is elusive at best.

Thus far, this Court itself has made little headway in defining the scope of the governmental functions deemed protected under National League of Cities. In that case the Court set forth examples of protected and unprotected functions, but provided no explanation of how those examples were identified. The only other case in which the Court has had occasion to address the problem is [Transportation Union v.] Long Island [1982]. We there observed: "The determination of whether a federal law impairs a state's authority with respect to 'areas of traditional [state] functions' may at times be a difficult one." The accuracy of that statement is demonstrated by this Court's own difficulties in Long Island in developing a workable standard for "traditional governmental function." We relied in large part there on "the *historical reality* that the operation of railroads is not among the functions *traditionally* performed by state and local governments," but we simultaneously disavowed "a static historical view of state functions generally immune from federal regulation." We held that the inquiry into a particular function's "traditional" nature was merely a means of determining whether the federal statute at issue unduly handicaps "basic state prerogatives," but we did not offer an explanation of what makes one state function a "basic prerogative" and another function not basic. Finally, having disclaimed a rigid reliance on the historical pedigree of state involvement in a particular area, we nonetheless found it appropriate to emphasize the extended historical record of *federal* involvement in the field of rail transportation.

Many constitutional standards involve "undoubte[d] . . . gray areas," and, despite the difficulties that this Court and other courts have encountered so far, it normally might be fair to venture the assumption that case-by-case development would lead to a workable standard for determining whether a particular governmental function should be immune from federal regulation under the Commerce Clause. A further cautionary note is sounded, however, by the Court's experience in the related field of state immunity from federal taxation. In South Carolina v. United States (1905), the Court held for the first time that the state tax immunity recognized in Collector v. Day, extended only to the "ordinary" and "strictly governmental" instrumentalities of state governments and not to instrumentalities "used by the State in the carrying on of an ordinary private business.'' While the Court applied the distinction outlined in South Carolina for the following 40 years, at no time during that period did the Court develop.a consistent formulation of the kinds of governmental functions that were entitled to immunity. . . .

If these tax immunity cases had any common thread, it was in the attempt to distinguish between "governmental" and "proprietary" functions. To say that the distinction between "governmental" and "proprietary" proved to be stable, however, would be something of an overstatement. . . .

Even during the heyday of the governmental/ proprietary distinction in inter-governmental tax immunity-doctrine the Court never explained the constitutional basis for that distinction. . . .

The distinction the Court discarded as unworkable in the field of tax immunity has proved no more fruitful in the field of regulatory immunity under the Commerce Clause. Neither do any of the alternative standards that might be employed to distinguish between protected and unprotected governmental functions appear manageable. We rejected the possibility of making immunity turn on a purely historical standard of "tradition" in Long Island, and properly so. The most obvious defect of a historical approach to state immunity is that it prevents a court from accommodating changes in the historical functions of States, changes that have resulted in a number of once-private functions like education being assumed by the States and their subdivisions. At the same time, the only apparent virtue of a rigorous historical standard, namely, its promise of a reasonably objective measure for state immunity, is illusory. Reliance on history as an organizing principle results in linedrawing of the most arbitrary sort; the genesis of state governmental functions stretches over a historical continuum from before the Revolution to the present, and courts would have to decide by fiat precisely how longstanding a pattern of state involvement had to be for federal regulatory authority to be defeated.* A nonhistorical standard for selecting immune governmental functions is likely to be just as unworkable as is a historical standard. The goal of identifying "uniquely" governmental functions, for example, has been rejected by the Court in the field of government tort liability in part because the notion of a "uniquely" governmental function is unmanageable. . . . Another possibility would be to confine immunity to "necessary" governmental services, that is, services that would be provided inadequately or not at all unless the government provided them. The set of services that fits into this category, however, may well be negligible. . . .

We believe, however, that there is a more fundamental problem at work here, a problem that explains why the Court was never able to provide a basis for the governmental/proprietary distinction in the intergovernmental tax immunity cases and why an attempt to draw similar distinctions with respect to federal regulatory authority under National League of Cities is unlikely to succeed regardless of how the distinctions are phrased. The problem is that neither the governmental/proprietary distinction nor any other that purports

---

*For much the same reasons, the existence vel non of a tradition of federal involvement in a particular area does not provide an adequate standard for state immunity. Most of the Federal Government's current regulatory activity originated less than 50 years ago with the New Deal, and a good portion of it has developed within the past two decades. The recent vintage of this regulatory activity does not diminish the strength of the federal interest in applying regulatory standards to state activities, nor does it affect the strength of the States' interest in being free from federal supervision. . . .

to separate out important governmental functions can be faithful to the role of federalism in a democratic society. The essence of our federal system is that within the realm of authority left open to them under the Constitution, the States must be equally free to engage in any activity that their citizens choose for the common weal, no matter how unorthodox or unnecessary anyone else—including the judiciary— deems state involvement to be. Any rule of state immunity that looks to the "traditional," "integral," or "necessary" nature of governmental functions inevitably invites an unelected federal judiciary to make decisions about which state policies it favors and which ones it dislikes. "The science of government . . . is the science of experiment," Anderson v. Dunn (1821), and the States cannot serve as laboratories for social and economic experiment . . . if they must pay an added price when they meet the changing needs of their citizenry by taking up functions that an earlier day and a different society left in private hands. . . .

We therefore now reject, as unsound in principle and unworkable in practice, a rule of state immunity from federal regulation that turns on a judicial appraisal of whether a particular governmental function is "integral" or "traditional." Any such rule leads to inconsistent results at the same time that it disserves principles of democratic self-governance, and it breeds inconsistency precisely because it is divorced from those principles. If there are to be limits on the Federal Government's power to interfere with state functions—as undoubtedly there are—we must look elsewhere to find them. We accordingly return to the underlying issue that confronted the Court in National League of Cities—the manner in which the Constitution insulates States from the reach of Congress' power under the Commerce Clause.

III.

The central theme of National League of Cities was that the States occupy a special position in our constitutional system and that the scope of Congress' authority under the Commerce Clause must reflect that position. Of course, the Commerce Clause by its specific language does not provide any special limitation on Congress' actions with respect to the States. . . . It is equally true, however, that the text of the Constitution provides the beginning rather than the final answer to every inquiry into questions of federalism, for "[b]ehind the words of the constitutional provisions are postulates which limit and control." . . . National League of Cities reflected the general conviction that the Constitution precludes, "the National Government [from] devouring the essentials of state sovereignty." Maryland v. Wirtz (dissenting opinion) [1968]. In order to be faithful to the underlying federal premises of the Constitution, courts must look for the "postulates which limit and control."

What has proved problematic is not the perception that the constitution's federal structure imposes limitations on the Commerce Clause, but rather the nature and content of those limitations. One approach . . . is to identify certain underlying elements of political sovereignty that are deemed essential to the States' "separate and independent existence." . . . This approach obviously underlay the Court's use of the "traditional governmental function" concept in National League of Cities. . . . In [that case], the Court concluded that decisions by a State concerning the wages and hours of its employees are an "undoubted attribute of state sovereignty.'' The opinion did not explain what aspects of such decision made them such an ''undoubted attribute,'' and the Court since then has remarked on the uncertain scope of the concept. See EEOC v. Wyoming (1983). The point of the inquiry, however, has remained to single out particular features of a State's internal governance that are deemed to be intrinsic parts of state sovereignty.

We doubt that courts ultimately can identify principled constitutional limitations on the scope of Congress' Commerce Clause powers over the States merely by relying on a priori definitions of state sovereignty. In part, this is because of the elusiveness of objective criteria for ''fundamental'' elements of state sovereignty, a problem we have witnessed in the search for ''traditional governmental functions.'' There is, however, a more fundamental reason: the sovereignty of the States is limited by the Constitution itself. A variety of sovereign powers . . . are withdrawn from the States. . . .

The States unquestionably do ''retai[n] a significant measure of sovereign authority.'' EEOC v. Wyoming (Powell, J., dissenting). They do so, however, only to the extent that the Constitution has not divested them of their original powers and transferred those powers to the Federal Government. . . ,

As a result, to say that the Constitution assumes the continued role of the States is to say little about the nature of that role. Only recently, this Court recognized that the purpose of the constitutional immunity recognized in National League of Cities is not to preserve ''a sacred province of state autonomy.'' EEOC v. Wyoming. . . ,

When we look for the States' ''residuary and inviolable sovereignty,'' The Federalist No. 39 (J. Madison), in the shape of the constitutional scheme rather than in predetermined notions of sovereign power, a different measure of state sovereignty emerges. Apart from the limitation on federal authority inherent in the delegated nature of Congress' Article I powers, the principal means chosen by the Framers to ensure the role of the States in the federal system lies in the structure of the Federal Government itself. It is no novelty to observe that the composition of the Federal Government was designed in large part to protect the States from overreaching by Congress. The Framers thus gave the States a role in the selection both of the Executive and the Legislative Branches of the Federal Government. The States were vested with indirect influence over the House of Representatives and the Presidency by their control of electoral qualifications and their role in presidential election. U. S. Const. Art. I, § 2, and Art. II, § 1. They were given more direct influence in the Senate, where each State received equal representation and each Senator was to be selected by the legislature of his State. Art. I, § 3. The significance attached to the States' equal representation in the Senate is underscored by the prohibition of any constitutional amendment divesting a State of equal representation without the State's consent. Art. V.

The extent to which the structure of the Federal Government itself was relied on to insulate the interests of the States is evident in the views of the Framers. . . . The Framers chose to rely on a federal system in which special restraints on federal power over the States inhered principally in the workings of the National Government itself, rather than in discrete limitations on the objects of federal authority. State sovereign interests, then, are more properly protected by procedural safeguards inherent in the structure of the federal system than by judicially created limitations on federal power.

The effectiveness of the federal political process in preserving the States' interests is apparent even today in the course of federal legislation. . . . At the same time that the States have exercised their influence to obtain federal support, they have been able to exempt themselves from a wide variety of obligations imposed by congress under the Commerce Clause. For example, the Federal Power Act, the National Labor Relations Act, the Labor-Management Reporting and Disclosure Act, the Occupational Safety and Health Act, the Employee Retirement Insurance Act, and the Sherman Act all contain express or implied exemptions for States and their subdivisions. The fact that some federal statutes such as FLSA extend general obligations to the States cannot obscure the extent to which the political position of the States in the federal system has served to minimize the burdens that the States bear under the Commerce Clause.

We realize that changes in the structure of the Federal Government have taken place since 1789, not the least of which has been the substitution of popular election of Senators by the adoption of the Seventeenth Amendment in 1913, and that these changes may work to alter the influence of the States in the federal political process. Nonetheless, against this background, we are convinced that the fundamental limitation that the constitutional scheme imposes on the Commerce Clause to protect the ''States as States'' is one of process rather than one of result. Any substantive restraint on the exercise of Commerce Clause powers must find its justification in the procedural nature of this basic limitation, and it must be tailored to compensate for possible failings in the political process rather than to dictate a ''sacred province of state autonomy.'' EEOC v. Wyoming.

In so far as the present cases are concerned, then, we need go no further than to state that we perceive nothing in the overtime and minimum-wage requirements of the FLSA, as applied to SAMTA, that is destructive of state sovereignty or violative of any constitutional provision. SAMTA faces nothing more than the same minimum-wage and overtime obligations that hundreds of thousands of other employers, public as well as private, have to meet. . . .

IV.

This analysis makes clear that Congress' action in affording SAMTA employees the protections of the wage and hour provisions of FLSA contravened no affirmative limit on Congress' power under the Commerce Clause. The judgment of the District Court therefore must be reversed.

Of course, we continue to recognize that the States occupy a special and specific position in our constitutional system and that the scope of Congress' authority under the Commerce Clause must reflect that position. But the principal and basic limit on the federal commerce power is that inherent in all congressional action—the built-in restraints that our system provides through state participation in federal governmental action. The political process ensures that laws that unduly burden the States will not be promulgated. In the factual setting of these cases the internal safeguards of the political process have performed as intended.

These cases do not require us to identify or define what affirmative limits the constitutional structure might impose on federal action affecting the States under the Commerce Clause. . . .

Though the separate concurrence providing the fifth vote in National League of Cities was ''not untroubled by certain possible implications'' of the decision, the Court in that case attempted to articulate affirmative limits on the Commerce Clause power in terms of core governmental functions and fundamental attributes of state sovereignty. But the model of democratic decisionmaking the Court there identified underestimated, in our view, the solicitude of the national political process for the continued vitality of the States. Attempts by other courts since then to draw guidance from this model have proved it both impracticable and doctrinally barren. In sum, in National League of Cities the Court tried to repair what did not need repair.

We do not lightly overrule recent precedent. . . . Due respect for the reach of congressional power within the federal system mandates that we do so now. National League of Cities v. Usery (1976) is overruled. The judgment of the District Court is reversed. . . .

Justice **Powell,** with whom the **Chief Justice,** Justice **Rehnquist,** and Justice **O'Connor** join, dissenting, said in part:

The Court today, in its 5–4 decision, overrules National League of Cities v. Usery, a case in which we held that Congress lacked authority to impose the requirements of the Fair Labor Standards Act on state and local governments. Because I believe this decision substantially alters the federal system embodied in the Constitution, I dissent.

I.

There are, of course, numerous examples over the history of this Court in which prior decisions have been reconsidered and overruled. There have been few cases, however, in which the principle of stare decisis and the rationale of recent decisions were ignored as abruptly as we now witness. . . .

Although the doctrine is not rigidly applied to constitutional questions, ''any departure from the doctrine of stare decisis demands special justification.'' . . . In the present case, the five Justices who compose the majority today participated in National League of Cities and the cases reaffirming it. The stability of judicial decision, and with it respect for the authority of this Court, are not served by the precipitous overruling of multiple precedents that we witness in this case.

Whatever effect the Court's decision may have in weakening the application of stare decisis, it is likely to be less important than what the Court has done to the Constitution itself. A unique feature of the United States is the *federal* system of government guaranteed by the Constitution and implicit in the very name of our country. Despite some genuflecting in the Court's opinion to the concept of federalism, today's decision effectively reduces the Tenth Amendment to meaningless rhetoric when Congress acts pursuant to the Commerce Clause. . . .

II. . . .

B.

Today's opinion does not explain how the States' role in the electoral process guarantees that particular exercises of the Commerce Clause power will not infringe on residual State sovereignty.* Members of Congress are elected from the various States, but once in office they are members of the federal government. Although the States participate in the Electoral College, this is hardly a reason to view the President as a representative of the States' interest against federal encroachment. . . .

. . . At least since Marbury v. Madison [1803] it has been the settled province of the federal judiciary "to say what the law is" with respect to the constitutionality of acts of Congress. In reflecting the role of the judiciary in protecting the States from federal overreaching, the Court's opinion offers no explanation for ignoring the teaching of the most famous case in our history. . . .

III. . . .

D

. . . The Court today propounds a view of federalism that pays only lip service to the role of the States. . . . Indeed, the Court barely acknowledges that the Tenth Amendment exists.† That Amendment states explicitly that "[t]he powers not delegated to the United States . . . are reserved to the States." U. S. Const. Amend. 10. The Court recasts this language to say that the States retain their sovereign powers "only to the extent that the Constitution has not divested them of their original powers and transferred those powers to the Federal Government." This rephrasing is not a distinction without a difference; rather, it reflects the Court's unprecedented view that Congress is free under the Commerce Clause to assume a State's traditional sovereign power, and to do so without judicial review of its action. Indeed, the Court's view of federalism appears to relegate the States to precisely the trivial role that opponents of the Constitution feared they would occupy.

Justice **Rehnquist** wrote a dissenting opinion.

---

*Late in its opinion, the Court suggests that after all there may be some "affirmative limits the constitutional structure might impose on federal action affecting the States under the Commerce Clause." . . . The Court's failure to specify the "affirmative limits" on federal power, or when and how these limits are to be determined, may well be explained by the transparent fact that any such attempt would be subject to precisely the same objections on which it relies to overrule National League of Cities.

†The Court's opinion mentions the Tenth Amendment only once, when it restates the question put to the parties for reargument in these cases.

Justice **O'Connor** wrote a dissenting opinion with which Justice **Powell** and Justice **Rehnquist** joined.

B. The Growth of Commerce Power

GIBBONS v. OGDEN

9 Wheaton 1; 6 L. Ed. 23 (1824)

In 1798 Robert R. Livingston secured from the New York legislature an exclusive twenty-year grant to navigate by steam the rivers and other waters of the state, provided that within two years he should build a boat which would make four miles an hour against the current of the Hudson River. The grant was made amidst the ribald jeers of the legislators, who had no faith whatever in the project. The terms of the grant were not met, however, and it was renewed in 1803—this time to Livingston together with his partner, Robert Fulton—and again for two years in 1807. In August, 1807, Fulton's steamboat made its first successful trip from New York to Albany, and steamboat navigation became a reality. The following year the legislature, now fully aware of the practical significance of Fulton's achievement, passed a law providing that for each new boat placed on New York waters by Fulton and Livingston they should be entitled to a five-year extension of their monopoly, which should, however, not exceed thirty years. The monopoly was made effective by further providing that no one should be allowed to navigate New York waters by steam without a license from Fulton and Livingston, and any unlicensed vessel should be forfeited to them. The business of steamboat navigation developed rapidly. Boats were put in operation between New York and Albany and intervening points, and steam ferries ran between Fulton Street, New York City, and points in New Jersey. In 1811 the partners obtained from the Territory of Orleans (later Louisiana) a monopoly of steam navigation on the waters of Louisiana similar to that granted by New York, thus assuring them a pivotal position in the two greatest ports of the land. Naturally the monopolistic nature of the Fulton-Livingston rights worked hardship on their would-be competitors, and neighboring states began to pass retaliatory laws directed against the New York partners. The New Jersey legislature in 1811 authorized the owner of any boat seized under the forfeiture clause of the Fulton-Livingston charter to capture and hold in retaliation any boat belonging to any New York citizen. Connecticut in 1822 forbade any vessel licensed by Fulton and Livingston to enter the waters of that state, and Ohio passed a somewhat similar law in the same year. Granting such exclusive franchises was a game at which more than one state could play; and such grants were made by Georgia, Massachusetts, Pennsylvania, Tennessee, New Hampshire, and Vermont. With the inevitable increase of feeling created by such policies, retaliatory acts became common. In short, an achievement of science which had seemed destined to enlarge the means of communication and develop the commerce of the nation appeared rather to be embroiling the states in bitter antagonisms and commercial warfare such as prevailed during the dismal period of the Confederation. It is against the background of this intensely acute economic situation that the case of Gibbons v. Ogden must be read.

Ogden had secured a license for steam navigation from Fulton and Livingston. Gibbons had originally been his partner but was now his rival and was operating steamboats between two points in New York under the authority of a coasting license obtained from the United States government. Upon Ogden's petition the New York court had enjoined Gibbons from continuing in business. The great jurist Chancellor James Kent wrote the opinion in this case claiming the whole Hudson River belonged to New York, upholding the validity of the New York statute establishing the monopoly and repudiating the idea that there was any conflict involved between federal and state authority. An appeal was taken by Gibbons to the Supreme Court of the United States, thus presenting to that tribunal its first case under the commerce clause of the Constitution.

So accustomed are we to the free flow of commerce among the states that it is hard to conceive how the nation might have developed had the arguments in favor of the monopoly prevailed, for it was urged that the powers of state and nation to regulate interstate commerce were concurrent; that in the absence of a conflicting congressional statute the state was free to exercise this concurrent power as it pleased; and the "commerce" which Congress may regulate was "the transportation and sale of commodities." Had that argument prevailed, the federal coasting license under which Gibbons operated would have given him no protection, since he was carrying passengers, not goods. But the most crucial argument of all was that the New York monopoly law was not a regulation of *interstate* commerce but was merely a regulation of commerce within the boundaries of the state of New York. "It [the law] does not deny the right of entry into its waters to any vessel navigated by steam; it only forbids such vessel, when within its waters and jurisdiction, to be moved by steam; but that vessel may still navigate by all other means; and it leaves the people of other states, or of New York, in full possession of the right of navigation, by all the means known or used at the time of the passage of the law. [Most early steam boats were also sailboats.] It is, therefore, strictly a regulation of internal trade and navigation, which belongs to the state. This may, indeed, indirectly affect the right of commercial intercourse between the states. But so do all other laws regulating internal trade." . . .

Webster's argument against the validity of the steamboat monopoly was perhaps his greatest effort before the Supreme Court, and some writers believe that Marshall's opinion invalidating the New York law is his greatest state paper; others would place it second only to the opinion in McCulloch v. Maryland (1819). It was perhaps the only genuinely popular decision which Marshall ever handed down. It was received with widespread expressions of approval, for it was, as one writer has put it, "the first great anti-trust decision." The economic consequences of it in freeing a developing commerce from the shackles of state monopoly can hardly be overestimated; and it established for all time the supremacy of the national government in all matters affecting interstate and foreign commerce.

Mr. Chief Justice **Marshall** delivered the opinion of the Court, saying in part:

The appellant contends that this decree is erroneous, because the laws which purport to give the exclusive privilege it sustains are repugnant to the constitution and laws of the United States.

They are said to be repugnant·

1st. To that clause in the constitution which authorizes Congress to regulate commerce.

2d. To that which authorizes Congress to promote the progress of science and useful arts. . . .

As preliminary to the very able discussions of the constitution which we have heard from the bar, and as having some influence on its construction, reference has been made to the political situation of these states, anterior to its formation. It has been said that they were sovereign, were completely independent, and were connected with each other only by a league. This is true. But when these allied sovereigns converted their league into a government, when they converted their congress of ambassadors, deputed to deliberate on their common concerns, and to recommend measures of general utility, into a legislature, empowered to enact laws on the most interesting subjects, the whole character in which the states appear, underwent a change, the extent of which must be determined by a fair consideration of the instrument by which that change was effected.

This instrument contains an enumeration of powers expressly granted by the people to their government. It has been said that these powers ought to be construed strictly. But why ought they to be so construed? Is there one sentence in the constitution which gives countenance to this rule? In the last of the enumerated powers, that which grants, expressly, the means for carrying all others into execution, Congress is authorized "to make all laws which shall be necessary and proper" for the purpose. But this limitation on the means which may be used, is not extended to the powers which are conferred; nor is there one sentence in the constitution, which has been pointed out by the gentlemen of the bar or which we have been able to discern, that prescribes this rule. We do not, therefore, think ourselves justified in adopting it. What do gentlemen mean by a strict construction? If they contend only against that enlarged construction which would extend words beyond their natural and obvious import, we might question the application of the term, but should not controvert the principle. If they contend for that narrow construction which, in support of some theory not to be found in the constitution, would deny to the government those powers which the words of the grant, as usually understood, import, and which are consistent with the general views and objects of the instrument; for the narrow construction, which would cripple the government and render it unequal to the objects for which it is declared to be instituted, and to which the powers given, as fairly understood, render it competent; then we cannot perceive the propriety of this strict construction, nor adopt it as the rule by which the constitution is to be expounded. As men, whose intentions require no concealment, generally employ the words which most directly and aptly express the ideas they intend to convey, the enlightened patriots who framed our constitution, and the people who adopted it, must be understood to have employed words in their natural sense, and to have intended what they have said. If, from the imperfection of human language, there should be serious doubts respecting the extent of any given power, it is a well-settled rule that the objects for which it was given, especially when those objects are expressed in the instrument itself, should have great influence in the construction. We know of no reason for excluding this rule from the present case. The grant does not convey power which might be beneficial to the grantor, if retained by himself, or which can enure solely to the benefit of the grantee; but is an investment of power for the general advantage, in the hands of agents selected for that purpose; which power can never be exercised by the people themselves, but must be placed in the hands of agents or lie dormant. We know of no rule for construing the extent of such powers, other than is given by the language of the instrument which confers them, taken in connection with the purposes for which they were conferred.

The words are: "Congress shall have power to regulate commerce with foreign nations, and among the several states, and with the Indian tribes."

The subject to be regulated is commerce; and our constitution being, as was aptly said at the bar, one of enumeration, and not of definition, to ascertain the extent of the power it becomes necessary to settle the meaning of the word. Counsel for the appellee would limit it to traffic, to buying and selling, or the interchange of commodities, and do not admit that it comprehends navigation. This would restrict a general term, applicable to many objects, to one of its significations. Commerce, undoubtedly, is traffic, but it is something more; it is intercourse. It describes the commercial intercourse between nations, and parts of nations, in all its branches, and regulated by prescribing rules for carrying on that intercourse. The mind can scarcely conceive a system for regulating commerce between nations, which shall exclude all laws concerning navigation, which shall be silent on the admission of the vessels of the one nation into the ports of the other, and be confined to prescribing rules for the conduct of individuals, in the actual employment of buying and selling, or of barter.

If commerce does not include navigation, the government of the Union has no direct power over that subject, and can make no law prescribing what shall constitute American vessels, or requiring that they shall be navigated by American seamen. Yet this power has been exercised from the commencement of the government, has been exercised with the consent of all, and has been understood by all to be a commercial regulation. All America understands, and has uniformly understood, the word "commerce" to comprehend navigation. It was so understood, and must have been so understood, when the constitution was framed. The power over commerce, including navigation, was one of the primary objects for which the people of America adopted their government, and must have been contemplated in forming it. The convention must have used the word in that sense, because all have understood it in that sense, and the attempt to restrict it comes too late. . . .

The word used in the constitution, then, comprehends, and has been always understood to comprehend, navigation within its meaning; and a power to regulate navigation is as expressly granted as if that term had been added to the word "commerce."

To what commerce does this power extend? The constitution informs us, to commerce "with foreign nations, and among the several states, and with the Indian tribes."

It has, we believe, been universally admitted that these words comprehend every species of commercial intercourse between the United States and foreign nations. No sort of trade can be carried on between this country and any other to which this power does not extend. It has been truly said that commerce, as the word is used in the constitution, is a unit, every part of which is indicated by the term.

If this be the admitted meaning of the word, in its application to foreign nations, it must carry the same meaning throughout the sentence, and remain a unit, unless there be some plain intelligible cause which alters it.

The subject to which the power is next applied, is to commerce "among the several states." The word "among" means intermingled with. A thing which is among others is intermingled with them. Commerce among the states cannot stop at the external boundary line of each state, but may be introduced into the interior.

It is not intended to say that these words comprehend that commerce which is completely internal, which is carried on between man and man in a state, or between different parts of the same state, and which does not extend to or affect other states. Such a power would be inconvenient, and is certainly unnecessary.

Comprehensive as the word "among" is, it may very properly be restricted to that commerce which concerns more states than one. . . . The completely internal commerce of a state, then, may be considered as reserved for the state itself.

But, in regulating commerce with foreign nations, the power of Congress does not stop at the jurisdictional lines of the several states. It would be a very useless power if it could not pass those lines. The commerce of the United States with foreign nations, is that of the whole United States. Every district has a right to participate in it. The deep streams which penetrate our country in every direction, pass through the interior of almost every state in the Union, and furnish the means of exercising this right. If Congress has the power to regulate it, that power must be exercised whenever the subject exists. If it exists within the states, if a foreign voyage may commence or terminate at a port within a state, then the power of Congress may be exercised within a state.

This principle is, if possible, still more clear when applied to commerce "among the several states." They either join each other, in which case they are separated by a mathematical line, or they are remote from each other, in which case other states lie between them. What is commerce "among" them; and how is it to be conducted? Can a trading expedition between two adjoining states commence and terminate outside of each? And if the trading intercourse be between two states remote from each other, must it not commence in one, terminate in the other, and probably pass through a third? Commerce among the states must, of necessity, be commerce with the states. In the regulation of trade with the Indian tribes, the action of the law, especially when the constitution was made, was chiefly within a state. The power of Congress, then, whatever it may be, must be exercised within the territorial jurisdiction of the several states. . . .

We are now arrived at the inquiry, What is this power?

It is the power to regulate; that is, to prescribe the rule by which commerce is to be governed. This power, like all others vested in Congress, is complete in itself, may be exercised to its utmost extent, and acknowledges no limitations other than are prescribed in the constitution. These are expressed in plain terms, and do not affect the questions which arise in this case, or which have been discussed at the bar. . . .

The power of Congress, then, comprehends navigation within the limits of every state in the Union, so far as that navigation may be, in any manner, connected with "commerce with foreign nations, or among the several states, or with the Indian tribes." It may, of consequence, pass the jurisdictional line of New York, and act upon the very waters to which the prohibition now under consideration applies.

But it has been urged with great earnestness, that although the power of Congress to regulate commerce with foreign nations, and among the several states, be co-extensive with the subject itself, and have no other limits than are prescribed in the constitution, yet the states may severally exercise the same power within their respective jurisdictions. In support of this argument, it is said that they possessed it as an inseparable attribute of sovereignty before the formation of the Constitution, and still retain it, except so far as they have surrendered it by that instrument; that this principle results from the nature of the government, and is secured by the tenth amendment; that an affirmative grant of power is not exclusive, unless in its own nature it be such that the continued exercise of it by the former possessor is inconsistent with the grant, and that this is not of that description.

The appellant, conceding these postulates, except the last, contends that full power to regulate a particular subject implies the whole power, and leaves no residuum; that a grant of the whole is incompatible with the existence of a right in another to any part of it. . . .

In discussing the question, whether this power is still in the states, in the case under consideration, we may dismiss from it the inquiry, whether it is surrendered by the mere grant to Congress, or is retained until Congress shall exercise the power. We may dismiss that inquiry, because it has been exercised, and the regulations which Congress deemed it proper to make, are now in full operation. The sole question is, can a state regulate commerce with foreign nations and among the states, while Congress is regulating it? . . .

The act passed in 1803, prohibiting the importation of slaves into any state which shall itself prohibit their importation, implies, it is said, an admission that the states possessed the power to exclude or admit them; from which it is inferred that they possess the same power with respect to other articles.

If this inference were correct; if this power was exercised, not under any particular clause in the constitution, but in virtue of a general right over the subject of commerce, to exist as long as the constitution itself, it might now be exercised. Any state might now import African slaves into its own territory. But it is obvious that the power of the states over this subject, previous to the year 1808, constitutes an exception to the power of Congress to regulate commerce, and the exception is expressed in such words as to manifest clearly the intention to continue the pre-existing right of the states to admit or exclude for a limited period. The words are: "The migration or importation of such persons as any of the states, now existing, shall think proper to admit, shall not be prohibited by the Congress prior to the year 1808." The whole object of the exception is to preserve the power to those states which might be disposed to exercise it; and its language seems to the court to convey this idea unequivocally. The possession of this particular power, then, during the time limited in the constitution, cannot be admitted to prove the possession of any other similar power.

It has been said that the act of August 7th, 1789, acknowledges a concurrent power in the states to regulate the conduct of pilots, and hence is inferred an admission of their concurrent right with Congress to regulate commerce with foreign nations and amongst the states. But this inference is not, we think, justified by the fact.

Although Congress cannot enable a state to legislate, Congress may adopt the provisions of a state on any subject. When the government of the Union was brought into existence, it found a system for the regulation of its pilots in full force in every state. The act which has been mentioned adopts this system, and gives it the same validity as if its provisions had been specially made by Congress. But the act, it may be said, is prospective also, and the adoption of laws to be made in future presupposes the right in the maker to legislate on the subject.

The act unquestionably manifests an intention to leave this subject entirely to the states, until Congress should think proper to interpose; but the very enactment of such a law indicates an opinion that it was necessary; that the existing system would not be applicable to the new state of things, unless expressly applied to it by Congress. . . .

These acts were cited at the bar for the purpose of showing an opinion in Congress that the states possess, concurrently with the legislature of the Union, the power to regulate commerce with foreign nations and among the states. Upon reviewing them, we think they do not establish the proposition they were intended to prove. They show the opinion that the states retain powers enabling them to pass the laws to which allusion has been made, not that those laws proceed from the particular power which has been delegated to Congress.

It has been contended by the counsel for the appellant, that, as the word "to regulate" implies in its nature full power over the thing to be regulated, it excludes, necessarily, the action of all others that would perform the same operation on the same thing. That regulation is designed for the entire result, applying to those parts which remain as they were, as well as to those which are altered. It produces a uniform whole, which is as much disturbed and deranged by changing what the regulating power designs to leave untouched, as that on which it has operated.

There is great force in this argument, and the court is not satisfied that it has been refuted.

Since, however, in exercising the power of regulating their own purely internal affairs, whether of trading or police, the states may sometimes enact laws, the validity of which depends on their interfering with, and being contrary to, an act of Congress passed in pursuance of the constitution, the court will enter upon the inquiry, whether the laws of New York, as expounded by the highest tribunal of that state, have, in their application to this case, come into collision with an act of Congress, and deprived a citizen of a right to which that act entitles him. Should this collision exist, it will be immaterial whether those laws were passed in virtue of a concurrent power "to regulate commerce with foreign nations and among the several states," or in virtue of a power to regulate their domestic trade and police. In one case and the other, the acts of New York must yield to the law of Congress; and the decision sustaining the privilege they confer, against a right given by a law of the Union, must be erroneous. . . .

The questions, then, whether the conveyance of passengers be a part of the coasting trade, and whether a vessel can be protected in that occupation by a coasting license, are not, and cannot be, raised in this case. The real and sole question seems to be, whether a steam machine, in actual use, deprives a vessel of the privileges conferred by a license.

In considering this question, the first idea which presents itself, is that the laws of Congress for the regulation of commerce, do not look to the principle by which vessels are moved. That subject is left entirely to individual discretion; and, in that vast and complex system of legislative enactment concerning it, which embraces everything that the legislature thought it necessary to notice, there is not, we believe, one word respecting the peculiar principle by which vessels are propelled through the water, except what may be found in a single act, granting a particular privilege to steamboats. With this exception, every act, either prescribing duties, or granting privileges, applies to every vessel, whether navigated by the instrumentality of wind or fire, of sails or machinery. The whole weight of proof, then, is thrown upon him who would introduce a distinction to which the words of the law give no countenance.

If a real difference could be admitted to exist between vessels carrying passengers and others, it has already been observed that there is no fact in this case which can bring up that question. And, if the occupation of steamboats be a matter of such general notoriety that the court may be presumed to know it, although not specially informed by the record, then we deny that the transportation of passengers is their exclusive occupation. It is a matter of general history, that, on our western waters, their principal employment is the transportation of merchandise; and all know, that in the waters of the Atlantic they are frequently so employed.

But all inquiry into this subject seems to the court to be put completely at rest by the act already mentioned, entitled, "An act for the enrolling and licensing of steamboats."

This act authorizes a steamboat employed, or intended to be employed, only in a river or bay of the United States, owned wholly or in part by an alien, resident within the United States, to be enrolled and licensed as if the same belonged to a citizen of the United States.

This act demonstrates the opinion of Congress, that steamboats may be enrolled and licensed, in common with vessels using sails. They are, of course, entitled to the same privileges, and can no more be restrained from navigating waters, and entering ports which are free to such vessels, than if they were wafted on their voyage by the winds, instead of being propelled by the agency of fire. The one element may be as legitimately used as the other, for every commercial purpose authorized by the laws of the Union; and the act of a state inhibiting the use of either to any vessel having a license under the act of Congress, comes, we think, in direct collision with that act.

As this decides the cause, it is unnecessary to enter in an examination of that part of the constitution which empowers Congress to promote the progress of science and the useful arts. . . .

UNITED STATES v. DARBY

312 U. S. 100; 85 L. Ed. 609; 61 S. Ct. 451 (1941)

It used to be said that the federal government has no police power. In a narrow sense this is true, for the police power is defined as the general power to pass regulatory laws for the protection of the health, morals, safety, good order, and general welfare of the community. The Constitution grants no such broad power to Congress, and so, by the operation of the Tenth Amendment, it is reserved to the states. Since the turn of the century, however, what may fairly be called a federal police power has come into existence through the use by Congress of certain of its delegated powers to achieve some of the same social objectives which the states achieve through the police power. Thus Congress has no delegated power to regulate local labor conditions, but if they can be shown to affect interstate commerce, then Congress can regulate them under the commerce power. It cannot punish ordinary business swindles, but it may make it a crime to use the mails for purposes of fraud. In this way Congress has been able to implement policies for the national welfare which it has no direct authority to adopt by hanging these policies on the "constitutional pegs" found in its powers to regulate interstate commerce, to operate the postal service, and to tax. By this somewhat indirect method Congress has come to exercise control over an ever-increasing number of social and economic problems. By far the largest part of this growing federal police power is based upon the commerce clause.

The use of the commerce power as a peg on which to hang social legislation developed in two somewhat different ways. The first of these involved the doctrine, first announced in the Lottery Case (Champion v. Ames, 1903), that Congress could validly bar from interstate commerce commodities which are dangerous or otherwise objectionable. In 1895 Congress forbade the sending of lottery tickets through interstate commerce or the mails. After holding that lottery tickets are articles of commerce, the Court decided that Congress had the power to guard the people of the United States from the "widespread pestilence of lotteries" by keeping lottery tickets out of the channels of interstate commerce over which Congress has undisputed control.

Congress was not slow to exercise the kind of power sustained in the Lottery Case. It excluded from interstate commerce impure or misbranded food and drugs, meat not properly inspected, obscene literature, prize fight films (later modified in part), and other injurious or fraudulent commodities. Under a somewhat similar sort of law, if fabrics shipped in interstate commerce are marked "all wool," they must in fact be all wool. It may be noted in passing that the power of Congress over the postal system has enabled it to exercise a wide police power by excluding objectionable articles from the mails and by forbidding the use of the mails for purposes of fraud.

The Court found no difference in principle between barring objectionable articles from interstate commerce and forbidding the use of the facilities of interstate commerce to aid immoral or criminal activities. In Hoke v. United States (1913) it held valid the Mann Act of 1910 which makes it a crime to transport women across a state line for immoral purposes. The act was not aimed at localized prostitution, but at the organized gangs of white slavers who carried on the interstate traffic in girls and women upon which commercialized vice depends. In 1925 Congress made it a crime knowingly to drive a stolen automobile across a state line, and this was upheld in Brooks v. United States (1925). Under the "anti-fence" laws, the same ban was put upon the interstate shipment of stolen goods in general. The so-called Lindbergh Act makes kidnapping a federal crime if the kidnapped person is carried across a state line (held valid in Gooch v. United States, 1936); and it is also a federal crime to use the mails, telephone, telegraph, or any system of interstate communication for purposes of extortion or blackmail. The Fleeing Felon Act of 1934 makes it a crime to travel in interstate commerce in order to escape from the criminal jurisdiction of a state, and in 1967 Congress forbade persons to travel in interstate commerce for the purpose of inciting a riot. The theory in all these cases is clear and convincing. Congress, which is responsible for interstate commerce and for the uses to which it is put, may punish those who use the facilities of that commerce for immoral or criminal purposes.

The federal police power development reviewed thus far had fairly plain sailing constitutionally. All the articles barred from commerce had been "bad" articles, and all the forbidden uses of the facilities of that commerce had been "bad" uses. In 1916, however, Congress pushed the police power theory somewhat further in passing the Child Labor Act of 1916. Congress was well aware that it lacked the power to forbid child labor throughout the country. What it did, therefore, was forbid the transportation in interstate commerce of the products of mines or factories in which children were employed in violation of the standards set up in this act. In other words, any employer who wished to market his goods through interstate commerce would have to stop employing children. It could not be claimed that the commodities produced in establishments using child labor were "bad" commodities, but merely that the conditions under which they were produced were "bad" conditions. The Supreme Court, split five to four, held the statute invalid in Hammer v. Dagenhart (1918). The majority opinion emphasized that the goods barred from interstate commerce by the act were harmless; that the effect of the act was to regulate, not interstate commerce, but the conditions under which goods entering that commerce were produced; and that it was, therefore, not a bona fide exercise of the commerce power. The Court rejected the argument that Congress could validly prevent those who produce goods under unsatisfactory labor conditions from using the channels of interstate commerce in order to compete with producers in other states who maintain decent labor conditions. It said: "Many causes may cooperate to give one state, by reason of local laws or conditions, an economic advantage over others. The commerce clause was not intended to give to Congress a general authority to equalize such conditions." Finally, the act was void under the Tenth Amendment because Congress was using its delegated power over commerce for the purpose of regulating child labor, a power which lies within the range of the powers reserved to the states.

Justice Holmes dissented in Hammer v. Dagenhart in a strong opinion in which he declared that the Child Labor Act was a clear and direct exercise of the commerce power and that it should not be held void because of its indirect effects upon state authority. "It does not matter," he said, "whether the supposed evil precedes or follows the transportation. It is enough that, in the opinion of Congress, the transportation encourages the evil. . . .

"The notion that prohibition is any less prohibition when applied to things now thought evil I do not understand. But if there is any matter upon which civilized countries have agreed,—far more unanimously than they have with regard to intoxicants and some other matters over which this country is now emotionally aroused,—it is the evil of premature and excessive child labor. I should have thought that if we were to introduce our own moral conceptions where, in my opinion, they do not belong, this was pre-eminently a case for upholding the exercise of all its powers by the United States.

"But I had thought that the propriety of the exercise of a power admitted to exist in some cases was for the consideration of Congress alone, and that this court always had disavowed the right to intrude its judgment upon questions of policy or morals. It is not for this court to pronounce when prohibition is necessary to regulation if it ever may be necessary,—to say that it is permissible as against strong drink, but not as against the product of ruined lives.

"The act does not meddle with anything belonging to the states. They may regulate their internal affairs and their domestic commerce as they like. But when they seek to send their products across the state line they are no longer within their rights."

In the 23 years between Hammer v. Dagenhart (1918) and the Darby case which overruled it, dramatic political changes swept the country. The Great Depression of the 1930's revealed that the laissez-faire economic theory which underlay most judicial thinking was unable to prevent economic disaster, and the state and local governments, upon which most of the burden fell, were unable to cope with the ensuing devastation. The result was a widespread change in attitude toward the role of government, particularly national government, in economic affairs. The election in 1932, and overwhelming reelection in 1936, of President Franklin D. Roosevelt was viewed as a mandate for his New Deal, a program of extensive government intervention in and control over the nation's economy.

Faced with an unsympathetic and intransigent Supreme Court, one of FDR's first moves upon reelection was to introduce in Congress a plan to enlarge the Court by one justice for every justice over the age of 70. Public opposition to the move was immediate and overwhelming and the so-called "court packing plan" was defeated. But from 1937 on, a majority of the Court (which included Justice Roberts, who had switched over), without alluding to the political pressures upon them, began holding valid measures very like those they had been finding invalid before.

In 1938 Congress enacted the Fair Labor Standards (Wages and Hours) Act, which provided the first comprehensive regulation of the working standards of persons engaged in interstate commerce or producing goods for that commerce. The act provided (the first year) for a minimum wage of 25 cents an hour and a maximum 44-hour week without overtime pay, and required employers subject to the act to keep records of the hours and pay of their workers. Prohibited, also, was the employment of children under 16 in manufacturing and mining, and under 18 in hazardous occupations. The act not only made it a crime to ship in interstate commerce goods manufactured in violation of these standards but, in addition, made it a crime to employ persons in the manufacture of goods for commerce under conditions which did not meet the prescribed standards. Darby, the president of a lumber company, was indicted for violating the wages, hours, and record-keeping provisions of the act.

Mr. Justice **Stone** delivered the opinion of the Court, saying in part:

The two principal questions raised by the record in this case are, *first,* whether Congress has constitutional power to prohibit the shipment in interstate commerce of lumber manufactured by employees whose wages are less than a prescribed minimum or whose weekly hours of labor at that wage are greater than a prescribed maximum, and, *second,* whether it has power to prohibit the employment of workmen in the production of goods "for interstate commerce" at other than prescribed wages and hours. A subsidiary question is whether in connection with such prohibitions Congress can require the employer subject to them to keep records showing the hours worked each day and week by each of his employees including those engaged "in the production and manufacture of goods to wit, lumber, for 'interstate commerce.' " . . .

The Fair Labor Standards Act set up a comprehensive legislative scheme for preventing the shipment in interstate commerce of certain products and commodities produced in the United States under labor conditions as respects wages and hours which fail to conform to standards set up by the Act. Its purpose, as we judicially know from the declaration of policy in § 2(a) of the Act, and the reports of Congressional committees proposing the legislation, . . . is to exclude from interstate commerce goods produced for the commerce and to prevent their production for interstate commerce, under conditions detrimental to the maintenance of the minimum standards of living necessary for health and general well-being; and to prevent the use of interstate commerce as the means of competition in the distribution of goods so produced, and as the means of spreading and perpetuating such substandard labor conditions among the workers of the several states. The Act also sets up an administrative procedure whereby those standards may from time to time be modified generally as to industries subject to the Act or within an industry in accordance with specified standards, by an administrator acting in collaboration with "Industry Committees" appointed by him. . . .

The indictment charges that appellee is engaged, in the state of Georgia, in the business of acquiring raw materials, which he manufactures into finished lumber with the intent, when manufactured, to ship it in interstate commerce to customers outside the state, and that he does in fact so ship a large part of the lumber so produced. There are numerous counts charging appellee with the shipment in interstate commerce from Georgia to points outside the state of lumber in the production of which, for interstate commerce, appellee has employed workmen at less than the prescribed minimum wage or more than the prescribed maximum hours without payment to them of any wage for overtime. Other counts charge the employment by appellee of workmen in the production of lumber for interstate commerce at wages [of] less than 25 cents an hour or for more than the maximum hours per week without payment to them of the prescribed overtime wage. Still another count charges appellee with failure to keep records showing the hours worked each day a week by each of his employees as required by § 11(c) and the regulation of the administrator, . . . and also that appellee unlawfully failed to keep such records of employees engaged "in the production and manufacture of goods, to-wit lumber, for interstate commerce." . . .

The case comes here on assignments by the Government that the district court erred in so far as it held that Congress was without constitutional power to penalize the acts set forth in the indictment, and appellee seeks to sustain the decision below on the grounds that the prohibition by Congress of those Acts is unauthorized by the commerce clause and is prohibited by the Fifth Amendment. . . . Hence we . . . confine our decision to the validity and construction of the statute.

The prohibition of shipment of the proscribed goods in interstate commerce. Section 15(a) (1) prohibits, and the indictment charges, the shipment in the interstate commerce, of goods produced for interstate commerce by employees whose wages and hours of employment do not conform to the requirements of the Act. Since this section is not violated unless the commodity shipped has been produced under labor conditions prohibited by § 6 and § 7, the only question arising under the commerce clause with respect to such shipments is whether Congress has the constitutional power to prohibit them.

While manufacture is not of itself interstate commerce the shipment of manufactured goods interstate is such commerce and the prohibition of such shipment by Congress is indubitably a regulation of the commerce. The power to regulate commerce is the power "to prescribe the rule by which commerce is governed." Gibbons v. Ogden [1824]. It extends not only to those regulations which aid, foster and protect the commerce, but embraces those which prohibit it. . . . It is conceded that the power of Congress to prohibit transportation in interstate commerce includes noxious articles, Lottery Case (Champion v. Ames) [1903] . . . ; stolen articles, Brooks v. United States [1925]; kidnapped persons, Gooch v. United States [1936] . . . and articles such as intoxicating liquor or convict made goods, traffic in which is forbidden or restricted by the laws of the state of destination. Kentucky Whip & Collar Co. v. Illinois C. R. Co. [1937].

But it is said that the present prohibition falls within the scope of none of these categories; that while the prohibition is nominally a regulation of the commerce its motive or purpose is regulation of wages and hours of persons engaged in manufacture, the control of which has been reserved to the states and upon which Georgia and some of the states of destination have placed no restriction; that the effect of the present statute is not to exclude the prescribed articles from interstate commerce in aid of state regulation as in Kentucky Whip & Collar Co. v. Illinois C. R. Co., but instead, under the guise of a regulation of interstate commerce, it undertakes to regulate wages and hours within the state contrary to the policy of the state which has elected to leave them unregulated.

The power of Congress over interstate commerce "is complete in itself, may be exercised to its utmost extent, and acknowledges no limitations other than are prescribed in the Constitution." Gibbons v. Ogden. That power can neither be enlarged nor diminished by the exercise or nonexercise of state power. . . . Congress, following its own conception of public policy concerning the restrictions which may appropriately be imposed on interstate commerce, is free to exclude from the commerce articles whose use in the states for which they are destined it may conceive to be injurious to the public health, morals or welfare, even though the state has not sought to regulate their use. . . .

Such regulation is not a forbidden invasion of state power merely because either its motive or its consequence is to restrict the use of articles of commerce within the states of destination and is not prohibited unless by other constitutional provisions. It is no objection to the assertion of the power to regulate interstate commerce that its exercise is attended by the same incidents which attend the exercise of the police power of the states. . . .

The motive and purpose of the present regulation are plainly to make effective the Congressional conception of public policy that interstate commerce should not be made the instrument of competition in the distribution of goods produced under substandard labor conditions, which competition is injurious to the commerce and to the states from and to which the commerce flows. The motive and purpose of a regulation of interstate commerce are matters for the legislative judgment upon the exercise of which the Constitution places no restriction and over which the courts are given no control. . . . "The judicial cannot prescribe to the legislative department of the government limitations upon the exercise of its acknowledged power." Veazie Bank v. Fenno [1869]. Whatever their motive and purpose, regulations of commerce which do not infringe some constitutional prohibition are within the plenary power conferred on Congress by the Commerce Clause. Subject only to that limitation, presently to be considered, we conclude that the prohibition of the shipment interstate of goods produced under the forbidden substandard labor conditions is within the constitutional authority of Congress.

In the more than a century which has elapsed since the decision of Gibbons v. Ogden, these principles of constitutional interpretation have been so long and repeatedly recognized by this Court as applicable to the Commerce Clause, that there would be little occasion for repeating them now were it not for the decision of this Court twenty-two years ago in Hammer v. Dagenhart [1918]. In that case it was held by a bare majority of the Court over the powerful and now classic dissent of Mr. Justice Holmes setting forth the fundamental issues involved, that Congress was without power to exclude the products of child labor from interstate commerce. The reasoning and conclusion of the Court's opinion there cannot be reconciled with the conclusion which we have reached, that the power of Congress under the Commerce Clause is plenary to exclude any article from interstate commerce subject only to the specific prohibitions of the Constitution.

Hammer v. Dagenhart has not been followed. The distinction on which the decision was rested that congressional power to prohibit interstate commerce is limited to articles which in themselves have some harmful or deleterious property—a distinction which was novel when made and unsupported by any provision of the Constitution—has long since been abandoned. Brooks v. United States; Kentucky Whip & Collar Co. v. Illinois C. R. Co.; . . . Mulford v. Smith [1939]. The thesis of the opinion that the motive of the prohibition or its effect to control in some measure the use or production within the states of the article thus excluded from the commerce can operate to deprive the regulation of its constitutional authority has long since ceased to have force. . . . And finally we have declared "The authority of the federal government over interstate commerce does not differ in extent or character from that retained by the states over intrastate commerce." United States v. Rock Royal Co-operative [1939].

The conclusion is inescapable that Hammer v. Dagenhart was a departure from the principles which have prevailed in the interpretation of the commerce clause both before and since the decision and that such vitality, as a precedent, as it then had has long since been exhausted. It should be and now is overruled.

Validity of the wage and hour requirements. Section 15(a) (2) and §§ 6 and 7 require employers to conform to the wage and hour provisions with respect to all employees engaged in the production of goods for interstate commerce. As appellee's employees are not alleged to be "engaged in interstate commerce" the validity of the prohibition turns on the question whether the employment, under other than the prescribed labor standards, of employees engaged in the production of goods for interstate commerce is so related to the commerce and so affects it as to be within the reach of the power of Congress to regulate it. . . .

. . . The power of Congress over interstate commerce is not confined to the regulation of commerce among the states. It extends to those activities intrastate which so affect interstate commerce or the exercise of the power of Congress over it as to make regulation of them appropriate means to the attainment of a legitimate end, the exercise of the granted power of Congress to regulate interstate commerce. . . .

. . . A recent example is the National Labor Relations Act for the regulation of employer and employee relations in industries in which strikes, induced by unfair labor practices named in the Act, tend to disturb or obstruct interstate commerce. See National Labor Relations Bd. v. Jones & L. Steel Corp. [1937]. . . . But long before the adoption of the National Labor Relations Act this Court had many times held that the power of Congress to regulate interstate commerce extends to the regulation through legislative action of activities intrastate which have a substantial effect on the commerce or the exercise of the Congressional power over it.

In such legislation Congress has sometimes left it to the courts to determine whether the intrastate activities have the prohibited effect on the commerce, as in the Sherman Act. It has sometimes left it to an administrative board or agency to determine whether the activities sought to be regulated or prohibited have such effect, as in the case of the Interstate Commerce Act, and the National Labor Relations Act or whether they come within the statutory definition of the prohibited Act as in the Federal Trade Commission Act. And sometimes Congress itself has said that a particular activity affects the commerce as it did in the present act, the Safety Appliance Act and the Railway Labor Act. In passing on the validity of legislation of the class last mentioned the only function of courts is to determine whether the particular activity regulated or prohibited is within the reach of the federal power. . . .

Congress having by the present Act adopted the policy of excluding from interstate commerce all goods produced for the commerce which do not conform to the specified labor standards, it may choose the means reasonably adapted to the attainment of the permitted end, even though they involve control of intrastate activities. . . . A familiar like exercise of power is the regulation of intrastate transactions which are so commingled with or related to interstate commerce that all must be regulated if the interstate commerce is to be effectively controlled. Shreveport Case [1914]. . . . Similarly Congress may require inspection and preventive treatment of all cattle in a disease infected area in order to prevent shipment in interstate commerce of some of the cattle without the treatment. . . . It may prohibit the removal, at destination, of labels required by the Pure Food & Drugs Act to be affixed to articles transported in interstate commerce, . . . And we have recently held that

Congress in the exercise of its power to require inspection and grading of tobacco shipped in interstate commerce may compel such inspection and grading of all tobacco sold at local auction rooms from which a substantial part but not all of the tobacco sold is shipped in interstate commerce. . . .

We think also that § 15(a) (2) now under consideration, is sustainable independently of § 15(a) (1), which prohibits shipment or transportation of the proscribed goods. As we have said the evils aimed at by the Act are the spread of substandard labor conditions through the use of the facilities of interstate commerce for competition by the goods so produced with those produced under the prescribed or better labor conditions; and the consequent disloca-tion of the commerce itself caused by the impairment or destruction of local businesses by competition made effective through interstate commerce. The Act is thus directed at the suppression of a method or kind of competition in interstate commerce which it has in effect condemned as "unfair," as the Clayton Act has condemned other "unfair methods of competition" made effective through interstate commerce. . . .

The Sherman Act and the National Labor Relations Act are familiar examples of the exertion of the commerce power to prohibit or control activities wholly intrastate because of their effect on interstate commerce. . . .

The means adopted by § 15(a) (2) for the protection of interstate commerce by the suppression of the production of the condemned goods for interstate commerce is so related to the commerce and so affects it as to be within the reach of the commerce power. . . . Congress, to attain its objective in the suppression of nation-wide competition in interstate commerce by goods produced under substandard labor conditions, has made no distinction as to the volume or amount of shipments in the commerce or of production for commerce by any particular shipper or producer. It recognized that in present day industry, competition by a small part may affect the whole and that the total effect of the competition of many small producers may be great. . . . The legislation aimed at a whole embraces all its parts.

So far as Carter v. Carter Coal Co. [1936] is inconsistent with this conclusion, its doctrine is limited in principle by the decisions under the Sherman Act and the National Labor Relations Act, which we have cited and which we follow. . . .

Our conclusion is unaffected by the Tenth Amendment which provides: "The powers not delegated to the United States by the Constitution nor prohibited by it to the states are reserved to the states respectively or to the people." The amendment states but a truism that all is retained which has not been surrendered. There is nothing in the history of its adoption to suggest that it was more than declaratory of the relationship between the national and state governments as it had been established by the Constitution before the amendment or that its purpose was other than to allay fears that the new national government might seek to exercise powers not granted, and that the states might not be able to exercise fully their reserved powers. . . .

From the beginning and for many years the amendment has been construed as not depriving the national government of authority to resort to all means for the exercise of a granted power which are appropriate and plainly adapted to the permitted end. . . . Whatever doubts may have arisen of the soundness of that conclusion they have been put at rest by the decisions under the Sherman Act and the National Labor Relations Act which we have cited. . . .

Reversed.

KATZENBACH v. McCLUNG

379 U. S. 294; 13 L. Ed. 2d 290; 85 S. Ct. 377 (1964)

In the preceding cases the Court permitted Congress to close the channels of interstate commerce to commodities and for purposes of which it disapproves. The effect is to permit a certain diversity of policy among the states without fear of out-of-state interference, as well as to aid in the capture of local criminals by helping to reduce their avenues of escape.

A quite different use of the commerce power, however, lies in the power of Congress to keep the channels of interstate commerce open and unimpeded. The development of this aspect of the commerce power into an effective weapon of social control came very slowly. For one hundred years prior to 1887, Congress made no attempt to regulate interstate commerce, and the Supreme Court was left to struggle alone with the question whether a particular activity was local, and hence subject to state control, or was interstate commerce and hence subject to no control at all.

With the passage of the Interstate Commerce Act in 1887 and the Sherman Act in 1890, Congress for the first time moved to regulate transportation and forbid monopoly in interstate commerce—only to find itself faced with a Supreme Court whose members showed little sympathy for government economic regulation of any kind. While the Court conceded Congress' right to provide for the safe movement of goods across state lines, it drew a sharp line between the control of things which had a direct effect on such commerce, and those whose effect was merely indirect.

Thus, in United States v. E. C. Knight Co. (1895), it denied the use of the Sherman Act to break up the powerful sugar trust which had been formed to control the manufacture and distribution of refined sugar throughout the United States. The Court held the Antitrust Act did not apply to combinations in restraint of manufacturing. "Doubtless the power to control the manufacture of a given thing involves in a certain sense the control of its disposition, but this is a secondary and not the primary sense; and although the exercise of that power may result in bringing the operation of commerce into play, it does not control it, and affects it only incidentally and indirectly. Commerce succeeds to manufacture, and is not a part of it. The power to regulate commerce is the power to prescribe the rule by which commerce shall be governed, and is a power independent of the power to suppress monopoly." In Oliver Iron Mining Co. v. Lord (1923) the Court held that mining, like manufacturing, was not interstate commerce.

Even where an interstate carrier was clearly involved, the power to regulate was limited to things directly affecting interstate movement. A federal statute outlawing so-called "yellow-dog contracts" (by which workmen were forced to agree not to join labor unions) was held void in Adair v. United States (1908) on the ground, among others, that there is no "possible legal or logical connection . . . between an employee's membership in a labor organization and the carrying on of interstate commerce."

In 1914, in the Shreveport Case, the Court abandoned this outmoded concept of two mutually exclusive areas of intrastate and interstate commerce, each clearly and safely under the control of state or federal government, and put in its place as a rule for measuring federal authority in the field of commerce, the realistic test of whether commercial or business activities—even though they be local—so impinge upon or affect interstate commerce as to bring them reasonably within the range of federal control. The Court recognized a functional relationship between local and interstate commerce and permitted the ICC to forbid a railroad to set local rates which discriminated against interstate rates which had been found by the commission to be reasonable.

In 1922 the doctrine of the Shreveport Case was extended to cover local businesses other than common carriers. In 1921 Congress had passed the Packers and Stockyards Act in an effort to break up discriminatory practices resulting from control of the stockyards by the "Big Five" meat packers: Swift, Armour, Cudahy, Wilson, and Morris. Livestock was shipped into Chicago from producers throughout the West and was received by brokers called "commission men," who unloaded the stock into pens in the stockyard, watered and cared for them, and then sold them on a commission basis, largely to the big meat packers. Most of the meat, either before or after packing, was shipped to eastern markets. The control of the stockyards by the packers and their resultant influence over the commission men resulted in discrimination against the western shipper as well as against other buyers. The act provided an elaborate scheme of regulation, including approval by the Secretary of Agriculture of all rates and charges for services and facilities in the stockyards.

In Stafford v. Wallace (1922) the Supreme Court sustained this regulation, rejecting the argument that Congress had no authority to control purely local sales of cattle after they had come to rest in the stockyards. "The stockyards," the Court said, "are not a place of rest or final destination. Thousands of head of live stock arrive daily by carloads and trainload lots, and must be promptly sold and disposed of and moved out to give place to the constantly flowing traffic that presses behind. The stockyards are but a throat through which the current flows, and the transactions which occur therein are only incident to this current from the West to the East, and from one State to another. Such transactions cannot be separated from the movement to which they contribute, and necessarily take on its character. . . ."

In 1935 the Court made clear that this reasoning did not apply to businesses handling commodities which had ceased their interstate journey and come to rest within a state. In Schechter Poultry Corp. v. United States (1935), the Court struck down the Live Poultry Code promulgated under the National Industrial Recovery Act which attempted to regulate hours, wages, and the conditions of sale of poultry which had moved in interstate commerce. Citing the "well-established distinction between direct and indirect effects," the Court found the business of selling chickens within the state had only an "indirect" effect on interstate commerce. "Where the effect of intrastate transactions upon interstate commerce is merely indirect, such transactions remain within the domain of State power." (At the same time the Court struck down the entire NIRA on the ground that it invalidly delegated legislative power to the President.)

In July, less than two months after the NIRA had been held void in the Schechter case, Congress passed the National Labor Relations Act (known as the Wagner Act, or NLRA), the first thoroughgoing and genuinely regulatory federal act to deal with the relations between labor and capital. The act was unique both in scope and in method. Its scope included all labor disputes which burdened or obstructed interstate commerce. Such burden or obstruction might take the form (1) of impairing the efficiency or safety of the instrumentalities of commerce, (2) of restraining the flow of raw materials or manufactured goods through interstate commerce, or controlling the prices thereof, (3) of reducing employment and wages sufficiently to reduce substantially the market for goods moving in interstate commerce, or (4) of obstructing directly the actual current of commerce. The method employed by the act was that of defining carefully seven or eight "unfair labor practices" which were forbidden, and of creating a new National Labor Relations Board with power upon investigation to issue "cease and desist orders," enforceable in the courts, against those guilty of these practices. This was the technique employed in the Federal Trade Commission Act under which the commission issued "cease and desist orders" against those found to be engaging in unfair competitive trade practices. The NLRB was, therefore, a very powerful body.

The Wagner Act clearly rested upon precarious footing, since its provisions extended to labor relations in the processes of manufacturing goods which were to be moved in interstate commerce. Ever since the E. C. Knight case (1895) the Court had insisted that manufacturing was antecedent to and clearly separate from the interstate commerce in which the manufactured goods later move, and while the Shreveport Case (1914) and Stafford v. Wallace (1922) indicated that the Court's attitude toward this distinction was becoming less rigid, the emphasis in the Schechter case upon "direct" and "indirect" effects which local activities produce on interstate commerce did not give supporters of the Wagner Act much encouragement. Moreover, in Carter v. Carter Coal Co. (1936), which held the Guffey Coal Act void, the Court said that the relations between employers and workmen in the coal industry did not directly affect interstate commerce in coal and could not therefore be regulated by Congress. The Court might very consistently have held the NLRA void in its application to labor relations in the field of manufacturing. But this it did not do.

The Wagner Act came before the Court in NLRB v. Jones & Laughlin Steel Corp. (1937). The NLRB had found that the Jones & Laughlin Steel Corporation had discharged some of its men because of their labor union activities. The board ordered the company to reinstate them and to cease such discrimination. The company was the fourth largest producer of steel in the country. It had 19 subsidiaries which comprised an integrated system. It owned mines, ships, railroads, furnaces, and mills. The board found that the plants in which the labor troubles occurred "might be likened to the heart of a self-contained, highly integrated body. They draw in the raw materials from Michigan, Minnesota, West Virginia, Pennsylvania in part through arteries and by means controlled by the respondent; they transform the materials and then pump them out to all parts of the nation through the vast mechanism which the respondent has elaborated."

The Court, with the about-face of March 1937 behind it (see the note to the Darby case), brushed aside arguments that the "stream of commerce" was broken, that this was manufacturing, and that its effect on interstate commerce was only indirect. "In view of respondent's far-flung activities, it is idle to say that the effect would be indirect or remote. It is obvious that it would be immediate and might be catastrophic. We are asked to shut our eyes to the plainest facts of our national life and to deal with the question of direct and indirect effects in an intellectual vacuum. When industries organize themselves on a national scale, making their relation to interstate commerce the dominant factor in their activities, how can it be maintained that their industrial labor relations constitute a forbidden field into which Congress may not enter when it is necessary to protect interstate commerce from the paralyzing consequences of industrial war?"

Perhaps even more striking than the extension of federal control in the field of labor relations has been the development of such control in the field of agriculture. The Agricultural Adjustment Act of 1933, which was held void in United States v. Butler (1936), had relied for its constitutional underpinnings upon the delegated powers of Congress to tax and to spend money. The Agricultural Adjustment Act of 1938, which aimed at similar objectives, was based on the commerce power. The act declared that its policy (in part) was: "to regulate interstate and foreign commerce in cotton, wheat, corn, tobacco and rice to the extent necessary to provide an orderly, adequate, and balanced flow of such commodities in interstate and foreign commerce through storage of reserve supplies, loans, marketing quotas, assisting farmers to obtain, in so far as practicable, parity prices for such commodities and parity of income, and assisting consumers to obtain an adequate and steady supply of such commodities at fair prices."

The attack upon the validity of the statute arose under the sections providing for the establishment of marketing quotas for flue-cured tobacco. There were similar sections dealing with cotton, wheat, corn, and rice. The act authorized the Secretary of Agriculture, when he found that the supply of tobacco had increased beyond a certain point, to put into effect a national marketing quota, provided that not more than one-third of the previous year's tobacco growers were opposed. The quotas were allocated in such a way that each grower was given a quota which he must not exceed. If tobacco in excess of the quota for a particular farm was marketed through a warehouse man, the latter paid to the Secretary a penalty equal to 50 percent of the market price of the excess, and might deduct this amount from the prices paid to the producer. In Mulford v. Smith (1939) the Supreme Court held the act valid. It was not, the Court said, a regulation of production but only a regulation of the interstate commerce in tobacco at the "throat where tobacco enters the stream of commerce,—the marketing warehouse." The fact that not all the tobacco was sold interstate was considered immaterial since the "regulation, to be effective, must, and therefore may constitutionally, apply to all sales."

A more extreme application of the 1938 statute was upheld in Wickard v. Filburn (1942). Quotas were established for the production of wheat, in order to prevent surpluses and maintain prices. Filburn raised 23 acres of wheat, none of which was intended for interstate commerce, and all of which he consumed or fed to his stock. The quota allotted to him, however, was 11.1 acres; and the Court held him validly liable to the statutory penalties on the wheat produced in excess of this quota. His production of this wheat affected interstate commerce "directly" just as much as though he had farmed 23,000 acres instead of 23.

In discussing the "judicial revolution of 1937" there will always be speculation as to the part played by public pressure and by President Franklin Roosevelt's threat to "pack" the Court, discussed more fully in the note to the Parrish case. But whether the Court responded to such pressure or whether its change of attitude was a spontaneous response to a new perception of social needs, its reversal in attitude was complete and permanent. While it is instructive to study the way in which the Court handled the change, and important to understand the reasoning upon which the post-1937 cases rest, today it is only with the greatest caution that one cites as authority cases from the earlier period. The Court had, in the economic sphere at least, turned over to the legislatures of the states and the nation the power to govern.

To a person unfamiliar with our institutions and constitutional history, it must seem strange that the national government, in its efforts to abolish race discrimination, should be forced to act under a grant of power to regulate interstate commerce. Of course, if a state government does the discriminating, either through its laws or its officials, the courts can interfere under the equal protection clause of the Fourteenth Amendment. But as early as 1883 in the Civil Rights Cases the Court made clear that private discrimination was not forbidden by the Fourteenth Amendment, and Congress had no "police power" under which it could outlaw it generally.

The passage of the Civil Rights Act of 1964, Title II of which was sustained in the present cases, brought to an all-time high congressional efforts to abolish race discrimination in the United States. The act itself was remarkable for a number of reasons. First, for the first time since the ill-fated Civil Rights Act of 1875, Congress made a sweeping attack on race discrimination. Second, the act commanded overwhelming bipartisan support. After five months of committee hearings, 2800 pages of testimony, and seven months of debates, the measure passed the House 289 to 126. In an unusual move, the Senate did not even send it to committee, but worked out a bill with informal bipartisan conferences. The House adopted the

Senate bill without change. Third, for the first time in history the Senate, with the all-out support of both majority and minority leaders, invoked cloture to stop a Southern filibuster on a civil rights measure.

In Heart of Atlanta Motel v. United States (1964), a companion to the present case, the Court held that discrimination against black guests by a motel serving interstate travellers was an impediment to the free movement of blacks among the several states.

Mr. Justice **Clark** delivered the opinion of the Court, saying in part:

This case was argued with Heart of Atlanta Motel v. United States in which we upheld the constitutional validity of Title II of the Civil Rights Act of 1964 against an attack by hotels, motels, and like establishments. This complaint for injunctive relief against appellants attacks the constitutionality of the Act as applied to a restaurant. . . .

2. The Facts

Ollie's Barbecue is a family-owned restaurant in Birmingham, Alabama, specializing in barbecued meats and homemade pies, with a seating capacity of 220 customers. It is located on a state highway 11 blocks from an interstate one and a somewhat greater distance from railroad and bus stations. The restaurant caters to a family and white-collar trade with a take-out service for Negroes. It employs 36 persons, two-thirds of whom are Negroes.

In the 12 months preceding the passage of the Act, the restaurant purchased locally approximately $150,000 worth of food, $69,683 or 46% of which was meat that it bought from a local supplier who had procured it from outside the State. The District Court expressly found that a substantial portion of the food served in the restaurant had moved in interstate commerce. The restaurant has refused to serve Negroes in its dining accommodations since its original opening in 1927, and since July 2, 1964, it has been operating in violation of the Act. The court below concluded that if it were required to serve Negroes it would lose a substantial amount of business.

On the merits, the District Court held that the Act could not be applied under the Fourteenth Amendment because it was conceded that the State of Alabama was not involved in the refusal of the restaurant to serve Negroes. . . . As to the Commerce Clause, the court found . . . that the clause was . . . a grant of power "to regulate intrastate activities, but only to the extent that action on its part is necessary or appropriate to the effective execution of its expressly granted power to regulate interstate commerce." There must be, it said, a close and substantial relation between local activities and interstate commerce which requires control of the former in the protection of the latter. The court concluded, however, that the Congress, rather than finding facts sufficient to meet this rule, had legislated a conclusive presumption that a restaurant affects interstate commerce if it serves or offers to serve interstate travelers or if a substantial portion of the food which it serves has moved in commerce. This, the court held, it could not do because there was no demonstrable connection between food purchased in interstate commerce and sold in a restaurant and the conclusion of Congress that discrimination in the restaurant would affect that commerce. . . .

3. The Act As Applied

Section 201 (a) of Title II commands that all persons shall be entitled to the full and equal enjoyment of the goods and services of any place of public accommodation without discrimination or segregation on the ground of race, color, religion, or national origin; and § 201 (b) defines establishments as places of public accommodation if their operations affect commerce or segregation by them as supported by state action. Sections 201 (b) (2) and (c) place any "restaurant . . . principally engaged in selling food for consumption on the premises" under the Act "if . . . it serves or offers to serve interstate travelers or a substantial portion of the food which it serves . . . has moved in commerce."

Ollie's Barbecue admits that it is covered by these provisions of the Act. The Government makes no contention that the discrimination at the restaurant was supported by the State of Alabama. There is no claim that interstate travelers frequented the restaurant. The sole question, therefore, narrows down to whether Title II, as applied to a restaurant annually receiving about $70,000 worth of food which has moved in commerce, is a valid exercise of the power of Congress. The Government has contended that Congress had ample basis upon which to find that racial discrimination at restaurants which receive from out of state a substantial portion of the food served does, in fact, impose commercial burdens of national magnitude upon interstate commerce. The appellees' major argument is directed to this premise. They urge that no such basis existed. It is to that question that we now turn.

4. The Congressional Hearings

As we noted in Heart of Atlanta Motel both houses of Congress conducted prolonged hearings on the Act. And, as we said there, while no formal findings were made, which of course are not necessary, it is well that we make mention of the testimony at these hearings the better to understand the problem before Congress and determine whether the Act is a reasonable and appropriate means toward its solution. The record is replete with testimony of the burdens placed on interstate commerce by racial discrimination in restaurants. A comparison of per capita spending by Negroes in restaurants, theaters, and like establishments indicated less spending, after discounting income differences, in areas where discrimination is widely practiced. This condition, which was especially aggravated in the South, was attributed in the testimony of the Under Secretary of Commerce to racial segregation. . . . This diminutive spending springing from a refusal to serve Negroes and their total loss as customers has, regardless of the absence of direct evidence, a close connection to interstate commerce. The fewer customers a restaurant enjoys the less food it sells and consequently the less it buys. . . . In addition, the Attorney General testified that this type of discrimination imposed "an artificial restriction on the market" and interfered with the flow of merchandise. . . . In addition, there were many references to discriminatory situations causing wide unrest and having a depressant effect on general business conditions in the respective communities. . . .

Moreover there was an impressive array of testimony that discrimination in restaurants had a direct and highly restrictive effect upon interstate travel by Negroes. This resulted, it was said, because discriminatory practices prevent Negroes from buying prepared food served on the premises while on a trip, except in isolated and unkempt restaurants and under most unsatisfactory and often unpleasant conditions. This obviously discourages travel and obstructs interstate commerce for one can hardly travel without eating. Likewise, it was said, that discrimination deterred professional, as well as skilled, people from moving into areas where such practices occurred and thereby caused industry to be reluctant to establish there. . . .

We believe that this testimony afforded ample basis for the conclusion that established restaurants in such areas sold less interstate goods because of the discrimination, that interstate travel was obstructed directly by it, that business in general suffered and that many new businesses refrained from establishing there as a result of it. Hence the District Court was in error in concluding that there was no connection between discrimination and the movement of interstate commerce. The court's conclusion that such a connection is outside "common experience" flies in the face of stubborn fact.

It goes without saying that, viewed in isolation, the volume of food purchased by Ollie's Barbecue from sources supplied from out of state was insignificant when compared with the total foodstuffs moving in commerce. But, as our late Brother Jackson said for the Court in Wickard v. Filburn (1942):

"That appellee's own contribution to the demand for wheat may be trivial by itself is not enough to remove him from the scope of federal regulation where, as here, his contribution, taken together with that of many others similarly situated, is far from trivial."

We noted in Heart of Atlanta Motel that a number of witnesses attested the fact that racial discrimination was not merely a state or regional problem but was one of nationwide scope. Against this background, we must conclude that while the focus of the legislation was on the individual restaurant's relation to interstate commerce, Congress appropriately considered the importance of that connection with the knowledge that the discrimination was but "representative of many others throughout the country, the total incidence of which if left unchecked may well become far-reaching in its harm to commerce." . . .

With this situation spreading as the record shows, Congress was not required to await the total dislocation of commerce. . . .

5. The Power of Congress to Regulate Local Activities

Article I, § 8, cl. 3, confers upon Congress the power "[t]o regulate Commerce . . . among the several States" and Clause 18 of the same Article grants it the power "[t]o make all Laws which shall be necessary and proper for carrying into Execution the foregoing Powers. . . ." This grant, as we have pointed out in Heart of Atlanta Motel "extends to those activities intrastate which so affect interstate commerce, or the exertion of the power of Congress over it, as to make regulation of them appropriate means to the attainment of a legitimate end, the effective execution of the granted power to regulate interstate commerce." . . . Much is said about a restaurant business being local but "even if appellee's activity be local and though it may not be regarded as commerce, it may still, whatever its nature, be reached by Congress if it exerts a substantial economic effect on interstate commerce. . . ." . . . The activities that are beyond the reach of Congress are "those which are completely within a particular State, which do not affect other States, and with which it is not necessary to interfere, for the purpose of executing some of the general powers of the government.'' ... This rule is as good today as it was when Chief Justice Marshall laid it down almost a century and a half ago. ...

Nor are the cases holding that interstate commerce ends when goods come to rest in the State of destination apposite here. That line of cases has been applied with reference to state taxation or regulation but not in the field of federal regulation.

The appellees contend that Congress has arbitrarily created a conclusive presumption that all restaurants meeting the criteria set out in the Act ''affect commerce.'' Stated another way, they object to the omission of a provision for a case-by-case determination—judicial or administrative—that racial discrimination in a particular restaurant affects commerce.

But Congress' action in framing this Act was not unprecedented. In United States v. Darby, this Court held constitutional the Fair Labor Standards Act of 1938. There Congress determined that the payment of substandard wages to employees engaged in the production of goods for commerce, while not itself commerce, so inhibited it as to be subject to federal regulation. The appellees in that case argued, as do the appellees here, that the Act was invalid because it included no provision for an independent inquiry regarding the effect on commerce of substandard wages in a particular business. ... But the Court rejected the argument, observing that:

''Sometimes Congress itself has said that a particular activity affects the commerce, as it did in the present Act, the Safety Appliance Act and the Railway Labor Act. In passing on the validity of legislation of the class last mentioned the only function of courts is to determine whether the particular activity regulated or prohibited is within the reach of the federal power.''

Here, as there, Congress has determined for itself that refusals of service to Negroes have imposed burdens both upon the interstate flow of food and upon the movement of products generally. Of course, the mere fact that Congress has said when particular activity shall be deemed to affect commerce does not preclude further examination by this Court. But where we find that the legislators, in light of the facts and testimony before them, have a rational basis for finding a chosen regulatory scheme necessary to the protection of commerce, our investigation is at an end. The only remaining question— one answered in the affirmative by the court below—is whether the particular restaurant either serves or offers to serve interstate travelers or serves food a substantial portion of which has moved in interstate commerce. ...

Confronted as we are with the facts laid before Congress, we must conclude that it had a rational basis for finding that racial discrimination in restaurants had a direct and adverse effect on the free flow of interstate commerce. Insofar as the sections of the Act here relevant are concerned, §§ 201 (b) (2) and (c), Congress prohibited discrimination only in those establishments having a close tie to interstate commerce, i.e., those, like the McClungs', serving food that has come from out of the State. We think in so doing that Congress acted well within its power to protect and foster commerce in extending the coverage of Title II only to those restaurants offering to serve interstate travelers or serving food, a substantial portion of which has moved in interstate commerce.

The absence of direct evidence connecting discriminatory restaurant service with the flow of interstate food, a factor on which the appellees place much reliance, is not, given the evidence as to the effect of such practices on other aspects of commerce, a crucial matter.

The power of Congress in this field is broad and sweeping; where it keeps within its sphere and violates no express constitutional limitation it has been the rule of this Court, going back almost to the founding days of the Republic, not to interfere. The Civil Rights Act of 1964, as here applied, we find to be plainly appropriate in the resolution of what the Congress found to be a national commercial problem of the first magnitude. We find it in no violation of any express limitations of the Constitution and we therefore declare it valid.

The judgment is therefore

Reversed.

Justices **Black, Douglas,** and **Goldberg** wrote concurring opinions.

3

The Nationalization
of the Bill of Rights

A. The Beginning

BARRON v. BALTIMORE

7 Peters 243; 8 L. Ed. 672 (1833)

One of the bitter criticisms of our federal Constitution as it came from the hands of the Convention was that it contained no bill of rights. It was feared that without specific guarantees the civil rights and liberties of the people and the states would be at the mercy of the proposed national government. Ratification was secured, but with a tacit understanding that a bill of rights should promptly be added which should restrict the national government in behalf of individual liberty. That the early statesmen thought of a federal bill of rights only in terms of restrictions on national power is emphasized by Hamilton's ingenious argument in *The Federalist* (No. 84) that since the proposed central government was one which possessed only the powers delegated to it, it would be not only unnecessary but unwise to prohibit it from doing things which were clearly outside the scope of its delegated authority.

When the First Congress convened, the House of Representatives proposed seventeen amendments in the nature of a bill of rights. One of these, the fourteenth, provided that "no *state* should infringe the right of trial by jury in criminal cases, nor the rights of conscience, nor the freedom of speech or of the press."(Emphasis added). This amendment, which was the only one restricting the powers of the states, was rejected by the Senate. The substance of the others was consolidated into twelve amendments, ten of which were finally ratified by the states.

The First Amendment indicates by its own language that it is directed only against the federal government, for it begins, "Congress shall make no law. . . ." The other amendments are couched in terms of general prohibition; and in spite of the perfectly clear historical evidence as to the intention of those who framed them, it came to be argued that these guarantees of civil liberty ought to be construed as restrictions upon state and federal governments alike. Whether this view is correct is the issue involved in Barron v. Baltimore, the last constitutional decision in which Chief Justice Marshall participated.

While paving its streets, the city of Baltimore had diverted from their natural courses certain streams, with the result that sand and gravel were deposited near Barron's wharf. The wharf, which had previously enjoyed the deepest water in the harbor, was rendered practically useless, for the deposits prevented the approach of vessels. A verdict of $4500 for Barron had been reversed by the state court of appeals, and a writ of error was taken to the Supreme Court of the United States. It was alleged by Barron that this action upon the part of the city constituted a violation of that clause of the Fifth Amendment which forbids taking private property for public use without just compensation. He insisted that this amendment, being a guarantee in behalf of individual liberty, ought to be construed to restrain the states as well as the national government.

The decision in Barron v. Baltimore has left an indelible impression on the development of civil rights in this country. While today Barron would have brought his case under the due process clause of the Fourteenth Amendment (which does restrict the states), the process of change by which parts of the Bill of Rights have come to be applicable to the states has been slow, uncertain, and confusing. Most rights in the Bill of Rights now do apply to the states, but they do so only because they are essential to due process of law. The ruling in the present case that the Bill of Rights does not apply *directly* to the states has never been overruled.

As a consequence of the Barron case, in the years prior to the Civil War the ordinary citizen looked to the state legislature to protect his person and property from private interference, and to the bill of rights in his state's constitution for protection against injury by his state government. Certainly he did not, and could not, expect the national government to step in and protect him either from his neighbor or from his state government.

At the close of the Civil War it seemed clear that without the intervention of the federal government the Southern states would by legislative restrictions strip the newly freed blacks of most of the ordinary rights and immunities of free citizens. To place the civil rights of blacks upon a firm basis Congress proposed the Fourteenth Amendment, authorizing the national government to step in and protect private persons against actions by his own state government. The states were forbidden to take life, liberty, or property without due process of law, or to deny anyone the equal protection of the laws. The amendment defined United States citizenship in terms which included blacks, and the states were forbidden to make laws abridging the privileges and immunities of that citizenship.

Exactly what the framers of the amendment intended to include in the phrase "privileges and immunities of citizens of the United States" is not altogether clear, and there is evidence to indicate that it was not clear even to the framers. Some apparently believed that the clause would include within its protection those basic rights enjoyed by all persons—such as the right to marry, to own property, to do business, and to move about freely. Others thought that it would include all or part of the protections listed in the federal Bill of Rights. In the Slaughter-House Cases the Court held that the privileges and immunities clause not only protected none of these rights, but by inference protected no rights that were not already amply protected elsewhere in the Constitution. With the exception of one case, mentioned below and later overruled, the Court has never held the clause to be violated.

The Slaughter-House Cases were the first cases brought under the Fourteenth Amendment, and they had nothing whatever to do with the rights of freedmen. The case arose on the following facts: the Reconstruction or "carpetbag" government in Louisiana, unquestionably under corrupt influence, had granted a monopoly of the slaughterhouse business to a single concern, thus preventing over one thousand other persons and firms from continuing in that business. The validity of the law was attacked under the Fourteenth Amendment. The case was argued before the Supreme Court twice and was decided by a majority of five to four.

In deciding the case the Court reasoned that the first section of the Fourteenth Amendment really defined two kinds of citizenship. United States citizens were those persons born or naturalized in the United States, while state citizens were such persons who were born within a particular state. Not only did the Court distinguish between state citizenship and national citizenship, but emphasized that those "fundamental" rights "which belong of right to the citizens of all free governments," such as the right to own property, and the right to pursue and obtain happiness and safety, are privileges of state citizenship. The privileges and immunities of United States citizenship are limited to those which one enjoys by virtue of his federal citizenship and "which owe their existence to the Federal government, its national character, its Constitution, or its laws."

The importance of the case can hardly be overestimated. By its definition the Court limited such privileges and immunities to things which the federal government had always had power to protect under the "supremacy clause" (see McCulloch v. Maryland, 1819) and thus, in effect, wrote the clause out of the Constitution. Certainly it averted, for the time being at least, the revolution in our constitutional system apparently intended by the framers of the amendment and reserved to the states the responsibility for protecting civil rights generally.

Nor has the Court been willing to expand the scope of the privileges and immunities clause beyond this early, limited interpretation. Five years before the Slaughter-House Cases the Supreme Court had held void, in Crandall v. Nevada (1868), a state tax on transporting persons out of the state, on the ground that such a tax would obstruct the citizen in his inherent federal right to come to the seat of his government. Two members of the Court, while concurring in the judgment, held the tax to be a violation of the commerce clause. In his opinion in the Slaughter-House Cases, Justice Miller cites this freedom of movement as an example of the privileges and immunities of United States citizens, and in 1941 in Edwards v. California, four members of the Court strongly urged that the California "anti-Okie" law should be held invalid on this ground. The majority had rested their decision, as had the minority in the Crandall case, upon the commerce power.

The Slaughter-House Cases held that the privileges and immunities of United States citizenship did not include the right to engage in a business of one's choice since such a privilege did not owe its existence to the national Constitution or laws. But did they include the rights listed in the Bill of Rights—rights which were certainly extended by the Constitution to United States citizens? The Court in Maxwell v. Dow (1900) held that they did not, reasoning that such privileges were those enjoyed exclusively by citizens, and since all persons enjoyed the protection of the Bill of Rights, its guarantees could not be considered privileges and immunities of that citizenship.

It looked for a time (1935–1940) as though the Court might broaden the scope and applicability of the privileges and immunities clause of the Fourteenth Amendment. In Colgate v. Harvey (1935) the Court held void a provision of a Vermont income tax law which taxed income from money loaned outside the state at a higher rate than that loaned inside the state. Besides denying the equal protection of the laws, this act was held to abridge the privileges and immunities of citizens of the United States. The right to carry on business freely across state lines was declared to be a privilege or immunity of federal citizenship, a doctrine sharply differing from the rule of the Slaughter-House Cases. In 1939, in Hague v. CIO, involving the validity under the Fourteenth Amendment of various repressions of free speech, assembly, etc., two justices of the Supreme Court from the majority held that the right of citizens to assemble and discuss their rights under the National Labor Relations Act was a privilege or immunity of citizens of the United States within the meaning of the Fourteenth Amendment. There was sharp dissent in both cases against this tendency to enlarge the scope of the privileges and immunities clause; and in Madden v. Kentucky (1940), in a case similar to Colgate v. Harvey, the Court specifically overruled that case and returned to the timeworn narrow construction of the privileges and immunities clause embodied in the Slaughter-House Cases.

The result of the Court's interpretation of the privileges and immunities clause is to equate those privileges to those of a member of an exclusive private club. Clearly membership in such a club does not entitle one to free speech or to own property, but it does entitle one to vote in the club elections and to the extent the club can and does extend exclusive privileges to its members, such as the right to hold parties in its clubhouse, these could be considered privileges and immunities of membership. As a matter of policy the United States has not generally limited its largesse to citizens, and many persons live their lives out as resident aliens barely conscious of any difference between themselves and their citizen neighbors. Even state attempts to discriminate against them must, in most instances, be justified by some "compelling state interest." (See the chapter on Equal Protection of the Laws.) They cannot vote (a privilege not exercised by some 60 percent of those who can) and they cannot homestead on federal land, but if these were to be viewed as the measure of the value of United States citizenship its importance to the thousands who seek it every year would be hard to understand. The single overriding value that such citizenship offers is not in anything tangible, but in the right to claim to be part of one of the richest, freest and most promising countries in the world.

Mr. Chief Justice **Marshall** delivered the opinion of the court:

The judgment brought up by this writ of error having been rendered by the court of a State, this tribunal can exercise no jurisdiction over it unless it be shown to come within the provisions of the twenty-fifth section of the Judicial Act.

The plaintiff in error contends that it comes within that clause in the fifth amendment to the Constitution which inhibits the taking of private property for public use without just compensation. He insists that this amendment, being in favor of the liberty of the citizen, ought to be so construed as to restrain the legislative power of a State, as well as that of the United States. If this proposition be untrue, the court can take no jurisdiction of the cause.

The question thus presented is, we think, of great importance, but not of much difficulty.

The Constitution was ordained and established by the people of the United States for themselves, for their own government, and not for the government of the individual States. Each State established a constitution for itself, and in that constitution provided such limitations and restrictions on the powers of its particular government as its judgment dictated. The people of the United States framed such a government for the United States as they supposed best adapted to their situation, and best calculated to promote their interests. The powers they conferred on this government were to be exercised by itself; and the limitations on power, if expressed in general terms, are naturally, and, we think, necessarily applicable to the government created by the instrument. They are limitations of power granted in the instrument itself; not of distinct governments, framed by different persons and for different purposes.

If these propositions be correct, the fifth amendment must be understood as restraining the power of the general government, not as applicable to the States. In their several constitutions they have imposed such restrictions on their respective governments as their own wisdom suggested; such as they deemed most proper for themselves. It is a subject on which they judge exclusively, and with which others interfere no farther than they are supposed to have a common interest.

The counsel for the plaintiff in error insists that the Constitution was intended to secure the people of the several States against the undue exercise of power by their respective State governments; as well as against that which might be attempted by their general government. In support of this argument he relies on the inhibitions contained in the tenth section of the first article.

We think that section affords a strong if not a conclusive argument in support of the opinion already indicated by the court.

The preceding section contains restrictions which are obviously intended for the exclusive purpose of restraining the exercise of power by the departments of the general government. Some of them use language applicable only to Congress; others are expressed in general terms. The third clause, for example, declares that ''no bill of attainder or ex post facto law shall be passed.'' No language can be more general; yet the demonstration is complete that it applies solely to the government of the United States. In addition to the general arguments furnished by the instrument itself, some of which have been already suggested, the succeeding section, the avowed purpose of which is to restrain State legislation, contains in terms the very prohibition. It declares that ''no State shall pass any bill of attainder or ex post facto law.'' This provision, then, of the ninth section, however comprehensive its language, contains no restriction on State legislation.

The ninth section having enumerated, in the nature of a bill of rights, the limitations intended to be imposed on the powers of the general government, the tenth proceeds to enumerate those which were to operate on the State legislatures. These restrictions are brought together in the same section, and are by express words applied to the States. ''No State shall enter into any treaty,'' etc. Perceiving that in a constitution framed by the people of the United States for the government of all, no limitation of the action of government on the people would apply to the State government, unless expressed in terms; the restrictions contained in the tenth section are in direct words so applied to the States.

It is worthy of remark, too, that these inhibitions generally restrain State legislation on subjects intrusted to the general government, or in which the people of all the States feel an interest.

A State is forbidden to enter into any treaty, alliance or confederation. If these compacts are with foreign nations, they interfere with the treaty-making power which is conferred entirely on the general government; if with each other, for political purposes, they can scarcely fail to interfere with the general purpose and intent of the Constitution. To grant letters of marque and reprisal would lead directly to war, the power of declaring which is expressly given to Congress. To coin money is also the exercise of a power conferred on Congress. It would be tedious to recapitulate the several limitations on the powers of the States which are contained in this section. They will be found, generally, to restrain State legislation on subjects intrusted to the government of the Union, in which the citizens of all the States are interested. In these alone were the whole people concerned. The question of their application to States is not left to construction. It is averred in positive words.

If the original Constitution, in the ninth and tenth sections of the first article, draws this plain and marked line of discrimination between the limitations it imposes on the powers of the general government and on those of the States; if in every inhibition intended to act on State power, words are employed which directly express that intent, some strong reason must be assigned for departing from this safe and judicious course in framing the amendments, before that departure can be assumed.

We search in vain for that reason.

Had the people of the several States, or any of them, required changes in their constitutions; had they required additional safeguards to liberty from the apprehended encroachments of their particular governments, the remedy was in their own hands, and would have been applied by themselves. A convention would have been assembled by the discontented State, and the required improvements would have been made by itself. The unwieldy and cumbrous machinery of procuring a recommendation from two-thirds of Congress, and the assent of three-fourths of their sister States, could never have occurred to any human being as a mode of doing that which might be effected by the State itself. Had the framers of these amendments intended them to be limitations on the powers of the State governments they would have imitated the framers of the original Constitution, and have expressed that intention. Had Congress engaged in the extraordinary occupation of improving the constitutions of the several States by affording the people additional protection from the exercise of power by their own governments in matters which concerned themselves alone, they would have declared this purpose in plain and intelligible language.

But it is universally understood, it is a part of the history of the day, that the great revolution which established the Constitution of the United States was not effected without immense opposition. Serious fears were extensively entertained that those powers which the patriot statesmen who then watched over the interests of our country, deemed essential to union, and to the attainment of those invaluable objects for which union was sought, might be exercised in a manner dangerous to liberty. In almost every convention by which the Constitution was adopted, amendments to guard against the abuse of power were recommended. These amendments demanded security against the apprehended encroachments of the general government—not against those of the local governments.

In compliance with a sentiment thus generally expressed, to quiet fears thus extensively entertained, amendments were proposed by the required majority in Congress, and adopted by the States. These amendments contain no expression indicating an intention to apply them to the State governments. This court cannot so apply them.

We are of opinion that the provision in the fifth amendment to the Constitution, declaring that private property shall not be taken for public use without just compensation, is intended solely as a limitation on the exercise of power by the government of the United States, and is not applicable to the legislation of the States. We are therefore of opinion that there is no repugnancy between the several acts of the General Assembly of Maryland, given in evidence by the defendants at the trial of this cause in the court of that State, and the Constitution of the United States.

This court, therefore, has no jurisdiction of the cause, and [it] is dismissed.

B. Economic Due Process

LOCHNER v. NEW YORK

198 U. S. 45; 49 L. Ed. 937; 25 S. Ct. 539 (1905)

At the time the Fourteenth Amendment was adopted the due process clause of the Fifth Amendment had been in effect against the federal government for three-quarters of a century. During that entire period the Supreme Court had decided only four or five cases interpreting the clause, but from Coke and Blackstone the ancient lineage and narrow meaning of the clause were abundantly clear. The clause traces its beginning to the guarantee embodied in Magna Charta that "no freeman shall be taken or imprisoned or deprived of his freehold or his liberties or free customs, or outlawed or exiled, or in any manner destroyed, nor shall we come upon him or send against him, except by a legal judgment of his peers or by the law of the land." With the reaffirmation of these guarantees in the Statute of Westminster (1354) Ed. III, "per legem terrae" became "due process of the law," although at the time of the adoption of the Bill of Rights the eight state constitutions providing such protection used the term "law of the land." Whichever words were used, the guarantee involved was the same: the government was forbidden to limit in any way the individual's personal or property rights unless it did so through proper procedures. In short, it was a check not on what the government could do but on the process it had to follow in order to do it.

This "procedural" due process was the only kind of due process there was until after the middle of the nineteenth century, when pressure from important property interests for a "substantive" content to the due process clause began to make itself felt. Among the leading purposes for which the United States Constitution had been framed was the protection of private property from the attacks of the "too popular" state governments. Hence those with vested property rights looked from the beginning to the judicially enforceable Constitution to protect them from legislation, particularly state legislation. They turned first to the protection against bills of attainder and ex post facto laws, but in Calder v. Bull (1798) the Supreme Court held that the ex post facto clause applied only to criminal legislation. Better luck was had with the contract clause, and in such cases as Fletcher v. Peck (1810) and the Dartmouth College Case (1819) the Court held that a vested right implied a contract not to divest it or interfere with its exercise. But with the passing of Chief Justice Marshall the strength of even this doctrine began to wane. In Charles River Bridge v. Warren Bridge (1837) the Court under Taney made clear that henceforth contracts would be strictly construed in favor of the people and against the vested interests; and much later, in Stone v. Mississippi (1880), the Court held that the police power to legislate in the public interest could not be limited by the contract clause.

So it was natural that pressure should mount to persuade the courts that the guarantee of due process of law should provide constitutional protection to the vested interests. In 1856 in Wynhammer v. New York a state court finally struck down a provision of a state prohibition statute as a denial of due process of law because the law provided for the confiscation of stocks of liquor in possession when the law took effect. The court's basic premise was that liquor was property which could not be transformed into a nuisance merely by the whim of the legislature; hence a statute providing for its confiscation was void, even though the procedures by which the confiscation took place followed "the forms which belong to due process of law." The court said, "The act . . . itself pronounces the sentence of condemnation, and the judicial machinery, such as it is, which it provides are agencies merely to insure the execution of the sentence."

This theory that the substance of a law itself could be held void for want of due process made its way slowly into the Supreme Court. In 1857, Chief Justice Taney in the Dred Scott case, after holding the Missouri Compromise Act void on a number of grounds, added that "an act of Congress which deprives a citizen of the United States of his liberty or property merely because he came himself or brought his property into a particular territory of the United States and who had committed no offense against the laws could hardly be dignified with the name of due process of law." But the Court was not yet ready to receive the doctrine. Justice Miller rejected it in the Slaughter-House Cases (1873); and in 1875 in Loan Association v. Topeka, the Court, completely ignoring the due process clause, held bad the expenditure of public money for a private purpose on the ground that this was a violation of those limits on governmental power "which grow out of the essential nature of all free governments; implied reservations of individual rights, without which the social compact could not exist. . . . " Again in 1878 in Davidson v. New Orleans, the Court made clear its attitude toward due process, going so far as to scold the bar for pressing upon them this new concept of due process. "There is here abundant evidence that there exists some strange misconception of the scope of this provision as found in the Fourteenth Amendment. In fact, it would seem, from the character of many of the cases before us, and the arguments made in them, that the clause under consideration is looked upon as a means of bringing to the test of the decision of this court the abstract opinions of every unsuccessful litigant in a State court of the justice of the decision against him, and of the merits of the legislation on which such a decision may be founded."

In 1877 there came before the Supreme Court a group of cases known as the "Granger Cases," in which the Supreme Court faced for the first time the important question of the right of a state legislature to regulate private business. The close of the Civil War ushered in a period of rapid railroad expansion. In the East, where industrial development tended to keep pace with the multiplication of transportation facilities, railroad building proved satisfactorily profitable. In the West, however, where new country was being opened up and population was sparse, the railroads had difficulty in paying dividends and frequently yielded to the temptation to indulge in stock-watering, questionable manipulation of credits, and doubtful practices in respect to grants of lands; to rebating and discrimination; and to other objectionable practices. Pitted against the desperate efforts of the railroads to make profits was the Western farmer, who wished to enjoy adequate railroad facilities at reasonable rates in order to facilitate the movement of crops in sparsely settled communities and who resented the unfair or dishonest methods of which some of the roads were known to be guilty. Out of this conflict of interests grew the Granger Movement, an organized effort on the part of the Western farmers which finally culminated in state legislation designed to cure the worst abuses. Starting in Illinois in 1871, the movement spread to other states; and soon railroads and warehousemen in Minnesota, Iowa, and Wisconsin found themselves subject to severe regulation with respect to rates and services. It was these laws which were challenged in the Granger Cases.

The first of these cases, Munn v. Illinois (1877), did not relate to railroad rate legislation but dealt rather with the question of the validity of an Illinois statute providing for the fixing of maximum charges for the storage of grain, in Chicago and other places having not less than one hundred thousand population, in warehouses "in which grain is stored in bulk, and in which the grain of different owners is mixed together, or in which grain is stored in such a manner that the identity of different lots or parcels cannot be accurately preserved." Here, as in the Slaughter-House Cases, an attempt was made to convince the Court that the legislation in question was in violation of the Fourteenth Amendment. It was urged that it involved a deprivation of property without due process of law and a denial of the equal protection of the laws. The Court again rejected the substantive due process argument, at least as applied to the regulatory measure before it. It held that terminal grain elevators were businesses sufficiently affected with a public interest to enable the legislature to regulate the charges which they made. It then went on to point out that the the Fourteenth Amendment provided no restriction upon burdensome or confiscatory rates; in cases where the legislature could regulate rates at all the degree of regulation was a matter of legislative discretion, and "for protection against abuses by legislatures the people must resort to the polls, not to the Courts."

The acceptance by the Supreme Court of "substantive" due process, in addition to the earlier exclusively "procedural" due process, took place gradually over a period of nearly 20 years as cases involving the validity of state laws came before it. The change came first in the area of rate controls. Within a decade after the Munn case (1877) the Court started to backtrack from Chief Justice Waite's dictum in that case—that the only appeal from an unjust rate was to elect a new legislature to enact a just one. In the Railroad Commission Cases (Stone v. Farmers' Loan & Trust Co., 1886) the Court, while confirming the legislature's power to regulate rates, added that "this power to regulate is not a power to destroy, and limitation is not the equivalent of confiscation. Under pretense of regulating fares and freights, the State cannot require a railroad corporation to carry persons or property without reward; neither can it do that which in law amounts to taking of private property for public use without just compensation, or without due process of law." Thus the legislature is apparently forbidden by due process to enact a regulatory measure which in substance is unreasonable. In Chicago, M. & St. P. R. Co. v. Minnesota (1890), the Court, abandoning the dictum of the Munn case, held that only by providing judicial review of the reasonableness of a rate, in contrast to an appeal to the legislature, could the requirement of due process of law be met.

For over 40 years the Supreme Court supervised with jealous care the rate regulation, whether by regulatory commission or by the legislature itself, of the nation's public utilities. Any rate which did not produce a fair return on a fair evaluation of the property was a denial of due process of law, and both the evaluation and the fairness of the return were subject, ultimately, to judicial review. It was not until 1944 in Federal Power Commission v. Hope Natural Gas Co. that the Court, noting that the value of a company depends on the rates it is allowed to charge, indicated that henceforth it would look to the overall reasonableness of the rate in terms of its general effect on the business, and leave to the proper agency the method by which the rate was to be set.

In Munn v. Illinois and the cases which followed it, the Court established the doctrine that the government could regulate prices and control terms of service (within limits) only of businesses which were "affected with a public interest." To impose these regulations upon a business not affected with a public interest was to deprive it of its liberty and property without due process of law. This doctrine seemed fair on its face and comported with the tradition of American individualism. But what is a business "affected with a public interest"? The Court found it difficult to answer this question because as cases involving it arose, it became obvious that there was no single characteristic by which a business so affected with a public interest could invariably be identified. Furthermore, even those businesses so affected could not necessarily be regulated in their entirety, but only in those aspects demanded by the need to protect the public interest. Thus, in the years in which the Court applied this elusive and difficult doctrine, it held void efforts to control wages in the meat packing business, the resale price of theater tickets, the price of gasoline, the rates charged by an employment agency, and the licensing of ice dealers. When, during the financial depression of the 1930's, New

York undertook to improve the lot of the dairy industry by setting a minimum price for milk, it was generally expected the Court would hold the price-fixing statute void. By none of the definitions in use could the milk industry be described as "affected with a public interest" and hence subject to price controls.

In Nebbia v. New York (1934) the Court held the New York statute valid. "The phrase 'affected with a public interest' can," said the Court, "in the nature of things, mean no more than that an industry, for adequate reason, is subject to control for the public good." Many facets of the milk industry were already subject to state regulation, and the Court saw no reason why prices should be "peculiarly sacrosanct." "So far as the requirement of due process is concerned, and in the absence of other constitutional restriction, a state is free to adopt whatever economic policy may reasonably be deemed to promote public welfare, and to enforce that policy by legislation adapted to its purpose. The courts are without authority either to declare such policy, or, when it is declared by the legislature, to override it. . . . "

What persuaded the Supreme Court to assert a supervisory power over the substance of state legislation which it had so carefully rejected in the Slaughter-House Cases (1873) is not difficult to surmise. During the two decades involved, the entire personnel of the Court, with the exception of Justice Field, had changed; and Field, who had dissented in the Slaughter-House Cases, had always been an apostle of the new faith. The new members coming onto the Court tended to reflect the social and economic pressures of the post-Civil War period: the tremendous expansion of the railroads and industry, the brawling struggle between management and labor with the growth of the trade union movement, and the increasing use of political power by the workingman to secure the enactment of protective labor legislation. Naturally, organized industry looked upon legislative efforts to ameliorate factory conditions and hours of labor as intolerable interferences with the employer's private affairs and a deprivation of his liberty and property. A generation of judges steeped in the individualism of the common law tended to share this view. Due process of law came to seem the completely appropriate and adequate constitutional weapon with which to combat the onward march of the new social control—the new police power.

This individualistic interpretation by the courts of due process of law found finally a definite basis in the development in the state courts during the 1880's of the doctrine of "liberty of contract," which was first introduced into the Supreme Court by Justice Peckham in Allgeyer v. Louisiana (1897), a case involving the right to buy insurance. There he interpreted due process as including "the right of the citizen . . . to live and work where he will; to earn his livelihood by any lawful calling; to pursue any livelihood or avocation, and for that purpose to enter into all contracts which may be proper, necessary, and essential to his carrying out to a successful conclusion the purposes above mentioned."

The concept of "liberty of contract" was both plausible and alluring. It asserted in substance that when two parties, neither of whom was under any legal disability, came together to make a contract which was not contrary to public policy, the legislature had no right to interfere and dictate the terms of the agreement. The application of this doctrine to the problem of protective labor legislation produced, however, some very startling results, due in large measure to the naïve assumption by the courts that the individual employee of a great industrial corporation possessed full liberty of contract and could dicker with his employer upon equal terms. Naturally, as time went on the courts found frequently that this vaunted liberty of contract was infringed by the laws regulating hours of labor, method and time of wage payment, employer's liability, factory conditions, and similar matters.

Sir Henry Maine's statement that "the movement of the progressive societies has hitherto been a movement from *status* to *contract*" marked this as a liberal doctrine which emancipated the individual, especially the laborer, from governmental controls and allowed him to bargain freely about his affairs. Hence it was only natural that it should receive a preferred place in the constitutional scheme. The normal presumption that a state statute is constitutional gradually gave way, and the burden of proof was placed upon those who would sustain a law alleged to limit such liberty of contract. The Court's insistence in Mugler v. Kansas (1887) that a state statute purporting to protect the public health, safety, and morals must bear a "real or substantial relation to those objects" meant that the Court had to be shown that such was the case before the act could be upheld.

The difficulty came in persuading the Court that such a relationship did in fact exist. In the Mugler case the Court had taken judicial notice of the evils of drink and had upheld the validity of a state prohibition statute; but the judges themselves had no knowledge of the social and economic conditions which led to the passage of laws regulating the hours of labor and working conditions. Nor was the bar, if it had such knowledge, in a position to transmit such knowledge to the bench, since the traditional method of arguing cases was to cite case precedents and attempt to show by rational analysis how the case at bar was similar. Thus the protagonists of protective labor laws found themselves with a strong presumption against the validity of the laws and no effective way to rebut the presumption.

If the burden of proof on those defending labor and social welfare legislation was unusually heavy, it was ultimately assumed in a novel and telling way. When Muller v. Oregon (1908), involving the validity of the Oregon ten-hour law for women, was argued before the Supreme Court, the justices had before them the first of the famous "Brandeis briefs." This brief, prepared by Louis D. Brandeis (later Justice Brandeis) set out very little in the way of strictly legal argument, but at great length presented documentary evidence of the social and economic facts and conditions which had led the legislature to pass the law. The Court was impressed, and while insisting that constitutional questions "are not settled by even a consensus of present public opinion . . . ," held that "at the same time, when a question of fact is debated and debatable, and the extent to which a special constitutional limitation goes is affected by the truth in respect to that fact, a widespread and long continued belief concerning it is worthy of consideration. We take judicial cognizance of all matters of general knowledge." The Court unanimously sustained the act.

A second break in the doctrine of the Lochner case came in 1917 in the case of Bunting v. Oregon, a case involving an Oregon statute providing a ten-hour day for all industrial workers. In a five-to-three decision the Court sustained the act and in doing so made it plain that the burden of proof had shifted to those who attacked its validity. "But we need not cast about for reasons for the legislative judgment. We are not required to be sure of the precise reasons for its exercise, or be convinced of the wisdom of its exercise. . . . It is enough for our decision if the legislation under review was passed in the exercise of an admitted power of government. . . . There is a contention made that the law . . . is not either necessary or useful 'for preservation of the health of employees. . . . ' The record contains no facts to support the contention, and against it is the judgment of the legislature and the supreme court. . . . " The same day the Court divided four to four to sustain the Oregon minimum wage law in Stettler v. O'Hara (1917). Justice Brandeis took no part in the decision of either of these cases. He had been counsel in the cases in the beginning, and with his appointment to the Supreme Court his place on the briefs had been taken by Felix Frankfurter, a professor in the Harvard Law School.

While the Court decided the Bunting case without any mention of the Lochner decision, it was widely assumed that the Lochner doctrine had been permanently abandoned. But in 1922 George Sutherland and Pierce Butler were appointed to the Court, and the following year the minimum wage statute of the District of Columbia was held void as a denial of due process of law. This was the case of Adkins v. Children's Hospital (1923). The Court divided five to three. Again Justice Brandeis did not sit, this time because his daughter was a member of the minimum wage commission. The majority opinion of Justice Sutherland reads like the opinion of the Court in the Lochner case, from which it quotes at length with approval. It held that there is no such connection between the wages women receive and their health, morals, or welfare as to justify destroying by law the freedom of contract of employers and the women who work for them. Furthermore, the Court said, the act does not guarantee that the minimum wage fixed shall not exceed the fair value of the service for which it is paid. Thus the Court returned to the old presumption of the invalidity of the statute and announced that while the materials in Professor Frankfurter's brief were useful enough to the legislature in passing the law, "they reflect no legitimate light upon the question of its validity." Chief Justice Taft and Justice Holmes wrote dissenting opinions. Justice Sanford concurred with the Chief Justice. In 1925 and in 1927 the Court without opinion ruled that the Adkins case rendered invalid the state minimum wage laws of Arizona and Arkansas respectively.

In 1933 New York passed a minimum wage law for women and children. Its framers sought to escape the ban of the Adkins decision by providing that the wages fixed should be based on the fair value of the labor paid for. The attempt failed. In Morehead v. New York ex rel. Tipaldo (1936) the Supreme Court in a five-to-four decision held the New York statute invalid. In the majority opinion Justice Butler stated that the statute was like the one held void in the Adkins case, but further said in substance that any minimum wage law, regardless of its provisions, would be invalid as a denial of due process of law. In a dissenting opinion Justice Stone observed: "It is difficult to imagine any grounds, other than our own personal economic predilections, for saying that the contract of employment is any the less an appropriate subject of legislation than are scores of others, in dealing with which this court has held that legislatures may curtail individual freedom in the public interest."

Public disenchantment with the Tipaldo decision was almost universal. Even the Republican Party repudiated it as it organized for the 1936 presidential campaign, and President Roosevelt, following his overwhelming reelection that November, immediately began laying plans for an attack on a Supreme Court he was convinced would ultimately strike down his entire New Deal program. On February 5, with his national prestige at an all-time high, he sent to Congress his ill-fated court-packing plan calling for the addition of a new justice to the Court for every justice over the age of 70 (of which there were six). While it presented no technical constitutional problems, since Congress sets the size of the Supreme Court, it aroused almost as much public antagonism as had the Tipaldo decision before it. A public which badly wanted New Deal legislation declared constitutional was clearly unprepared to sacrifice the independence of the Supreme Court to get it.

During all this time Washington's minimum wage law of 1913 had been in force and the case of West Coast Hotel v. Parrish challenging its validity was on the docket at the time the Tipaldo case was decided. At the opening of the new term in October 1936, the Court refused to rehear the Tipaldo case, and the West Coast Hotel case was argued in December. On March 29, 1937, with the court-packing battle in full swing, Justice Roberts switched his vote. The Court overruled Adkins and Tipaldo and sustained the Washington statute. Justices Sutherland, Van Devanter, McReynolds and Butler dissented. To the chant of "a switch in time saves nine," the country watched with relief as one New Deal statute after another was held valid. The Supreme Court, in a philosophical about-face, had returned to the political branches of government the power to regulate the nation's economy.

The Lochner case is presented here because it is, in a sense, a museum piece. The archaic opinion of Justice Peckham for the majority expresses with accuracy the dominant judicial doctrine of that period, with its reliance upon the concept of "liberty of contract," a doctrine which was widely believed to be essential to stability and good order in our economic and social life. The classic dissenting opinion of Justice Holmes, however, laid down the challenge which was to revolutionize judicial thinking with respect to the state's power to legislate in behalf of the economic and social welfare of its citizens.

Lochner was convicted of violating a New York statute called the Labor Law which provided that no employee should be "required or permitted to work in a biscuit, bread or cake bakery, or confectionery establishment more than sixty hours in any one week, or more than ten hours in any one day unless for the purpose of making a shorter day on the last day of the week." The legislature had proceeded upon the assumption that the conditions in the baking industry were such as to demand the intervention of the state in behalf of the employees. The majority of the Supreme Court did not agree that such protection was reasonably necessary and accordingly held that there was no adequate justification for this infringement of the private rights of the employer. Four justices dissented on the ground that there was sufficient support for the view of the legislature to make it a debatable question whether the law was arbitrary or not and that when such was the case, the courts should not override the legislative judgment. The dissenting opinion of Justice Holmes has become almost a classic as a statement of the more liberal judicial attitude toward the question of the validity of social and economic legislation under the Fourteenth Amendment.

Mr. Justice **Peckham** delivered the opinion of the Court, saying in part:

The statute necessarily interferes with the right of contract between the employer and employees, concerning the number of hours in which the latter may labor in the bakery of the employer. The general right to make a contract in relation to his business is part of the liberty of the individual protected by the 14th Amendment of the Federal Constitution. . . . , Under that provision no state can deprive any person of life, liberty, or property without due process of law. The right to purchase or to sell labor is part of the liberty protected by this amendment, unless there are circumstances which exclude the right. There are, however, certain powers, existing in the sovereignty of each state in the Union, somewhat vaguely termed police powers, the exact description and limitation of which have not been attempted by the courts. Those powers, broadly stated, and without, at present, any attempt at a more specific limitation, relate to the safety, health, morals, and general welfare of the public. Both property and liberty are held on such reasonable conditions as may be imposed by the governing power of the state in the exercise of those powers, and with such conditions the 14th Amendment was not designed to interfere. . . .

The state, therefore, has power to prevent the individual from making certain kinds of contracts, and in regard to them the Federal Constitution offers no protection. If the contract be one which the state, in the legitimate exercise of its police power, has the right to prohibit, it is not prevented from prohibiting it by the 14th Amendment. Contracts in violation of a statute, either of the Federal or state government, or a contract to let one's property for immoral purposes, or to do any other unlawful act, could obtain no protection from the Federal Constitution, as coming under the liberty of person or of free contract. Therefore, when the state, by its legislature, in the assumed exercise of its police powers, has passed an act which seriously limits the right to labor or the right of contract in regard to their means of livelihood between persons who are sui juris (both employer and employee), it becomes of great importance to determine which shall prevail,—the right of the individual to labor for such time as he may choose, or the right of the state to prevent the individual from laboring, or from entering into any contract to labor, beyond a certain time prescribed by the state. . . .

It must, of course, be conceded that there is a limit to the valid exercise of the police power by the state. There is no dispute concerning this general proposition. Otherwise the 14th Amendment would have no efficacy and the legislatures of the states would have unbounded power, and it would be enough to say that any piece of legislation was enacted to conserve the morals, the health, or the safety of the people; such legislation would be valid, no matter how absolutely without foundation the claim might be. The claim of the police power would be a mere pretext,—become another and delusive name for the supreme sovereignty of the state to be exercised free from constitutional restraint. This is not contended for. In every case that comes before this court, therefore, where legislation of this character is concerned, and where the protection of the Federal Constitution is sought, the question necessarily arises: Is this a fair, reasonable, and appropriate exercise of the police power of the state, or is it an unreasonable, unnecessary, and arbitrary interference with the right of the individual to his personal liberty, or to enter into those contracts in relation to labor which may seem to him appropriate or necessary for the support of himself and his family? Of course the liberty of contract relating to labor includes both parties to it. The one has as much right to purchase as the other to sell labor.

This is not a question of substituting the judgment of the court for that of the legislature. If the act be within the power of the state it is valid, although the judgment of the court might be totally opposed to the enactment of such a law. But the question would still remain: Is it within the police power of the state? and that question must be answered by the court.

The question whether this act is valid as a labor law, pure and simple, may be dismissed in a few words. There is no reasonable ground for interfering with the liberty of person or the right of free contract, by determining the hours of labor, in the occupation of a baker. There is no contention that bakers as a class are not equal in intelligence and capacity to men in other trades or manual occupations, or that they are not able to assert their rights and care for themselves without the protecting arm of the state, interfering with their independence of judgment and of action. They are in no sense wards of the state. Viewed in the light of a purely labor law, with no reference whatever to the question of health, we think that a law like the one before us involves neither the safety, the morals, nor the welfare, of the public, and that the interest of the public is not in the slightest degree affected by such an act. The law must be upheld, if at all, as a law pertaining to the health of the individual engaged in the occupation of a baker. It does not affect any other portion of the public than those who are engaged in that occupation. Clean and wholesome bread does not depend upon whether the baker works but ten hours per day or only sixty hours a week. The limitation of the hours of labor does not come within the police power on that ground.

It is a question of which of two powers or rights shall prevail,—the power of the state to legislate or the right of the individual to liberty of person and freedom of contract. The mere assertion that the subject relates, though but in a remote degree, to the public health, does not necessarily render the enactment valid. The act must have a more direct relation, as a means to an end, and the end itself must be appropriate and legitimate, before an act can be held to be valid which interferes with the general right of an individual to be free in his person and in his power to contract in relation to his own labor. . . .

We think the limit of the police power has been reached and passed in this case. There is, in our judgment, no reasonable foundation for holding this to be necessary or appropriate as a health law to safeguard the public health, or the health of the individuals who are following the trade of a baker. If this statute be valid, and if, therefore, a proper case is made out in which to deny the right of an individual, sui juris, as employer or employee, to make contracts for the labor of the latter under the protection of the provisions of the Federal Constitution, there would seem to be no length to which legislation of this nature might not go. . . .

We think that there can be no fair doubt that the trade of a baker, in and of itself, is not an unhealthy one to that degree which would authorize the legislature to interfere with the right to labor, and with the right of free contract on the part of the individual, either as employer or employee. In looking through statistics regarding all trades and occupations, it may be true that the trade of a baker does not appear to be as healthy as some other trades, and is also vastly more healthy than still others. To the common understanding the trade of a baker has never been regarded as an unhealthy one. Very likely physicians would not recommend the exercise of that or of any other trade as a remedy for ill health. Some occupations are more healthy than others, but we think there are none which might not come under the power of the legislature to supervise and control the hours of working therein, if the mere fact that the occupation is not absolutely and perfectly healthy is to confer that right upon the legislative department of the government. It might be safely affirmed that almost all occupations more or less affect the health. There must be more than the mere fact of the possible existence of some small amount of unhealthiness to warrant legislative interference with liberty. It is unfortunately true that labor, even in any department, may possibly carry with it the seeds of unhealthiness. But are we all, on that account, at the mercy of legislative majorities? A printer, a tinsmith, a locksmith, a carpenter, a cabinetmaker, a dry goods clerk, a bank's, a lawyer's, or a physician's clerk, or a clerk in almost any kind of business, would all come under the power of the legislature, on this assumption. No trade, no occupation, no mode of earning one's living, could escape this all-pervading power, and the acts of the legislature in limiting the hours of labor in all employments would be valid, although such limitation might seriously cripple the ability of the laborer to support himself and his family. In our large cities there are many buildings into which the sun penetrates for but a short time in each day, and these buildings are occupied by people carrying on the business of bankers, brokers, lawyers, real estate, and many other kinds of business, aided by many clerks, messengers, and other employees. Upon the assumption of the validity of this act under review, it is not possible to say that an act, prohibiting lawyers' or bank clerks, or others, from contracting to labor for their employers more than eight hours a day would be invalid. It might be said that it is unhealthy to work more than that number of hours in an apartment lighted by artificial light during the working hours of the day; that the occupation of the bank clerk, the lawyer's clerk, the real-estate clerk, or the broker's clerk, in such offices is therefore unhealthy, and the legislature, in its paternal wisdom, must, therefore, have the right to legislate on the subject of and to limit, the hours for such labor; and, if it exercises that power, and its validity be questioned, it is sufficient to say, it has reference to the public health; it has reference to the health of the employees condemned to labor day after day in buildings where the sun never shines; it is a health law, and therefore it is valid, and cannot be questioned by the courts.

It is also urged, pursuing the same line of argument, that it is to the interest of the state that its population should be strong and robust, and therefore any legislation which may be said to tend to make people healthy must be valid as health laws, enacted under the police power. If this be a valid argument and a justification for this kind of legislation, it follows that the protection of the Federal Constitution from undue interference with liberty of person and freedom of contract is visionary, wherever the law is sought to be justified as a valid exercise of the police power. Scarcely any law but might find shelter under such assumptions, and conduct, properly so called, as well as contract, would come under the restrictive sway of the legislature. Not only the hours of employees, but the hours of employers, could be regulated, and doctors, lawyers, scientists, all professional men, as well as athletes and artisans, could be forbidden to fatigue their brains and bodies by prolonged hours of exercise, lest the fighting strength of the state be impaired. We mention these extreme cases because the contention is extreme. We do not believe in the soundness of the views which uphold this law. On the contrary, we think that such a law as this, although passed in the assumed exercise of the police power, and as relating to the public health, or the health of the employees named, is not within that power, and is invalid. The act is not, within any fair meaning of the term, a health law, but is an illegal interference with the rights of individuals, both employers and employees, to make contracts regarding labor upon such terms as they may think best, or which they may agree upon with the other parties to such contracts. Statutes of the nature of that under review, limiting the hours in which grown and intelligent men may labor to earn their living, are mere meddlesome interferences with the rights of the individual, and they are not saved from condemnation by the claim that they are passed in the exercise of the police power and upon the subject of the health of the individual whose rights are interfered with, unless there be some fair ground, reasonable in and of itself, to say that there is material danger to the public health, or to the health of the employees, if the hours of labor are not curtailed. . . .

It was further urged on the argument that restricting the hours of labor in the case of bakers was valid because it tended to cleanliness on the part of the workers, as a man was more apt to be cleanly when not overworked, and if cleanly then his ''output'' was also more likely to be so. . . . The connection, if any exist, is too shadowy and thin to build any argument for the interference of the legislature. If the man works ten hours a day it is all right, but if ten and a half or eleven his health is in danger and his bread may be unhealthy, and, therefore, he shall not be permitted to do it. This, we think, is unreasonable and entirely arbitrary. . . .

. . . It seems to us that the real object and purpose were simply to regulate the hours of labor between the master and his employees (all being men, sui juris), in a private business, not dangerous in any degree to morals, or in any real and substantial degree to the health of the employees. Under such circumstances the freedom of master and employee to contract with each other in relation to their employment, and in defining the same, cannot be prohibited or interfered with, without violating the Federal Constitution.

The judgment . . . must be reversed. . . .

Mr. Justice **Harlan,** with whom Mr. Justice **White** and Mr. Justice **Day** concurred in dissenting, said in part:

. . . I find it impossible, in view of common experience, to say that there is here no real or substantial relation between the means employed by the state and the end sought to be accomplished by its legislation. . . .

We judicially know that the question of the number of hours during which a workman should continuously labor has been, for a long period, and is yet, a subject of serious consideration among civilized peoples, and by those having special knowledge of the laws of health. Suppose the statute prohibited labor in bakery and confectionery establishments in excess of eighteen hours each day. No one, I take it, could dispute the power of the state to enact such a statute. But the statute before us does not embrace extreme or exceptional cases. It may be said to occupy a middle ground in respect of the hours of labor. What is the true ground for the state to take between legitimate protection, by legislation, of the public health and liberty of contract is not a question easily solved, nor one in respect of which there is or can be absolute certainty. There are very few, if any, questions in political economy about which entire certainty may be predicated. . . .

I do not stop to consider whether any particular view of this economic question presents the sounder theory. What the precise facts are it may be difficult to say. It is enough for the determination of this case, and it is enough for this court to know, that the question is one about which there is room for debate and for an honest difference of opinion. There are many reasons of a weighty, substantial character, based upon the experience of mankind, in support of the theory that, all things considered, more than ten hours steady work each day, from week to week, in a bakery or confectionery establishment, may endanger the health and shorten the lives of the workmen, thereby diminishing their physical and mental capacity to serve the state and to provide for those dependent upon them.

If such reasons exist that ought to be the end of this case, for the state is not amenable to the judiciary, in respect of its legislative enactments, unless such enactments are plainly, palpably, beyond all question, inconsistent with the Constitution of the United States. . . .

Mr. Justice **Holmes** dissenting:

I regret sincerely that I am unable to agree with the judgment in this case, and I think it my duty to express my dissent.

This case is decided upon an economic theory which a large part of the country does not entertain. If it were a question whether I agreed with that theory, I should desire to study it further and long before making up my mind. But I do not conceive that to be my duty, because I strongly believe that my agreement or disagreement has nothing to do with the right of a majority to embody their opinions in law. It is settled by various decisions of this court that state constitutions and state laws may regulate life in many ways which we as legislators might think as injudicious, or if you like as tyrannical, as this, and which equally with this, interfere with the liberty to contract. Sunday laws and usury laws are ancient examples. A more modern one is the prohibition of lotteries. The liberty of the citizen to do as he likes so long as he does not interfere with the liberty of others to do the same, which has been a shibboleth for some well-known writers, is interfered with by school laws, by the Postoffice, by every state or municipal institution which takes his money for purposes thought desirable, whether he likes it or not. The 14th Amendment does not enact Mr. Herbert Spencer's Social Statics. The other day we sustained the Massachusetts vaccination law. Jacobson v. Massachusetts [1905]. United States and state statutes and decisions cutting down the liberty to contract by way of combination are familiar to this court. Northern Securities Co. **v.** United States [1904]. Two years ago we upheld the prohibition of sales of stock on margins, or for future delivery, in the Constitution of California. . . . The decision sustaining an eight-hour law for miners is still recent. Holden v. Hardy [1898]. Some of these laws embody convictions or prejudices which judges are likely to share. Some may not. But a constitution is not intended to embody a particular economic theory, whether of paternalism and the organic relation of the citizen to the state or of laissez faire. It is made for people of fundamentally differing views, and the accident of our finding certain opinions natural and familiar, or novel, and even shocking, ought not to conclude our judgment upon the question whether statutes embodying them conflict with the Constitution of the United States.

General propositions do not decide concrete cases. The decision will depend on a judgment or intuition more subtle than any articulate major premise. But I think that the proposition just stated, if it is accepted, will carry us far toward the end. Every opinion tends to become a law. I think that the word "liberty," in the 14th Amendment, is perverted when it is held to prevent the natural outcome of a dominant opinion, unless it can be said that a rational and fair man necessarily would admit that the statute proposed would infringe fundamental principles as they have been understood by the traditions of our people and our law. It does not need research to show that no such sweeping condemnation can be passed upon the statute before us. A reasonable man might think it a proper measure on the score of health. Men whom I certainly could not pronounce unreasonable would uphold it as a first instalment of a general regulation of the hours of work. Whether in the latter aspect it would be open to the charge of inequality I think it unnecessary to discuss.

C. The Theory of "Incorporation" of the Bill of Rights

HURTADO v. CALIFORNIA

110 U. S. 516; 28 L. Ed. 232; 4 S. Ct. 111 (1884)

While the due process clauses of the Fifth and Fourteenth Amendments came to be restrictions by which the validity of the substance of legislation was tested in the courts, it should not be forgotten that originally due process was construed only as a limitation on governmental procedure. Whatever the government did, it had to do in accordance with the "process" which was "due" under the law of the land. But what, concretely, did such process include? To nonprofessionals, thinking in terms of criminal procedure, it undoubtedly included the common-law procedures with which they were familiar— procedures spelled out in detail in the Bill of Rights. The Supreme Court, however, rejected the idea that due process required adherence to a fixed list of prescribed procedures, and in Davidson v. New Orleans (1878) it explained that the meaning of the clause would be determined "by the gradual process of judicial inclusion and exclusion, as the cases presented for decision shall require, with the reasoning on which such decisions may be founded."

The Court had already decided, in the case of Murray's Lessee v. Hoboken Land and

Improvement Co. (1856), that "due" process did not always mean "judicial" process; and an administrative agency could employ procedures which had the sanction of long-established custom. In this case an administrative warrant authorizing the seizure of a man's property to satisfy a debt to the government was found to be a well-established procedure and hence due process of law.

But if old established procedures were due process of law, then surely those common-law procedures listed in the Bill of Rights were due process of law. And if this were the case, why were they not guaranteed by the Fourteenth Amendment in state criminal cases? This was the argument of Hurtado in the present case. He had been convicted of murder by the state of California and sentenced to be hanged. He claimed a denial of due process because instead of a grand jury indictment, to which he would have been entitled under the common law, he had been charged by an information prepared by the prosecuting attorney—a form of charge authorized by the state of California, but limited at common law to misdemeanors.

Mr. Justice **Matthews** delivered the opinion of the Court, saying in part:

. . . The proposition of law we are asked to affirm is, that an indictment or presentment by a grand jury, as known to the common law of England, is essential to that "due process of law," when applied to prosecutions for felonies, which is secured and guaranteed by this provision of the Constitution of the United States, and which accordingly it is forbidden to the States respectively to dispense with in the administration of criminal law.

. . . It is maintained on behalf of the plaintiff in error that the phrase "due process of law" is equivalent to "law of the land," as found in the [thirty-]ninth chapter of Magna Charta; that, by immemorial usage, it has acquired a fixed, definite and technical meaning; that it refers to and includes, not only the general principles of public liberty and private right, which lie at the foundation of all free government, but the very institutions which, venerable by time and custom, have been tried by experience and found fit and necessary for the preservation of those principles, and which, having been the birthright and inheritance of every English subject, crossed the Atlantic with the colonists and were transplanted and established in the fundamental laws of the State; that, having been originally introduced into the Constitution of the United States as a limitation upon the powers of the government, brought into being by that instrument, it has now been added as an additional security to the individual against oppression by the States themselves; that one of these institutions is that of the grand jury, an indictment or presentment by which against the accused in cases of alleged felonies is an essential part of due process of law, in order that he may not be harassed or destroyed by prosecutions founded only upon private malice or popular fury. . . .

It is urged upon us, however, in argument, that the claim made in behalf of the plaintiff in error is supported by the decision of this court in Murray's Lessee v. Hoboken Land & Improvement Company [1856]. There, Mr. Justice Curtis delivering the opinion of the court, after showing that due process of law must mean something more than the actual existing law of the land, for otherwise it would be no restraint upon legislative power, proceeds as follows: "To what principle, then, are we to resort to ascertain whether this process, enacted by Congress, is due process? To this the answer must be twofold. We must examine the Constitution itself to see whether this process be in conflict with any of its provisions. If not found to be so, we must look to those settled usages and modes of proceeding existing in the common and statute law of England before the emigration of our ancestors, and which are shown not to have been unsuited to their civil and political condition by having been acted on by them after the settlement of this country.''

This, it is argued, furnishes an indispensable test of what constitutes ''due process of law''; that any proceeding otherwise authorized by law, which is not thus sanctioned by usage, or which supersedes and displaces one that is, cannot be regarded as due process of law.

But this inference is unwarranted. The real syllabus of the passage quoted is, that a process of law, which is not otherwise forbidden, must be taken to be due process of law, if it can show the sanction of settled usage both in England and in this country; but it by no means follows, that nothing else can be due process of law. The point in the case cited arose in reference to a summary proceeding, questioned on that account, as not due process of law. The answer was: however exceptional it may be, as tested by definitions and principles of ordinary procedure, nevertheless, this, in substance, has been immemorially the actual law of the land, and, therefore, is due process of law. But to hold that such a characteristic is essential to due process of law, would be to deny every quality of the law but its age, and to render it incapable of progress or improvement. It would be to stamp upon our jurisprudence the unchangeableness attributed to the laws of the Medes and Persians.

This would be all the more singular and surprising, in this quick and active age, when we consider that, owing to the progressive development of legal ideas and institutions in England, the words of Magna Charta stood for very different things at the time of the separation of the American Colonies from what they represented originally. . . .

The Constitution of the United States was ordained, it is true, by descendants of Englishmen, who inherited the traditions of English law and history; but it was made for an undefined and expanding future, and for a people gathered and to be gathered from many Nations and of many tongues. And while we take just pride in the principles and institutions of the common law, we are not to forget that in lands where other systems of jurisprudence prevail, the ideas and processes of civil justice are also not unknown. Due process of law, in spite of the absolutism of continental governments, is not alien to that Code which survived the Roman Empire as the foundation of modern civilization in Europe, and which has given us that fundamental maxim of distributive justice, *suum cuique tribuere*. There is nothing in Magna Charta, rightly construed as a broad charter of public right and law, which ought to exclude the best ideas of all systems and of every age; and as it was the characteristic principle of the common law to draw its inspiration from every fountain of justice, we are not to assume that the sources of its supply have been exhausted. On the contrary, we should expect that the new and various experiences of our own situation and system will mold and shape it into new and not less useful forms. . . .

We are to construe this phrase in the 14th Amendment by the usus loquendi of the Constitution itself. The same words are contained in the 5th Amendment. That article makes specific and express provision for perpetuating the institution of the grand jury, so far as relates to prosecutions, for the more aggravated crimes under the laws of the United States. It declares that ''No person shall be held to answer for a capital or otherwise infamous crime, unless on a presentment or indictment of a grand jury, except in cases arising in the land or naval forces, or in the militia when in actual service in time of war or public danger; nor shall any person be subject for the same offense to be twice put in jeopardy of life or limb; nor shall he be compelled in any criminal case to be a witness against himself.'' It then immediately adds: ''nor be deprived of life, liberty or property, without due process of law.'' According to a recognized canon interpretation, especially applicable to formal and solemn instruments of constitutional law, we are forbidden to assume, without clear reason to the contrary, that any part of this most important Amendment is superfluous. The natural and obvious inference is, that in the sense of the Constitution, ''due process of law'' was not meant or intended to include, ex vi termini, the institution and procedure of a grand jury in any case. The conclusion is equally irresistible, that when the same phrase was employed in the 14th Amendment to restrain the action of the States, it was used in the same sense and with no greater extent; and that if in the adoption of that Amendment it had been part of its purpose to perpetuate the institution of the grand jury in all the States, it would have embodied, as did the 5th Amendment, express declarations to that effect. Due process of law in the latter refers to that law of the land, which derives its authority from the legislative powers conferred upon Congress by the Constitution of the United States, exercised within the limits therein prescribed, and interpreted according to the principles of the common law. In the 14th Amendment, by parity of reason, it refers to that law of the land in each State, which derives its authority from the inherent and reserved powers of the State, exerted within the limits of those fundamental principles of liberty and justice which lie at the base of all our civil and political institutions, and the greatest security for which resides in the right of the people to make their own laws, and alter them at their pleasure. ''The 14th Amendment,'' as was said by Mr. Justice Bradley in Mo. v. Lewis [1880], ''does not profess to secure to all persons in the United States the benefit of the same laws and the same remedies. Great diversities in these respects may exist in two States separated only by an imaginary line. On one side of this line there may be a right of trial by jury, and on the other side no such right. Each State prescribes its own modes of judicial proceeding.''

But it is not to be supposed that these legislative powers are absolute and despotic, and that the Amendment prescribing due process of law is too vague and indefinite to operate as a practical restraint. It is not every Act, legislative in form, that is law. Law is something more than mere will exerted as an act of power. . . . Arbitrary power, enforcing its edicts to the injury of the persons and property of its subjects, is not law, whether manifested as the decree of a personal monarch or of an impersonal multitude. And the limitations imposed by our constitutional law upon the action of the governments, both state and national, are essential to the preservation of public and private rights, notwithstanding the representative character of our political institutions. . . .

It follows that any legal proceeding enforced by public authority, whether sanctioned by age and custom, or newly devised in the discretion of the legislative power, in furtherance of the general public good, which regards and preserves these principles of liberty and justice, must be held to be due process of law. . .

Tried by these principles, we are unable to say that the substitution for a presentment or indictment by a grand jury of the proceeding by information, after examination and commitment by a magistrate, certifying to the probable guilt of the defendant, with the right on his part to the aid of counsel, and to the cross-examination of the witnesses produced for the prosecution, is not due process of law. It is, as we have seen, an ancient proceeding at common law, which might include every case of an offense of less grade than a felony, except misprision of treason; and in every circumstance of its administration, as authorized by the

Statute of California, it carefully considers and guards the substantial interest of the prisoner. It is merely a preliminary proceeding, and can result in no final judgment, except as the consequence of a regular judicial trial, conducted precisely as in cases of indictments. . . .

For these reasons, finding no error therein, the judgment of the Supreme Court of California is affirmed.

Mr. Justice **Harlan,** dissenting, said in part:

. . I cannot agree that the State may, consistently with due process of law, require a person to answer for a capital offense, except upon the presentment or indictment of a grand jury. . . .

. . . To what principles are we to resort to ascertain whether this process . . . is due process? To this the answer must be twofold. We must examine the Constitution itself to see whether this process be in conflict with any of its provisions. If not found to be so, we must look *"to those settled usages and modes of proceeding existing in the common and statute law of England before the emigration of our ancestors, and which are shown not to have been unsuited to their civil and political condition by having been acted on by them after the settlement of this country."* . . .

. . . Let us inquire (and no other inquiry is at all pertinent) whether according to the settled usages and modes of proceeding to which, this court has said, reference must be had, an information for a capital offense was, prior to the adoption of our Constitution, regarded as due process of law. . . . [Justice Harlan here reviews the authorities and finds it was not.]

My brethren concede that there are principles of liberty and justice, lying at the foundation of our civil and political institutions, which no State can violate consistently with that due process of law required by the 14th Amendment in proceedings involving life, liberty or property. Some of these principles are enumerated in the opinion of the court. But, for reasons which do not impress my mind as satisfactory, they exclude from that enumeration the exemption from prosecution, by information, for a public offense involving life. By what authority is that exclusion made? Is it justified by the settled usages and modes of procedure, existing under the common and statute law of England at the emigration of our ancestors or at the foundation of our government? Does not the fact that the people of the original States required an amendment of the National Constitution, securing exemption from prosecution, for a capital offense, except upon the indictment or presentment of a grand jury, prove that, in their judgment, such an exemption was essential to protection against accusation and unfounded prosecution and, therefore, was a fundamental principle in liberty and justice? . . .

But it is said that the framers of the Constitution did not suppose that due process of law necessarily required for a capital offense the institution and procedure of a grand jury, else they would not in the same amendment prohibiting the deprivation of life, liberty or property without due process of law, have made specific and express provision for a grand jury where the crime is capital or otherwise infamous; therefore, it is argued, the requirement by the 14th Amendment, of due process of law in all proceedings involving life, liberty and property, without specific reference to grand juries in any case whatever, was not intended as a restriction upon the power which it is claimed that the States previously had, so far as the express restrictions of the National Constitution are concerned, to dispense altogether with grand juries.

The line of argument, it seems to me, would lead to results which are inconsistent with the vital principles of republican government. If the presence in the 5th Amendment of a specific provision for grand juries in capital cases, alongside the provision for due process of law in proceedings involving life, liberty or property, is held to prove that due process of law did not, in the judgment of the framers of the Constitution, necessarily require a grand jury in capital cases, inexorable logic would require it to be, likewise, held that the right not to be put twice in jeopardy of life and limb for the same offense, nor compelled in a criminal case to testify against one's self (rights and immunities also specifically recognized in the 5th Amendment) were not protected by that due process of law required by the settled usages and proceedings existing under the common and statute law of England at the settlement of this country. More than that, other Amendments of the Constitution proposed at the same time, expressly recognize the right of persons to just compensation for private property taken for public use; their right, when accused of crime, to be informed of the nature and cause of the accusation against them, and to a speedy and public trial, by an impartial jury of the State and district wherein the crime was committed; to be confronted by the witnesses against them; and to have compulsory process for obtaining witnesses in their favor. Will it be claimed that these rights were not secured by the "law of the land" or by "due process of law," as declared and established at the foundation of our government? Are they to be excluded from the enumeration of the fundamental principles of liberty and justice and, therefore, not embraced by "due process of law?" ...

It seems to me that too much stress is put upon the fact that the framers of the Constitution made express provision for the security of those rights which at common law were protected by the requirement of due process of law and, in addition, declared, generally, that no person shall "be deprived of life, liberty or property without due process of law." The rights, for the security of which these express provisions were made, were of a character so essential to the safety of the people that it was deemed wise to avoid the possibility that Congress, in regulating the processes of law, would impair or destroy them. Hence their specific enumeration in the earlier Amendments of the Constitution. ...

POWELL v. ALABAMA

287 U. S. 45; 77 L. Ed. 158; 53 S. Ct. 55 (1932)

The Court in the Hurtado case (1884) not only rejected the idea that the protections listed in the Bill of Rights are included in due process, but the reasoning on which the decision was based made logically impossible their inclusion in the future. In 1897, however, following the advent of the concept of substantive due process in Munn v. Illinois (1877), the Court held that due process forbade a state to seize private property without just compensation; see Chicago, B. & Q. R. Co. v. Chicago. Justice Harlan, who had dissented in Hurtado, wrote the opinion of the Court without alluding to that case or calling attention to the fact that the right was one listed in the Bill of Rights. He held, simply, that the right to compensation was a right "founded in natural equity" and "laid down as a principle of universal law. Indeed, in a free government almost all other rights would become worthless if the government possessed an uncontrollable power over the private fortune of every citizen." He emphasized that "in determining what is due process of law regard must be had to substance, not to form," and pointed out that while "the legislature may prescribe a form of procedure to be observed in the taking of private property for public use, . . . it is not due process of law if provision be not made for compensation."

The C. B. & Q. decision had not overruled Hurtado, but since the two cases were in some ways incompatible, it seemed plausible to suppose that some of the Bill of Rights guarantees for persons accused of crime might also be found essential to due process. In Twining v. New Jersey (1908), however, the Court rejected the notion. The right to just compensation, it noted, was part of due process because of its fundamental nature, not because it was listed in the Bill of Rights. Not only was the guarantee against self-incrimination not of this fundamental nature, as Twining claimed, but added that the Court had never held void any state criminal procedure for want of due process of law. "Salutary as the principle [self-incrimination] may seem to the great majority, it cannot be ranked with the right to hearing before condemnation, the immunity from arbitrary power not acting by general laws, and the inviolability of private property." Clearly, the rights protected by due process were property rights—not rights involving criminal procedure. It was not until 1964, in Malloy v. Hogan, that the Court overruled Twining and held the protection against self-incrimination essential to due process.

With the rise of the doctrine of substantive due process it was increasingly urged on the Court that the "liberty" protected by the due process clause of the Fourteenth Amendment should include, at the very least, the freedom of speech and press mentioned in the First Amendment. The pressure was not only from members of the bar, but from the Court itself. In 1907 Justice Harlan, in a dissenting opinion in Patterson v. Colorado, declared, "I go further and hold that the privileges of free speech and a free press, belonging to every citizen of the United States, constitute essential parts of every man's liberty, and are protected against violation by that clause of the Fourteenth Amendment forbidding a state to deprive any person of his liberty without due process of law." Essentially the same view was expressed by Justice Brandeis in his dissenting opinion in Gilbert v. Minnesota (1920), a case in which the Court assumed for the sake of argument that freedom of speech was "a natural and inherent" right but held that it had not been violated. Although in Prudential Insurance Co. v. Cheek (1922) the Court insisted that "neither the Fourteenth Amendment nor any other provision of the Constitution of the United States imposes upon the states any restrictions about 'freedom of speech,' " the following year it began to show signs of conversion to a broader conception of the term "liberty." In Meyer v. Nebraska (1923) Justice McReynolds, in an opinion holding invalid a Nebraska statute forbidding the teaching of any subject in any language but English in any private, parochial, or public school, defined the "liberty" protected by the due process clause as follows: "Without doubt, it denotes not merely freedom from bodily restraint, but also the right of the individual to contract, to engage in any of the common occupations of life, to acquire useful knowledge, to marry, establish a home and bring up children, to worship God according to the dictates of his own conscience, and, generally, to enjoy those privileges long recognized at common law as essential to the orderly pursuit of happiness by free men."

Two years later, in what was in fact a constitutional revolution, the Court, in Gitlow v. New York (1925), reversed its stand. Gitlow had challenged a state statute as violating his freedom of speech and thereby denying him due process; the Supreme Court took jurisdiction under the due process clause, declaring that "For present purposes we may and do assume that freedom of speech and of the press—which are protected by the First Amendment from abridgment by Congress—are among the fundamental personal rights and 'liberties' protected by the due process clause of the Fourteenth Amendment from impairment by the states." In Gitlow's case the Court held the state statute valid and upheld Gitlow's conviction; but in 1931, in Near v. Minnesota, the Court held a state statute void on the ground that it denied due process by unreasonably restricting freedom of speech and press. With these two cases these important liberties became effectively "nationalized," and the states came under federal judicial scrutiny and discipline in dealing with freedom of speech and press.

The other liberties mentioned in the First Amendment followed in due course. In Hamilton v. Board of Regents of the University of California (1934) freedom of religion was held to be protected by the Fourteenth Amendment, although the Court held that Hamilton's religious liberty was not abridged by making him take military drill as a condition of attending the state university. In De Jonge v. Oregon (1937) freedom of assembly was added to the list. The assimilation of the First Amendment into the Fourteenth was completed in Everson v. Board of Education (1947). The preceding cases were decided on the theory that the due process clause protects "liberty" and that "liberty" includes freedom of speech, press, religion, and assembly. The Everson case, however, which involved state aid to parochial school pupils, raised no question of "freedom" of religion but the question of whether the state action amounted to an "establishment" of religion. It could be argued that a state-supported religion does not abridge freedom of religion and hence is not an abridgment of "liberty" protected by due process of law, but the Supreme Court in the Everson case did not argue the point; it simply declared that "the First Amendment, as made applicable to the states by the Fourteenth . . . commands that a state 'shall make no law respecting an establishment of religion. . . .' "

With the incorporation of First Amendment rights into the due process clause of the Fourteenth, pressure was brought on the Court to reconsider its stand in Hurtado (1884) and Twining (1908) to find other rights in the Bill of Rights to be "essential to due process" and hence applicable to the states. The present case, one of the famous Scottsboro Cases, raises the question of whether the right to counsel, guaranteed against federal infringement by the Sixth Amendment, is applicable to the states through the Fourteenth.

Mr. Justice **Sutherland** delivered the opinion of the Court, saying in part:

The petitioners, hereinafter referred to as defendants, are negroes charged with the crime of rape, committed upon the persons of two white girls. The crime is said to have been committed on March 25, 1931. The indictment was returned in a state court of first instance on March 31, and the record recites that on the same day the defendants were arraigned and entered pleas of not guilty. There is a further recital to the effect that upon the arraignment they were represented by counsel. But no counsel had been employed, and aside from a statement made by the trial judge several days later during a colloquy immediately preceding the trial, the record does not disclose when, or under what circumstances, an appointment of counsel was made, or who was appointed. During the colloquy referred to, the trial judge, in response to a question, said that he had appointed all the members of the bar for the purpose of arraigning the defendants and then of course anticipated that the members of the bar would continue to help the defendants if no counsel appeared. Upon the argument here both sides accepted that as a correct statement of the facts concerning the matter.

There was a severance upon the request of the state, and the defendants were tried in three several groups, as indicated above. As each of the three cases was called for trial, each defendant was arraigned, and, having the indictment read to him, entered a plea of not guilty.

Whether the original arraignment and pleas were regarded as ineffective is not shown. Each of the three trials was completed within a single day. Under the Alabama statute the punishment for rape is to be fixed by jury, and in its discretion may be from ten years' imprisonment to death. The juries found defendants guilty and imposed the death penalty upon all. The trial court overruled motions for new trials and sentenced the defendants in accordance with the verdicts. The judgments were affirmed by the state supreme court. Chief Justice Anderson thought the defendants had not been accorded a fair trial and strongly dissented.

In this court the judgments are assailed upon the grounds that the defendants, and each of them, were denied due process of law and the equal protection of the laws, in contravention of the Fourteenth Amendment, specifically as follows: (1) They were not given a fair, impartial and deliberate trial; (2) they were denied the right of counsel, with the accustomed incidents of consultation and opportunity of preparation for trial; and (3) they were tried before juries from which qualified members of their own race were systematically excluded. These questions were properly raised and saved in the courts below.

The only one of the assignments which we shall consider is the second, in respect of the denial of counsel; and it becomes unnecessary to discuss the facts of the case or the circumstances surrounding the prosecution except in so far as they reflect light upon that question.

The record shows that on the day when the offense is said to have been committed, these defendants, together with a number of other negroes, were upon a freight train on its way through Alabama. On the same train were seven white boys and two white girls. A fight took place between the negroes and the white boys, in the course of which the white boys, with the exception of one named Gilley, were thrown off the train. A message was sent ahead, reporting the fight and asking that every negro be gotten off the train. The participants in the fight, and the two girls, were in an open gondola car. The two girls testified that each of them was assaulted by six different negroes in turn, and they identified the seven defendants as having been among the number. None of the white boys was called to testify, with the exception of Gilley, who was called in rebuttal.

Before the train reached Scottsboro, Alabama, a sheriff's posse seized the defendants and two other negroes. Both girls and the negroes then were taken to Scottsboro, the county seat. Word of their coming and of the alleged assault had preceded them, and they were met at Scottsboro by a large crowd. It does not sufficiently appear that the defendants were seriously threatened with, or that they were actually in danger of, mob violence; but it does appear that the attitude of the community was one of great hostility. The sheriff thought it necessary to call for the militia to assist in safeguarding the prisoners. Chief Justice Anderson pointed out in his opinion that every step taken from the arrest and arraignment to the sentence was accompanied by the military. Soldiers took the defendants to Gadsden for safekeeping, brought them back to Scottsboro for arraignment, returned them to Gadsden for safekeeping while awaiting trial, escorted them to Scottsboro for trial a few days later, and guarded the courthouse and grounds at every stage of the proceedings. It is perfectly apparent that the proceedings, from beginning to end, took place in an atmosphere of tense, hostile and excited public sentiment. During the entire time, the defendants were closely confined or were under military guard. The record does not disclose their ages, except that one of them was nineteen; but the record clearly indicates that most, if not all, of them were youthful, and they are constantly referred to as "the boys." They were ignorant and illiterate. All of them were residents of other states, where alone members of their families or friends resided.

However guilty defendants, upon due inquiry might prove to have been, they were, until convicted, presumed to be innocent. It was the duty of the court having their cases in charge to see that they were denied no necessary incident of a fair trial. With any error of the state court involving alleged contravention of the state statutes or constitution we, of course, have nothing to do. The sole inquiry which we are permitted to make is whether the federal Constitution was contravened ... and as to that, we confine ourselves, as already suggested, to the inquiry whether the defendants were in substance denied the right of counsel, and if so, whether such denial infringes the due process clause of the Fourteenth Amendment.

First. The record shows that immediately upon the return of the indictment defendants were arraigned and pleaded not guilty. Apparently they were not asked whether they had, or were able to employ, counsel, or wished to have counsel appointed; or whether they had friends or relatives who might assist in that regard if communicated with. That it would not have been an idle ceremony to have given the defendants reasonable opportunity to communicate with their families and endeavor to obtain counsel is demonstrated by the fact that very soon after conviction able counsel appeared in their behalf. . . .

It is hardly necessary to say that the right to counsel being conceded, a defendant should be afforded a fair opportunity to secure counsel of his own choice. Not only was that not done here, but such designation of counsel as was attempted was either so indefinite or so close upon the trial as to amount to a denial of effective and substantial aid in that regard. This will be amply demonstrated by a brief review of the record.

April 6, six days after indictment, the trials began. When the first case was called, the court inquired whether the parties were ready for trial. The state's attorney replied that he was ready to proceed. No one answered for the defendants or appeared to represent or defend them. Mr. Roddy, a Tennessee lawyer not a member of the local bar, addressed the court, saying that he had not been employed, but that people who were interested had spoken to him about the case. He was asked by the court whether he intended to appear for the defendants, and answered that he would like to appear along with counsel that the court might appoint. . . .

It thus will be seen that until the very morning of the trial no lawyer had been named or definitely designated to represent the defendants. Prior to that time, the trial judge had "appointed all the members of the bar" for the limited "purpose of arraigning the defendants." Whether they would represent the defendants thereafter if no counsel appeared in their behalf, was a matter of speculation only, or, as the judge indicated, of mere anticipation on the part of the court. Such a designation, even if made for all purposes, would, in our opinion, have fallen far short of meeting, in any proper sense, a requirement for the appointment of counsel. How many lawyers were members of the bar does not appear; but, in the very nature of things, whether many or few, they would not, thus collectively named, have been given that clear appreciation of responsibility or impressed with that individual sense of duty which should and naturally would accompany the appointment of a selected member of the bar, specifically named and assigned. . . . ,

. . . In any event, the circumstance lends emphasis to the conclusion that during perhaps the most critical period of the proceedings against these defendants, that is to say, from the time of their arraignment until the beginning of their trial, when consultation, thoroughgoing investigation and preparation were vitally important, the defendants did not have the aid of counsel in any real sense, although they were as much entitled to such aid during that period as at the trial itself. . . .

Second. The Constitution of Alabama provides that in all criminal prosecutions the accused shall enjoy the right to have the assistance of counsel; and a state statute requires the court in a capital case, where the defendant is unable to employ counsel, to appoint counsel for him. The state supreme court held that these provisions had not been infringed, and with that holding we are powerless to interfere. The question, however, which it is our duty, and within our power, to decide, is whether the denial of the assistance of counsel contravenes the due process clause of the Fourteenth Amendment to the federal Constitution. . . .

One test which has been applied to determine whether due process of law has been accorded in given instances is to ascertain what were the settled usages and modes of proceeding under the common and statute law of England before the Declaration of Independence, subject, however, to the qualification that they be shown not to have been unsuited to the civil and political conditions of our ancestors by having been followed in this country after it became a nation. . . . Plainly, as appears from the foregoing, this test, as thus qualified, has not been met in the present case.

We do not overlook the case of Hurtado v. California [1884], where this court determined that due process of law does not require an indictment by a grand jury as a prerequisite to prosecution by a state for murder. In support of that conclusion the court referred to the fact that the Fifth Amendment, in addition to containing the due process of law clause, provides in explicit terms that "No person shall be held to answer for a capital, or otherwise infamous crime, unless on a presentment or indictment of a grand jury," and said that since no part of this important amendment could be regarded as superfluous, the obvious inference is that in the sense of the Constitution due process of law was not intended to include, ex vi termini, the institution and procedure of a grand jury in any case; and that the same phrase, employed in the Fourteenth Amendment to restrain the action of the states, was to be interpreted as having been used in the same sense and with no greater extent; and that if it had been the purpose of that Amendment to perpetuate the institution of the grand jury in the states, it would have embodied, as did the Fifth Amendment, an express declaration to that effect.

The Sixth Amendment, in terms, provides that in all criminal prosecutions the accused shall enjoy the right "to have the assistance of counsel for his defense." In the face of the reasoning of the Hurtado Case, if it stood alone, it would be difficult to justify the conclusion that the right to counsel, being thus specifically granted by the Sixth Amendment, was also within the intendment of the due process of law clause. But the Hurtado Case does not stand alone. In the later case of Chicago, B. & Q. R. Co. v. Chicago [1897], this court held that a judgment of a state court, even though authorized by statute, by which private property was taken for public use without just compensation, was in violation of the due process of law required by the Fourteenth Amendment, notwithstanding that the Fifth Amendment explicitly declares that private property shall not be taken for public use without just compensation. . . .

Likewise, this court has considered that freedom of speech and of the press are rights protected by the due process clause of the Fourteenth Amendment, although in the First

Amendment, Congress is prohibited in specific terms from abridging the right. Gitlow v. New York [1925]. . . .

These later cases establish that notwithstanding the sweeping character of the language in the Hurtado Case, the rule laid down is not without exceptions. The rule is an aid to construction, and in some instances may be conclusive; but it must yield to more compelling considerations whenever such considerations exist. The fact that the right involved is of such a character that it cannot be denied without violating those "fundamental principles of liberty and justice which lie at the base of all our civil and political institutions" (Hebert v. Louisiana [1926]), is obviously one of those compelling considerations which must prevail in determining whether it is embraced within the due process clause of the Fourteenth Amendment, although it be specifically dealt with in another part of the federal Constitution. Evidently this court, in the later cases enumerated, regarded the rights there under consideration as of this fundamental character. That some such distinction must be observed is foreshadowed in Twining v. New Jersey [1908], where Mr. Justice Moody, speaking for the court, said that ". . . it is possible that some of the personal rights safeguarded by the first eight Amendments against national action may also be safeguarded against state action, because a denial of them would be a denial of due process of law. Chicago, B. & Q. R. Co. v. Chicago [1897]. If this is so, it is not because those rights are enumerated in the first eight Amendments, but because they are of such a nature that they are included in the conception of due process of law." While the question has never been categorically determined by this court, a consideration of the nature of the right and a review of the expressions of this and other courts, make it clear that the right to the aid of counsel is of this fundamental character.

It never has been doubted by this court, or any other so far as we know, that notice and hearing are preliminary steps essential to the passing of an enforceable judgment, and that they, together with a legally competent tribunal having jurisdiction of the case, constitute basic elements of the constitutional requirement of due process of law. . . .

What, then, does a hearing include? Historically and in practice, in our own country at least, it has always included the right to the aid of counsel when desired and provided by the party asserting the right. The right to be heard would be, in many cases, of little avail if it did not comprehend the right to be heard by counsel. Even the intelligent and educated layman has small and sometimes no skill in the science of law. If charged with crime, he is incapable, generally, of determining for himself whether the indictment is good or bad. He is unfamiliar with the rules of evidence. Left without the aid of counsel he may be put on trial without a proper charge, and convicted upon incompetent evidence, or evidence irrelevant to the issue or otherwise inadmissible. He lacks both the skill and knowledge adequately to prepare his defense, even though he have a perfect one. He requires the guiding hand of counsel at every step in the proceedings against him. Without it, though he be not guilty, he faces the danger of conviction because he does not know how to establish his innocence. If that be true of men of intelligence, how much more true is it of the ignorant and illiterate, or those of feeble intellect. If in any case, civil or criminal, a state or federal court were arbitrarily to refuse to hear a party by counsel, employed by and appearing for him, it reasonably may not be doubted that such a refusal would be a denial of a hearing, and, therefore, of due process in the constitutional sense.

The decisions all point to that conclusion. . . . In Ex parte Chin Loy You (D. C.) 223 Fed. 833 [1915], also a deportation case, the district judge held that under the particular circumstances of the case the prisoner, having reasonably made demand, was entitled to confer with and have the aid of counsel. Pointing to the fact that the right to counsel as secured by the Sixth Amendment relates only to criminal prosecutions, the judge said, ''But it is equally true that the provision was inserted in the Constitution because the assistance of counsel was recognized as essential to any fair trial of a case against a prisoner.'' . . .

In the light of the facts outlined in the forepart of this opinion—the ignorance and illiteracy of the defendants, their youth, the circumstances of public hostility, the imprisonment and the close surveillance of the defendants by the military forces, the fact that their friends and families were all in other states and communication with them necessarily difficult, and above all that they stood in deadly peril of their lives—we think the failure of the trial court to give them reasonable time and opportunity to secure counsel was a clear denial of due process.

But passing that, and assuming their inability, even if opportunity had been given, to employ counsel, as the trial court evidently did assume, we are of opinion that, under the circumstances just stated, the necessity of counsel was so vital and imperative that the failure of the trial court to make an effective appointment of counsel was likewise a denial of due process within the meaning of the Fourteenth Amendment. Whether this would be so in other criminal prosecutions, or under other circumstances, we need not determine. All that it is necessary now to decide, as we do decide, is that in a capital case, where the defendant is unable to employ counsel, and is incapable adequately of making his own defense because of ignorance, feeblemindedness, illiteracy, or the like, it is the duty of the court, whether requested or not, to assign counsel for him as a necessary requisite of due process of law; and that duty is not discharged by an assignment at such a time or under such circumstances as to preclude the giving of effective aid in the preparation and trial of the case. To hold otherwise would be to ignore the fundamental postulate, already adverted to, ''that there are certain immutable principles of justice which inhere in the very idea of free government which no member of the Union may disregard.'' . . . In a case such as this, whatever may be the rule in other cases, the right to have counsel appointed, when necessary, is a logical corollary from the constitutional right to be heard by counsel. . . .

The United States by statute and every state in the Union by express provision of law, or by the determination of its courts, make it the duty of the trial judge, where the accused is unable to employ counsel, to appoint counsel for him. In most states the rule applies broadly to all criminal prosecutions, in others it is limited to the more serious crimes, and in a very limited number, to capital cases. A rule adopted with such unanimous accord reflects, if it does not establish, the inherent right to have counsel appointed at least in cases like the present, and lends convincing support to the conclusion we have reached as to the fundamental nature of that right.

The judgments must be reversed and the causes remanded for further proceedings not inconsistent with this opinion.

Judgments reversed.

Mr. Justice **Butler** wrote a dissenting opinion in which Mr. Justice **McReynolds** concurred.

PALKO v. CONNECTICUT

302 U. S. 319; 82 L. Ed. 288; 58 S. Ct. 149 (1937)

With the decision in Powell v. Alabama (1932) it appeared that the long struggle to nationalize the Bill of Rights might at last be bearing fruit. The Court had acknowledged that it no longer felt bound by the Hurtado reasoning; the application to the states of the Fifth Amendment right to just compensation and the First Amendment rights of free speech, press, religion, and assembly showed that some of the Bill of Rights guarantees could be applied to the states through due process of law. And now, in Powell, the Court for the first time had found one of the rights of persons accused of crime to be essential to due process.

The Palko case, printed below, made clear that the Court was not prepared to abandon earlier decisions such as Hurtado and Twining. Instead, it undertook to explain why some rights, such as the rights to counsel and free speech, are absorbed into due process; and why others, like jury trial and grand jury indictment, are not. It should be emphasized that the cases "absorbing" rights into the Fourteenth Amendment do not overrule Barron v. Baltimore (1833). The provisions of the federal Bill of Rights still limit directly only the federal government; it is the Fourteenth Amendment which limits the states. What the Court has done is to reverse the practical effect of the rule in Barron v. Baltimore with respect to part, but not all, of the Bill of Rights. Some of these rights are still not considered by the Court to be so fundamental as to be required by due process of law. The Court in case after case has been classifying the provisions of the Bill of Rights into those which are essential to due process of law and thus bind the states through the operation of the Fourteenth Amendment, and those which are not essential to due process and by which the states are not bound. In effect, the Court has established an "honor roll" of superior rights which bind both state and national governments. The opinion in the present case is important since it gives an official summary of this classification up to 1937 and states clearly the principles upon which the classification rests.

One question which the Palko case failed to answer satisfactorily was what was meant by "absorption" or "incorporation" of a Bill of Rights guarantee into due process. Did it mean that the right, as listed in the Bill of Rights and interpreted by the Supreme Court in federal cases, was made applicable to the states? Or was the right as applied to the states a more general right, less clearly defined and permitting more leeway and discretion on the part of the states? Clearly, incorporation of the First Amendment has meant its application to the states exactly as it is applied to the national government. Justices Brandeis and Holmes, in their dissent in the Gitlow case, suggested that the free speech applicable to the states perhaps "may be accepted with a somewhat larger latitude of interpretation than is allowed to Congress by the sweeping language that governs or ought to govern the laws of the United States." The Court, however, with the exception of whether jury verdicts must be unanimous (see Apodoca v. Oregon, 1972), has never acknowledged such a distinction, and the same rules for deciding such cases are applied to the states and the nation alike.

With the gradual extension of due process to include other rights, an important controversy developed as to how these rights would apply to the states. This problem is discussed in connection with the specific rights in the chapter below.

Mr. Justice **Cardozo** delivered the opinion of the Court, saying in part:

. . . Appellant was indicted . . . for the crime of murder in the first degree. A jury found him guilty of murder in the second degree, and he was sentenced to confinement in the state prison for life. Thereafter the state of Connecticut, with the permission of the judge presiding at the trial, gave notice of appeal to the Supreme Court of Errors. This it did pursuant to an act adopted in 1886 which is printed in the margin.* . . . Upon such appeal, the Supreme Court of Errors reversed the judgment and ordered a new trial. . . . It found that there had been error of law to the prejudice of the state. . . .

. . . [The] defendant was brought to trial again. Before a jury was impaneled and also at later stages of the case he made the objection that the effect of the new trial was to place him twice in jeopardy for the same offense, and in so doing to violate the Fourteenth Amendment of the Constitution of the United States. Upon the overruling of the objection the trial proceeded. The jury returned a verdict of murder in the first degree, and the court sentenced the defendant to the punishment of death. . . . The case is here upon appeal.

1. The execution of the sentence will not deprive appellant of his life without the process of law assured to him by the Fourteenth Amendment of the Federal Constitution.

The argument for appellant is that whatever is forbidden by the Fifth Amendment is forbidden by the Fourteenth also. The Fifth Amendment, which is not directed to the states, but solely to the federal government, creates immunity from double jeopardy. No person shall be "subject for the same offense to be twice put in jeopardy of life or limb." The Fourteenth Amendment ordains, "nor shall any state deprive any person of life, liberty, or property, without due process of law." To retry a defendant, though under one indictment and only one, subjects him, it is said, to double jeopardy in violation of the Fifth Amendment, if the prosecution is one on behalf of the United States. From this the consequence is said to follow that there is a denial of life or liberty without due process of law, if the prosecution is one on behalf of the People of a State. . . .

We have said that in appellant's view the Fourteenth Amendment is to be taken as embodying the prohibitions of the Fifth. His thesis is even broader. Whatever would be a violation of the original bill of rights (Amendments 1 to 8) if done by the federal government is now equally unlawful by force of the Fourteenth Amendment if done by a state. There is no such general rule.

The Fifth Amendment provides, among other things, that no person shall be held to answer for a capital or otherwise infamous crime unless on presentment or indictment of a grand jury. This court has held that, in prosecutions by a state, presentment or indictment by a grand jury may give way to informations at the instance of a public officer. Hurtado v. California [1884]. . . . The Fifth Amendment provides also that no person shall be compelled in any criminal case to be a witness against himself. This court has said that, in prosecutions by a state, the exemption will fail if the state elects to end it. Twining v. New Jersey [1908]. . . . The Sixth Amendment calls for a jury trial in criminal cases and the Seventh for a jury trial in civil cases at common law where the value in controversy shall exceed twenty dollars.

---

*"Sec. 6494, *Appeals by the state in criminal cases.* Appeals from the rulings and decisions of the superior court or of any criminal court of common pleas, upon all questions of law arising on the trial of criminal cases, may be taken by the state, with the permission of the presiding judge, to the supreme court of errors, in the same manner and to the same effect as if made by the accused. . . ."

This court has ruled that consistently with those amendments trial by jury may be modified by a state or abolished altogether. Walker v. Sauvinet [1876]; Maxwell v. Dow [1900]. . . . As to the Fourth Amendment, one should refer to Weeks v. United States [1914] and as to other provisions of the Sixth, to West v. Louisiana [1904].

On the other hand, the due process clause of the Fourteenth Amendment may make it unlawful for a state to abridge by its statutes the freedom of speech which the First Amendment safeguards against encroachment by the Congress (De Jonge v. Oregon [1937]) or the like freedom of the press . . . (Near v. Minnesota [1931]), or the free exercise of religion (Hamilton v. University of California [1934]); . . ., or the right of peaceable assembly, without which speech would be unduly trammeled (De Jonge v. Oregon), or the right of one accused of crime to the benefit of counsel (Powell v. Alabama [1932]). In these and other situations immunities that are valid as against the federal government by force of the specific pledges of particular amendments have been found to be implicit in the concept of ordered liberty, and thus, through the Fourteenth Amendment, become valid as against the states.

The line of division may seem to be wavering and broken if there is a hasty catalogue of the cases on the one side and the other. Reflection and analysis will induce a different view. There emerges the perception of a rationalizing principle which gives to discrete instances a proper order and coherence. The right to trial by jury and the immunity from prosecution except as the result of an indictment may have value and importance. Even so, they are not of the very essence of a scheme of ordered liberty. To abolish them is not to violate a "principle of justice so rooted in the traditions and conscience of our people as to be ranked as fundamental." . . . Few would be so narrow or provincial as to maintain that a fair and enlightened system of justice would be impossible without them. What is true of jury trials and indictments is true also, as the cases show, of the immunity from compulsory self-incrimination. Twining v. New Jersey. This too might be lost, and justice still be done. Indeed, today as in the past there are students of our penal system who look upon the immunity as a mischief rather than a benefit, and who would limit its scope or destroy it altogether. . . . The exclusion of these immunities and privileges from the privileges and immunities protected against the action of the states has not been arbitrary or casual. It has been dictated by a study and appreciation of the meaning, the essential implications, of liberty itself.

We reach a different plane of social and moral values when we pass to the privileges and immunities that have been taken over from the earlier articles of the federal bill of rights and brought within the Fourteenth Amendment by a process of absorption. These in their origin were effective against the federal government alone. If the Fourteenth Amendment has absorbed them, the process of absorption has had its source in the belief that neither liberty nor justice would exist if they were sacrificed. Twining v. New Jersey. This is true, for illustration, of freedom of thought and speech. Of that freedom one may say that it is the matrix, the indispensable condition, of nearly every other form of freedom. With rare aberrations a pervasive recognition of that truth can be traced in our history, political and legal. So it has come about that the domain of liberty, withdrawn by the Fourteenth Amendment from encroachment by the states, has been enlarged by latter-day judgments to include liberty of the mind as well as liberty of action. . . . Fundamental too in the concept of due process, and so in that of liberty, is the thought that condemnation shall be rendered only after trial. . . . The hearing, moreover, must be a real one, not a sham or a pretense. Moore v.

Dempsey [1923]. . . . For that reason, ignorant defendants in a capital case were held to have been condemned unlawfully when in truth, though not in form, they were refused the aid of counsel. Powell v. Alabama. The decision did not turn upon the fact that the benefit of counsel would have been guaranteed to the defendants by the provisions of the Sixth Amendment if they had been prosecuted in a federal court. The decision turned upon the fact that in the particular situation laid before us in the evidence the benefit of counsel was essential to the substance of a hearing.

Our survey of the cases serves, we think, to justify the statement that the dividing line between them, if not unfaltering throughout its course, has been true for the most part to a unifying principle. On which side of the line the case made out by the appellant has appropriate location must be the next inquiry and the final one. Is that kind of double jeopardy to which the statute has subjected him a hardship so acute and shocking that our polity will not endure it? Does it violate those "fundamental principles of liberty and justice which lie at the base of all our civil and political institutions?" . . . The answer surely must be "no." What the answer would have to be if the state were permitted after a trial free from error to try the accused over again or to bring another case against him, we have no occasion to consider. We deal with the statute before us and no other. The state is not attempting to wear the accused out by a multitude of cases with accumulated trials. It asks no more than this, that the case against him shall go on until there shall be a trial free from the corrosion of substantial legal error. . . . This is not cruelty at all, nor even vexation in any immoderate degree. If the trial had been infected with error adverse to the accused, there might have been review at his instance, and as often as necessary to purge the vicious taint. A reciprocal privilege, subject at all times to the discretion of the presiding judge . . . , has now been granted to the state. There is here no seismic innovation. The edifice of justice stands, in its symmetry, to many, greater than before.

2. The conviction of appellant is not in derogation of any privileges or immunities that belong to him as a citizen of the United States. . . .

Maxwell v. Dow [1900], gives all the answer that is necessary.

The judgment is affirmed.

Mr. Justice **Butler** dissents.

GIDEON v. WAINWRIGHT

372 U. S. 335; 9 L. Ed. 2d 799; 83 S. Ct. 792 (1963)

While it is clear that rights not mentioned in the Bill of Rights must be protected, if at all, through the "fundamental fairness" concept implicit in due process of law, what of those rights that *are* listed in the Bill of Rights but which are not (as are the First Amendment rights) incorporated into due process? The decision in Powell v. Alabama (1932) was widely regarded as incorporating the Sixth Amendment right to counsel into due process, and this assumption was bolstered by its inclusion in Palko in the list of rights "that have been taken over from the earlier articles of the federal Bill of Rights and brought within the Fourteenth Amendment by a process of absorption." In 1942, however, the Supreme Court made clear that this was not the case. In Betts v. Brady it emphasized that "the due process clause of the Fourteenth Amendment does not incorporate, as such, the specific guarantees found in the Sixth Amendment although a denial by a state of rights or privileges specifically embodied in that and others of the first eight amendments may, in certain circumstances, or in connection with other elements, operate, in a given case, to deprive a litigant of due process of law. . . . That which may, in one setting, constitute a denial of fundamental fairness, shocking to the universal sense of justice, may, in other circumstances, and in the light of other considerations, fall short of such denial."

There thus appeared a sharp distinction between the two kinds of rights. Rights like those in the First Amendment were apparently "incorporated" or "absorbed" into due process so that they were applied against the states exactly as they were against the federal government, and state and federal cases served interchangeably as precedent. Rights not so incorporated were protected by the flexible "fundamental fairness" rule that any state conduct which is grossly unfair denies due process of law. The language used by the Court to describe these two aspects of due process is often confusing. While it will describe a right listed in the Bill of Rights as sufficiently "fundamental" to be incorporated into due process, it also uses "fundamental" to describe the level of fairness demanded of the states in its exercise of those procedures not so incorporated.

The disagreement on the Court both over the implications of incorporation and what language was needed to accomplish it, made it difficult to tell when a right had, in fact, been incorporated. In Louisiana ex rel. Francis v. Resweber (1947), for instance, the Court held it was not a cruel and unusual punishment to try a second time to electrocute a person after the first attempt had failed to kill him. But while four members of the majority stated somewhat ambiguously that the "Fourteenth [Amendment] would prohibit by its due process clause execution by a state in a cruel manner," Justice Frankfurter wrote a concurring opinion to explain that in his view "the penology of a state is not to be tested by the scope of the Eighth Amendment."

In 1949 the Court appeared to incorporate into due process the protection in the Fourth Amendment against unreasonable searches and seizures. In Wolf v. Colorado (1949) it held that "the security of one's privacy against arbitrary intrusion by the police—which is at the core of the Fourth Amendment—is basic to a free society. It is therefore implicit in 'the concept of ordered liberty' and as such enforceable against the States through the Due Process Clause." Despite Justice Frankfurter's later protestation that this did not result in incorporation, it was clear that at least four members of the Court assumed it did. Whatever the merits of this, the Court in Wolf effectively nullified such protection as it had extended by refusing to apply a rule, developed years before in Weeks v. United States (1914), that forbade the admission in court of evidence gotten by unreasonable searches and seizures. This rule, concededly the only real deterrent to unlawful police searches, was held to be merely a rule of evidence, and not a requirement of the Fourth Amendment.

The attitude of judicial self-restraint under which the states had been shaping their own standards of fair criminal procedure came to an abrupt halt in 1961. In Mapp v. Ohio the Court overruled Wolf v. Colorado (1949) and clearly made the Fourth Amendment, together with its exclusionary rule, applicable to the states. Then in 1962 it removed all doubt about the "incorporation" of cruel and unusual punishments when it used the formula, made familiar by First Amendment cases, that the state had violated the "Eighth and Fourteenth Amendments"; see Robinson v. California. The following year any lingering doubts about the meaning of "incorporation" were dispelled when eight members of the Court in Ker v. California (1963) agreed that federal constitutional standards of reasonableness of searches "is the same under the Fourth and Fourteenth Amendments." Only Justice Harlan clung to the view that "the more flexible concept of 'fundamental fairness' " should apply to the states.

The incorporation of other rights came rapidly. In 1964 following the decision in the present case, the Court in Malloy v. Hogan incorporated the Fifth Amendment privilege against self-incrimination. This was followed in 1965 by the right to confront one's accusers (Pointer v. Texas), in 1966 by an impartial jury (Parker v. Gladden), and in 1967 by speedy trial (Klopfer v. North Carolina), and the right to subpoena witnesses (Washington v. Texas). In 1968 the Court added the Sixth Amendment right to a jury trial in a criminal case (Duncan v. Louisiana) and in 1969, in Benton v. Maryland, it finally overruled Palko v. Connecticut (1937) and incorporated the protection against double jeopardy. "Palko's roots," the Court explained, "had been cut away years ago. We today only recognize the inevitable."

The decision in Duncan v. Louisiana inaugurated an unforeseen development in the doctrine of incorporation. Incorporation had long been viewed as a way of forcing the states to adhere to a higher standard of conduct than was required by mere "fundamental fairness," and was hence a step in the civilizing process of treating more fairly those who were accused of crime. But following the Duncan case two decisions by the Supreme Court began reducing the requirements traditionally thought of as part of the jury trial. In Williams v. Florida (1970) the Court held a six-man jury met the requirements of the Sixth Amendment, and in Apodoca v. Oregon (1972) it held the Amendment did not required a unanimous verdict. The decisions were reached by reviewing the history of the Amendment's adoption, but while eight justices agreed that it had been incorporated into the Fourteenth and therefore applied to the states, four of them dissented on the ground that it required 12 men and a unanimous verdict.

Justice Powell, who had replaced Justice Harlan in 1971, agreed with Justices White, Burger, Blackmun and Rehnquist that "a defendant in a state court may constitutionally be convicted by less than a unanimous verdict." He agreed with his predecessor, however, that not "all elements of jury trial within the meaning of the Sixth Amendment are necessarily embodied in or incorporated into the Due Process Clause of the Fourteenth Amendment," and added "that unanimity is one of the indispensable features of *federal* jury trial." Thus, while eight members agreed that the Eighth Amendment requires the same standards of both state and nation, Justice Powell's position threatened to "disincorporate" the Amendment by applying a different standard to each. The threat, however, was short-lived. Justice Brennan switched over, and in 1973, speaking for a five-man majority, held the Seventh Amendment requirement of a civil jury did not preclude a six-person federal jury; see Colegrove v. Battin (1973).

Five years later, in Ballew v. Georgia (1978), the Court held void a six-person jury which required only a vote of five to convict. The Court agreed unanimously in both cases that the smaller size defeated the purpose of the jury, but Justices Burger and Rehnquist joined Justice Powell in rejecting the idea that the Sixth Amendment was "incorporated" into the Fourteenth.

Following the reversal of his conviction in the present case, Gideon was retried by the state of Florida in the same courtroom, before the same judge, with the same witnesses, but with a lawyer appointed by the Court a Gideon's request. This time he was acquitted.

Mr. Justice **Black** delivered the opinion of the Court, saying in part:

Petitioner was charged in a Florida state court with having broken and entered a pool-room with intent to commit a misdemeanor. This offense is a felony under Florida law. Appearing in court without funds and without a lawyer, petitioner asked the court to appoint counsel for him, whereupon the following colloquy took place:

"The Court: Mr. Gideon, I am sorry, but I cannot appoint Counsel to represent you in this case. Under the laws of the State of Florida, the only time the Court can appoint Counsel to represent a Defendant is when that person is charged with a capital offense. I am sorry, but I will have to deny your request to appoint Counsel to defend you in this case.

"The Defendant: The United States Supreme Court says I am entitled to be represented by Counsel."

Put to trial before a jury, Gideon conducted his defense about as well as could be expected from a layman. He made an opening statement to the jury, cross-examined the State's witnesses, presented witnesses in his own defense, declined to testify himself, and made a short argument "emphasizing his innocence to the charge contained in the Information filed in this case." The jury returned a verdict of guilty, and petitioner was sentenced to serve five years in the state prison. . . . Since 1942, when Betts v. Brady was decided by a divided Court, the problem of a defendant's federal constitutional right to counsel in a state court has been a continuing source of controversy and litigation in both state and federal courts. To give this problem another review here, we granted certiorari. Since Gideon was proceeding in forma pauperis, we appointed counsel to represent him and requested both sides to discuss in their briefs and oral arguments the following: "Should this Court's holding in Betts v. Brady be reconsidered?"

I.

The facts upon which Betts claimed that he had been unconstitutionally denied the right to have counsel appointed to assist him are strikingly like the facts upon which Gideon here bases his federal constitutional claim. Betts was indicted for robbery in a Maryland state court. On arraignment, he told the trial judge of his lack of funds to hire a lawyer and asked the court to appoint one for him. Betts was advised that it was not the practice in that county to appoint counsel for indigent defendants except in murder and rape cases. He then pleaded not guilty, had witnesses summoned, cross-examined the State's witnesses, examined his own, and chose not to testify himself. He was found guilty by the judge, sitting without a jury, and sentenced to eight years in prison. Like Gideon, Betts sought release by habeas corpus, alleging that he had been denied the right to assistance of counsel in violation of the Fourteenth Amendment. Betts was denied any relief, and on review this Court affirmed. It was held that a refusal to appoint counsel for an indigent defendant charged with a felony did not necessarily violate the Due Process Clause of the Fourteenth Amendment, which for reasons given the Court deemed to be the only applicable federal constitutional provision. The Court said:

"Asserted denial [of due process] is to be tested by an appraisal of the totality of facts in a given case. That which may, in one setting, constitute a denial of fundamental fairness, shocking to the universal sense of justice, may, in other circumstances, and in the light of other considerations, fall short of such denial.''

Treating due process as ''a concept less rigid and more fluid than those envisaged in other specific and particular provisions of the Bill of Rights,'' the Court held that refusal to appoint counsel under the particular facts and circumstances in the Betts Case was not so ''offensive to the common and fundamental ideas of fairness'' as to amount to a denial of due process. Since the facts and circumstances of the two cases are so nearly indistinguishable, we think the Betts v. Brady holding if left standing would require us to reject Gideon's claim that the Constitution guarantees him the assistance of counsel. Upon full reconsideration we conclude that Betts v. Brady should be overruled.

II.

The Sixth Amendment provides, ''In all criminal prosecutions, the accused shall enjoy the right . . . to have the Assistance of Counsel for his defence.'' We have construed this to mean that in federal courts counsel must be provided for defendants unable to employ counsel unless the right is competently and intelligently waived. Betts argued that this right is extended to indigent defendants in state courts by the Fourteenth Amendment. In response the Court stated that, while the Sixth Amendment laid down ''no rule for the conduct of the States, the question recurs whether the constraint laid by the Amendment upon the national courts expresses a rule so fundamental and essential to a fair trial, and so, to due process of law, that it is made obligatory upon the States by the Fourteenth Amendment.'' In order to decide whether the Sixth Amendment's guarantee of counsel is of this fundamental nature, the Court in Betts set out and considered ''[r]elevant data on the subject . . . afforded by constitutional and statutory provisions subsisting in the colonies and the States prior to the inclusion of the Bill of Rights in the national Constitution, and in the constitutional, legislative, and judicial history of the States to the present date.'' On the basis of this historical data the Court concluded that ''appointment of counsel is not a fundamental right, essential to a fair trial.'' It was for this reason the Betts Court refused to accept the contention that the Sixth Amendment's guarantee of counsel for indigent federal defendants was extended to or, in the words of that Court, ''made obligatory upon the States by the Fourteenth Amendment.'' Plainly, had the Court concluded that appointment of counsel for indigent criminal defendant was ''a fundamental right, essential to a fair trial,'' it would have held that the Fourteenth Amendment requires appointment of counsel in a state court, just as the Sixth Amendment requires in a federal court.

We think the Court in Betts had ample precedent for acknowledging that those guarantees of the Bill of Rights which are fundamental safeguards of liberty immune from federal abridgment are equally protected against state invasion by the Due Process Clause of the Fourteenth Amendment. This same principle was recognized, explained and applied in Powell v. Alabama (1932), a case upholding the right of counsel, where the Court held that despite sweeping language to the contrary in Hurtado v. California (1884), the Fourteenth Amendment ''embraced'' those ''fundamental principles of liberty and justice which lie at the base of all our civil and political institutions,'' even though they had been ''specifically dealt with in another part of the federal Constitution.'' In many cases other than Powell and Betts, this Court has looked to the fundamental nature of original Bill of Rights guarantees to decide whether the Fourteenth Amendment makes them obligatory on the States. Explicitly recognized to be of this ''fundamental nature'' and therefore made immune from state invasion by the Fourteenth, or some part of it, are the First Amendment's freedoms of speech, press, religion, assembly, association, and petition for redress of grievances. For the same reason, though not always in precisely the same terminology, the Court has made obligatory on the States the Fifth Amendment's command that private property shall not be taken for public use without just compensation, the Fourth Amendment's prohibition of unreasonable searches and seizures, and the Eighth's ban on cruel and unusual punishment. On the other hand, this Court in Palko v. Connecticut (1937), refused to hold that the Fourteenth Amendment made the double jeopardy provision of the Fifth Amendment obligatory on the States. In so refusing, however, the Court, speaking through Mr. Justice Cardozo, was careful to emphasize that ''immunities that are valid as against the federal government by force of the specific pledges of particular amendments have been found to be implicit in the concept of ordered liberty, and thus, through the Fourteenth Amendment, become valid as against the states'' and that guarantees ''in their origin ... effective against the federal government alone'' had by prior cases ''been taken over from the earlier articles of the federal bill of rights and brought within the Fourteenth Amendment by a process of absorption.''

We accept Betts v. Brady's assumption, based as it was on our prior cases, that a provision of the Bill of Rights which is ''fundamental and essential to a fair trial'' is made obligatory upon the States by the Fourteenth Amendment. We think the Court in Betts was wrong, however, in concluding that the Sixth Amendment's guarantee of counsel is not one of these fundamental rights. Ten years before Betts v. Brady, this Court, after full consideration of all the historical data examined in Betts, had unequivocally declared that ''the right to the aid of counsel is of this fundamental character.'' . . . While the Court at the close of its Powell opinion did by its language, as this Court frequently does, limit its holding to the particular facts and circumstances of that case, its conclusions about the fundamental nature of the right to counsel are unmistakable. Several years later, in 1936, the Court reemphasized what it had said about the fundamental nature of the right to counsel in this language:

''We concluded that certain fundamental rights, safeguarded by the first eight amendments against federal action, were also safeguarded against state action by the due process of law clause of the Fourteenth Amendment, and among them the fundamental right of the accused to the aid of counsel in a criminal prosecution.'' Grosjean v. American Press Co. (1936).

And again in 1938 this Court said:

''[The assistance of counsel] is one of the safeguards of the Sixth Amendment deemed necessary to insure fundamental human rights of life and liberty. . . . The Sixth Amendment stands as a constant admonition that if the constitutional safeguards it provides be lost, justice will not 'still be done,' '' Johnson v. Zerbst (1938). . . .

In light of these many other prior decisions of this Court, it is not surprising that the Betts Court, when faced with the contention that ''one charged with crime, who is unable to obtain counsel, must be furnished counsel by the State,'' conceded that ''[e]xpressions in the opinions of this court lend color to the argument. . . .'' The fact is that in deciding as it did—that ''appointment of counsel is not a fundamental right, essential to a fair trial''—the

Court in Betts v. Brady made an abrupt break with its own well-considered precedents. In returning to these old precedents, sounder we believe than the new, we but restore constitutional principles established to achieve a fair system of justice. Not only these precedents but also reason and reflection require us to recognize that in our adversary system of criminal justice, any person haled into court, who is too poor to hire a lawyer, cannot be assured a fair trial unless counsel is provided for him. This seems to us to be an obvious truth. Governments, both state and federal, quite properly spend vast sums of money to establish machinery to try defendants accused of crime. Lawyers to prosecute are everywhere deemed essential to protect the public's interest in an orderly society. Similarly, there are few defendants charged with crime, few indeed, who fail to hire the best lawyers they can get to prepare and present their defenses. That government hires lawyers to prosecute and defendants who have the money hire lawyers to defend are the strongest indications of the widespread belief that lawyers in criminal courts are necessities, not luxuries. The right of one charged with crime to counsel may not be deemed fundamental and essential for fair trials in some countries, but it is in ours. From the very beginning, our state and national constitutions and laws have laid great emphasis on procedural and substantive safeguards designed to assure fair trials before impartial tribunals in which every defendant stands equal before the law. This noble ideal cannot be realized if the poor man charged with crime has to face his accusers without a lawyer to assist him. A defendant's need for a lawyer is nowhere better stated than in the moving words of Mr. Justice Sutherland in Powell v. Alabama:

"The right to be heard would be, in many cases, of little avail if it did not comprehend the right to be heard by counsel. Even the intelligent and educated layman has small and sometimes no skill in the science of law. If charged with crime, he is incapable, generally, of determining for himself whether the indictment is good or bad. He is unfamiliar with the rules of evidence. Left without the aid of counsel he may be put on trial without a proper charge, and convicted upon incompetent evidence, or evidence irrelevant to the issue or otherwise inadmissible. He lacks both the skill and knowledge adequately to prepare his defense, even though he have a perfect one. He requires the guiding hand of counsel at every step in the proceedings against him. Without it, though he be not guilty, he faces the danger of conviction because he does not know how to establish his innocence."

The Court in Betts v. Brady departed from the sound wisdom upon which the Court's holding in Powell v. Alabama rested. Florida, supported by two other States, has asked that Betts v. Brady be left intact. Twenty-two States, as friends of the Court, argue that Betts was "an anachronism when handed down" and that it should now be overruled. We agree.

The judgment is reversed and the cause is remanded to the Supreme Court of Florida for further action not inconsistent with this opinion.

Reversed.

Mr. Justice **Douglas,** while joining the opinion of the Court, wrote a separate opinion, saying in part:

My Brother Harlan is of the view that a guarantee of the Bill of Rights that is made applicable to the States by reason of the Fourteenth Amendment is a lesser version of that same guarantee as applied to the Federal Government. Mr. Justice Jackson shared the view. But that view has not prevailed and rights protected against state invasion by the Due Process

Clause of the Fourteenth Amendment are not watered-down versions of what the Bill of Rights guarantees.

Mr. Justice **Clark,** concurring in the result, wrote a separate opinion.

Mr. Justice **Harlan,** concurring, said in part:

I agree that Betts v. Brady should be overruled, but consider it entitled to a more respectful burial than has been accorded, at least on the part of those of us who were not on the Court when that case was decided.

I cannot subscribe to the view that Betts v. Brady represented "an abrupt break with its own well-considered precedents." In 1932, in Powell v. Alabama, a capital case, this Court declared that under the particular facts there presented—"the ignorance and illiteracy of the defendants, their youth, the circumstances of public hostility . . . and above all that they stood in deadly peril of their lives"—the state court had a duty to assign counsel for the trial as a necessary requisite of due process of law. It is evident that these limiting facts were not added to the opinion as an afterthought; they were repeatedly emphasized, and were clearly regarded as important to the result.

Thus when this Court, a decade later, decided Betts v. Brady, it did no more than to admit of the possible existence of special circumstances in noncapital as well as capital trials, while at the same time insisting that such circumstances be shown in order to establish a denial of due process. The right to appointed counsel had been recognized as being considerably broader in federal prosecutions, see Johnson v. Zerbst, but to have imposed these requirements on the States would indeed have been "an abrupt break" with the almost immediate past. The declaration that the right to appointed counsel in state prosecutions, as established in Powell v. Alabama, was not limited to capital cases was in truth not a departure from, but an extension of, existing precedent. . . .

[Mr. Justice Harlan here notes the "troubled journey" of the Powell and Betts doctrines and concedes that since 1950 no "special circumstances" have been found to justify the absence of counsel.]

. . . The Court has come to recognize, in other words, that the mere existence of a serious criminal charge constituted in itself special circumstances requiring the services of counsel at trial. In truth the Betts v. Brady rule is no longer a reality.

This evaluation, however, appears not to have been fully recognized by many state courts, in this instance charged with the front-line responsibility for the enforcement of constitutional rights. To continue a rule which is honored by this Court only with lip service is not a healthy thing and in the long run will do disservice to the federal system. . . .

In agreeing with the Court that the right to counsel in a case such as this should now be expressly recognized as a fundamental right embraced in the Fourteenth Amendment, I wish to make a further observation. When we hold a right or immunity, valid against the Federal Government, to be "implicit in the concept of ordered liberty" and thus valid against the States, I do not read our past decisions to suggest that by so holding, we automatically carry over an entire body of federal law and apply it in full sweep to the States. Any such concept would disregard the frequently wide disparity between the legitimate interests of the States and of the Federal Government, the divergent problems that they face, and the significantly different consequences of their actions. . . . In what is done today I do not understand the Court to depart from the principles laid down in Palko v. Connecticut, or to embrace the concept that the Fourteenth Amendment "incorporates" the Sixth Amendment as such.

On these premises I join in the judgment of the Court.

D. The Concept of "Fundamental Fairness"

ROCHIN v. CALIFORNIA

342 U.S. 165; 96 L. Ed. 183; 72 S. Ct. 205 (1952)

Despite its obvious reluctance to incorporate the specific guarantees of the Bill of Rights, the Court did take increasing interest in state procedures and machinery, and grew more watchful lest they not meet the requirements of fundamental fairness. Such insistence on fundamental fairness, especially for persons accused of crime, was bound to bring before the Court the widest variety of state activities. In 1927, for instance, the Court in Tumey v. Ohio reversed the conviction of a bootlegger who had been tried before the mayor of a small town. An ordinance provided that the mayor should retain the court costs as payment for his judicial work, but no costs were paid if the defendant were acquitted. Tumey had been fined one hundred dollars, and the costs involved were twelve dollars. The Supreme Court held it to be a denial of due process to "subject his liberty or property to the judgment of a court, the judge of which has a direct, personal, substantial pecuniary interest in reaching a conclusion against him in his case. . . . There are doubtless mayors," the Court conceded, "who would not allow such a consideration as twelve dollar costs in each case to affect their judgment in it, but the requirement of due process of law in judicial procedure is not satisfied by the argument that men of the highest honor and the greatest self-sacrifice could carry it on without danger of injustice. Every procedure which would offer a possible temptation to the average man as a judge to forget the burden of proof required to convict the defendant, or which might lead him not to hold the balance nice, clear and true between the state and the accused denies the latter due process of law." The doctrine of Tumey was reaffirmed as recently as 1977 when the Court in Connally v. Georgia held void a search warrant issued by a justice of the peace. The justice received five dollars if he issued the warrant but nothing if he didn't.

Nor are jury members expected to be persons of unrestrained self-sacrifice, and a trial conducted in an atmosphere of mob violence is inherently unfair. In Moore v. Dempsey (1923) five blacks were convicted in an Arkansas court of the murder of a white man and sentenced to death. The Court described the trial in these words: "The court and the neighborhood were thronged with an adverse crowd that threatened the most dangerous consequences to any one interfering with the desired result. The counsel did not venture to demand delay or a change of venue, to challenge a juryman, or to ask for separate trials. He had had no preliminary consultation with the accused, called no witnesses for the defense, although they could have been produced, and did not put the defendants on the stand. The trial lasted about three quarters of an hour, and in less than five minutes the jury brought in a verdict of murder in the first degree. According to the allegations and affidavits there never was a chance for the petitioners to be acquitted; no juryman could have voted for an acquittal and continued to live in Phillips County, and if any prisoner, by any chance, had been acquitted by a jury, he could not have escaped the mob." Under these conditions no trial in the true sense was possible and the defendants were denied due process of law.

The Supreme Court has made it clear that due process is denied by an attempt to punish a person for a crime which is not clearly defined. In 1934 New Jersey passed an act punishing by $10,000 or twenty years or both the crime of being "a gangster." A gangster was defined as "any person not engaged in any lawful occupation, known to be a member of any gang consisting of two or more persons, who has been convicted at least three times of being a disorderly person, or who has been convicted of any crime. . . ." In Lanzetta v. New Jersey (1939) the Court held the statute void, noting that "no one may be required at peril of his life, liberty or property to speculate as to the meaning of penal statutes. All are entitled to be informed as to what the State commands or forbids."

In 1972 the Supreme Court struck down a Jacksonville vagrancy ordinance which, in the archaic language of the Elizabethan Poor Law, defines as vagrants (among others) "rogues and vagabonds, or dissolute persons who go about begging, . . . common night walkers, . . . common railers and brawlers, persons wandering or strolling around from place to place without any lawful purpose or object, habitual loafers, [and] . . . persons able to work but habitually living upon the earnings of their wives or minor children. . . ." Two white girls and their black dates were arrested on the main thoroughfare in Jacksonville and convicted of "prowling by auto." In Papachristou v. Jacksonville (1972) a unanimous Court found the ordinance "void for vagueness both in the sense that it 'fails to give a person of ordinary intelligence fair notice that his contemplated conduct is forbidden by the statute,' . . . and because it encourages arbitrary arrests and convictions." Not only does it make "criminal activities which by modern standards are normally innocent," but it puts "unfettered discretion in the hands of the Jacksonville police. . . . Those generally implicated by the imprecise terms of the ordinance—poor people, nonconformists, dissenters, idlers—may be required to comport themselves according to the lifestyle deemed appropriate by the Jacksonville police and the courts. Where, as here, there are no standards governing the exercise of the discretion granted by the ordinance, the scheme permits and encourages an arbitrary and discriminatory enforcement of the law . . . It results in a regime in which the poor and unpopular are permitted to 'stand on a public sidewalk . . . only at the whim of any police officer.' Shuttlesworth v. Birmingham [1969]." In 1983 the case was reaffirmed in Kolender v. Lawson where the Court struck down a California statute making it a crime to be unable to produce "credible and reliable" identification when asked to do so by a police officer. The statute was violated unless "the officer [is] satisfied that the identification is reliable."

Nor can a state through its criminal procedure favor the wealthy over the poor. In order to carry an appeal to the supreme court of Illinois in a criminal case it is necessary to have a stenographic transcript of the trial proceedings. Only an indigent defendant who had been sentenced to death was provided with a free transcript; all other defendants had to buy it. As a result, a poor person convicted of a *noncapital* crime and therefore *not* entitled to a free transcript would be deprived of the right to appeal because of poverty—a right easily available to the well-to-do convict. In Griffin v. Illinois (1956) the Supreme Court held this to be a violation of due process and equal protection of the laws. "In criminal trials," the Court said, "a State can no more discriminate on account of poverty than on account of religion, race, or color. Plainly the ability to pay costs in advance bears no rational relationship to a defendant's guilt or innocence and could not be used as an excuse to deprive a defendant of a fair trial. . . , There is no meaningful distinction between a rule which would deny the poor the right to defend themselves in a trial court and one which effectively denies the poor an adequate appellate review accorded to all who have money enough to pay the costs in advance." In Mayer v. Chicago (1972) the Court extended the rule to include persons charged with a misdemeanor and liable only to a fine. "Griffin," it emphasized, ". . . is a flat protection against pricing indigent defendants out of as effective an appeal as would be available to others able to pay their own way."

Mr. Justice **Frankfurter** delivered the opinion of the Court, saying in part:

Having "some information that [the petitioner here] was selling narcotics," three deputy sheriffs of the County of Los Angeles, on the morning of July 1, 1949, made for the two-story dwelling house in which Rochin lived with his mother, common-law wife, brothers and sisters. Finding the outside door open, they entered and then forced open the door to Rochin's room on the second floor. Inside they found petitioner sitting partly dressed on the side of the bed, upon which his wife was lying. On a "night stand" beside the bed the deputies spied two capsules. When asked "Whose stuff is this?" Rochin seized the capsules and put them in his mouth. A struggle ensued, in the course of which the three officers "jumped upon him" and attempted to extract the capsules. The force they applied proved unavailing against Rochin's resistance. He was handcuffed and taken to a hospital. At the direction of one of the officers a doctor forced an emetic solution through a tube into Rochin's stomach against his will. This "stomach pumping" produced vomiting. In the vomited matter were found two capsules which proved to contain morphine.

Rochin was brought to trial before a California Superior Court, sitting without a jury, on the charge of possessing "a preparation of morphine" in violation of the California Health and Safety Code. Rochin was convicted and sentenced to sixty days' imprisonment. The chief evidence against him was the two capsules. They were admitted over petitioner's objection, although the means of obtaining them was frankly set forth in the testimony by one of the deputies, substantially as here narrated. . . .

. . . Regard for the requirements of the Due Process Clause "inescapably imposes upon this Court an exercise of judgment upon the whole course of the proceedings [resulting in a conviction] in order to ascertain whether they offend those canons of decency and fairness which express the notions of justice of English-speaking peoples even toward those charged with the most heinous offenses." Malinski v. New York [1945]. These standards of justice are not authoritatively formulated anywhere as though they were specifics. Due process of law is a summarized constitutional guarantee of respect for those personal immunities which, as Mr. Justice Cardozo twice wrote for the Court, are "so rooted in the traditions and conscience of our people as to be ranked as fundamental," Snyder v. Massachusetts [1934], or are "implicit in the concept of ordered liberty." Palko v. Connecticut [1937].

The Court's function in the observance of this settled conception of the Due Process Clause does not leave us without adequate guides in subjecting State criminal procedures to constitutional judgment. In dealing not with the machinery of government but with human rights, the absence of formal exactitude, or want of fixity of meaning, is not an unusual or even regrettable attribute of constitutional provisions. Words being symbols do not speak without a gloss. On the one hand the gloss may be the deposit of history, whereby a term gains technical content. Thus the requirements of the Sixth and Seventh Amendments for trial by jury in the Federal courts have a rigid meaning. No changes or chances can alter the content of the verbal symbol of "jury"—a body of twelve men who must reach a unanimous conclusion if the verdict is to go against the defendant. On the other hand, the gloss of some of the verbal symbols of the Constitution does not give them a fixed technical content. It exacts a continuing process of application.

When the gloss has thus not been fixed but is a function of the process of judgment, the judgment is bound to fall differently at different times and differently at the same time through different judges. Even more specific provisions, such as the guaranty of freedom of speech and the detailed protection against unreasonable searches and seizures, have inevitably evoked as sharp divisions in this Court as the least specific and most comprehensive protection of liberties, the Due Process Clause.

The vague contours of the Due Process Clause do not leave judges at large. We may not draw on our merely personal and private notions and disregard the limits that bind judges in their judicial function. Even though the concept of due process of law is not final and fixed, these limits are derived from considerations that are fused in the whole nature of our judicial process. See Cardozo, The Nature of the Judicial Process; The Growth of the Law; The Paradoxes of Legal Science. These are considerations deeply rooted in reason and in the compelling traditions of the legal profession. The Due Process Clause places upon this Court the duty of exercising a judgment, within the narrow confines of judicial power in reviewing State convictions, upon interests of society pushing in opposite directions.

Due process of law thus conceived is not to be derided as resort to a revival of "natural law." To believe that this judicial exercise of judgment could be avoided by freezing "due process of law" at some fixed stage of time or thought is to suggest that the most important aspect of constitutional adjudication is a function for inanimate machines and not for judges, for whom the independence safeguarded by Article 3 of the Constitution was designed and who are presumably guided by established standards of judicial behavior. Even cybernetics has not yet made that haughty claim. To practice the requisite detachment and to achieve sufficient objectivity no doubt demands of judges the habit of self-discipline and self-criticism, incertitude that one's own views are incontestable and alert tolerance toward views not shared. But these are precisely the presuppositions of our judicial process. They are precisely the qualities society has a right to expect from those entrusted with ultimate judicial power.

Restraints on our jurisdiction are self-imposed only in the sense that there is from our decisions no immediate appeal short of impeachment or constitutional amendment. But that does not make due process of law a matter of judicial caprice. The faculties of the Due Process Clause may be indefinite and vague, but the mode of their ascertainment is not self-willed. In each case "due process of law" requires an evaluation based on a disinterested inquiry pursued in the spirit of science, on a balanced order of facts exactly and fairly stated, on the detached consideration of conflicting claims, . . . on a judgment not ad hoc and episodic but duly mindful of reconciling the needs both of continuity and of change in a progressive society.

Applying these general considerations to the circumstances of the present case, we are compelled to conclude that the proceedings by which this conviction was obtained do more than offend some fastidious squeamishness or private sentimentalism about combatting crime too energetically. This is conduct that shocks the conscience. Illegally breaking into the privacy of the petitioner, the struggle to open his mouth and remove what was there, the forcible extraction of his stomach's contents—this course of proceeding by agents of government to obtain evidence is bound to offend even hardened sensibilities. They are methods too close to the rack and the screw to permit of constitutional differentiation.

It has long since ceased to be true that due process of law is heedless of the means by which otherwise relevant and credible evidence is obtained. This was not true even before the series of recent cases enforced the constitutional principle that the States may not base convictions upon confessions, however much verified, obtained by coercion. These decisions are not arbitrary exceptions to the comprehensive right of States to fashion their own rules of evidence for criminal trials. They are not sports in our constitutional law but applications of a general principle. They are only instances of the general requirement that States in their prosecutions respect certain decencies of civilized conduct. Due process of law, as a historic and generative principle, precludes defining, and thereby confining, these standards of conduct more precisely than to say that convictions cannot be brought about by methods that offend ''a sense of justice.'' See Mr. Chief Justice Hughes, speaking for a unanimous Court in Brown v. Mississippi [1936]. It would be a stultification of the responsibility which the course of constitutional history has cast upon this Court to hold that in order to convict a man the police cannot extract by force what is in his mind but can extract what is in his stomach.

To attempt in this case to distinguish what lawyers call ''real evidence'' from verbal evidence is to ignore the reasons for excluding coerced confessions. Use of involuntary verbal confessions in State criminal trials is constitutionally obnoxious not only because of their unreliability. They are inadmissible under the Due Process Clause even though statements contained in them may be independently established as true. Coerced confessions offend the community's sense of fair play and decency. So here, to sanction the brutal conduct which naturally enough was condemned by the court whose judgment is before us, would be to afford brutality the cloak of law. Nothing would be more calculated to discredit law and thereby to brutalize the temper of a society. . . .

On the facts of this case the conviction of the petitioner has been obtained by methods that offend the Due Process Clause. The judgment below must be

Reversed.

Mr. Justice **Minton** took no part in the consideration or decision of this case.

Mr. Justice **Black**, concurring, said in part:

Adamson v. California [1947] sets out reasons for my belief that state as well as federal courts and law enforcement officers must obey the Fifth Amendment's command that ''No person . . . shall be compelled in any criminal case to be a witness against himself.'' I think a person is compelled to be a witness against himself not only when he is compelled to testify, but also when as here, incriminating evidence is forcibly taken from him by a contrivance of modern science. . . .

Mr. Justice **Douglas** wrote a concurring opinion.

DeSHANEY v. WINNEBAGO SOC. SERV.

489 U. S. 189; 103 L. Ed. 2d 249; 109 S. Ct. 998 (1989)

While the phrase "fundamental fairness" has a certain alluring simplicity to it, the Court not only has disagreed on its content but has not adopted it as an accepted description of the doctrine. In Hurtado v. California (1884) this level of fairness was described as "those fundamental principles of liberty and justice which lie at the base of all our civil and political institutions." In 1943 Justice Frankfurter described it as "those minimal historic safeguards for securing trial by reason . . . below which we reach what is really trial by force"; see McNabb v. United States (1943). And in the Rochin case, above, he described it as a level below which state conduct "shocks the conscience" and is "too close to the rack and the screw to permit of constitutional differentiation." Whatever the language chosen, the underlying concept remains the same. There is a level of state conduct toward persons accused or convicted of crime that is so offensive to the Court that it denies those persons due process of law. How offensive this conduct must be in any particular case depends upon the justices making the decision.

Two years after the decision in Rochin the Court faced a case so shocking that two of the justices suggested federal prosecution of the state authorities involved and four noted that "few police measures have come to our attention that more flagrantly, deliberately, and persistently violated the fundamental principles declared by the Fourth Amendment." The California police, alerted by the purchase of a federal gambling tax stamp, broke into Irvine's private home and planted microphones. For a month they listened to conversations within the house, including those in his bedroom, and finally obtained enough evidence to convict him of bookmaking. In Irvine v. California (1954) the Court held the use of the evidence valid. Since, under Wolf v. Colorado (1949), the actual entry and bugging were constitutional, the validity of the evidence turned on the degree of "shock" involved in obtaining it. Over the bitter dissent of Justice Frankfurter the Court rejected the unrestrained "shock the conscience" doctrine of Rochin, pointing out that such a rule gave no guidance to state police or law makers as to which kinds of conduct were permissible. It returned to the pattern of providing specific rules of guidance; in Rochin there had been physical coercion and in Irvine there had not.

Probably the major difference between a legislative enactment and a constitutional provision is that the former is designed to regulate the conduct of individuals while the purpose of the latter is to indicate how the government is to be organized and to impose limits upon its powers. So well accepted is this distinction that provisions in the federal constitution forbidding individuals to hold slaves or (in the Eighteenth Amendment) manufacture liquor are viewed as legislation and hence anomalies in the constitutional scheme. Generally speaking, our constitutions neither restrict the behavior of private individuals nor guarantee affirmative aid from the government. Constitutions merely protect them from certain forms of government interference with their liberty.

When the Framers met in Philadelphia it was generally accepted that "that government was best which governs least." Nobody looked to the government to help them in times of trouble. All that was required was a regulated society in which people, especially those with property, could conduct their affairs as they were accustomed to do and be protected from those who wished to interfere with them. To savor the Court's attitude toward the rights of businessmen, see Lochner v. New York (1905).

The twentieth century, however, has seen dramatic and wholly unforseen changes in the relations between the people and their government. Triggered by a demand for protection from unscrupulous business magnates, and later by the desperate need for government help to survive the horrors of the Great Depression, the governments, both state and federal, have become increasingly the beneficent protectors to which the people look for help of all kinds. Private enterprise in such crucial areas as care for the aged, welfare for the poor, fire protection and ambulance service, hospitals, child care centers, to name a few, has given way to a reliance on government.

The failure of government to deal adequately with the increasing incidence of street crime, battered women, and injury by drunken, unlicensed, or uninsured drivers appears to have generated two answers by the public. One is illustrated by the New York City subway rider who shot a number of attackers and was convicted merely of carrying a gun without a license. The other is an increasing insistence that individuals should have a constitutional right to protection by the government itself against such threats. The Court's implicit rejection of the latter claim in the case below represents a conscious refusal to extend the "fundamental fairness" doctrine to this contentious area.

Chief Justice **Rehnquist** delivered the opinion of the Court.

Petitioner is a boy who was beaten and permanently injured by his father, with whom he lived. The respondents are social workers and other local officials who received complaints that petitioner was being abused by his father and had reason to believe that this was the case, but nonetheless did not act to remove petitioner from his father's custody. Petitioner sued respondents claiming that their failure to act deprived him of his liberty in violation of the Due Process Clause of the Fourteenth Amendment to the United States Constitution. We hold that it did not.

I.

The facts of this case are undeniably tragic. Petitioner Joshua DeShaney was born in 1979. In 1980, a Wyoming court granted his parents a divorce and awarded custody of Joshua to his father, Randy DeShaney. The father shortly thereafter moved to Neenah, a city located in Winnebago County, Wisconsin, taking the infant Joshua with him. There he entered into a second marriage, which also ended in divorce.

The Winnebago County authorities first learned that Joshua DeShaney might be a victim of child abuse in January 1982, when his father's second wife complained to the police, at the time of their divorce, that he had previously "hit the boy causing marks and

[was] a prime case for child abuse." The Winnebago County Department of Social Services (DSS) interviewed the father, but he denied the accusations, and DSS did not pursue them further. In January 1983, Joshua was admitted to a local hospital with multiple bruises and abrasions. The examining physician suspected child abuse and notified DSS, which immediately obtained an order from a Wisconsin juvenile court placing Joshua in the temporary custody of the hospital. Three days later, the county convened an ad hoc "Child Protection Team"—consisting of a pediatrician, a psychologist, a police detective, the county's lawyer, several DSS caseworkers, and various hospital personnel—to consider Joshua's situation. At this meeting, the Team decided that there was insufficient evidence of child abuse to retain Joshua in the custody of the court. The Team did, however, decide to recommend several measures to protect Joshua, including enrolling him in a preschool program, providing his father with certain counselling services, and encouraging his father's girlfriend to move out of the home. Randy DeShaney entered into a voluntary agreement with DSS in which he promised to cooperate with them in accomplishing these goals.

Based on the recommendations of the Child Protection Team, the juvenile court dismissed the child protection case and returned Joshua to the custody of his father. A month later, emergency room personnel called the DSS caseworker handling Joshua's case to report that he had once again been treated for suspicious injuries. The caseworker concluded that there was no basis for action. For the next six months, the caseworker made monthly visits to the DeShaney home, during which she observed a number of suspicious injuries on Joshua's head; she also noticed that he had not been enrolled in school and that the girlfriend had not moved out. The caseworker dutifully recorded these incidents in her files, along with her continuing suspicions that someone in the DeShaney household was physically abusing Joshua, but she did nothing more. In November 1983, the emergency room notified DSS that Joshua had been treated once again for injuries that they believed to be caused by child abuse. On the caseworker's next two visits to the DeShaney home, she was told that Joshua was too ill to see her. Still DSS took no action.

In March 1984, Randy DeShaney beat 4-year-old Joshua so severely that he fell into a life-threatening coma. Emergency brain surgery revealed a series of hemorrhages caused by traumatic injuries to the head inflicted over a long period of time. Joshua did not die, but he suffered brain damage so severe that he is expected to spend the rest of his life confined to an institution for the profoundly retarded. Randy DeShaney was subsequently tried and convicted of child abuse.

Joshua and his mother brought this action under 42 USC § 1983 in the United States District Court for the Eastern District of Wisconsin against respondents Winnebago County, its Department of Social Services, and various individual employees of the Department. The complaint alleged that respondents had deprived Joshua of his liberty without due process of law, in violation of his rights under the Fourteenth Amendment, by failing to protect him against a risk of violence at his father's hands of which they knew or should have known. The District Court granted summary judgment for respondents.

The Court of Appeals for the Seventh Circuit affirmed . . . .

Because of the inconsistent approaches taken by the lower courts in determining when, if ever, the failure of a state or local governmental entity or its agents to provide an individual with adequate protective services constitutes a violation of the individuals due process rights

. . . and the importance of the issue to the administration of state and local governments, we granted certiorari. We now affirm.

II.

The Due Process Clause of the Fourteenth Amendment provides that ''[n]o State shall . . . deprive any person of life, liberty, or property, without due process of law.'' Petitioners contend that the State deprived Joshua of his liberty interest in ''free[dom] from . . . unjustified intrusions on person security,'' . . . by failing to provide him with adequate protection against his father's violence. The claim is one invoking the substantive rather than procedural component of the Due Process Clause; petitioners do not claim that the State denied Joshua protection without according him appropriate procedural safeguards, . . . but that it was categorically obliged to protect him in these circumstances, see Youngberg v. Romeo (1982).

But nothing in the language of the Due Process Clause itself requires the State to protect the life, liberty, and property of its citizens against invasion by private actors. The Clause is phrased as a limitation on the State's power to act, not as a guarantee of certain minimal levels of safety and security. It forbids the State itself to deprive individuals of life, liberty or property without ''due process of law,'' but its language cannot fairly be extended to impose an affirmative obligation on the State to ensure that those interests do not come to harm through other means. Nor does history support such an expansive reading of the constitutional text. Like its counterpart in the Fifth Amendment, the Due Process Clause of the Fourteenth Amendment was intended to prevent government ''from abusing [its] power, or employing it as an instrument of oppression." . . . Its purpose was to protect the people of the State, not to ensure that the State protected them from each other. The Framers were content to leave the extent of governmental obligation in the latter area to the democratic political processes.

Consistent with these principles, our cases have recognized that the Due Process Clauses generally confer no affirmative right to governmental aid, even where such aid may be necessary to secure life, liberty or property interest of which the government itself may not deprive the individual. See, e. g., Harris v. McRae (1980) (no obligation to fund abortions or other medical services) (discussing Due Process Clause of Fifth Amendment); Lindsey v. Normet (1972) (no obligation to provide adequate housing) (discussing Due Process Clause of Fourteenth Amendment); see also Youngberg v. Romeo [1982] (''As a general matter, a State is under no constitutional duty to provide substantive services for those within its border.''). As we said in Harris v. McRae, ''[a]lthough the liberty protected by the Due Process Clause affords protection against unwarranted *government* interference . . ., it does not confer an entitlement to such [governmental aid] as may be necessary to realize all the advantages of that freedom.'' (emphasis added). If the Due Process Clause does not require the State to provide its citizens with particular protective services, it follows that the State cannot be held liable under the Clause for injuries that could have been averted had it chosen to provide them. As a general matter, then, we conclude that a State's failure to protect an individual against private violence simply does not constitute a violation of the Due Process Clause.

Petitioners contend, however, that even if the Due Process Clause imposes no affirmative obligation on the State to provide the general public with adequate protective services, such a duty may arise out of certain "special relationships" created or assumed by the State with respect to particular individuals. Petitioners argue that such a "special relationship" existed here because the State knew that Joshua faced a special danger of abuse at his father's hands, and specifically proclaimed, by word and by deed, its intention to protect him against that danger. Having actually undertaken to protect Joshua from this danger—which petitioner concedes the State played no part in creating—the State acquired an affirmative "duty," enforceable through the Due Process Clause, to do so in a reasonably competent fashion. Its failure to discharge that duty, so the argument goes, was an abuse of governmental power that so "shocks the conscience," Rochin v. California (1952), as to constitute a substantive due process violation.

We reject this argument. It is true that in certain limited circumstances the Constitution imposes upon the State affirmative duties of care and protection with respect to particular individuals. In Estelle v. Gamble (1976), we recognized that the Eighth Amendment's prohibition against cruel and unusual punishment, made applicable to the States through the Fourteenth Amendment's Due Process Clause, ... requires the State to provide adequate medical care to incarcerated prisoners. We reasoned that because the prisoner is unable " 'by reason of the deprivation of his liberty [to] care for himself,' " it is only " 'just' " that the State be required to care for him.

In Youngberg v. Romeo (1982), we extended this analysis beyond the Eighth Amendment setting, holding that the substantive component of the Fourteenth Amendment's Due Process Clause requires the State to provide involuntarily committed mental patients with such services as are necessary to ensure their "reasonable safety" from themselves and others. ... As we explained, "[i]f it is cruel and unusual punishment to hold convicted criminals in unsafe conditions, it must be unconstitutional [under the Due Process Clause] to confine the involuntarily committed—who may not be punished at all—in unsafe conditions." ...

But these cases afford petitioners no help. Taken together, they stand only for the proposition that when the State takes a person into its custody and holds him there against his will, the Constitution imposes upon it a corresponding duty to assume some responsibility for his safety and general well-being. ... The rationale for this principle is simple enough: when the State by the affirmative exercise of its power so restrains an individual's liberty that it renders him unable to care for himself, and at the same time fails to provide for his basic human needs—e.g., food, clothing, shelter, medical care, and reasonable safety—it transgresses the substantive limits on state action set by the Eighth Amendment and the Due Process Clause. ... The affirmative duty to protect arises not from the State's knowledge of the individual's predicament or from its expressions of intent to help him, but from the limitations which it has imposed on his freedom to act on his own behalf. ... In the substantive due process analysis, it is the State's affirmative act of restraining the individual's freedom to act on his own behalf—through incarceration, institutionalization, or other similar restraint of personal liberty—which is the "deprivation of liberty" triggering the protections of the Due Process Clause, not its failure to act to protect his liberty interests against harms inflicted by other means.

The Estelle-Youngberg analysis simply has no applicability in the present case.

Petitioners concede that the harms Joshua suffered did not occur while he was in the State's custody, but while he was in the custody of his natural father, who was in no sense a state actor. While the State may have been aware of the dangers that Joshua faced in the free world, it played no part in their creation, nor did it do anything to render him any more vulnerable to them. That the State once took temporary custody of Joshua does not alter the analysis, for when it returned him to his father's custody, it placed him in no worse position than that in which he would have been had it not acted at all; the State does not become the permanent guarantor of an individual's safety by having once offered him shelter. Under these circumstances, the State had no constitutional duty to protect Joshua. . . . A state may, through its courts and legislatures, impose such affirmative duties of care and protection upon its agents as it wishes. But not "all common-law duties owed by government actors were . . . constitutionalized by the Fourteenth Amendment." Because, as explained above, the State had no constitutional duty to protect Joshua against his father's violence, its failure to do so—though calamitous in hindsight—simply does not constitute a violation of the Due Process Clause.

Judges and lawyers, like other humans, are moved by natural sympathy in a case like this to find a way for Joshua and his mother to receive adequate compensation for the grievous harm inflicted upon them. But before yielding to that impulse, it is well to remember once again that the harm was inflicted not by the State of Wisconsin, but by Joshua's father. The most that can be said of the state functionaries in this case is that they stood by and did nothing when suspicious circumstances dictated a more active role for them. In defense of them it must also be said that had they moved too soon to take custody of the son away from the father, they would likely have been met with charges of improperly intruding into the parent-child relationship, charges based on the same Due Process Clause that forms the basis for the present charge of failure to provide adequate protection.

The people of Wisconsin may well prefer a system of liability which would place upon the State and its officials the responsibility for failure to act in situations such as the present one. They may create such a system, if they do not have it already, by changing the tort law of the State in accordance with the regular law-making process. But they should not have it thrust upon them by this Court's expansion of the Due Process Clause of the Fourteenth Amendment.

Affirmed.

Justice **Brennan**, with whom Justice **Marshall** and Justice **Blackmun** joined, dissented, saying in part:

"The most that can be said of the state functionaries in this case," the Court today concludes, "is that they stood by and did nothing when suspicious circumstances dictated a more active role for them." Because I believe that this description of respondents' conduct tells only part of the story and that, accordingly, the Constitution itself "dictated a more active role" for respondents in the circumstances presented here, I cannot agree that respondents had no constitutional duty to help Joshua DeShaney. . . .

The Court's baseline is the absence of positive rights in the Constitution and a concomitant suspicion of any claim that seems to depend on such rights. From this perspective, the DeShaney's claim is first and foremost about inaction (the failure, here, of respondents to take steps to protect Joshua), and only tangentially about action (the establishment of a state program specifically designed to help children like Joshua.) And from this perspective, holding these Wisconsin officials liable—where the only difference between this case and one involving a general claim to protective services is Wisconsin's establishment and operation of a program to protect children—would seem to punish an effort that we should seek to promote. . . .

Because of the Court's initial fixation on the general principle that the Constitution does not establish positive rights, it is unable to appreciate our recognition in Estelle and Youngberg that this principle does not hold true in all circumstances. Thus, in the Court's view, Youngberg can be explained (and dismissed) in the following way: "In the substantive due process analysis, it is the State's affirmative act of restraining the individual's freedom to act on his own behalf—through incarceration, institutionalization, or other similar restraint of personal liberty—which is the 'deprivation of liberty' triggering the protection of the Due Process Clause, not its failure to act to protect his liberty interests against harms inflicted by other means." This restatement of Youngberg's holding should come as a surprise when one recalls our explicit observation in that case that Romeo did not challenge his commitment to the hospital, but instead "argue[d] that he had a constitutionally protected liberty interest in safety, freedom of movement, and training within the institution; and that petitioners infringed these rights *by failing to provide* constitutionally required conditions of confinement." (emphasis added). I do not mean to suggest that "the State's affirmative act of restraining the individual's freedom to act on his own behalf" was irrelevant in Youngberg; rather I emphasize that this conduct would have led to no injury, and consequently no cause of action under § 1983, unless the State then had failed to take steps to protect Romeo from himself and from others. In addition, the Court's exclusive attention to State-imposed restraints of "the individual's freedom to act on his own behalf" suggests that it was the State that rendered Romeo unable to care for himself, whereas in fact—with an I. Q. of between 8 and 10, and the mental capacity of an 18-month-old child—he had been quite incapable of taking care of himself long before the State stepped into his life. Thus, the fact of hospitalization was critical in Youngberg not because it rendered Romeo helpless to help himself, but because it separated him from other sources of aid that, we held, the State was obligated to replace. Unlike the Court, therefore, I am unable to see in Youngberg a neat and decisive divide between action and inaction.

Moreover, to the Court, the only fact that seems to count as an "affirmative act of restraining the individual's freedom to act on his own behalf" is direct physical control. . . . I would not, however, give Youngberg and Estelle such a stingy scope. I would recognize, as the Court apparently cannot, that "the State's knowledge of [an] individual's predicament [and] its expression of intent to help him" can amount to a "limitation of his freedom to act on his own behalf" or to obtain help from others. Thus, I would read Youngberg and Estelle to stand for a much more generous proposition that, if a State cuts off private sources of aid and then refuses aid itself, it cannot wash its hands of the harm that results from its inaction. . . .

Wisconsin has established a child-welfare system specifically designed to help children like Joshua. Wisconsin law places upon the local department of social services such as respondent (DSS or Department) a duty to investigate reported instances of child abuse. While other governmental bodies and private persons are largely responsible for the reporting of possible cases of child abuse, Wisconsin law channels all such reports to the local department of social services for evaluation and, if necessary, further action. Even when it is the sheriff's office or police department that receives a report of suspected child abuse, that report is referred to local social services departments for action; the only exception to this occurs when the reporter fears for the child's *immediate* safety. In this way, Wisconsin law invites—indeed, directs—citizens and other governmental entities to depend on local departments of social services such as respondent to protect children from abuse.

The specific facts before us bear out this view of Wisconsin's system of protecting children. Each time someone voiced a suspicion that Joshua was being abused, that information was relayed to the Department for investigation and possible action. When Randy DeShaney's second wife told the police that he had " 'hit the boy causing marks and [was] a prime case for child abuse,' " the police referred her complaint to DSS. When, on three separate occasions, emergency room personnel noticed suspicious injuries on Joshua's body, they went to DSS with this information. When neighbors informed the police that they had seen or heard Joshua's father or his father's lover beating or otherwise abusing Joshua, the police brought these reports to the attention of DSS. And when respondent Kemmeter, through these reports and through her own observations in the course of nearly 20 visits to the DeShaney home, compiled growing evidence that Joshua was being abused, that information stayed within the Department—chronicled by the social worker in detail that seems almost eerie in light of her failure to act upon it. (As to the extent of the social worker's involvement in and knowledge of Joshua's predicament, her reaction to the news of Joshua's last and most devastating injuries is illuminating: "I just knew the phone would ring some day and Joshua would be dead.")

Even more telling than these examples is the Department's control over the decision whether to take steps to protect a particular child from suspected abuse. While many different people contributed information and advice to this decision, it was up the people at DSS to make the ultimate decision (subject to the approval of the local government's Corporation Counsel) whether to disturb the family's current arrangements. When Joshua first appeared at a local hospital with injuries signaling physical abuse, for example, it was DSS that made the decision to take him into temporary custody for the purpose of studying his situation—and it was DSS, acting in conjunction with the Corporation Counsel, that returned him to his father. Unfortunately for Joshua DeShaney, the buck effectively stopped with the Department.

In these circumstances, a private citizen, or even a person working in a government agency other than DSS, would doubtless feel that her job was done as soon as she had reported her suspicions of child abuse to DSS. Through its child-welfare program, in other words, the State of Wisconsin has relieved ordinary citizens and governmental bodies other than the Department of any sense of obligation to do anything more than report their suspicions of child abuse to DSS. If DSS ignores or dismisses these suspicions, no one will step in to fill the gap. Wisconsin's child-protection program thus effectively confined Joshua DeShaney within the walls of Randy DeShaney's violent home until such time as DSS took action to remove him. Conceivably, then, children like Joshua are made worse off by the existence of this program when the persons and entities charged with carrying it out fail to do their jobs.

It simply belies reality, therefore, to contend that the State "stood by and did nothing" with respect to Joshua. Through its child-protection program, the State actively intervened in Joshua's life and, by virtue of this intervention, acquired ever more certain knowledge that Joshua was in grave danger. These circumstances, in my view, plant this case solidly within the tradition of cases like Youngberg and Estelle.

Justice **Blackmun**, dissenting, said in part:

Today, the Court purports to be the dispassionate oracle of the law, unmoved by "natural sympathy." But, in this pretense, the Court itself retreats into a sterile formalism which prevents it from recognizing either the facts of the case before it or the legal norms that should apply to those facts. As Justice Brennan demonstrates, the facts here involve not merely passivity, but active state intervention in the life of Joshua DeShaney—intervention that triggered a fundamental duty to aid the by once the State learned of the severe danger to which he was exposed.

The Court fails to recognize this duty because it attempts to draw a sharp and rigid line between action and inaction. But such formalistic reasoning has no place in the interpretation of the broad and stirring clauses of the Fourteenth Amendment. Indeed, I submit that these clauses were designed, at least in part, to undo the formalistic legal reasoning that infected antebellum jurisprudence, which the late Professor Robert Cover analyzed so effectively in his significant work entitled Justice Accused (1975).

Like the antebellum judges who denied relief to fugitive slaves, the Court today claims that its decision, however harsh, is compelled by existing legal doctrine. On the contrary, the question presented by this case is an open one, and our Fourteenth Amendment precedents may be read more broadly or narrowly depending upon how one chooses to read them. Faced with the choice, I would adopt a "sympathetic" reading, one which comports with dictates of fundamental justice and recognizes that compassion need not be exiled from the province of judging.

E. The Changing Nature of Human Rights

ROE v. WADE

410 U. S. 113; 35 L. Ed. 2d 147; 93 S. Ct. 705 (1973)

"The Court today does *not* pick out particular human activities, characterize them as 'fundamental,' and give them added protection. . . . To the contrary, the Court simply recognizes, as it must, an established constitutional right, and gives to that right no less protection than the Constitution itself demands."

Although this quotation from Justice Stewart by the Court in San Antonio v. Rodriguez

(1973) states the orthodox view of the Court's role, few scholars today would subscribe to it. While in theory all rights in the Constitution are of equal value (the Constitution nowhere suggests that some rights are more important than others), over the years the Court has always cherished certain rights which it considered more important than other rights and hence entitled to greater constitutional protection. The rights so honored have changed from time to time as the Court perceived changes in basic social values. In the early days private property was given special consideration, and later this came to include the rights of businessmen and "liberty of contract." Then in the 1930s and 1940s, while the economic rights fell from grace, the rights listed in the First Amendment rose to favor. In recent years the rights of privacy and the right to vote have vied for membership in the ranks of the elite.

Since the ranking of these rights is a matter of value judgment, it has been condemned by those who disapproved the particular ranking as "judicial legislation," "substituting judicial values for those of the community," a "violation of the democratic process," and a "lack of proper judicial restraint." While such attacks seem to challenge the role of the Court in this area, in fact few justices have rejected philosophically the idea that some rights are more important than others. The classic example is Justice Holmes, who condemned the judicial favoritism shown to economic rights (see Lochner v. New York, 1905) while insisting that speech could be curtailed only if it presented a "clear and present danger" (see his dissent in Gitlow v. New York, 1925).

Perhaps the easiest method of giving added protection to a right, once it is identified, is to clothe it in language that nullifies the normal presumption in favor of legislative acts and forces the government to show that its laws are reasonable and necessary. Such language abounds in the areas of the First Amendment: the "clear and present danger" test, the statement that First Amendment rights are in a "preferred position" (Murdock v. Pennsylvania, 1943) and the rule (since modified) that publications cannot be condemned as obscene unless they are utterly without redeeming social value—all serve to tip the scales in favor of the right and against the government wishing to suppress or regulate it.

In 1960 in Bates v. Little Rock a new phrase made its appearance. The Court held bad the demand of the city of Little Rock for the publication of the membership lists of the NAACP on the ground that it would destroy the group's organizational privacy and impair its operations. "Where there is a significant encroachment upon personal liberty, the State may prevail only upon showing a subordinating interest which is compelling." This "compelling state interest" phrase appeared again in several cases in 1963 (see Gibson v. Florida Investigating Committee), where its impact was to make the state produce evidence that it had a compelling interest which could be met only by infringing a claimed right of association. In none of the cases was sufficient interest shown.

In 1969 the "compelling state interest" doctrine was applied to the equal protection clause. The Court in this area had long granted favored status to certain bases of classification, such as race and religion, holding that legislative distinctions based on them were, if not "invidious," at least "inherently suspect." But with Shapiro v. Thompson and Kramer v. U.S.F.D. the Court looked not at the bases of classification alone, but at the aims sought to be achieved by these bases. In striking down the requirement of a year's residence to receive welfare and the requirement of taxpayer (or parental) status to vote in school board elections, the Court found that where a classification limits the right to move freely across state lines or the right to vote, it could only be justified by a compelling state interest.

In the case below, the phrase is moved again—this time into the area of privacy protected by the Constitution. Here the Court not only upholds the right of a mother to decide, in consultation with her doctor, whether or not to have an abortion, but spells out the "compelling points" at which the state's "compelling interest" permits it to undertake regulation of abortions.

One of the anomalies of the Court's technique of expanding the protection of human rights has been its unwillingness to use those clauses of the Constitution that seem to provide the most flexibility. As early as 1873 in the Slaughter-House Cases it rejected the idea that the "privileges and immunities" clause of the Fourteenth Amendment had any substantive content and all efforts to persuade it to open up this clause have failed. In contrast, two years later, when what the Court considered to be an important right could not be brought under any existing constitutional guarantee, the Court turned to what it conceived to be the general or fundamental principles of the Constitution to supply the necessary protection. In Loan Association v. Topeka (1875) the Court forbade spending tax money for private purposes on the ground that it violated limits on governmental power that "grow out of the essential nature of all free governments." With the evolution of the due process clause, this right became an element of due process of law.

Even more anomalous has been its total unwillingness to give content to the Ninth Amendment. This Amendment, the last of the personal guarantees of the Bill of Rights, provides that "the enumeration in the Constitution, of certain rights, shall not be construed to deny or disparage others retained by the people." By implication certain unnamed rights are retained by the people and presumably entitled to the same protection by the Court as those which were enumerated. But while the Court has willingly given the widest interpretation to a legalistic phrase like "due process of law," it has never handed down a decision interpreting the Ninth Amendment.

The closest the Court has come to giving substance to this amendment came in Griswold v. Connecticut (1965), a case in which the Court extended judicial protection to a "right of privacy." This right, the Court found, was the cumulative result of "penumbras, formed by emanations from those [Bill of Rights] guarantees that help give them life and substance. . . . Various guarantees create zones of privacy. The right of association contained in the penumbra of the First Amendment is one . . . . The Third Amendment in its prohibition against the quartering of soldiers 'in any house' in time of peace without the consent of the owner is another facet of that privacy. The Fourth Amendment explicitly affirms the 'right of the people to be secure in their persons, houses, papers, and effects, against unreasonable searches and seizures.' The Fifth Amendment in its Self-Incrimination Clause enables the citizen to create a zone of privacy which government may not force him to surrender to his detriment. The Ninth Amendment provides: 'The enumeration in the Constitution, of certain rights, shall not be construed to deny or disparage others retained by the people.' . . . The present case, then, concerns a relationship lying within the zone of privacy created by several fundamental constitutional guarantees."

Griswold involved the validity of a Connecticut statute which forbade the use of birth control techniques, or giving aid or advice to persons regarding their use. In holding the statute void the Court rejected out of hand the idea that the police "would be allowed to search the sacred precincts of marital bedrooms for telltale signs of the use of contraceptives." Three members of the majority noted that ignoring a "right so basic and fundamental and so deep-rooted in our society as the right of privacy in marriage" would be to "ignore the Ninth Amendment and to give it no effect whatsoever." They stressed, however, that the Ninth Amendment did not constitute an independent source of rights protected from either state or federal government, but merely that "fundamental rights exist that are not expressly enumerated in the first eight amendments" and that "the list of rights included there [should] not be deemed exhaustive."

The extension of the right to privacy to include a woman's right to have an abortion triggered a highly emotional nationwide political battle. With the political and financial support of "anti-abortion" and "right to life" groups, efforts were made to overturn or undo the effects of the case by constitutional amendment, by Congressional statutes defining a fetus as a "person" entitled to due process of law, and by various procedural statutes designed to prevent federal courts from enforcing its ruling.

While such direct limitations were generally unavailing, an approach which struck at the public financing of such abortions proved remarkably successful. In Beal v. Doe (1977), the Court held the Medicaid provisions of the Social Security Act did not require the financing of nontherapeutic abortions, although a state was free to provide such funding under Medicaid if it wished; then in Maher v. Roe, decided the same day, it held that a state was under no obligation to finance therapeutic abortions merely because it elected to finance normal childbirth. And in Poelker v. Doe (1977), it held that a city hospital had no constitutional obligation to provide nontherapeutic abortions. "We merely hold, for the reasons stated in Maher, that the Constitution does not forbid a State or city, pursuant to democratic processes, from expressing a preference for normal childbirth as St. Louis has done."

So successful was the technique of withholding funding in the actual limitation of abortions that in 1976 Representative Hyde of Illinois introduced the first of the so-called "Hyde Amendments" to the appropriation acts providing funding for Medicaid, a scheme by which the federal government provides financial help to states that volunteer to provide to the needy certain medically necessary professional services. The 1980 version of the amendment forbids the use of federal funds to perform abortions except "where the life of the mother would be endangered if the fetus were carried to term" or the pregnancy was the result of rape or incest promptly reported to the proper authorities. The result was to forbid the financing of abortions even when they are deemed "medically necessary."

Many states passed their own version of the Hyde Amendment to stop the funding of abortions. In Harris v. McRae (1980) the Court upheld one such state law, holding that the state's obligation to provide necessary medical services "does not require a participating State to pay for those medically necessary abortions for which federal reimbursement is unavailable under the Hyde Amendment." Quoting with approval from Maher, the Court again stressed that "although Congress has opted to subsidize medically necessary services generally, but not certain medically necessary abortions, the fact remains that the Hyde Amendment leaves an indigent woman with at least the same range of choice in deciding whether to obtain a medically necessary abortion as she would have had if Congress had chosen to subsidize no health care costs at all."

Although these "funding" cases authorized the states effectively to deny abortions to the largest group of women seeking them—the poor, the Court in 1983 reaffirmed Roe v. Wade. At the same time, however, the Court permitted additional limitations on the right. Justice Powell, speaking for six members of the Court in Akron v. Akron Center for Reproductive Health, noted that "the doctrine of stare decisis . . . demands respect in a society governed by the rule of law," and in a footnote added: "There are especially compelling reasons for adhering to stare decisis in applying the principles of Roe v. Wade. That case was considered with special care. It was first argued during the 1971 Term, and reargued—with extensive briefing—the following term. The decision was joined by the Chief Justice and six other Justices. Since Roe was decided in February 1973, the Court repeatedly and consistently has accepted and applied the basic principle that a woman has a fundamental right to make the highly personal choice whether or not to terminate her pregnancy. . . ."

In Planned Parenthood v. Ashcroft (1983) the Court conceded that the compelling interest of the state entitled it to ban abortions entirely once the fetus became viable, and Missouri had done so except to preserve the life or health of the mother. Hence it was not unreasonable to require the presence of a second physician to care for the fetus, since the attending physician would be occupied with the care of the mother. Moreover, the requirement of parental or judicial consent for a minor to have an abortion and the further requirement that the court deny such request only for "good cause," was valid since it sufficiently protected both the interest of the pregnant minor herself and the state's legitimate interest in protecting immature minors generally.

The retirement of Chief Justice Burger and Justice Powell and their replacement by Justices Scalia and Kennedy drastically altered the prognosis for Roe v. Wade. In Webster v. Reproductive Services (1989) the Court confronted a challenge to a Missouri statute avowedly designed to limit the right of abortion as much as possible. While the statute forbade the use of public money or personnel to either encourage or perform abortions not necessary to the life of the mother, its critical provision required the performance of elaborate and expensive tests on a woman 20 weeks or more pregnant to determine if the fetus were viable. Since this involved tests during the second trimester when few if any fetuses are viable, Justices Rehnquist, White and Kennedy felt that Roe's rigid trimester rule should be abandoned, while Justice Scalia felt Roe should be overruled. Justice O'Connor, while holding that the tests were not unduly burdensome and therefore valid, felt Roe should not be disturbed. Justice Blackmun, writing for Justices Brennan, Marshall, and (on the crucial issue) Stevens, argued that permitting Missouri to regulate abortions during the second trimester "in the interest of potential life" effectively overruled Roe v. Wade.

Justice Brennan, one of the Court's staunchest defenders of Roe v. Wade, retired from the Court at the close of the 1989 term. On October 8, 1990, he was replaced by Justice David H. Souter.

In the present case an unidentified unmarried pregnant woman (called Jane Roe) was confronted with a Texas law which made it a crime to procure an abortion, or attempt one, except with respect to "an abortion procured or attempted by medical advice for the purpose of saving the life of the mother." She asked a declaratory judgment that the law was void and an injunction against its enforcement.

Mr. Justice **Blackmun** delivered the opinion of the Court, saying in part:

V.

The principal thrust of appellant's attack on the Texas statutes is that they improperly invade a right, said to be possessed by the pregnant woman, to choose to terminate her pregnancy. Appellant would discover this right in the concept of personal ''liberty'' embodied in the Fourteenth Amendment's Due Process Clause; or in personal, marital, familial, and sexual privacy said to be protected by the Bill of Rights or its penumbras, see Griswold v. Connecticut (1965); Eisenstadt v. Baird (1972) (White, J., concurring); or among those rights reserved to the people by the Ninth Amendment, Griswold v. Connecticut (Goldberg, J., concurring). Before addressing this claim, we feel it desirable briefly to survey, in several aspects, the history of abortion, for such insight as that history may afford us, and then to examine the state purposes and interests behind the criminal abortion laws.

VI.

It perhaps is not generally appreciated that the restrictive criminal abortion laws in effect in a majority of States today are of relatively recent vintage. Those laws, generally proscribing abortion or its attempt at any time during pregnancy except when necessary to preserve the pregnant woman's life, are not of ancient or even of common law origin. Instead, they derive from statutory changes effected, for the most part, in the latter half of the 19th century. . . .

[The Court here reviews the history of attitudes toward abortion and abortion laws since ancient times.]

VII.

Three reasons have been advanced to explain historically the enactment of criminal abortion laws in the 19th century and to justify their continued existence.

It has been argued occasionally that these laws were the product of a Victorian social concern to discourage illicit sexual conduct. Texas, however, does not advance this justification in the present case, and it appears that no court or commentator has taken the argument seriously. The appellants and amici contend, moreover, that this is not a proper state purpose at all and suggest that, if it were, the Texas statutes are overbroad in protecting it since the law fails to distinguish between married and unwed mothers.

A second reason is concerned with abortion as a medical procedure. When most criminal abortion laws were first enacted, the procedure was a hazardous one for the woman. This was particularly true prior to the development of antisepsis. Antiseptic techniques, of course, were based on discoveries by Lister, Pasteur, and others first announced in 1867, but were not generally accepted and employed until about the turn of the century. Abortion mortality was high. Even after 1900, and perhaps until as late as the development of antibiotics in the 1940's, standard modern techniques such as dilation and curettage were not nearly so safe as they are today. Thus it has been argued that a State's real concern in enacting a criminal abortion law was to protect the pregnant woman, that is, to restrain her from submitting to a procedure that placed her life in serious jeopardy.

Modern medical techniques have altered this situation. Appellants and various amici refer to medical data indicating that abortion in early pregnancy, that is, prior to the end of first trimester, although not without its risk, is now relatively safe. Mortality rates for women undergoing early abortions, where the procedure is legal, appear to be as low as or lower than the rates for normal childbirth. Consequently, any interest of the State in protecting the woman from an inherently hazardous procedure, except when it would be equally dangerous for her to forego it, has largely disappeared. Of course, important state interests in the area of health and medical standards do remain. The State has a legitimate interest in seeing to it that abortion, like any other medical procedure, is performed under circumstances that insure maximum safety for the patient. This interest obviously extends at least to the performing physician and his staff, to the facilities involved, to the availability of after-care, and to adequate provision for any complication or emergency that might arise. The prevalence of high mortality rates at illegal "abortion mills" strengthens, rather than weakens, the State's interest in regulating the conditions under which abortions are performed. Moreover, the risk to the woman increases as her pregnancy continues. Thus the State retains a definite interest in protecting the woman's own health and safety when an abortion is proposed at a late stage of pregnancy.

The third reason is the State's interest—some phrase it in terms of duty—in protecting prenatal life. Some of the argument for this justification rests on the theory that a new human life is present from the moment of conception. The State's interest and general obligation to protect life then extends, it is argued, to prenatal life. Only when the life of the pregnant mother herself is at stake, balanced against the life she carries within her, should the interest of the embryo or fetus not prevail. Logically, of course, a legitimate State interest in this area need not stand or fall on acceptance of the belief that life begins at conception or at some other point prior to live birth. In assessing the State's interest, recognition may be given to the less rigid claim that as long as at least *potential* life is involved, the State may assert interests beyond the protection of the pregnant woman alone.

Parties challenging state abortion laws have sharply disputed in some courts the contention that a purpose of these laws, when enacted, was to protect prenatal life. . . .

It is with these interests, and the weight to be attached to them, that this case is concerned.

VIII.

The Constitution does not explicitly mention any right of privacy. In a line of decisions, however, going back perhaps as far as Union Pacific R. Co. v. Botsford (1891), the Court has recognized that a right of personal privacy, or a guarantee of certain areas or zones of privacy, does exist under the Constitution. In varying contexts the Court or individual Justices have indeed found at least the roots of that right in the First Amendment, Stanley v. Georgia (1969); in the Fourth and Fifth Amendments, Terry v. Ohio (1968), Katz v. United States (1967) . . . ; in the penumbras of the Bill of Rights, Griswold v. Connecticut (1965); in the Ninth Amendment; or in the concept of liberty guaranteed by the first section of the Fourteenth Amendment, see Meyer v. Nebraska (1923). These decisions make it clear that only personal rights that can be deemed "fundamental" or "implicit in the concept of ordered liberty," Palko v. Connecticut (1937), are included in this guarantee of personal privacy. They also make it clear that the right has some extension to activities relating to marriage, Loving v. Virginia (1967), procreation, Skinner v. Oklahoma (1942), contraception, Eisenstadt v. Baird (1972). . . .

This right of privacy, whether it be founded in the Fourteenth Amendment's concept of personal liberty and restrictions upon state action, as we feel it is, or, as the District Court determined, in the Ninth Amendment's reservation of rights to the people, is broad enough to encompass a woman's decision whether or not to terminate her pregnancy. The detriment that the State would impose upon the pregnant woman by denying this choice altogether is apparent. Specific and direct harm medically diagnosable even in early pregnancy may be involved. Maternity, or additional offspring, may force upon the woman a distressful life and future. Psychological harm may be imminent. Mental and physical health may be taxed by child care. There is also the distress, for all concerned, associated with the unwanted child, and there is the problem of bringing a child into a family already unable, psychologically and otherwise, to care for it. In other cases, as in this one, the additional difficulties and continuing stigma of unwed motherhood may be involved. All these are factors the woman and her responsible physician necessarily will consider in consultation.

On the basis of elements such as these, appellants and some amici argue that the woman's right is absolute and that she is entitled to terminate her pregnancy at whatever time, in whatever way, and for whatever reason she alone chooses. With this we do not agree. Appellants' arguments that Texas either has no valid interest at all in regulating the abortion decision, or no interest strong enough to support any limitation upon the woman's sole determination, is unpersuasive. The Court's decisions recognizing a right of privacy also acknowledge that some state regulation in areas protected by that right is appropriate. As noted above, a State may properly assert important interests in safeguarding health, in maintaining medical standards, and in protecting potential life. At some point in pregnancy, these respective interests become sufficiently compelling to sustain regulation of the factors that govern the abortion decision. The privacy right involved, therefore, cannot be said to be absolute. In fact, it is not clear to us that the claim asserted by some amici that one has an unlimited right to do with one's body as one pleases bears a close relationship to the right of privacy previously articulated in the Court's decisions. The Court has refused to recognize an unlimited right of this kind in the past. Jacobson v. Massachusetts (1905) (vaccination); Buck v. Bell (1927) (sterilization).

We therefore conclude that the right of personal privacy includes the abortion decision, but that this right is not unqualified and must be considered against state interests in regulation.

Where certain ''fundamental rights'' are involved, the Court has held that regulation limiting these rights may be justified only by a ''compelling state interest,'' Kramer v. Union Free School District (1969), Shapiro v. Thompson (1969), . . . , and that legislative enactments must be narrowly drawn to express only the legitimate state interests at stake. Griswold v. Connecticut (1965). . . .

IX.

The District Court held that the appellee failed to meet his burden of demonstrating that the Texas statute's infringement upon Roe's rights was necessary to support a compelling state interest. . . . Appellee argues that the State's determination to recognize and protect prenatal life from and after conception constitutes a compelling state interest. As noted above, we do not agree fully with either formulation.

A. The appellee and certain amici argue that the fetus is a ''person'' within the language and meaning of the Fourteenth Amendment. In support of this they outline at length and in detail the well-known facts of fetal development. If this suggestion of personhood is established, the appellant's case, of course, collapses, for the fetus' right to life is then guaranteed specifically by the Amendment. The appellant conceded as much on reargument. On the other hand, the appellee conceded on reargument that no case could be cited that holds that a fetus is a person within the meaning of the Fourteenth Amendment.

The Constitution does not define ''person'' in so many words. Section 1 of the Fourteenth Amendment contains three references to "person." The first, in defining "citizens," speaks of "persons born or naturalized in the United States." The word also appears both in the Due Process Clause and in the Equal Protection Clause. "Person" is used in other places in the Constitution. . . . But in nearly all these instances, the use of the word is such that it has application only postnatally. None indicates, with any assurance, that it has any possible pre-natal application.* All this, together with our observation, that throughout the major portion of the 19th century prevailing legal abortion practices were far freer than they are today, persuades us that the word "person," as used in the Fourteenth Amendment, does not include the unborn. . . .

B. The pregnant woman cannot be isolated in her privacy. She carries an embryo and, later, a fetus, if one accepts the medical definitions of the developing young in the human uterus. . . . The situation therefore is inherently different from marital intimacy, or bedroom possession of obscene material, or marriage, or procreation, or education, with which Eisenstadt, Griswold, Stanley, Loving, Skinner, Pierce, and Meyer were respectively concerned. As we have intimated above, it is reasonable and appropriate for a State to decide that at some point in time another interest, that of health of the mother or that of potential human life, becomes significantly involved. The woman's privacy is no longer sole and any right of privacy she possesses must be measured accordingly.

Texas urges that, apart from the Fourteenth Amendment, life begins at conception and is present throughout pregnancy, and that, therefore, the State has a compelling interest in protecting that life from and after conception. We need not resolve the difficult question of when life begins. When those trained in the respective disciplines of medicine, philosophy, and theology are unable to arrive at any consensus, the judiciary, at this point in the development of man's knowledge, is not in a position to speculate as to the answer.

It should be sufficient to note briefly the wide divergence of thinking on this most sensitive and difficult question. . . .

X.

In view of all this, we do not agree that, by adopting one theory of life, Texas may override the rights of the pregnant woman that are at stake. We repeat, however, that the State does have an important and legitimate interest in preserving and protecting the health of the pregnant woman, whether she be a resident of the State or a nonresident who seeks medical consultation and treatment there, and that it has still *another* important and legitimate interest in protecting the potentiality of human life. These interests are separate and distinct. Each grows in substantiality as the woman approaches term and, at a point during pregnancy, each becomes "compelling."

With respect to the State's important and legitimate interest in the health of the mother,

---

*When Texas urges that a fetus is entitled to Fourteenth Amendment protection as a person, it faces a dilemma. Neither in Texas nor in any other State are all abortions prohibited. Despite broad proscription, an exception always exists. The exception contained in Art. 1196, for an abortion procured or attempted by medical advice for the purpose of saving the life of the mother, is typical. But if the fetus is a person who is not to be deprived of life without due process of law, and if the mother's condition is the sole determinant, does not the Texas exception appear to be out of line with the Amendment's command? . . .

the "compelling" point, in the light of present medical knowledge, is at approximately the end of the first trimester. This is so because of the now established medical fact, referred to above . . . that until the end of the first trimester mortality in abortion is less than mortality in normal childbirth. It follows that, from and after this point, a State may regulate the abortion procedure to the extent that the regulation reasonably relates to the preservation and protection of maternal health. Examples of permissible state regulation in this area are requirements as to the qualifications of the person who is to perform the abortion; as to the licensure of that person; as to the facility in which the procedure is to be performed, that is, whether it must be a hospital or may be a clinic or some other place of less-than-hospital status; as to the licensing of the facility; and the like.

This means, on the other hand, that, for the period of pregnancy prior to this "compelling" point, the attending physician, in consultation with his patient, is free to determine, without regulation by the State, that in his medical judgment the patient's pregnancy should be terminated. If that decision is reached, the judgment may be effectuated by an abortion free of interference by the State.

With respect to the State's important and legitimate interest in potential life, the "compelling" point is at viability. This is so because the fetus then presumably has the capability of meaningful life outside the mother's womb. State regulation protective of fetal life after viability thus has both logical and biological justifications. If the State is interested in protecting fetal life after viability, it may go so far as to proscribe abortion during that period except when it is necessary to preserve the life or health of the mother.

Measured against these standards, the Texas Penal Code, in restricting legal abortions to those "procured or attempted by medical advice for the purpose of saving the life of the mother," sweeps too broadly. The statute makes no distinction between abortions performed early in pregnancy and those performed later, and it limits to a single reason, "saving" the mother's life, the legal justification for the procedure. The statute, therefore, cannot survive the constitutional attack made upon it here. . . .

XI.

To summarize and to repeat:

1. A state criminal abortion statute of the current Texas type, that excepts from criminality only a *life saving* procedure on behalf of the mother, without regard to pregnancy stage and without recognition of the other interests involved, is violative of the Due Process Clause of the Fourteenth Amendment.

(a) For the stage prior to approximately the end of the first trimester, the abortion decision and its effectuation must be left to the medical judgment of the pregnant woman's attending physician.

(b) For the stage subsequent to approximately the end of the first trimester, the State, in promoting its interest in the health of the mother, may, if it chooses, regulate the abortion procedure in ways that are reasonably related to maternal health.

(c) For the stage subsequent to viability the State, in promoting its interest in the potentiality of human life, may, if it chooses, regulate, and even proscribe, abortion except where it is necessary, in appropriate medical judgment, for the preservation of the life or health of the mother.

2. The State may define the term "physician," as it has been employed in the preceding numbered paragraphs of this Part XI of this opinion, to mean only a physician currently licensed by the State, and may proscribe any abortion by a person who is not a physician as so defined.

In Doe v. Bolton procedural requirements contained in one of the modern abortion statutes are considered. That opinion and this one, of course, are to be read together. . . .

Mr. Chief Justice **Burger** concurred.

Mr. Justice **Douglas** concurred.

Mr. Justice **Stewart,** concurring said in part:

In 1963, this Court, in Ferguson v. Skrupa, purported to sound the death knell for the doctrine of substantive due process, a doctrine under which many state laws had in the past been held to violate the Fourteenth Amendment. As Mr. Justice Black's opinion for the Court in Skrupa put it: "We have returned to the original constitutional proposition that courts do not substitute their social and economic beliefs for the judgment of legislative bodies, who are elected to pass laws."

Barely two years later, in Griswold v. Connecticut, the Court held a Connecticut birth control law unconstitutional. In view of what had been so recently said in Skrupa, the Court's opinion in Griswold understandably did its best to avoid reliance on the Due Process Clause of the Fourteenth Amendment as the ground for decision. Yet, the Connecticut law did not violate any provision of the Bill of Rights, nor any other specific provision of the Constitution. So it was clear to me then, and it is equally clear to me now, that the Griswold decision can be rationally understood only as a holding that the Connecticut statute substantively invaded the "liberty" that is protected by the Due Process Clause of the Fourteenth Amendment. As so understood, Griswold stands as one in a long line of pre-Skrupa cases decided under the doctrine of substantive due process, and I now accept it as such.

"In a Constitution for a free people, there can be no doubt that the meaning of 'liberty' must be broad indeed." . . . The Constitution nowhere mentions a specific right of personal choice in matters of marriage and family life, but the "liberty" protected by the Due Process Clause of the Fourteenth Amendment covers more than those freedoms explicitly named in the Bill of Rights. . . .

Several decisions of this Court make clear that freedom of personal choice in matters of marriage and family life is one of the liberties protected by the Due Process Clause of the Fourteenth Amendment. Loving v. Virginia, Griswold v. Connecticut . . . . That right necessarily includes the right of a woman to decide whether or not to terminate her pregnancy. "Certainly the interests of a woman in giving of her physical and emotional self during pregnancy and the interests that will be affected throughout her life by the birth and raising of a child are of a far greater degree of significance and personal intimacy than the right to send a child to private school protected in Pierce v. Society of Sisters (1925), or the right to teach a foreign language protected in Meyer v. Nebraska (1923)." . . .

Mr. Justice **Rehnquist,** dissenting, said in part:

. . . I have difficulty in concluding, as the Court does, that the right of "privacy" is involved in this case. Texas by the statute here challenged bars the performance of a medical abortion by a licensed physician on a plaintiff such as Roe. A transaction resulting in an operation such as this is not "private" in the ordinary usage of that word. . . .

If the Court means by the term "privacy" no more than that the claim of a person to be free from unwanted state regulation of consensual transactions may be a form of "liberty" protected by the Fourteenth Amendment, there is no doubt that similar claims have been upheld in our earlier decisions on the basis of that liberty. I agree with the statement of Mr. Justice Stewart in his concurring opinion that the "liberty," against deprivation of which without due process the Fourteenth Amendment protects, embraces more than the rights found in the Bill of Rights. But that liberty is not guaranteed absolutely against deprivation, but only against deprivation without due process of law. The test traditionally applied in the area of social and economic legislation is whether or not a law such as that challenged has a rational relation to a valid state objective. . . . But the Court's sweeping invalidation of any restrictions on abortion during the first trimester is impossible to justify under that standard, and the conscious weighing of competing factors which the Court's opinion apparently substitutes for the established test is far more appropriate to a legislative judgment than to a judicial one.

The Court eschews the history of the Fourteenth Amendment in its reliance on the "compelling state interest" test. . . . But the Court adds a new wrinkle to this test by transposing it from the legal considerations associated with the Equal Protection Clause of the Fourteenth Amendment to this case arising under the Due Process Clause of the Fourteenth Amendment. Unless I misapprehend the consequences of this transplanting of the "compelling state interest test," the Court's opinion will accomplish the seemingly impossible feat of leaving this area of the law more confused than it found it.

While the Court's opinion quotes from the dissent of Mr. Justice Holmes in Lochner v. New York (1905), the result it reaches is more closely attuned to the majority opinion of Mr. Justice Peckham in that case. As in Lochner and similar cases applying substantive due process standards to economic and social welfare legislation, the adoption of the compelling state interest standard will inevitably require this Court to examine the legislative policies and pass on the wisdom of these policies in the very process of deciding whether a particular state interest put forward may or may not be "compelling." . . .

The fact that a majority of the States, reflecting after all the majority sentiment in those States, have had restrictions on abortions for at least a century is a strong indication, it seems to me, that the asserted right to an abortion is not "so rooted in the traditions and conscience of our people as to be ranked as fundamental," Snyder v. Massachusetts (1934). . . .

Mr. Justice **White,** with whom Mr. Justice **Rehnquist** joins, dissented.

BOWERS v. HARDWICK

478 U. S. 186; 92 L. Ed. 2d 140; 106 S. Ct. 2841 (1986)

While the right to sell obscene material enjoys no protection under the First Amendment, the freedom of thought implicitly guaranteed by that provision ensures the right of persons to enjoy such material in the privacy of their own homes. Relying on the Court's statement in Roth that "obscenity is not within the area of constitutionally protected speech or press," the state of Georgia made the mere possession of obscene material a crime. In Stanley v. Georgia (1969), the Court held the statute void. It conceded the wording of Roth v. United States (1957), but pointed out that it and other obscenity cases all involved the sale and distribution of obscene materials to others, and should be read in that context. "This right to receive information and ideas, regardless of their social worth, . . . is fundamental to our free society," and "also fundamental is the right to be free, except in very limited circumstances, from unwanted governmental intrusions into one's privacy."

The Court rejected outright the idea that Georgia had a right to "control the moral content of a person's thoughts." "Whatever may be the justification for other statutes regulating obscenity, we do not think they reach into the privacy of one's own home. If the First Amendment means anything, it means that a State has no business telling a man, sitting alone in his own house, what books he may read or what films he may watch. Our whole constitutional heritage rebels at the thought of giving government the power to control men's minds." Nor could Georgia justify its statute on the ground that the possession of pornography led to antisocial conduct. "Given the present state of knowledge, the State may no more prohibit mere possession of obscenity on the ground that it may lead to antisocial conduct than it may prohibit possession of chemistry books on the ground that they may lead to the manufacture of home-made spirits."

The present case brought to the Court for the first time the question whether a state could punish homosexual conduct. At least two lines of precedent were arguably relevant. First, the privacy cases from Griswold to Roe, which emphasized the intensely personal nature of consensual sexual behavior among adults (including unmarried adults), and the right to make choices affecting this conduct free of government intrusion. Second, the obscenity cases, which, while also involving privacy concerns, were grounded in the First Amendment and thus provided a minimal protection for conduct as opposed to speech or thought. The choice between these two lines of precedents is critical: put simply, seeing homosexual conduct as akin to heterosexual conduct suggests one result, while seeing it as akin to obscenity suggests another. In the case below the Court leaned heavily on the obscenity cases, emphasizing that Stanley involved First Amendment materials while here physical activity was involved. In contrast, the dissent drew more heavily on the heterosexual cases and thus did not get entangled in the problems of protecting conduct under the First Amendment. The two approaches result not only in different conclusions; they tell fundamentally different stories about both the nature of homosexual conduct and the appropriate stance of the government and heterosexual individuals toward the gay community. A *Newsweek* poll taken shortly after the Bowers decision revealed that over half those answering the question disapproved the outcome. But while the trend seems to be in favor of making sodomy legal, the apparent relationship between sodomy and the AIDS epidemic (Acquired Immunity Deficiency Syndrome, a fatal and incurable disease) which first burgeoned in the homosexual community, has added to the difficulties of those pressing for legalization. As of January 1990, 25 states and the District of Columbia still had laws against sodomy.

Justice **White** delivered the opinion of the Court, saying in part:

In August 1982, respondent Hardwick (hereafter respondent) was charged with violating the Georgia statute criminalizing sodomy by committing that act with another adult male in the bedroom of respondent's home. After a preliminary hearing, the District Attorney decided not to present the matter to the grand jury unless further evidence developed.

Respondent then brought suit in the Federal District Court, challenging the constitutionality of the statute insofar as it criminalized consensual sodomy. He asserted that he was a practicing homosexual, that the Georgia sodomy statute, as administered by the defendants, placed him in imminent danger of arrest, and that the statute for several reasons violates the Federal Constitution. . . .

. . . Relying on our decisions in Griswold v. Connecticut (1965), Eisenstadt v. Baird (1972), Stanley v. Georgia (1969), and Roe v. Wade (1973), the [court of appeals held] that the Georgia statute violated respondent's fundamental rights because his homosexual activity is a private and intimate association that is beyond the reach of state regulation by reason of the Ninth Amendment and the Due Process Clause of the Fourteenth Amendment. The case was remanded for trial, at which, to prevail, the State would have to prove that the statute is supported by a compelling interest and is the most narrowly drawn means of achieving that end.

. . . We agree with the petitioner that the Court of Appeals erred, and hence reverse its judgment.

This case does not require a judgment on whether laws against sodomy between consenting adults in general, or between homosexuals in particular, are wise or desirable. It raises no question about the right or propriety of state legislative decisions to repeal their laws that criminalize homosexual sodomy, or of state-court decisions invalidating those laws on state constitutional grounds. The issue presented is whether the Federal Constitution confers a fundamental right upon homosexuals to engage in sodomy and hence invalidates the laws of the many States that still make such conduct illegal and have done so for a very long time. The case also calls for some judgment about the limits of the Court's role in carrying out its constitutional mandate.

We first register our disagreement with the Court of Appeals and with respondent that the Court's prior cases have construed the Constitution to confer a right of privacy that extends to homosexual sodomy and for all intents and purposes have decided this case. [The Court here notes a series of cases dealing with child rearing, procreation, marriage, contraception and abortion.]

Accepting the decisions in these cases and the above description of them, we think it evident that none of the rights announced in those cases bears any resemblance to the claimed constitutional right of homosexuals to engage in acts of sodomy that is asserted in this case. No connection between family, marriage, or procreation on the one hand and homosexual activity on the other has been demonstrated, either by the Court of Appeals or by respondent. Moreover, any claim that these cases nevertheless stand for the proposition that any kind of private sexual conduct between consenting adults is constitutionally insulated from state proscription is unsupportable. . . .

Precedent aside, however, respondent would have us announce, as the Court of Appeals did, a fundamental right to engage in homosexual sodomy. This we are quite unwilling to do. It is true that despite the language of the Due Process Clauses of the Fifth and Fourteenth Amendments, which appears to focus only on the processes by which life, liberty or property is taken, the cases are legion in which those Clauses have been interpreted to have substantive content, subsuming rights that to a great extent are immune from federal or state regulation or proscription. Among such cases are those recognizing rights that have little or no textual support in the constitutional language. . . .

Striving to assure itself and the public that announcing rights not readily identifiable in the Constitution's text involves much more than the imposition of the Justices' own choice of values on the States and the Federal Government, the Court has sought to identify the nature of the rights qualifying for heightened judicial protection. In Palko v. Connecticut (1937) it was said that this category includes those fundamental liberties that are "implicit in the concept of ordered liberty," such that "neither liberty nor justice would exist if [they] were sacrificed." A different description of fundamental liberties appeared in Moore v. East Cleveland (1977) (opinion of Powell, J.), where they are characterized as those liberties that are "deeply rooted in this nation's history and tradition." . . .

It is obvious to us that neither of these formulations would extend a fundamental right to homosexuals to engage in acts of consensual sodomy. Proscriptions against that conduct have ancient roots. Sodomy was a criminal offense at common law and was forbidden by the laws of the original 13 States when they ratified the Bill of Rights. In 1868, when the Fourteenth Amendment was ratified, all but 5 of the 37 States in the Union had criminal sodomy laws. In fact, until 1961, all 50 States outlawed sodomy, and today, 25 States and the District of Columbia continue to provide criminal penalties for sodomy performed in private and between consenting adults. Against this background, to claim that a right to engage in such conduct is "deeply rooted in this nation's history and tradition" or "implicit in the concept of ordered liberty" is, at best, facetious.

Nor are we inclined to take a more expansive view of our authority to discover new fundamental rights imbedded in the Due Process Clause. The Court is most vulnerable and comes nearest to illegitimacy when it deals with judge-made constitutional law having little or no cognizable roots in the language or design of the Constitution. That this is so was painfully demonstrated by the face-off between the Executive and the Court in the 1930's, which resulted in the repudiation of much of the substantive gloss that the Court had placed on the Due Process Clause of the Fifth and Fourteenth Amendments. There should be, therefore, great resistance to expand the substantive reach of those Clauses, particularly if it requires redefining the category of rights deemed to be fundamental. Otherwise, the Judiciary necessarily takes to itself further authority to govern the country without express constitutional authority. The claimed right pressed on us today falls far short of overcoming this resistance.

Respondent, however, asserts that the result should be different where the homosexual conduct occurs in the privacy of the home. He relies on Stanley v. Georgia (1969) where the Court held that the First Amendment prevents conviction for possessing and reading obscene material in the privacy of one's home. "If the First Amendment means anything, it means that a State has no business telling a man, sitting alone in his house, what books he may read or what films he may watch.''

Stanley did protect conduct that would not have been protected outside the home, and it partially prevented the enforcement of state obscenity laws; but the decision was firmly grounded in the First Amendment. The right pressed upon us here has no similar support in the text of the Constitution, and it does not qualify for recognition under the prevailing principles for construing the Fourteenth Amendment. Its limits are also difficult to discern. Plainly enough, otherwise illegal conduct is not always immunized whenever it occurs in the home. Victimless crimes, such as the possession and use of illegal drugs, do not escape the law where they are committed at home. Stanley itself recognized that its holding offered no protection for the possession in the home of drugs, firearms, or stolen goods. And if respondent's submission is limited to the voluntary sexual conduct between consenting adults, it would be difficult, except by fiat, to limit the claimed right to homosexual conduct while leaving exposed to prosecution adultery, incest, and other sexual crimes even though they are committed in the home. We are unwilling to start down that road. . . .

Chief Justice **Burger**, concurring, said in part:

I join the Court's opinion, but I write separately to underscore my view that in constitutional terms there is no such thing as a fundamental right to commit homosexual sodomy. . . .

This is essentially not a question of personal ''preferences'' but rather of the legislative authority of the State. I find nothing in the Constitution depriving a State of the power to enact the statute challenged here.

Justice **Powell**, concurring, said in part:

I join the opinion of the Court. . . . This is not to suggest, however, that respondent may not be protected by the Eighth Amendment of the Constitution. The Georgia statute at issue in this case authorizes a court to imprison a person for up to 20 years for a single private, consensual act of sodomy. In my view, a prison sentence for such conduct—certainly a sentence of long duration — would create a serious Eighth Amendment issue. . . .

Justice **Blackmun**, with whom Justice **Brennan**, Justice **Marshall** and Justice **Stevens** join, dissenting, said in part:

This case is no more about ''a fundamental right to engage in homosexual sodomy,'' as the Court purports to declare, than Stanley v. Georgia (1969) was about a fundamental right to watch obscene movies, or Katz v. United States (1967) was about a fundamental right to place interstate bets from a telephone booth. Rather, this case is about ''the most comprehensive of rights and the right most valued by civilized men,'' namely, ''the right to be let alone.'' Olmstead v. United States (1928) (Brandeis, J., dissenting).

The statute at issue denies individuals the right to decide for themselves whether to engage in particular forms of private, consensual sexual activity. The Court concludes that § 16-6-2 is valid essentially because ''the laws of . . . many States . . . still make such conduct illegal and have done so for a very long time.'' But the fact that the moral judgments expressed by statutes like § 16-6-2 may be '' 'natural and familiar . . . ought not to conclude our judgment upon the question whether statutes embodying them conflict with the Constitution of the United States.' '' Roe v. Wade (1973), quoting Lochner v. New York (1905) (Holmes, J., dissenting). Like Justice Holmes, I believe that ''[i]t is revolting to have no better reason for a rule of law than that so it was laid down in the time of Henry IV. It is still more revolting if the grounds upon which it was laid down have vanished long since, and the rule simply persists from blind imitation of the past.'' . . . I believe we must analyze respondent Hardwick's claim in the light of the values that underlie the constitutional right to privacy. If that right means anything, it means that, before Georgia can prosecute its citizens for making choices about the most intimate aspects of their lives, it must do more than assert that the choice they have made is an '' 'abominable crime not fit to be named among Christians.' '' Herring v. State, 119 Ga. 709 (1904).

I.

. . . A fair reading of the statute and of the complaint clearly reveals that the majority has distorted the question this case presents.

First, the Court's almost obsessive focus on homosexual activity is particularly hard to justify in light of the broad language Georgia has used. Unlike the Court, the Georgia Legislature has not proceeded on the assumption that homosexuals are so different from other citizens that their lives may be controlled in a way that would not be tolerated if it limited the choices of those other citizens. . . . Michael Hardwick's standing may rest in significant part on Georgia's apparent willingness to enforce against homosexuals a law it seems not to have any desire to enforce against heterosexuals. But his claim that § 16-6-2 involves an unconstitutional intrusion into his privacy and his right of intimate association does not depend in any way on his sexual orientation. . . .

II. . . .

A. . . .

Only the most willful blindness could obscure the fact that sexual intimacy is ''a sensitive, key relationship of human existence, central to family life, community welfare, and the development of human personality.'' Paris Adult Theatre I v. Slaton (1973) . . . . The fact that individuals define themselves in a significant way through their intimate sexual relationships with others suggests, in a Nation as diverse as ours, that there may be many ''right'' ways of conducting those relationships, and that much of the richness of a relationship will come from the freedom an individual has to *choose* the form and nature of these intensely personal bonds. . . .

In a variety of circumstances we have recognized that a necessary corollary of giving individuals freedom to choose how to conduct their lives is acceptance of the fact that different individuals will make different choices. For example, in holding that the clearly important state interest in public education should give way to a competing claim by the Amish to the effect that extended formal schooling threatened their way of life, the Court declared: "There can be no assumption that today's majority is 'right' and the Amish and others like them are 'wrong.' A way of life that is odd or even erratic but interferes with no rights or interests of others is not to be condemned because it is different." Wisconsin v. Yoder (1972). The Court claims that its decision today merely refuses to recognize a fundamental right to engage in homosexual sodomy; what the Court really has refused to recognize is the fundamental interest all individuals have in controlling the nature of their intimate associations with others.

B.

The behavior for which Hardwick faces prosecution occurred in his own home, a place to which the Fourth Amendment attaches special significance. The Court's treatment of this aspect of the case is symptomatic of its overall refusal to consider the broad principles that have informed our treatment of privacy in specific cases. Just as the right to privacy is more than the mere aggregation of a number of entitlements to engage in specific behavior, so too, protecting the physical integrity of the home is more than merely a means of protecting specific activities that often take place there. . . .

The Court's interpretation of the pivotal case of Stanley v. Georgia (1969) is entirely unconvincing. Stanley held that Georgia's undoubted power to punish the public distribution of constitutionally unprotected, obscene material did not permit the State to punish the private possession of such material. According to the majority here, Stanley relied entirely on the First Amendment, and thus, it is claimed, sheds no light on cases not involving printed materials. But that is not what Stanley said. Rather, the Stanley Court anchored its holding in the Fourth Amendment's special protection for the individual in his home: " 'The makers of our Constitution undertook to secure conditions favorable to the pursuit of happiness. They recognized the significance of man's spiritual nature, of his feelings and of his intellect. They knew that only a part of the pain, pleasure and satisfactions of life are to be found in material things. They sought to protect Americans in their beliefs, their thoughts, their emotions and their sensations.' . . .

"These are the rights that appellant is asserting in the cases before us. He is asserting the right to read or observe what he pleases—the right to satisfy his intellectual and emotional needs in the privacy of his own home." (Quoting Olmstead v. United States [1928], Brandeis, J., dissenting).

The central place that Stanley gives Justice Brandeis' dissent in Olmstead, a case raising *no* First Amendment claim, shows that Stanley rested as much on the Court's understanding of the Fourth Amendment as it did on the First. Indeed, in Paris Adult Theatre I v. Slaton (1973), the Court suggested that reliance on the Fourth Amendment not only supported the Court's outcome in Stanley but actually was *necessary* to it: "If obscene material unprotected by the First Amendment in itself carried with it a 'penumbra' of constitutionally protected privacy, this Court would not have found it necessary to decide Stanley on the narrow basis of the 'privacy of the home,' which was hardly more than a reaffirmation that 'a man's home is his castle.' " "The right of the people to be secure in their . . . houses," expressly guaranteed by the Fourth Amendment, is perhaps the most "textual" of the various constitutional provisions that inform our understanding of the right to privacy, and thus I cannot agree with the Court's statement that "[t]he right pressed upon us here has no . . . support in the text of the Constitution." Indeed, the right of an individual to conduct intimate relationships in the intimacy of his or her own home seems to me to be the heart of the Constitution's protection of privacy. . . .

III. . . .

The core of petitioner's defense of § 16-6-2 . . . is that respondent and others who engage in the conduct prohibited by § 16-6-2 interfere with Georgia's exercise of the " 'right of the Nation and of the States to maintain a decent society.' " Paris Adult Theatre I v. Slaton . . . . Essentially, petitioner argues, and the Court agrees, that the fact that the acts described in § 16-6-2 "for hundreds of years, if not thousands, have been uniformly condemned as immoral" is a sufficient reason to permit a State to ban them today. . . .

I cannot agree that either the length of time a majority has held its convictions or the passions with which it defends them can withdraw legislation from this Court's scrutiny. . . . As Justice Jackson wrote so eloquently for the Court in West Virginia Board of Education v. Barnette (1943), " . . . [F]reedom to differ is not limited to things that do not matter much. That would be a mere shadow of freedom. The test of its substance is the right to differ as to things that touch the heart of the existing order." It is precisely because the issue raised by this case touches the heart of what makes individuals what they are that we should be especially sensitive to the rights of those whose choices upset the majority.

The assertion that "traditional Judeo-Christian values proscribe" the conduct involved cannot provide an adequate justification for § 16-6-2. That certain, but by no means all, religious groups condemn the behavior at issue gives the State no license to impose their judgments on the entire citizenry. The legitimacy of secular legislation depends instead on whether the State can advance some justification for its law beyond its conformity to religious doctrine. . . . Thus, far from buttressing his case, petitioner's invocation of Leviticus, Romans, St. Thomas Aquinas, and sodomy's heretical status during the Middle Ages undermines his suggestion that § 16-6-2 represents a legitimate use of secular coercive power.

Justice **Stevens,** with whom Justice **Brennan** and Justice **Marshall** joined, wrote a dissenting opinion.

4

First Amendment Rights

GITLOW v. NEW YORK

268 U. S. 652; 69 L. Ed. 1138; 45 S. Ct. 625 (1925)

Freedom of speech and press are not absolute rights and were never intended to be so. They are relative, in the sense that they are limited by the coexisting rights of others (as in the matter of libel) and by the demands of national security and public decency. As Justice Holmes put it (below), "The most stringent protection of free speech would not protect a man in falsely shouting fire in a theatre and causing a panic." Free-speech and free-press cases present to the courts difficult questions of degree: questions involved in drawing the line that separates the speech and publication which government must suppress in order to be safe and decent from that which it must allow and protect in order to be free and democratic.

Perhaps the most conspicuous and interesting instance in our history of interference with freedom of expression never came before the Supreme Court of the United States. The Sedition Act of 1798 provided among other things for the severe punishment of false, scandalous, and malicious writings against the government, either house of Congress, or the President if published with intent to defame any of them, or to excite against them the hatred of the people, or to stir up sedition. It was limited in operation to two years. Ten persons were convicted under it, and many others were indicted but not tried. Its enactment and enforcement called forth great popular indignation, and President Jefferson upon assuming office pardoned all persons still imprisoned under its provisions. Many years later Congress refunded with interest the fines which had been imposed.

The relative character of the right of free speech and press becomes particularly obvious in time of war. Where is the line to be drawn between legitimate and salutary freedom of discussion and utterances which, by reason of their disloyal or seditious character, must be deemed incompatible with the public safety? This is a delicate and important question. During the Civil War such interferences with freedom of speech and press as occurred were perpetrated by military officers under the sanction of martial law; and no question of the validity of these acts of repression ever came squarely before the Supreme Court. World War I brought forth a large grist of restrictive legislation, both state and federal, and numerous judicial questions arose as to the validity of these acts and their application to specific cases. Most conspicuous of these laws were the Espionage Act of 1917—which penalized any circulation of false statements made with intent to interfere with military success, as well as any attempt to cause disloyalty in the Army or Navy or to obstruct recruiting—and the Sedition Act of 1918—which made it a crime to say or do anything which could obstruct the sale of government bonds, or to utter or publish words intended to bring into contempt or disrepute the form of government of the United States, the Constitution, flag, uniform, etc., or to incite resistance to the government or promote the cause of its enemies. Nearly a thousand persons were convicted under these two acts. Their validity was sustained in six cases coming to the Supreme Court after the close of the war.

Schenck v. United States (1919) was the first of these cases, and in it Justice Holmes announced the now famous "clear and present danger" test. "The question in every case is whether the words used are used in such circumstances and are of such a nature as to create a clear and present danger that they will bring about the substantive evils that Congress has a right to prevent. It is a question of proximity and degree." Schenck had been convicted of circulating pamphlets urging resistance to the draft, and the Court found that they presented a clear and present danger of achieving this result. A week later the Court decided two more cases, Frohwerk v. United States (1919), involving a pro-German newspaper man, and Debs v. United States (1919), involving the famous Socialist leader. Holmes wrote the opinions sustaining the convictions of the two men on the grounds that their writings and speeches met the test of clear and present danger.

The Espionage Act of 1917 forbade certain kinds of action, such as causing or attempting to cause insubordination or obstructing the draft. It did not expressly limit freedom of speech; it limited it only when speech amounted to the kind of action forbidden by the statute. In order to determine when a particular speech became "action" and thus punishable under the statute, the Court resorted to two tests, the "bad tendency" test and the "clear and present danger" test.

The "bad tendency" test was designed, as Professor Chafee put it, "to kill the serpent in the egg" by preventing all speech which had a tendency, however remote, to bring about acts in violation of the law. It had its roots in the doctrine of constructive treason, so infamous in English history, under which criticism of the government was construed as an attempt to accomplish the overthrow of that government and was punished as treason. The "clear and present danger" test, devised by Justice Holmes in the Schenck case (1919), held that speech becomes punishable as action only when there is a danger, clear and present, that it will bring the action about. If there is no clear and present danger the speech does not amount to action, and the statute forbidding the action has not been violated. Holmes's doctrine was not intended as a test of the validity of the statute itself, since presumably the "action" which the statute forbids is, like obstructing the draft, something Congress could legitimately prohibit.

The clear and present danger test is not simple to apply. It is, for instance, difficult to apply to a statute which by its language forbids certain kinds of speech. If a person makes the kind of speech thus forbidden, then he has violated the statute; in other words, once the legislature has decided for itself what kind of speech is dangerous and forbidden it, the courts can hold the statute unconstitutional but they cannot say it has not been violated. Holmes and Brandeis apparently felt that statutes of this kind could not constitutionally be applied to cases in which there was no clear and present danger of serious substantive evil. See Whitney v. California (1927).

In the present case Benjamin Gitlow was prosecuted under the New York Criminal Anarchy Act of 1902 for distributing a document similar to the Communist Manifesto of Marx and Engels (1848). This statute, which formed the model for the federal Smith Act, punishes certain kinds of speech and publication regardless of the intent of the speaker or publisher.

Not until 1965 was the New York act again invoked successfully, when William Epton was convicted of criminal anarchy for conspiring to instigate and inflame the Harlem race riots that followed the killing by a policeman of a fifteen-year-old black boy.

Mr. Justice **Sanford** delivered the opinion of the Court, saying in part:

Benjamin Gitlow was indicted in the supreme court of New York, with three others, for the statutory crime of criminal anarchy. . . .

The contention here is that the statute, by its terms and as applied in this case, is repugnant to the due process clause of the 14th Amendment. Its material provisions are:

"§ 160. Criminal anarchy defined.—Criminal anarchy is the doctrine that organized government should be overthrown by force or violence, or by assassination of the executive head or of any of the executive officials of government, or by any unlawful means. The advocacy of such doctrine either by word of mouth or writing is a felony.

"§ 161. Advocacy of criminal anarchy.—Any person who:

"**1.** By word of mouth or writing advocates, advises or teaches the duty, necessity or propriety of overthrowing or overturning organized government by force or violence, or by assassination of the executive head or of any of the executive officials of government, or by any unlawful means; or

"**2.** Prints, publishes, edits, issues or knowingly circulates, sells, distributes or publicly displays any book, paper, document, or written or printed matter in any form, containing or advocating, advising or teaching the doctrine that organized government should be overthrown by force, violence or any unlawful means . . . ,

"Is guilty of a felony and punishable" by imprisonment or fine, or both.

The indictment was in two counts. The first charged that the defendants had advocated, advised, and taught the duty, necessity, and propriety of overthrowing and overturning organized government by force, violence, and unlawful means, by certain writings therein set forth, entitled, "The Left Wing Manifesto"; the second, that he had printed, published, and knowingly circulated and distributed a certain paper called "The Revolutionary Age," containing the writings set forth in the first count, advocating, advising, and teaching the doctrine that organized government should be overthrown by force, violence, and unlawful means.

. . . It was admitted that the defendant signed a card subscribing to the Manifesto and Program of the Left Wing, which all applicants were required to sign before being admitted to membership; that he went to different parts of the state to speak to branches of the Socialist party about the principles of the Left Wing, and advocated their adoption; and that he was responsible [as business manager] for the Manifesto as it appeared, that "he knew of the publication, in a general way, and he knew of its publication afterwards, and is responsible for its circulation."

There was no evidence of any effect resulting from the publication and circulation of the Manifesto.

No witnesses were offered in behalf of the defendant.

Extracts from the Manifesto are set forth in the margin. Coupled with a review of the rise of Socialism, it condemned the dominant "moderate Socialism" for its recognition of the necessity of the democratic parliamentary state; repudiated its policy of introducing

Socialism by legislative measures; and advocated, in plain and unequivocal language, the necessity of accomplishing the "Communist Revolution" by a militant and "revolutionary Socialism," based on "the class struggle" and mobilizing the "power of the proletariat in action," through mass industrial revolts developing into mass political strikes and "revolutionary mass action" for the purpose of conquering and destroying the parliamentary state and establishing in its place, through a "revolutionary dictatorship of the proletariat," the system of Communist Socialism. The then recent strikes in Seattle and Winnipeg were cited as instances of a development already verging on revolutionary action and suggestive of proletarian dictatorship, in which the strike workers were "trying to usurp the functions of municipal government"; and Revolutionary Socialism, it was urged, must use these mass industrial revolts to broaden the strike, make it general and militant, and develop it into mass political strikes and revolutionary mass action for the annihilation of the parliamentary state.

... The sole contention here is, essentially, that, as there was no evidence of any concrete result flowing from the publication of the Manifesto, or of circumstances showing the likelihood of such result, the statute as construed and applied by the trial court penalizes the mere utterance, as such, of "doctrine" having no quality of incitement, without regard either to the circumstances of its utterance or to the likelihood of unlawful sequences; and that, as the exercise of the right of free expression with relation to government is only punishable "in circumstances involving likelihood of substantive evil," the statute contravenes the due process clause of the Fourteenth Amendment. The argument in support of this contention rests primarily upon the following propositions: 1st, that the "liberty" protected by the 14th Amendment includes the liberty of speech and of the press; and 2nd, that while liberty of expression "is not absolute," it may be restrained "only in circumstances where its exercise bears a causal relation with some substantive evil, consummated, attempted, or likely"; and as the statute "takes no account of circumstances," it unduly restrains this liberty, and is therefore unconstitutional.

The precise question presented, and the only question which we can consider under this writ of error, then, is whether the statute, as construed and applied in this case by the state courts, deprived the defendant of his liberty of expression, in violation of the due process clause of the 14th Amendment.

The statute does not penalize the utterance or publication of abstract "doctrine" or academic discussion having no quality of incitement to any concrete action. It is not aimed against mere historical or philosophical essays. It does not restrain the advocacy of changes in the form of government by constitutional and lawful means. What it prohibits is language advocating, advising, or teaching the overthrow of organized government by unlawful means. These words imply urging to action. Advocacy is defined in the Century Dictionary as: "1. The act of pleading for, supporting, or recommending; active espousal." It is not the abstract "doctrine" of overthrowing organized government by unlawful means which is denounced by the statute, but the advocacy of action for the accomplishment of that purpose. ...

The Manifesto, plainly, is neither the statement of abstract doctrine nor, as suggested by counsel, mere prediction that industrial disturbances and revolutionary mass strikes will result spontaneously in an inevitable process of evolution in the economic system. It advocates and urges in fervent language mass action which shall progressively foment industrial disturbances, and, through political mass strikes and revolutionary mass action, overthrow and destroy organized parliamentary government. It concludes with a call to action in these words: "The proletariat revolution and the Communist reconstruction of society—*the struggle for these*—is now indispensable. . . . The Communist International calls the proletariat of the world to the final struggle!" This is not the expression of philosophical abstraction, the mere prediction of future events: it is the language of direct incitement.

The means advocated for bringing about the destruction of organized parliamentary government, namely, mass industrial revolts usurping the functions of municipal government, political mass strikes directed against the parliamentary state, and revolutionary mass action for its final destruction, necessarily imply the use of force and violence, and in their essential nature are inherently unlawful in a constitutional government of law and order. That the jury were warranted in finding that the Manifesto advocated not merely the abstract doctrine of overwhelming organized government by force, violence, and unlawful means, but action to that end, is clear.

For present purposes we may and do assume that freedom of speech and of the press— which are protected by the 1st Amendment from abridgment by Congress— are among the fundamental personal rights and "liberties" protected by the due process clause of the 14th Amendment from impairment by the states. . . .

It is a fundamental principle, long established, that freedom of speech and of the press which is secured by the Constitution does not confer an absolute right to speak or publish, without responsibility, whatever one may choose, or an unrestricted and un-bridled license that gives immunity for every possible use of language, and prevents the punishment of those who abuse this freedom. 2 Story, Const. 5th ed. § 1580, p. 634. . . . Reasonably limited, it was said by Story in the passage cited, this freedom is an inestimable privilege in a free government; without such limitation, it might become the scourge of the Republic.

That a state, in the exercise of its police power, may punish those who abuse this freedom by utterances inimical to the public welfare, tending to corrupt public morals, incite to crime, or disturb the public peace, is not open to question. . . . Thus it was held by this court in the Fox Case [Fox v. Washington, 1915], that a state may punish publications advocating and encouraging a breach of its criminal laws; and, in the Gilbert Case [Gilbert v. Minnesota, 1920], that a state may punish utterances teaching or advocating that its citizens should not assist the United States in prosecuting or carrying on war with its public enemies.

And, for yet more imperative reasons, a state may punish utterances endangering the foundations of organized government and threatening its overthrow by unlawful means. These imperil its own existence as a constitutional state. Freedom of speech and press, said Story (supra), does not protect disturbances of the public peace or the attempt to subvert the government. It does not protect publications or teachings which tend to subvert or imperil the government, or to impede or hinder it in the performance of its governmental duties. . . . It does not protect publications prompting the overthrow of government by force; the punishment of those who publish articles which tend to destroy organized society being essential to the security of freedom and the stability of the state. . . . And a state may penalize utterances which openly advocate the overthrow of the representative and constitutional form of government of the United States and the several states, by violence or other unlawful means. . . . In short, this freedom does not deprive a state of the primary and essential right of self-preservation, which, so long as human governments endure, they cannot be denied. . . .

By enacting the present statute the state has determined, through its legislative body, that utterances advocating the overthrow of organized government by force, violence, and unlawful means, are so inimical to the general welfare, and involve such danger of substantive evil, that they may be penalized in the exercise of its police power. That determination must be given great weight. Every presumption is to be indulged in favor of the validity of the statute. . . . That utterances inciting to the overthrow of organized government by unlawful means present a sufficient danger of substantive evil to bring their punishment within the range of legislative discretion is clear. Such utterances, by their very nature, involve danger to the public peace and to the security of the state. They threaten breaches of the peace and ultimate revolution. And the immediate danger is none the less real and substantial because the effect of a given utterance cannot be accurately foreseen. The state cannot reasonably be required to measure the danger from every such utterance in the nice balance of a jeweler's scale. A single revolutionary spark may kindle a fire that, smoldering for a time, may burst into a sweeping and destructive conflagration. It cannot be said that the state is acting arbitrarily or unreasonably when, in the exercise of its judgment as to the measures necessary to protect the public peace and safety, it seeks to extinguish the spark without waiting until it has enkindled the flame or blazed into the conflagration. It cannot reasonably be required to defer the adoption of measures for its own peace and safety until the revolutionary utterances lead to actual disturbances of the public peace or imminent and immediate danger of its own destruction; but it may, in the exercise of its judgment, suppress the threatened danger in its incipiency. . . .

We cannot hold that the present statute is an arbitrary or unreasonable exercise of the police power of the state, unwarrantably infringing the freedom of speech or press; and we must and do sustain its constitutionality.

This being so it may be applied to every utterance—not too trivial to be beneath the notice of the law—which is of such a character and used with such intent and purpose as to bring it within the prohibition of the statute. . . . In other words, when the legislative body has determined generally, in the constitutional exercise of its discretion, that utterances of a certain kind involve such danger of substantive evil that they may be punished, the question whether any specific utterance coming within the prohibited class is likely, in and of itself, to bring about the substantive evil, is not open to consideration. It is sufficient that the statute itself be constitutional, and that the use of the language comes within its prohibition.

It is clear that the question in such cases is entirely different from that involved in those cases where the statute merely prohibits certain acts involving the danger of substantive evil, without any reference to language itself, and it is sought to apply its provisions to language used by the defendant for the purpose of bringing about prohibited results. There, if it be contended that the statute cannot be applied to the language used by the defendant because of its protection by the freedom of speech or press, it must necessarily be found, as an original question, without any previous determination by the legislative body, whether the specific language used involved such likelihood of bringing about the substantive evil as to deprive it of the constitutional protection. In such cases it has been held that the general provisions of the statute may be constitutionally applied to the specific utterance of the defendant if its natural tendency and probable effect were to bring about the substantive evil which the legislative body might prevent. Schenck v. United States [1919]; Debs v. United States [1919]. And the general statement in the Schenck Case that the "question in every case is whether the words are used in such circumstances and are of such a nature as to create a clear and present danger that they will bring about the substantive evils,"—upon which great reliance is placed in the defendant's argument,—was manifestly intended, as shown by the context, to apply only in cases of this class, and has no application to those like the present, where the legislative body itself has previously determined the danger of substantive evil arising from utterances of a specified character. . . .

And finding, for the reasons stated, that the statute is not in itself unconstitutional, and that it has not been applied in the present case in derogation of any constitutional right, the judgment of the Court of Appeals is affirmed.

Mr. Justice **Holmes** dissented:

Mr. Justice Brandeis and I are of the opinion that this judgment should be reversed. The general principle of free speech, it seems to me, must be taken to be included in the 14th Amendment, in view of the scope that has been given to the word "liberty" as there used, although perhaps it may be accepted with a somewhat larger latitude of interpretation than is allowed to Congress by the sweeping language that governs, or ought to govern, the laws of the United States. If I am right, then I think that the criterion sanctioned by the full court in Schenck v. United States, applies: "The question in every case is whether the words used are used in such circumstances and are of such a nature as to create a clear and present danger that they will bring about the substantive evils that [the state] has a right to prevent." It is true that in my opinion this criterion was departed from in Abrams v. United States [1919] but the convictions that I expressed in that case are too deep for it to be possible for me as yet to believe that it and Schaefer v. United States [1920] have settled the law. If what I think the correct test is applied, it is manifest that there was no present danger of an attempt to overthrow the government by force on the part of the admittedly small minority who shared the defendant's views. It is said that this Manifesto was more than a theory, that it was an incitement. Every idea is an incitement. It offers itself for belief, and, if believed, it is acted on unless some other belief outweighs it, or some failure of energy stifles the movement at its birth. The only difference between the expression of an opinion and an incitement in the narrower sense is the speaker's enthusiasm for the result. Eloquence may set fire to reason. But whatever may be thought of the redundant discourse before us, it had no chance of starting a present conflagration. If, in the long run, the beliefs expressed in proletarian dictatorship are destined to be accepted by the dominant forces of the community, the only meaning of free speech is that they should be given their chance and have their way.

If the publication of this document had been laid as an attempt to induce an uprising against government at once, and not at some indefinite time in the future, it would have presented a different question. The object would have been one with which the law might deal, subject to the doubt whether there was any danger that the publication could produce any result; or, in other words, whether it was not futile and too remote from possible conse-quences. But the indictment alleges the publication and nothing more.

DENNIS v. UNITED STATES

341 U. S. 494; 95 L. Ed. 1137; 71 S. Ct. 857 (1951)

The Smith Act of 1940, which in 1948 became § 2385 of Title 18 of the United States Code, directs a five-pronged attack against subversion. First, it punishes anyone who "know-ingly or willfully advocates . . . or teaches the duty . . . or propriety of overthrowing . . . the government of the United States . . . by force or violence. . . ." Second, it punishes the dis-semination of literature advocating such overthrow "with intent to cause such overthrow." Third, it punishes anyone who "organizes . . . any society, group or assembly of persons to teach, advocate or encourage" such overthrow. Fourth, it punishes anyone who "becomes or is a member of . . . any such society, group or assembly . . . knowing the purposes thereof." Finally, it makes it a separate offense to conspire to do any of the above things.

The validity of the act was considered by the Supreme Court for the first time in the Dennis case below. In 1948, the 11 top leaders of the American Communist party were indicted under the act for willfully and knowingly conspiring to teach and advocate the over-throw of government by force and violence, and to organize the Communist party for the purpose of so doing. The trial in District Judge Medina's court in New York ran from January 20 to September 23, 1949, and resulted in conviction. Judge Medina's charge to the jury included two important interpretations of the law. First, he ruled out the possibility that "teaching" or "conspiring to teach" alone would violate the statute. "You must be satisfied from the evidence beyond a reasonable doubt that the defendants had an intent to cause the overthrow or destruction of the Government of the United States by force and violence, and that it was with this intent and for the purpose of furthering that objective that they conspired both (1) to organize the Communist Party . . . and (2) to teach and advocate. . . ." Second, should the jury find that the statute as so construed had been violated, it was their duty to find the defendants guilty. "I find as a matter of law that there is sufficient danger of a substantive evil that the Congress has a right to prevent to justify the application of the statute under the First Amendment. . . ."

Both the conviction and this charge to the jury were upheld by the court of appeals in an opinion by Judge Learned Hand. The Supreme Court limited the scope of its review to the constitutional questions raised, chief of which was the First Amendment question of free speech. It did not review the sufficiency of the evidence to support the verdict.

In the five opinions written in the Dennis case, there are four interpretations of the clear and present danger test. Chief Justice Vinson, speaking for four members of the Court, paid allegiance to Holmes's statement and application of the test, but in reality adopted in its place Judge Hand's test of " *clear and probable* danger." The danger need not be imminent; it is enough that there is a group willing to attempt the overthrow of government if and when possible. The Chief Justice read the time element out of clear and present danger.

Justice Frankfurter had always rejected the idea that a law which on its face invades free speech must be presumed to be unconstitutional, or that the First Amendment occupies any "preferred position." See Thomas v. Collins (1945). He felt that free-speech cases call for .

the weighing of competing interests, and that the legislative judgment embodied in the Smith Act, that the Communist threat to the security of the country justifies punitive action, is amply supported by evidence.

In an incisive concurring opinion Justice Jackson bluntly declared that the test of clear and present danger has no applicability to a criminal conspiracy such as that carried on by the Communist party. It was never intended to be applied in a case like this, and should be reserved for cases involving restrictions upon speeches and publications.

Justices Black and Douglas, dissenting, felt that the clear and present danger test had been destroyed. Justice Douglas emphasized that the defendants were charged with no overt acts, only with speeches and publications. He also felt that the question of clear and present danger should be decided by the jury and not by the court.

The decision in the Dennis case provided for the first time a legal basis for the idea that the Communist party is a criminal conspiracy dedicated to overthrowing the government of the United States by force and violence. It therefore seemed logical to suppose that any official of the party, and probably any member who was familiar with the aims of the party, could be convicted for his part in the conspiracy. Acting upon this assumption the government moved against 14 second-string Communist leaders, and in Yates v. United States (1957) the Supreme Court reversed their convictions, acquitting five of them outright and remanding the other nine for retrial. The District Court, it explained, had failed to charge the jury that in order to convict it must find the defendants guilty of advocating "action" in the "language of incitement." "The essence of the Dennis holding," the Court said, "was that indoctrination of a group in preparation for future violent action, as well as exhortation to immediate action, by advocacy found to be directed to 'action for the accomplishment' of forcible overthrow, to violence 'as a rule or principle of action,' and employing 'language of incitement,' is not constitutionally protected when the group is of sufficient size and cohesiveness, is sufficiently oriented towards action, and other circumstances are such as reasonably to justify apprehension that action will occur. This is quite a different thing from the view of the District Court here that mere doctrinal justification of forcible overthrow, if engaged in with the intent to accomplish overthrow, is punishable per se under the Smith Act. That sort of advocacy, even though uttered with the hope that it may ultimately lead to violent revolution, is too remote from concrete action to be regarded as the kind of indoctrination preparatory to action which was condemned in Dennis."

Although Justice Harlan stresses that he is merely applying the doctrine of the Dennis case, it seems apparent that in insisting in Yates that advocacy amount to incitement to action, he is, without actually using the well-known phrase, moving back toward the clear and present danger rule of Holmes and Brandeis. The Dennis case was widely believed to have modified and weakened that rule.

Four years after Yates, in Scales v. United States (1961), the Supreme Court passed on the validity of the membership section for the first time, and in a five-to-four decision held it valid as applied to Scales. It stated that this was not mere "guilt by association." The guilt was personal and punishable under the act if it were "active membership in an organization [in this case the Communist party] engaged in illegal advocacy by one having guilty knowledge and intent." Scales had been convicted first in 1955, and after a second trial and two full arguments before the Court his case was finally heard and considered in conjunction with Communist Party v. Subversive Activities Control Board (1961). Scales argued that the membership section of the Smith Act had been repealed by the section of the Subversive Activities Control Act of 1950 (requiring registration of Communists), which provides that : "Neither the holding of office nor membership in any Communist organization by any person shall constitute per se a violation of subsection (a) or subsection (c) of this section or any other criminal statute." Justice Harlan's opinion for the majority held that the section quoted from the act of 1950 clarified, rather than repealed, the membership section of the Smith Act; and he emphasized the difference between punishing a man for membership per se and punishing him for membership with guilty knowledge and with intent to aid in the violent overthrow of government. In the dissenting opinions it was urged that the act of 1950 had repealed the Smith Act provision and that the membership section violated the First Amendment.

The clear and present danger test was described by Justice Brandeis as "rule of reason" (Schaefer v. United States, 1920), and it is used by the Court to determine that point at which speech becomes so entwined with action, or so likely to bring about action, as to be punishable under a statute which forbids such action. It was for this reason that the Court refused to apply it in the Gitlow case, where the statute forbade speech, rather than action.

But some social interests are relatively of such slight value that the right of free speech apparently outweighs them even though there is a clear and present danger, and in Schneider v. Irvington (1939) the Court said that keeping the streets clean was such a value. "We are of opinion that the purpose to keep the streets clean and of good appearance is insufficient to justify an ordinance which prohibits a person rightfully on a public street from handing literature to one willing to receive it." The Court assumed there was a clear and present danger the streets would be littered. Thus the Court not only must find a speech presents a clear and present danger, but under what has come to be known as the "balancing of interests" doctrine, must weigh the social value of the restriction against the seriousness of the threat to free speech.

One of the difficulties involved in applying the "balancing of interests" doctrine is the determination of exactly what interests are at stake. When the Supreme Court decides a case arising under the First Amendment, it is deciding between the right of the government to protect some social value from attack, and the right of an individual to attack it. It is easy to argue, in such circumstances, that the interest of the one should yield to the interests of the many—overlooking the fact that there is a vital social value in the right of the individual to make his challenge. Such an argument is especially persuasive where the social value involved is, or can be made to appear to be, the very security of the nation itself. In this situation the individual interest is bound to yield.

To avoid this almost inevitable result in cases where both the public and individual interests are important ones, the Court has devised a new approach which, for the sake of convenience, we will call the "minimum infringement" doctrine. Under this doctrine the government has an obligation to achieve its social goals with the least possible infringement of First Amendment rights, and where it appears to the Court that this standard has not been met, the statute will be held void.

In United States v. Robel (1967) the Court upheld the right of Robel, an avowed though passive Communist, to work in a shipyard despite a federal statute forbidding such employment to a member of the Communist Party. The Court declined to read the statute as applying only to "active" membership and refused to apply the "balancing of interests" test. Instead it applied the "minimum infringement" test, holding the statute void on its face because it "casts its net across a broad range of associational activities, indiscriminately trapping membership which can be constitutionally punished and membership which cannot be so proscribed." While Congress is clearly entitled to protect sensitive activities from spies and saboteurs, it "must achieve its goal by means which have a 'less drastic' impact on the continued vitality of First Amendment freedoms."

Mr. Chief Justice **Vinson** announced the judgment of the Court and an opinion in which Mr. Justice **Reed**, Mr. Justice **Burton**, and Mr. Justice **Minton** join, saying in part:

I.

It will be helpful in clarifying the issues to treat next the contention that the trial judge improperly interpreted the statute by charging that the statute required an unlawful intent before the jury could convict. . . .

. . . The structure and purpose of the statute demand the inclusion of intent as an element of the crime. Congress was concerned with those who advocate and organize for the overthrow of the Government. Certainly those who recruit and combine for the purpose of advocating overthrow intend to bring about that overthrow. We hold that the statute required as an essential element of the crime proof of the intent of those who are charged with its violation to overthrow the Government by force and violence. . . .

II.

The obvious purpose of the statute is to protect existing Government, not from change by peaceable, lawful and constitutional means, but from change by violence, revolution and terrorism. That it is within the *power* of the Congress to protect the Government of the United States from armed rebellion is a proposition which requires little discussion. Whatever theoretical merit there may be to the argument that there is a "right" to rebellion against dictatorial governments is without force where the existing structure of the government provides for peaceful and orderly change. We reject any principle of governmental helplessness in the face of preparation for revolution, which principle, carried to its logical conclusion, must lead to anarchy. No one could conceive that it is not within the power of Congress to prohibit acts intended to overthrow the Government by force and violence. The question with which we are concerned here is not whether Congress has such *power*, but whether the *means* which it has employed conflict with the First and Fifth Amendments to the Constitution.

One of the bases for the contention that the means which Congress has employed are invalid takes the form of an attack on the face of the statute on the grounds that by its terms it prohibits academic discussion of the merits of Marxism-Leninism, that it stifles ideas and is contrary to all concepts of a free speech and a free press. Although we do not agree that the language itself has that significance, we must bear in mind that it is the duty of the federal courts to interpret federal legislation in a manner not inconsistent with the demands of the Constitution. . . . This is a federal statute which we must interpret as well as judge. . . .

The very language of the Smith Act negates the interpretation which petitioners would have us impose on the Act. It is directed at advocacy, not discussion. Thus, the trial judge properly charged the jury that they could not convict if they found that petitioners did "no more than pursue peaceful studies and discussions or teaching and advocacy in the realm of ideas." He further charged that it was not unlawful "to conduct in an American college and university a course explaining the philosophical theories set forth in the books which have been placed in evidence." Such a charge is in strict accord with the statutory language, and illustrates the meaning to be placed on those words. Congress did not intend to eradicate the free discussion of political theories, to destroy the traditional rights of Americans to discuss and evaluate ideas without fear of governmental sanction. Rather Congress was concerned with the very kind of activity in which the evidence showed these petitioners engaged.

III.

But although the statute is not directed at the hypothetical cases which petitioners have conjured, its application in this case has resulted in convictions for the teaching and advocacy of the overthrow of the Government by force and violence, which, even though coupled with the intent to accomplish that overthrow, contains an element of speech. For this reason, we must pay special heed to the demands of the First Amendment marking out the boundaries of speech.

We pointed out in [American Communications Ass'n v. Douds, 1950] that the basis of the First Amendment is the hypothesis that speech can rebut speech, propaganda will answer propaganda, free debate of ideas will result in the wisest governmental policies. It is for this reason that this Court has recognized the inherent value of free discourse. An analysis of the leading cases in this Court which have involved direct limitations on speech, however, will demonstrate that both the majority of the Court and the dissenters in particular cases have recognized that this is not an unlimited, unqualified right, but that the societal value of speech must, on occasion, be subordinated to other values and considerations.

No important case involving free speech was decided by this Court prior to Schenck v. United States (1919). . . . Writing for a unanimous Court, Justice Holmes states that the "question in every case is whether the words used are used in such circumstances and are of such a nature as to create a clear and present danger that they will bring about the substantive evils that Congress has a right to prevent." . . . The fact is inescapable, too, that the phrase bore no connotation that the danger was to be any threat to the safety of the Republic. The charge was causing and attempting to cause insubordination in the military forces and obstruct recruiting. The objectionable document denounced conscription and its most inciting sentence was, "You must do your share to maintain, support and uphold the rights of the people of this country." Fifteen thousand copies were printed and some circulated. This insubstantial gesture toward insubordination in 1917 during war was held to be a clear and present danger of bringing about the evil of military insubordination.

In several later cases involving convictions under the Criminal Espionage Act, the nub of the evidence the Court held sufficient to meet the "clear and present danger" test enunciated in Schenck was as follows: [Five cases, 1919–1920, are here discussed.] . . .

The rule we deduce from these cases is that where an offense is specified by a statute in nonspeech or nonpress terms, a conviction relying upon speech or press as evidence of violation may be sustained only when the speech or publication created a "clear and present danger" of attempting or accomplishing the prohibited crime, e. g., interference with enlistment. The dissents, we repeat, in emphasizing the value of speech, were addressed to the argument of the sufficiency of the evidence.

The next important case before the Court in which free speech was the crux of the conflict was Gitlow v. New York [1925]. There New York had made it a crime to "advocate ... the necessity or propriety of overthrowing ... the government by force. ..." The evidence of violation of the statute was that the defendant had published a Manifesto attacking the Government and capitalism. The convictions were sustained, Justices Holmes and Brandeis dissenting. The majority refused to apply the "clear and present danger" test to the specific utterance. Its reasoning was as follows: The "clear and present danger" test was applied to the utterance itself in Schenck because the question was merely one of sufficiency of evidence under an admittedly constitutional statute. Gitlow, however, presented a different question. There a legislature had found that a certain kind of speech was, itself, harmful and unlawful. The constitutionality of such a state statute had to be adjudged by this Court just as it determined the constitutionality of any state statute, namely, whether the statute was "reasonable." Since it was entirely reasonable for a state to attempt to protect itself from violent overthrow, the statute was perforce reasonable. The only question remaining in the case became whether there was evidence to support the conviction, a question which gave the majority no difficulty. Justices Holmes and Brandeis refused to accept this approach, but insisted that wherever speech was the evidence of the violation, it was necessary to show that the speech created the "clear and present danger" of the substantive evil which the legislature had the right to prevent. Justices Holmes and Brandeis, then, made no distinction between a federal statute which made certain acts unlawful, the evidence to support the conviction being speech, and a statute which made speech itself the crime. This approach was emphasized in Whitney v. California [1927], where the Court was confronted with a conviction under the California Criminal Syndicalist statute. The Court sustained the conviction, Justices Brandeis and Holmes concurring in the result. In their concurrence they repeated that even though the legislature had designated certain speech as criminal, this could not prevent the defendant from showing that there was no danger that the substantive evil would be brought about.

Although no case subsequent to Whitney and Gitlow has expressly overruled the majority opinions in those cases, there is little doubt that subsequent opinions have inclined toward the Holmes-Brandeis rationale. And in American Communications Ass'n v. Douds ... we pointed out that Congress did not intend to punish belief, but rather intended to regulate the conduct of union affairs. We therefore held that any indirect sanction on speech which might arise from the oath requirement did not present a proper case for the "clear and present danger" test, for the regulation was aimed at conduct rather than speech. In discussing the proper measure of evaluation of this kind of legislation, we suggested that the Holmes-Brandeis philosophy insisted that where there was a direct restriction upon speech, a "clear and present danger" that the substantive evil would be caused was necessary before the statute in question could be constitutionally applied. And we stated, "[The First] Amendment requires that one be permitted to believe what he will. It requires that one be permitted to advocate what he will unless there is a clear and present danger that a substantial public evil will result therefrom." But we further suggested that neither Justice Holmes nor Justice Brandeis ever envisioned that a shorthand phrase should be crystallized into a rigid rule to be applied inflexibly without regard to the circumstances of each case. Speech is not an absolute, above and beyond control by the legislature when its judgment, subject to review here, is that certain kinds of speech are so undesirable as to warrant criminal sanction. Nothing is more certain in modern society than the principle that there are no absolutes, that a name, a phrase, a standard has meaning only when associated with the considerations which gave birth to the nomenclature. . . . To those who would paralyze our Government in the face of impending threat by encasing it in a semantic straitjacket we must reply that all concepts are relative.

In this case we are squarely presented with the application of the "clear and present danger" test, and must decide what that phrase imports. We first note that many of the cases in which this Court has reversed convictions by use of this or similar tests have been based on the fact that the interest which the State was attempting to protect was itself too insubstantial to warrant restriction of speech. . . . Overthrow of the Government by force and violence is certainly a substantial enough interest for the Government to limit speech. Indeed, this is the ultimate value of any society, for if a society cannot protect its very structure from armed internal attack, it must follow that no subordinate value can be protected. If, then, this interest may be protected, the literal problem which is presented is what has been meant by the use of the phrase "clear and present danger" of the utterances bringing about the evil within the power of Congress to punish.

Obviously, the words cannot mean that before the Government may act, it must wait until the *putsch* is about to be executed, the plans have been laid and the signal is awaited. If Government is aware that a group aiming at its overthrow is attempting to indoctrinate its members and to commit them to a course whereby they will strike when the leaders feel the circumstances permit, action by the Government is required. The argument that there is no need for Government to concern itself, for Government is strong, it possesses ample powers to put down a rebellion, it may defeat the revolution with ease needs no answer. For that is not the question. Certainly an attempt to overthrow the Government by force, even though doomed from the outset because of inadequate numbers or power of the revolutionists, is a sufficient evil for Congress to prevent. The damage which such attempts create both physically and politically to a nation makes it impossible to measure the validity in terms of the probability of success, or the immediacy of a successful attempt. In the instant case the trial judge charged the jury that they could not convict unless they found that petitioners intended to overthrow the Government "as speedily as circumstances would permit." This does not mean, and could not properly mean, that they would not strike until there was certainty of success. What was meant was that the revolutionists would strike when they thought the time was ripe. We must therefore reject the contention that success or probability of success is the criterion.

The situation with which Justices Holmes and Brandeis were concerned in Gitlow was a comparatively isolated event, bearing little relation in their minds to any substantial threat to the safety of the community. . . . They were not confronted with any situation comparable to the instant one—the development of an apparatus designed and dedicated to the overthrow of the Government, in the context of world crisis after crisis.

Chief Judge Learned Hand, writing for the majority below, interpreted the phrase as follows: "In each case [courts] must ask whether the gravity of the 'evil,' discounted by its improbability, justifies such invasion of free speech as is necessary to avoid the danger." We adopt this statement of the rule. As articulated by Chief Judge Hand, it is as succinct and inclusive as any other we might devise at this time. It takes into consideration those factors which we deem relevant, and relates their significances. More we cannot expect from words.

Likewise, we are in accord with the court below, which affirmed the trial court's finding that the requisite danger existed. The mere fact that from the period 1945 to 1948 petitioners' activities did not result in an attempt to overthrow the Government by force and violence is of course no answer to the fact that there was a group that was ready to make the attempt. The formation by petitioners of such a highly organized conspiracy, with rigidly disciplined members subject to call when the leaders, these petitioners, felt that the time had come for action, coupled with the inflammable nature of world conditions, similar uprisings in other countries, and the touch-and-go nature of our relations with countries with whom petitioners were in the very least ideologically attuned, convince us that their convictions were justified on this score. And this analysis disposes of the contention that a conspiracy to advocate, as distinguished from the advocacy itself, cannot be constitutionally restrained, because it comprises only the preparation. It is the existence of the conspiracy which creates the danger. . . . If the ingredients of the reaction are present, we cannot bind the Government to wait until the catalyst is added.

IV.

[The Court here considers whether the trial court was correct in not submitting to the jury the question of the existence of clear and present danger.]
. . . The argument that the action of the trial court is erroneous, in declaring as a matter of law that such violation shows sufficient danger to justify the punishment despite the First Amendment, rests on the theory that a jury must decide a question of the application of the First Amendment. We do not agree.

When facts are found that establish the violation of a statute, the protection against conviction afforded by the First Amendment is a matter of law. The doctrine that there must be a clear and present danger of a substantive evil that Congress has a right to prevent is a judicial rule to be applied as a matter of law by the courts. The guilt is established by proof of facts. Whether the First Amendment protects the activity which constitutes the violation of the statute must depend upon a judicial determination of the scope of the First Amendment applied to the circumstances of the case. . . .

V

There remains to be discussed the question of vagueness—whether the statute as we have interpreted it is too vague, not sufficiently advising those who would speak of the limitations upon their activity. . . .

We hold that §§ 2(a) (1), (2)(a) (3) and 3 of the Smith Act, do not inherently, or as construed or applied in the instant case, violate the First Amendment and other provisions of the Bill of Rights, or the First and Fifth Amendments because of indefiniteness. Petitioners intended to overthrow the Government of the United States as speedily as the circumstances would permit. Their conspiracy to organize the Communist Party and to teach and advocate the overthrow of the Government of the United States by force and violence created a "clear and present danger" of an attempt to overthrow the Government by force and violence. They were properly and constitutionally convicted for violation of the Smith Act. The judgments of conviction are

Affirmed.

Mr. Justice **Clark** took no part in this case.

Mr. Justice **Frankfurter** wrote a concurring opinion.

Mr. Justice **Jackson** wrote a concurring opinion.

Mr. Justice **Black** wrote a dissenting opinion.

Mr. Justice **Douglas** wrote a dissenting opinion.

NEAR v. MINNESOTA

283 U. S. 697; 75 L. Ed. 1357; 51 S. Ct. 625 (1931)

The struggle to achieve freedom of the press has been long and difficult. Once the invention of the printing press made possible the dissemination of information to the people generally, it became painfully clear to the monarchs of Europe that here lay a serious threat to their absolute powers. Their first reaction was to outlaw and destroy this new engine of seditious propaganda. Failing in this, they resorted to a system of licensing under which all publications, before being released to the public, had to be submitted to the King's Licenser. Serious penalties were meted out to those whose publications did not bear the official imprimatur. Obviously no criticism of the sovereign or government, whether just or unjust, could be published under such a system; and the long fight against the official licenser was a major part of the fight to establish democratic institutions.

It is against this background that the case of Near v. Minnesota must be read. The law involved had been dubbed the "Minnesota gag law." It provided for the "padlocking," by injunctive process, of a newspaper for printing matter which was scandalous, malicious, defamatory, or obscene. Such a "padlock" injunction, enforceable by the customary process of summary punishment for contempt of court, could be lifted only by convincing the judge who issued it that the publication would, in the future, be unobjectionable. This, in the judgment of the majority of the Court, amounted to previous censorship of publication and a violation of long-established canons of free speech and press.

The present case represents the climax of a striking evolution in our constitutional law whereby freedom of speech and press was at last effectively "nationalized" or confided to the protection of the federal courts against both national and state impairment. The steps in that evolution are traced in the note to Powell v. Alabama (1932). The case of Near v. Minnesota was the first case in which a state law was held unconstitutional as violating that freedom of press protected by the due process clause of the Fourteenth Amendment.

In contrast to the experience in Europe where books and periodicals had been the subject of censorship, the only focus of overt and systematic censorship in the United States was the motion picture. Early movies were largely thought of as entertainment subject to the same police control as stage shows and a number of cities and states censored them for anti-social content. It was not until 1952 that the Supreme Court finally held them to be part of the press of the country protected by the First Amendment, and even then it refused to outlaw their censorship entirely. In Burstyn v. Wilson (1952) it held void New York's censorship of *The Miracle* for being sacrilegious and while it made clear that "the state has no legitimate interest in protecting any or all religions from views distasteful to them," it also emphasized that "it does not follow that the Constitution requires absolute freedom to exhibit every motion picture of every kind at all times and places."

For nearly a decade after Burstyn the Court held void all challenged exercises of censorship without forbidding censorship in theory but without saying what kind of censorship would be upheld. Although the Court had insisted as early as Near v. Minnesota that "the protection even as to previous restraint is not absolutely unlimited," no scheme of previous censorship had ever been found valid and the Court had never undertaken to explain just what this dictum meant. It had spoken of "exceptional" circumstances that might justify such censorship, but it had defined them, not in terms of when or how the state could censor, but in terms of the kinds of ideas that could be suppressed. But how, without resorting to a general scheme of censorship and licensing, were these suppressible ideas to be located? How was a state to identify and suppress "utterances creating a hindrance to the . . . war effort," or which offended "the primary requirements of decency," without examining all utterances before they were published? Since it was this very "examining" before publication that the Court held void in the Near case, the theory underlying the dictum seemed incompatible with the holding of the case.

Doubts arose as to whether *any* censorship would be approved, until finally a case came to the Court where the film was not submitted to the censor and a direct challenge was made to the censorship as censorship. In Times Film Corp. v. Chicago (1961) the Court held the censorship valid. A five-man majority pointed out that "one of the exceptional cases" mentioned in Near where prior censorship might be permitted included " 'the primary requirements of decency [that] may be enforced against obscene publications,' " and refused to hold, under "petitioner's broadside attack," that "the State is stripped of all constitutional power to prevent, in the most effective fashion, the utterance of this class of speech." The dissenting justices complained that the Court was abandoning the restraints on prior censorship "without requiring any demonstration that this is an exceptional case, whatever that might be, and without any indication that Chicago has sustained the 'heavy burden' which was supposed to have been placed upon it. Clearly, this is neither an exceptional case nor has Chicago sustained any burden. . . ." By holding valid previous censorship in the Times Film case while citing this incompatible dictum in Near as authority, the Court raised serious doubts whether or not the basic hold of the Near case had been abandoned.

Closely allied to the problem of movie censorship is the problem presented by the publication of obscene material generally, and the constitutional theories involved are closely intertwined. Although a state may not resort to prior censorship of the press, it does have authority to punish the publication of matter offensive to public morals and decency. While it had long been assumed that clearly obscene publications could validly be punished, the question was never squarely decided by the Supreme Court until 1957 in the case of Roth v.

United States. There two cases were combined: one involved the prosecution of one Alberts by the state of California for publishing obscene matter; the other, the prosecution of Roth by the federal government for violation of the law forbidding the sending of obscene matter through the mails. On historical grounds the Court decided that the First Amendment was not intended to protect obscenity, and therefore the question of whether an obscene publication presented a clear and present danger of "antisocial conduct" was entirely irrelevant.

In Kingsley Books v. Brown (1957), decided the same day as the Roth case, the Court had found a procedure that met the requirements of the First Amendment. New York laws provided a municipality with a "limited injunctive remedy" under which the government requests in court an injunction against the sale of an allegedly obscene book until the matter of obscenity can be determined judicially. The bookseller against whom the injunction is sought is entitled to bring the issues before the court within one day and a decision shall be rendered by the court within two days of the conclusion of the trial. Only a person disobeying an injunction issued after such a trial would be subject to criminal penalty. The Court pointed out that the procedure had marked advantages over the simple criminal prosecution for selling obscene matter. It advanced the public interest by preventing the sale of something already adjudged obscene, at the same time it enabled a bookseller to avoid selling a book which may "without prior warning subject him to a criminal prosecution with the hazard of imprisonment." Moreover, since the act "studiously withholds restraint upon matters not already published and not yet found to be offensive," it avoids any limitation on the sale of nonobscene material. In Freedman v. Maryland (1956) the Court extended this doctrine of expeditious judicial review to the censorship of movies.

In other First Amendment areas, the Court distinguishes between protected and unprotected speech on the basis of its potential for actual harm. In most areas this is articulated by the clear and present danger test. Justice Holmes's wise rule that only those utterances should be suppressed that present a clear and present danger of bringing about some substantive evil probably expresses the ideal of free speech in a democracy. It is, in essence, a reflection of the doctrine that that government is best which governs least. But few people live easily with such a rule when it involves expressions of which they disapprove. There is a natural tendency in most of us to feel that the First Amendment should protect the right to say those things we want to say or hear, while permitting the government to suppress those expressions which we find offensive. Thus, those who find attacks on their religious beliefs offensive see no merit in having "that sort of thing" protected by the First Amendment; at the same time they feel their own beliefs and practices should be immune from governmental interference. Those who find what they consider disloyal or subversive utterances a threat to their way of life see no reason why they should not be suppressed—as long as their own right to complain about the government and agitate for change is not restricted.

The clear and present danger test protects against the suppression of speech based on the estimated impact of what is spoken or printed. The test is not, however, used in obscenity cases. There is no apparent agreement that reading pornography increases sex crimes or has any other injurious effect. Such material is suppressed by law, not because it produces injurious results, but because many people find it offensive, and especially do not want their children exposed to it. The obscenity cases illustrate the kind of judgment the Supreme Court has to make when it abandons the clear and present danger philosophy and substitutes a judgment on the merits of certain kinds of speech. Is there any constitutional reason why those who enjoy the "titillation" of erotic literature shouldn't be allowed to obtain it? But then why shouldn't those who find such material offensive be allowed to raise the moral tone of the community by suppressing it? The same question might be asked regarding rock music. By deciding to judge obscenity by its distastefulness rather than by its potential for tangible harm, the Court has made it almost impossible to judge the validity of censorship in terms of the purpose to be served. Probably nothing vital is lost whichever way a particular matter is decided—so few expressions are in themselves really valuable or important—but in the long run the spirit of freedom in a society may well depend on whether the question ceases to be "Why shouldn't he speak?" and becomes instead "Why shouldn't he be suppressed?" It is with this in mind that the role of the Court in deciding most First Amendment cases, but especially obscenity cases, should be judged.

In the Roth case, five members of the Court agreed that obscene material was that "which deals with sex in a manner appealing to prurient interest." Such material, it was emphasized, does not enjoy constitutional protection because it is "utterly without social importance." The Court in Roth found that the jury had been properly instructed on the standards, so the conviction was valid.

In the years following Roth the court attempted and failed to agree on a definition of obscenity. In Jacobellis v. Ohio (1964) two members of the Court stated that a national, not a local definition should prevail, and in Memoirs v. Massachusetts (1966) six members agreed that the book *Fanny Hill* was not obscene since, despite the fact it was found to appeal to prurient interests and be patently offensive, it was not utterly without redeeming social value.

Finally, in Miller v. California (1973), the Court reached a measure of agreement. It reaffirmed that obscene material was outside the First Amendment, but abandoned the "redeeming social value" test and substituted another: "The basic guidelines for the trier of fact must be: (a) whether "the average person, applying contemporary community standards" would find that the work, taken as a whole, appeals to the prurient interest. . . . (b) whether the work depicts or describes, in a patently offensive way, sexual conduct specifically defined by the applicable state law, and (c) whether the work, taken as a whole, lacks serious literary, artistic, political, or scientific value."

Paris Adult Theater 1 v. Slaton (1973) raised the question whether the government could censor pornographic films shown in "adult only" theaters devoid of offensive advertising. Using procedures which met the test of Freedman v. Maryland (1965), the city of Atlanta, Georgia had moved to enjoin the exhibition of two "adult" films in such theaters and the Court in a five-to-four decision held that such censorship was constitutionally permissible. While apparently recognizing an adult person's right to see and read what he chooses, the Court found that the " 'right of the nation and of the states to maintain a decent society' " may legitimately outweigh the individual's right to do what he will in private.

Writing for the majority, Chief Justice Burger stated, "we hold that there are legitimate state interests at stake in stemming the tide of commercialized obscenity, even assuming it is feasible to enforce effective safeguards against exposure to juveniles and to the passerby. . . . These [legitimate state interests] include the interest of the public in the quality of life and the total community environment, the tone of commerce in the great city centers, and, possibly, the public safety itself."

The Court was not troubled by the lack of conclusive scientific data to show that obscene materials adversely affect individuals or society. "Although there is no conclusive proof of a connection between antisocial behavior and obscene material, the legislature of Georgia could quite reasonably determine that such a connection does or might exist."

Justice Brennan's dissent was based in large part on the Court's experience with obscenity cases since Roth. After reviewing those cases, Brennan concluded "that the concept of 'obscenity' cannot be defined with sufficient specificity and clarity to provide fair notice to persons who create and distribute sexually oriented materials, to prevent substantial erosions of protected speech as a by-product of the attempt to suppress unprotected speech, and to avoid very costly institutional harms." For Brennan, the consequences of censoring obscenity were severe enough to make such censorship unconstitutional unless the state possessed a "very substantial interest" in suppressing such speech. Brennan contended that there was no very substantial state interest in censoring obscene material distributed only to consenting adults and, "would hold, therefore, that at least in the absence of distribution to juveniles or obtrusive exposure to unconsenting adults, the First and Fourteenth Amendments prohibit the state and federal governments from attempting wholly to suppress sexually oriented materials . . . ."

One of Brennan's major objections to the majority's approach in Paris and Miller was that the standards enunciated in those cases do nothing to alleviate the uncertainty about what is obscene, leaving it to judges and justices to decide this question subjectively on a case-by-case basis. As Justice Steward conceded in Jacobellis, he might never be able to define it, "but I know it when I see it." As if to prove Brennan's point, one year after Paris and Miller a unanimous Court reversed the conviction of a theater operator for showing a movie which dealt with sex, but without showing "hard core" explicit sexual conduct. "Our own view of the film satisfies us that 'Carnal Knowledge' could not be found under the Miller standards to depict sexual conduct in a patently offensive way." See Jenkins v. Georgia (1974).

Mr. Chief Justice **Hughes** delivered the opinion of the Court, saying in part:

Chapter 285 of the Session Laws of Minnesota for the year 1925 provides for the abatement, as a public nuisance, of a "malicious, scandalous and defamatory newspaper, magazine or other periodical." Section one of the act is as follows:

"Section 1: Any person who, as an individual, or as a member or employee of a firm, or association or organization, or as an officer, director, member or employee of a corporation, shall be engaged in the business of regularly or customarily producing, publishing or circulating, having in possession, selling or giving away,

(a) an obscene, lewd and lascivious newspaper, magazine, or other periodical, or

(b) a malicious, scandalous and defamatory newspaper, magazine or other periodical,

is guilty of a nuisance, and all persons guilty of such nuisance may be enjoined, as hereinafter provided.

Participation in such business shall constitute a commission of such nuisance and render the participant liable and subject to the proceedings, orders and judgments provided for in this act. Ownership, in whole or in part, directly or indirectly, of any such periodical, or of any stock or interest in any corporation or organization which owns the same in whole or in part, or which publishes the same, shall constitute such participation." . . .

Section two provides that whenever any such nuisance is committed or exists, the county attorney of any county where any such periodical is published or circulated, or, in case of his failure or refusal to proceed upon written request in good faith of a reputable citizen, the attorney general, or upon like failure or refusal of the latter, any citizen of the county, may maintain an action in the district court of the county in the name of the state to enjoin perpetually the persons committing or maintaining any such nuisance from further committing or maintaining it. Upon such evidence as the court shall deem sufficient, a temporary injunction may be granted. The defendants have the right to plead by demurrer or answer, and the plaintiff may demur or reply as in other cases.

The action, by section three, is to be "governed by the practice and procedure applicable to civil actions for injunctions," and after trial the court may enter judgment permanently enjoining the defendants found guilty of violating the act from continuing the violation and, "in and by such judgment, such nuisance may be wholly abated." The court is empowered, as in other cases of contempt, to punish disobedience to a temporary or permanent injunction by fine of not more than $1000 or by imprisonment in the county jail for not more than twelve months.

Under this statute, (section one, clause (b)), the county attorney of Hennepin county brought this action to enjoin the publication of what was described as a "malicious, scandalous and defamatory newspaper, magazine and periodical," known as "The Saturday Press," published by the defendants in the city of Minneapolis. . . .

Without attempting to summarize the contents of the voluminous exhibits attached to the complaint, we deem it sufficient to say that the articles charged in substance that a Jewish gangster was in control of gambling, bootlegging and racketeering in Minneapolis, and that law enforcing officers and agencies were not energetically performing their duties. Most of the charges were directed against the chief of police; he was charged with gross neglect of duty, illicit relations with gangsters, and with participation in graft. The county attorney was charged with knowing the existing conditions and with failure to take adequate measures to remedy them. The mayor was accused of inefficiency and dereliction. One member of the grand jury was stated to be in sympathy with the gangsters. A special grand jury and a special prosecutor were demanded to deal with the situation in general, and, in particular, to investigate an attempt to assassinate one Guilford, one of the original defendants, who, it appears from the articles, was shot by gangsters after the first issue of the periodical had been published. There is no question but that the articles made serious accusations against the public officers named and others in connection with the prevalence of crimes and the failure to expose and punish them. . . .

[Upon complaint the state court ordered Near to show cause why a temporary injunction should not be issued and forbade, meanwhile, further publication of the periodical. Near demurred on constitutional grounds. The district court certified the question of the constitutionality of the statute to the state supreme court, which held it valid. Near then answered the complaint but presented no evidence, and a permanent injunction was issued.]

From the judgment as thus affirmed, the defendant Near appeals to this court.

This statute, for the suppression as a public nuisance of a newspaper or periodical, is unusual, if not unique, and raises questions of grave importance transcending the local interests involved in the particular action. It is no longer open to doubt that the liberty of the press, and of speech, is within the liberty safeguarded by the due process clause of the 14th Amendment from invasion by state action. . . . In maintaining this guaranty, the authority of the State to enact laws to promote the health, safety, morals and general welfare of its people is necessarily admitted. The limits of this sovereign power must always be determined with appropriate regard to the particular subject of its exercise. . . . Liberty of speech and of the press is also not an absolute right, and the state may punish its abuse. . . . Liberty, in each of its phases, has its history and connotation and, in the present instance, the inquiry is as to the historic conception of the liberty of the press and whether the statute under review violates the essential attributes of that liberty. . . .

With respect to these contentions it is enough to say that in passing upon constitutional questions the court has regard to substance and not to mere matters of form, and that, in accordance with familiar principles, the statute must be tested by its operation and effect. . . . That operation and effect we think are clearly shown by the record in this case. We are not concerned with mere errors of the trial court, if there be such, in going beyond the direction of the statute as construed by the supreme court of the state. It is thus important to note precisely the purpose and effect of the statute as the state court has construed it.

First. The statute is not aimed at the redress of individual or private wrongs. Remedies for libel remain available and unaffected. The statute, said the state court, "is not directed at threatened libel but at an existing business which, generally speaking, involves more than libel." It is aimed at the distribution of scandalous matter as "detrimental to public morals and to the general welfare," tending "to disturb the peace of the community" and "to provoke assaults and the commission of crime." In order to obtain an injunction to suppress the future publication of the newspaper or periodical, it is not necessary to prove the falsity of the charges that have been made in the publication condemned. In the present action there was no allegation that the matter published was not true. It is alleged, and the statute requires the allegation, that the publication was "malicious." But, as in prosecutions for libel, there is no requirement of proof by the state of malice in fact as distinguished from malice inferred from the mere publication of the defamatory matter. The judgment in this case proceeded upon the mere proof of publication. The statute permits the defense, not of the truth alone, but only that the truth was published with good motives and for justifiable ends. It is apparent that under the statute the publication is to be regarded as defamatory if it injures reputation, and that it is scandalous if it circulates charges of reprehensible conduct, whether criminal or otherwise, and the publication is thus deemed to invite public reprobation and to constitute a public scandal. The court sharply defined the purpose of the statute, bringing out the precise point, in these words: "There is no constitutional right to publish a fact merely because it is true. It is a matter of common knowledge that prosecutions under the criminal libel statutes do not result in efficient repression or suppression of the evils of scandal. Men who are the victims of such assaults seldom resort to the courts. This is especially true if their sins are exposed and the only question relates to whether it was done with good motives and for justifiable ends. This law is not for the protection of the person attacked nor to punish the wrongdoer. It is for the protection of the public welfare."

Second. The statute is directed not simply at the circulation of scandalous and defamatory statements with regard to private citizens, but at the continued publication by newspapers and periodicals of charges against public officers of corruption, malfeasance in office, or serious neglect of duty. Such charges by their very nature create a public scandal. They are scandalous and defamatory within the meaning of the statute, which has its normal operation in relation to publications dealing prominently and chiefly with the alleged derelictions of public officers.

Third. The object of the statute is not punishment, in the ordinary sense, but suppression of the offending newspaper or periodical. The reason for the enactment, as the state court has said, is that prosecutions to enforce penal statutes for libel do not result in "efficient repression or suppression of the evils of scandal." Describing the business of publication as a public nuisance, does not obscure the substance of the proceeding which the statute authorizes. It is the continued publication of scandalous and defamatory matter that constitutes the business and the declared nuisance. In the case of public officers, it is the reiteration of charges of official misconduct, and the fact that the newspaper or periodical is principally devoted to that purpose, that exposes it to suppression. In the present instance, the proof was that nine editions of the newspaper or periodical in question were published on successive dates, and that they were chiefly devoted to charges against public officers and in relation to the prevalence and protection of crime. In such a case, these officers are not left to their ordinary remedy in a suit for libel, or the authorities to a prosecution for criminal libel. Under this statute, a publisher of a newspaper or periodical, undertaking to conduct a campaign to expose and to censure official derelictions, and devoting his publication principally to that purpose, must face not simply the possibility of a verdict against him in a suit or prosecution for libel, but a determination that his newspaper or periodical is a public nuisance to be abated, and that this abatement and suppression will follow unless he is prepared with legal evidence to prove the truth of the charges and also to satisfy the court that, in addition to being true, the matter was published with good motives and for justifiable ends.

This suppression is accomplished by enjoining publications and that restraint is the object and effect of the statute.

Fourth. The statute not only operates to suppress the offending newspaper or periodical but to put the publisher under an effective censorship. When a newspaper or periodical is found to be "malicious, scandalous and defamatory," and is suppressed as such, resumption of publication is punishable as a contempt of court by fine or imprisonment. Thus, where a newspaper or periodical has been suppressed because of the circulation of charges against public officers of official misconduct, it would seem to be clear that the renewal of the publication of such charges would constitute a contempt and that the judgment would lay a permanent restraint upon the publisher, to escape which he must satisfy the court as to the character of a new publication. Whether he would be permitted again to publish matter deemed to be derogatory to the same or other public officers would depend upon the court's ruling. In the present instance the judgment restrained the defendants from "publishing, circulating, having in their possession, selling or giving away any publication whatsoever which is a malicious, scandalous or defamatory newspaper, as defined by law." The law gives no definition except that covered by the words "scandalous and defamatory," and publications charging official misconduct are of that class. While the court, answering the objection that the judgment was too broad, saw no reason for construing it as restraining the defendants "from operating a newspaper in harmony with the public welfare to which all must yield," and said that the defendants had not indicated "any desire to conduct their business in the usual and legitimate manner," the manifest inference is that, at least with respect to a new publication directed against official misconduct, the defendant would be held, under penalty of punishment for contempt as provided in the statute, to a manner of publication which the court considered to be "usual and legitimate" and consistent with the public welfare.

If we cut through mere details of procedure, the operation and effect of the statute in substance is that public authorities may bring the owner or publisher of a newspaper or periodical before a judge upon a charge of conducting a business of publishing scandalous and defamatory matter—in particular that the matter consists of charges against public officers of official dereliction—and unless the owner or publisher is able and disposed to bring competent evidence to satisfy the judge that the charges are true and are published with good motives and for justifiable ends, his newspaper or periodical is suppressed and further publication is made punishable as a contempt. This is of the essence of censorship.

The question is whether a statute authorizing such proceedings in restraint of publication is consistent with the conception of the liberty of the press as historically conceived and guaranteed. In determining the extent of the constitutional protection, it has been generally, if not universally, considered that it is the chief purpose of the guaranty to prevent previous restraints upon publication. The struggle in England, directed against the legislative power of the licenser, resulted in renunciation of the censorship of the press. The liberty deemed to be established was thus described by Blackstone: "The liberty of the press is indeed essential to the nature of a free state; but this consists in laying no *previous* restraints upon publications, and not in freedom from censure for criminal matter when published. Every freeman has an undoubted right to lay what sentiments he pleases before the public; to forbid this, is to destroy the freedom of the press; but if he publishes what is improper, mischievous or illegal, he must take the consequence of his own temerity." . . .

The criticism upon Blackstone's statement has not been because immunity from previous restraint upon publication has not been regarded as deserving of special emphasis, but chiefly because that immunity cannot be deemed to exhaust the conception of the liberty guaranteed by state and Federal constitutions. The point of criticism has been "that the mere exemption from previous restraints cannot be all that is secured by the constitutional provisions;" and that "the liberty of the press might be rendered a mockery and a delusion, and the phrase itself a by-word, if, while every man was at liberty to publish what he pleased, the public authorities might nevertheless punish him for harmless publications." . . . But it is recognized that punishment for the abuse of the liberty accorded to the press is essential to the protection of the public, and that the common law rules that subject the libeler to responsibility for the public offense, as well as for the private injury, are not abolished by the protection extended in our constitutions. . . . In the present case, we have no occasion to inquire as to the permissible scope of subsequent punishment: For whatever wrong the appellant has committed or may commit, by his publications, the state appropriately affords both public and private redress by its libel laws. As has been noted, the statute in question does not deal with punishments; it provides for no punishment, except in case of contempt for violation of the court's order, but for suppression and injunction, that is, for restraint upon publication.

The objection has also been made that the principle as to immunity from previous restraint is stated too broadly, if every such restraint is deemed to be prohibited. That is undoubtedly true; the protection even as to previous restraint is not absolutely unlimited. But the limitation has been recognized only in exceptional cases. "When a nation is at war many things that might be said in time of peace are such a hindrance to its effort that their utterance will not be endured so long as men fight and that no court could regard them as protected by any constitutional right." Schenck v. United States [1919]. No one would question but that a government might prevent actual obstruction to its recruiting service or the publication of the sailing dates of transports or the number and location of troops. On similar grounds, the primary requirements of decency may be enforced against obscene publications. The security of the community life may be protected against incitements to acts of violence and the overthrow by force of orderly government. The constitutional guaranty of free speech does not "protect a man from an injunction against uttering words that may have all the effect of force. . . ."

The exceptional nature of its limitations places in a strong light the general conception that liberty of the press, historically considered and taken up by the Federal Constitution, has meant, principally although not exclusively, immunity from previous restraints or censorship. The conception of the liberty of the press in this country had broadened with the exigencies of the colonial period and with the efforts to secure freedom from oppressive administration. That liberty was especially cherished for the immunity it afforded from previous restraint of the publication of censure of public officers and charges of official misconduct. . . .

The importance of this immunity has not lessened. While reckless assaults upon public men, and efforts to bring obloquy upon those who are endeavoring faithfully to discharge official duties, exert a baleful influence and deserve the severest condemnation in public opinion, it cannot be said that this abuse is greater, and it is believed to be less, than that which characterized the period in which our institutions took shape. Meanwhile, the administration of government has become more complex, the opportunities for malfeasance and corruption have multiplied, crime has grown to most serious proportions, and the danger of its protection by unfaithful officials and of the impairment of the fundamental security of life and property by criminal alliances and official neglect, emphasizes the primary need of a vigilant and courageous press, especially in great cities. The fact that the liberty of the press may be abused by miscreant purveyors of scandal does not make any the less necessary the immunity of the press from previous restraint in dealing with official misconduct. Subsequent punishment for such abuses as may exist is the appropriate remedy, consistent with constitutional privilege. . . .

The statute in question cannot be justified by reason of the fact that the publisher is permitted to show, before injunction issues, that the matter published is true and is published with good motives and for justifiable ends. If such a statute, authorizing suppression and injunction on such a basis, is constitutionally valid, it would be equally permissible for the legislature to provide that at any time the publisher of any newspaper could be brought before a court, or even an administrative officer (as the constitutional protection may not be regarded as resting on mere procedural details) and required to produce proof of the truth of his publication, or of what he intended to publish, and of his motives, or stand enjoined. If this can be done, the legislature may provide machinery for determining in the complete exercise of its discretion what are justifiable ends and restrain publication accordingly. And it would be but a step to a complete system of censorship. The recognition of authority to impose previous restraint upon publication in order to protect the community against the circulation of charges of misconduct, and especially of official misconduct, necessarily would carry with it the admission of the authority of the censor against which the constitutional barrier was erected. The preliminary freedom, by virtue of the very reason for its existence, does not depend, as this court has said, on proof of truth. . . .

Equally unavailing is the insistence that the statute is designed to prevent the circulation of scandal which tends to disturb the public peace and to provoke assaults and the commission of crime. Charges of reprehensible conduct, and in particular of official malfeasance, unquestionably create a public scandal, but the theory of the constitutional guaranty is that even a more serious public evil would be caused by authority to prevent publication. . . . There is nothing new in the fact that charges of reprehensible conduct may create resentment and the disposition to resort to violent means of redress, but this well-understood tendency did not alter the determination to protect the press against censorship and restraint upon publication. . . . The danger of violent reactions becomes greater with effective organization of defiant groups resenting exposure, and if this consideration warranted legislative interference with the initial freedom of publication, the constitutional protection would be reduced to a mere form of words.

For these reasons we hold the statute, so far as it authorized the proceedings in this action under clause (b) of section one, to be an infringement of the liberty of the press guaranteed by the 14th Amendment. We should add that this decision rests upon the operation and effect of the statute, without regard to the question of the truth of the charges contained in the particular periodical. The fact that the public officers named in this case, and those associated with the charges of official dereliction, may be deemed to be impeccable, cannot affect the conclusion that the statute imposes an unconstitutional restraint upon publication.

Judgment reversed.

Mr. Justice **Butler** dissented in an opinion in which Justices **Van Devanter, McReynolds,** and **Sutherland** concurred.

RICHMOND NEWSPAPERS, INC. v. VIRGINIA

488 U. S. 555; 65 L. Ed. 2d 973; 100 S. Ct. 2814 (1980)

On Sunday Morning, June 13, 1971, *The New York Times* ran on its front page a modest headline spanning columns five, six, and seven:
Vietnam Archive: Pentagon Study Traces
3 Decades of Growing U. S. Involvement
A small box underneath said, "Three pages of documentary material from the Pentagon study begin on page 35."
In this unobtrusive way, the reading public was introduced to what was to become one of the most dramatic and sensational cases ever to reach the Supreme Court. The study, tracing the deliberate involvement of the United States in Vietnam during the administrations of four presidents, was based on a 7000-page top secret study made by the Pentagon and was turned over to the *Times* by Daniel Ellsberg, a Pentagon employee, as an act of conscience.
The following Monday night, just as the third in the series was about to appear, the Justice Department called the *Times* and asked them to desist from further publication on the ground that publication violated the Espionage Act. The *Times* refused, and Tuesday afternoon the Attorney General filed a motion for an injunction in the district court in New York. That afternoon District Judge Gurfein, who just that day had started work as a federal judge, issued the first federal injunction against a newspaper publication in the history of the nation.

He revoked the order a few days later, only to have the revocation set aside by the court of appeals on June 23. Three days later the Supreme Court heard oral argument and on June 30 it decided in New York Times Co. v. United States (1971) that the injunction could not stand. Nine opinions accompanied the short per curiam opinion of the Court, with Justices Burger, Harlan, and Blackmun dissenting, largely on the ground that no one, not even the government, had had time to learn the facts of the case. The orderly thing, they felt, was to delay publication until the impact of the release of the material could be assessed.

While it is perhaps true, as Justice Holmes said, that great cases make bad law, the importance of the Supreme Court's decision in the present case would be hard to overstate. Over the past forty years, the growing complexity and pervasiveness of government have resulted in a steady increase in presidential power at the expense of congressional power. Nowhere is this more apparent than in the areas of foreign affairs and national defense, in which the President has special constitutional authority, and it is widely assumed that constitutional limitations on presidential prerogatives in these areas should bow to presidential determinations of what the national security requires. The Supreme Court has apparently agreed, and not since Ex parte Milligan (1866), except for the Steel Seizure Case in 1952, has the Supreme Court said "no" to the President on matters of this kind. It thus came as a shock to those who approve such presidential authority that the Court should refuse to prevent the publication of material which the government deemed harmful to the national interest despite the refusal of Congress to provide such a remedy.

While Justice Black was probably right in saying that the First Amendment was drafted to prevent just such assumptions of governmental power over the press, his contention that the Amendment should be applied absolutely literally was so at odds with its judicial development that it attracted few adherents. Far more impressive were the votes of Justices Stewart and White, who felt that the publication was certainly wrong and might even be a crime, but refused to enjoin it because the "heavy burden" borne by the government under the First Amendment had not been met.

In a far less spectacular case decided some six weeks before the Pentagon Papers case the Court also held void an injunction against publication—in this case the distribution of pamphlets in the home neighborhood of an Illinois realtor accused of "block-busting." The leaflets were designed to let "his neighbors know what he was doing to us" in the hope he would agree to stop such tactics. Rejecting the argument that the purpose of the leaflets was to force "rather than inform" and that the injunction was a valid protection for the realtor's right of privacy, the Court held it void as a previous restraint on speech and publication. "The claim that the expressions were intended to exercise a coercive impact on respondent does not remove them from the reach of the First Amendment. Petitioners plainly intended to influence respondent's conduct by their activities; this is not fundamentally different from the function of a newspaper. . . . But so long as the means are peaceful, the communication need not meet standards of acceptability." See Organization for a Better Austin v. Keefe (1971).

The cardinal value which we attach to freedom of speech and press in a democratic society sometimes tends to obscure the fact that the use of these freedoms may jeopardize other civil liberties of the individual. One of these is the right of a litigant in a court of law to have his case tried by an impartial judge or jury. The conflict arises when unrestrained newspaper comment on a pending or current trial threatens the impartiality of any jury which could be drawn, or brings pressure upon judge or jury to reach a particular decision. An essential phase of judicial power has always been the power of a judge to protect the administration of justice in his court by punishing for contempt those who would interfere with it. In England, this power has always been very sternly used, and as recently as 1949 the Lord Chief Justice fined the London *Daily Mirror* £10,000 and sentenced the editor to three months in jail for the paper's lurid comments on the crimes of the so-called "English Bluebeard" who was then on trial for murder.

In dealing with this conflict, courts in the United States have been far more lenient to questionable newspaper comment than have courts in England. In three cases decided in the 1940's, the Court struck down judicial efforts to curb the press. In Bridges v. California (1941) it set aside the contempt conviction of union leader Harry Bridges who had released to the press a threat that he would close down the West Coast ports if the court tried to enforce a decision against him. In Pennekamp v. Florida (1946) it quashed a contempt resulting from editorials and cartoons appearing in the *Miami Herald* which accused the local judge of playing into the hands of criminal elements and thwarting the efforts of the district attorney to enforce the law. In Craig v. Harney (1947) it set aside a contempt conviction where the newspaper, by a bitter attack on a trial judge, had tried to alter his decision. In all three cases the Court stressed the importance of an unfettered press and added in Craig that "the law of contempt is not made for the protection of judges who may be sensitive to the winds of public opinion. Judges are supposed to be men of fortitude, able to thrive in a hardy climate. . . . Nor can we assume that the trial judge was not a man of fortitude."

While the Court has been unwilling to permit the punishment of newspapers for trying to influence the course of justice, it has not hesitated to reverse the conviction of persons whose trials were clearly so influenced. In Irvin v. Dowd (1961) the police issued a press release stating that Irvin had confessed to six murders. The one change of venue allowed by the state law merely took him into the next county—a county so blanketed by the adverse publicity that nearly 90 percent of the prospective jurors, and eight of the 12 members of the actual jury, believed the defendant was guilty before the trial even started. And in Rideau v. Louisiana (1963) police permitted the filming of a twenty-minute interview between Rideau and the sheriff, in which Rideau confessed to robbery, kidnapping, and murder. He was denied a change of venue despite the fact that three television broadcasts had carried the "interview," and three members of the jury had seen it. The Supreme Court reversed both convictions.

The cooperation between police and the news media following President Kennedy's assassination, which culminated in the murder of Lee Harvey Oswald before a nationwide television audience, brought public demand for reform. In 1964 the New Jersey supreme court ordered a ban on pretrial statements to newsmen by prosecutors, police, and defense attorneys, while the Judicial Conference of the United States recommended to Congress the passage of a bill prohibiting the release of information to the press which had not previously been filed with the trial court. And in 1966 a committee of the American Bar Association recommended strong limits on pretrial reporting by both prosecutors and defense attorneys. While official moves of this kind met considerable opposition from the organized press, informal codes of conduct, such as those adopted in Nebraska in the case below, have been worked out in conference among the industry, the bar associations, and the courts.

Strong impetus was given the reform movement by the decision in Sheppard v. Maxwell (1966) overturning the conviction of Dr. Sam Sheppard for the murder of his wife. "Doctor Sam," a prominent Cleveland physician, was tried in a suburban court in what the Supreme Court described as a "carnival atmosphere." The press, convinced of his guilt, demanded his conviction and innundated the community with highly inflamatory, prejudicial statements which the judge, who refused to sequester the jury or grant a change of venue, was unable to keep from reaching the jury. The Court noted that "every court that has considered this case, save the court that tried it, has deplored the manner in which the news media inflamed and prejudiced the public." As for the trial itself, "the fact is that bedlam reigned at the courthouse during the trial, and newsmen took over practically the entire courtroom hounding most of the participants in the trial, especially Sheppard." After a careful review of the authority of a trial court to control the conduct of the trials before it, the Court concluded that they were adequate to protect the fairness of the trial. Strict rules of press behavior were enforced when Dr. Sheppard was retried by Ohio in 1966. An unspectacular trial resulted in his acquittal.

The result of the efforts at reform has been to shift the constitutional battle between the courts and the press to new ground as courts have tried to devise ways of preventing the publication of prejudicial news comments. In 1975, Erwin Simants was arrested and prosecuted for the brutal murder of six members of the Henry Kellie family in their home in Sutherland, Nebraska, a town of about 850 people. The crime attracted nationwide attention, and both Simant's attorney and the county attorney, fearing the "reasonable likelihood of prejudicial news which would make difficult, if not impossible, the impaneling of an impartial jury and tend to prevent a fair trial," obtained from the county court an order restricting press coverage. The news media asked the United States district court to vacate the order, but that court issued an order of its own prohibiting reporting on five subjects: "(1) the existence or contents of a confession Simants had made to law enforcement officers, which had been introduced in open court at arraignment; (2) the fact or nature of statements Simants had made to other persons; (3) the contents of a note he had written the night of the crime; (4) certain aspects of the medical testimony at the preliminary hearing; (5) the identity of the victims of the alleged sexual assault and the nature of the assault."

In Nebraska Press Asso. v. Stuart (1976), the Supreme Court unanimously held the court's order void. While conceding that the trial judge was justified in concluding there would be intense pretrial publicity, it found no evidence that the restraining order, on its face a serious limit on freedom of the press, was the only or even an effective way of guaranteeing an impartial jury. Not only did the trial court not explore other alternatives open to it, but in a town of 850 there was no reason to suppose the press accounts would be any more damaging than the rumors that were bound to circulate. As far as the material that had been introduced in open court, the Court reiterated its statement in Sheppard v. Maxwell (1966) that "there is nothing that proscribes the press from reporting events that transpire in the courtroom." In 1979, this latter point was reaffirmed and extended to information obtained by normal reporting techniques—in this case the name of a juvenile killer obtained by merely querying witnesses. The Court held the state's interest in protecting the privacy of juveniles insufficient to justify punishing the paper for publishing the name, especially since the law did not apply to either radio or television. See Smith v. Daily Mail Publishing Co. (1979).

To what extent do the news media, as the eyes and ears of a public that can rarely if ever witness events and conditions first hand, have a right of access to information not available to the public at large? In Branzburg v. Hayes (1972) the Supreme Court refused to create a constitutional privilege under the First Amendment for newsmen to withhold confidential sources of information from a grand jury investigating crime. The case involved newspaper reporters who had won the confidence of drug users and of the Black Panther Party and had written behind-the-scenes stories about them. Grand juries investigating these matters subpoenaed the reporters to testify and they refused on the ground that to do so would dry up their news sources and obstruct the free flow of news protected by the First Amendment. A five-man majority rejected their claim, holding that "the First Amendment does not guarantee the press a constitutional right of special access to information not available to the public generally."

In a series of cases the Supreme Court used this statement to justify forbidding the press access to prison facilities not available to the public at large. In Pell v. Procunier (1974), it upheld rules adopted by a California prison forbidding interviews with selected inmates on the ground that the inmates so selected became celebrities and posed a disciplinary problem.

The Court noted that the rules reflected no intention to conceal conditions within the prison and that members of the press were free to visit the prison and speak with prisoners they happened to meet. In Saxbe v. Washington Post Co. (1974), the Court extended the same rule to federal prisons, and in Houchins v. KQED, Inc. (1978), in a four-to-three decision, it extended it to a California jail where it seemed apparent that the authorities were trying to conceal conditions within the jail from public scrutiny.

The first suggestion that the Court might be rethinking the question of access came in Gannett v. DePasquale (1979). Following the apparent murder of an upstate New York man, three suspects were apprehended in Michigan with the victim's pickup truck and gun. They were returned to New York for trial, and following their arraignment asked for a pretrial hearing to argue the inadmissibility in evidence of the gun and certain statements made to the Michigan police that they claimed were involuntary. Arguing that the "unabated buildup of adverse publicity had jeopardized the ability of the defendants to receive a fair trial," they moved that the hearings be closed to the public and the press. Without objection from the press the hearing was closed but the trial judge later held a full hearing on whether or not the transcript of the hearing should be released. The trial judge presumed a constitutional right of access on the part of the press but after finding on the record that an open suppression hearing would pose a "reasonable probability of prejudice to these defendants," he refused to release the transcript.

In a five-to-four decision, the Court upheld the trial judge. Justice Stewart's opinion reviewed the commentaries and precedents and concluded that the Sixth Amendment guarantee of a public trial was for the benefit of the accused, not the public. While he conceded the importance of open trials to the public, he made clear that "recognition of an independent public interest in the enforcement of Sixth Amendment guarantees is a far cry . . . from the creation of a constitutional right on the part of the public." Furthermore, while "there is no question that the Sixth Amendment permits and even assumes open trials as a norm," historically the public had no right to attend *pretrial* proceedings. In addition, even assuming a constitutional right of access on the part of the press, it had not been violated in this case because the trial court had properly "balanced the 'constitutional rights of the press and public' against the 'defendants' right to a fair trial.' " In 1965 in Estes v. Texas the Court had held that televising a sensational trial had denied the defendant due process of law, noting that the "public trial" guaranteed by the Sixth Amendment was not the equivalent of a day in a "stadium . . . or nationwide arena." In 1981, however, the Court in Chandler v. Florida construed Estes as not banning all television coverage, although a defendant clearly had a right (which had not been exercised in this case) to try to show that media coverage had an adverse affect upon the fairness of his trial.

Following the Richmond case below the Court moved to restrict still further the right of courts to close the judicial process to the press. In Globe Newspaper Co. v. Superior Court (1982) it held void a Massachusetts statute requiring all rape trials involving a minor victim to be closed to the public. Acknowledging that Richmond had raised the right of access to constitutional stature, the Court made clear that the rule was not an absolute and that a state could close a trial if it could show a compelling governmental interest which "is narrowly tailored to serve that interest." Massachusetts argued that the law would spare the minor victim embarrassment and trauma, and would encourage witnesses to come forward who might otherwise be reluctant to testify. The Court rejected both justifications, noting that the first goal could be met equally well with a discretionary power to close the trial, and the second was vitiated by the fact that the transcript of the testimony and other sources of information about it were available to the press, so that secrecy as a motive to testify was not advanced by the law. In Press-Enterprise Co. v. Superior Court (1984) the Court struck down a court order barring the press from the voir dire examination of a criminal jury without carefully supported findings that such closure was necessary to protect the privacy values of individual talesmen and without examining other alternative ways of protecting them. In this case three days of the voir dire had been open to the press and six weeks of it had been closed.

In the present case, the state's prosecution of the defendant for murder had resulted in three mistrials, at least one of which was apparently the result of a prospective juror reading about inadmissible evidence. At the start of the fourth trial, the defendant asked that the trial be closed. A hearing was held from which the press was excluded and the judge ruled that the press and public be excluded from the trial.

Mr. Chief Justice **Burger** announced the judgment of the Court and delivered an opinion in which Mr. Justice **White** and Mr. Justice **Stevens** joined, saying in part:

II.

We begin consideration of this case by noting that the precise issue presented here has not previously been before this Court for decision. In Gannett Co., Inc. v. DePasquale (1979), the Court was not required to decide whether a right of access to *trials,* as distinguished from hearings on *pre*trial motions, was constitutionally guaranteed. The Court held that the Sixth Amendment's guarantee to the accused of a public trial gave neither the public nor the press an enforceable right of access to a *pre*trial suppression hearing. One concurring opinion specifically emphasized that ''a hearing on a motion before trial to suppress evidence is not a *trial*. . . .'' (Burger, C.J., concurring). Moreover, the Court did not decide whether the First and Fourteenth Amendments guarantee a right of the public to attend trials: nor did the dissenting opinion reach this issue.

In prior cases the Court has treated questions involving conflicts between publicity and a defendant's right to a fair trial; as we observed in Nebraska Press Asso. v. Stuart (1976), ''[t]he problems presented by this [conflict] are almost as old as the Republic.'' . . . But here for the first time the Court is asked to decide whether a criminal trial itself may be closed to the public upon the unopposed request of a defendant, without any demonstration that closure is required to protect the defendant's superior right to a fair trial, or that some other overriding consideration requires closure.

A.

The origins of the proceeding which has become the modern criminal trial in Anglo-American justice can be traced back beyond reliable historical records. We need not here review all details of its development, but a summary of that history is instructive. What is significant for present purposes is that throughout its evolution, the trial has been open to all who cared to observe. . . .

[The Court here traced the development of the English court system from the days before the Norman Conquest down to the sixteenth century, noting the uniform openness of the criminal trial.] Three centuries later, Sir Frederic Pollock was able to state of the "rule of publicity" that, "[h]ere we have one tradition, at any rate, which has persisted through all changes." . . . See also E. Jenks, The Book of English Law 73-74 (6th ed. 1967): "[O]ne of the most conspicuous features of English justice, that all judicial trials are held in open court, to which the public have free access, . . . appears to have been the rule in England from time immemorial."

We have found nothing to suggest that the presumptive openness of the trial, which English courts were later to call "one of the essential qualities of a court of justice," . . . was not also an attribute of the judicial systems of colonial America. In Virginia, for example, such records as there are of early criminal trials indicate that they were open, and nothing to the contrary has been cited. . . . Indeed, when in the mid-1600's the Virginia Assembly felt that the respect due the courts was "by the clamorous unmannerlyness of the people lost, and order, gravity and decoram which should manifest the authority of a court in the court it selfe neglicted," the response was not to restrict the openness of the trials to the public, but instead to prescribe rules for the conduct of those attending them. . . .

In some instances, the openness of trials was explicitly recognized as part of the fundamental law of the colony. . . .

B.

As we have shown, and as was shown in both the Court's opinion and the dissent in Gannett, the historical evidence demonstrates conclusively that at the time when our organic laws were adopted, criminal trials both here and in England had long been presumptively open. This is no quirk of history; rather, it has long been recognized as an indispensible attribute of an Anglo-American trial. Both Hale in the 17th century and Blackstone in the 18th saw the importance of openness to the proper functioning of a trial; it gave assurance that the proceedings were conducted fairly to all concerned, and it discouraged perjury, the misconduct of participants, and decisions based on secret bias or partiality. . . . The nexus between openness, fairness, and the perception of fairness was not lost on [foreign observers]: "[T]he judge, the counsel, and the jury, are constantly exposed to public animadversion; and this greatly tends to augment the extraordinary confidence, which the English repose in the administration of justice."

This observation raises the important point that "[t]he publicity of a judicial proceeding is a requirement of much broader bearing than its mere effect on the quality of testimony." . . . The early history of open trials in part reflects the wide spread acknowledgement, long before there were behavioral scientists, that public trials had significant community therapeutic value. Even without such experts to frame the concept in words, people sensed from experience and observation that, especially in the administration of criminal justice, the means used to achieve justice must have the support derived from public acceptance of both the process and its results.

When a shocking crime occurs, a community reaction of outrage and public protest often follows. . . . Thereafter the open processes of justice serve an important prophylactic purpose, providing an outlet for community concern, hostility, and emotion. Without an awareness that society's responses to criminal conduct are underway, natural human reactions of outrage and protest are frustrated and may manifest themselves in some form of vengeful "self-help," as indeed they did regularly in the activities of vigilante "committees" on our frontiers. . . .

Civilized societies withdraw both from the victim and the vigilante the enforcement of criminal laws, but they cannot erase from people's consciousness the fundamental, natural yearning to see justice done—or even the urge for retribution. The crucial prophylactic aspects of the administration of justice cannot function in the dark; no community catharsis can occur if justice is "done in a corner [or] in any covert manner." It is not enough to say that results alone will satiate the natural community desire for "satisfaction." A result considered untoward may undermine public confidence, and where the trial has been concealed from public view an unexpected outcome can cause a reaction that the system at best has failed and at worst has been corrupted. To work effectively, it is important that society's criminal process "satisfy the appearance of justice," . . . and the appearance of justice can best be provided by allowing people to observe it.

Looking back, we see that when the ancient "town meeting" form of trial became too cumbersome, twelve members of the community were delegated to act as its surrogates, but the community did not surrender its right to observe the conduct of trials. The people retained a "right of visitation" which enabled them to satisfy themselves that justice was in fact being done. . . .

In earlier times, both in England and America, attendance at court was a common mode of "passing the time." . . . With the press, cinema, and electronic media now supplying the representations or reality of the real life drama once available only in the courtroom, attendance at court is no longer a widespread pastime. Yet "[i]t is not unrealistic even in this day to believe that public inclusion affords citizens a form of legal education and hopefully promotes confidence in the fair administration of justice." . . . Instead of acquiring information about trials by firsthand observation or by word of mouth from those who attended, people now acquire it chiefly through the print and electronic media. In a sense, this validates the media claim of functioning as surrogates for the public. While media representatives enjoy the same right of access as the public, they often are provided special seating and priority of entry so that they may report what people in attendance have seen and heard. This "contributes[s] to public understanding of the rule of law and to comprehension of the functioning of the entire criminal justice system. . . ." Nebraska Press Asso. v. Stuart (Brennan, J., concurring).

C.

From this unbroken, uncontradicted history, supported by reasons as valid today as in centuries past, we are bound to conclude that a presumption of openness inheres in the very nature of a criminal trial under our system of justice. This conclusion is hardly novel; without a direct holding on the issue, the Court has voiced its recognition of it in a variety of contexts over the years. . . . Recently in Gannett Co. Inc. v. DePasquale (1979), both the majority and dissenting opinions agreed that open trials were part of the common law tradition.

Despite the history of criminal trials being presumptively open since long before the

Constitution, the State presses its contention that neither the Constitution nor the Bill of Rights contains any provision which by its terms guarantees to the public the right to attend criminal trials. Standing alone, this is correct, but there remains the question whether, absent an explicit provision, the Constitution affords protection against exclusion of the public from criminal trials.

III.

A.

The First Amendment, in conjunction with the Fourteenth, prohibits governments from "abridging the freedom of speech, or of the press; or the right of the people peaceably to assemble, and to Petition the Government for a redress of grievances." These expressly guaranteed freedoms share a common core purpose of assuring freedom of communication on matters relating to the functioning of government. Plainly it would be difficult to single out any aspect of government of higher concern and importance to the people than the manner in which criminal trials are conducted; as we have shown, recognition of this pervades the centuries-old history of open trials and the opinions of this Court.

The Bill of Rights was enacted against the backdrop of the long history of trials being presumptively open. Public access to trials was then regarded as an important aspect of the process itself; the conduct of trials "before as many of the people as chuse to attend" was regarded as one of "the inestimable advantages of a free English constitution of government." . . . In guaranteeing freedoms such as those of speech and press, the First Amendment can be read as protecting the right of everyone to attend trials so as to give meaning to those explicit guarantees. "[T]he First Amendment goes beyond protection of the press and the self-expression of individuals to prohibit government from limiting the stock of information from which members of the public may draw." First National Bank of Boston v. Bellotti (1978). Free speech carries with it some freedom to listen. "In a variety of contexts this Court has referred to a First Amendment right to 'receive information and ideas.' " Kleindienst v. Mandel (1972). What this means in the context of trials is that the First Amendment guarantees of speech and press, standing alone, prohibit government from summarily closing courtroom doors which had long been open to the public at the time that amendment was adopted. "For the First Amendment does not speak equivocally. . . . It must be taken as a command of the broadest scope that explicit language, read in the context of a liberty-loving society, will allow." Bridges v. California (1941).

It is not crucial whether we describe this right to attend criminal trials to hear, see, and communicate observations concerning them as a "right of access," cf. Gannett (Powell, J., concurring); Saxbe v. Washington Post Co. (1974); Pell v. Procunier (1974)* or a "right to gather information," for we have recognized that "without some protection for seeking out the news, freedom of the press could be eviscerated." Branzburg v. Hayes (1972). The

---

*Procunier and Saxbe, supra, are distinguishable in the sense that they were concerned with penal institutions which, by definition, are not "open" or public places. Penal institutions do not share the long tradition of openness. . . .

explicit, guaranteed rights to speak and to publish concerning what takes place at a trial would lose much meaning if access to observe the trial could, as it was here, be foreclosed arbitrarily.

B.

The right of access to places traditionally open to the public, as criminal trials have long been, may be seen as assured by the amalgam of the First Amendment guarantees of speech and press; and their affinity to the right of assembly is not without relevance. From the outset, the right of assembly was regarded not only as an independent right but also as a catalyst to augment the free exercise of the other First Amendment rights with which it was deliberately linked by the draftsmen. "The right of peaceable assembly is a right cognate to those of free speech and free press and is equally fundamental." DeJonge v. Oregon (1937). People assemble in public places not only to speak or to take action, but also to listen, observe, and learn; indeed, they may "assembl[e] for any lawful purpose," Hague v. C.I.O. (1939) (opinion of Stone, J.). Subject to the traditional time, place and manner restrictions, . . . streets, sidewalks, and parks are places traditionally open, where First Amendment rights may be exercised . . . ; a trial courtroom also is a public place where the people generally—and representatives of the media—have a right to be present, and where their presence historically has been thought to enhance the integrity and quality of what takes place.

C.

The State argues that the Constitution nowhere spells out a guarantee for the right of the public to attend trials, and that accordingly no such right is protected. The possibility that such a contention could be made did not escape the notice of the Constitution's draftsmen; they were concerned that some important rights might be thought disparaged because not specifically guaranteed. . . .

But arguments such as the State makes have not precluded recognition of important rights not enumerated. Notwithstanding the appropriate caution against reading into the Constitution rights not explicitly defined, the Court has acknowledged that certain unarticulated rights are implicit in enumerated guarantees. For example, the rights of association and of privacy, the right to be presumed innocent and the right to be judged by a standard of proof beyond a reasonable doubt in a criminal trial, as well as the right to travel, appear nowhere in the Constitution or Bill of Rights. Yet these important, but unarticulated rights have nonetheless been found to share constitutional protection in common with explicit guarantees. The concerns expressed by Madison and others have thus been resolved; fundamental rights, even though not expressly guaranteed, have been recognized by the Court as indispensable to the enjoyment of rights explicitly defined.

We hold that the right to attend criminal trials is implicit in the guarantees of the First Amendment; without the freedom to attend such trials, which people have exercised for centuries, important aspects of freedom of speech and "of the press could be eviscerated." . . .

D.

. . . Despite the fact that this was the fourth trial of the accused, the trial judge made no findings to support closure; no inquiry was made as to whether alternative solutions would have met the need to ensure fairness; there was no recognition of any right under the Constitution for the public or press to attend the trial. In contrast to the proceeding dealt with in Gannett, there exist in the context of the trial itself various tested alternatives to satisfy the constitutional demands of fairness. See, e.g., Nebraska Press Association v. Stuart, Sheppard v. Maxwell. There was no suggestion that any problems with witnesses could not have been dealt with by their exclusion from the courtroom or their sequestration during the trial. Nor is there anything to indicate that sequestration of the jurors would not have guarded against their being subjected to any improper information. All of the alternatives admittedly present difficulties for trial courts, but none of the factors relied on here was beyond the realm of the manageable. Absent an overriding interest articulated in findings, the trial of a criminal case must be open to the public. Accordingly, the judgment under review is reversed.

Reversed.

Mr. Justice **Powell** took no part in the consideration or decision of this case.

Mr. Justice **White** wrote a short concurring opinion.

Mr. Justice **Stevens,** concurring, said in part:

This is a watershed case. Until today the Court has accorded virtually absolute protection to the dissemination of ideas, but never before has it squarely held that the acquisition of newsworthy matter is entitled to any constitutional protection whatsoever. An additional word of emphasis is therefore appropriate. . . .

. . . In Houchins v. KQED, Inc. [1978], I explained at length why Mr. Justice Brennan, Mr. Justice Powell, and I were convinced that "[a]n official prison policy of concealing . . . knowledge from the public by arbitrarily cutting off the flow of information at its source abridges the freedom of speech and of the press protected by the First and Fourteenth Amendments to the Constitution." . . .

It is somewhat ironic that the Court should find more reason to recognize a right of access today than it did in Houchins. For Houchins involved the plight of a segment of society least able to protect itself, an attack on a longstanding policy of concealment, and an absence of any legitimate justification for abridging public access to information about how government operates. In this case we are protecting the interests of the most powerful voices in the community, we are concerned with an almost unique exception to an established tradition of openness in the conduct of criminal trials, and it is likely that the closure order was motivated by the judge's desire to protect the individual defendant from the burden of a fourth criminal trial.

Mr. Justice **Brennan,** with whom Mr. Justice **Marshall** joins, concurring in the judgment, said in part:

Gannett Co. v. DePasquale (1979), held that the Sixth Amendment right to a public trial was personal to the accused, conferring no right of access to pretrial proceedings that is separately enforceable by the public or the press. The instant case raises the question whether the First Amendment, of its own force and as applied to the States through the Fourteenth Amendment, secures the public an independent right of access to trial proceedings. Because I believe that the First Amendment—of itself and as applied to the States through the Fourteenth Amendment—secures such a public right of access, I agree with those of my Brethren who hold that, without more, agreement of the trial judge and the parties cannot constitutionally close a trial to the public.

Mr. Justice **Blackmun,** concurring in the judgment, said in part:

II.

The Court's ultimate ruling in Gannett, with such clarification as is provided by the opinions in this case today, apparently is now to the effect that there is no *Sixth* Amendment right on the part of the public—or the press—to an open hearing on a motion to suppress. I, of course, continue to believe that Gannett was in error, both in its interpretation of the Sixth Amendment generally, and in its application to the suppression hearing, for I remain convinced that the right to a public trial is to be found where the constitution explicitly placed it—in the Sixth Amendment.

The Court, however, has eschewed the Sixth Amendment route. The plurality turns to other possible constitutional sources and invokes a veritable potpourri of them—the speech clause of the First Amendment, the press clause, the assembly clause, the Ninth Amendment, and a cluster of penumbral guarantees recognized in past decisions. This course is troublesome, but it is the route that has been selected, and, at least for now, we must live with it. . . .

Having said all this, and with the Sixth Amendment set to one side in this case, I am driven to conclude, as a secondary position, that the First Amendment must provide some measure of protection for public access to the trial. The opinion in partial dissent in Gannett explained that the public has an intense need and a deserved right to know about the administration of justice in general; about the prosecution of local crimes in particular; about the conduct of the judge, the prosecutor, defense counsel, police officers, other public servants, and all the actors in the judicial arena; and about the trial itself. . . . It is clear and obvious to me, on the approach the Court has chosen to take, that, by closing this criminal trial, the trial judge abridged these First Amendment interests of the public.

I also would reverse, and I join the judgment of the Court.

Mr. Justice **Rehnquist,** dissenting, said in part:

For the reasons stated in my separate concurrence in Gannett Co., Inc. v. DePasquale, I do not believe that either the First or Sixth Amendments as made applicable to the States by the Fourteenth, require that a State's reasons for denying public access to a trial, where both the prosecuting attorney and the defendant have consented to an order of closure approved by the judge, are subject to any additional constitutional review at our hands. And I most certainly do not believe that the Ninth Amendment confers upon us any such power to review orders of state trial judges closing trials in such situations. . . .

The proper administration of justice in any nation is bound to be a matter of the highest concern to all thinking citizens. But to gradually rein in, as this Court has done over the past generation, all of the ultimate decision-making power over how justice shall be administered, not merely in the federal system but in each of the 50 States, is a task that no Court consisting of nine persons, however gifted, is equal to. Nor is it desirable that such authority be exercised by such a tiny numerical fragment of the 220 million people who compose the population of this country.

WALKER v. BIRMINGHAM

388 U. S. 307; 18 L. Ed. 2d 1210; 87 S. Ct. 1824 (1967)

During the late 1950's and early 1960's Southern blacks, led by such people as Martin Luther King, Jr., undertook to bring an end to segregation by nonviolent means. This was to be done by attracting public attention to segregation policies in the hope that the public conscience would be aroused and demand their abolition.

Against these efforts the Southern communities rolled out a battery of legal field pieces, some of them dating back to the early days of the common law. One of these was a prosecution for criminal trespass. Among the techniques employed to publicize segregation was the "sit-in" demonstration, in which blacks, sometimes accompanied by sympathetic whites, would enter a restaurant or lunch counter with a **WHITE ONLY** sign in the window and ask to be served. When service was denied, they refused to leave, and the police would be called to arrest them for trespass.

In five cases decided in 1964 the Supreme Court reversed on nonconstitutional grounds convictions for sit-in demonstrations. Although the Court carefully avoided the issue of whether state enforcement of trespass laws to effect private discrimination made the state a party to the discrimination, six justices in separate opinions indicated their stand on this issue. Justices Black, Harlan, and White argued that in the absence of a statute forbidding such discrimination, the impartial enforcement of trespass statutes does not make the state a party to the discrimination and hence does not deny equal protection, while Justices Warren, Goldberg, and Douglas argued that the framers of the Fourteenth Amendment had assumed the continued existence of the right of all citizens to enter places of public accommodation, and the refusal of the state to enforce that right as to blacks denies them the equal protection of the law. See Bell v. Maryland, Bouie v. Columbia, Griffin v. Maryland, Robinson v. Florida, and Barr v. Columbia.

The final chapter in the sit-in cases was written in Hamm v. Rock Hill (1964), decided the same day as Heart of Atlanta Motel v. United States. Again the Court failed to reach the constitutional issue but concluded that the Civil Rights Act of 1964, by making sit-ins no longer a crime, had abated sit-in prosecutions then in progress, since the states no longer had a policy to be served by such prosecutions. Federal statutes would decree this result as far as federal crimes were concerned, and the supremacy clause dictated the same result for state crimes. The effect of the decision was to stop the prosecution of some 3,000 sit-in demonstrators.

A second technique relied upon by the Southern communities was the well-established right of any organized community to protect itself from a breach of the peace. Such a breach is "a substantive evil which the state can prevent" through the exercise of its police power; therefore a speech which presents a "clear and present danger" of causing a breach of the peace is punishable. Although the use of such statutes against demonstrations and "marches" presented some novel features, the general rules regarding them had been laid down years before. The Supreme Court, in reviewing cases which allege a violation of freedom of speech on this ground must determine (1) that the statute, as interpreted by the state court or by the judge in his charge to the jury, really defines a breach of the peace, and (2) that a clear and present danger of such breach actually exists.

In Chaplinsky v. New Hampshire (1942) a Jehovah's Witness called a police officer "a God damned racketeer" and "a damned Fascist," in violation of a state statute whose purpose, the state court said, was to forbid words "such as have a direct tendency to cause acts of violence by the persons to whom, individually, the remark is addressed." The Court agreed that such speech could constitutionally be punished: "There are certain well-defined and narrowly limited classes of speech, the prevention and punishment of which have never been thought to raise any constitutional problem. These include the lewd and obscene, the profane, the libelous, and the insulting or 'fighting' words—those which by their very utterance inflict injury or tend to incite an immediate breach of the peace. . . . 'Resort to epithets or personal abuse is not in any proper sense communication of information or opinion safeguarded by the Constitution. . . .' " There was, moreover, a clear and present danger: ". . . the appellations 'damned racketeer' and 'damned Fascist' are epithets likely to provoke the average person to retaliation, and thereby cause a breach of the peace."

Another case in which the making of a speech was punished by the city as a breach of the peace was Terminiello v. Chicago (1949), a case which remains bitterly controversial. Terminiello (who denied he was a Fascist) was introduced by Gerald L. K. Smith and spoke in an auditorium in Chicago to a crowd of about 800 persons, under the sponsorship of the Christian Veterans of America. Outside, a protesting crowd of over a thousand (who denied they were Communist-led) milled about, yelling and throwing stones at the windows. Inside Terminiello spoke despite the tumult, linking Democrats, Jews, and Communists together in a speech filled with race hatred. A cordon of policemen assigned to the meeting was unable to prevent several outbreaks of violence, including the smashing of doors and windows.

Terminiello was found guilty of inciting a breach of the peace and fined $100. The trial court charged the jury that " 'breach of the peace' consists of any 'misbehavior which violates the public peace and decorum'; and that the 'misbehavior may constitute a breach of the peace if it stirs the public to anger, invites dispute, brings about a condition of unrest, or creates a disturbance. . . .' " The Supreme Court never reached the question whether the speech itself might be punishable, because it found that the statute as interpreted by the trial judge permitted the punishment of speech that was protected by the Constitution: ". . . A function of free speech under our system of government is to invite dispute. It may indeed best serve its high purpose when it induces a condition of unrest, creates dissatisfaction with conditions as they are, or even stirs people to anger. Speech is often provocative and challenging. It may strike at prejudices and preconceptions and have profound unsettling effects as it presses for acceptance of an idea. . . . The ordinance as construed by the trial court seriously invaded this province."

In contrast to the Terminiello decision, the Court in Feiner v. New York (1951) upheld the disorderly conduct conviction of a Syracuse University student for a street-corner speech in which he was apparently "endeavoring to arouse the Negro people against the whites, urging that they rise up in arms and fight for equal rights." The two policemen present later testified that the mixed crowd of 75 to 80 persons "was restless and there was some pushing, shoving, and milling around." Fearful that they could not control the crowd if violence erupted, they asked Feiner to stop speaking and arrested him when he refused. The Court held the trial court justified in finding a clear and present danger of causing a riot.

In 1963 in Edwards v. South Carolina the Court upheld the right to demonstrate on public property. A group of black students had gathered on the statehouse lawn to protest state segregation policies. The pickets listened to a religious harangue, sang, stamped their feet, and clapped. They refused to disperse when ordered and were arrested for a breach of the peace. The Court held that "the Fourteenth Amendment does not permit a State to make criminal the peaceful expression of unpopular views. . ." and the breach of the peace statute was so vague as to "permit punishment of the fair use of this opportunity." In this case "there was no violence or threat of violence on their part, or on the part of any member of the crowd watching them. Police protection was ample. . . . And the record is barren of any evidence of 'fighting words.' "

The courageous efforts of Southern blacks to achieve racial equality through nonviolent means won widespread admiration and support from the liberal white community and strong encouragement was given the National Association for the Advancement of Colored People (NAACP) in its efforts to win recognition for black rights in the courts. Since the average victim of race discrimination was ill equipped to fight for his legal rights, the NAACP shouldered his financial burden and provided him with legal assistance, with the result that a number of Southern states made serious efforts to oust or cripple the organization. The result was a series of Supreme Court holdings that the organization need not divulge its membership lists either as a condition of doing business in the state (NAACP v. Alabama, 1958), or to a legislative committee investigating Communism in civil rights organizations (Gibson v. Florida Investigation Committee, 1963). Nor was its bringing of test cases punishable as barratry (NAACP v. Button, 1963), and it could not be forbidden to do business in the state (NAACP v. Alabama, 1964). All of these decisions rested on a freedom of association held to be protected by the First Amendment and made applicable to the states by the Fourteenth.

With the outbreak of racial violence in Northern cities in the summer of 1965 and with the breach between the conservative, law-oriented NAACP on the one hand and the more militant Congress of Racial Equality (CORE) and Student Nonviolent Coordinating Committee (SNCC) on the other, Northern white support for the civil rights movement fell off sharply. The 1966 civil rights bill with provisions against anti-civil rights terrorism and an open housing provision failed to pass Congress, and in the fall elections of that year a number of congressional candidates and advocates of referendum measures exploited the fear of "black power" and looked, in some cases successfully, to a "white backlash" for support.

In Adderley v. Florida (1966) the Supreme Court for the first time held valid a state criminal trespass statute against black demonstrators. A group of some 200 students from Florida A&M had marched to the jail in Tallahassee to protest the arrest of some of their body for trying to integrate public theaters, as well as against segregation policies generally. Over 100 remained after being ordered to leave, and were arrested for trespass. In contrast to Edwards, the Court held the trespass statute was not too broad to be valid. "It is aimed at conduct of one limited kind, that is for one person or persons to trespass upon the property of another with a malicious and mischievous intent. There is no lack of notice in this law, nothing to entrap or fool the unwary." Moreover, the demonstration was found to be on "that part of the jail grounds reserved for jail uses," and "the State, no less than a private owner of property, has power to preserve the property under its control for the use to which it is lawfully dedicated. . . . The United States Constitution does not forbid a State to control the use of its own property for its own lawful nondiscriminatory purpose."

The difficulties that confront a state in imposing those "reasonable" limits on free speech which the Constitution allows are illustrated by cases involving the suppression of public nuisances. The Supreme Court held that a statute which forbade entirely the distribution of literature was unconstitutional. In Jamison v. Texas (1943) an ordinance forbade the distribution of handbills on the streets of Dallas. Mrs. Jamison, a member of Jehovah's Witnesses, was convicted of violating the ordinance and fined $5.00. The Court held that "one who is rightfully on a street which the state has left open to the public carries with him there as elsewhere the constitutional right to express his views in an orderly fashion. . . . The right to distribute handbills concerning religious subjects on the streets may not be prohibited at all times, at all places, and under all circumstances."

In 1983 the Court extended this rule to include the sidewalks surrounding the Supreme Court building itself. In Grace v. United States it held void a federal statute forbidding picketing on the premises of the Supreme Court, including the sidewalk immediately surrounding the building but not the sidewalks across the street. Noting that sidewalks "traditionally have been held open to the public for expressive activities" the Court held that Congress could not, without adequate justification, withdraw their "public forum" status. It conceded the right to maintain proper order and decorum within the Court grounds, but held that sidewalks were sidewalks and "a total ban on [picketing] is no more necessary for the maintenance of peace and tranquility on the public sidewalks surrounding the building than on any other sidewalks in the city." Grace had been convicted of carrying a sign bearing the words of the First Amendment.

The state may, on the other hand, place freedom of speech under reasonable police regulations for the protection of the recognized social interests of the community. In Kovacs v. Cooper (1949) the Court upheld a Trenton, New Jersey, ordinance which forbade the use on the streets of a sound-truck which emitted "loud and raucous noises." The Court found that "loud and raucous" was a sufficiently clear definition of the crime, since it has "through daily use acquired a content that conveys to any interested person a sufficiently accurate concept of what is forbidden." Moreover, the restriction was a reasonable one, since "the unwilling listener is not like the passer-by who may be offered a pamphlet in the street but cannot be made to take it." However, while a city may legitimately regulate the display of billboards within its jurisdiction in the interest of traffic safety and the appearance of the city, it may not validly permit exemptions which favor commercial messages over non-commercial messages; see Metromedia, Inc. v. San Diego (1981).

What a state may not limit directly by statute, it may not permit a policeman or other officer to limit under a grant of administrative discretion which amounts to censorship. Many municipalities have used the device of requiring a license for all public modes of expression, and making it a crime to violate the license requirement. The Supreme Court has almost uniformly held these ordinances to be unconstitutional limitations on freedom of speech and press. If the licensing officer has authority to pass on the desirability of the intended speech, or has authority broad enough to forbid a speech protected by the First Amendment, the ordinance is void on its face because it establishes previous censorship, condemned by the Court in Near v. Minnesota (1931). Thus in Saia v. New York (1948) the Court held void an ordinance which forbade the use of a sound-truck on the streets without the permission of the chief of police: "There are no standards prescribed for the exercise of his discretion. The statute is not narrowly drawn to regulate the hours or places of use of loud-speakers, or the volume of sound. . . ."

However, what the state may do directly by statute it may also do through the device of administrative discretion provided the discretion is so narrow that the administrator may not censor speech or press. In Cox v. New Hampshire (1941) the Court sustained an ordinance that required a permit from a license board in order to parade in the streets. A group of Jehovah's Witnesses staged an "information march" without applying for a permit and were convicted of violating the ordinance; the state court held that any other form of expression was open to them, and "the defendants, separately, or collectively in groups not constituting a parade or procession" were "under no contemplation of the Act." Furthermore, the discretion of the license board had to be exercised with "uniformity of method of treatment upon the facts of each application, free from improper or inappropriate considerations and from unfair discrimination." The statutory mandate was held to be a "systematic consistent and just order of treatment, with reference to the convenience of public use of the highways." This, the Supreme Court found, was a valid use of the authority to "control the use of its public streets for parades or processions."

But if a state may not deny a person a license to speak, may it, nevertheless, enjoin a person from speaking and then punish him when he violates the injunction? This problem first arose in the case of Thomas v. Collins (1945). A Texas statute required every labor union organizer operating in the state to secure from the secretary of state an organizer's card before soliciting any members for his union. In order to get the card he had to give his name and his union affiliations and show his credentials. The secretary of state had no discretion to refuse to register such an organizer if he met these requirements. When registered, he was given a card which he was required to carry with him and show to any person whom he solicited for membership. R. J. Thomas, president of the United Automobile Workers, went to Texas after the passage of this act for the express purpose of contesting its validity. He announced his intention to address a labor union meeting, and this plan was widely advertised in advance. He did not apply for registration as a labor organizer as required by the statute. He addressed a meeting of union men and he specifically invited any nonunion person present to join the union. Prior to the meeting, a restraining order was served on Thomas, forbidding him to address the meeting in the capacity of an organizer since he had not registered; and he was later cited for contempt for a deliberate and willful violation of the order.

The Court held the statute void on two grounds. First, the statute was so broad as to make possible the punishment of legitimate speech. It forbade soliciting members, and "how," the Court said, "one might 'laud unionism,' as the State and the State Supreme Court conceded Thomas was free to do, yet in these circumstances not imply an invitation, is hard to conceive. . . . The restriction's effect, as applied, in a very practical sense was to prohibit Thomas not only to solicit members and memberships, but also to speak in advocacy of the cause of trade unionism. . . ." In the second place, there was not a clear and present danger of bringing about a sufficiently substantial injury to the public to justify the restriction: "We cannot say that 'solicit' in this setting is such a dangerous word. So far as free speech alone is concerned, there can be no ban or restriction or burden placed on the use of such a word except on showing of exceptional circumstances where the public safety, morality or health is involved or some other substantial interest of the community is at stake. . . . A restriction so destructive of the right of public discussion, without greater or more imminent danger to the public interest than existed in this case, is incompatible with the freedoms secured by the

First Amendment. . . . If the exercise of the rights of free speech and free assembly cannot be made a crime, we do not think this can be accomplished by the device of requiring previous registration as a condition for exercising them and making such a condition the foundation for restraining in advance their exercise and for imposing a penalty for violating such a restraining order."

A similar problem was presented in Poulos v. New Hampshire (1953), which arose under an ordinance like the one involved in the Cox case. Poulos, a Jehovah's Witness, applied for a permit to speak in Goodwin Park in Portsmouth on a particular Sunday and was refused; Poulos spoke without the permit and was arrested. The state court interpreted the statute as it had in the Cox case, as requiring uniformity and impartiality of treatment. It found that Poulos had not received such treatment, and that the denial of the license had been arbitrary and unreasonable. It held, however, that Poulos was properly convicted; he had no right to violate the ordinance, but should have brought a civil suit in the courts to compel the issuance of a license.

The Supreme Court sustained the conviction on the ground that the ordinance was valid and the state could validly require that arbitrary administrative action be corrected by orderly court procedure: "It must be admitted that judicial correction of arbitrary refusal by administrators to perform official duties under valid laws is exulcerating and costly. But to allow applicants to proceed without the required permits to run businesses, erect structures, purchase firearms, transport or store explosives or inflammatory products, hold public meetings without prior safety arrangements or take other unauthorized action is apt to cause breaches of the peace or create public dangers. The valid requirements of license are for the good of the applicants and the public. It would be unreal to say that such official failures to act in accordance with state law, redressable by state judicial procedures, are state acts violative of the Federal Constitution. Delay is unfortunate, but the expense and annoyance of litigation is a price citizens must pay for life in an orderly society where the rights of the First Amendment have a real and abiding meaning. Nor can we say that a state's requirement that redress must be sought through appropriate judicial procedure violates due process." The Court distinguished this case from Thomas v. Collins, holding that there the statute was void on its face, while here the ordinance was valid.

While Thomas v. Collins suggests that a person is free to ignore a judicial restraining order if the statute under which it is issued is void on its face, the case printed below cast serious doubt upon the vitality of this holding. In April of 1963, Martin Luther King, Jr., together with two other ministers, Wyatt T. Walker and Fred L. Shuttlesworth, announced plans for a "march" on Good Friday. They requested, and were denied, a permit for the march under § 1159 of the Birmingham city code which provided that the city commission "shall grant a written permit for such parade, procession or other public demonstration, prescribing the streets or other public ways which may be used therefor, unless in its judgment the public welfare, peace, safety, health, decency, good order, morals or convenience require that it be refused."

Apparently fearing the march would take place without a permit, city officials applied the Wednesday before Good Friday for an injunction against "participating in or encouraging mass street parades or mass processions without a permit." The injunction was served the following day, and that night a meeting was held at which one of the petitioners announced that "injunction or no injunction we are going to march tomorrow." No attempt was made to seek judicial review of the injunction, and the petitioners marched both on Good Friday and again on Easter Sunday, leading a group of 50 to 60 followers each time.

In two separate cases the petitioners were convicted (1) of disobeying the injunction and (2) of marching without a license, receiving sentences of five days in jail and a $50 fine for the first and 90 days at hard labor (plus 48 days at hard labor in default of payment of a $75 fine and $24 costs) for the second. Because of their different rates of movement through the judicial labyrinth, the case below, involving the validity of the injunction, reached the Supreme Court almost two years before Shuttlesworth v. Birmingham (1969) involving the marching without a license. It is interesting to speculate what the outcomes might have been had Shuttlesworth been decided before Walker, rather than the other way around. In Shuttlesworth the Court found that the ordinance requiring a license to march was void as lacking "the narrow, objective, and definite standards to guide the licensing authority." It reviewed the testimony that efforts to apply for a license a week before the march had been met by the police commissioner with a "No, you will not get a permit in Birmingham, Alabama, to picket," and concluded "the petitioner was clearly given to understand that under no circumstances would he and his group be permitted to demonstrate in Birmingham, not that a demonstration would be approved if a time and place were selected that would minimize traffic problems." While the Court properly noted (in a footnote) that the issues in Walker were different from those in Shuttlesworth, it did not have to face quite as baldly the judicial enforcement of an injunction enforcing an ordinance it had already held void as a denial of freedom of speech.

Mr. Justice **Stewart** delivered the opinion of the Court, saying in part:

. . . On Easter Sunday, April 14, a crowd of between 1,500 and 2,000 people congregated in the midafternoon in the vicinity of Seventh Avenue and Eleventh Street North in Birmingham. One of the petitioners was seen organizing members of the crowd in formation. A group of about 50, headed by three other petitioners, started down the sidewalk two abreast. At least one other petitioner was among the marchers. Some 300 or 400 people from among the onlookers followed in a crowd that occupied the entire width of the street and overflowed onto the sidewalks. Violence occurred. Members of the crowd threw rocks that injured a newspaperman and damaged a police motorcycle.

The next day the city officials who had requested the injunction applied to the state circuit court for an order to show cause why the petitioners should not be held in contempt for violating it. At the ensuing hearing the petitioners sought to attack the constitutionality of the injunction on the ground that it was vague and overbroad, and restrained free speech. They also sought to attack the Birmingham parade ordinance upon similar grounds, and upon the further ground that the ordinance had previously been administered in an arbitrary and discriminatory manner.

The circuit judge refused to consider any of these contentions, pointing out that there had been neither a motion to dissolve the injunction, nor an effort to comply with it by applying for a permit from the city commission before engaging in the Good Friday and Easter Sunday parades. Consequently, the court held that the only issues before it were whether it had jurisdiction to issue the temporary injunction, and whether thereafter the petitioners had knowingly violated it. Upon these issues the court found against the petitioners, and imposed upon each of them a sentence of five days in jail and a $50 fine, in accord with an Alabama statute.

The Supreme Court of Alabama affirmed. . . .

Howat v. Kansas [1922] was decided by this Court almost 50 years ago. That was a case in which people had been punished by a Kansas trial court for refusing to obey an anti-strike injunction issued under the state industrial relations act. They had claimed a right to disobey the court's order upon the ground that the state statute and the injunction based upon it were invalid under the Federal Constitution. The Supreme Court of Kansas had affirmed the judgment, holding that the trial court "had general power to issue injunctions in equity and that, even if its exercise of the power was erroneous, the injunction was not void, and the defendants were precluded from attacking it in this collateral proceeding . . . that, if the injunction was erroneous, jurisdiction was not thereby forfeited, that the error was subject to correction only by the ordinary method of appeal, and disobedience to the order constituted contempt."

This Court, in dismissing the writ of error, not only unanimously accepted but fully approved the validity of the rule of state law upon which the judgment of the Kansas court was grounded:

"An injunction duly issuing out of a court of general jurisdiction with equity powers upon pleadings properly invoking its action, and served upon persons made parties therein and within the jurisdiction, must be obeyed by them however erroneous the action of the court may be, even if the error be in the assumption of the validity of a seeming but void law going to the merits of the case. It is for the court of first instance to determine the question of the validity of the law, and until its decision is reversed for error by orderly review, either by itself or by a higher court, its orders based on its decision are to be respected, and disobedience of them is contempt of its lawful authority, to be punished."

The rule of state law accepted and approved in Howat v. Kansas is consistent with the rule of law followed by the federal courts.

In the present case, however, we are asked to hold that this rule of law, upon which the Alabama courts relied, was constitutionally impermissible. We are asked to say that the Constitution compelled Alabama to allow the petitioners to violate this injunction, to organize and engage in these mass street parades and demonstrations, without any previous effort on their part to have the injunction dissolved or modified, or any attempt to secure a parade permit in accordance with its terms. Whatever the limits of Howat v. Kansas, we cannot accept the petitioners' contentions in the circumstances of this case.

Without question the state court that issued the injunction had, as a court of equity, jurisdiction over the petitioners and over the subject matter of the controversy. And this is not a case where the injunction was transparently invalid or had only a frivolous pretense to validity. We have consistently recognized the strong interest of state and local governments in regulating the use of their streets and other public places. Cox v. New Hampshire [1941]; Kovacs v. Cooper [1949]; Poulos v. New Hampshire [1953]; Adderley v. Florida [1966]. When protest takes the form of mass demonstrations, parades, or picketing on public streets and sidewalks, the free passage of traffic and the prevention of public disorder and violence become important objects of legitimate state concern. As the Court stated, in Cox v. Louisiana, "We emphatically reject the notion . . . that the First and Fourteenth Amendments afford the same kind of freedom to those who would communicate ideas by conduct such as patrolling, marching, and picketing on streets and highways, as these amendments afford to those who communicate ideas by pure speech." . . .

. . . The generality of the language contained in the Birmingham parade ordinance upon which the injunction was based would unquestionably raise substantial constitutional issues concerning some of its provisions. . . . The petitioners, however, did not even attempt to apply to the Alabama courts for an authoritative construction of the ordinance. Had they done so, those courts might have given the licensing authority granted in the ordinance a narrow and precise scope, as did the New Hampshire courts in Cox v. New Hampshire and Poulos v. New Hampshire. . . . Here, just as in Cox and Poulos, it could not be assumed that this ordinance was void on its face.

The breadth and vagueness of the injunction itself would also unquestionably be sub-ject to substantial constitutional question. But the way to raise that question was to apply to the Alabama courts to have the injunction modified or dissolved. The injunction in all events clearly prohibited mass parading without a permit, and the evidence shows that the petitioners fully understood that prohibition when they violated it.

. . . The petitioners also claim that they were free to disobey the injunction because the parade ordinance on which it was based had been administered in the past in an arbitrary and discriminatory fashion. In support of this claim they sought to introduce evidence that, a few days before the injunction issued, requests for permits to picket had been made to a member of the city commission. One request had been rudely rebuffed, and this same official had later made clear that he was without power to grant the permit alone, since the issuance of such permits was the responsibility of the entire city commission. Assuming the truth of this proffered evidence, it does not follow that the parade ordinance was void on its face. The petitioners, moreover, did not apply for a permit either to the commission itself or to any commissioner after the injunction issued. Had they done so, and had the permit been refused, it is clear that their claim of arbitrary or discriminatory administration of the ordinance would have been considered by the state circuit court upon a motion to dissolve the injunction.

This case would arise in quite a different constitutional posture if the petitioners, before disobeying the injunction, had challenged it in the Alabama courts, and had been met with delay or frustration of their constitutional claims. But there is no showing that such would have been the fate of a timely motion to modify or dissolve the injunction. There was an interim of two days between the issuance of the injunction and the Good Friday march. The petitioners give absolutely no explanation of why they did not make some application to the state court during that period. The injunction had issued ex parte; if the court had been presented with the petitioners' contentions, it might well have dissolved or at least modified its order in some respects. If it had not done so, Alabama procedure would have provided for an expedited process of appellate review. It cannot be presumed that the Alabama courts would have ignored the petitioners' constitutional claims. Indeed, these contentions were accepted in another case by an Alabama appellate court that struck down on direct review the conviction under this very ordinance of one of these same petitioners. . . .

The rule of law that Alabama followed in this case reflects a belief that in the fair administration of justice no man can be judge in his own case, however exalted his station, however righteous his motives, and irrespective of his race, color, politics, or religion. This Court cannot hold that the petitioners were constitutionally free to ignore all the procedures of the law and carry their battle to the streets. One may sympathize with the petitioners' impatient commitment to their cause. But respect for judicial process is a small price to pay for the civilizing hand of law, which alone can give abiding meaning to constitutional freedom.

Affirmed.

Mr. Chief Justice **Warren,** whom Mr. Justice **Brennan** and Mr. Justice **Fortas** join, dissenting, said in part:

Petitioners in this case contend that they were convicted under an ordinance that is unconstitutional on its face because it submits their First and Fourteenth Amendment rights to free speech and peaceful assembly to the unfettered discretion of local officials. They further contend that the ordinance was unconstitutionally applied to them because the local officials used their discretion to prohibit peaceful demonstrations by a group whose political viewpoint the officials opposed. The Court does not dispute these contentions, but holds that petitioners may nonetheless be convicted and sent to jail because the patently unconstitutional ordinance was copied into an injunction—issued ex parte without prior notice or hearing on the request of the Commissioner of Public Safety—forbidding all persons having notice of the injunction to violate the ordinance without any limitation of time. I dissent because I do not believe that the fundamental protections of the Constitution were meant to be so easily evaded, or that "the civilizing hand of law" would be hampered in the slightest by enforcing the First Amendment in this case. . . .

The salient facts can be stated very briefly. Petitioners are Negro ministers who sought to express their concern about racial discrimination in Birmingham, Alabama, by holding peaceful protest demonstrations in that city on Good Friday and Easter Sunday, 1963. For obvious reasons, it was important for the significance of the demonstrations that they be held on those particular dates. A representative of petitioners' organization went to the City Hall and asked "to see the person or persons in charge to issue permits, permits for parading, picketing, and demonstrating." She was directed to Public Safety Commissioner Connor, who denied her request for a permit in terms that left no doubt that petitioners were not going to be issued a permit under any circumstances. "He said, 'No, you will not get a permit in Birmingham, Alabama to picket. I will picket you over to the City Jail,' and he repeated that twice." A second, telegraphic request was also summarily denied, in a telegram signed by "Eugene 'Bull' Connor," with the added information that permits could be issued only by the full City Commission, a three-man body consisting of Commissioner Connor and two others.* According to petitioners' offer of proof, the truth of which is assumed for purposes of this case, parade permits had uniformly been issued for all other groups by the city clerk on the request of the traffic bureau of the police department, which was under Commissioner

---

*. . . The attitude of the city administration in general and of its Public Safety Commissioner in particular are a matter of public record, of course, and are familiar to this Court from previous litigation. See Shuttlesworth v. City of Birmingham (1965); Shuttlesworth v. City of Birmingham (1964); Shuttlesworth v. City of Birmingham (1963); Gober v. City of Birmingham (1963); In Re Shuttlesworth (1962). The United States Commission on Civil Rights found continuing abuse of civil rights protestors by the Birmingham police, including use of dogs, clubs, and firehoses. . . . Commissioner Eugene "Bull" Connor, a self-proclaimed white supremacist, . . . made no secret of his personal attitude toward the rights of Negroes and the decisions of this Court. He vowed that racial integration would never come to Birmingham, and wore a button inscribed "Never" to advertise that vow. Yet the Court indulges in speculation that these civil rights protesters might have obtained a permit from this city and this man had they made enough repeated applications.

Connor's direction. The requirement that the approval of the full Commission be obtained was applied only to this one group.

Understandably convinced that the City of Birmingham was not going to authorize their demonstrations under any circumstances, petitioners proceeded with their plans despite Commissioner Connor's orders. On Wednesday, April 10, at 9 in the evening, the city filed in a state circuit court a bill of complaint seeking an ex parte injunction. . . .

. . . The Circuit Court issued the injunction in the form requested, and in effect ordered petitioners and all other persons having notice of the order to refrain for an unlimited time from carrying on any demonstrations without a permit. A permit, of course, was clearly unobtainable; the city would not have sought this injunction if it had any intention of issuing one.

Petitioners were served with copies of the injunction at various times on Thursday and on Good Friday. Unable to believe that such a blatant and broadly drawn prior restraint on their First Amendment rights could be valid, they announced their intention to defy it and went ahead with the planned peaceful demonstrations on Easter weekend. On the following Monday, when they promptly filed a motion to dissolve the injunction, the court found them in contempt, holding that they had waived all their First Amendment rights by disobeying the court order.

These facts lend no support to the court's charges that petitioners were presuming to act as judges in their own case, or that they had a disregard for the judicial process. They did not flee the jurisdiction or refuse to appear in the Alabama courts. Having violated the injunction, they promptly submitted themselves to the courts to test the constitutionality of the injunction and the ordinance it parroted. They were in essentially the same position as persons who challenge the constitutionality of a statute by violating it, and then defend the ensuing criminal prosecution on constitutional grounds. It has never been thought that violation of a statute indicated such a disrespect for the legislature that the violator always must be punished even if the statute was unconstitutional. . . .

I do not believe that giving this Court's seal of approval to such a gross misuse of the judicial process is likely to lead to greater respect for the law any more than it is likely to lead to greater protection for First Amendment freedoms. The ex parte temporary injunction has a long and odious history in this country, and its susceptibility to misuse is all too apparent from the facts of the case. As a weapon against strikes, it proved so effective in the hands of judges friendly to employers that Congress was forced to take the drastic step of removing from federal district courts the jurisdiction to issue injunctions in labor disputes. The labor injunction fell into disrepute largely because it was abused in precisely the same way that the injunctive power was abused in this case. Judges who were not sympathetic to the union cause commonly issued, without notice or hearing, broad restraining orders addressed to large numbers of persons and forbidding them to engage in acts that were either legally permissible or, if illegal, that could better have been left to the regular course of criminal prosecution. The injunctions might later be dissolved, but in the meantime strikes would be crippled because the occasion on which concerted activity might have been effective had passed. Such injunctions, so long discredited as weapons against concerted labor activities, have now been given new life by this Court as weapons against the exercise of First Amendment freedoms. Respect for the courts and for judicial process was not increased by the history of the labor injunction. . . .

. . . The majority opinion in this case rests essentially on a single precedent, and that a case the authority of which has clearly been undermined by subsequent decisions. Howat v. Kansas (1922), was decided in the days when the labor injunction was in fashion. . . .

It is not necessary to question the continuing validity of the holding in Howat v. Kansas, however, to demonstrate that neither it nor the Mine Workers [United States v. United Mine Workers (1947)] case supports the holding of the majority in this case. In Howat the subpoena and injunction were issued to enable the Kansas Court of Industrial Relations to determine an underlying labor dispute. In the Mine Workers case, the District Court issued a temporary anti-strike injunction to preserve existing conditions during the time it took to decide whether it had authority to grant the Government relief in a complex and difficult action of enormous importance to the national economy. In both cases the orders were of questionable legality, but in both cases they were reasonably necessary to enable the court or administrative tribunal to decide an underlying controversy of considerable importance before it at the time. This case involves an entirely different situation. The Alabama Circuit Court did not issue this temporary injunction to preserve existing conditions while it proceeded to decide some underlying dispute. There was no underlying dispute before it, and the court in practical effect merely added a judicial signature to a pre-existing criminal ordinance. Just as the court had no need to issue the injunction to preserve its ability to decide some underlying dispute, the city had no need of an injunction to impose a criminal penalty for demonstrating on the streets without a permit. The ordinance already accomplished that. In point of fact, there is only one apparent reason why the city sought this injunction and why the court issued it: to make it possible to punish petitioners for contempt rather than for violating the ordinance, and thus to immunize the unconstitutional statute and its unconstitutional application from any attack. I regret that this strategy has been so successful. . . .

Mr. Justice **Douglas,** with whom **The Chief Justice,** Mr. Justice **Brennan,** and Mr. Justice **Fortas** concur, dissenting, said in part:

The right to defy an unconstitutional statute is basic in our scheme. Even when an ordinance requires a permit to make a speech, to deliver a sermon, to picket, to parade, or to assemble, it need not be honored when it is invalid on its face. Lovell v. Griffin [1938] . . . Thomas v. Collins [1945]. . . .

Mr. Justice **Brennan,** with whom **The Chief Justice,** Mr. Justice **Douglas,** and Mr. Justice **Fortas** joined, wrote a dissenting opinion.

UNITED STATES v. EICHMAN

110 L. Ed. 2d 287 (1990)

A great many groups in American society rely heavily upon symbols to personify or embody the organization. While the organization itself, with its political structure, its rules and its procedures is difficult for people to feel close to, a symbol representing the organization can evoke tremendous emotional involvement and loyalty. Since prehistoric times, mankind has used idols as symbols to denote its deities and many churches today rely on physical representations to epitomize the spiritual essence of their beliefs. In this way the difficulty of relating to a complex and often contradictory set of beliefs is avoided. The symbol supports the group or community by keeping alive the myth and promise of a known and shared normative vision.

Few problems would exist were these symbols merely the property of private groups, limited in use to the members of those groups. The meaning of an icon used by a secret society does not concern the public at large. When a symbol, such as a flag, is used to represent a nation, however, a very different situation exists. What the adopted symbol represents, among the varied and diverse beliefs present in the nation, can become a very serious question indeed. To what is one subscribing when he pays homage to the flag of a country? Which of the many beliefs in a country is one showing loyalty to when he salutes the British flag? The flag of the Confederate States?

The first major constitutional challenge to saluting the American flag involved, not the beliefs for which the flag stood, but whether one could be *required* to give homage to any symbol. In the 1940s in a small town in West Virginia the Jehovah's Witnesses challenged the requirement that their children salute the flag on the ground that this constituted bowing down to a graven image contrary to the Second Commandment. In West Virginia State Board of Education v. Barnette (1943) the Court held the children involved could not be compelled to salute the flag. Conceding the right of the government to try to foster a spirit of national unity, the Court clearly forbade the use of force to achieve it. "Those who begin coercive elimination of dissent soon find themselves exterminating dissenters. Compulsory unification of opinion achieves only the unanimity of the graveyard.

"It seems trite but necessary to say that the First Amendment to our Constitution was designed to avoid these ends by avoiding these beginnings. There is no mysticism in the American concept of the State or of the nature or origin of its authority. We set up government by consent of the governed, and the Bill of Rights denies those in power any legal opportunity to coerce that consent. Authority here is to be controlled by public opinion, not public opinion by authority. The case is made difficult not because the principles of its decision are obscure but because the flag involved is our own."

The use of the American flag by a number of conservative organizations to symbolize their beliefs has resulted in the unfortunate conclusion by others that that is what the flag does stand for. In Texas v. Johnson (1989) a group of demonstrators burned an American flag to "protest the policies of the Reagan administration and certain Dallas-based corporations." Johnson, who actually did the burning, was convicted of desecrating a flag in violation of Texas law. In a five-to-four decision the Court found the burning to be an "expression of dissatisfaction with the policies of this country" and therefore protected by the First and Fourteenth Amendments. Following this decision Congress passed the Flag Protection Act of 1989 challenged in the case below.

Justice **Brennan** delivered the opinion of the Court, saying in part:

In these consolidated appeals, we consider whether appellees' prosecution for burning a United States flag in violation of the Flag Protection Act of 1989 is consistent with the First Amendment. Applying our recent decision in Texas v. Johnson (1989), the District Courts held that the Act cannot constitutionally be applied to appellees. We affirm.

II.

Last Term in Johnson, we held that a Texas statute criminalizing the desecration of venerated objects, including the United States flag, was unconstitutional as applied to an individual who had set such a flag on fire during a political demonstration. The Texas statute provided that ''[a] person commits an offense if he intentionally or knowingly desecrates ... [a] national flag,'' where ''desecrate'' meant to ''deface, damage, or otherwise physically mistreat in a way that the actor knows will seriously offend one or more persons likely to observe or discover his action.'' We first held that Johnson's flag-burning was ''conduct 'sufficiently imbued with elements of communication' to implicate the First Amendment.'' We next considered and rejected the State's contention that, under United States v. O'Brien (1968), we ought to apply the deferential standard with which we have reviewed Government regulations of conduct containing both speech and nonspeech elements where ''the governmental interest is unrelated to the suppression of free expression.'' We reasoned that the State's asserted interest ''in preserving the flag as a symbol of nationhood and national unity,'' was an interest ''related 'to the suppression of free expression' within the meaning of O'Brien'' because the State's concern with protecting the flag's symbolic meaning is implicated ''only when a person's treatment of the flag communicates some message.'' Johnson, supra. We therefore subjected the statute to '' 'the most exacting scrutiny,' '' and we concluded that the State's asserted interests could not justify the infringement on the demonstrator's First Amendment rights.

After our decision in Johnson, Congress passed the Flag Protection Act of 1989. The Act provides in relevant part:

''(a)(1) Whoever knowingly mutilates, defaces, physically defiles, burns, maintains on the floor or ground, or tramples upon any flag of the United States shall be fined under this title or imprisoned for not more than one year, or both.

''(2) This subsection does not prohibit any conduct consisting of the disposal of a flag when it has become worn or soiled.

''(b) As used in this section, the term 'flag of the United States' means any flag of the United States, or any part thereof, made or any substance, of any size, in a form that is commonly displayed.''

The Government concedes in this case, as it must, that appellees' flag-burning constituted expressive conduct ... but invites us to reconsider our rejection in Johnson of the claim that flag-burning as a mode of expression, like obscenity or ''fighting words,'' does not enjoy the full protection of the First Amendment. Cf. Chaplinsky v. New Hampshire (1942). This we decline to do. The only remaining question is whether the Flag Protection Act is sufficiently distinct from the Texas statute that it may constitutionally be applied to proscribe appellees' expressive conduct.

The Government contends that the Flag Protection Act is constitutional because, unlike the statute addressed in Johnson, the Act does not target expressive conduct on the basis of the content of its message. The Government asserts an interest in ''protect[ing] the physical integrity of the flag under all circumstances'' in order to safeguard the flag's identity '' 'as the unique and unalloyed symbol of the Nation.' '' The Act proscribes conduct (other than disposal) that damages or mistreats a flag, without regard to the actor's motive, his intended message, or the likely effects of his conduct on onlookers. By contrast, the Texas statute expressly prohibited only those acts of physical flag desecration "that the actor knows will seriously offend" onlookers, and the former federal statue prohibited only those acts of desecration that "cas[t] contempt upon" the flag.

Although the Flag Protection Act contains no explicit content-based limitation on the scope of prohibited conduct, it is nevertheless clear that the Government's asserted interest is "related 'to the suppression of free expression,' " and concerned with the content of such expression. The Government's interest in protecting the "physical integrity" of a privately owned flag rests upon a perceived need to preserve the flag's status as a symbol of our Nation and certain national ideals. But the mere destruction or disfigurement of a particular physical manifestation of the symbol, without more, does not diminish or otherwise affect the symbol itself in any way. For example, the secret destruction of a flag in one's own basement would not threaten the flag's recognized meaning. Rather, the Government's desire to preserve the flag as a symbol for certain national ideals is implicated "only when a person's treatment of the flag communicates [a] message" to others that is inconsistent with those ideals.*

Moreover, the precise language of the Act's prohibitions confirms Congress' interest in the communicative impact of flag destruction. The Act criminalizes the conduct of anyone who "knowingly mutilates, defaces, physically defiles, burns, maintains on the floor or ground, or tramples upon any flag." Each of the specific terms—with the possible exception of "burns"—unmistakably connotes disrespectful treatment of the flag and suggests a focus on those acts likely to damage the flag's symbolic value. And the explicit exemption in § 700(a)(2) for disposal of "worn or soiled" flags protects certain acts traditionally associated with patriotic respect for the flag.

As we explained in Johnson, "[I]f we were to hold that a State may forbid flag-burning wherever it is likely to endanger the flag's symbolic role, but allow it wherever burning a flag promotes that role—as where, for example, a person ceremoniously burns a dirty flag— we would be . . . permitting a State to 'prescribe what shall be orthodox' by saying that one may burn the flag to convey one's attitude toward it and its referents only if one does not endanger the flag's representation of nationhood and national unity." Although Congress cast the Flag Protection Act in somewhat broader terms than the Texas statute at issue in Johnson, the Act still suffers from the same fundamental flaw: it suppresses expression out of concern for its likely communicative impact. Despite the Act's wider scope, its restriction

---

*Aside from the flag's association with particular ideals, at some irreducible level the flag is emblematic of the Nation as a sovereign entity. Appellant's amicus asserts that the Government has a legitimate nonspeech-related interest in safeguarding this "eminently practical legal aspect of the flag, as an incident of sovereignty." Brief for the Speaker and the Leadership Group of the United States House of Representatives. This interest has firm historical roots: "While the symbolic role of the flag is now well-established, the flag was an important incident of sovereignty before it was used for symbolic purposes by patriots and others. When the nation's founders first determined to adopt a national flag, they intended to serve specific functions relating to our status as a sovereign nation." . . .

We concede that the Government has a legitimate interest in preserving the flag's function as an "incident of sovereignty," though we need not address today the extent to which this interest may justify any laws regulating conduct that would thwart this core function, as might a commercial or like appropriation of the image of the United States flag. Amicus does not, and cannot, explain how a statute that penalizes anyone who knowingly burns, mutilates, or defiles any American flag is designed to advance this asserted interest in maintaining the association between the flag and the Nation. Burning a flag does not threaten to interfere with this association in any way; indeed, the flag-burner's message depends in part on the viewer's ability to make this very association.

on expression cannot be " 'justified without reference to the content of the regulated speech.' " The Act therefore must be subjected to "the most exacting scrutiny" and for the reasons stated in Johnson the Government's interest cannot justify its infringement on First Amendment rights. We decline the Government's invitation to reassess this conclusion in light of Congress' recent recognition of a purported "national consensus" favoring a prohibition on flag-burning. Even assuming such a consensus exists, any suggestion that the Government's interest in suppressing speech becomes more weighty as popular opposition to that speech grows is foreign to the First Amendment.

III.

" 'National unity as an end which officials may foster by persuasion and example is not in question.' " Johnson, supra, quoting West Virginia Board of Education v. Barnette (1943). Government may create national symbols, promote them, and encourage their respectful treatment. But the Flag Protection Act goes well beyond this by criminally proscribing expressive conduct because of its likely communicative impact.

We are aware that desecration of the flag is deeply offensive to many. But the same might be said, for example, of virulent ethnic and religious epithets, see Terminiello v. Chicago (1949), vulgar repudiations of the draft, see Cohen v. California (1971), and scurrilous caricatures. . . . "If there is a bedrock principle underlying the First Amendment, it is that the government may not prohibit the expression of an idea simply because society finds the idea itself offensive or disagreeable." Johnson, supra. Punishing desecration of the flag dilutes the very freedom that makes this emblem so revered, and worth revering. The judgments are

Affirmed.

Justice **Stevens**, with whom The **Chief Justice**, Justice **White** and Justice **O'Connor** join, dissenting.

The Court's opinion ends where proper analysis of the issue should begin. Of course "the Government may not prohibit the expression of an idea simply because society finds the idea itself offensive or disagreeable." None of us disagrees with that proposition. But it is equally well settled that certain methods of expression may be prohibited if (a) the prohibition is supported by a legitimate societal interest that is unrelated to suppression of the ideas the speaker desires to express; (b) the prohibition does not entail any interference with the speaker's freedom to express those ideas by other means; and (c) the interest in allowing the speaker complete freedom of choice among alternative methods of expression is less important than the societal interest supporting the prohibition.

Contrary to the position taken by counsel for the flag burners in Texas v. Johnson, it is now conceded that the Federal Government has a legitimate interest in protecting the symbolic value of the American flag. Obviously that value cannot be measured, or even described, with any precision. It has at least these two components: in times of national crisis, it inspires and motivates the average citizen to make personal sacrifices in order to achieve societal goals of overriding importance; at all times, it serves as a reminder of the paramount importance of pursuing the ideals that characterize our society.

The first question the Court should consider is whether the interest in preserving the value of that symbol is unrelated to suppression of the ideas that flag burners are trying to express. In my judgment the answer depends, at least in part, on what those ideas are. A flag burner might intend various messages. The flag burner may wish simply to convey hatred, contempt, or sheer opposition directed at the United States. This might be the case if the flag were burned by an enemy during time of war. A flag burner may also, or instead, seek to convey the depth of his personal conviction about some issue, by willingly provoking the use of force against himself. In so doing, he says that "my disagreement with certain policies is so strong that I am prepared to risk physical harm (and perhaps imprisonment) in order to call attention to my views." This second possibility apparently describes the expressive conduct of the flag burners in these cases. Like the protesters who dramatized their opposition to our engagement in Vietnam by publicly burning their draft cards—and who were punished for doing so—their expressive conduct is consistent with affection for this country and respect for the ideals that the flag symbolizes. There is at least one further possibility: a flag burner may intend to make an accusation against the integrity of the American people who disagree with him. By burning the embodiment of America's collective commitment to freedom and equality, the flag burner charges that the majority has forsaken that commitment—that continued respect for the flag is nothing more than hypocrisy. Such a charge may be made even if the flag burner loves the country and zealously pursues the ideals that the country claims to honor.

The idea expressed by a particular act of flag burning is necessarily dependent on the temporal and political context in which it occurs. In the 1960's it may have expressed opposition to the country's Vietnam policies, or at least to the compulsory draft. In Texas v. Johnson, it apparently expressed opposition to the platform of the Republican Party. In these cases, the respondents have explained that it expressed their opposition to racial discrimination, to the failure to care for the homeless, and of course to statutory prohibitions of flag burning. In any of these examples, the protestors may wish both to say that their own position is the only one faithful to liberty and equality, and to accuse their fellow citizens of hypocritical indifference to—or even of a selfish departure from—the ideals which the flag is supposed to symbolize. The ideas expressed by flag burners are thus various and often ambiguous.

The Government's legitimate interest in preserving the symbolic value of the flag is, however, essentially the same regardless of which of many different ideas may have motivated a particular act of flag burning. As I explained in my dissent in Johnson, the flag uniquely symbolizes the ideas of liberty, equality, and tolerance—ideas that Americans have passionately defended and debated throughout our history. The flag embodies the spirit of our national commitment to those ideals. The message thereby transmitted does not take a stand upon our disagreements, except to say that those disagreements are best regarded as competing interpretations of shared ideals. It does not judge particular policies, except to say that they command respect when they are enlightened by the spirit of liberty and equality. To the world, the flag is our promise that we will continue to strive for these ideals. To us, the flag is a reminder both that the struggle for liberty and equality is unceasing, and that our obligation of tolerance and respect for all of our fellow citizens encompasses those who disagree with us—indeed, even those whose ideas are disagreeable or offensive.

Thus, the Government may—indeed, it should—protect the symbolic value of the flag without regard to the specific content of the flag burners' speech. The prosecution in this case does not depend upon the object of the defendants' protest. It is, moreover, equally clear that the prohibition does not entail any interference with the speaker's freedom to express his or her ideas by other means. It may well be true that other means of expression may be less effective in drawing attention to those ideas, but that is not itself a sufficient reason for immunizing flag burning. Presumably a gigantic fireworks display or a parade of nude models in a public park might draw even more attention to a controversial message, but such methods of expression are nevertheless subject to regulation.

This case therefore comes down to a question of judgment. Does the admittedly important interest in allowing every speaker to choose the method of expressing his or her ideas that he or she deems most effective and appropriate outweigh the societal interest in preserving the symbolic value of the flag? This question, in turn, involves three different judgments: (1) The importance of the individual interest in selecting the preferred means of communication; (2) the importance of the national symbol; and (3) the question whether tolerance of flag burning will enhance or tarnish that value. The opinions in Texas v. Johnson demonstrate that reasonable judges may differ with respect to each of these judgments.

The individual interest is unquestionably a matter of great importance. Indeed, it is one of the critical components of the idea of liberty that the flag itself is intended to symbolize. Moreover, it is buttressed by the societal interest in being alerted to the need for thoughtful response to voices that might otherwise go unheard. The freedom of expression protected by the First Amendment embraces not only the freedom to communicate particular ideas, but also the right to communicate them effectively. That right, however, is not absolute—the communicative value of a well-placed bomb in the Capitol does not entitle it to the protection of the First Amendment.

Burning a flag is not, of course, equivalent to burning a public building. Assuming that the protester is burning his own flag, it causes no physical harm to other persons or to their property. The impact is purely symbolic, and it is apparent that some thoughtful persons believe that impact, far from depreciating the value of the symbol, will actually enhance its meaning. I most respectfully disagree. Indeed, what makes this case particularly difficult for me is what I regard as the damage to the symbol that has already occurred as a result of this Court's decision to place its stamp of approval on the act of flag burning. A formerly dramatic expression of protest is now rather commonplace. In today's marketplace of ideas, the public burning of a Vietnam draft card is probably less provocative than lighting a cigarette. Tomorrow flag burning may produce a similar reaction. There is surely a direct relationship between the communicative value of the act of flag burning and the symbolic value of the object being burned.

The symbolic value of the American flag is not the same today as it was yesterday. Events during the last three decades have altered the country's image in the eyes of numerous Americans, and some now have difficulty understanding the message that the flag conveyed to their parents and grandparents—whether born abroad and naturalized or native born. Moreover, the integrity of the symbol has been compromised by those leaders who seem to advocate compulsory worship of the flag even by individuals whom it offends, or who seem to manipulate the symbol of national purpose into a pretext for partisan disputes about meaner ends. And, as I have suggested, the residual value of the symbol after this Court's decision in Texas v. Johnson is surely not the same as it was a year ago.

Given all these considerations, plus the fact that the Court today is really doing nothing more than reconfirming what it has already decided, it might be appropriate to defer to the judgment of the majority and merely apply the doctrine of stare decisis to the case at hand. That action, however, would not honestly reflect my considered judgment concerning the relative importance of the conflicting interests that are at stake. I remain persuaded that the considerations identified in my opinion in Texas v. Johnson are of controlling importance in this case as well.

Accordingly, I respectfully dissent.

LYNCH v. DONNELLY

465 U. S. 668; 79 L. Ed. 2d 604; 104 S. Ct. 1355 (1984)

In its first 150 years the Supreme Court decided but one important case which dealt with freedom of religion. In 1879 the case of Reynolds v. United States reached the conclusion that the religious liberty protected by the First Amendment does not include the right to commit immoral or criminal acts, even though these are sanctioned by religious doctrine. Thus Reynolds, a Mormon in the Territory of Utah, was held properly convicted of the crime of polygamy in spite of the fact that the Mormon religion held polygamy to be proper and desirable. Supreme Court cases involving religious liberty were rare because the First Amendment, which protects freedom of religion, was construed to apply only to Congress and not to the states; see Barron v. Baltimore (1833). Congress had little opportunity and less inclination to violate the First Amendment, and what the states did by way of dealing with religious matters was their own business so far as the federal Constitution was concerned.

By the 1930s this situation had begun to change. As we have seen in Near v. Minnesota (1931), the Court had by this time held that certain of the civil liberties (freedom of speech and press) which are protected by the First Amendment against invasion by the federal government are also part of the liberty which the due process clause of the Fourteenth Amendment forbids the states to abridge. This suggested that state action dealing with religious matters could also be attacked on constitutional grounds in the Supreme Court. Thus in 1934 the Court passed upon the question whether a student who had religious scruples against bearing arms could be compelled, under penalty of expulsion, to take military drill in the University of California. It held in Hamilton v. Regents of University of California (1934) that while the religious beliefs of Hamilton were protected by due process of law, he was not being compelled to attend the university and could assert no constitutional right to do so without complying with the state's requirement of military training.

In the early 1930s the Jehovah's Witnesses, a religious group, began an aggressive nationwide campaign to spread their religious doctrines. In this enterprise every Witness regards himself as a minister of the gospel. The doctrines themselves were grounded on calculations as to the second coming of Christ and the battle of Armageddon, but they also include virulent condemnation of all organized religion and churches, especially the Roman Catholic Church. These were denounced as the works of Satan. The Jehovah's Witnesses spread their teachings by personal appeals, by the sale or free distribution of literature, and by canvassing house to house asking permission to play phonograph records, one of which, called "Enemies," was a bitter attack on religious organizations. Community resentment against the Witnesses and their methods was often intense; it expressed itself at first in a good deal of mob violence, and later in resort to a variety of legal measures designed to discourage the Witnesses and curb their more unpopular activities. With fanatical zeal the Witnesses fought every legal attempt to restrict their freedom of action. As a result they have brought to the Supreme Court since 1938 some 30 major cases involving religious liberty issues. In a majority of these they have been successful. These decisions have done much to clarify our constitutional law relating to freedom of religion.

The most spectacular issue of religious liberty to be raised by the Jehovah's Witnesses was that of the compulsory flag salute. The Witnesses refuse to salute the flag or permit their children to do so, because they believe that this violates the First Commandment. This refusal caused bitter resentment, and some 17 states passed statutes requiring all school children to salute the flag and providing for the expulsion of those who refused. The question of whether these acts unconstitutionally restricted freedom of religion came to the Court in Minersville School District v. Gobitis (1940). With one judge dissenting, the Court held that it did not. In an opinion by Justice Frankfurter it was stated that freedom of religion is not absolute, and that some compromises may be necessary in order to secure the national unity, which is the basis of national security. In West Virginia State Board of Education v. Barnette (1943), discussed in the note to the Eichman case, the Court overruled Gobitis on the ground that the state's requirement violated freedom of speech.

In Sherbert v. Verner (1963) the free exercise clause was held violated where un-employment compensation was denied a Seventh Day Adventist who refused "suitable" work which required her to work on Saturday. Such a rule, the Court held, "forces her to choose between following the precepts of her religion and forfeiting benefits, on the one hand, and abandoning one of the precepts of her religion in order to accept work on the other hand. Governmental imposition of such a choice puts the same kind of burden upon the free exer-cise of religion as would a fine imposed against appellant for her Saturday worship." The holding was reaffirmed in Thomas v. Review Board (1981) where a Jehovah's Witness was held entitled to unemployment insurance after quitting for religious reasons a job which in-volved making weapons. The steel company for which he worked had closed the roll foundry where he worked and transferred him to a department making gun turrets. It was reaffirmed again in Frazee v. Employment Security Dept. (1989) and extended to a professed Christian who belonged to no particular sect but established a sincerely held religious belief against working on Sunday.

In two cases the Court dealt with the unusual demands of the Old Order Amish, a plain people who lead a simple, rural farm life in cohesive, self-supporting religious communities, stressing "a life of 'goodness,' rather than a life of intellect; wisdom, rather than technical knowledge; community welfare rather than competition; and separation from, rather than integration with, contemporary worldly society." They dress plainly, do not use machinery or electricity and their transportation consists of horse-drawn wagons and buggies lighted at night with a lantern. In Wisconsin v. Yoder (1972) they resisted the efforts of the state to make their children attend school past the eighth grade. They argued that by sending their children to high school "they would not only expose themselves to the danger of the censure of the church community, but . . . endanger their own salvation and that of their children." The Court held that in view of the kind of life for which the Amish children were being trained and the unquestioned success of the Amish society, the state did not have sufficiently compelling interest in the additional years of schooling to warrant interfering with the free exercise of their religion. In United States v. Lee (1982), however, the Court held that Amish employers and employees had to pay into the social security system despite the self-sufficiency of the Amish and the fact "that both payment and receipt of social security benefits is forbidden by the Amish faith." The Court found mandatory participation essential to the fiscal vitality of the system and noted the lack of difference in principle between this and the payment of income taxes which any number of religious groups might object to paying through religious objection to the purposes for which the money was spent.

Although most of the Court's early cases involved the free exercise clause of the First Amendment, a number of difficult problems have arisen in recent years under the provision that "Congress shall make no law respecting an establishment of religion." The free exercise and no establishment clauses of the First Amendment were the framers' answer to the place of religion in the highly pluralistic social structures of the time. Religion was to be a private affair; the heavy thumb of the government was to be used neither to aid nor hinder, lest man's freedom to worship as he chose and the right to support only the church of his choice be jeopardized. But even as the framers wrote, many of the practices of the time made clear that the "separation of church and state" would not entail the government ignoring the existence of religion. Both houses of the Congress employed a chaplain; "In God We Trust" was embossed on our coins; and the help and understanding of God were exhorted on all public occasions. In general the people thought of themselves as religious, mostly Christian, and a government recognition of that fact did not seem in any way inconsistent with the doctrines of the First Amendment.

With the gradual diversification of religious beliefs many well-accepted religious practices and manifestations were challenged in the courts, and with the application to the states of the religion clauses of the First Amendment, these challenges raised potential federal questions.

The Supreme Court has shown considerable reluctance to review many activities that have been part of our historical heritage. In November 1964, it left untouched a New York decision upholding the words "under God" in the pledge of allegiance; in 1966 (Murray v. Goldstein) it declined to review a Maryland case upholding the validity of tax exemption for church buildings, and as recently as 1971 it let stand the rejection by a district court of an effort to stop the astronauts from praying over television on their way to the moon (O'Hair v. Paine, 1971).

However, in Walz v. Tax Commission (1970) the Court accepted a case challenging the validity of tax exemption for church property. The case was brought by a reclusive New York attorney who was a Christian, but not a member of any religious organization. He owned a 22 x 29-foot plot of land on Staten Island which, with neither buildings nor street access, was assessed by the City of New York at $100. Walz refused to pay the $5.24 a year property tax on the ground that he was being forced to support churches and synagogues, which pay no taxes. The Court recognized its past struggles to "find a neutral course between the two Religion Clauses, both of which are cast in absolute terms, and either of which, if expanded to a logical extreme, would tend to clash with the other." It concluded that "no perfect or absolute separation is really possible," that both had to coexist, and the real function of the Court was to prevent "excessive entanglement" between the two. Since tax exemption for churches had been in existence since the formation of the Union, it posed no real threat to the separation of church and state. "The exemption creates only a minimal and remote involvement between church and state and far less than the taxation of churches. It restricts the fiscal relationship between church and state, and tends to complement and reinforce the desired separation insulating each from the other."

In Marsh v. Chambers (1983) the Court held valid the employment of a chaplain for the state legislature noting that the framers had employed one for Congress at the same time they were proposing the First Amendment, and "the practice of opening legislative sessions with prayer has become part of the fabric of our society."

It seems apparent that while the early governments in this country tended to let the individual fend for himself as far as his economic welfare went, they did not take any such hands-off policy with regard to his spiritual welfare. Even those colonies that did not have established religions tended to encourage religion, usually a Protestant Christianity. Among the most common forms of such encouragement were the so-called Sunday Blue Laws, or Sunday Closing Laws, adopted to advance "the true and sincere worship of God according to his holy will" (New York) or "to the end that the Sabbath may be celebrated in a religious manner" (Massachusetts Bay Colony). Such laws, which were adopted in every state but Alaska, forbid to a greater or lesser extent various forms of physical or economic activity on Sunday. Some merely forbid the selling of liquor, while others forbid all economic activity and then set up elaborate exceptions to the rule. In four cases in 1961 the Court held valid the Sunday closing laws of Maryland and Pennsylvania. In two of the cases the defendants alleged that the laws constituted an establishment of religion. The Court rejected this contention. Conceding that the origin of such laws was undoubtedly religious and that the day chosen favored the dominant Christian sects, the Court pointed out that such laws had long since ceased to be religiously inspired and were merely an exercise of the police power of the state to provide the community a day of rest, amusement, and family togetherness. The state, the Court held, could reasonably decide that everyone should rest on the same day (rather than let each individual choose his own day) and it was not an establishment of religion to pick the day that most people thought of as a "day off," even though it had a religious origin. See McGowan v. Maryland (1961) and Two Guys from Harrison-Allentown, Inc. v. McGinley (1961).

In two of the cases the Court faced the additional question of the free exercise of religion. Gallagher v. Crown Kosher Super Market (1961) and Braunfeld v. Brown (1961) involved Orthodox Jews who closed their businesses on Saturday, the Jewish Sabbath, and claimed that forcing them to close on Sunday, too, was in effect to place an economic burden upon them because of their religion. Although the six members of the majority could not agree on an opinion, they did agree that since the laws were valid under the police power and were not intended to discriminate against persons on religious grounds, the indirect economic disadvantage visited on persons because of their religious beliefs did not render the law a violation of their religious liberties. In illustration they pointed to the validity of laws against polygamy, held valid in Reynolds v. United States (1879).

In 1977 Connecticut amended its Sunday-closing law to provide that "no person who states that a particular day of the week is observed as his Sabbath may be required by his employer to work on such day. An employee's refusal to work on his Sabbath shall not constitute grounds for dismissal." In Thornton v. Caldor (1985) the Court held the statute a violation of the establishment clause because it had no secular purpose. "The State . . . commands that Sabbath religious concerns automatically control over all secular interests at the work place; the statute takes no account of the convenience or interests of the employer or those of other employees who do not observe a Sabbath. . . . There is no exception under the statute for special circumstances, such as the Friday Sabbath observer employed in an occupation with a Monday through Friday schedule—a school teacher, for example . . . . This unyielding weighting in favor of Sabbath observers over all other interests contravenes a fundamental principle of the Religion Clauses . . . ." In Texas Monthly v. Bullock (1989) the Court held void a Texas tax exemption for religious periodicals on the ground it violated the establishment clause.

Five years after the present case was decided the Court faced a case involving the placing of a crèche on the grand staircase of the county office building by a Roman Catholic group and a 45-foot Christmas tree and an 18-foot Chanukah menorah outside the building. In Allegheny County v. Pittsburgh ACLU (1989) a divided Court held void the crèche within the building but approved the Christmas tree and menorah on the ground they were related to holidays rather than religious ceremonies. Justices Blackmun, O'Connor, Kennedy, Rehnquist, White and Scalia agreed the menorah did not advance religion, the latter four on the ground that none of the displays did so. Justices Blackmun, O'Connor, Marshall, Stevens and Brennan agreed the crèche was an aid to religion, while the latter three agreed both the crèche and the menorah were such an aid.

The present case involves a challenge to the inclusion of a crèche in a city owned Christmas display on the ground that "the erection of the crèche has the real and substantial effect of affiliating the City with the Christian beliefs that the crèche represents."

Chief Justice **Burger** delivered the opinion of the Court, saying in part:

We granted certiorari to decide whether the Establishment Clause of the First Amendment prohibits a municipality from including a crèche, or Nativity scene, in its annual Christmas display.

I.

Each year, in cooperation with the downtown retail merchants' association, the city of Pawtucket, R. I., erects a Christmas display as part of its observance of the Christmas holiday season. The display is situated in a park owned by a nonprofit organization and located in the heart of the shopping district. The display is essentially like those to be found in hundreds of towns or cities across the Nation—often on public grounds—during the Christmas season. The Pawtucket display comprises many of the figures and decorations traditionally associated with Christmas, including, among other things, a Santa Claus house, reindeer pulling Santa's sleigh, candy-striped poles, a Christmas tree, carolers, cutout figures representing such characters as a clown, an elephant, and a teddy bear, hundreds of colored lights, a large banner that reads "SEASONS GREETINGS," and the crèche at issue here. All components of this display are owned by the city.

The crèche, which has been included in the display for 40 or more years, consists of the traditional figures, including the Infant Jesus, Mary and Joseph, angels, shepherds, kings, and animals, all ranging in height from 5" to 5'. In 1973, when the present crèche was acquired, it cost the city $1365; it now is valued at $200. The erection and dismantling of the crèche costs the city about $20 per year; nominal expenses are incurred in lighting the crèche. No money has been expended on its maintenance for the past 10 years. . . .

II.

A.

This Court has explained that the purpose of the Establishment and Free Exercise Clauses of the First Amendment is "to prevent, as far as possible, the intrusion of either [the church or the state] into the precincts of the other." Lemon v. Kurtzman (1971). At the same time, however, the Court has recognized that "total separation is not possible in an absolute sense. Some relationship between government and religious organizations is inevitable." In every Establishment Clause case, we must reconcile the inescapable tension between the objective of preventing unnecessary intrusion of either the church or the state upon the other, and the reality that, as the Court has so often noted, total separation of the two is not possible.

The Court has sometimes described the Religion Clauses as erecting a "wall" between church and state, see, e.g., Everson v. Board of Education (1947). The concept of a "wall" of separation is a useful figure of speech probably deriving from views of Thomas Jefferson. The metaphor has served as a reminder that the Establishment Clause forbids an established church or anything approaching it. But the metaphor itself is not a wholly accurate description of the practical aspects of the relationship that in fact exists between church and state.

No significant segment of our society and no institution within it can exist in a vacuum or in total or absolute isolation from all the other parts, much less from government. "It has never been thought either possible or desirable to enforce a regime of total separation. . . ." . . . Nor does the Constitution require complete separation of church and state; it affirmatively mandates accommodation, not merely tolerance, of all religions, and forbids hostility toward any. . . . Anything less would require the "callous indifference" we have said was never intended by the Establishment Clause. Zorach [v. Clauson (1952)]. Indeed, we have observed, such hostility would bring us into "war with our national tradition as embodied in the First Amendment's guaranty of the free exercise of religion." , . . .

B.

The Court's interpretation of the Establishment Clause has comported with what history reveals was the contemporaneous understanding of its guarantees. A significant example of the contemporaneous understanding of that Clause is found in the events of the first week of the First Session of the First Congress in 1789. In the very week that Congress approved the Establishment Clause as part of the Bill of Rights for submission to the states, it enacted legislation providing for paid chaplains for the House and Senate. . . .

The interpretation of the Establishment Clause by Congress in 1789 takes on special significance in light of the Court's emphasis that the First Congress "was a Congress whose constitutional decisions have always been regarded, as they should be regarded, as of the greatest weight in the interpretation of that fundamental instrument," Myers v. United States (1926).

It is clear that neither the 17 draftsmen of the Constitution who were Members of the First Congress, nor the Congress of 1789, saw any establishment problem in the employment of congressional Chaplains to offer daily prayers in the Congress, a practice that has continued for nearly two centuries. It would be difficult to identify a more striking example of the accommodation of religious belief intended by the Framers.

C. . . .

Other examples of reference to our religious heritage are found in the statutorily prescribed national motto "In God We Trust," which Congress and the President mandated for our currency, and in the language "One nation under God," as part of the Pledge of Allegiance to the American flag. That pledge is recited by many thousands of public school children—and adults—every year.

Art galleries supported by public revenues display religious paintings of the 15th and 16th centuries, predominantly inspired by one religious faith. . . . The very chamber in which oral arguments on this case were heard is decorated with a notable and permanent—not seasonal—symbol of religion: Moses with the Ten Commandments. Congress has long provided chapels in the Capitol for religious worship and meditation. . . .

III.

This history may help explain why the Court consistently has declined to take a rigid, absolutist view of the Establishment Clause. We have refused "to construe the Religion Clauses with a literalness that would undermine the ultimate constitutional objective *as illuminated by history*." Walz v. Tax Commission (1970) (Emphasis added). In our modern, complex society, whose traditions and constitutional underpinnings rest on and encourage diversity and pluralism in all areas, an absolutist approach in applying the Establishment Clause is simplistic and has been uniformly rejected by the Court.

Rather than mechanically invalidating all governmental conduct or statutes that confer benefits or give special recognition to religion in general or to one faith—as an absolutist approach would dictate—the Court has scrutinized challenged legislation or official conduct to determine whether, in reality, it establishes a religion or religious faith, or tends to do so. . . .

In the line-drawing process we have often found it useful to inquire whether the challenged law or conduct has a secular purpose, whether its principal or primary effect is to advance or inhibit religion, and whether it creates an excessive entanglement of government with religion. But, we have repeatedly emphasized our unwillingness to be confined to any single test or criterion in this sensitive area. . . .

In this case, the focus of our inquiry must be on the crèche in the context of the Christmas season. . . . Focus exclusively on the religious component of any activity would inevitably lead to its invalidation under the Establishment Clause.

The Court has invalidated legislation or governmental action on the ground that a secular purpose was lacking, but only when it has concluded there was no question that the statute or activity was motivated wholly by religious considerations. . . .

The District Court inferred from the religious nature of the crèche that the city has no secular purpose for the display. In so doing, it rejected the city's claim that its reasons for including the crèche are essentially the same as its reasons for sponsoring the display as a whole. . . . The city, like the Congresses and Presidents, . . . has principally taken note of a significant historical religious event long celebrated in the Western World. The crèche in the display depicts the historical origins of this traditional event long recognized as a National Holiday. . . .

The narrow question is whether there is a secular purpose for Pawtucket's display of the crèche. The display is sponsored by the city to celebrate the Holiday and to depict the origins of that Holiday. These are legitimate secular purposes. The District Court's inference, drawn from the religious nature of the crèche, that the city has no secular purpose was, on this record, clearly erroneous. . . .

The dissent asserts some observers may perceive that the city has aligned itself with the Christian faith by including a Christian symbol in its display and that this serves to advance religion. We can assume, arguendo, that the display advances religion in a sense; but our precedents plainly contemplate that on occasion some advancement of religion will result from governmental action. The Court has made it abundantly clear, however, that "not every law that confers an 'indirect,' 'remote,' or 'incidental' benefit upon [religion] is, for that reason alone, constitutionally invalid." [Committee for Public Education v.] Nyquist [1973]. . . .

The District Court found that there had been no administrative entanglement between religion and state resulting from the city's ownership and use of the crèche. But it went on to hold that some political divisiveness was engendered by this litigation. Coupled with its finding of an impermissible sectarian purpose and effect, this persuaded the court that there was "excessive entanglement." . . .

The Court of Appeals correctly observed that this Court has not held that political divisiveness alone can serve to invalidate otherwise permissible conduct. And we decline to so hold today. . . . In any event, apart from this litigation there is no evidence of political friction or divisiveness over the crèche in the 40-year history of Pawtucket's Christmas celebration. . . . A litigant cannot, by the very act of commencing a lawsuit . . . create the appearance of divisiveness and then exploit it as evidence of entanglement.

We are satisfied that the city has a secular purpose for including the crèche, that the city has not impermissibly advanced religion, and that including the crèche does not create excessive entanglement between religion and government. . . .

Justice **O'Connor,** concurring, said in part:

I concur in the opinion of the Court. I write separately to suggest a clarification of our Establishment Clause doctrine. . . .

I.

The Establishment Clause prohibits government from making adherence to a religion relevant in any way to a person's standing in the political community. Government can run afoul of that prohibition in two principal ways. One is excessive entanglement with religious institutions, which may interfere with the independence of the institutions, give the institutions access to government or governmental powers not fully shared by nonadherents of the religion, and foster the creation of political constituencies defined along religious lines. . . . The second and more direct infringement is government endorsement or disapproval of religion. Endorsement sends a message to nonadherents that they are outsiders, not full members of the political community, and an accompanying message to adherents that they are insiders, favored members of the political community. Disapproval sends the opposite message. . . .

III. . . .

B. . . .

Pawtucket's display of its crèche, I believe, does not communicate a message that the government intends to endorse the Christian beliefs represented by the crèche. Although the religious and indeed sectarian significance of the crèche, as the district court found, is not neutralized by the setting, the overall holiday setting changes what viewers may fairly understand to be the purpose of the display—as a typical museum setting, though not neutralizing the religious content of a religious painting, negates any message of endorsement of that content. The display celebrates a public holiday, and no one contends that declaration of that holiday is understood to be an endorsement of religion. . . .

Justice **Brennan,** with whom Justice **Marshall,** Justice **Blackmun** and Justice **Stevens** join, dissenting, said in part:

The principles announced in the compact phrases of the Religion Clauses have, as the Court today reminds us, proved difficult to apply. Faced with that uncertainty, the Court properly looks for guidance to the settled test announced in Lemon v. Kurtzman (1971). . . .

I. . . .

A. . . .

This well-defined three-part test expresses the essential concerns animating the Establishment Clause. Thus, the test is designed to ensure that the organs of government remain strictly separate and apart from religious affairs, for "a union of government and religion tends to destroy government and degrade religion." . . .

Applying the three-part test to Pawtucket's crèche, I am persuaded that the city's inclusion of the crèche in its Christmas display simply does not reflect a "clearly . . . secular purpose." . . . Here we have no explicit statement of purpose by Pawtucket's municipal government accompanying its decision to purchase, display, and maintain the crèche. Governmental purpose may nevertheless be inferred. . . . In the present case, the city claims that its purposes were exclusively secular. Pawtucket sought, according to this view, only to participate in the celebration of a national holiday and to attract people to the downtown area in order to promote pre-Christmas retail sales and to help engender the spirit of goodwill and neighborliness commonly associated with the Christmas season.

Despite these assertions, two compelling aspects of this case indicate that our generally prudent "reluctance to attribute unconstitutional motives" to a governmental body . . . should be overcome. First, . . . all of Pawtucket's "valid secular objectives can be readily accomplished by other means." Plainly, the city's interest in celebrating the holiday and in promoting both retail sales and goodwill are fully served by the elaborate display of Santa Claus, reindeer, and wishing wells that are already a part of Pawtucket's annual Christmas display. More importantly, the nativity scene, unlike every other element of the Hodgson Park display, reflects a sectarian exclusivity that the avowed purposes of celebrating the holiday season and promoting retail commerce simply do not encompass. To be found constitutional, Pawtucket's seasonal celebration must at least be nondenominational and not serve to promote religion. The inclusion of a distinctively religious element like the crèche, however, demonstrates that a narrower sectarian purpose lay behind the decision to include a nativity scene. That the crèche retained this religious character for the people and municipal government of Pawtucket is suggested by the Mayor's testimony at trial in which he stated that for him, as well as others in the city, the effort to eliminate the nativity scene from Pawtucket's Christmas celebration "is a step towards establishing another religion, nonreligion that it may be." Plainly, the city and its leaders understood that the inclusion of the crèche in its display would serve the wholly religious purpose of "keep[ing] 'Christ in Christmas.' " From this record, therefore, it is impossible to say with the kind of confidence that was possible in McGowan v. Maryland (1961) that a wholly secular goal predominates.

The "primary effect" of including a nativity scene in the city's display is, as the District Court found, to place the government's imprimatur of approval on the particular religious beliefs exemplified by the crèche. Those who believe in the message of the nativity receive the unique and exclusive benefit of public recognition and approval of their views. For many, the city's decision to include the crèche as part of its extensive and costly efforts to celebrate Christmas can only mean that the prestige of the government has been conferred on the beliefs associated with the crèche, thereby providing "a significant symbolic benefit to religion. . . ." . . . The effect on minority religious groups, as well as on those who may reject all religion, is to convey the message that their views are not similarly worthy of public recognition nor entitled to public support. It was precisely this sort of religious chauvinism that the Establishment Clause was intended forever to prohibit. . . .

Finally, it is evident that Pawtucket's inclusion of a crèche as part of its annual Christmas display does pose a significant threat of fostering "excessive entanglement." . . . It is worth noting that after today's decision, administrative entanglements may well develop. Jews and other non-Christian groups, prompted perhaps by the Mayor's remark that he will include a Menorah in future displays, can be expected to press government for inclusion of their symbols, and faced with such requests, government will have to become involved in accommodating the various demands. . . . More importantly, although no political divisiveness was apparent in Pawtucket prior to the filing of respondents' lawsuit, that act, as the District Court found, unleashed powerful emotional reactions which divided the city along religious lines. The fact that calm had prevailed prior to this suit does not immediately suggest the absence of any division on the point for, as the District Court observed, the quiescence of those opposed to the crèche may have reflected nothing more than their sense of futility in opposing the majority. Of course, the Court is correct to note that we have never held that the potential for divisiveness alone is sufficient to invalidate a challenged governmental practice; we have, nevertheless, repeatedly emphasized that "too close a proximity" between religious and civil authorities . . . may represent a "warning signal" that the values embodied in the Establishment Clause are at risk. . . .

B. . . .

. . . I refuse to accept the notion implicit in today's decision that non-Christians would find that the religious content of the crèche is eliminated by the fact that it appears as part of the city's otherwise secular celebration of the Christmas holiday. The nativity scene is clearly distinct in its purpose and effect from the rest of the Hodgson Park display for the simple reason that it is the only one rooted in a biblical account of Christ's birth. It is the chief symbol of the characteristically Christian belief that a divine Savior was brought into the world and that the purpose of this miraculous birth was to illuminate a path toward salvation and redemption. For Christians, that path is exclusive, precious, and holy. But for those who do not share these beliefs, the symbolic reenactment of the birth of a divine being who has been miraculously incarnated as a man stands as a dramatic reminder of their differences with Christian faith. When government appears to sponsor such religiously inspired views, we cannot say that the practice is " 'so separate and so indisputably marked off from the religious function,' . . . that [it] may fairly be viewed as reflect[ing] a neutral posture toward religious institutions." . . . To be so excluded on religious grounds by one's elected government is an insult and an injury that, until today, could not be countenanced by the Establishment Clause.

Second. . . . The Court apparently believes that once it finds that the designation of Christmas as a public holiday is constitutionally acceptable, it is then free to conclude that virtually every form of governmental association with the celebration of the holiday is also constitutional. The vice of this dangerously superficial argument is that it overlooks the fact that the Christmas holiday in our national culture contains both secular and sectarian elements. To say that government may recognize the holiday's traditional, secular elements of gift-giving, public festivities, and community spirit, does not mean that government may indiscriminately embrace the distinctively sectarian aspects of the holiday. Indeed, in its eagerness to approve the crèche, the Court has advanced a rationale so simplistic that it would appear to allow the Mayor of Pawtucket to participate in the celebration of a Christmas Mass, since this would be just another unobjectionable way for the city to "celebrate the holiday." As is demonstrated below, the Court's logic is fundamentally flawed both because it obscures the reason why public designation of Christmas Day as a holiday is constitutionally acceptable, and blurs the distinction between the secular aspects of Christmas and its distinctively religious character, as exemplified by the crèche. . . .

III.

The American historical experience concerning the public celebration of Christmas, if carefully examined, provides no support for the Court's decision. The opening sections of the Court's opinion, while seeking to rely on historical evidence, do no more than recognize the obvious: because of the strong religious currents that run through our history, an inflexible or absolutistic enforcement of the Establishment Clause would be both imprudent and impossible. This observation is at once uncontroversial and unilluminating. Simply enumerating the various ways in which the Federal Government has recognized the vital role religion plays in our society does nothing to help decide the question presented in *this* case.

Indeed, the Court's approach suggests a fundamental misapprehension of the proper uses of history in constitutional interpretation. Certainly, our decisions reflect the fact that an awareness of historical practice often can provide a useful guide in interpreting the abstract language of the Establishment Clause. . . . But historical acceptance of a particular practice alone is never sufficient to justify a challenged governmental action, since, as the Court has rightly observed, ''no one acquires a vested or protected right in violation of the Constitution by long use, even when that span of time covers our entire national existence and indeed predates it.'' . . .

In McGowan, for instance, the Court carefully canvassed the entire history of Sunday Closing Laws from the colonial period up to modern times. On the basis of this analysis, we concluded that while such laws were rooted in religious motivations, the current purpose was to serve the wholly secular goal of providing a uniform day of rest for all citizens. Our inquiry in Walz was similarly confined to the special history of the practice under review. There the Court found a pattern of ''undeviating acceptance'' over the entire course of the Nation's history of according property-tax exemptions to religious organizations, a pattern which supported our finding that the practice did not violate the Religion Clauses. Finally, where direct inquiry into the Framer's intent reveals that the First Amendment was not understood to prohibit a particular practice, we have found such an understanding compelling. Thus, in Marsh v. Chambers, after marshaling the historical evidence which indicated that the First Congress had authorized the appointment of paid chaplains for its own proceedings only three days before it reached agreement on the final wording of the Bill of Rights, the Court concluded on the basis of this ''unique history'' that the modern-day practice of opening legislative sessions with prayer was constitutional.

Although invoking these decisions in support of its result, the Court wholly fails to discuss the history of the public celebration of Christmas or the use of publicly displayed nativity scenes. The Court, instead, simply asserts, without any historical analysis or support whatsoever, that the now familiar celebration of Christmas springs from an unbroken history of acknowledgement ''by the people, by the Executive Branch, by the Congress, and the courts for two centuries. . . .'' The Court's complete failure to offer any explanation of its assertion is perhaps understandable, however, because the historical record points in precisely the opposite direction. Two features of this history are worth noting. First, at the time of the adoption of the Constitution and the Bill of Rights, there was no settled pattern of celebrating Christmas, either as a purely religious holiday or as a public event. Second, the historical evidence, such as it is, offers no uniform pattern of widespread acceptance of the holiday and indeed suggests that the development of Christmas as a public holiday is a comparatively recent phenomenon.* . . .

Furthermore, unlike the religious tax exemptions upheld in Walz, the public display of nativity scenes as part of governmental celebrations of Christmas does not come to us supported by an unbroken history of widespread acceptance. It was not until 1836 that a State first granted legal recognition to Christmas as a public holiday. This was followed in the period between 1845 and 1865, by 28 jurisdictions which included Christmas Day as a legal holiday. Congress did not follow the States' lead until 1870 when it established December 25th, along with the Fourth of July, New Year's Day, and Thanksgiving, as a legal holiday in the District of Columbia. This pattern of legal recognition tells us only that public acceptance of the holiday was gradual and that the practice—in stark contrast to the record presented in either Walz or Marsh—did not take on the character of a widely recognized holiday until the middle of the nineteenth century. . . .

In sum, there is no evidence whatsoever that the Framers would have expressly approved a federal celebration of the Christmas holiday including public displays of a nativity scene; accordingly, the Court's repeated invocation of the decision in Marsh is not only baffling, it is utterly irrelevant. Nor is there any suggestion that publicly financed and supported displays of Christmas crèches are supported by a record of widespread, undeviating acceptance that extends throughout our history. Therefore, our prior decisions which relied upon concrete, specific historical evidence to support a particular practice simply have no bearing on the question presented in this case. Contrary to today's careless decision, those prior cases have all recognized that the "illumination" provided by history must always be focused on the particular practice at issue in a given case. Without that guiding principle and the intellectual discipline it imposes, the Court is at sea, free to select random elements of America's varied history solely to suit the views of five Members of this Court.

Justice **Blackmun,** with whom Justice **Stevens** joins, dissenting, said in part:

Not only does the Court's resolution of this controversy make light of our precedents, but also, ironically, the majority does an injustice to the crèche and the message it manifests. While certain persons, including the Mayor of Pawtucket, undertook a crusade to "keep 'Christ' in Christmas," the Court today has declared that presence virtually irrelevant. The majority urges that the display, "with or without a crèche," "recall[s] the religious nature of the Holiday," and "engenders a friendly community spirit of good will in keeping with the season." Before the District Court, an expert witness for the city made a similar, though perhaps more candid, point, stating that Pawtucket's display invites people "to participate in the Christmas spirit, brotherhood, peace, and let loose with their money." The crèche has been relegated to the role of a neutral harbinger of the holiday season, useful for commercial

---

*The Court's insistence upon pursuing this vague historical analysis is especially baffling since even the petitioners and their supporting amici concede that no historical evidence equivalent to that relied upon in Marsh, McGowan, or Walz supports publicly sponsored Christmas displays. . . .

purposes, but devoid of any inherent meaning and incapable of enhancing the religious tenor of a display of which it is an integral part. The city has its victory—but it is a Pyrrhic one indeed.

EDWARDS v. AGUILLARD

482 U. S. 578; 96 L. Ed. 2d 510; 107 S. Ct. 2573 (1987)

"Well, in *our* country," said Alice, still panting a little, "You'd generally get to somewhere else—if you ran very fast for a long time as we've been doing."

"A slow sort of country!" said the Queen. "Now, *here*, you see, it takes all the running *you* can do, to keep in the same place."

Lewis Carroll, *Through the Looking Glass*

This sums up the plight of religious education in the United States. Early education in America was religious education, supported by the civil government in the Bible-common-wealth of Massachusetts, and by the various church groups in the Middle and Southern colonies. In the early nineteenth century the demand for free public education resulted in a system of public schools free from religious control and largely free from sectarian influence, a situation wholly satisfactory to an overwhelmingly Protestant nation. Waves of Catholic immigration injected a new element into the picture. The Catholic Church regards the teaching of religion as a primary function of education. Unwilling to send their children to the public schools, which they regarded as either devoid of all religious influence or tainted with Protestantism, Catholics felt obliged to build and maintain a system of parochial schools at their own expense. When these parochial schools met the state's educational standards they were accredited as schools in which the requirements of the compulsory education laws could be satisfied.

In 1922 the state of Oregon passed a law requiring all parents to send their children to the public schools of the state. The Supreme Court, in Pierce v. Society of Sisters (1925), held that the statute denied due process of law by taking from parents their freedom to "direct the upbringing and education" of their children by sending them either to parochial or to private nonsectarian schools of approved educational standards. It is not surprising that Catholic citizens, who paid taxes to support public schools which they did not use, should try to secure some public aid for the parochial schools; and they exerted a good deal of pressure to bring this about. Opposition to this was, however, bitter and widespread; and by the end of the nineteenth century practically every state had adopted some kind of prohibition against the use of state funds for the support of religious education. In numerous cases the state courts held void attempts to extend direct or indirect aid to parochial schools.

Born in an era when school teachers were poorly paid, school facilities simple and inexpensive, and extracurricular activities virtually nonexistent, the religious school had little difficulty keeping up with its public counterpart. But time has seen marked changes in the public schools. The curriculum, once limited to the three "R's," now includes a wide and sophisticated group of subjects; organized athletics have replaced the simple playground games; pupils are transported to school, fed lunch in school, and transported home again;

expensive electronic teaching devices have replaced or supplemented the traditional classroom teacher, and even that teacher comes to his job more completely and expensively educated, asking and receiving more money. The religious school must compete with all of this if it is to "keep in the same place."

Can the state, if it desires, also give these benefits to children attending parochial or private schools? It was argued on the one hand that to do so would not only violate the state constitutional clauses which forbid the use of public money in aid of religion or religious education, but would violate also the clause of the First Amendment which forbids "an establishment of religion," a clause now carried over into the Fourteenth Amendment as a limitation on the states. It was argued on the other side that in providing these services and benefits the state was aiding the child and not the school which he attends. Most state courts accepted this latter reasoning, which came to be known as the "child benefit theory"; and the Supreme Court, in Cochran v. Louisiana State Board of Education (1930), held valid a state law authorizing the use of public funds to supply "school books to the school children of the state," including children in parochial and private nonsectarian schools. The Court agreed that "the school children and the state alone are beneficiaries" of these appropriations, and not the schools which the children attend. The Supreme Court again applied the theory in Everson v. Board of Education (1947) to hold valid the provision of free bus transportation to children attending parochial schools, and yet again in Board of Education v. Allen (1968) to uphold providing secular textbooks to students in parochial schools.

Unfortunately, the child benefit theory, while giving a plausible explanation for the results reached, does not provide any real test for reaching those results in the first place. If the fact that a child is benefitted makes an expenditure valid, it is hard to see why the state cannot build and support religious schools. On the other hand, if anything that aids religion is forbidden by the First Amendment, why are not fire and police protection for churches unconstitutional? What the Constitution demands is state neutrality toward religion, but what constitutes neutrality in a society where governmental aid and supervision are almost ubiquitous? How is the line to be drawn between neutrality and impermissible state aid to religion?

In Lemon v. Kurtzman (1971) the Court added a new way of distinguishing neutral treatment from unconstitutional aid to religion. The case involved efforts by Pennsylvania and Rhode Island to pay part of the salaries of teachers in parochial schools—plans which the Court held void. Conceding that it could "only dimly perceive the lines of demarcation in this extraordinarily sensitive area of constitutional law," the Court identified three tests to be applied. "First, the statute must have a secular legislative purpose; second, its principal or primary effect must be one that neither advances nor inhibits religion, Board of Education v. Allen (1968); finally, the statute must not foster 'an excessive government entanglement with religion.' Walz [1970]. . . . " It was the last of these tests which the Court found to be violated by the teacher payment plans. Since the money was to be used to pay only for secular teaching, "a comprehensive, discriminating, and continuing state surveillance will inevitably be required to ensure that these restrictions are obeyed and the First Amendment otherwise respected. Unlike a book, a teacher cannot be inspected once so as to determine the extent and intent of his or her personal beliefs and subjective acceptance of the limitations imposed by the First Amendment. These prophylactic contacts will involve excessive and enduring entanglement between state and church. . . . "

The Court found an even "broader base of entanglement . . . presented by the divisive political potential of these state programs." "Political division along religious lines was one of the principal evils against which the First Amendment was intended to protect," and in this case the inevitable religious divisiveness would be aggravated by "the need for continuing annual appropriations and the likelihood of larger and larger demands as costs and populations grow."

While early efforts to provide aid to religious schools which did not entail such entanglement were not notably successful, as time passed such efforts met with approval more and more often. Thus, while the Higher Education Facilities Act of 1963 provided building grants and loans to colleges and universities, in Tilton v. Richardson (1971) the Court held void a provision that limited the use of such buildings for religous purposes for only 20 years. A decade later the Court, in Valley Forge Christian College v. Americans United (1982), without reference to the Tilton case, held that an outright grant of property to a religious school did not afford a taxpayer standing to complain about a violation of the First Amendment.

Finally, the state of Minnesota devised a method of giving direct financial aid to persons sending their children to private schools. It amended its income tax law to allow a deduction of up to $700 for monies actually spent on "tuition, textbooks and transportation" for elementary school pupils regardless of the school they attended. In Mueller v. Allen (1982) the Court held the statute valid since it met the three tests laid down in Lemon. Acknowledging its "reluctance to attribute unconstitutional motives to the states," and recognizing the states' interest in maintaining the strength of private schools which educated so many of the states' children, it held that any move to defray the cost of education served a secular purpose.

While the Everson and Allen cases involving school buses and textbooks for parochial schools had held valid certain kinds of aid to children attending religious schools, it did not answer the needs of parents whose children were getting what was reviewed as a "Godless" education in the public schools. Churches, whose success in competing for the time and interest of children has never been outstanding, and parents who wanted their child to have religious training but could no longer get him to go to Sunday School finally devised a scheme of "released time," whereby the child could get such religious training during his "working day" rather than after school or on weekends. One such program was set up in Champaign, Illinois. Public school pupils whose parents signed "request cards" attended religious-instruction classes conducted during regular school hours in the school building, but taught by outside teachers (chosen by a religious council representing the various faiths) who were subject to the approval and supervision of the superintendent of schools. These teachers were not paid from public funds. Records of attendance at these classes were kept and reported to the school authorities, and pupils who did not attend them spent their time on their ordinary studies. The Supreme Court held the plan void in Illinois ex rel. McCollum v. Board of Education (1948). The Court said that the facts "show the use of tax-supported property for religious instruction and the close cooperation between the school authorities and the religious council in promoting religious education. The operation of the State's compulsory education system thus assists and is integrated with the program of religious instruction carried on by separate religious sects. Pupils compelled by law to go to school for secular education are released in part from their legal duty upon the condition that they attend the religious classes. This is beyond all question a utilization of the tax-established and tax-supported public school system to aid religious groups to spread their faith."

New York faced the problem presented by McCollum by having the children bused off the school grounds for religious instruction and having the religious groups pay for the application blanks and any other costs involved. While those pupils not attending religious instruction remained in school, the Court found there was no coercion on these children to attend religious classes and in Zorach v. Clauson held the plan valid. "[While] the government must be neutral when it comes to competition between sects . . . it can close its doors or suspend its operations as to those who want to repair to their religious sanctuary for worship or instruction. No more than that is undertaken here." In oft-quoted language the

Court pointed out that "we are a religious people whose institutions presuppose a Supreme Being. . . . When the state encourages religious instruction or cooperates with religious authorities by adjusting the schedule of public events to sectarian needs, it follows the best of our traditions. For it then respects the religious nature of our people and accommodates the public service to their spiritual needs." It also stated that "the First Amendment . . . does not say that in every and all respects there shall be a separation of Church and State" and that government need not show "a callous indifference" to religious groups. Justice Douglas, who wrote the opinion, later recanted, but while the Court has often made clear that the First Amendment protects the rights of Atheists as well as the religious, the Court has never overruled this language.

In Widmar v. Vincent (1981) the problems of McCollum and Zorach came back to haunt the Court in a different form. Here a group of students at the University of Missouri at Kansas City wanted to use for a meeting of "evangelical Christian students" one of the rooms assigned for the use of the one-hundred-odd student organizations on the campus. The University denied the request on the ground that it would constitute aid to religion while the students argued that their freedom of speech was being abridged on account of its content. The Supreme Court upheld the students. It agreed that two of the three tests for establishment were easily met. A nondiscriminatory open-forum policy, including nondiscrimination against religious speech, would have a secular purpose and would avoid entanglement with religion. Nor was it persuaded that "the primary effect of the public forum, open to all forms of discourse, would be to advance religion. . . . This Court has explained that a religious organization's enjoyment of merely "incidental" benefits does not violate the prohibition against the "primary advancement" of religion. Here, any religious benefits would be "incidental." A similar result was reached in Westside Community Schools v. Mergens (1990) when the Court held the federal Equal Access Act forbade a school to deny a proposed "Christian club" which was open to all students the same right to use school rooms after school hours as was accorded any "noncurriculum related" club, such as the chess club.

Those who felt that the public schools were becoming "Godless," and for whom released time was not an available or desirable solution, undertook a campaign to retain some religion in the public schools. In most public schools it was long the custom to begin the day with a short religious exercise. This usually consisted of reading excerpts from the Protestant Bible and sometimes of singing hymns and repeating the Lord's Prayer. Usually those children whose parents objected were excused from these exercises, although this was not always the case. State court decisions on the validity of these exercises were in sharp conflict, and this specific question never reached the Supreme Court.

In 1962 in Engel v. Vitale, the Supreme Court held void the following prayer composed by the New York Board of Regents for use in the public schools. "Almighty God, we acknowledge our dependence upon Thee, and we beg Thy blessings upon us, our parents, our teachers and our Country." The Court conceded that no issue of religious freedom was involved, since no one was forced to hear or say the prayer. It emphasized, however, that under the establishment clause, "government in this country, be it state or federal, is without power to prescribe by law any particular form of prayer which is to be used as an official prayer in carrying on any program of governmentally sponsored religious activity." The decision aroused a storm of protest. Members in both Houses of Congress began work on a constitutional amendment which would nullify the decision, while school boards throughout the country sought ways of avoiding the impact of the decision. Some required students to recite stanzas of "America" and "The Star Spangled Banner" in which there is reference to God; while others, evidently assuming that it was official participation that made the Regents' Prayer bad, merely authorized children to bring prayers to school and take turns reciting them "voluntarily." One common solution was the adoption of a "moment of silence," which a student could use for silent prayer or not, as he wished.

By 1965 the storm had largely abated. The proposed constitutional amendment had been opposed by most religious groups and was conceded to be dead; legal attempts to reverse New York's prohibition on "voluntary" prayers and the singing of the fourth stanza of "America" as a devotional (rather than a patriotic) exercise had failed; Chief Justice Warren had successfully opposed a House proposal to inscribe "In God We Trust" above the Supreme Court bench. On the other hand, a legal attack on the inclusion of "under God" in the pledge of allegiance had also failed, and the Supreme Court continued to open its sessions with the marshal asking that "God save the United States and this honorable Court."

In Abington School District v. Schempp (1963) the Court for the first time held the use of the Bible in morning devotionals to be in violation of the First Amendment. The state of Pennsylvania required by law that "at least ten verses from the Holy Bible shall be read, without comment, at the opening of each public school on each school day. Any child shall be excused from such Bible reading . . . upon the written request of his parent or guardian." The Schempps were Unitarians who objected to some doctrines purveyed by a literal reading of the Bible, but who declined to ask that their children be excused because they would not only have to stand out in the hall during the exercise but would probably miss the school announcements which followed immediately after. A three-judge federal district court held the practice void on the basis of the Vitale case, and enjoined its continuance. In 1980 the doctrine was applied to hold void a Kentucky law requiring the posting in every classroom of a copy of the Ten Commandments. The Court found the document had "no secular legislative purpose." See Stone v. Graham.

In Wallace v. Jaffree (1985) the state of Alabama had sequentially adopted three statutes apparently designed to get as much prayer in the public schools as possible. The first statute, passed in 1978, merely authorized a one-minute period of silence in all public schools "for meditation." The second, passed in 1981, authorized a period of silence "for meditation or voluntary prayer," while the third, passed the following year, authorized teachers to lead "willing students" in a prescribed prayer to "Almighty God . . . the Creator and Supreme Judge of the world."

At trial the district judge found all three statutes valid. Relying on what he perceived to be newly discovered historical evidence, he held that, in his opinion, "Alabama has the power to establish a state religion if it chooses to do so." The court of appeals rejected this approach and the Supreme Court found it "unnecessary to comment at length on the District Court's remarkable conclusion that the Federal Constitution imposes no obstacle to Alabama's establishment of a state religion." The court of appeals also found the last two statutes void under the establishment clause, but no argument was made that the statute merely requiring "meditation" was in any way invalid.

A number of religions rely upon a literal interpretation of the Bible as the word of God. In their view the Darwinian theory that humans, like the earth and all forms of life upon it, have evolved over hundreds of thousands of years, is a contradiction of the Book of Genesis which states that God created the world and all its creatures in six days in the forms in which they appear today.

The year after the decision of the Tennessee courts upholding that state's so-called "monkey law" which banned the teaching of evolution (see Scopes v. State, 154 Tenn. 105 (1927)), members of these religious groups secured the enactment of a similar law in Arkansas. In Epperson v. Arkansas (1968) the Supreme Court struck down the Arkansas statute as an establishment of religion. "There can be no doubt that Arkansas has sought to prevent its teachers from discussing the theory of evolution because it is contrary to the belief of some that the Book of Genesis must be the exclusive source of doctrine as to the origin of man. No suggestion has been made that Arkansas' law may be justified by considerations of state policy other than the religious views of some of its citizens. It is clear that fundamentalist sectarian conviction was and is the law's reason for existence. Its antecedent, Tennessee's 'monkey law,' candidly stated its purpose: to make it unlawful 'to teach any theory that denies the story of the Divine Creation of man as taught in the Bible, and to teach instead that man has descended from a lower order of animals'. Perhaps the sensational publicity attendant upon the Scopes trial induced Arkansas to adopt less explicit language. It eliminated Tennessee's reference to 'the story of the Divine Creation of man' as taught in the Bible, but there is no doubt that the motivation for the law was the same: to suppress the teaching of a theory which, it was thought, 'denied' the divine creation of man."

Justice **Brennan** delivered the opinion of the Court, saying in part:

The question for decision is whether Louisiana's "Balanced Treatment for Creation-Science and Evoluation-Science in Public School Instruction" Act (Creationism Act), is facially invalid as violative of the Establishment Clause of the First Amendment.

I.

The Creationism Act forbids the teaching of the theory of evolution in public schools unless accompanied by instruction in "creation science." No school is required to teach evolution or creation science. If either is taught, however, the other must also be taught. The theories of evolution and creation science are statutorily defined as "the scientific evidences for [creation or evolution] and inferences from those scientific evidences."

Appellees, who include parents of children attending Louisiana public schools, Louisiana teachers, and religious leaders, challenged the constitutionality of the Act in District Court, seeking an injunction and declaratory relief. Appellants, Louisiana officials charged with implementing the Act, defended on the ground that the purpose of the Act is to protect a legitimate secular interest, namely, academic freedom. Appellees attacked the Act as facially invalid because it violated the Establishment Clause and made a motion for summary judgment. . . .

II.

The Establishment Clause forbids the enactment of any law "respecting an establishment of religion." The Court has applied a three-pronged test to determine whether legislation comports with the Establishment Clause. First, the legislature must have adopted the law with a secular purpose. Second, the statute's principal or primary effect must be one that neither advances nor inhibits religion. Third, the statute must not result in an excessive entanglement of government with religion. Lemon v. Kurtzman [1971]. State action violates the Establishment Clause if it fails to satisfy any of these prongs. . . .

The Court has been particularly vigilant in monitoring compliance with the Establishment Clause in elementary and secondary schools. Families entrust public schools with the education of their children, but condition their trust on the understanding that the classroom will not purposely be used to advance religious views that may conflict with the private beliefs of the student and his or her family. Students in such institutions are impressionable and their attendance is involuntary. . . . The State exerts great authority and coercive power through mandatory attendance requirements, and because of the students' emulation of teachers as role models and the children's susceptibility to peer pressure. . . .

Therefore, in employing the three-pronged Lemon test, we must do so mindful of the particular concerns that arise in the context of public elementary and secondary schools. We now turn to the evaluation of the Act under the Lemon test.

III.

Lemon's first prong focuses on the purpose that animated adoption of the Act. "The purpose prong of the Lemon test asks whether government's actual purpose is to endorse or disapprove of religion." Lynch v. Donnelly [1984] (O'Connor, J., concurring). A governmental intention to promote religion is clear when the State enacts a law to serve a religious purpose. . . .

True, the Act's stated purpose is to protect academic freedom. This phrase might, in common parlance, be understood as referring to enhancing the freedom of teachers to teach what they will. The Court of Appeals, however, correctly concluded that the Act was not designed to further that goal. We find no merit in the State's argument that the "legislature may not [have] use[d] the terms 'academic freedom' in the correct legal sense. They might have [had] in mind, instead, a basic concept of fairness; teaching all of the evidence." Even if "academic freedom" is read to mean "teaching all of the evidence" with respect to the origin of human beings, the Act does not further this purpose. The goal of providing a more comprehensive science curriculum is not furthered either by outlawing the teaching of evolution or by requiring the teaching of creation science.

A.

While the Court is normally deferential to a State's articulation of a secular purpose, it is required that the statement of such purpose be sincere and not a sham. . . . As Justice O'Connor stated in Wallace: "It is not a trivial matter, however, to require that the legislature manifest a secular purpose and omit all sectarian endorsements from its laws. That requirement is precisely tailored to the Establishment Clause's purpose of assuring that Government not intentionally endorse religion or a religious practice."

It is clear from the legislative history that the purpose of the legislative sponsor, Senator Bill Keith, was to narrow the science curriculum. During the legislative hearings, Senator Keith stated: "My preference would be that neither [creationism nor evolution] be taught." Such a ban on teaching does not promote—indeed, it undermines—the provision of a comprehensive scientific education.

It is equally clear that requiring schools to teach creation science with evolution does not advance academic freedom. The Act does not grant teachers a flexibility that they did not already possess to supplant the present science curriculum with the presentation of theories, besides evolution, about the origin of life. Indeed, the Court of Appeals found that no law prohibited Louisiana public schoolteachers from teaching any scientific theory. As the president of the Louisiana Science Teachers Association testified, "[a]ny scientific concept that's based on established fact can be included in our curriculum already, and no legislation allowing this is necessary." The Act provides Louisiana schoolteachers with no new authority. Thus the stated purpose is not furthered by it.

The Alabama statute held unconstitutional in Wallace v. Jaffree [1985] is analogous. In Wallace, the State characterized its new law as one designed to provide a 1-minute period for meditation. We rejected that stated purpose as insufficient, because a previously adopted Alabama law already provided for such a 1-minute period. Thus, in this case, as in Wallace, "[a]ppellants have not identified any secular purpose that was not fully served by [existing state law] before the enactment of [the statute in question]."

Furthermore, the goal of basic "fairness" is hardly furthered by the Act's discriminatory preference for the teaching of creation science and against the teaching of evolution. While requiring that curriculum guides be developed for creation science, the Act says nothing of comparable guides for evolution. Similarly, resource services are supplied for creation science but not for evolution. Only "creation scientists" can serve on the panel that supplies the resource services. The Act forbids school boards to discriminate against anyone who "chooses to be a creation-scientist" or to teach "creationism," but fails to protect those who choose to teach evolution or any other non-creation science theory, or who refuse to teach creation science.

If the Louisiana Legislature's purpose was solely to maximize the comprehensiveness and effectiveness of science instruction, it would have encouraged the teaching of all scientific theories about the origins of humankind. But under the Act's requirements, teachers who were once free to teach any and all facets of this subject are now unable to do so. Moreover, the Act fails even to ensure that creation science will be taught, but instead requires the teaching of this theory only when the theory of evolution is taught. Thus we agree with the Court of Appeals' conclusion that the Act does not serve to protect academic freedom, but has the distinctly different purpose of discrediting "evolution by counterbalancing its teaching at every turn with the teaching of creationism. . . ."

B.

. . . We need not be blind in this case to the legislature's preeminent religious purpose in enacting this statute. There is a historic and contemporary link between the teachings of certain religious denominations and the teaching of evolution. It was this link that concerned the court in Epperson v. Arkansas (1968) which also involved a facial challenge to a statute regulating the teaching of evolution. In that case, the Court reviewed an Arkansas statute that made it unlawful for an instructor to teach evolution or to use a textbook that referred to this scientific theory. Although the Arkansas anti-evolution law did not explicitly state its predominate religious purpose, the Court could not ignore that "[t]he statute was a product of the upsurge of 'fundamentalist' religious fervor" that has long viewed this particular scientific theory as contradicting the literal interpretation of the Bible. After reviewing the history of anti-evolution statutes, the Court determined that "there can be no doubt that the motivation for the [Arkansas] law was the same [as other anti-evolution statutes]: to suppress the teaching of a theory which, it was thought, 'denied' the divine creation of man." The Court found that there can be no legitimate state interest in protecting particular religions from scientific views "distasteful to them," and concluded "that the First Amendment does not permit the State to require that teaching and learning must be tailored to the principles or prohibitions of any religious sect or dogma."

These same historic and contemporaneous antagonisms between the teachings of certain religious denominations and the teaching of evolution are present in this case. The preeminent purpose of the Louisiana Legislature was clearly to advance the religious viewpoint that a supernatural being created humankind. . . .

Furthermore, it is not happenstance that the legislature required the teaching of a theory that coincided with religious view. The legislative history documents that the Act's primary purpose was to change the science curriculum of public schools in order to provide persuasive advantage to a particular religious doctrine that rejects the factual basis of evolution in its entirety. The sponsor of the Creationism Act, Senator Keith, explained during the legislative hearings that his disdain for the theory of evolution resulted from the support that evolution supplied to views contrary to his own religious beliefs. According to Senator Keith, the theory of evolution was consonant with the "cardinal principle[s] of religious humanism, secular humanism, theological liberalism, aetheistism [sic]." The state senator repeatedly stated that scientific evidence supporting his religious views should be included in the public school curriculum to redress the fact that the theory of evolution incidentally coincided with what he characterized as religious beliefs antithetical to his own. The legislation therefore sought to alter the science curriculum to reflect endorsement of a religious view that is antagonistic to the theory of evolution.

In this case, the purpose of the Creationism Act was to restructure the science curriculum to conform with a particular religious viewpoint. Out of many possible science subjects taught in the public schools, the legislature chose to affect the teaching of the one scientific theory that historically has been opposed by certain religious sects. . . . Because the primary purpose of the Creationism Act is to advance a particular religious belief, the Act endorses religion in violation of the First Amendment. . . .

V.

The Louisiana Creationism Act advances a religious doctrine by requiring either the banishment of the theory of evolution from public school classrooms or the presentation of a religious viewpoint that rejects evolution in its entirety. The Act violates the Establishment Clause of the First Amendment because it seeks to employ the symbolic and financial support of government to achieve a religious purpose. The judgment of the Court of Appeals therefore is affirmed.

Justice **Powell**, with whom Justice **O'Connor** joins, wrote a concurring opinion.

Justice **White**, concurring in the judgment, said in part:

As it comes to us, this is not a difficult case. Based on the historical setting and plain language of the Act both courts construed the statutory words "creation-science" to refer to a religious belief, which the Act required to be taught if evolution was taught. In other words, the teaching of evolution was conditioned on the teaching of a religious belief. Both courts concluded that the state legislature's primary purpose was to advance religion and that the statute was therefore unconstitutional under the Establishment Clause.

... Unless ... we are to reconsider the Court's decisions interpreting the Establishment Clause, I agree that the judgment of the Court of Appeals must be affirmed.

Justice **Scalia**, with whom Chief Justice **Rehnquist** joined, dissented, saying in part:

Even if I agreed with the questionable premise that legislation can be invalidated under the Establishment Clause on the basis of its motivation alone, without regard to its effects, I would still find no justification for today's decision. The Louisiana legislators who passed the "Balanced Treatment for Creation-Science and Evolution-Science Act" (Balanced Treatment Act), each of whom had sworn to support the Constitution, were well aware of the potential Establishment Clause problems and considered that aspect of the legislation with great care. After seven hearings and several months of study, resulting in substantial revision of the original proposal, they approved the Act overwhelmingly and specifically articulated the secular purpose they meant it to serve. Although the record contains abundant evidence of the sincerity of that purpose (the only issue pertinent to this case), the Court today holds, essentially on the basis of "its visceral knowledge regarding what *must* have motivated the legislators" that the members of the Louisiana Legislature knowingly violated their oaths and then lied about it. I dissent. ...

I.

... The only evidence in the record of the "received meaning and acceptation" of "creation science" is found in five affidavits filed by appellants. In those affidavits, two scientists, a philosopher, a theologian, and an educator, all of whom claim extensive knowledge of creation science, swear that it is essentially a collection of scientific data supporting the theory that the physical universe and life within it appeared suddenly and have not changed substantially since appearing. These experts insist that creation science is a strictly scientific concept that can be presented without religious references. At this point, then, we must assume that the Balanced Treatment Act does *not* require the presentation of religious doctrine.

Nothing in today's opinion is plainly to the contrary, but what the statute means and what it requires are of rather little concern to the Court. Like the Court of Appeals, the Court finds it necessary to consider only the motives of the legislators who supported the

Balanced Treatment Act. After examining the statute, its legislative history, and its historical and social context, the Court holds that the Louisiana Legislature acted without "a secular legislative purpose" and that the Act therefore fails the "purpose" prong of the three-part test set forth in Lemon v. Kurtzman (1971). As I explain below, I doubt whether that "purpose" requirement of Lemon is a proper interpretation of the Constitution; but even if it were, I could not agree with the Court's assessment that the requirement was not satisfied here.

This Court has said little about the first component of the Lemon test. Almost invariably, we have effortlessly discovered a secular purpose for measures challenged under the Establishment Clause . . . . [Justice Scalia here lists a dozen cases, most of which turned on the "entanglement" prong of Lemon.] In fact, only once before deciding Lemon, and twice since, have we invalidated a law for lack of a secular purpose. See Wallace v. Jaffree (1985); Stone v. Graham (1980) (per curiam); Epperson v. Arkansas (1968).

Nevertheless, a few principles have emerged from our cases, principles which should, but to an unfortunately large extent do not, guide the Court's application of Lemon today. It is clear, first of all, that regardless of what "legislative purpose" may mean in other contexts, for the purpose of the Lemon test it means the "actual" motives of those responsible for the challenged action. . . . Thus, if those legislators who supported the Balanced Treatment Act in fact acted with a "sincere" secular purpose, the Act survives the first component of the Lemon test, regardless of whether that purpose is likely to be achieved by the provisions they enacted.

Our cases have also confirmed that when the Lemon Court referred to "a secular . . . purpose," it meant "*a* secular purpose." The author of Lemon, writing for the Court, has said that invalidation under the purpose prong is appropriate when "there [is] *no question* that the statute or activity was motivated *wholly* by religious considerations." Lynch v. Donnelly (1984) (Burger, C.J.) (emphasis added); see also Wallace v. Jaffree ("the First Amendment requires that a statute must be invalidated if it is *entirely* motivated by a purpose to advance religion") (emphasis added). In all three cases in which we struck down laws under the Establishment Clause for lack of a secular purpose, we found that the legislature's sole motive was to promote religion. . . . Thus, the majority's invalidation of the Balanced Treatment Act is defensible only if the record indicates that the Louisiana Legislature had no secular purpose.

It is important to stress that the purpose forbidden by Lemon is the purpose to "advance religion." . . . Our cases in no way imply that the Establishment Clause forbids legislators merely to act upon their religious convictions. We surely would not strike down a law providing money to feed the hungry or shelter the homeless if it could be demonstrated that, but for the religious beliefs of the legislators, the funds would not have been approved. Also, political activism by the religiously motivated is part of our heritage. Notwithstanding the majority's implication to the contrary, we do not presume that the sole purpose of a law is to advance religion merely because it was supported strongly by organized religions or by adherents of particular faiths. . . . To do so would deprive religious men and women of their right to participate in the political process. Today's religious activism may give us the Balanced Treatment Act, but yesterday's resulted in the abolition of slavery, and tomorrow's may bring relief for famine victims. . . .

II.

A.

We have relatively little information upon which to judge the motives of those who supported the Act. About the only direct evidence is the statute itself and transcripts of the seven committee hearings at which it was considered. . . . Nevertheless, there is ample evidence that the majority is wrong in holding that the Balanced Treatment Act is without secular purpose.

. . . The Act had its genesis (so to speak) in legislation introduced by Senator Bill Keith in June 1980. . . .

Before summarizing the testimony of Senator Keith and his supporters, I wish to make clear that I by no means intend to endorse its accuracy. But my views (and the views of this Court) about creation science and evolution are (or should be) beside the point. Our task is not to judge the debate about teaching the origins of life, but to ascertain what the members of the Louisiana Legislature believed. The vast majority of them voted to approve a bill which explicitly stated a secular purpose; what is crucial is not their *wisdom* in believing that purpose would be achieved by the bill, but their *sincerity* in believing it would be.

Most of the testimony in support of Senator Keith's bill came from the Senator himself and from scientists and educators he presented, many of whom enjoyed academic credentials that may have been regarded as quite impressive by members of the Louisiana Legislature. To a substantial extent, their testimony was devoted to lengthy, and, to the layman, seemingly expert scientific expositions on the origin of life. These scientific lectures touched upon, inter alia, biology, paleontology, genetics, astronomy, astrophysics, probability analysis, and biochemistry. The witnesses repeatedly assured committee members that "hundreds and hundreds" of highly respected, internationally renowned scientists believed in creation science and would support their testimony.

Senator Keith and his witnesses testified essentially as set forth in the following numbered paragraphs:

(1) There are two and only two scientific explanations for the beginning of life—evolution and creation science. . . . Evolution posits that life arose out of inanimate chemical compounds and has gradually evolved over millions of years. Creation science posits that all life forms now on earth appeared suddenly and relatively recently and have changed little. . . .

(2) The body of scientific evidence supporting creation science is as strong as that supporting evolution. In fact, it may be *stronger*. The evidence for evolution is far less compelling than we have been led to believe. Evolution is not a scientific "fact," since it cannot actually be observed in a laboratory. Rather, evolution is merely a scientific theory or "guess." . . .

(3) Creation science is educationally valuable. Students exposed to it better understand the current state of scientific evidence about the origin of life. Those students even have a better understanding of evolution. . . .

(4) Although creation science is educationally valuable and strictly scientific, it is now being censored from or misrepresented in the public schools. . . . Teachers have been brain-

washed by an entrenched scientific establishment composed almost exclusively of scientists to whom evolution is like a "religion." These scientists discriminate against creation scientists so as to prevent evolution's weaknesses from being exposed.

(5) The censorship of creation science has at least two harmful effects. First, it deprives students of knowledge of one of the two scientific explanations for the origin of life and leads them to believe that evolution is proven fact; thus, their education suffers and they are wrongly taught that science has proved their religious beliefs false. Second, it violates the Establishment Clause. The United States Supreme Court has held that secular humanism is a religion. Belief in evolution is a central tenet of that religion. Thus, by censoring creation science and instructing students that evolution is fact, public school teachers are now advancing religion in violation of the Establishment Clause. . . .

We have no way of knowing, of course, how many legislators believed the testimony of Senator Keith and his witnesses. But in the absence of evidence to the contrary, we have to assume that many of them did. Given that assumption, the Court today plainly errs in holding that the Louisiana Legislature passed the Balanced Treatment Act for exclusively religious purposes.

B.

. . . Even if the legislative history were silent or ambiguous about the existence of a secular purpose—and here it is not—the statute should survive Lemon's purpose test. But even more validation than mere legislative history is present here. The Louisiana Legislature explicitly set forth its secular purpose ("protecting academic freedom") in the very test of the Act. . . .

The Court seeks to evade the force of this expression of purpose by stubbornly misinterpreting it, and then finding that the provisions of the Act do not advance that misinterpreted purpose, thereby showing it to be a sham. The Court first surmises that "academic freedom" means "enhancing the freedom of teachers to teach what they will," even though "academic freedom" in that sense has little scope in the structured elementary and secondary curriculums with which the Act is concerned. Alternatively, the Court suggests that it might mean "maximiz[ing] the comprehensiveness and effectiveness of science instruction," though that is an exceedingly strange interpretation of the words, and one that is refuted on the very face of the statute. Had the Court devoted to this central question of the meaning of the legislatively expressed purpose a small fraction of the research into legislative history that produced its quotations of religiously motivated statements by individual legislators, it would have discerned quite readily what "academic freedom" meant: *students'* freedom from *indoctrination*. The legislature wanted to ensure that students would be free to decide for themselves how life began, based upon a fair and balanced presentation of the scientific evidence—that is, to protect "the right of each [student] voluntarily to determine what to believe (and what not to believe) free of any coercive pressures from the State." . . .

In sum, even if one concedes, for the sake of argument, that a majority of the Louisiana Legislature voted for the Balanced Treatment Act partly in order to foster (rather than merely eliminate discrimination against) Christian fundamentalist beliefs, our cases establish that that alone would not suffice to invalidate the Act, so long as there was a genuine secular purpose as well. We have, moreover, no adequate basis for disbelieving the secular purpose set forth in the Act itself, or for concluding that it is a sham enacted to conceal the legislators' violation of their oaths of office. I am astonished by the Court's unprecedented readiness to reach such a conclusion, which I can only attribute to an intellectual predisposition created by the facts and the legend of Scopes v. State, 154 Tenn. 105 (1927)—an instinctive reaction that any governmentally imposed requirements bearing upon the teaching of evolution must be a manifestation of Christian fundamentalist repression. In this case, however, it seems to me the Court's position is the repressive one. The people of Louisiana, including those who are Christian fundamentalists, are quite entitled, as a secular matter, to have whatever scientific evidence there may be against evolution presented in their schools, just as Mr. Scopes was entitled to present whatever scientific evidence there was for it. Perhaps what the Louisiana Legislature has done is unconstitutional because there *is* no such evidence, and the scheme they have established will amount to no more than a presentation of the Book of Genesis. But we cannot say that on the evidence before us in this summary judgment context, which includes ample uncontradicted testimony that ''creation science'' is a body of scientific knowledge rather than revealed belief. *Infinitely less* can we say (or should we say) that the scientific evidence for evolution is so conclusive that no one could be gullible enough to believe that there is any real scientific evidence to the contrary, so that the legislation's stated purpose must be a lie. Yet that illiberal judgment, that Scopes-in-reverse, is ultimately the basis on which the Court's facile rejection of the Louisiana Legislature's purpose must rest. . . .

III.

I have to this point assumed the validity of the Lemon ''purpose'' test. In fact, however, I think the pessimistic evaluation that the Chief Justice [Rehnquist] made of the totality of Lemon is particularly applicable to the ''purpose'' prong: it is ''a constitutional theory [that] has no basis in the history of the amendment it seeks to interpret, is difficult to apply and yields unprincipled results . . . .'' Wallace v. Jaffree (Rehnquist, J., dissenting). . . .

Given the many hazards involved in assessing the subjective intent of governmental decisionmakers, the first prong of Lemon is defensible, I think, only if the text of the Establishment Clause demands it. That is surely not the case. . . .

5

Rights of Persons
Accused of Crime

A. The Exclusion of
Unconstitutional Evidence

WEEKS v. UNITED STATES

232 U. S. 383; 58 L. Ed. 652; 34 S. Ct. 341 (1914)

At common law whether evidence was admissible in court had nothing to do with whether the police secured the evidence legally or not. A lawyer could argue that certain evidence was incompetent, irrelevant, and immaterial; but if the court found it wasn't, it was admissible. The court was not concerned with the legality of the methods used to obtain it. If it had been stolen, either by a private person or by a police officer, the common law provided for prosecution of the thief or a civil action for trespass and the return of the property.

With the growth of professional police forces and the burgeoning of personal rights against searches and seizures and compulsory self-incrimination it became clear that these approaches were not effective restraints on enthusiastic police investigation. Not only were juries, who as individuals depended on these same police for the protection of themselves and their homes, reluctant to convict an officer who had turned up evidence of crime or induced a confession, but such financial awards as were made were normally not large enough to serve as a serious deterrent. It was long argued, therefore, that evidence illegally obtained should not be admitted in court, because refusal to admit it provided the only effective deterrent to the illegal conduct. This argument was slow to find favor, and for years most of the states continued to follow the common-law rule. The Supreme Court itself apparently adhered to it until the decision in the present case. See Adams v. New York (1904).

The areas in which the Supreme Court has had the most difficulty agreeing on a consistent philosophy are those of unreasonable searches and seizures and compulsory self-incrimination (discussed in the Miranda case, below). In part this is merely a reflection of the conflicting values in the country as a whole, but it is also the result of the methods by which the guarantees are enforced. Individual rights can be divided into two types. Those like free speech and religion have intrinsic value to the individual and are thought of as "substantive" rights, while those like the right to counsel and a jury trial are termed "procedural" because their purpose is to ensure that one will only be convicted of crime on the basis of true evidence fairly presented and impartially appraised. Appellate courts will normally enforce the substantive rights by ordering the government either to stop interfering with their exercise or to grant those which are being withheld. The procedural rights, on the other hand, are usually policed by ordering a new, untainted trial to take the place of the unfair one.

The guarantee against unreasonable searches and seizures and the protection against compulsory self-incrimination are in the anomalous position of being *substantive* rights, of value to the individual for their own sake, but enforceable by the courts only through the procedural technique of ordering excluded at a new trial the evidence gotten by their violation. The result in those cases where the tainted evidence was essential to conviction is the release of a person who has been found guilty on the basis of probative evidence fairly appraised, not because he might be innocent, but because the police have violated his rights. In Justice Cardozo's famous phrase, "the criminal is to go free because the constable has blundered." People v. Defore, 242 N. Y. 13 (1926). While Supreme Court justices are not supposed to be influenced in constitutional judgments by the apparent guilt or innocence of a particular defendant, it is hard to escape the conclusion that a more consistent concern for the rights of the accused might emerge if the price were not the freeing of so many obviously guilty defendants.

Despite the acceptance of the Weeks "exclusion of evidence" doctrine in the federal system, two problems have plagued the Supreme Court: (1) how, as a rational matter, can the rule be justified, and (2) is it really a constitutional requirement or is it just a convenient rule of evidence promulgated by the Court and which the Court could change at will?

One justification for the rule, characterized as the "imperative of judicial integrity," was expressed in two classic dissents in Olmstead v. United States (1928). In the words of Justice Holmes, "We have to choose, and for my part I think it a less evil that some criminals should escape than that the government should play an ignoble part." Or, as Justice Brandeis put it, "Decency, security, and liberty alike demand that government officials shall be subjected to the same rules of conduct that are commands to the citizen. In a government of laws, existence of the government will be imperiled if it fails to observe the law scrupulously. Our government is the potent, the omnipresent, teacher. For good or for ill, it teaches the whole people by its example. Crime is contagious. If the government becomes a law-breaker, it breeds contempt for the law; it invites every man to become a law unto himself; it invites anarchy. To declare that in the administration of the criminal law the end justifies the means—to declare that the government may commit crimes in order to secure the conviction of a private criminal—would bring terrible retribution. Against that pernicious doctrine this court should resolutely set its face." The underlying assumption that makes these two classic statements relevant here is that a court which makes use of illegally or unconstitutionally gotten evidence, like a fence who receives stolen goods, shares in the criminality of the original theft.

The second justification, the "deterrent effect" argument, is the one on which the Court has clearly placed its reliance. Since it is apparent that the traditional common-law actions against a police officer by the victim of an unreasonable search are totally ineffective in preventing such searches, the Court has concluded that only by making it unrewarding to search illegally will the practice be abandoned. Although persuasive in theory, two things have made the technique less effective than it might have been. In the first place many investigative goals, such as the location and identification of witnesses, conspirators, and investigative leads, are furthered by illegal searches even though the results cannot be used in court. In the second place, the Court has not set the kind of comprehensive ban on the use of unconstitutional searches that would produce a really deterrent effect. Clearly it has not been designed to deter stealing evidence in general, as shown both by the fact the Court admits evidence stolen by private individuals and by the Weeks case itself, in which evidence stolen by the state police was held admissible. This "silver platter" doctrine was later abandoned as to evidence stolen by state officials; see Benanti v. United States (1957) and Elkins v. United States (1960).

Nor has the Court held inadmissible evidence gotten unconstitutionally, even by federal officers, where it was not used directly against the victim of the search. In Goldstein v. United States (1942) the telephones of Goldstein's accomplices had been illegally tapped and when they were confronted with the transcript of their conversation, they agreed to testify against Goldstein. The Court upheld the use of the testimony on the ground that the protection against unconstitutional search and seizure, like that against self-incrimination, was a purely personal right.

There are, in addition, purposes for which illegally gotten evidence may be used even against the victim himself. Thus, in Walder v. United States (1954) the Court held that narcotics which had been unreasonably seized from the defendant could be used to impeach his credibility at a later (and unrelated) trial at which he had testified broadly that he had never possessed narcotics before. The Court distinguished between using the evidence to convict him and using it to make him out a liar. In 1971 in Harris v. New York, the Court reaffirmed the Walder doctrine and permitted statements taken from the accused without the warnings required by Miranda v. Arizona (1966) to be used to impeach his credibility. In both cases the accused had taken the stand in his own defense, but unlike Walder, the statements introduced in Harris contradicted his protestations of innocence. The jury had been instructed to use the statement only to assess the defendant's credibility and not as evidence of guilt, and there was no denial that the statements made were voluntary. "The shield provided by Miranda," said Chief Justice Burger, "cannot be perverted into a license to use perjury by way of a defense, free from the risk of confrontation with prior inconsistent utterances."

Whether the language of the Weeks case meant that the "exclusionary rule" was required by the Constitution has been debated by the Court over the years. In Wolf v. Colorado (1949) the Court held that it was not, and found that while due process in the Fourteenth Amendment forbade a state to search and seize unreasonably, it did not forbid it to use the evidence obtained by such searches. Twelve years later the Court in Mapp v. Ohio (1961) abandoned this interpretation and extended the exclusionary rule to the states. While a plurality made clear that the "exclusionary rule is an essential part of both the Fourth and Fourteenth Amendments," Justice Black, the majority's fifth vote, held that it was not the Fourth alone, but the combination of the Fourth and Fifth that dictated exclusion. Either way, however, the rule was declared to be of constitutional origin.

In 1965, in a case holding the Mapp rule was not retroactive, the Court avoided saying that it was a constitutional rule and found that Mapp, like all the cases since Wolf, was "based on the necessity for an effective deterrent to illegal police action." It found that the cause of deterrence would not be advanced by making the rule retroactive, since not only had the misconduct of the police prior to Mapp already occurred, but at the time it occurred it had been sanctioned by Wolf. See Linkletter v. Walker (1965).

In the years that followed there was no suggestion that the exclusionary rule was required by the Fourth Amendment, and the Court leaned increasingly on the deterrent purpose of the rule in deciding whether or not it should be applied. In United States v. Calandra (1974), referring to the rule as "a judicially created remedy designed to safeguard Fourth Amendment rights generally through its deterrent effect," the Court described its application as a "balancing process" in which the effectiveness of the deterrence was weighed against the loss to society of valuable probative evidence. There the Court found the deterrent effect of excluding unconstitutionally gotten evidence from a grand jury investigation was "uncertain at best," since it was unlikely that the police would search and seize evidence merely to obtain an indictment if they could not use it later at the trial.

Two years later, in United States v. Janis (1976), the Court relied on this balancing process to justify the admission of unconstitutionally seized evidence in a federal civil trial. In this case the state had seized bookmaking equipment and records pursuant to a search warrant later found to be invalid, and the Court held they could be introduced by the Internal Revenue Service in a suit for unpaid wagering taxes. Since they were inadmissible in the state criminal proceedings for which they had originally been sought, the Court felt that the state agents had been "punished" enough.

The same day the Court decided Janis, it dealt a body blow to those who had come to look upon the Supreme Court as a protector of rights against infringement by the states. Voting six to three, the Court in Stone v. Powell (1976) held a federal writ of habeas corpus (a remedy traditionally available where a person is held by a state in violation of his federal constitutional rights) should no longer be issued to review claims that evidence should have been excluded from a trial as unconstitutionally obtained where there had been adequate state consideration of the claims. The Court rejected the "judicial integrity" rationale, noting that it "has limited force as a justification for the exclusion of highly probative evidence," and that it "becomes minimal where the federal habeas corpus relief is sought by a prisoner who previously had been afforded the opportunity for full and fair consideration of his search-and-seizure claim at trial and on direct review."

In the case which follows, Weeks was arrested by a city police officer at his place of business and indicted in a federal court on a charge of sending lottery tickets through the mails. The police also searched his house and turned over to a United States marshal papers and articles found there. Thereupon the marshal himself, accompanied by police officers, searched Weeks's room and carried away other documents and letters. No warrants had been obtained either for the arrest or for the search by the police or marshal. Before the trial Weeks petitioned the federal district court to return all the papers and articles seized by the various officers. The district court, however, allowed the papers to be used against Weeks at the trial.

Mr. Justice **Day** delivered the opinion of the Court, saying in part:

The defendant assigns error, among other things, in the court's refusal to grant his petition for the return of his property, and in permitting the papers to be used at the trial. . . .

. . . The tendency of those who execute the criminal laws of the country to obtain conviction by means of unlawful seizures and enforced confessions, the latter often obtained after subjecting accused persons to unwarranted practices destructive of rights secured by the federal Constitution, should find no sanction in the judgments of the courts, which are charged at all times with the support of the Constitution, and to which people of all conditions have a right to appeal for the maintenance of such fundamental rights. . . .

. . . If letters and private documents can thus be seized and held and used in evidence against a citizen accused of an offense, the protection of the 4th Amendment, declaring his right to be secure against such searches and seizures, is of no value, and, so far as those thus placed are concerned, might as well be stricken from the Constitution. The efforts of the courts and their officials to bring the guilty to punishment, praiseworthy as they are, are not to be aided by the sacrifice of those great principles established by years of endeavor and suffering which have resulted in their embodiment in the fundamental law of the land. . . .

. . . While there is no opinion in the case, the court in this proceeding doubtless relied upon what is now contended by the government to be the correct rule of law under such circumstances, that the letters having come into the control of the court, it would not inquire into the manner in which they were obtained, but, if competent, would keep them and permit their use in evidence. . . .

The right of the court to deal with papers and documents in the possession of the district attorney and other officers of the court, and subject to its authority, was recognized in Wise v. Henkel [1911]. That papers wrongfully seized should be turned over to the accused has been frequently recognized in the early as well as later decisions of the courts.

We therefore reach the conclusion that the letters in question were taken from the house of the accused by an official of the United States, acting under color of his office in direct violation of the constitutional rights of the defendant; that having made a seasonable application for their return, which was heard and passed upon by the court, there was involved in the order refusing the application a denial of the constitutional rights of the accused, and that the court should have restored these letters to the accused. In holding them and permitting their use upon the trial, we think prejudicial error was committed. As to the papers and property seized by the policemen, it does not appear that they acted under any claim of federal authority such as would make the amendment applicable to such unauthorized seizures. The record shows that what they did by way of arrest and search and seizure was done before the finding of the indictment in the Federal court; under what supposed right or authority does not appear. What remedies the defendant may have against them we need not inquire, as the 4th Amendment is not directed to individual misconduct of such officials. Its limitations reach the Federal government and its agencies. . . .

Reversed.

B. Exclusion in Action: Searches and Seizures

TERRY v. OHIO

392 U. S. 1; 20 L. Ed. 2d 889; 88 S. Ct. 1868 (1968)

The flexibility needed by the Court to provide reasoned arguments to go with its ever-changing views on searches and seizures has been provided by what has become known as the "talismanic" approach. Essentially this involves taking a constitutional theory, giving it a short-hand name, then using that name until it comes to have an entity of its own quite unrelated to the theory from which it sprang. When using the talisman the Court does not look back to the original theory, but interprets the talisman as though it were the true statement of the rule. This has the advantage of freeing it from the restraints of the rule without apparently abandoning the rule itself.

For example, the basic constitutional theory underlying the Fourth Amendment is that a magistrate, not a policeman, should decide when a person's privacy should yield to a search and that a search without a magistrate's warrant is "unreasonable" *unless it can be justified by some "exigent circumstance"* that makes getting a warrant impractical. Two such exceptions are the warrantless search of an automobile before it can escape and the warrantless search of a person by an arresting officer to protect both himself and the evidence of the crime. However, since probable cause is necessary to get a search warrant, there must be probable cause to search without a warrant; and the arresting officer must be prepared to satisfy the court that the probable cause existed before the search was made.

The talismans that have evolved from these two exceptions to the warrant requirement are the "Carroll" and the "search incident" doctrines. Carroll v. United States (1925) involved stopping and searching without a warrant a bootlegger's car. The Supreme Court upheld the search, but emphasized that "where the securing of a warrant is reasonably practicable it must be used. . . . In cases where seizure is impossible except without a warrant, the seizing officer acts unlawfully and at his peril unless he can show the court probable cause." In its talismanic form these last requirements are dropped and the Carroll doctrine becomes the right to search a car without a warrant.

The common law authorized a policeman to conduct a limited search, or "frisk," at the time of a lawful arrest. The obvious justification was that an arrested person might have on his person either a weapon with which he could effect his escape, or evidence which he might find an opportunity to destroy. On this theory the extent of a search, both in time and space, is limited to what is necessary to protect the arresting officer or the evidence. But "search incident," once it had been given a name, took on a life of its own and in its talismanic form became an automatic right to search any arrested person. While the original theory had built-in limits stemming from the need that gave rise to it, the talismanic form knew no limits at all.

In the past half-century the Supreme Court has wandered back and forth between the theory and the talisman like a restless ghost. In Agnello v. United States (1925) it said that a search incident could extend "to the place where the arrest is made," but held it could not extend to another house several blocks away, and in Harris v. United States (1947) it upheld the search of Harris' four-room apartment because it was "under his immediate control." In neither case could the defendant have threatened the police officers or destroyed evidence.

A year later, in Trupiano v. United States (1948), the talismanic approach was abandoned. Revenue agents had watched an illegal still being constructed and put into operation for a period of several weeks, during which they could have obtained both search and arrest warrants. When they finally closed in, one man was engaged in running the still and the Court sustained his arrest. But it held that since there had been plenty of time to obtain a warrant to seize the still the seizure was void without one.

Two years later in United States v. Rabinowitz (1950) the Court abruptly overruled Trupiano and held valid a widespread search of a defendant's property on the strength of his lawful arrest alone. Noting that the Constitution required only that a search be reasonable, not that it be made with a warrant if practicable, the Court found that, considering all the circumstances, this search was reasonable. The impact of this holding was to make possible a much broader search in conjunction with lawful arrest than could be made under a search warrant—as long as the arrest took place on the premises to be searched—since there were no limits, as in the case of search warrants, as to "places to be searched" or "things to be seized." This was so much easier that in some communities the traditional search warrant became virtually extinct.

After nearly 20 years of this approach the Supreme Court overruled Harris and

Rabinowitz and returned to the restrictive doctrines of Trupiano. In Chimel v. California (1969) the police had, as incident to arrest, searched an entire house including a garage and workshop. The Court declined to draw distinctions based on the size of the area involved. "The only reasoned distinction is one between a search of the person arrested and the area within his reach on the one hand, and more extensive searches on the other." Furthermore, the theory justifying the search incident to arrest, the Court explained, itself marks its proper extent. "When an arrest is made, it is reasonable for the arresting officer to search the person arrested in order to remove any weapons that the latter might seek to use in order to resist arrest or effect his escape. Otherwise, the officer's safety might well be endangered, and the arrest itself frustrated. In addition, it is entirely reasonable for the arresting officer to search and seize any evidence on the arrestee's person in order to prevent its concealment or destruction. And the area into which an arrestee might reach in order to grab a weapon or evidentiary items must, of course, be governed by a like rule. A gun on a table or in a drawer in front of one who is arrested can be as dangerous to the arresting officer as one concealed in the clothing of the person arrested. There is ample justification, therefore, for a search of the arrestee's person and the area 'within his immediate control'—construing that phrase to mean the area from within which he might gain possession of a weapon or destructible evidence.

"There is no comparable justification, however, for routinely searching rooms other than that in which an arrest occurs—or, for that matter, for searching through all the desk drawers or other closed or concealed areas in that room itself. Such searches, in the absence of well-recognized exceptions, may be made only under the authority of a search warrant. The 'adherence to judicial processes' mandated by the Fourth Amendment requires no less."

Any idea that the Court had abandoned the talismanic approach to the search incident doctrine was destined to be short-lived. It rejected it in 1971 in Coolidge v. New Hampshire and refused to allow the warrantless search of a car whose owner was arrested inside the house, but by 1974 it was back in full force in United States v. Edwards where it permitted the warrantless search of defendant's clothes a full day after he had been jailed for his offense. In upholding the validity of the search, the Court, dividing five to four, argued that the mere fact of a full "custodial" arrest justified a complete warrantless search of his clothing, and since they could have searched him that night, it was not unreasonable to wait until the next morning when substitute clothes could be made available. Referring with approval to a case decided two years prior to Chimel, the Court noted that "it was no answer [in that case] to say that the police could have obtained a search warrant, for the Court held the test to be not whether it was reasonable to procure a search warrant, but whether the search itself was reasonable, which it was." Four dissenting justices pointed out that this language had been expressly rejected in Chimel and that, in view of the time lapse, "the considerations that typically justify a warrantless search incident to a lawful arrest were wholly absent here. . . . The police had ample time to seek a warrant, and no exigent circumstances were present to excuse their failure to do so."

The persistent attractiveness of the talismanic approach is exemplified by New York v. Belton (1981). There four men were stopped for speeding and when the police smelled burned marijuana in the car they ordered them out of the car, arrested them for possession and separated them from one another along the thruway. They then searched the car and found heroin in the pocket of a jacket left on the back seat. The Court converted the Chimel doctrine into a "workable rule" by holding that "when a policeman has made a lawful custodial arrest of the occupant of an automobile, he may, as a contemporaneous incident of that arrest, search the passenger compartment of that automobile." He may "also examine the contents of any containers found within the passenger compartment, for if the passenger compartment is within reach of the arrestee, so also will containers in it be within his reach."

The right of the police to arrest a person, like any other "seizure," has to be made on probable cause. If the arrest is to be made by warrant the magistrate who is to issue it must be told the facts so he can decide if there is probable cause. This does not necessarily mean sufficient evidence to obtain a conviction. It is enough that it reflect the "practical considerations of everyday life on which reasonable and prudent men, not legal technicians, act"; see Brinegar v. United States (1949). Where a police officer actually sees a felony being committed, or where he knows a felony has been committed and has probable cause to believe the suspect committed it, he may arrest the person without a warrant. These situations, however, involve the actual commission of a felony and it is this that is involved when the search incident doctrine speaks of a search incident to a "valid arrest." The policeman in the case below was not witnessing the commission of a crime, nor even overt preparations for the commission of a crime. There was nothing he could have taken to a magistrate to obtain either a search or arrest warrant based upon probable cause.

The Court, in holding valid the "frisk" in this case, opened up an entirely new dimension to the law of search and seizure. Never before had there been a valid way in which an officer could stop persons against their will and conduct a quick, superficial check to see if they passed some elementary test. The result of the change was to insist that an officer have probable cause, not to *believe* that a crime was in progress, but merely to *suspect* this. The nature and amount of evidence needed to justify such suspicion was determined by balancing the individual right of privacy sacrificed against the public good to be served should the suspicion prove to be correct. Thus, while in United States v. Brignoni-Ponce (1975) the brief stop of a car near the Mexican border to check the citizenship of its occupants was held valid, in United States v. Place (1983) a 90-minute detention at an airport while a suspect's luggage was subjected to a "sniff" test by narcotic-hunting dogs was well beyond the limits in both time and personal inconvenience permitted by Terry. In United States v. Martinez-Fuerte (1976) the doctrine of Brignoni-Ponce was extended to cover a permanent routine border check stop, and in Michigan State Police v. Sitz (1990) it was extended again to cover a roving road-block check for driver sobriety.

Perhaps the most complex set of facts involving the sufficiency of "reasonable suspicion" to search without a warrant arose in United States v. Sokolow (1989). Andrew Sokolow (together with a Janet Norian) flew from Honolulu to Miami and back, and upon his return was stopped by Drug Enforcement Administration agents. The agents found 1,063 grams of cocaine in his carry-on luggage.

Evidence leading to the decision to stop him included the fact that prior to departing Hawaii he paid $2,100 for two round-trip tickets from a roll of $20 bills containing nearly twice that amount; he travelled under a name that did not match his telephone listing; that he flew to Miami, a "source city" for illicit drugs, and returned within 48 hours, despite the fact the flight took 20 hours each way. In addition he appeared nervous, wore a black jumpsuit and gold jewelry, appeared about 25 years old and checked none of his luggage. Some of these characteristics matched a "drug courier profile" drawn up to aid DEA agents in identifying possible smugglers. In a seven-to-two decision the Court upheld the search. "Any one of these factors is not by itself proof of any illegal conduct and is quite consistent with innocent travel. But we think taken together they amount to reasonable suspicion." Justice Marshall and Brennan dissented, condemning the use of "profiles" by the DEA on the ground that they "can only dull the officer's ability and determination to make sensitive and fact-specific inferences 'in light of his experience,' . . . a risk enhanced by the profile's 'chameleon-like way of adapting to any particular set of observations.' "

Mr. Chief Justice **Warren** delivered the opinion of the Court, saying in part:

This case presents serious questions concerning the role of the Fourth Amendment in the confrontation on the street between the citizen and the policeman investigating suspicious circumstances.

Petitioner Terry was convicted of carrying a concealed weapon and sentenced to the statutorily prescribed term of one to three years in the penitentiary. Following the denial of a pretrial motion to suppress, the prosecution introduced in evidence two revolvers and a number of bullets seized from Terry and a codefendant, Richard Chilton, by Cleveland Police Detective Martin McFadden. At the hearing on the motion to suppress this evidence, Officer McFadden testified that while he was patrolling in plain clothes in downtown Cleveland at approximately 2:30 in the afternoon of October 31, 1963, his attention was attracted by two men, Chilton and Terry, standing on the corner of Huron Road and Euclid Avenue. He had never seen the two men before, and he was unable to say precisely what first drew his eye to them. However, he testified that he had been a policeman for 39 years and a detective for 35 and that he had been assigned to patrol this vicinity of downtown Cleveland for shoplifters and pickpockets for 30 years. He explained that he had developed routine habits of observation over the years and that he would "stand and watch people or walk and watch people at many intervals of the day." He added: "Now, in this case when I looked over they didn't look right to me at the time."

His interest aroused, Officer McFadden took up a post of observation in the entrance to a store 300 to 400 feet away from the two men. "I got more purpose to watch them when I seen their movements," he testified. He saw one of the men leave the other one and walk southwest on Huron Road, past some stores. The man paused for a moment and looked in a store window, then walked on a short distance, turned around and walked back toward the corner, pausing once again to look in the same store window. He rejoined his companion at the corner, and the two conferred briefly. Then the second man went through the same series of motions, strolling down Huron Road, looking in the same window, walking on a short distance, turning back, peering in the store window again, and returning to confer with the first man at the corner. The two men repeated this ritual alternately between five and six times apiece—in all, roughly a dozen trips. At one point, while the two were standing together on the corner, a third man approached them and engaged them briefly in conversation. This man then left the two others and walked west on Euclid Avenue. Chilton and Terry resumed their measured pacing, peering, and conferring. After this had gone on for 10 to 12 minutes, the two men walked off together, heading west on Euclid Avenue, following the path taken earlier by the third man.

By this time Officer McFadden had become thoroughly suspicious. He testified that after observing their elaborately casual and oft-repeated reconnaissance of the store window on Huron Road, he suspected the two men of "casing a job, a stick-up," and that he considered it his duty as a police officer to investigate further. He added that he feared "they may have a gun." Thus, Officer McFadden followed Chilton and Terry and saw them stop in front of Zucker's store to talk to the same man who had conferred with them earlier on the street corner. Deciding that the situation was ripe for direct action, Officer McFadden approached the three men, identified himself as a police officer and asked for their names. At this point his knowledge was confined to what he had observed. He was not acquainted with any of the three men by name or by sight, and he had received no information concerning them from any other source. When the men "mumbled something" in response to his inquiries, Officer McFadden grabbed petitioner Terry, spun him around so that they were facing the other two, with Terry between McFadden and the others, and patted down the outside of his clothing. In the left breast pocket of Terry's overcoat Officer McFadden felt a pistol. He reached inside the overcoat pocket, but was unable to remove the gun. At this point, keeping Terry between himself and the others, the officer ordered all three men to enter Zucker's store. As they went in, he removed Terry's overcoat completely, retrieved a .38 caliber revolver from the pocket and ordered all three men to face the wall with their hands raised. Officer McFadden proceeded to pat down the outer clothing of Chilton and the third man, Katz. He discovered another revolver in the outer pocket of Chilton's overcoat, but no weapons were found on Katz. The officer testified that he only patted the men down to see whether they had weapons, and that he did not put his hands beneath the outer garments of either Terry or Chilton until he felt their guns. So far as appears from the record, he never placed his hands beneath Katz's outer garments. Officer McFadden seized Chilton's gun, asked the proprietor of the store to call a police wagon, and took all three men to the station, where Chilton and Terry were formally charged with carrying concealed weapons.

On the motion to suppress the guns the prosecution took the position that they had been seized following a search incident to a lawful arrest. The trial court rejected this theory, stating that it "would be stretching the facts beyond reasonable comprehension" to find that Officer McFadden had had probable cause to arrest the men before he patted them down for weapons. However, the court denied the defendant's motion on the ground that Officer McFadden, on the basis of his experience, "had reasonable cause to believe . . . that the defendants were conducting themselves suspiciously, and some interrogation should be made of their action." Purely for his own protection, the court held, the officer had the right to pat down the outer clothing of these men, whom he had reasonable cause to believe might be armed. The court distinguished between an investigatory "stop" and an arrest, and between a "frisk" of the outer clothing for weapons and a full-blown search for evidence of crime. The frisk, it held, was essential to the proper performance of the officer's investigatory duties, for without it "the answer to the police officer may be a bullet, and a loaded pistol discovered during the frisk is admissible."

After the court denied their motion to suppress, Chilton and Terry waived jury trial and pleaded not guilty. The court adjudged them guilty. . . . We granted certiorari (1967) to determine whether the admission of the revolvers in evidence violated petitioner's rights under the Fourth Amendment, made applicable to the States by the Fourteenth, Mapp v. Ohio (1961). We affirm the conviction. . . .

II.

Our first task is to establish at what point in this encounter the Fourth Amendment becomes relevant. That is, we must decide whether and when Officer McFadden "seized" Terry and whether and when he conducted a "search." There is some suggestion in the use of such terms as "stop" and "frisk" that such police conduct is outside the purview of the

Fourth Amendment because neither action rises to the level of a "search" or "seizure" within the meaning of the Constitution. We emphatically reject this notion. It is quite plain that the Fourth Amendment governs "seizures" of the person which do not eventuate in a trip to the station house and prosecution for crime—"arrests" in traditional terminology. It must be recognized that whenever a police officer accosts an individual and restrains his freedom to walk away, he has "seized" that person. And it is nothing less than sheer torture of the English language to suggest that a careful exploration of the outer surfaces of a person's clothing all over his or her body in an attempt to find weapons is not a "search." Moreover, it is simply fantastic to urge that such a procedure performed in public by a policeman while the citizen stands helpless, perhaps facing a wall with his hands raised, is a "petty indignity." It is a serious intrusion upon the sanctity of the person, which may inflict great indignity and arouse strong resentment, and it is not to be undertaken lightly.

The danger in the logic which proceeds upon distinctions between a "stop" and an "arrest," or "seizure" of the person, and between a "frisk" and a "search" is twofold. It seeks to isolate from constitutional scrutiny the initial stages of the contact between the policeman and the citizen. And by suggesting a rigid all-or-nothing model of justification and regulation under the Amendment, it obscures the utility of limitations upon the scope, as well as the initiation, of police action as a means of constitutional regulation. This Court has held in the past that a search which is reasonable at its inception may violate the Fourth Amendment by virtue of its intolerable intensity and scope. . . . The scope of the search must be "strictly tied to and justified by" the circumstances which rendered its initiation permissible. Warden v. Hayden (1967) (Mr. Justice Fortas, concurring). . . .

The distinctions of classical "stop-and-frisk" theory thus serve to divert attention from the central inquiry under the Fourth Amendment—the reasonableness in all the circumstances of the particular governmental invasion of a citizen's personal security. "Search" and "seizure" are not talismans. We therefore reject the notions that the Fourth Amendment does not come into play at all as a limitation upon police conduct if the officers stop short of something called "technical arrest" or a "full-blown search."

In this case there can be no question, then, that Officer McFadden "seized" petitioner and subjected him to a "search" when he took hold of him and patted down the outer surfaces of his clothing. We must decide whether at that point it was reasonable for Officer McFadden to have interfered with petitioner's personal security as he did.* And in determining whether the seizure and search were "unreasonable" our inquiry is a dual one—whether the officer's action was justified at its inception, and whether it was reasonably related in scope to the circumstances which justified the interference in the first place.

---

*We thus decide nothing today concerning the constitutional propriety of an investigative "seizure" upon less than probable cause for purposes of "detention" and/or interrogation. Obviously, not all personal intercourse between policemen and citizens involves "seizures" of persons. Only when the officer, by means of physical force or show of authority, has in some way restrained the liberty of a citizen may we conclude that a "seizure" has occurred. We cannot tell with any certainty upon this record whether any such "seizure" took place here prior to Officer McFadden's initiation of physical contact for purposes of searching Terry for weapons, and we thus may assume that up to that point no intrusion upon constitutionally protected rights had occurred.

III.

If this case involved police conduct subject to the Warrant Clause of the Fourth Amendment, we would have to ascertain whether "probable cause" existed to justify the search and seizure which took place. However, that is not the case. We do not retreat from our holdings that the police must, whenever practicable, obtain advance judicial approval of searches and seizures through the warrant procedure, see, e. g., Katz v. United States (1967); Beck v. Ohio (1964); Chapman v. United States (1961), or that in most instances failure to comply with the warrant requirement can only be excused by exigent circumstances, see, e. g., Warden v. Hayden (1967) (hot pursuit); cf. Preston v. United States (1964). But we deal here with an entire rubric of police conduct—necessarily swift action predicated upon the on-the-spot observations of the officer on the beat—which historically has not been, and as a practical matter could not be, subjected to the warrant procedure. Instead, the conduct involved in this case must be tested by the Fourth Amendment's general proscription against unreasonable searches and seizures.

Nonetheless, the notions which underlie both the warrant procedure and the requirement of probable cause remain fully relevant in this context. In order to assess the reasonableness of Officer McFadden's conduct as a general proposition, it is necessary "first to focus upon the governmental interest which allegedly justifies official intrusion upon the constitutionally protected interests of the private citizen," for there is "no ready test for determining reasonableness other than by balancing the need to search [or seize] against the invasion which the search [or seizure] entails." Camara v. Municipal Court (1967). And in justifying the particular intrusion the police officer must be able to point to specific and articulate facts which, taken together with rational inferences from those facts, reasonably warrant that intrusion. . . .

Applying these principles to this case, we consider first the nature and extent of the governmental interests involved. One general interest is of course that of effective crime prevention and detection; it is this interest which underlies the recognition that a police officer may in appropriate circumstances and in an appropriate manner approach a person for purposes of investigating possibly criminal behavior even though there is no probable cause to make an arrest. It was this legitimate investigative function Officer McFadden was discharging when he decided to approach petitioner and his companions. He had observed Terry, Chilton, and Katz go through a series of acts, each of them perhaps innocent in itself, but which taken together warranted further investigation . . .

The crux of this case, however, is not the propriety of Officer McFadden's taking steps to investigate petitioner's suspicious behavior, but rather, whether there was justification for McFadden's invasion of Terry's personal security by searching him for weapons in the course of that investigation. . . .

Petitioner does not argue that a police officer should refrain from making any investigation of suspicious circumstances until such time as he has probable cause to make an arrest; nor does he deny that police officers in properly discharging their investigative function may find themselves confronting persons who might well be armed and dangerous. Moreover, he does not say that an officer is always unjustified in searching a suspect to discover weapons. Rather, he says it is unreasonable for the policeman to take that step until such time as the situation evolves to a point where there is probable cause to make an arrest.

When that point has been reached, petitioner would concede the officer's right to conduct a search of the suspect for weapons, fruits or instrumentalities of the crime, or "mere" evidence, incident to the arrest.

There are two weaknesses in this line of reasoning, however. First, it fails to take account of traditional limitations upon the scope of searches, and thus recognizes no distinction in purpose, character, and extent between a search incident to an arrest and a limited search for weapons. The former, although justified in part by the acknowledged necessity to protect the arresting officer from assault with a concealed weapon . . . , is also justified on other grounds and can therefore involve a relatively extensive exploration of the person. A search for weapons in the absence of probable cause to arrest, however, must, like any other search, be strictly circumscribed by the exigencies which justify its initiation. . . . Thus it must be limited to that which is necessary for the discovery of weapons which might be used to harm the officer or others nearby, and may realistically be characterized as something less than a "full" search, even though it remains a serious intrusion.

A second, and related, objection to petitioner's argument is that it assumes that the law of arrest has already worked out the balance between the particular interests involved here— the neutralization of danger to the policeman in the investigative circumstance and the sanctity of the individual. But this is not so. An arrest is a wholly different kind of intrusion upon individual freedom from a limited search for weapons, and the interests each is designed to serve are likewise quite different. An arrest is the initial stage of a criminal prosecution. It is intended to vindicate society's interest in having its laws obeyed, and it is inevitably accompanied by future interference with the individual's freedom of movement, whether or not trial or conviction ultimately follows. The protective search for weapons, on the other hand, constitutes a brief, though far from inconsiderable, intrusion upon the sanctity of the person. It does not follow that because an officer may lawfully arrest a person only when he is apprised of facts sufficient to warrant a belief that the person has committed or is committing a crime, the officer is equally unjustified, absent that kind of evidence, in making any intrusions short of an arrest. Moreover, a perfectly reasonable apprehension of danger may arise long before the officer is possessed of adequate information to justify taking a person into custody for the purpose of prosecuting him for a crime. Petitioner's reliance on cases which have worked out standards of reasonableness with regard to "seizures" constituting arrests and searches incident thereto is thus misplaced. It assumes that the interests sought to be vindicated and the invasions of personal security may be equated in the two cases, and thereby ignores a vital aspect of the analysis of the reasonableness of particular types of conduct under the Fourth Amendment.

Our evaluation of the proper balance that has to be struck in this type of case leads us to conclude that there must be a narrowly drawn authority to permit a reasonable search for weapons for the protection of the police officer, where he has reason to believe that he is dealing with an armed and dangerous individual, regardless of whether he has probable cause to arrest the individual for a crime. The officer need not be absolutely certain that the individual is armed; the issue is whether a reasonably prudent man in the circumstances would be warranted in the belief that his safety or that of others was in danger. . . . And in determining whether the officer acted reasonably in such circumstances, due weight must be given, not to his inchoate and unparticularized suspicion or "hunch," but to the specific reasonable inferences which he is entitled to draw from the facts in light of his experience. . . .

IV.

We must now examine the conduct of Officer McFadden in this case to determine whether his search and seizure of petitioner were reasonable, both at their inception and as conducted. He had observed Terry, together with Chilton and another man, acting in a manner he took to be preface to a "stick-up." We think on the facts and circumstances Officer McFadden detailed before the trial judge a reasonably prudent man would have been warranted in believing petitioner was armed and thus presented a threat to the officer's safety while he was investigating his suspicious behavior. . . .

The scope of the search in this case presents no serious problem in light of these standards. Officer McFadden patted down the outer clothing of petitioner and his two companions. He did not place his hands in their pockets or under the outer surface of their garments until he had felt weapons, and then he merely reached for and removed the guns. He never did invade Katz's person beyond the outer surfaces of his clothes, since he discovered nothing in his pat down which might have been a weapon. Officer McFadden confined his search strictly to what was minimally necessary to learn whether the men were armed and to disarm them once he discovered the weapons. He did not conduct a general exploratory search for whatever evidence of criminal activity he might find.

V.

We conclude that the revolver seized from Terry was properly admitted in evidence against him. At the time he seized petitioner and searched him for weapons, Officer McFadden had reasonable grounds to believe that petitioner was armed and dangerous, and it was necessary for the protection of himself and others to take swift measures to discover the true facts and neutralize the threat of harm if it materialized. The policeman carefully restricted his search to what was appropriate to the discovery of the particular items which he sought. Each case of this sort will, of course, have to be decided on its own facts. We merely hold today that where a police officer observes unusual conduct which leads him reasonably to conclude in light of his experience that criminal activity may be afoot and that the persons with whom he is dealing may be armed and presently dangerous; where in the course of investigating this behavior he identifies himself as a policeman and makes reasonable inquiries; and where nothing in the initial stages of the encounter serves to dispel his reasonable fear for his own or others' safety, he is entitled for the protection of himself and others in the area to conduct a carefully limited search of the outer clothing of such persons in an attempt to discover weapons which might be used to assault him. Such a search is reasonable search under the Fourth Amendment, and any weapons seized may properly be introduced in evidence against the person from whom they were taken.

Affirmed.

Mr. Justice **Black** concurs in the judgment and the opinion except where the opinion quotes from and relies upon this Court's opinion in Katz v. United States and the concurring opinion in Warden v. Hayden.

Justices **Harlan** and **White** wrote concurring opinions.

Mr. Justice **Douglas,** dissenting, said in part:

I agree that petitioner was "seized" within the meaning of the Fourth Amendment. I also agree that frisking petitioner and his companions for guns was a "search." But it is a mystery how that "search" and that "seizure" can be constitutional by Fourth Amendment standards, unless there was "probable cause" to believe that (1) a crime had been committed or (2) a crime was in the process of being committed or (3) a crime was about to be committed.

The opinion of the Court disclaims the existence of "probable cause." If loitering were an issue and that was the offense charged, there would be "probable cause" shown. But the crime here is carrying concealed weapons; and there is no basis for concluding that the officer had "probable cause" for believing that crime was being committed. Had a warrant been sought, a magistrate would, therefore, have been unauthorized to issue one, for he can act only if there is a showing of "probable cause." We hold today that the police have greater authority to make a "seizure" and conduct a "search" than a judge has to authorize such action. We have said precisely the opposite over and over again.

MIRANDA v. ARIZONA

384 U. S. 436; 16 L. Ed. 2d 694; 86 S. Ct. 1602 (1966)

The privilege against compulsory self-incrimination grew up in England as a revolt against procedures, especially those in the ecclesiastical courts and the Court of Star Chamber, whereby persons were questioned by the judges in order both to get evidence on which to accuse them and to secure a confession from them after they were accused. Immunity from such questioning gradually became established in the common law, and it was this immunity that was written into the Fifth Amendment of the Constitution. Over the years it has been one of the most controversial guarantees in the Bill of Rights. At the time the first colonists came to America it was still not universally accepted in England, and important deviations occurred during the colonial period, notably in the Salem "witch trials." Throughout much of its history the desirability of the protection has been questioned by various bodies of opinion on two grounds: First, it is considered no longer a necessary protection; modern courts would prevent any attempt to get evidence from an accused by means of torture or intimidation. The second ground is that the protection is a shield only to the guilty, since only a guilty person can legitimately refuse to give evidence on the ground that his testimony would tend to incriminate him. This position is bolstered by the historical fact that prominent among those who brought about the adoption of the protection in England were the early Puritans, who were obviously guilty of heresy but who objected to being forced to provide the only testimony upon which they could be convicted in the ecclesiastical courts and the Court of Star Chamber.

Despite these attacks, the protection against compulsory self-incrimination continues to command strong support. There is a strong moral sense which regards it as uncivilized to put a person, whether innocent or guilty, through the degrading process of having to give the evidence upon which he may be convicted of crime. The protection is also felt to promote sound police methods by preventing the lazy prosecutor from relying upon evidence he can secure by the relatively easy method of torturing his suspects. Sir James Fitzjames Stephens illustrates this point by quoting an Indian policeman who said, "It is far pleasanter to sit comfortably in the shade rubbing red pepper into a poor devil's eyes than to go about in the sun hunting up evidence." Wigmore, the great authority on evidence, while criticizing many aspects of the guarantee, supported it on the ground that it protected innocent and guilty alike from the overzealousness of prosecuting officials who are forced by public opinion to maintain a high conviction record if they are to continue to hold their offices.

Unlike the protection against unreasonable searches and seizures, the protection against self-incrimination contains what amounts to a built-in exclusionary rule. Evidence that is coerced from a person cannot be used in court to convict him. The Court had always made clear that the right not to be a witness against one's self was not limited to being excused from taking the witness stand at one's criminal trial. Any statement coerced from a person by the government, wherever the coercion took place, constituted self-incrimination and in addition any information gotten by the government as a result of such coerced statements was excluded from court as "fruit of the poisoned tree." Since statements could be gotten from a person under an almost unlimited range of circumstances, the Court was continually faced with the question whether they were voluntary or coerced. As a result of the slow convergence of two very different doctrines the Court finally arrived at what it hoped would be a solution to its problem. Have a lawyer on hand when the person makes his statement!

Before this solution could be brought to pass the right to a lawyer had to be made applicable to the states and in 1963, in the celebrated case of Gideon v. Wainwright, the Supreme Court held applicable to trials in state courts the Sixth Amendment right to counsel. In the years following it decided a series of cases, some of them highly controversial, extending that right to points both earlier and later in the criminal process than the trial itself. In Hamilton v. Alabama (1961) it held that an accused was entitled to counsel (at state expense, if necessary) at the time of his arraignment and in White v. Maryland (1963) it was pushed back to the preliminary hearing stage. Then in Douglas v. California (1963) it was moved forward to cover the first appeal from a criminal conviction which is normally given by the state as a matter of right. The rationale behind all of these cases was that these were "critical stages" in the criminal process. It was at these points that a person might do or fail to do, or say or fail to say, something that could irrevocably prejudice his chances of acquittal. It was at these points that the "guiding hand of counsel" was vital if his rights were to receive full protection. In United States v. Wade (1967) and Gilbert v. California (1967) the Court extended the right of counsel to include that point where an accused is identified as a wanted suspect by being picked out of a police line-up by an eyewitness, although it did hold in Gilbert that taking a handwriting sample from a man before he saw his lawyer did not violate his rights. Here, too, the suspect's right to an unprejudiced identification may easily be jeopardized by an excess of police enthusiasm.

While these changes were going on the Court was also struggling with the somewhat unrelated problem of coerced confessions. Although it had held in Brown v. Mississippi (1936) that a confession based on coercion—in this case physical torture—was void, it was continually plagued by the problem of what constituted coercion. It conceded that coercion could be psychological as well as physical, but it was haunted by the fact so clearly stated in Stein v. New York (1953), that "no criminal confession is voluntary" in the "sense that petitioners wanted to make them." A definition of "voluntary" that meant some pressure could be used, but not too much, raised endless difficulties for the Court. Since most confessions are secured before a person is formally charged with crime, the Court had managed to solve much of the problem in the *federal* courts by requiring that an accused be taken immediately before a committing magistrate. But this ruling rested on the supervisory authority of the Court over the administration of federal justice and so could not be extended to the states. Consequently the Court had to trace a guideline for the states as cases came before it, and as the Court noted in Spano v. New York (1959), as "the methods used to extract confessions become more sophisticated, our duty . . . only becomes more difficult because of the more delicate judgments to be made." In the Spano case the defendant was persuaded to confess by fatigue and the false sympathy aroused by a boyhood friend on the police force, while in subsequent cases the techniques used included threatening to bring the defendant's wife in for questioning (Rogers v. Richmond, 1961), threatening to take her infant children from her and give them to strangers (Lynumn v. Illinois, 1963), injecting "truth serum" into his veins (Townsend v. Sain, 1963), and refusing to let him call his wife or lawyer until he had confessed (Haynes v. Washington, 1963). While in some of these cases the police disputed the defendant's version, in all of them the defendants were denied access to counsel who might have given them moral support and perhaps furnished a dispassionate version of the proceedings. Claims that the right to counsel was being denied were noted by the Court but not reached because the confessions were held to be coerced. Clearly the amount of "pressure" a state could use to invoke a confession was getting less and less.

Then in 1964 the Court moved sharply to merge these two lines of development, extending the right to counsel, but in such a way that would serve also as a protection against forced confessions. In Massiah v. United States (1964) the government was forbidden to question an accused, who was under indictment, in the absence of his lawyer, and in Escobedo v. Illinois (1964) it held that where "the investigation is no longer a general inquiry into an unsolved crime but has begun to focus on a particular suspect, the suspect has been taken into police custody, the police carry out a process of interrogations that lends itself to eliciting incriminating statements, the suspect has requested and been denied an opportunity to consult with his lawyer, and the police have not effectively warned him of his absolute constitutional right to remain silent, the accused has been denied 'the Assistance of Counsel' in violation of the Sixth Amendment to the Constitution as 'made obligatory upon the States by the Fourteenth Amendment.' "

Not until 1971 in Harris v. New York did the Court move to reduce the impact of Miranda by permitting the use in court of evidence gotten in violation of the rule. Harris, on trial for a narcotics violation, took the stand and testified that a bag of powder he had sold to an undercover agent was baking powder rather than heroin. He was asked on cross-examination if this did not contradict statements made to the police at the time of his arrest. These statement had been made without the Miranda warnings and were then read back to him. The jury was instructed that they could not be used to determine his guilt, but only his credibility. In a five-to-four decision the Court held this use of the statements valid. Conceding that "some comments in the Miranda opinion can indeed be read as indicating a bar to use of any uncounseled statement for any purpose," they were only dicta and "it does not follow from Miranda that evidence inadmissible against an accused in the prosecution's case in chief is barred for all purposes, provided of course that the trustworthiness of the evidence satisfies legal standards." The Court reaffirmed Walder v. United States (1954) in which a similar decision had been reached with regard to illegally seized evidence (see the note to Weeks v. United States, 1914) and added, "the shield provided by Miranda cannot be perverted into a license to use perjury by way of a defense, free from the risk of confrontation with prior inconsistent utterances." In James v. Illinois (1990), however, the Court made clear that such illegally gotten evidence could not be used to impeach the testimony of anyone except the defendant himself.

In Oregon v. Hass (1975) the Court not only reaffirmed Harris but extended it to a defendant who had been given the Miranda warnings and had his request for an attorney ignored. "One might concede that when proper Miranda warnings have been given, and the officer then continues his interrogation after the suspect asks for an attorney, the officer may be said to have little to lose and perhaps something to gain by way of possibly uncovering impeachment material. . . . In any event, the balance was struck in Harris, and we are not disposed to change it now." Where the testimony is used to convict, however, the Court has adhered firmly to Miranda. In Edwards v. Arizona (1981) Edwards' request for a lawyer was ignored and a resumption of questioning produced a confession. The Court held he had not waived his right to counsel.

Miranda v. Arizona was decided in 1966 by a Court headed by Chief Justice Earl Warren. Its purpose was to ensure that the underprivileged, uneasy in the presence of the police and unfamiliar with their rights under the law, would be told of their right to legal counsel and assured that they did not need to answer questions until such counsel was provided. Police and prosecutors alike viewed this class of people as providing the bulk of the "criminal element" and were concerned that providing them with lawyers would make it exceedingly difficult if not impossible to get them to confess to their crimes and would thus reduce the number of convictions. The political pressure provided by the law enforcement agencies, abetted by those who viewed themselves as possible victims of crime, has resulted over the years in a watering down of the protections afforded by the Miranda rule.

In New York v. Quarles (1984) the Court held the Miranda warnings unnecessary in cases in which the public safety was at stake. The police had cornered a suspected criminal in a supermarket at about 12:30 A.M., handcuffed him and frisked him and found an empty shoulder holster under his arm. They asked him where the gun was and he nodded in the direction of some empty cartons and said, "The gun is over there." The police retrieved the gun and then read the defendant his Miranda rights. He waived right to counsel, answered the questions asked, and was convicted with the use of the statements given both before and after the Miranda warnings were given.

In holding valid the use of the statements the Court announced and justified what it called a "public safety" exception to the Miranda rule. "In such a situation, if the police are required to recite the familiar Miranda warnings before asking the whereabouts of the gun, suspects in Quarles' position might well be deterred from responding. Procedural safeguards that deter a suspect from responding were deemed acceptable in Miranda in order to protect the Fifth Amendment privilege; when the primary social cost of those added protections is the possibility of fewer convictions, the Miranda majority was willing to bear that cost. Here, had Miranda warnings deterred Quarles from responding . . . the cost would have been something more than merely the failure to obtain evidence. . . . Officer Kraft needed an answer to his question not simply to make his case against Quarles but to ensure that additional danger to the public did not result from the concealment of the gun in a public area. We conclude that the need for answers to questions in a situation posing a threat to the public safety outweighs the need for the prophylactic rule protecting the Fifth Amendment's privilege against self-incrimination."

In Oregon v. Elstad (1985) a defendant argued that, since he had confessed without being given his Miranda warnings, all his confessions, even those given after being warned, were tainted by the first (invalid) confession and were therefore void. The Court rejected his contention.

In addition to weakening Miranda by devising exceptions to it, the Court drastically reduced its effectiveness in providing legal help for needy defendants by adopting a rigid, technical approach to its interpretation. There is no better illustration of this than the case of Moran v. Burbine (1986). Burbine had been picked up by the Cranston, Rhode Island, police for breaking and entering, and while he was in their custody they learned that he might be implicated in a recent murder in Providence. The Providence police immediately sent over three men to question him. About two hours later Burbine's sister, not knowing anything about the murder charge, obtained a public defender to represent him in the breaking and entering inquiry. She phoned the Cranston police and notified them that she would represent Burbine if the police intended to put him in a lineup or question him. The police informed her that he would not be questioned until the next day. Burbine was not notified that his sister had obtained counsel or the substance of the phone conversation.

Less than an hour later the police began a series of interrogations, following properly administered Miranda warnings, which ultimately produced three signed confessions admitting the murder. The trial court ruled that the constitutional right to request a lawyer was personal to the defendant and could not be exercised by the lawyer. Since Burbine had never requested a lawyer, the phone call was irrelevant.

Justice O'Connor, joined by justices Burger, White, Blackmun, Powell and Rehnquist, upheld Burbine's conviction. They concluded that whatever the motives or conduct of the police, the freely signed confessions following valid Miranda warnings made the conviction constitutional. "Events occurring outside of the presence of the suspect and entirely unknown to him surely can have no bearing on the capacity to comprehend and knowingly relinquish a constitutional right. Under the analysis of the Court of Appeals, the same defendant, armed with the same information and confronted with precisely the same police conduct, would have knowingly waived his Miranda rights had a lawyer not telephoned the police station to inquire about his status. Nothing in any of our waiver decisions or in our understanding of the essential components of a valid waiver requires so incongruous a result. No doubt the additional information would have been useful to respondent; perhaps even it might have affected his decision to confess. But we have never read the Constitution to require that the police supply a suspect with a flow of information to help him calibrate his self-interest in deciding whether to speak or stand by his rights."

Justices Stevens, Brennan and Marshall addressed the ethical aspects of the case in their dissent. "The Court concludes that the police may deceive an attorney by giving her false information about whether her client will be questioned, and that the police may deceive a suspect by failing to inform him of his attorney's communications and efforts to represent him. For the majority, this conclusion, though "distaste[ful]," is not even debatable. The deception of the attorney is irrelevant because the attorney has no right to information, accuracy, honesty, or fairness in the police response to her questions about her client. The deception of the client is acceptable, because, although the information would affect the client's assertion of his rights, the client's actions in ignorance of the availability of his attorney are voluntary, knowing, and intelligent; additionally, society's interest in apprehending, prosecuting, and punishing criminals outweighs the suspect's interest in information regarding his attorney's efforts to communicate with him. Finally, even mendacious police interference in the communications between a suspect and his lawyer does not violate any notion of fundamental fairness because it does not shock the conscience of the majority."

Mr. Chief Justice **Warren** delivered the opinion of the Court, saying in part:

The cases before us raise questions which go to the roots of our concepts of American criminal jurisprudence: the restraints society must observe consistent with the Federal Constitution in prosecuting individuals for crime. More specifically, we deal with the admissibility of statements obtained from an individual who is subjected to custodial police interrogation and the necessity for procedures which assure that the individual is accorded his privilege under the Fifth Amendment to the Constitution not to be compelled to incriminate himself. . . .

Our holding will be spelled out with some specificity in the pages which follow but briefly stated it is this: the prosecution may not use statements, whether exculpatory or inculpatory, stemming from custodial interrogation of the defendant unless it demonstrates the use of procedural safeguards effective to secure the privilege against self-incrimination. By custodial interrogation, we mean questioning initiated by law enforcement officers after a person has been taken into custody or otherwise deprived of his freedom of action in any significant way. As for the procedural safeguards to be employed, unless other fully effective means are devised to inform accused persons of their right of silence and to assure a continuous opportunity to exercise it, the following measures are required. Prior to any questioning, the person must be warned that he has a right to remain silent, that any statement he does make may be used as evidence against him, and that he has a right to the presence of an attorney, either retained or appointed. The defendant may waive effectuation of these rights, provided the waiver is made voluntarily, knowingly and intelligently. If, however, he indicates in any manner and at any stage of the process that he wishes to consult with an attorney before speaking there can be no questioning. Likewise, if the individual is alone and indicates in any manner that he does not wish to be interrogated, the police may not question him. The mere fact that he may have answered some questions or volunteered some statements on his own does not deprive him of the right to refrain from answering any further inquiries until he has consulted with an attorney and thereafter consents to be questioned.

I.

The constitutional issue we decide in each of these cases is the admissibility of statements obtained from a defendant questioned while in custody or otherwise deprived of his freedom of action in any significant way. In each, the defendant was questioned by police officers, detectives, or a prosecuting attorney in a room in which he was cut off from the outside world. In none of these cases was the defendant given a full and effective warning of his rights at the outset of the interrogation process. In all the cases, the questioning elicited oral admissions, and in three of them, signed statements as well which were admitted at their trials. They all thus share salient features—incommunicado interrogation of individuals in a police-dominated atmosphere, resulting in self-incriminating statements without full warnings of constitutional rights.

. . . The use of physical brutality and violence is not, unfortunately, relegated to the past. . . .

. . . Unless a proper limitation upon custodial interrogation is achieved—such as these decisions will advance—there can be no assurance that practices of this nature will be eradicated in the foreseeable future. . . .

Again we stress that the modern practice of in-custody interrogation is psychologically rather than physically oriented. As we have stated before, "Since Chambers v. Florida [1940] this Court has recognized that coercion can be mental as well as physical, and that the blood of the accused is not the only hallmark of an unconstitutional inquisition." Blackburn v. Alabama (1960). Interrogation still takes place in privacy. Privacy results in secrecy and this in turn results in a gap in our knowledge as to what in fact goes on in the interrogation rooms. A valuable source of information about present police practices, however, may be found in various police manuals and texts which document procedures employed with success in the past, and which recommend various other effective tactics. These texts are used by law enforcement agencies themselves as guides. It should be noted that these texts professedly present the most enlightened and effective means presently used to obtain statements through custodial interrogation. By considering these texts and other data, it is possible to describe procedures observed and noted around the country. . . . [The Court here quotes at length from a number of books on criminal investigation.]

From these representative samples of interrogation techniques, the setting prescribed by the manuals and observed in practice becomes clear. In essence, it is this: To be alone with the subject is essential to prevent distraction and to deprive him of any outside support. The aura of confidence in his guilt undermines his will to resist. He merely confirms the preconceived story the police seek to have him describe. Patience and persistence, at times relentless questioning are employed. To obtain a confession, the interrogator must "patiently maneuver himself or his quarry into a position from which the desired objective may be obtained." When normal procedures fail to produce the needed result, the police may resort to deceptive stratagems such as giving false legal advice. It is important to keep the subject off balance, for example, by trading on his insecurity about himself or his surroundings. The police then persuade, trick, or cajole him out of exercising his constitutional rights.

Even without employing brutality, the "third degree" or the specific stratagems described above, the very fact of custodial interrogation exacts a heavy toll on individual liberty and trades on the weakness of individuals. This fact may be illustrated simply by referring to three confession cases decided by this Court in the Term immediately preceding our Escobedo decision. In Townsend v. Sain (1963), the defendant was a 19 year-old heroin addict, described as a "near mental defective." The defendant in Lynumn v. Illinois (1963), was a woman who confessed to the arresting officer after being importuned to "cooperate" in order to prevent her children from being taken by relief authorities. This Court as in those cases reversed the conviction of a defendant in Haynes v. Washington (1963), whose persistent request during his interrogation was to phone his wife or attorney. In other settings, these individuals might have exercised their constitutional rights. In the incommunicado police-dominated atmosphere, they succumbed.

[The Court here discusses the facts of the cases before it, noting that in each the questioning in an "incommunicado police-dominated atmosphere" had resulted in a confession.]

In these cases, we might not find the defendant's statements to have been involuntary in traditional terms. Our concern for adequate safeguards to protect precious Fifth Amendment rights is, of course, not lessened in the slightest. In each of the cases, the defendant was thrust into an unfamiliar atmosphere and run through menacing police interrogation procedures. The potentiality for compulsion is forcefully apparent, for example, in Miranda, where the indigent Mexican defendant was a seriously disturbed individual with pronounced sexual fantasies, and in Stewart, in which the defendant was an indigent Los Angeles Negro who had dropped out of school in the sixth grade. To be sure, the records do not evince overt physical coercion or patent psychological ploys. The fact remains that in none of these cases did the officers undertake to afford appropriate safeguards at the outset of the interrogation to insure that the statements were truly the product of free choice.

It is obvious that such an interrogation environment is created for no purpose other than to subjugate the individual to the will of his examiner. This atmosphere carries its own badge of intimidation. To be sure, this is not physical intimidation, but it is equally destructive of human dignity. The current practice of incommunicado interrogation is at odds with one of our Nation's most cherished principles—that the individual may not be compelled to incriminate himself. Unless adequate protective devices are employed to dispel the compulsion inherent in custodial surroundings, no statement obtained from the defendant can truly be the product of his free choice.

From the foregoing, we can readily perceive an intimate connection between the privilege against self-incrimination and police custodial questioning. . . .

II.

. . . We have recently noted that the privilege against self-incrimination—the essential mainstay of our adversary system—is founded on a complex of values. . . . All these policies point to one overriding thought: the constitutional foundation underlying the privilege is the respect a government—state or federal—must accord to the dignity and integrity of its citizens. To maintain a "fair state-individual balance," to require the government "to shoulder the entire load," . . . to respect the inviolability of the human personality, our accusatory system of criminal justice demands that the government seeking to punish an individual produce the evidence against him by its own independent labors, rather than by the cruel, simple expedient of compelling it from his own mouth. . . . In sum, the privilege is fulfilled only when the person is guaranteed the right "to remain silent unless he chooses to speak in the unfettered exercise of his will." . . .

The question in these cases is whether the privilege is fully applicable during a period of custodial interrogation. . . . We are satisfied that all the principles embodied in the privilege apply to informal compulsion exerted by law-enforcement officials during in-custody questioning. An individual swept from familiar surroundings into police custody, surrounded by antagonistic forces, and subjected to the techniques of persuasion described above cannot be otherwise than under compulsion to speak. As a practical matter, the compulsion to speak in the isolated setting of the police station may well be greater than in courts or other official investigations, where there are often impartial observers to guard against intimidation or trickery.

This question, in fact, could have been taken as settled in federal courts almost 70 years go, when, in Bram v. United States (1897), this Court held:

"In criminal trials, in the courts of the United States, wherever a question arises whether a confession is incompetent because not voluntary, the issue is controlled by that portion of the Fifth Amendment . . . commanding that no person 'shall be compelled in any criminal case to be a witness against himself.' '' . . .

III. . . .

It is impossible for us to foresee the potential alternatives for protecting the privilege which might be devised by Congress or the States in the exercise of their creative rule-making capacities. Therefore we cannot say that the Constitution necessarily requires adherence to any particular solution for the inherent compulsions of the interrogation process as it is presently conducted. Our decision in no way creates a constitutional straitjacket which will handicap sound efforts at reform, nor is it intended to have this effect. We encourage Congress and the States to continue their laudable search for increasingly effective ways of protecting the rights of the individual while promoting efficient enforcement of our criminal laws. However, unless we are shown other procedures which are at least as effective in apprising accused persons of their right of silence and in assuring a continuous opportunity to exercise it, the following safeguards must be observed. . . .

[The Court here elaborates on and justifies the requirements summarized at the beginning of the opinion.]

If the interrogation continues without the presence of an attorney and a statement is taken, a heavy burden rests on the government to demonstrate that the defendant knowingly and intelligently waived his privilege against self-incrimination and his right to retained or appointed counsel. . . . This Court has always set high standards of proof for the waiver of constitutional rights, Johnson v. Zerbst (1938), and we reassert these standards as applied to in-custody interrogation. Since the State is responsible for establishing the isolated circumstances under which the interrogation takes place and has the only means of making available corroborated evidence of warnings given during incommunicado interrogation, the burden is rightly on its shoulders. . . .

The warnings required and the waiver necessary in accordance with our opinion today are, in the absence of a fully effective equivalent, pre-requisites to the admissibility of any statement made by a defendant. No distinction can be drawn between statements which are direct confessions and statements which amount to ''admissions'' of part or all of an offense. The privilege against self-incrimination protects the individual from being compelled to incriminate himself in any manner; it does not distinguish degrees of incrimination. Similarly for precisely the same reason, no distinction may be drawn between inculpatory statements and statements alleged to be merely ''exculpatory.'' If a statement made were in fact truly exculpatory it would, of course, never be used by the prosecution. In fact, statements merely intended to be exculpatory by the defendant are often used to impeach his testimony at trial or to demonstrate untruths in the statement given under interrogation and thus to prove guilt by implication. These statements are incriminating in any meaningful sense of the word and may not be used without the full warnings and effective waiver required for any other statements. In Escobedo itself, the defendant fully intended his accusation of another as the slayer to be exculpatory as to himself.

The principles announced today deal with the protection which must be given to the privilege against self-incrimination when the individual is first subjected to police interrogation while in custody at the station or otherwise deprived of his freedom of action in any significant way. It is at this point that our adversary system of criminal proceedings commences, distinguishing itself at the outset from the inquisitorial system recognized in some countries. Under the system of warnings we delineate today or under any other system which may be devised and found effective, the safeguards to be erected about the privilege must come into play at this point. . . .

In dealing with statements obtained through interrogation, we do not purport to find all confessions inadmissible. Confessions remain a proper element in law enforcement. Any statement given freely and voluntarily without any compelling influences is, of course, admissible in evidence. The fundamental import of the privilege while an individual is in custody is not whether he is allowed to talk to the police without the benefit of warnings and counsel, but whether he can be interrogated. There is no requirement that police stop a person who enters a police station and states that he wishes to confess to a crime, or a person who calls the police to offer a confession or any other statement he desires to make. Volunteered statements of any kind are not barred by the Fifth Amendment and their admissibility is not affected by our holding today. . . .

IV.

A recurrent argument made in these cases is that society's need for interrogation outweighs the privilege. This argument is not unfamiliar to this Court. . . . The whole thrust of our foregoing discussion demonstrates that the Constitution has prescribed the rights of the individual when confronted with the power of government when it provided in the Fifth Amendment that an individual cannot be compelled to be a witness against himself. That right cannot be abridged. As Mr. Justice Brandeis once observed:

"Decency, security and liberty alike demand that government officials shall be subjected to the same rules of conduct that are commands to the citizen. In a government of laws, existence of the government will be imperilled if it fails to observe the law scrupulously. Our Government is the potent, the omnipresent teacher. For good or for ill, it teaches the whole people by its example.

Crime is contagious. If the Government becomes a lawbreaker, it breeds contempt for law; it invites every man to become a law unto himself; it invites anarchy. To declare that in the administration of the criminal law the end justifies the means . . . would bring terrible retribution. Against that pernicious doctrine this Court should resolutely set its face." Olmstead v. United States [1928] (dissenting opinion). . . .

V.

Because of the nature of the problem and because of its recurrent significance in numerous cases, we have to this point discussed the relationship of the Fifth Amendment privilege to police interrogation without specific concentration on the facts of the cases before us. We turn now to these facts to consider the application to these cases of the constitutional principles discussed above. In each instance, we have concluded that statements were obtained from the defendant under circumstances that did not meet constitutional standards for protection of the privilege.

[The Court here reviews in detail the facts of the four cases and concludes either that the defendant did not waive his right to silence, or was not informed that he had a right to silence or to counsel.]

Mr. Justice **Clark** dissented in part.

Mr. Justice **Harlan,** whom Mr. Justice **Stewart** and Mr. Justice **White** joined, dissented, saying in part:

I believe the decision of the Court represents poor constitutional law and entails harmful consequences for the country at large. How serious these consequences may prove to be only time can tell. But the basic flaws in the Court's justification seem to me readily apparent now once all sides of the problem are considered. . . .

While the fine points of this scheme are far less clear than the Court admits, the tenor is quite apparent. The new rules are not designed to guard against police brutality or other unmistakably banned forms of coercion. Those who use third-degree tactics and deny them in court are equally able and destined to lie as skillfully about warnings and waivers. Rather, the thrust of the new rules is to negate all pressures, to reinforce the nervous or ignorant suspect, and ultimately to discourage any confession at all. The aim in short is toward ''voluntariness'' in a utopian sense, or to view it from a different angle, voluntariness with a vengeance. . . .

What the Court largely ignores is that its rules impair, if they will not eventually serve wholly to frustrate, an instrument of law enforcement that has long and quite reasonably been thought worth the price paid for it. There can be little doubt that the Court's new code would markedly decrease the number of confessions. To warn the suspect that he may remain silent and remind him that his confession may be used in court are minor obstructions. To require also an express waiver by the suspect and an end to questioning whenever he demurs must heavily handicap questioning. And to suggest or provide counsel for the suspect simply invites the end of the interrogation.

How much harm this decision will inflict on law enforcement cannot fairly be predicted with accuracy. Evidence on the role of confessions is notoriously incomplete, . . . and little is added by the Court's reference to the FBI experience and the resources believed wasted in interrogation. . . . We do know that some crimes cannot be solved without confessions, that ample expert testimony attests to their importance in crime control, and that the Court is taking a real risk with society's welfare in imposing its new regime on the country. The social costs of crime are too great to call the new rules anything but a hazardous experimentation.

While passing over the costs and risks of its experiment, the Court portrays the evils of normal police questioning in terms which I think are exaggerated. Albeit stringently confined by the due process standards interrogation is no doubt often inconvenient and unpleasant for the suspect. However, it is not less so for a man to be arrested and jailed, to have his house searched, or to stand trial in court, yet all this may properly happen to the most innocent given probable cause, a warrant, or an indictment. Society has always paid a stiff price for law and order, and peaceful interrogation is not one of the dark moments of the law. . . .

Mr. Justice **White,** with whom Mr. Justice **Harlan** and Mr. Justice **Stewart** joined, dissented, saying in part:

The proposition that the privilege against self-incrimination forbids in-custody interrogation without the warnings specified in the majority opinion and without a clear waiver of counsel has no significant support in the history of the privilege or in the language of the Fifth Amendment. As for the English authorities and the common-law history, the privilege, firmly established in the second half of the seventeenth century, was never applied except to prohibit compelled judicial interrogations. The rule excluding coerced confessions matured about 100 years later, ''[b]ut there is nothing in the reports to suggest that the theory has its roots in the privilege against self-incrimination. And so far as the cases reveal, the privilege, as such, seems to have been given effect only in judicial proceedings, including the preliminary examinations by authorized magistrates.'' . . .

UNITED STATES v. LEON

468 U. S. 897; 82 L. Ed. 2d 677; 104 S. Ct. 3424 (1984)

Over the years in a wide variety of decisions the Court had manifested a basic discontent with the exclusionary rule of Weeks v. United States. The Court seemed to agree that blatant violations of the right of personal privacy could only be discouraged by the use of the doctrine, yet it balked at having to exclude from court unimpeachable evidence of a person's guilt simply because of some legal flaw in the way it was obtained. It had vacillated in its application of the Carroll and "search incident" doctrines and in Terry v. Ohio it had eased dramatically the restrictions on warrantless searches. But it had still failed to find a doctrine that would let it ban illegal evidence gotten in ways it found objectionable, while admitting equally illegal evidence whose admission seemed to promote the cause of justice.

Curiously enough, it was in the context of the retroactivity question that the Court finally devised a theory that it hoped would provide this flexibility. The abrupt reversal of many long-standing constitutional rules in the years of the Warren Court brought to the fore a new kind of problem: To what extent were the new interpretations of the constitution to be made retroactive so as to free prisoners held under the old interpretations? The traditional rule had always been to apply any new interpretation retroactively, but faced with the spectre of thousands of retrials, the Court reexamined this doctrine and in Linkletter v. Walker (1965) set a precedent for limiting the retroactivity of certain rights. Whether a holding is to be applied retroactively depends on the nature of the right and the purposes it is designed to serve. In its decision in United States v. Calandra (1974) the Court had leaned heavily on the "deterrent effect" of the exclusionary rule and concluded that if in fact excluding the evidence would not have deterred the police conduct, there was no point in excluding the evidence through a retroactive application of the rule.

A year later in United States **v.** Peltier (1975) the Court refined the doctrine into what has become known as the "good faith" exception to the exclusion rule. Bluntly stated, if the purpose of the exclusion of evidence is to deter the police from making illegal searches, there is no point in excluding the evidence if the police did not know the search was illegal. Why punish a policeman if he does not know he is misbehaving? If he is acting "in good faith," then the evidence should be admissible.

The Peltier case arose out of the enforcement of legislation regulating our border patrols and again involved the questions of the retroactivity of a newly announced interpretation of the law. The Court found that the guards along the Mexican border were relying on what they believed to be valid rules regarding the stopping and searching of vehicles near the border and there was no point in "punishing" them by refusing to admit their evidence simply because the rules had been changed.

Four years later, in Michigan v. Defillippo (1979), the Court extended the "good faith" doctrine of Peltier beyond the confines of the retroactivity question to hold admissible evidence gotten by a search incident to an unconstitutional arrest. Defillippo was stopped by the police in a Detroit alley under suspicious circumstances and asked to identify himself. When he refused he was arrested under a city ordinance that made it a crime to refuse such identification, was searched incident to the arrest, and marijuana was found in his pocket. He was charged with possession but the Michigan court, holding the identification ordinance void for vagueness and hence the arrest invalid, held the evidence inadmissible as the product of an invalid search.

The Supreme Court reversed. A police officer, it held, has a duty to enforce a law until it is held void unless it is "so grossly and flagrantly unconstitutional that any person of reasonable prudence would be bound to see its flaws." Such was not the case here, and since the refusal to give his name was a crime being committed in the presence of the officer, the arrest and incident search were valid. The unconstitutionality of the ordinance under which DeFillipo had been arrested was stressed in a companion case holding void on its face an El Paso ordinance making it a crime for a person to refuse to identify himself to a police officer; see Brown v. Texas (1979).

Originally limited to evidence gotten by an unreasonable search and seizure, the "good faith" doctrine moved within a year into the area of evidence obtained by questioning suspects. After giving a murder suspect Miranda warnings, three police officers were taking him to the police station for questioning. During the ride, two of them discussed the danger posed to the community by the fact that the murder gun was still missing. A school for hand-icapped children was nearby "and God forbid one of them might find a weapon with shells and might hurt themselves." The suspect interrupted and asked the officers to return to the scene of the crime. There he produced the hidden weapon because " 'he wanted to get the gun out of the way because of the kids in the area in the school.' " The Court upheld the admission of the gun and the defendant's statements pointing out that the officers, acting in good faith, had not intended their conversation as interrogation and they could not have known of the defendant's sensitivity where handicapped children were concerned. See Rhode Island v. Innis (1980).

In the present case a confidential informant of unproven reliability tipped off the police of Burbank, Calif., that Leon and others were selling cocaine and methaqualone from their home and other places. The police watched the comings and goings of the five or six persons involved, some of whom were known to have been involved in the drug traffic, and concluded that they were engaged in a drug smuggling operation. Several district attorneys reviewed the evidence collected by the police and at their request a state judge issued a warrant to search a number of residences and vehicles. The defendants were indicted on drug charges. They filed a motion to suppress the evidence seized under the warrant and the district court granted the motion on the ground that the reliability and credibility of the informant had not been established. "I just cannot find this warrant sufficient for a showing of probable cause" for the issuance of a search warrant.

Justice **White** delivered the opinion of the Court, saying in part:

This case presents the question whether the Fourth Amendment exclusionary rule should be modified so as not to bar the use in the prosecutions's case-in-chief of evidence obtained by officers acting in reasonable reliance on a search warrant issued by a detached and neutral magistrate but ultimately found to be unsupported by probable cause. To resolve this question, we must consider once again the tension between the sometimes competing goals of, on the one hand, deterring official misconduct and removing inducements to unreasonable invasions of privacy and, on the other, establishing procedures under which criminal defendants are "acquitted or convicted on the basis of all the evidence which exposes the truth." . . .

I. . . .

We have concluded that, in the Fourth Amendment context, the exclusionary rule can be modified somewhat without jeopardizing its ability to perform its intended functions. . . .

II. . . .

A.

The Fourth Amendment contains no provision expressly precluding the use of evidence obtained in violation of its commands, and an examination of its origin and purposes makes clear that the use of fruits of a past unlawful search or seizure "work[s] no new Fourth Amendment wrong." United States v. Calandra (1974). The wrong condemned by the Amendment is "fully accomplished" by the unlawful search or seizure itself, and the exclusionary rule is neither intended nor able to "cure the invasion of the defendant's rights which he has already suffered." . . . The rule thus operates as "a judicially created remedy designed to safeguard Fourth Amendment rights generally through its deterrent effect, rather than a personal constitutional right of the person aggrieved." . . .

Whether the exclusionary sanction is appropriately imposed in a particular case, our decisions make clear, is "an issue separate from the question whether the Fourth Amendment rights of the party seeking to invoke the rule were violated by police conduct." Illinois v. Gates [1983]. Only the former question is currently before us, and it must be resolved by weighing the costs and benefits of preventing the use in the prosecution's case-in-chief ot inherently trustworthy tangible evidence obtained in reliance on a search warrant issued by a detached and neutral magistrate that ultimately is found to be defective.

The substantial social costs exacted by the exclusionary rule for the vindication of Fourth Amendment rights have long been a source of concern. "Our cases have consistently recognized that unbending application of the exclusionary sanction to enforce ideals of government rectitude would impede unacceptably the truth-finding functions of judge and jury." ... An objectionable collateral consequence of this interference with the criminal justice system's truth-finding function is that some guilty defendants may go free or receive reduced sentences as a result of favorable plea bargains. Particularly when law enforcement officers have acted in objective good faith or their transgressions have been minor, the magnitude of the benefit conferred on such guilty defendants offends basic concepts of the criminal justice system. ... Indiscriminate application of the exclusionary rule, therefore, may well "generat[e] disrespect for the law and the administration of justice." ...

B.

... The Court has, to be sure, not seriously questioned, "in the absence of a more efficacious sanction, the continued application of the rule to suppress evidence from the [prosecution's] case where a Fourth Amendment violation has been substantial and deliberate...." Nevertheless, the balancing approach that has evolved in various contexts—including criminal trials—"forcefully suggest[s] that the exclusionary rule be more generally modified to permit the introduction of evidence obtained in the reasonable good-faith belief that a search or seizure was in accord with the Fourth Amendment." ...

[The Court here reviews the past cases and the exceptions to the exclusionary rule.]

As yet, we have not recognized any form of good-faith exception to the Fourth Amendment exclusionary rule. But the balancing approach that has evolved during the years of experience with the rule provides strong support for the modification currently urged upon us. As we discuss below, our evaluation of the costs and benefits of suppressing reliable physical evidence seized by officers reasonably relying on a warrant issued by a detached and neutral magistrate leads to the conclusion that such evidence should be admissible in the prosecution's case-in-chief.

III.

A.

Because a search warrant "provides the detached scrutiny of a neutral magistrate, which is a more reliable safeguard against improper searches than the hurried judgment of a law enforcement officer 'engaged in the often competitive enterprise of ferreting out crime,' " ... we have expressed a strong preference for warrants and declared that "in a doubtful or marginal case a search under a warrant may be sustainable where without one it would fail." ... Reasonable minds frequently may differ on the question whether a particular affidavit establishes probable cause, and we have thus concluded that the preference for warrants is most appropriately effectuated by according "great deference" to a magistrate's determination. . . .

Deference to the magistrate, however, is not boundless. It is clear, first, that the deference accorded to a magistrate's finding of probable cause does not preclude inquiry into the knowing or reckless falsity of the affidavit on which that determination was based. . . . Second, the courts must also insist that the magistrate purport to "perform his 'neutral and detached' function and not serve merely as a rubber stamp for the police." . . . A magistrate failing to "manifest that neutrality and detachment demanded of a judicial officer when presented with a warrant application" and who acts instead as "an adjunct law enforcement officer" cannot provide valid authorization for an otherwise unconstitutional search. . . .

Third, reviewing courts will not defer to a warrant based on an affidavit that does not "provide the magistrate with a substantial basis for determining the existence of probable cause." Illinois v. Gates. "Sufficient information must be presented to the magistrate to allow that official to determine probable cause; his action cannot be a mere ratification of the bare conclusions of others." . . . Even if the warrant application was supported by more than a "bare bones" affidavit, a reviewing court may properly conclude that, notwithstanding the deference that magistrates deserve, the warrant was invalid because the magistrate's probable-cause determination reflected an improper analysis of the totality of the circumstances . . . or because the form of the warrant was improper in some respect.

Only in the first of these three situations, however, has the Court set forth a rationale for suppressing evidence obtained pursuant to a search warrant; in the other areas, it has simply excluded such evidence without considering whether Fourth Amendment interests will be advanced. To the extent that proponents of exclusion rely on its behavioral effects on judges and magistrates in these areas, their reliance is misplaced. First, the exclusionary rule is designed to deter police misconduct rather than to punish the errors of judges and magistrates. Second, there exists no evidence suggesting that judges and magistrates are inclined to ignore or subvert the Fourth Amendment or that lawlessness among these actors requires application of the extreme sanction of exclusion.

Third, and most important, we discern no basis, and are offered none, for believing that exclusion of evidence seized pursuant to a warrant will have a significant deterrent effect on the issuing judge or magistrate. Many of the factors that indicate that the exclusionary rule cannot provide an effective "special" or "general" deterrent for individual offending law enforcement officers apply as well to judges or magistrates. And, to the extent that the rule is thought to operate as a "systemic" deterrent on a wider audience, it clearly can have no such effect on individuals empowered to issue search warrants. Judges and magistrates are not adjuncts to the law enforcement team; as neutral judicial officers, they have no stake in the outcome of particular criminal prosecutions. The threat of exclusion thus cannot be expected significantly to deter them. Imposition of the exclusionary sanction is not necessary meaningfully to inform judicial officers of their errors, and we cannot conclude that admitting evidence obtained pursuant to a warrant while at the same time declaring that the warrant was somehow defective will in any way reduce judicial officers' professional incentives to comply with the Fourth Amendment, encourage them to repeat their mistakes, or lead to the granting of all colorable warrant requests.

B.

If exclusion of evidence obtained pursuant to a subsequently invalidated warrant is to have any deterrent effect, therefore, it must alter the behavior of individual law enforcement officers or the policies of their departments. One could argue that applying the exclusionary rule in cases where the police failed to demonstrate probable cause in the warrant application deters future inadequate presentations or "magistrate shopping" and thus promotes the ends of the Fourth Amendment. Suppressing evidence obtained pursuant to a technically defective warrant supported by probable cause also might encourage officers to scrutinize more closely the form of the warrant and to point out suspected judicial errors. We find such arguments speculative and conclude that suppression of evidence obtained pursuant to a warrant should be ordered only on a case-by-case basis and only in those unusual cases in which exclusion will further the purposes of the exclusionary rule.

We have frequently questioned whether the exclusionary rule can have any deterrent effect when the offending officers acted in the objectively reasonable belief that their conduct did not violate the Fourth Amendment. "No empirical researcher, proponent or opponent of the rule, has yet been able to establish with any assurance whether the rule has a deterrent effect. . . ." . . . But even assuming that the rule effectively deters some police misconduct and provides incentives for the law enforcement profession as a whole to conduct itself in accord with the Fourth Amendment, it cannot be expected, and should not be applied, to deter objectively reasonable law enforcement activity. . . .

This is particularly true, we believe, when an officer acting with objective good faith has obtained a search warrant from a judge or magistrate and acted within its scope. In most such cases, there is no police illegality and thus nothing to deter. It is the magistrate's responsibility to determine whether the officer's allegations establish probable cause and, if so, to issue a warrant comporting in form with the requirements of the Fourth Amendment. In the ordinary case, an officer cannot be expected to question the magistrate's probable-cause determination or his judgment that the form of the warrant is technically sufficient. . . . Penalizing the officer for the magistrate's error, rather than his own, cannot logically contribute to the deterrence of Fourth Amendment violations.

C.

We conclude that the marginal or nonexistent benefits produced by suppressing evidence obtained in objectively reasonable reliance on a subsequently invalidated search warrant cannot justify the substantial costs of exclusion. We do not suggest, however, that exclusion is always inappropriate in cases where an officer has obtained a warrant and abided by its terms. . . .

Suppression . . . remains an appropriate remedy if the magistrate or judge in issuing a warrant was misled by information in an affidavit that the affiant knew was false or would have known was false except for his reckless disregard of the truth. . . . The exception we recognize today will also not apply in cases where the issuing magistrate wholly abandoned his judicial role . . . ; in such circumstances, no reasonably well-trained officer should rely on the warrant. Nor would an officer manifest objective good faith in relying on a warrant based on an affidavit "so lacking in indicia of probable cause as to render official belief in its existence entirely unreasonable." ... Finally, depending on the circumstances of the particular case, a warrant may be so facially deficient—i.e., in failing to particularize the place to be searched or the things to be seized—that the executing officers cannot reasonably presume it to be valid. ...

Justice **Blackmun,** concurring, said in part:

... I write separately ... to underscore what I regard as the unavoidably provisional nature of today's decisions. ...

What must be stressed ... is that any empirical judgment about the effect of the exclusionary rule in a particular class of cases necessarily is a provisional one. By their very nature, the assumptions on which we proceed today cannot be cast in stone. To the contrary, they now will be tested in the real world of state and federal law enforcement, and this Court will attend to the results. If it should emerge from experience that, contrary to our expectations, the good faith exception to the exclusionary rule results in a material change in police compliance with the Fourth Amendment, we shall have to reconsider what we have undertaken here. The logic of a decision that rests on untested predictions about police conduct demands no less.

Justice **Brennan**, with whom Justice **Marshall** joins, dissenting said in part:

I. ...

A.

... Because seizures are executed principally to secure evidence, and because such evidence generally has utility in our legal system only in the context of a trial supervised by a judge, it is apparent that the admission of illegally obtained evidence implicates the same constitutional concerns as the initial seizure of that evidence. Indeed, by admitting unlawfully seized evidence, the judiciary becomes a part of what is in fact a single governmental action prohibited by the terms of the Amendment. ...

It is difficult to give any meaning at all to the limitations imposed by the Amendment if they are read to proscribe only certain conduct by the police but to allow other agents of the same government to take advantage of evidence secured by the police in violation of its requirements. The Amendment therefore must be read to condemn not only the initial unconstitutional invasion of privacy—which is done, after all, for the purpose of securing evidence—but also the subsequent use of any evidence so obtained.

The Court evades this principle by drawing an artificial line between the constitutional rights and responsibilities that are engaged by actions of the police and those that are engaged when a defendant appears before the courts. According to the Court, the substantive protections of the Fourth Amendment are wholly exhausted at the moment when police unlawfully invade an individual's privacy and thus no substantive force remains to those protections at the time of trial when the government seeks to use evidence obtained by the police.

I submit that such a crabbed reading of the Fourth Amendment casts aside the teaching of those Justices who first formulated the exclusionary rule, and rests ultimately on an impoverished understanding of judicial responsibility in our constitutional scheme. For my part, "[t]he right of the people to be secure in their persons, houses, papers and effects, against unreasonable searches and seizures" comprises a personal right to exclude all evidence secured by means of unreasonable searches and seizures. The right to be free from the initial invasion of privacy and the right of exclusion are coordinate components of the central embracing right to be free from unreasonable searches and seizures. . . .

B.

. . . The Court since Calandra has gradually pressed the deterrence rationale for the rule back to center stage. . . . The various arguments advanced by the Court in this campaign have only strengthened my conviction that the deterrence theory is both misguided and unworkable. First, the Court has frequently bewailed the "cost" of excluding reliable evidence. In large part, this criticism rests upon a refusal to acknowledge the function of the Fourth Amendment itself. If nothing else, the Amendment plainly operates to disable the government from gathering information and securing evidence in certain ways. In practical terms, of course, this restriction of official power means that some incriminating evidence inevitably will go undetected if the government obeys these constitutional restraints. It is the loss of that evidence that is the "price" our society pays for enjoying the freedom and privacy safeguarded by the Fourth Amendment. Thus, some criminals will go free *not*, in Justice (then Judge) Cardozo's misleading epigram, "because the constable has blundered," People v. Defore, 242 N. Y. 13 (1926), but rather because official compliance with Fourth Amendment requirements makes it more difficult to catch criminals. Understood in this way, the Amendment directly contemplates that some reliable and incriminating evidence will be lost to the government; therefore, it is not the exclusionary rule, but the Amendment itself that has imposed this cost.

In addition, the Court's decisions over the past decade have made plain that the entire enterprise of attempting to assess the benefits and costs of the exclusionary rule in various contexts is a virtually impossible task for the judiciary to perform honestly or accurately. Although the Court's language in those cases suggests that some specific empirical basis may support its analyses, the reality is that the Court's opinions represent inherently unstable compounds of intuition, hunches, and occasional pieces of partial and often inconclusive data. In Calandra, for example, the Court, in considering whether the exclusionary rule should apply in grand jury proceedings, had before it no concrete evidence whatever concerning the impact that application of the rule in such proceedings would have either in terms of the long-term costs or the expected benefits. To the extent empirical data is available regarding the general costs and benefits of the exclusionary rule, it has shown, on the one hand, as the Court acknowledges today, that the costs are not as substantial as critics have asserted in the past, and, on the other hand, that while the exclusionary rule may well have certain deterrent effects, it is extremely difficult to determine with any degree of precision whether the incidence of unlawful conduct by police is now lower than it was prior to Mapp. . . . The Court has sought to turn this uncertainty to its advantage by casting the burden of proof upon proponents of the rule. . , . "Obviously," however, "the assignment of the burden of proof on an issue where evidence does not exist and cannot be obtained is outcome determinative. [The] assignment of the burden is merely a way of announcing a predetermined conclusion."* By remaining within its redoubt of empiricism and by basing the rule solely on the deterrence rationale, the Court has robbed the rule of legitimacy. A doctrine that is explained as if it were an empirical proposition but for which there is only limited empirical support is both inherently unstable and an easy mark for critics. The extent of this Court's fidelity to Fourth Amendment requirements, however, should not turn on such statistical uncertainties. . . .

III.

Even if I were to accept the Court's general approach to the exclusionary rule, I could not agree with today's result. There is no question that in the hands of the present Court the deterrence rationale has proved to be a powerful tool for confining the scope of the rule. In Calandra, for example, the Court concluded that the "speculative and undoubtedly minimal advance in the deterrence of police misconduct," was insufficient to outweigh the "expense of substantially impeding the grand jury." In Stone v. Powell [1976], the Court found that "the additional contribution, if any, of the consideration of search-and-seizure claims of state prisoners on collateral review is small in relation to the costs." In United States v. Janis (1976), the Court concluded that "exclusion from federal civil proceedings of evidence unlawfully seized by a state criminal enforcement officer has not been shown to have a sufficient likelihood of deterring the conduct of the state police so that it outweighs the societal costs imposed by the exclusion." And in an opinion handed down today, the Court finds that the "balance between costs and benefits comes out against applying the exclusionary rule in civil deportation hearings held by the Immigration and Naturalization Service." INS v. Lopez-Mendoza [1984]. . , ,

At the outset, the Court suggests that society has been asked to pay a high price—in terms either of setting guilty persons free or of impeding the proper functioning of trials—as a result of excluding relevant physical evidence in cases where the police, in conducting searches and seizing evidence, have made only an "objectively reasonable" mistake concerning the constitutionality of their actions. But what evidence is there to support such a claim?

Significantly, the Court points to none, and, indeed, as the Court acknowledges, recent studies have demonstrated that the "costs" of the exclusionary rule—calculated in terms of dropped prosecutions and lost convictions—are quite low. Contrary to the claims of the rule's critics that exclusion leads to "the release of countless guilty criminals," . , . these studies have demonstrated that federal and state prosecutors very rarely drop cases because of potential search and seizure problems. For example, a 1979 study prepared at the request

---

*Dworkin, Fact Style Adjudication and the Fourth Amendment: The Limits of Lawyering, 48 Ind. L. J. 329, 332-333 (1973). . , .

of Congress by the General Accounting Office reported that only 0.4% of all cases actually declined for prosecution by federal prosecutors were declined primarily because of illegal search problems....

What then supports the Court's insistence that this evidence be admitted? Apparently, the Court's only answer is that even though the costs of exclusion are not very substantial, the potential deterrent effect in these circumstances is so marginal that exclusion cannot be justified....

... But what the Court overlooks is that the deterrence rationale for the rule is not designed to be, nor should it be thought of as, a form of "punishment" of individual police officers for their failures to obey the restraints imposed by the Fourth Amendment. ... Instead, the chief deterrent function of the rule is its tendency to promote institutional compliance with Fourth Amendment requirements on the part of law enforcement agencies generally. Thus, as the Court has previously recognized, "over the long term, [the] demonstration [provided by the exclusionary rule] that our society attaches serious consequences to violations of constitutional rights is thought to encourage those who formulate law enforcement policies, and the officers who implement them, to incorporate Fourth Amendment ideals into their value system." ... It is only through such an institution-wide mechanism that information concerning the Fourth Amendment standards can be effectively communicated to rank and file officers....

After today's decision, however, that institutional incentive will be lost. Indeed, the Court's "reasonable mistake" exception to the exclusionary rule will tend to put a premium on police ignorance of the law....

... A chief consequence of today's decision will be to convey a clear and unambiguous message to magistrates that their decisions to issue warrants are now insulated from subsequent judicial review. Creation of this new exception for good faith reliance upon a warrant implicitly tells magistrates that they need not take much care in reviewing warrant applications, since their mistakes will from now on have virtually no consequences: If their decision to issue a warrant was correct, the evidence will be admitted; if their decision was incorrect but the police relied in good faith on the warrant, the evidence will also be admitted. Inevitably, the care and attention devoted to such an inconsequential chore will dwindle.

6

Right to Equal Protection of the Law

A. Race

DRED SCOTT v. SANDFORD

19 How. 393; 15 L. Ed. 691 (1857)

It is a curious fact that while the Constitution carefully outlined the basic structure of the United States government and spelled out both its powers and limitations, nowhere did it indicate who were to be citizens of the newly formed nation. Clearly the idea of citizenship was not simply overlooked. Article I requires that senators and representatives shall have been citizens for a term of years and Article II provides that "no person except a natural born citizen" shall be President. But the document was silent as to who such citizens were to be. In the absence of such provision it was generally assumed that the English rule of "jus soli," whereby a person born in a country was a citizen, would prevail—in contrast to the rule of "jus sanguinis" of the European continent where citizenship came from one's parents. However, in 1790 Congress by law extended United States citizenship to those born of American parents outside the country.

Even less helpful was the reference to state citizenship. Article IV, in what is known as the "comity clause," provided that "the citizens of each State shall be entitled to all the privileges and immunities of citizens of the several States." But who were these citizens and how was such citizenship acquired? Could a person be a citizen of a state without being a citizen of the United States? Some 20 states have at one time or another permitted aliens (from the federal point of view) to vote provided they had applied for United States citizenship. Were they then citizens of the state? These questions have never been answered by the Supreme Court.

It is against this background that the present case must be viewed. Prior to the adoption of the Fourteenth Amendment the prevailing view probably was that, save in cases of naturalization, persons were automatically citizens of the United States if they were citizens of a state. This had been the view of Calhoun, and also of such constitutional authorities as Story and Rawle. The Court in the present case recognized state citizenship as the source of federal citizenship, but insisted that the state had no further power to confer federal citizenship on persons by making them state citizens.

The Dred Scott decision is probably the most notorious one ever handed down by the Supreme Court, and certainly brought the prestige of that institution to an all-time low. Further, it destroyed the reputation of Chief Justice Taney, until that time widely regarded as an effective and respected jurist. The issue could have been decided without raising the constitutional issue by finding, as the Court had done in previous cases, that whatever Scott's status while in a free state or territory, upon his return to a slave state with his master he had again become a slave. Justice Nelson had written what was to be the Court opinion based on this argument, but when it was learned that Justices McLean and Curtis were raising the constitutional issue in their dissents, Chief Justice Taney wrote a new Court opinion dealing with the points raised.

The facts of the case were these: Dred Scott had been taken by his master from Missouri into Illinois—a free state—and later into federal territory (now Minnesota) made free by the Missouri Compromise of 1820. When Scott was returned to Missouri his new owner, an abolitionist, arranged to be sued for Scott's freedom in a Missouri court—an early example of a test case—and while Scott won his freedom, he lost it again on appeal. To bring the issue to a federal court, a fictitious sale was arranged to a New Yorker named Sandford. The legal issue before the Court was whether Dred Scott was a citizen of Missouri and thus could sue in the federal courts on the ground of diversity of citizenship.

Nearly 150 years later it is easy to overlook a number of facts regarding the case. Chief Justice Taney, a resident of Maryland, shared with the entire Court a deep concern over the tension within the country raised by the existence of slavery that carried with it the threat of secession, if not civil war. He hoped that if the Court made a definitive decision it would not only solve the problem but preserve the Union as well. Interesting, too, is the fact that, by deciding the case as it did, the Court effectively banned all blacks, free or not, from appealing to the courts to protect their liberty and property.

Mr. Chief Justice **Taney** delivered the opinion of the Court, saying in part:

The question is simply this: can a negro, whose ancestors were imported into this country and sold as slaves, become a member of the political community formed and brought into existence by the Constitution of the United States, and as such become entitled to all the rights, and privileges, and immunities, guarantied by that instrument to the citizen. One of these rights is the privilege of suing in a court of the United States in the cases specified in the Constitution.

It will be observed, that the plea applies to that class of persons only whose ancestors were negroes of the African race, and imported into this country, and sold and held as slaves. The only matter in issue before the court, therefore, is, whether the descendants of such slaves, when they shall be emancipated, or who are born of parents who had become free before their birth, are citizens of a state, in the sense in which the word "citizen" is used in the Constitution of the United States. And this being the only matter in dispute on the pleadings, the court must be understood as speaking in this opinion of that class only; that is, of those persons who are the descendants of Africans who were imported into this country and sold as slaves. . . .

The words "people of the United States" and "citizens" are synonymous terms, and mean the same thing. They both describe the political body, who, according to our republican institutions, form the sovereignty, and who hold the power and conduct the government through their representatives. They are what we familiarly call the "sovereign people," and every citizen is one of this people, and a constituent member of this sovereignty. The question before us is, whether the class of persons described in the plea in abatement compose a portion of this people, and are constituent members of this sovereignty. We think they are not, and that they are not included, and were not intended to be included, under the word "citizens" in the Constitution, and can, therefore, claim none of the rights and privileges which that instrument provides for and secures to citizens of the United States. On the contrary, they were at that time considered as a subordinate and inferior class of beings, who had been subjugated by the dominant race, and whether emancipated or not, yet remained subject to their authority, and had no rights or privileges but such as those who held the power and the government might choose to grant them. . . .

In discussing this question, we must not confound the rights of citizenship which a state may confer within its own limits, and the rights of citizenship as a member of the Union. It does not by any means follow, because he has all the rights and privileges of a citizen of a State, that he must be a citizen of the United States. He may have all the rights and privileges of the citizen of a State, and yet not be entitled to the rights and privileges of a citizen in any other State. For, previous to the adoption of the Constitution of the United States, every State had the undoubted right to confer on whomsoever it pleased the character of a citizen, and to endow him with all its rights. But this character, of course, was confined to the boundaries of the State, and gave him no rights or privileges in other States beyond those secured to him by the laws of nations and the comity of States. Nor have the several States surrendered the power of conferring these rights and privileges by adopting the Constitution of the United States. Each State may still confer them upon an alien, or any one it thinks proper, or upon any class or description of persons; yet he would not be a citizen in the sense in which that word is used in the Constitution of the United States, nor entitled to sue as such in one of its courts, nor to the privileges and immunities of a citizen in the other States. The rights which he would acquire would be restricted to the State which gave them. The Constitution has conferred on Congress the right to establish an uniform rule of naturalization, and this right is evidently exclusive, and has always been held by this court to be so. Consequently, no State, since the adoption of the Constitution, can, by naturalizing an alien, invest him with the rights and privileges secured to a citizen of a State under the federal government, although, so far as the State alone was concerned, he would undoubtedly be entitled to the rights of a citizen, and clothed with all the rights and immunities which the Constitution and laws of the State attached to that character.

It is very clear, therefore, that no State can, by any Act or law of its own, passed, since the adoption of the Constitution, introduce a new member into the political community created by the Constitution of the United States. It cannot make him a member of this community by making him a member of its own. And for the same reason it cannot introduce any person, or description of persons, who were not intended to be embraced in this new political family, which the Constitution brought into existence, but were intended to be excluded from it. . . .

It is true, every person, and every class and description of persons, who were at the time of the adoption of the Constitution recognized as citizens in the several States, became also citizens of this new political body; but none other; it was formed by them, and for them and their posterity, but for no one else. And the personal rights and privileges guarantied to citizens of this new sovereignty were intended to embrace those only who were then members of the several state communities, or who should afterwards, by birthright or otherwise, become members, according to the provisions of the Constitution and the principles on which it was founded. . . .

It becomes necessary, therefore, to determine who were citizens of the several States when the Constitution was adopted. And in order to do this, we must recur to the governments and institutions of the thirteen Colonies, when they separated from Great Britain and formed new sovereignties, and took their places in the family of independent nations. We must inquire who, at that time, were recognized as the people or citizens of a State, whose rights and liberties had been outraged by the English Government; and who declared their independence, and assumed the powers of government to defend their rights by force of arms.

In the opinion of the court, the legislation and histories of the times, and the language used in the Declaration of Independence, show, that neither the class of persons who had been imported as slaves, nor their descendants, whether they had become free or not, were then acknowledged as a part of the people, nor intended to be included in the general words used in that memorable instrument.

It is difficult at this day to realize the state of public opinion in relation to that unfortunate race, which prevailed in the civilized and enlightened portions of the world at the time of the Declaration of Independence, and when the Constitution of the United States was framed and adopted. But the public history of every European nation displays it, in a manner too plain to be mistaken.

They had for more than a century before been regarded as beings of an inferior order; and altogether unfit to associate with the white race, either in social or political relations; and so far inferior, that they had no rights which the white man was bound to respect; and that the negro might justly and lawfully be reduced to slavery for his benefit. He was bought and sold, and treated as an ordinary article of merchandise and traffic, whenever a profit could be made by it. This opinion was at that time fixed and universal in the civilized portion of the white race. It was regarded as an axiom in morals as well as in politics, which no one thought of disputing, or supposed to be open to dispute; and men in every grade and position in society daily and habitually acted upon it in their private pursuits, as well as in matters of public concern, without doubting for a moment the correctness of this opinion.

And in no nation was this opinion more firmly fixed or more uniformly acted upon than by the English government and English people. They not only seized them on the coast of Africa, and sold them or held them in slavery for their own use; but they took them as ordinary articles of merchandise to every country where they could make a profit on them, and were far more extensively engaged in this commerce than any other nation in the world.

The opinion thus entertained and acted upon in England was naturally impressed upon the colonies they founded on this side of the Atlantic. And, accordingly, a negro of the African race was regarded by them as an article of property, and held, and bought and sold as such, in every one of the thirteen Colonies which united in the Declaration of Independence, and afterwards formed the Constitution of the United States. The slaves were more or less numerous in the different Colonies, as slave labor was found more or less profitable. But no one seems to have doubted the correctness of the prevailing opinion of the time.

The legislation of the different Colonies furnishes positive and indisputable proof of this fact. . . . [The Court here reviews this legislation.]

We refer to these historical facts for the purpose of showing the fixed opinions concerning that race, upon which the statesmen of that day spoke and acted. It is necessary to do this, in order to determine whether the general terms used in the Constitution of the United States, as to the rights of man and the rights of the people, was intended to include them, or to give to them or their posterity the benefit of any of its provisions. . . .

No one, we presume, supposes that any change in public opinion or feeling in relation to this unfortunate race, in the civilized nations of Europe or in this country, should induce the court to give to the words of the Constitution a more liberal construction in their favor than they were intended to bear when the instrument was framed and adopted. Such an argument would be altogether inadmissible in any tribunal called on to interpret it. If any of its provisions are deemed unjust, there is a mode prescribed in the instrument itself by which it may be amended; but while it remains unaltered, it must be construed now as it was understood at the time of its adoption. It is not only the same in words, but the same in meaning, and delegates the same powers to the government, and reserves and secures the same rights and privileges to the citizen; and as long as it continues to exist in its present form, it speaks not only in the same words, but with the same meaning and intent with which it spoke when it came from the hands of its framers, and was voted on and adopted by the people of the United States. Any other rule of construction would abrogate the judicial character of this court, and make it the mere reflex of the popular opinion or passion of the day. This court was not created by the Constitution for such purposes. Higher and graver trusts have been confided to it, and it must not falter in the path of duty. . . .

And upon a full and careful consideration of the subject, the court is of opinion that, upon the facts stated in the plea in abatement, Dred Scott was not a citizen of Missouri within the meaning of the Constitution of the United States, and not entitled as such to sue in its courts; and, consequently, that the Circuit Court had no jurisdiction of the case, and that the judgment on the plea in abatement is erroneous. . . .

It is true that the result either way, by dismissal or by a judgment for the defendant, makes very little, if any difference in a pecuniary or personal point of view to either party. But the fact that the result would be very nearly the same to the parties in either form of judgment, would not justify this court in sanctioning an error in the judgment which is patent on the record, and which, if sanctioned, might be drawn into precedent, and lead to serious mischief and injustice in some future suit.

We proceed, therefore, to inquire whether the facts relied on by the plaintiff entitled him to his freedom. . . .

In considering this part of the controversy, two questions arise: 1st. Was he, together with his family, free in Missouri by reason of the stay in the territory of the United States hereinbefore mentioned? And 2d. If they were not, is Scott himself free by reason of his removal to Rock Island, in the State of Illinois, as stated in the above admissions?

We proceed to examine the first question.

The Act of Congress, upon which the plaintiff relies, declares that slavery and involuntary servitude, except as a punishment for crime, shall be forever prohibited in all that part of that territory ceded by France, under the name of Louisiana, which lies north of thirty-six degrees thirty minutes north latitude, and not included within the limits of Missouri. And the difficulty which meets us at the threshold of this part of the inquiry is, whether Congress was authorized to pass this law under any of the powers granted to it by the Constitution; for if the authority is not given by that instrument, it is the duty of this court to declare it void and inoperative, and incapable of conferring freedom upon one who is held as a slave under the laws of any one of the States.

The counsel for the plaintiff has laid much stress upon that article in the Constitution which confers on Congress the power "to dispose of and make all needful rules and regulations respecting the territory or other property belonging to the United States;" but, in the judgment of the court, that provision has no bearing on the present controversy, and the power there given, whatever it may be, is confined, and was intended to be confined, to the territory which at that time belonged to, or was claimed by, the United States, and was within their boundaries as settled by the Treaty with Great Britain, and can have no influence upon a territory afterwards acquired from a foreign government. It was a special provision for a known and particular Territory, and to meet a present emergency, and nothing more.

A brief summary of the history of the times, as well as the careful and measured terms in which the article is framed, will show the correctness of this proposition. . . .

This brings us to examine by what provision of the Constitution the present Federal Government under its delegated and restricted powers, is authorized to acquire territory outside of the original limits of the United States, and what powers it may exercise therein over the person or property of a citizen of the United States, while it remains a territory, and until it shall be admitted as one of the States of the Union.

There is certainly no power given by the Constitution to the Federal Government to establish or maintain Colonies bordering on the United States or at a distance, to be ruled and governed at its own pleasure; nor to enlarge its territorial limits in any way, except by the admission of new States. . . .

We do not mean, however, to question the power of Congress in this respect. The power to expand the territory of the United States by the admission of new States is plainly given; and in the construction of this power by all the departments of the government, it has been held to authorize the acquisition of territory, not fit for admission at the time, but to be admitted as soon as its population and situation would entitle it to admission. It is acquired to become a State, and not to be held as a colony and governed by Congress with absolute authority. . . .

. . . And when the territory becomes a part of the United States, the Federal Government enters into possession in the character impressed upon it by those who created it. It enters upon it with its powers over the citizen strictly defined, and limited by the Constitution, from which it derives its own existence, and by virtue of which alone it continues to exist and act as a government and sovereignty. It has no power of any kind beyond it; and it cannot, when it enters a territory of the United States, put off its character, and assume discretionary or despotic powers which the Constitution has denied to it. . . .

A reference to a few of the provisions of the Constitution will illustrate this proposition.

For example, no one, we presume, will contend that Congress can make any law in a territory respecting the establishment of religion or the free exercise thereof, or abridging the freedom of speech or of the press, or the right of the people of the territory peaceably to assemble and to petition the government for the redress of grievances.

Nor can Congress deny to the people the right to keep and bear arms, nor the right to trial by jury, nor compel anyone to be a witness against himself in a criminal proceeding.

These powers, and others in relation to rights of person, which it is not necessary here to enumerate, are, in express and positive terms, denied to the general government; and the rights of private property have been guarded with equal care. Thus the rights of property are united with the rights of person, and placed on the same ground by the fifth amendment to the Constitution, which provides that no person shall be deprived of life, liberty and property, without due process of law. And an Act of Congress which deprives a citizen of the United States of his liberty or property, merely because he came himself or brought his property into a particular Territory of the United States, and who had committed no offense against the laws, could hardly be dignified with the name of due process of law. . . .

Now, as we have already said in an earlier part of this opinion, upon a different point, the right of property in a slave is distinctly and expressly affirmed in the Constitution. The right to traffic in it, like an ordinary article of merchandise and property, was guaranteed to the citizens of the United States, in every State that might desire it, for twenty years. And the government in express terms is pledged to protect it in all future time, if the slave escapes from his owner. This is done in plain words—too plain to be misunderstood. And no word can be found in the Constitution which gives Congress a greater power over slave property, or which entitles property of that kind to less protection than property of any other description. The only power conferred is the power coupled with the duty of guarding and protecting the owner in his rights.

Upon these considerations, it is the opinion of the court that the Act of Congress which prohibited a citizen from holding and owning property of this kind in the territory of the United States north of the line therein mentioned, is not warranted by the Constitution, and is therefore void; and that neither Dred Scott himself, nor any of his family, were made free by being carried into this territory; even if they had been carried there by the owner, with the intention of becoming a permanent resident. . . .

But there is another point in the case which depends on state power and state law. And it is contended, on the part of the plaintiff, that he is made free by being taken to Rock Island, in the State of Illinois, independently of his residence in the territory of the United States; and being so made free he was not again reduced to a state of slavery by being brought back to Missouri.

Our notice of this part of the case will be very brief; for the principle on which it depends was decided in this court, upon much consideration, in the case of Strader et al. v. Graham [1850]. In that case, the slaves had been taken from Kentucky to Ohio, with the consent of the owner, and afterwards brought back to Kentucky. And this court held that their status or condition, as free or slave, depended upon the laws of Kentucky, when they were brought back into that State, and not of Ohio; and that this court had no jurisdiction to revise the judgment of a state court upon its own laws. This was the point directly before the court, and the decision that this court had not jurisdiction, turned upon it, as will be seen by the report of the case.

So in this case: as Scott was a slave when taken into the State of Illinois by his owner, and was there held as such, and brought back in that character, his status, as free or slave, depended on the laws of Missouri, and not of Illinois. . . .

Upon the whole, therefore, it is the judgment of this court, that it appears by the record before us that the plaintiff in error is not a citizen of Missouri, in the sense in which that word is used in the Constitution; and that the Circuit Court of the United States, for that reason, had no jurisdiction in the case, and could give no judgment in it.

Its judgment for the defendant must, consequently, be reversed, and a mandate issued directing the suit to be dismissed for want of jurisdiction.

Mr. Justice **Wayne** wrote a concurring opinion.

Mr. Justice **Nelson** wrote a concurring opinion.

Mr. Justice **Grier** concurred with Mr. Justice **Nelson,** and also wrote a concurring opinion.

Mr. Justice **Daniels** wrote a concurring opinion.

Mr. Justice **Campbell** wrote a concurring opinion.

Mr. Justice **Catron** wrote a concurring opinion.

Mr. Justice **McLean** wrote a dissenting opinion.

Mr. Justice **Curtis,** dissenting, said in part:

To determine whether any free persons, descended from Africans held in slavery, were citizens of the United States under the Confederation, and consequently at the time of the adoption of the Constitution of the United States, it is only necessary to know whether any such persons were citizens of either of the States under the Confederation at the time of the adoption of the Constitution.

Of this there can be no doubt. At the time of the ratification of the Articles of Confederation, all free native-born inhabitants of the States of New Hampshire, Massachusetts, New York, New Jersey and North Carolina, though descended from African slaves, were not only citizens of those States, but such of them as had the other necessary qualifications possessed the franchise of electors on equal terms with other citizens. . . .

Did the Constitution of the United States deprive them or their descendants of citizenship?

That Constitution was ordained and established by the people of the United States through the action, in each State, of those persons who were qualified by its laws to act thereon, in behalf of themselves and all other citizens of that State. In some of the States, as we have seen, colored persons were among those qualified by law to act on this subject. These colored persons were not only included in the body of "the people of the United States by whom the Constitution was ordained and established," but in at least five of the States they had the power to act, and doubtless did act, by their suffrages, upon the question of its adoption. It would be strange, if we were to find in that instrument anything which deprived of their citizenship any part of the people of the United States who were among those by whom it was established.

I can find nothing in the Constitution which, proprio vigore, deprives of their citizenship any class of persons who were citizens of the United States at the time of its adoption, or who should be native-born citizens of any State after its adoption; nor any power enabling Congress to disfranchise persons born on the soil of any State, and entitled to citizenship of such State by its constitution and laws. And my opinion is, that, under the Constitution of the United States, every free person born on the soil of a State, who is a citizen of that State by force of its Constitution or laws, is also a citizen of the United States. . . .

PLESSY v. FERGUSON

163 U. S. 537; 41 L. Ed. 256; 16 S. Ct. 1138 (1896)

During the Reconstruction era which followed the death of President Lincoln, blacks in the South had enjoyed many of the rights and privileges possessed by whites. But with the return of "white man's government" to the Southern states, state laws were again adopted reminiscent of the "Black Codes" which had been passed right after the Civil War to "keep the Negro in his place." These laws established, and enforced by criminal penalties, a system of racial segregation under which members of the black and white races were required to be separated in the enjoyment of public and semi-public facilities. Separate schools, parks, waiting rooms, bus and railroad accommodations were required by law to be furnished each race; and where completely separate facilities later on proved to be not feasible, as in a dining car, a curtained partition served to separate the races.

Where racial segregation was accomplished through private action, as in the case of stores or clubs, no constitutional issue could be raised after the decision in the Civil Rights Cases in 1883. Where the segregation was required by law, however, the question arose whether it violated the rights guaranteed to the newly freed black by the Fourteenth Amendment. This problem came to the Court for the first time in the present case, 28 years after the Amendment had been adopted. The legislature of Louisiana had passed in 1890 a statute providing "that all railway companies carrying passengers in their coaches in this state shall provide equal but separate accommodations for the white and colored races, by providing two or more passenger coaches for each passenger train, or by dividing the passenger coaches by a partition so as to secure separate accommodations. . . ." A fine of $25 or 20 days in jail was the penalty for sitting in the wrong compartment. Plessy, a person who was one-eighth black, refused to vacate a seat in the white compartment of a railway car and was arrested for violating the statute.

The Plessy case made lawful for nearly 60 years the doctrine that blacks were not denied the equal protection of the laws by compelling them to accept "separate but equal" accommodations. There is a bit of irony in the fact that the majority opinion in the Plessy case was written by Justice Brown, a Yale man from the state of Michigan, while the eloquent protest against racial discrimination is found in the dissenting opinion of Justice Harlan, a Southerner from Kentucky.

While it is clear that the Court in Plessy employs the "rational basis" test in its most lenient form, it is included here as a necessary prelude to the Brown case which follows.

Although Plessy involved segregation only in the use of railroad facilities, there was no reason to doubt that the Court would uphold segregation in other areas as well, especially education. This became clear when the Court, in Berea College v. Kentucky (1908), held that the state could validly forbid a college, even though a private institution, to teach whites and blacks at the same time and place. This left no doubt of the validity of the Southern laws requiring the education of white and black children in separate tax-supported schools.

While the segregation of whites and blacks was valid, it was valid only on the theory that the facilities offered were equal, since it is the "equal" protection of the laws that is guaranteed by the Fourteenth Amendment. In common usage there are no degrees of equality; things or conditions are either equal or they are not equal. But the Supreme Court has not taken this view. It has held, rather, that equality in accommodations means not exact or mathematical equality, but only "substantial" equality. In earlier cases the Court was extremely lenient in construing what "equality" required in the segregated school systems of the South. In Cumming v. County Board of Education (1899) it found no denial of equal protection of the laws in the failure of a Southern county to provide a high school for 60 black children, although it maintained a high school for white children. The Court seemed satisfied with the county's defense that it could not afford to build a high school for black children. In Gong Lum v. Rice (1927) the Court held that a Chinese girl could validly be required to attend a school for black children in a neighboring school district, rather than be allowed to attend the nearby school for white children.

Gradually the Court began to adopt a tougher attitude, requiring the states to approximate equal conditions in segregated accommodations. This tougher attitude was made abundantly clear in 1938 in the leading case of Missouri ex rel. Gaines v. Canada (1938). Gaines, a black graduate of Lincoln University and a citizen of Missouri, applied for admission to the University of Missouri law school. Blacks were barred from the law school at the state university; but in order to give them "equal" treatment, the state would pay their tuition in any out-of-state law school which would admit them. Gaines refused to accept this plan, and Chief Justice Hughes held that Gaines was "entitled to be admitted to the law school of the state university in the absence of other and proper provisions for his legal training within the state . . . ."

In Sweatt v. Painter (1950) the state of Texas claimed that its new law school for blacks afforded educational opportunities essentially equal to those at the University of Texas Law School. The Court rejected this claim of equality on very significant grounds. The law school for white students, it said, "possesses to a far greater degree those qualities which are incapable of objective measurement but which make for greatness in a law school. . . . The law school, the proving ground for legal learning and practice, cannot be effective in isolation from the individuals and institutions with which the law interacts. . . . The [black] law school . . . excludes from its student body members of racial groups which number 85% of the population of the State and include most of the lawyers, judges and other officials with whom petitioner will inevitably be dealing when he becomes a member of the Texas bar. With such a substantial and significant segment of society excluded, we cannot conclude that the education offered petitioner is substantially equal to that which he would receive if admitted to the University of Texas Law School."

In the cases dealing with black segregation which reached the Supreme Court after Plessy the doctrine of that case was followed and never reexamined. The Court seemed content with the "separate but equal" rule of that case, which, as someone aptly put it, guaranteed to the black "the equal, but different, protection of the laws." During the forty-year period beginning with McCabe v. Atchison, T. & S. F. Ry. Co. (1914), the Court, applying ever more rigid standards of equality under segregation, found that black plaintiffs in each case had in fact been denied equality of treatment; and so the Court, following the rule that it will not decide constitutional issues if it can avoid doing so, continued to grant relief to blacks not because segregation was unconstitutional but because they were unequally treated under segregation. While in the Texas Law School case and McCabe, involving segregated dining cars, the Court virtually stated that there were circumstances in which segregation in itself resulted in inequality of treatment, the rule of Plessy v. Ferguson remained intact.

It is interesting to speculate what might have been the outcome had the Court, while upholding "separate but equal" as a doctrine, taken the words "equal protection" seriously and found that Plessy, who was seven-eighths white, was to be considered white.

Mr. Justice **Brown** delivered the opinion of the Court, saying in part:

The object of the [Fourteenth] amendment was undoubtedly to enforce the absolute equality of the two races before the law, but in the nature of things it could not have been intended to abolish distinctions based upon color, or to enforce social, as distinguished from political, equality, or a commingling of the two races upon terms unsatisfactory to either. Laws permitting, and even requiring their separation in places where they are liable to be brought into contact do not necessarily imply the inferiority of either race to the other, and have been generally, if not universally, recognized as within the competency of the state legislatures in the exercise of their police power. The most common instance of this is connected with the establishment of separate schools for white and colored children, which [has] been held to be a valid exercise of the legislative power even by courts of states where the political rights of the colored race have been longest and most earnestly enforced.

One of the earliest of these cases is that of Roberts v. Boston, 5 Cush. (Mass.) 198 [1849] in which the supreme judicial court of Massachusetts held that the general school committee of Boston had power to make provision for the instruction of colored children in separate schools established exclusively for them, and to prohibit their attendance upon the other schools. . . . Similar laws have been enacted by Congress under its general power of legislation over the District of Columbia, as well as by the legislatures of many of the states, and have been generally, if not uniformly, sustained by the courts. . . .

Laws forbidding the intermarriage of the two races may be said in a technical sense to interfere with the freedom of contract, and yet have been universally recognized as within the police power of the state. . . .

The distinction between laws interfering with the political equality of the negro and those requiring the separation of the two races in schools, theatres, and railway carriages, has been frequently drawn by this court. . . .

In this connection, it is also suggested by the learned counsel for the plaintiff in error that the same argument that will justify the state legislature in requiring railways to provide separate accommodations for the two races will also authorize them to require separate cars to be provided for people whose hair is of a certain color, or who are aliens, or who belong to certain nationalities, or to enact laws requiring colored people to walk upon one side of the street, and white people upon the other, or requiring white men's houses to be painted white, and colored men's black, or their vehicles or business signs to be of different colors, upon the theory that one side of the street is as good as the other, or that a house or vehicle of one color is as good as one of another color. The reply to all this is that every exercise of the police power must be reasonable, and extend only to such laws as are enacted in good faith for the promotion of the public good, and not for the annoyance or oppression of a particular class. . . .

So far, then, as a conflict with the 14th Amendment is concerned, the case reduces itself to the question whether the statute of Louisiana is a reasonable regulation, and with respect to this there must necessarily be a large discretion on the part of the legislature. In determining the question of reasonableness it is at liberty to act with reference to the established usages, customs, and traditions of the people, and with a view to the promotion of their comfort, and the preservation of the public peace and good order. Gauged by this standard, we cannot say that a law which authorizes or even requires the separation of the two races in public conveyances is unreasonable, or more obnoxious to the 14th Amendment than the acts of Congress requiring separate schools for colored children in the District of Columbia, the constitutionality of which does not seem to have been questioned, or the corresponding acts of state legislatures.

We consider the underlying fallacy of the plaintiff's argument to consist in the assumption that the enforced separation of the two races stamps the colored race with a badge of inferiority. If this be so, it is not by reason of anything found in the act, but solely because the colored race chooses to put that construction upon it. The argument necessarily assumes that if, as has been more than once the case, and is not unlikely to be so again, the colored race should become the dominant power in the state legislature, and should enact a law in precisely similar terms, it would thereby relegate the white race to an inferior position. We imagine that the white race, at least, would not acquiesce in this assumption. The argument also assumes that social prejudices may be overcome by legislation, and that equal rights cannot be secured to the negro except by an enforced commingling of the two races. We cannot accept this proposition. If the two races are to meet on terms of social equality, it must be the result of natural affinities, a mutual appreciation of each other's merits and a voluntary consent of individuals. . . . Legislation is powerless to eradicate racial instincts or to abolish distinctions based upon physical differences, and the attempt to do so can only result in accentuating the difficulties of the present situation. If the civil and political rights of both races be equal, one cannot be inferior to the other civilly or politically. If one race be inferior to the other socially, the Constitution of the United States cannot put them upon the same plane. . . .

The judgment of the court below is therefore affirmed.

Mr. Justice **Brewer** took no part in the decision of this case.

Mr. Justice **Harlan** wrote a dissenting opinion, saying in part:

While there may be in Louisiana persons of different races who are not citizens of the United States, the words in the act, ''white and colored races,'' necessarily include all citizens of the United States of both races residing in that state. So that we have before us a state enactment that compels, under penalties, the separation of the two races in railroad passenger coaches, and makes it a crime for a citizen of either race to enter a coach that has been assigned to citizens of the other race.

Thus the state regulates the use of a public highway by citizens of the United States solely upon the basis of race.

However apparent the injustice of such legislation may be, we have only to consider whether it is consistent with the Constitution of the United States. . . .

In respect of civil rights, common to all citizens, the Constitution of the United States does not, I think, permit any public authority to know the race of those entitled to be protected in the enjoyment of such rights. Every true man has pride of race, and under appropriate circumstances, when the rights of others, his equals before the law, are not to be affected, it is his privilege to express such pride and to take such action based upon it as to him seems proper. But I deny that any legislative body or judicial tribunal may have regard to the race of citizens when the civil rights of those citizens are involved. Indeed such legislation as that here in question is inconsistent, not only with that equality of rights which pertains to citizenship, national and state, but with the personal liberty enjoyed by every one within the United States. . . .

The white race deems itself to be the dominant race in this country. And so it is, in prestige, in achievements, in education, in wealth and in power. So, I doubt not that it will continue to be for all time, if it remains true to its great heritage and holds fast to the principles of constitutional liberty. But in view of the Constitution, in the eye of the law, there is in this country no superior, dominant, ruling class of citizens. There is no caste here. Our Constitution is color-blind, and neither knows nor tolerates classes among citizens. In respect of civil rights, all citizens are equal before the law. The humblest is the peer of the most powerful. The law regards man as man, and takes no account of his surroundings or of his color when his civil rights as guaranteed by the supreme law of the land are involved. It is therefore to be regretted that this high tribunal, the final expositor of the fundamental law of the land, has reached the conclusion that it is competent for a state to regulate the enjoyment by citizens of their civil rights solely upon the basis of race.

In my opinion, the judgment this day rendered will, in time, prove to be quite as pernicious as the decision made by this tribunal in the Dred Scott Case. It was adjudged in that case that the descendants of Africans who were imported into this country and sold as slaves were not included nor intended to be included under the word "citizens" in the Constitution, and could not claim any of the rights and privileges which that instrument provided for and secured to citizens of the United States; that at the time of the adoption of the Constitution they were "considered as a subordinate and inferior class of beings, who had been subjugated by the dominant race, and, whether emancipated or not, yet remained subject to their authority, and had no rights or privileges but such as those who held the power and the government might choose to grant them." The recent amendments of the Constitution, it was supposed, had eradicated these principles from our institutions. But it seems that we have yet, in some of the states, a dominant race, a superior class of citizens, which assumes to regulate the enjoyment of civil rights, common to all citizens, upon the basis of race. The present decision, it may well be apprehended, will not [only] stimulate aggressions, more or less brutal and irritating, upon the admitted rights of colored citizens, but will encourage the belief that it is possible, by means of state enactments, to defeat the beneficent purposes which the people of the United States had in view when they adopted the recent amendments of the Constitution, by one of which the blacks of this country were made citizens of the United States and of the states in which they respectively reside and whose privileges and immunities, as citizens, the states are forbidden to abridge. Sixty millions of whites are in no danger from the presence here of eight millions of blacks. The destinies of the two races in this country are indissolubly linked together, and the interests of both require that the common government of all shall not permit the seeds of race hate to be planted under the sanction of law. What can more certainly arouse race hate, what more certainly create and perpetuate a feeling of distrust between these races, than State enactments which in fact proceed on the ground that colored citizens are so inferior and degraded that they cannot be allowed to sit in public coaches occupied by white citizens? That, as all will admit, is the real meaning of such legislation as was enacted in Louisiana.

The sure guarantee of the peace and security of each race is the clear, distinct, unconditional recognition by our governments, national and state, of every right that inheres in civil freedom, and of the equality before the law of all citizens of the United States without regard to race. State enactments, regulating the enjoyment of civil rights, upon the basis of race, and cunningly devised to defeat legitimate results of the war, under the pretense of recognizing equality of rights, can have no other result than to render permanent peace impossible and to keep alive a conflict of races, the continuance of which must do harm to all concerned. This question is not met by the suggestion that social equality cannot exist between the white and black races in this country. That argument, if it can be properly regarded as one, is scarcely worthy of consideration, for social equality no more exists between two races when travelling in a passenger coach or a public highway than when members of the same races sit by each other in a street car or in the jury box, or stand or sit with each other in a political assembly, or when they use in common the streets of a city or town, or when they are in the same room for the purpose of having their names placed on the registry of voters, or when they approach the ballot-box in order to exercise the high privilege of voting. . . .

The arbitrary separation of citizens, on the basis of race, while they are on a public highway, is a badge of servitude wholly inconsistent with the civil freedom and the equality before the law established by the Constitution. It cannot be justified upon any legal grounds.

If evils will result from the commingling of the two races upon public highways established for the benefit of all, they will be infinitely less than those that will surely come from state legislation regulating the enjoyment of civil rights upon the basis of race. We boast of the freedom enjoyed by our people above all other peoples. But it is difficult to reconcile that boast with a state of the law which, practically, puts the brand of servitude and degradation upon a large class of our fellow citizens, our equals before the law. The thin disguise of ''equal'' accommodations for passengers in railroad coaches will not mislead any one, or atone for the wrong this day done. . . .

I am of opinion that the statute of Louisiana is inconsistent with the personal liberty of citizens, white and black, in that state, and hostile to both the spirit and letter of the Constitution of the United States. If laws of like character should be enacted in the several states of the Union, the effect would be in the highest degree mischievous. Slavery as an institution tolerated by law would, it is true, have disappeared from our country, but there would remain a power in the states, by sinister legislation, to interfere with the full enjoyment of the blessings of freedom; to regulate civil rights, common to all citizens, upon the basis of race; and to place in a condition of legal inferiority a large body of American citizens, now constituting a part of the political community, called the people of the United States, for whom and by whom, through representatives, our government is administered. Such a system is inconsistent with the guarantee given by the Constitution to each state of a republican form of government, and may be stricken down by congressional action, or by the courts in the discharge of their solemn duty to maintain the supreme law of the land, anything in the Constitution or laws of any state to the contrary notwithstanding.

For the reasons stated, I am constrained to withhold my assent from the opinion and judgment of the majority.

BROWN v. BOARD OF EDUCATION OF TOPEKA

347 U. S. 483; 98 L. Ed. 873; 74 S. Ct. 686 (1954)

In the fall of 1952 the Supreme Court had on its docket cases from four states (Kansas, South Carolina, Virginia, and Delaware), and from the District of Columbia, directly challenging the constitutionality of racial segregation in public schools. In all of these cases the facts showed that "the Negro and white schools involved have been equalized, or are being equalized, with respect to buildings, curricula, qualifications and salaries of teachers, and other 'tangible' factors." After nearly 60 years the Court again had squarely before it the question of the constitutionality of segregation per se—the question of whether the doctrine of Plessy v. Ferguson should be affirmed or reversed.

The five cases were argued together in December 1952, and the country waited with tense interest for the Court's decision. On June 8, 1953, the Court restored the cases to the docket for reargument in the fall and issued a list of questions which it wished counsel to address. The Court asked for enlightenment on two main points. First, is there historical evidence which shows the intentions of those who framed and ratified the Fourteenth Amendment with respect to the impact of that amendment upon racial segregation in the public schools? Second, if the Court finds racial segregation violates the Fourteenth Amendment, what kind of decree could and should be issued to bring about an end of segregation?

The cases were reargued in December 1953. Elaborate briefs set forth in great detail the background of the Fourteenth Amendment and the intentions of its framers and ratifiers. The negative result of this historical research is commented on in the opinion below. Some of the briefs, including the one filed by the Attorney General, presented suggestions on the form of the court decree by which segregation might best be ended should the Court hold it to be invalid. Counsel for the National Association for the Advancement of Colored People, which had played a major part in the instigation of these cases, declined to deal with this point. In their counsel's view, segregation, if held invalid, should be abolished completely and without delay.

Again the Court moved with deliberation, and its decision was not handed down until May 17, 1954. It is doubtful if the Supreme Court in its entire history has rendered a decision of greater social and ideological significance than this one. Three things in the present case indicate the high sense of responsibility felt by the justices of the Supreme Court in deciding a case of such vital national importance. First, the Court was unanimous. Second, one opinion was written, and not half a dozen. Third, the Court set for argument in the fall of 1954 the problem of the nature of the decree by which its decision that segregation is invalid might best be given effect. Disagreement in the Court on the decision, or disagreement on the reasons for the decision, would have aided those who resented the Court's ruling and have sought to thwart it. There was wisdom in announcing the constitutional ruling and then allowing a breathing spell during which ways and means of implementing the decision might be carefully and deliberately studied.

Because the Supreme Court wanted a full bench to hear argument on the nature of the decrees necessary to implement its May 17 decision and the Senate marked time on the confirmation of John Marshall Harlan to succeed Justice Robert Jackson on the Court, the argument set for the fall of 1954 was postponed until the spring of 1955. The Court allowed an almost unprecedented 14 hours of oral argument. On May 31, the Court handed down its decision remanding the cases back to the lower courts, which were directed to fashion decrees in accordance with "equitable principles." While recognizing that to abolish segregation "may call for the elimination of a variety of obstacles in making the transition," the Court declared that the district "courts will require that the defendants make a prompt and reasonable start toward full compliance with our May 17, 1954, ruling. Once such a start has been made, the courts may find that additional time is necessary to carry out the ruling in an effective manner. The burden rests upon the defendants to establish that such time is necessary in the public interest and is consistent with good faith compliance at the earliest practicable date. . . . The cases are remanded to the District Courts to take such proceedings and enter such orders and decrees consistent with this opinion as are necessary and proper to admit to public schools on a racially nondiscriminatory basis with all deliberate speed the parties to these cases."

Faced with the desegregation order, Prince Edward County closed its public schools and provided various kinds of financial support for privately operated segregated schools. In Griffin v. School Board of Prince Edward County (1964) the Court held that the plan denied equal protection of the law. Noting that "the case has been delayed since 1951 by resistance at the state and county level, by legislation, and by law suits," it emphasized that "there has been entirely too much deliberation and not enough speed." The Court conceded to the state a "wide discretion" in deciding whether state laws should operate statewide or only in some counties, "but the record in the present case could not be clearer that Prince Edward's public schools were closed and private schools operated in their place with state and county assistance, for one reason, and one reason only: to ensure, through measures taken by the county and the State, that white and colored children in Prince Edward County would not, under any circumstances, go to the same school. Whatever nonracial grounds might support a State's allowing a county to abandon public schools, the object must be a constitutional one, and grounds of race and opposition to desegregation do not qualify as constitutional." The district court was told to "enter a decree which will guarantee that these petitioners will get the kind of education that is given in the State's public schools" even if it had to order the Board of Supervisors to levy taxes to do it. After trying in vain to discover what the penalties for refusal would be, the supervisors finally decided to obey, and in the fall of 1964 Prince Edward County reopened its schools on an integrated basis.

Meanwhile the political branches of government had taken a hand in speeding integration, and threats by the department of Health, Education and Welfare (HEW) to withhold federal aid to segregated schools under the Civil Rights Act of 1964 resulted in widespread token compliance, largely by offering blacks "freedom of choice" among schools. Yet with the start of the 1965-66 school year fewer than 10 percent of the South's blacks were attending desegregated schools. In March of 1966 HEW announced new guidelines designed to desegregate all 12 grades by the fall of 1967. Protracted litigation culminated in an announcement by the court of appeals in a Georgia case in December 1968, that all schools in the states of the fifth circuit—Alabama, Florida, Louisiana, Mississippi, and Texas—be integrated by the fall of 1969 or abandoned.

In July 1969 it became apparent that some 30 schools in Mississippi would not be ready for integration with the opening of the fall term, and the government suddenly announced that it would no longer try to hold the South to "arbitrary" deadlines for desegregation. At the same time the United States Court of Appeals for the Fifth Circuit reaffirmed its policy and ordered full integration, by September, and the Justice Department replied by asking for a delay until December 1.

The announced change in policy came as a shock to the lawyers of the NAACP Legal Defense Fund who, after working for many years in partnership with government attorneys for full integration suddenly found themselves carrying on the fight alone. Even the government attorneys themselves had trouble accepting the sudden switch, and a large number of them signed a statement of protest against the new policy. In spite of this the court of appeals granted the requested delay, and the Legal Defense Fund appealed to the Supreme Court. In a brief per curiam opinion, one of the first in which Chief Justice Burger participated, the Court unanimously rejected the government's request for a delay. The "continued operation of segregated schools under a standard of allowing 'all deliberate speed' for desegregation" said the Court, "is no longer constitutionally permissible. Under explicit holdings of this Court the obligation of every school district is to terminate dual school systems at once and to operate now and hereafter only unitary schools." See Alexander v. Holmes County Board of Education (1969).

Despite this rebuff by the Supreme Court, the Justice Department promptly announced that it would no longer push for more rapid desegregation in over 100 schools in the Deep South. The Justice Department's position, however, did not matter much because HEW, with its authority to withhold funds from schools that were not desegregating, effectively had become the principal administrative support for the courts' orders. The Mississippi school districts did integrate, but many whites in heavily black areas transferred to hastily created all white "private academies." HEW promptly urged the Internal Revenue Service (IRS) to withhold tax exemption from such schools, and in July 1970 the IRS complied.

Bob Jones University v. United States (1983) brought to the Court the issue whether the IRS could validly withhold the normally available tax exemption from a private educational institution simply because it discriminated against blacks. The case, which turned primarily on the intent of Congress in adopting the statute, was given a bizarre twist when President Reagan ordered the government to change sides after certiorari had been granted. The case was kept from becoming moot when the court of appeals enjoined the government's grant of tax immunity, and since the Attorney General was now on the side of Bob Jones, the Court appointed outside counsel to defend the government's position. It found the IRS interpretation to be correct and held that "the Government has a fundamental, overriding interest in eradicating racial discrimination in education—discrimination that prevailed, with official approval, for the first 165 years of this Nation's history."

While apparently most rural and small town school districts moved peacefully toward integration in 1970, in big cities a new cry was heard. To desegregate urban schools located in the center of black or white neighborhoods, it was necessary to transport students out of their home neighborhoods by school bus. As district courts prepared plans calling for busing between pairs of black and white schools, community voices rose in defense of their "neighborhood schools." In Florida, Governor Claude Kirk seized physically the Bradenton schools to prevent busing and relinquished them only when faced with a $10,000-a-day fine. In both the House and Senate, amendments passed to prevent HEW guidelines from requiring busing, only to have them fail when the act finally passed.

And in Charlotte-Mecklenburg, the country's 43rd largest school district, an "antibusing" school board was elected. The district court rejected a plan devised by the Board as not producing sufficient integration at the elementary level and accepted in its place a plan prepared by an outside expert which called for the pairing and grouping of elementary schools and the busing of pupils between them. In upholding the validity of the district court's plan the Supreme Court, in Swann v. Charlotte-Mecklenburg Board of Education (1971) and the companion case of Davis v. Board of Commissioners (1971), spelled out the lengths to which district courts can go to achieve an integrated school system. In Nyquist v. Lee (1971) the Court held void without opinion New York's 1969 antibusing statute upon which most of the Southern antibusing statutes had been patterned.

As the long fight to integrate Southern schools achieved increasing success, attention was turned to Northern cities in which segregation was as complete in many cases as it had ever been in the South. While segregation in the South had its genesis in laws providing separate facilities for the two races (de jure), in the big cities of the North an equally effective segregation (de facto) came about as a by-product of the development of single-race neighborhoods. The creation of these neighborhoods, while in part probably the result of personal preferences, has been fostered by both a tacit unwillingness of whites to sell to blacks and a system of economic zoning that puts the cost of homes in middle-class white communities beyond the financial reach of blacks whose economic opportunities are in turn restricted by both the inferior "ghetto" education afforded them and the hiring policies of business which reserves the best-paid jobs for whites. Thus, while in Charlotte-Mecklenburg only two-thirds of the black pupils were in schools that were 99 percent black and a quarter of them attended schools more than half white, in Chicago three-quarters of the black children went to all-black schools and only three percent went to schools that were mostly white.

Even systematic desegregation, however, does not always provide a permanent solution to the segregation problem. Experience has shown that the migration that tends to follow desegregation orders in big cities merely converts de jure patterns into de facto ones. The most striking illustration is the District of Columbia school system, which integrated in 1956; in subsequent years so many whites with school-age children left the District that only five percent of the pupils in the system are white.

This situation faced the cities of Detroit, Michigan, and Richmond, Virginia. The school districts in those cities had such a high concentration of blacks that no amount of line-drawing or busing could change their racial composition. In contrast, the school districts in the surrounding suburban counties were almost entirely white. Where, as in Pontiac, Michigan and in Denver, Colorado school board action in locating schools and in drawing attendance lines had encouraged segregation in part of the school system, the Court viewed this as de jure segregative action which created a presumption that the entire system was unlawfully segregated; see Keyes v. School District (1973).

On the other hand, where only the city school district was found guilty of segregation, the remedy could not validly involve the surrounding white suburban school districts which had not acted unconstitutionally. In Milliken v. Bradley (1974) the district court and court of appeals had found that Detroit, with the aid of the state itself, had engaged in deliberate segregation within Detroit and that the only remedy, since Detroit was so largely black, was to bus students between Detroit and the nearby white suburbs. The Supreme Court, voting five to four, struck down the district court's "inter-district" plan and ordered a plan which involved "Detroit only." "Before the boundaries of separate and autonomous school districts may be set aside by consolidating the separate units for remedial purposes or by imposing a cross-district remedy, it must first be shown that there has been a constitutional violation within one district that produces a significant segregative effect in another district. . . . The constitutional right of the Negro respondents residing in Detroit is to attend a unitary school system in that district. Unless petitioners drew the district lines in a discriminatory fashion, or arranged for white students residing in the Detroit district to attend schools in Oakland and Macomb Counties, they were under no constitutional duty to make provisions for Negro students to do so."

Justices White, Douglas, Brennan and Marshall dissented, arguing that it was the constitutional obligation of the *state*, not the school district, to provide equal protection, and since the state had engaged in segregation it had an obligation to desegregate—an obligation it could not avoid by pleading the sanctity of its school district lines or the administrative inconvenience of inter-district cooperation.

The extension of the Brown doctrine to other areas of segregation was done by the Court largely through the technique of affirming lower court decisions without opinion. In Baltimore v. Dawson (1955) the desegregation ruling was held applicable to public beaches, and in Holmes v. Atlanta (1955), to public golf courses. In 1963, in deciding Watson v. Memphis, the Court held that recreation facilities, like universities, must be desegregated at once. On the strength of this rule, the city of Jackson, Mississippi desegregated its parks and golf links but decided instead to close its five swimming pools. In Palmer v. Thompson (1971) the Court upheld the move, noting that a statute could not be held void because of the motivations of the legislature which adopted it, and there was no evidence that the city was "now covertly aiding the maintenance and operation of pools which are private in name only. It shows no state action affecting blacks differently from whites." Three of the four dissenting justices argued that the city action was a public stand against desegregating public facilities and the forbidding of blacks to swim because of their color—both denials of equal protection.

Because Brown was based on the Fourteenth Amendment, which applies only to the states, a separate opinion was necessary to invalidate segregation in the schools of the District of Columbia, which is under congressional authority. In Bolling v. Sharpe, the Court held that the due process clause of the Fifth Amendment forbids racial segregation by the federal government.

Mr. Chief Justice **Warren**, delivering the opinion of the Court in the Brown case, said in part:

These cases come to us from the States of Kansas, South Carolina, Virginia, and Delaware. They are premised on different facts and different local conditions, but a common legal question justifies their consideration together in this consolidated opinion.

In each of the cases, minors of the Negro race, through their legal representatives, seek the aid of the courts in obtaining admission to the public schools of their community on a nonsegregated basis. In each instance, they had been denied admission to schools attended by white children under laws requiring or permitting segregation according to race. This segregation was alleged to deprive the plaintiffs of the equal protection of the laws under the Fourteenth Amendment. . . .

The plaintiffs contend that segregated public schools are not "equal" and cannot be made "equal," and that hence they are deprived of the equal protection of the laws. Because of the obvious importance of the question presented, the Court took jurisdiction. Argument was heard in the 1952 Term, and reargument was heard this Term on certain questions propounded by the Court.

Reargument was largely devoted to the circumstances surrounding the adoption of the Fourteenth Amendment in 1868. It covered exhaustively consideration of the Amendment in Congress, ratification by the states, then existing practices in racial segregation, and the views of proponents and opponents of the Amendment. This discussion and our own investigation convince us that, although these sources cast some light, it is not enough to resolve the problem with which we are faced. At best, they are inconclusive. The most avid proponents of the post-War Amendments undoubtedly intended them to remove all legal distinctions among "all persons born or naturalized in the United States." Their opponents, just as certainly, were antagonistic to both the letter and the spirit of the Amendments and wished them to have the most limited effect. What others in Congress and the state legislatures had in mind cannot be determined with any degree of certainty.

An additional reason for the inconclusive nature of the Amendment's history, with respect to segregated schools, is the status of public education at that time. In the South, the movement toward free common schools, supported by general taxation, had not yet taken hold. Education of white children was largely in the hands of private groups. Education of Negroes was almost nonexistent, and practically all of the race were illiterate. In fact, any education of Negroes was forbidden by law in some states. Today, in contrast, many Negroes have achieved outstanding success in the arts and sciences as well as in the business and professional world. It is true that public school education at the time of the Amendment had advanced further in the North, but the effect of the Amendment on Northern States was generally ignored in the congressional debates. Even in the North, the conditions of public education did not approximate those existing today. The curriculum was usually rudimentary; ungraded schools were common in rural areas; the school term was but three months a year in many states; and compulsory school attendance was virtually unknown. As a consequence, it is not surprising that there should be so little in the history of the Fourteenth Amendment relating to its intended effect on public education.

In the first cases in this Court construing the Fourteenth Amendment, decided shortly after its adoption the Court interpreted it as proscribing all state-imposed discriminations against the Negro race. The doctrine of "separate but equal" did not make its appearance in this Court until 1896 in the case of Plessy v. Ferguson, involving not education but transportation. American courts have since labored with the doctrine for over half a century. In this Court, there have been six cases involving the "separate but equal" doctrine in the field of public education. In Cumming v. Board of Education of Richmond County [1899] and Gong Lum v. Rice [1927] the validity of the doctrine itself was not challenged. In more recent cases, all on the graduate school level, inequality was found in that specific benefits enjoyed by white students were denied to Negro students of the same educational qualifications. State of Missouri ex rel. Gaines v. Canada [1938], Sipuel v. Board of Regents of University of Oklahoma [1948], Sweatt v. Painter [1950], McLaurin v. Oklahoma State Regents [1950]. In none of these cases was it necessary to reexamine the doctrine to grant relief to the Negro plaintiff. And in Sweatt v. Painter the Court expressly reserved decision on the question whether Plessy v. Ferguson should be held inapplicable to public education.

In the instant cases, that question is directly presented. Here, unlike Sweatt v. Painter, there are findings below that the Negro and white schools involved have been equalized, or are being equalized, with respect to buildings, curricula, qualifications and salaries of teachers, and other "tangible" factors. Our decision, therefore, cannot turn on merely a comparison of these tangible factors in the Negro and white schools involved in each of the cases. We must look instead to the effect of segregation itself on public education.

In approaching this problem, we cannot turn the clock back to 1868 when the Amendment was adopted, or even to 1896 when Plessy v. Ferguson was written. We must consider public education in the light of its full development and its present place in American life throughout the Nation. Only in this way can it be determined if segregation in public schools deprives these plaintiffs of the equal protection of the laws.

Today, education is perhaps the most important function of state and local governments. Compulsory school attendance laws and the great expenditures for education both demonstrate our recognition of the importance of education to our democratic society. It is required in the performance of our most basic public responsibilities, even service in the armed forces. It is the very foundation of good citizenship. Today it is a principal instrument in awakening the child to cultural values, in preparing him for later professional training, and in helping him to adjust normally to his environment. In these days, it is doubtful that any child may reasonably be expected to succeed in life if he is denied the opportunity of an education. Such an opportunity, where the state has undertaken to provide it, is a right which must be made available to all on equal terms.

We come then to the question presented: Does segregation of children in public schools solely on the basis of race, even though the physical facilities and other "tangible" factors may be equal, deprive the children of the minority group of equal educational opportunities? We believe that it does.

In Sweatt v. Painter, in finding that a segregated law school for Negroes could not provide them equal educational opportunities, this Court relied in large part on "those qualities which are incapable of objective measurement but which make for greatness in a law school." In McLaurin v. Oklahoma State Regents, the Court, in requiring that a Negro admitted to a white graduate school be treated like all other students, again resorted to intangible considerations: ". . . his ability to study, to engage in discussions and exchange views with other students, and, in general, to learn his profession." Such considerations apply with added force to children in grade and high schools. To separate them from others of similar age and qualifications solely because of their race generates a feeling of inferiority as to their status in the community that may affect their hearts and minds in a way unlikely ever to be undone. The effect of this separation on their educational opportunities was well stated by a finding in the Kansas case by a court which nevertheless felt compelled to rule against the Negro plaintiffs:

"Segregation of white and colored children in public schools has a detrimental effect upon the colored children. The impact is greater when it has the sanction of the law; for the policy of separating the races is usually interpreted as denoting the inferiority of the Negro group. A sense of inferiority affects the motivation of a child to learn. Segregation with the sanction of law, therefore, has a tendency to [retard] the educational and mental development of Negro children and to deprive them of some of the benefits they would receive in a racial[ly] integrated school system." Whatever may have been the extent of psychological knowledge at the time of Plessy v. Ferguson, this finding is amply supported by modern authority.* Any language in Plessy v. Ferguson contrary to this finding is rejected.

We conclude that in the field of public education the doctrine of "separate but equal" has no place. Separate educational facilities are inherently unequal. Therefore, we hold that the plaintiffs and others similarly situated for whom the actions have been brought are, by reason of the segregation complained of, deprived of the equal protection of the laws guaranteed by the Fourteenth Amendment. This disposition makes unnecessary any discussion whether such segregation also violates the Due Process Clause of the Fourteenth Amendment.

Because these are class actions, because of the wide applicability of this decision, and because of the great variety of local conditions, the formulation of decrees in these cases presents problems of considerable complexity. On reargument, the consideration of appropriate relief was necessarily subordinated to the primary question—the constitutionality of segregation in public education. We have now announced that such segregation is a denial of the equal protection of the laws. In order that we may have the full assistance of the parties in formulating decrees, the cases will be restored to the docket, and the parties are requested to present further argument on Questions 4 and 5 previously propounded by the Court for the reargument this Term.†

The Attorney General of the United States is again invited to participate. The Attorneys General of the states requiring or permitting segregation in public education will also be permitted to appear as amici curiae upon request to do so by September 15, 1954, and submission of briefs by October 1, 1954.

It is so ordered.

---

*K. B. Clark, Effect of Prejudice and Discrimination on Personality Development (Midcentury White House Conference on Children and Youth, 1950); Witmer and Kotinsky, Personality in the Making (1952), ch VI; Deutscher and Chein, The Psychological Effects of Enforced Segregation: A Survey of Social Science Opinion, 26 J Psychol 259 (1948); Chein, What are the Psychological Effects of Segregation Under Conditions of Equal Facilities?, 3 Int J Opinion and Attitude Res 229 (1949); Brameld, Educational Costs, in Discrimination and National Welfare (MacIver, ed, 1949), 44 –48; Frazier, The Negro in the United States (1949), 674 –681. And see generally Myrdal, An American Dilemma (1944).

†"4. Assuming it is decided that segregation in public schools violates the Fourteenth Amendment

"(a) would a decree necessarily follow providing that, within the limits set by normal geographic school districting, Negro children should forthwith be admitted to schools of their choice, or

"(b) may this Court, in the exercise of its equity powers, permit an effective gradual adjustment to be brought about from existing segregated systems to a system not based on color distinctions?

"5. On the assumption on which questions 4(a) and (b) are based, and assuming further that this Court will exercise its equity powers to the end described in question 4(b),

"(a) should this Court formulate detailed decrees in these cases;

"(b) if so, what specific issues should the decrees reach;

"(c) should this Court appoint a special master to hear evidence with a view to recommending specific terms for such decrees;

"(d) should this Court remand to the courts of first instance with directions to frame decrees in these cases, and if so, what general directions should the decrees of this Court include and what procedures should the courts of first instance follow in arriving at the specific terms of more detailed decrees?"

RICHMOND v. CROSON

488 U.S. 469; 102 L. Ed. 2d 854; 109 S. Ct. 706 (1989)

A major factor in maintaining the intellectual and cultural disadvantage of blacks has been an almost universal discrimination against them economically. White small businesses and professionals simply did not hire blacks, however well qualified. Large employers hired some, but they were systematically left in the servile or menial positions represented by Pullman porters in the railroad industry and the janitorial staff of industry generally. Labor unions of skilled workers ordinarily discriminated against blacks. Even where whites and blacks could compete for the same jobs, whites were better paid for the same work and their chances for promotion were better. And when technological advances displaced workers, it was the unskilled black workers who most often were out of jobs.

During most of our constitutional history Congress and the Court have left this problem to the states, and only a handful of states forbade discrimination in private employment. During World War II the President's Fair Employment Practices Committee achieved significant results, but with the return to a peace-time economy and the abolition of the Committee, much of the progress was lost. It was not until the Civil Rights Act of 1964, held valid in Heart of Atlanta Motel v. United States (1964), that a systematic national attack on the problem was made. Title VII of the act forbade race discrimination in hiring and the classification of employees in such a way as to "adversely affect" their status because of their race, color, sex, religion, or national origin.

Although the act permitted the use of professionally constructed ability tests provided they were not used to discriminate, in Griggs v. Duke Power Co. (1971) the Court found that the company had violated the act by using a high school diploma and an intelligence test to qualify workers for all but manual labor jobs. The Court noted that the tests bore no demonstrable relationship to the jobs for which they were required, and since blacks had long received an inferior education, the tests could be presumed to, and did in fact, discriminate against them. Speaking for a unanimous Court, Chief Justice Burger emphasized that "Congress has not commanded that the less qualified be preferred over the better qualified simply because of minority origins. Far from disparaging job qualifications as such, Congress had made such qualifications the controlling factor, so that race, religion, nationality and sex become irrelevant."

In Washington v. Davis (1976), however, the Court increased substantially the difficulty of showing that an employer's job qualification tests were discriminatory. It conceded that under Title VII, a job test or other qualification could be invalid even though it was not adopted with the *intent* to discriminate. Merely showing that a test had a discriminatory *effect* was enough to switch the burden to the employer to show that the test was valid under Title VII. However, the court made it relatively easy for the employer to meet this burden. Under the statute a test was valid if it were "job-related," but the Court said "job related" did not mean mere ability to perform the job. It could also include the ability to enter a required training program, even though some of that program was unrelated to the job. Washington v. Davis itself, however, involved a test required by the government and thus raised constitutional issues. In this situation, what the Court described as the "more rigorous standard" for tests under Title VII was one which the Court was "not disposed to adopt . . . for the purposes of applying the Fifth and Fourteenth Amendments. . . .

The case involved two blacks who had failed to pass a verbal ability test required as a condition of admission to the Washington, D.C., police department. There was neither evidence nor claim of purposeful discrimination, and the Court declined to hold the test void despite the fact that four times as many blacks as whites failed it. Noting that in both jury cases and in de jure school segregation cases there had been purposeful discrimination, the Court said: "As an initial matter, we have difficulty understanding how a law establishing a racially neutral qualification for employment is nevertheless racially discriminatory and denies 'any person . . . equal protection of the law' simply because a greater proportion of Negroes fail to qualify than members of other racial or ethnic groups. . . . Test 21, which is administered generally to prospective Government employees, concededly seeks to ascertain whether those who take it have acquired a particular level of verbal skill; and it is untenable that the Constitution prevents the Government from seeking modestly to upgrade the communicative abilities of its employees rather than to be satisfied with some lower level of competence, particularly where the job requires special ability to communicate orally and in writing. Respondents, as Negroes, could no more successfully claim that the test denied them equal protection than could white applicants who also failed."

Where both the Constitution and the law look to a policy of nondiscrimination and desegregation, what steps may be taken to bring about the desired result? Can blacks be identified and considered as blacks? And if so, for what purposes? May an employer who has always hired whites now consider only black applicants until the balance is redressed? If he may not, and due to educational background white applicants are better qualified, how is the balance ever to be redressed? If he may, is he not illegally discriminating in favor of blacks over whites? The question is the difficult one of defining equality of racial treatment in the context of a society in which nearly every institution is structured to favor whites.

In University of California v. Bakke (1978) the University of California Medical School at Davis had set aside sixteen of its 100 entering seats for minority and disadvantaged applicants. The medical school was created in 1968, had no history of purposeful discrimination and adopted this minority program to increase the number of minority students attending the school. Allan Bakke, a 37-year-old white engineer was denied admission and brought suit against the University claiming he was better qualified than some of the sixteen minority students and was being discriminated against because of his race.

In a five-to-four decision with six opinions the Court held void the Davis set-aside program but refused to hold that race could not be a legitimate consideration in admitting students. Justices Burger, Stewart, Rehnquist and Stevens held that Title VI of the Civil Rights Act of 1964 flatly forbade any discrimination whatsoever based on race. Justice Powell, the swing vote, argued that if race were merely one of a number of considerations used to determine admission, as it was at Harvard, it would not violate the equal protection clause. But to establish a fixed quota to aid "persons perceived as members of relatively victimized groups at the expense of other innocent individuals in the absence of judicial, legislative, or administrative findings of constitutional or statutory violations" would be such a denial.

Justices Brennan, White, Marshall and Blackmun joined Justice Powell on the use of race, holding that as a classification it could be used for benign purposes. "Unquestionably we have held that a government practice or statute which restricts 'fundamental rights' or which contains 'suspect classifications' is to be subjected to 'strict scrutiny' and can be justified only if it furthers a compelling government purpose and, even then, only if no less restrictive alternative is available. . . . But no fundamental right is involved here. . . . Nor do whites as a class have any of the 'traditional indicia of suspectness: the class is not saddled with such disabilities, or subjected to such a history of purposeful unequal treatment, or relegated to such a position of political powerlessness as to command extraordinary protection from the majoritarian political process.' "

In the years following the Bakke decision a divided Court whose membership was changing struggled with interpretations both of the Constitution and of §§ 703 (a) and (d) of Title VII of the Civil Rights Act of 1964, all of which, to some ill- defined extent, forbade race discrimination in employment. The question raised by the cases was the extent to which various employers, public and private, could undertake "affirmative action" or "reverse discrimination" to bring more minority personnel into what were largely all-white or all-male work forces.

While the mixture of constitutional and statutory issues and the wide variations among the facts of the cases make generalization virtually impossible, the cases appear to fall into three roughly defined categories:

First, where the group, whether public or private, had a long established record of discrimination and had defied court orders to desegregate, the Court held valid the court-ordered affirmative action. In Sheet Metal Workers v. EEOC (1976) a labor union with a long record of deliberate race discrimination was ordered to mend its ways and fined for contempt when it failed to do so. And in United States v. Paradise (1987) the Court found that Alabama state troopers had ignored for over a dozen years court orders to appoint or promote blacks to the force and upheld a court-devised affirmative action plan. With Justices O'Connor, White, Rehnquist and Burger dissenting, Justice Powell cast the deciding vote.

A second pair of cases involved firefighting organizations in two cities. In both cases, to avoid going to trial and risking a court order requiring the adoption of an affirmative action plan, the city fire departments settled by means of a "consent decree"—an official settlement whose terms are approved by the court. In Firefighters v. Stotts (1984), the city of Memphis agreed in the consent decree to hire more blacks, but denied having engaged in discrimination. Since there was no showing of deliberate discrimination, and since the consent decree made no mention of a union contract providing "first on, last off" in case of layoffs, the majority upheld the laying off of the last hired, most of whom were black. On the other hand, in Firefighters v. Cleveland (1986), the city admitted to a long and serious record of race discrimination and in a six-to-three decision the Court upheld the consent decree, which provided a quota of minority promotions. The court further held that the decree was not a court "order" and hence not limited by the sections of Title VII limiting certain race-conscious relief after trial.

In the third category are four cases in which affirmative action was taken voluntarily, rather than as a result of a court finding of discrimination or a consent decree agreed to in order to avoid a finding of such discrimination. Two of these case involved public agencies, and both held the affirmative action void. The first, of course, was the Bakke decision printed below. The second was Wygant v. Jackson Board of Education (1986) in which a Union-School Board agreement gave probationary blacks preference over tenured whites at lay-off time in order to maintain a black quota. The presence of a state agency brought the equal protection clause into play and a four-member plurality applied the "strict scrutiny" test. "Societal discrimination, without more, is too amorphous a basis for imposing a racially classified remedy. The role model theory announced by the District Court and the resultant holding typify this indefiniteness."

Also in the third category are two cases involving voluntary affirmative action plans that the court considered solely under Title VII, not the equal protection clause. In both of these the Court upheld the affirmative action. The language of § 703 (a) made it illegal "to fail or refuse to hire or to discharge any individual, or otherwise to discriminate against any individual with respect to his compensation, terms, conditions, or privileges of employment, because of such individual's race, color, religion, sex, or national origin. . . ." In Steelworkers v. Weber (1979) a majority of the Court found that the intent of Title VII was to improve the lot of blacks and "we cannot agree with respondent that Congress intended to prohibit the private sector from taking effective steps to accomplish the goal that Congress designed Title VII to achieve."

It reached the same result in Johnson v. Transportation Agency (1987). Diane Joyce was appointed to the position of road dispatcher despite the fact a man had scored slightly higher on one of the tests. Prior to her appointment, none of the 238 Skilled Craft Worker positions in the Agency was held by a woman, although the Court conceded that this was a result of societal discrimination and not the deliberate policy of the Agency and that in promoting qualified applicants sex was only one of the factors to be considered. The dissenting justices in both cases argued that the language of . . . 703 forbade discriminating in favor of minorities as well as against them. [While one party in the Johnson case was a government agency, no constitutional issue was raised or considered.]

In Fullilove v. Klutznick (1980), a case raising a different constitutional issue, a badly divided Court held valid a Congressional statute requiring that ten percent of money granted to the states for public works be set aside for minority contractors. Justices White, Burger, and Powell agreed that the law's purpose was to prevent the perpetuation of discriminatory practices, and that Congress could act both under its spending power and under Section 5 of the Fourteenth Amendment, while Justice Powell, speaking for himself, argued that because an appropriate governmental authority had identified the need for such affirmative action the law met the strict scrutiny test he had relied on in Bakke.

The present case arose when Richmond, Virginia, a city with a 50 percent black population with no record of discrimination against minority contractors, undertook to offset (so far as it could within its jurisdiction) the effect of such discrimination in the construction industry. Evidence revealed that only .67 percent of the city's construction contracts went to minority-owned business enterprises (MBEs), that only 4.7 percent of the construction firms throughout the country were minority owned, and of these 41 percent were located in California, New York, Illinois, Florida and Hawaii. Testimony indicated that "the general conduct of the construction industry in this area, in the State, and around the nation, is one in which race discrimination and exclusion on the basis of race is widespread." The city adopted a "remedial" plan providing that henceforth 30 percent of the money for such contracts should go to MBEs.

In 1983 the city went out on bid for toilet fixtures for the jail and Croson, a local contractor, found that under the terms of the law the fixtures would have to be supplied by an MBE. One local MBE appeared the day before the bids were due and asked to be considered as a subcontractor. The difficulty he faced getting credit both delayed and raised the amount of the bid. Since Croson was the only bidder, the city decided to rebid the contract and Croson sued on the ground that the set-aside plan was unconstitutional.

It has long been the policy of the Federal Communications Commission to promote minority ownership of radio and television stations, but as recently as 1986 they owned less than 2.1 percent of these facilities. In 1978, with the explicit approval of Congress, the FCC began considering minority ownership among the factors to be considered in the awarding of licenses. It also announced a plan under which the reassignment of an existing license was easier if the new owner were a member of a minority group.

In Metro Broadcasting v. FCC (1990) the Supreme Court upheld the validity of these policies against the challenge that they violated the equal protection component of the Fifth Amendment. It reaffirmed its decision in Fullilove v. Klutznick (1980), noting that that case did not apply "strict scrutiny" to race-based classifications. "We apply [the Klutznick] standard today. We hold that benign race-conscious measures mandated by Congress—even if those measures are not 'remedial' in the sense of being designed to compensate victims of past governmental or societal discrimination—are constitutionally permissible to the extent that they serve important governmental objectives within the power of Congress and are substantially related to achievement of those objectives." It held the goal of broadcast diversity was "an important governmental objective," and the plans were substantially related to achieving that goal. Justices O'Connor, Rehnquist, Scalia and Kennedy dissented, arguing that "strict scrutiny" should be applied to all race classifications.

Justice **O'Connor** announced the judgment of the Court and delivered an opinion concurred in as indicated below, saying in part:

In this case, we confront once again the tension between the Fourteenth Amendment's guarantee of equal treatment to all citizens, and the use of race-based measures to ameliorate the effects of past discrimination on the opportunities enjoyed by members of minority groups in our society. In Fullilove v. Klutznick (1980) we held that a congressional program requiring that 10% of certain federal construction grants be awarded to minority contractors did not violate the equal protection principles embodied in the Due Process Clause of the Fifth Amendment. Relying largely on our decision in Fullilove, some lower federal courts have applied a similar standard of review in assessing the constitutionality of state and local minority set-aside provisions under the Equal Protection Clause of the Fourteenth Amendment. . . . Since our decision two Terms ago in Wygant v. Jackson Board of Education (1986) the lower federal courts have attempted to apply its standards in evaluating the constitutionality of state and local programs which allocate a portion of public contracting opportunities exclusively to minority-owned businesses. . . . We noted probable jurisdiction in this case to consider the applicability of our decision in Wygant to a minority set-aside program adopted by the city of Richmond, Virginia. . . .

II. [Joined by Justices **Rehnquist** and **White**]

The parties and their supporting amici fight an initial battle over the scope of the city's power to adopt legislation designed to address the effects of past discrimination. Relying on our decision in Wygant, appellee argues that the city must limit any race-based remedial efforts to eradicating the effects of its own prior discrimination. This is essentially the position taken by the Court of Appeals below. Appellant argues that our decision in Fullilove is controlling, and that as a result the city of Richmond enjoys sweeping legislative power to define and attack the effects of prior discrimination in its local construction industry. We find that neither of these two rather stark alternatives can withstand analysis.

In Fullilove, we upheld the minority set-aside contained in § 103(f)(2) of the Public Works Employment Act of 1977 against a challenge based on the equal protection component of the Due Process Clause. The Act authorized a four billion [dollar] appropriation for federal grants to state and local governments for use in public works projects. The primary purpose of the Act was to give the national economy a quick boost in a recessionary period; funds had to be committed to state or local grantees by September 30, 1977. The Act also contained the following requirement: '' 'Except to the extent the Secretary determines otherwise, no grant shall be made under this Act . . . unless the applicant gives satisfactory assurance to the Secretary that at least 10 per centum of the amount of each grant shall be expended for minority business enterprises.' ''

The principal opinion in Fullilove, written by Chief Justice Burger, did not employ ''strict scrutiny'' or any other traditional standard of equal protection review. The Chief Justice noted at the outset that although racial classifications call for close examination, the Court was at the same time, ''bound to approach [its] task with appropriate deference to the Congress, a co-equal branch charged by the Constitution with the power to 'provide for the . . . general Welfare of the United States' and 'to enforce by appropriate legislation,' the equal protection guarantees of the Fourteenth Amendment.'' The principal opinion asked two questions: first, were the objectives of the legislation within the powers of Congress? Second, was the limited use of racial and ethnic criteria a permissible means for Congress to carry out its objectives within the constraints of the Due Process Clause?

On the issue of congressional power, the Chief Justice found that Congress' commerce power was sufficiently broad to allow it to reach the practices of prime contractors on federally funded local construction projects. Congress could mandate state and local government compliance with the set-aside program under its § 5 power to enforce the Fourteenth Amendment.

The Chief Justice next turned to the constraints on Congress' power to employ race-conscious remedial relief. His opinion stressed two factors in upholding the MBE set-aside. First was the unique remedial powers [sic] of Congress under § 5 of the Fourteenth Amendment: ''Here we deal . . . not with the limited remedial powers of a federal court, for example, but with the broad remedial powers of Congress. It is fundamental that *in no organ of government, state or federal, does there repose a more comprehensive remedial power than in the Congress,* expressly charged by the Constitution with competence and authority to enforce equal protection guarantees.'' (plurality opinion)(emphasis added).

Because of these unique powers, the Chief Justice concluded that ''Congress not only may induce voluntary action to assure compliance with existing federal statutory or constitutional antidiscrimination provisions, but also, where Congress has authority to *declare certain conduct unlawful,* it may, as here, authorize and induce state action to avoid such conduct.'' (emphasis added).

In reviewing the legislative history behind the Act, the principal opinion focused on the evidence before Congress that a nationwide history of past discrimination had reduced minority participation in federal construction grants. . . . The Chief Justice concluded that ''Congress had abundant historical basis from which it could conclude that traditional procurement practices, when applied to minority businesses, could perpetuate the effects of prior discrimination.''

The second factor emphasized by the principal opinion in Fullilove was the flexible nature of the 10% set-aside. Two ''congressional assumptions'' underlay the MBE program: first, that the effects of past discrimination had impaired the competitive position of minority businesses, and second, that ''adjustment for the effects of past discrimination'' would assure that at least 10% of the funds from the federal grant program would flow to minority businesses. The Chief Justice noted that both of these ''assumptions'' could be ''rebutted'' by a grantee seeking a waiver of the 10% requirement. Thus a waiver could be sought where minority businesses were not available to fill the 10% requirement or, more importantly, where an MBE attempted "to exploit the remedial aspects of the program by charging an unreasonable price, i.e., a price not attributable to the present effects of prior discrimination." The Chief Justice indicated that without this fine tuning to remedial purpose, the statute would not have "pass[ed] muster." . . .

Appellant and its supporting amici rely heavily on Fullilove for the proposition that a city council, like Congress, need not make specific findings of discrimination to engage in race-conscious relief. Thus, appellant argues "[i]t would be a perversion of federalism to hold that the federal government has a compelling interest in remedying the effects of racial discrimination in its own public works program, but a city government does not."

What appellant ignores is that the Congress, unlike any State or political subdivision, has a specific constitutional mandate to enforce the dictates of the Fourteenth Amendment. The power to "enforce" may at times also include the power to define situations which *Congress* determines threaten principles of equality and to adopt prophylactic rules to deal with those situations. ("Correctly viewed, § 5 is a positive grant of legislative power authorizing Congress to exercise its discretion in determining whether and what legislation is needed to secure the guarantees of the Fourteenth Amendment"). . . .

That Congress may identify and redress the effects of society-wide discrimination does not mean that, a fortiori, the States and their political subdivisions are free to decide that such remedies are appropriate. Section 1 of the Fourteenth Amendment is an explicit *constraint* on state power, and the States must undertake any remedial efforts in accordance with that provision. To hold otherwise would be to cede control over the content of the Equal Protection Clause to the 50 state legislatures and their myriad political subdivisions. The mere recitation of a benign or compensatory purpose for the use of a racial classification would essentially entitle the States to exercise the full power of Congress under § 5 of the Fourteenth Amendment and insulate any racial classification from judicial scrutiny under § 1. We believe that such a result would be contrary to the intentions of the Framers of the Fourteenth Amendment, who desired to place clear limits on the States' use of race as a criterion for legislative action, and to have the federal courts enforce those limitations. . . .

It would seem equally clear, however, that a state or local subdivision (if delegated the authority from the State) has the authority to eradicate the effects of private discrimination within its own legislative jurisdiction. This authority must, of course, be exercised within the constraints of § 1 of the Fourteenth Amendment. Our decision in Wygant is not to the contrary. Wygant addressed the constitutionality of the use of racial quotas by local school authorities pursuant to an agreement reached with the local teachers' union. It was in the context of addressing the school board's power to adopt a race-based layoff program affecting its own work force that the Wygant plurality indicated that the Equal Protection Clause required "some showing of prior discrimination by the governmental unit involved." Wygant. As a matter of state law, the city of Richmond has legislative authority over its procurement policies, and can use its spending powers to remedy private discrimination, if it identifies that discrimination with the particularity required by the Fourteenth Amendment. To this extent, on the question of the city's competence, the Court of Appeals erred in following Wygant by rote in a case involving a state entity which has state-law authority to address discriminatory practices within local commerce under its jurisdiction.

Thus, if the city could show that it had essentially become a "passive participant" in a system of racial exclusion practiced by elements of the local construction industry, we think it clear that the city could take affirmative steps to dismantle such a system. It is beyond dispute that any public entity, state or federal, has a compelling interest in assuring that public dollars, drawn from the tax contributions of all citizens, do not serve to finance the evil of private prejudice. . . .

III.

A. [Joined by Justices **Rehnquist, White, Stevens** and **Kennedy.**]

The Equal Protection Clause of the Fourteenth Amendment provides that "[N]o State shall . . . deny to *any person* within its jurisdiction the equal protection of the laws." (emphasis added.) As this Court has noted in the past, the "rights created by the first section of the Fourteenth Amendment are, by its terms, guaranteed to the individual. The rights established are personal rights." Shelley v. Kraemer (1948). The Richmond Plan denies certain citizens the opportunity to compete for a fixed percentage of public contracts based solely upon their race. To whatever racial group these citizens belong, their "personal rights" to be treated with equal dignity and respect are implicated by a rigid rule erecting race as the sole criterion in an aspect of public decisionmaking.

Absent searching judicial inquiry into the justification for such race-based measures, there is simply no way of determining what classifications are "benign" or "remedial" and what classifications are in fact motivated by illegitimate notions of racial inferiority or simple racial politics. Indeed, the purpose of strict scrutiny is to "smoke out" illegitimate uses of race by assuring that the legislative body is pursuing a goal important enough to warrant use of a highly suspect tool. The test also ensures that the means chosen "fit" this compelling goal so closely that there is little or no possibility that the motive for the classification was illegitimate racial prejudice or stereotype.

Classifications based on race carry a danger of stigmatic harm. Unless they are strictly reserved for remedial settings, they may in fact promote notions of racial inferiority and lead to a politics of racial hostility. See University of California Regents v. Bakke [1978] (opinion of Powell, J.). ("[P]referential programs may only reinforce common stereotypes holding that certain groups are unable to achieve success without special protection based on a factor having no relation to individual worth"). We thus reaffirm the view expressed by the plurality in Wygant that the standard of review under the Equal Protection Clause is not dependent on the race of those burdened or benefited by a particular classification. . . .

Our continued adherence to the standard of review employed in Wygant, does not, as Justice Marshall's dissent suggests, indicate that we view "racial discrimination as largely a phenomenon of the past" or that "government bodies need no longer preoccupy themselves with rectifying racial injustice.'' As we indicate, States and their local subdivisions have many legislative weapons at their disposal both to punish and prevent present discrimination and to remove arbitrary barriers to minority advancement. Rather, our interpretation of § 1 stems from our agreement with the view expressed by Justice Powell in Bakke, that ''[t]he guarantee of equal protection cannot mean one thing when applied to one individual and something else when applied to a person of another color.''

... See Weinberger v. Wiesenfeld (1975) (''[T]he mere recitation of a benign, compensatory purpose is not an automatic shield which protects against any inquiry into the actual purposes underlying a statutory scheme''). The dissent's watered-down version of equal protection review effectively assures that race will always be relevant in American life, and that the ''ultimate goal'' of ''eliminat[ing] entirely from governmental decisionmaking such irrelevant factors as a human being's race,'' Wygant, (Stevens, J., dissenting) will never be achieved.

Even were we to accept a reading of the guarantee of equal protection under which the level of scrutiny varies according to the ability of different groups to defend their interests in the representative process, heightened scrutiny would still be appropriate in the circumstances of this case. One of the central arguments for applying a less exacting standard to ''benign'' racial classifications is that such measures essentially involve a choice made by dominant racial groups to disadvantage themselves. If one aspect of the judiciary's role under the Equal Protection Clause is to protect ''discrete and insular minorities'' from majoritarian prejudice or indifference, see United States v. Carolene Products Co. (1938), some maintain that these concerns are not implicated when the ''white majority'' places burdens upon itself.

In this case, blacks comprise approximately 50% of the population of the city of Richmond. Five of the nine seats on the City Council are held by blacks. The concern that a political majority will more easily act to the disadvantage of a minority based on unwarranted assumptions or incomplete facts would seem to militate for, not against, the application of heightened judicial scrutiny in this case. (''Of course it works both ways: a law that favors Blacks over Whites would be suspect if it were enacted by a predominantly Black legislature'').

In Bakke the Court confronted a racial quota employed by the University of California at Davis Medical School. . . .

Justice Powell's opinion applied heightened scrutiny under the Equal Protection Clause to the racial classification at issue. His opinion decisively rejected the first justification for the racially segregated admissions plan. The desire to have more black medical students or doctors, standing alone, was not merely insufficiently compelling to justify a racial classification, it was ''discrimination for its own sake,'' forbidden by the Constitution. Nor could the second concern, the history of discrimination in society at large, justify a racial quota in medical school admissions. Justice Powell contrasted the ''focused'' goal of remedying ''wrongs worked by specific instances of racial discrimination'' with ''the remedying of the effects of 'societal discrimination,' an amorphous concept of injury that may be ageless in its reach into the past.'' He indicated that for the governmental interest in remedying past discrimination to be triggered ''judicial, legislative, or administrative findings of constitutional or statutory violations'' must be made. Only then does the Government have a compelling interest in favoring one race over another.

In Wygant (1986), four Members of the Court applied heightened scrutiny to a race-based system of employee layoffs. Justice Powell, writing for the plurality, again drew the distinction between "societal discrimination" which is an inadequate basis for race-conscious classifications, and the type of identified discrimination that can support and define the scope of race-based relief. The challenged classification in that case tied the layoff of minority teachers to the percentage of minority students enrolled in the school district. The lower courts had upheld the scheme, based on the theory that minority students were in need of "role models" to alleviate the effects of prior discrimination in society. This Court reversed, with a plurality of four Justices reiterating the view expressed by Justice Powell in Bakke that "[s]ocietal discrimination, without more, is too amorphous a basis for imposing a racially classified remedy." Wygant (plurality opinion).

The role model theory employed by the lower courts failed for two reasons. First, the statistical disparity between students and teachers had no probative value in demonstrating the kind of prior discrimination in hiring or promotion that would justify race-based relief. (O'Connor, J., concurring in part and concurring in judgment) ("The disparity between the percentage of minorities on the teaching staff and the percentage of minorities in the student body is not probative of employment discrimination"). Second, because the role model theory had no relation to some basis for believing a constitutional or statutory violation had occurred, it could be used to "justify" race-based decisionmaking essentially limitless in scope and duration. ("In the absence of particularized findings, a court could uphold remedies that are ageless in their reach into the past, and timeless in their ability to affect the future").

B. [Joined by Justices **Rehnquist, White, Stevens, Scalia** and **Kennedy.**]

We think it clear that the factual predicate offered in support of the Richmond Plan suffers from the same two defects identified as fatal in Wygant. The District Court found the city council's "findings sufficient to ensure that, in adopting the Plan, it was remedying the present effects of past discrimination in the *construction industry*." (emphasis added). Like the "role model" theory employed in Wygant, a generalized assertion that there has been past discrimination in an entire industry provides no guidance for a legislative body to determine the precise scope of the injury it seeks to remedy. It "has no logical stopping point." Wygant (plurality opinion). "Relief" for such an ill-defined wrong could extend until the percentage of public contracts awarded to MBEs in Richmond mirrored the percentage of minorities in the population as a whole.

Appellant argues that it is attempting to remedy various forms of past discrimination that are alleged to be responsible for the small number of minority businesses in the local contracting industry. Among these the city cites the exclusion of blacks from skilled construction trade unions and training programs. This past discrimination has prevented them "from following the traditional path from laborer to entrepreneur." . . .

While there is no doubt that the sorry history of both private and public discrimination in this country has contributed to a lack of opportunities for black entrepreneurs, this observation, standing alone, cannot justify a rigid racial quota in the awarding of public contracts in Richmond, Virginia. . . .

It is sheer speculation how many minority firms there would be in Richmond absent past societal discrimination, just as it was sheer speculation how many minority medical students would have been admitted to the medical school at Davis absent past discrimination in educational opportunities. Defining these sorts of injuries as "identified discrimination" would give local governments license to create a patchwork of racial preferences based on statistical generalizations about any particular field of endeavor.

These defects are readily apparent in this case. The 30% quota cannot in any realistic sense be tied to any injury suffered by anyone. . . .

The District Court accorded great weight to the fact that the city council designated the Plan as "remedial." But the mere recitation of a "benign" or legitimate purpose for a racial classification is entitled to little or no weight. . . .

. . . The history of racial classifications in this country suggests that blind judicial deference to legislative or executive pronouncements of necessity has no place in equal protection analysis. See Korematsu v. United States (1944) (Murphy, J., dissenting).

. . . There is no doubt that "[w]here gross statistical disparities can be shown, they alone in a proper case may constitute prima facie proof of a pattern or practice of discrimination" under Title VII. Hazelwood School Dist. v. United States (1977). But it is equally clear that "[w]hen special qualifications are required to fill particular jobs, comparisons to the general population (rather than to the smaller group of individuals who possess the necessary qualifications) may have little probative value." . . .

In this case, the city does not even know how many MBE's in the relevant market are qualified to undertake prime or subcontracting work in public construction projects. . . . Nor does the city know what percentage of total city construction dollars minority firms now receive as subcontractors on prime contracts let by the city.

To a large extent, the set-aside of subcontracting dollars seems to rest on the unsupported assumption that white prime contractors simply will not hire minority firms. See Associated General Contractors of Cal. v. City and Cty. of San Francisco ("There is no finding—and we decline to assume—that male caucasian constructors will award contracts only to other male caucasians"). . . . Without any information on minority participation in subcontracting, it is quite simply impossible to evaluate overall minority representation in the city's construction expenditures. . . .

Justice Marshall apparently views the requirement that Richmond identify the discrimination it seeks to remedy in its own jurisdiction as a mere administrative headache, an "onerous documentary obligatio[n]." We cannot agree. In this regard, we are in accord with Justice Stevens' observation in Fullilove, that "[b]ecause racial characteristics so seldom provide a relevant basis for disparate treatment, and because classifications based on race are potentially so harmful to the entire body politic, it is especially important that the reasons for any such classification be clearly identified and unquestionably legitimate." Fullilove (dissenting opinion). The "evidence" relied upon by the dissent, the history of school desegregation in the Richmond and numerous congressional reports, does little to define the scope of any injury to minority contractors in Richmond or the necessary remedy. The factors relied upon by the dissent could justify a preference of any size or duration. . . .

In sum, none of the evidence presented by the city points to any identified discrimination in the Richmond construction industry. We, therefore, hold that the city has failed to demonstrate a compelling interest in apportioning public contracting opportunities on the basis of race. . . .

IV. [Joined by Justices **Rehnquist, White, Stevens, Scalia** and **Kennedy.**]

As noted by the court below, it is almost impossible to assess whether the Richmond Plan is narrowly tailored to remedy prior discrimination since it is not linked to identified discrimination in any way. We limit ourselves to two observations in this regard.

First, there does not appear to have been any consideration of the use of race-neutral means to increase minority business participation in city contracting. . . . Many of the barriers to minority participation in the construction industry relied upon by the city to justify a racial classification appear to be race neutral. If MBE's disproportionately lack capital or cannot meet bonding requirements, a race-neutral program of city financing for small firms would, a fortiori, lead to greater minority participation. The principal opinion in Fullilove found that Congress had carefully examined and rejected race-neutral alternatives before enacting the MBE set-aside. . . . There is no evidence in this record that Richmond City Council has considered any alternatives to a race-based quota.

Second, the 30% quota cannot be said to be narrowly tailored to any goal, except perhaps outright racial balancing. It rests upon the "completely unrealistic" assumption that minorities will choose a particular trade in lockstep proportion to their representation in the local population. . . .

Given the existence of an individualized procedure, the city's only interest in maintaining a quota system rather than investigating the need for remedial action in particular cases would seem to be simple administrative convenience. But the interest in avoiding the bureaucratic effort necessary to tailor remedial relief to those who truly have suffered the effects of prior discrimination cannot justify a rigid line drawn on the basis of a suspect classification. . . . Under Richmond's scheme, a successful black, Hispanic, or Oriental entrepreneur from anywhere in the country enjoys an absolute preference over other citizens based solely on their race. We think it obvious that such a program is not narrowly tailored to remedy the effects of prior discrimination.

V. . . . [Joined by Justices **Rehnquist, White** and **Kennedy.**]

[The Court here assures cities the right to deal with "identified" discrimination and points out nondiscriminatory ways in which small contractors could legitimately be aided.]

. . . Accordingly, the judgment of the Court of Appeals for the Fourth Circuit is affirmed.

Justice **Stevens**, concurring in part and concurring in the judgment, said in part:

A central purpose of the Fourteenth Amendment is to further the national goal of equal opportunity for all our citizens. In order to achieve that goal we must learn from our past mistakes, but I believe the Constitution requires us to evaluate our policy decisions—including those that govern the relationships among different racial and ethnic groups—primarily by studying their probable impact on the future. I therefore do not agree with the premise that seems to underlie today's decision, as well as the decision in Wygant v. Jackson Board of Education (1986), that a governmental decision that rests on a racial classification is never permissible except as a remedy for a past wrong. I do, however, agree with the Court's explanation of why the Richmond ordinance cannot be justified as a remedy for past discrimination, and therefore join Parts I, III-B, and IV of its opinion. I write separately to emphasize three aspects of the case that are of special importance to me. . . .

Justice **Kennedy**, concurring in part and concurring in the judgment, said in part:

I join all but Part II of Justice O'Connor's opinion and give this further explanation.

Part II examines our case law upholding Congressional power to grant preferences based on overt and explicit classification by race. See Fullilove v. Klutznick (1980). With the acknowledgment that the summary in Part II is both precise and fair, I must decline to join it. The process by which a law that is an equal protection violation when enacted by a State becomes transformed to an equal protection guarantee when enacted by Congress poses a difficult proposition for me; but as it is not before us, any reconsideration of that issue must await some further case. For purposes of the ordinance challenged here, it suffices to say that the State has the power to eradicate racial discrimination and its effects in both the public and private sectors, and the absolute duty to do so where those wrongs were caused intentionally by the State itself. The Fourteenth Amendment ought not to be interpreted to reduce a State's authority in this regard, unless, of course, there is a conflict with federal law or a state remedy is itself a violation of equal protection. The latter is the case presented here.

Justice **Scalia**, concurring in the judgment, said in part:

I agree with much of the Court's opinion, and, in particular, with Justice O'Connor's conclusion that strict scrutiny must be applied to all governmental classification by race, whether or not its asserted purpose is "remedial" or "benign." I do not agree, however, with Justice O'Connor's dictum suggesting that, despite the Fourteenth Amendment, state and local governments may in some circumstances discriminate on the basis of race in order (in a broad sense) "to ameliorate the effects of past discrimination." The benign purpose of compensating for social disadvantages, whether they have been acquired by reason of prior discrimination or otherwise, can no more be pursued by the illegitimate means of racial discrimination than can other assertedly benign purposes we have repeatedly rejected.

Justice **Marshall**, with whom Justice **Brennan** and Justice **Blackmun** join, dissenting, said in part:

It is a welcome symbol of racial progress when the former capital of the Confederacy acts forthrightly to confront the effects of racial discrimination in its midst. In my view, nothing in the Constitution can be construed to prevent Richmond, Virginia, from allocating a portion of its contracting dollars for businesses owned or controlled by members of minority groups. Indeed, Richmond's set-aside program is indistinguishable in all meaningful respects from—and in fact was patterned upon—the federal set-aside plan which this Court upheld in Fullilove v. Klutznick (1980).

A majority of this Court holds today, however, that the Equal Protection Clause of the Fourteenth Amendment blocks Richmond's initiative. The essence of the majority's position* is that Richmond has failed to catalogue adequate findings to prove that past discrimination has impeded minorities from joining or participating fully in Richmond's construction contracting industry. I find deep irony in second-guessing Richmond's judgment on this point. As much as any municipality in the United States, Richmond knows what racial discrimination is; a century of decisions by this and other federal courts has richly documented the city's disgraceful history of public and private racial discrimination. In any event, the Richmond City Council *has* supported its determination that minorities have been wrongly excluded from local construction contracting. Its proof includes statistics showing that minority-owned businesses have received virtually no city contracting dollars and rarely if ever belonged to area trade associations; testimony by municipal officials that discrimination has been widespread in the local construction industry; and the same exhaustive and widely publicized federal studies relied on in Fullilove, studies which showed that pervasive discrimination in the Nation's tight-knit construction industry had operated to exclude minorities from public contracting. These are precisely the types of statistical and testimonial evidence which, until today, this Court had credited in cases approving of race-conscious measures designed to remedy past discrimination.

More fundamentally, today's decision marks a deliberate and giant step backward in this Court's affirmative-action jurisprudence. Cynical of one municipality's attempt to redress the effects of past racial discrimination in a particular industry, the majority launches a grapeshot attack on race-conscious remedies in general. The majority's unnecessary pronouncements will inevitably discourage or prevent governmental entities, particularly States and localities, from acting to rectify the scourge of past discrimination. This is the harsh reality of the majority's decision, but it is not the Constitution's command.

I.

As an initial matter, the majority takes an exceedingly myopic view of the factual predicate on which the Richmond city council relied when it passed the Minority Business Utilization Plan. The majority analyzes Richmond's initiative as if it were based solely upon the facts about local construction and contracting practices adduced during the city council session at which the measure was enacted. In so doing, the majority downplays the fact that the City Council had before it a rich trove of evidence that discrimination in the Nation's construction industry had seriously impaired the competitive position of businesses owned or controlled by members of minority groups. It is only against this backdrop of documented national discrimination, however, that the local evidence adduced by Richmond can be

---

*In the interests of convenience I refer to the opinion in this case authored by Justice O'Connor as "the majority", recognizing that certain portions of that opinion have been joined by only a plurality of the Court.

properly understood. The majority's refusal to recognize that Richmond has proved itself no exception to the dismaying pattern of national exclusion which Congress so painstakingly identified infects its entire analysis of this case. . . .

. . . "The effects of past inequities stemming from racial prejudice have not remained in the past. The Congress has recognized the reality that past discriminatory practices have, to some degree, adversely affected our present economic system.

"While minority persons comprise about 16 percent of the Nation's population, of the 13 million businesses in the United States, only 382,000, or approximately 3.0 percent, are owned by minority individuals. The most recent data from the Department of Commerce also indicates that the gross receipts of all businesses in this country totals about $2,540.8 billion, and of this amount only $16.6 billion, or about 0.65 percent was realized by minority business concerns.

"These statistics are not the result of random chance. *The presumption must be made that past discriminatory systems have resulted in present economic inequities.*' " (quoted in Fullilove) (opinion of Burger, C.J.) (emphasis deleted and added). A 1977 Report by the same [congressional] Committee concluded: "[O]ver the years, there has developed a business system which has traditionally excluded measurable minority participation. In the past more than the present, this system of conducting business transactions overtly precluded minority input. Currently, we more often encounter a business system which is racially neutral on its face, but because of past overt social and economic discrimination is presently operating, in effect, to perpetuate these past inequities. Minorities, until recently, have not participated to any measurable extent, in our total business system generally, or in the construction industry in particular." (quoted in Fullilove). . . .

II.

"Agreement upon a means for applying the Equal Protection Clause to an affirmative-action program has eluded this Court every time the issue has come before us." Wygant v. Jackson Bd. of Education (1986) (Marshall, J., dissenting). My view has long been that race-conscious classifications designed to further remedial goals "must serve important governmental objectives and must be substantially related to achievement of those objectives" in order to withstand constitutional scrutiny. University of California Regents v. Bakke (1978) . . . .

A.

1.

Turning first to the governmental interest inquiry, Richmond has two powerful interests in setting aside a portion of public contracting funds for minority-owned enterprises. The first is the city's interest in eradicating the effects of past racial discrimination. It is far too late in the day to doubt that remedying such discrimination is a compelling, let alone an important, interest. In Fullilove, six Members of this Court deemed this interest sufficient to support a race-conscious set-aside program governing federal contract procurement. The decision, in holding that the federal set-aside provision satisfied the Equal Protection Clause under any level of scrutiny, recognized that the measure sought to remove "barriers to competitive access which had their roots in racial and ethnic discrimination, and which continue today, even absent any intentional discrimination or unlawful conduct." . . .

Richmond has a second compelling interest in setting aside, where possible, a portion of its contracting dollars. That interest is the prospective one of preventing the city's own spending decisions from reinforcing and perpetuating the exclusionary effects of past discrimination. . . .

The majority pays only lip service to this additional governmental interest. But our decisions have often emphasized the danger of the government tacitly adopting, encouraging, or furthering racial discrimination even by its own routine operations. In Shelley v. Kraemer (1948), this Court recognized this interest as a constitutional command, holding unanimously that the Equal Protection Clause forbids courts to enforce racially restrictive covenants even where such covenants satisfied all requirements of state law and where the State harbored no discriminatory intent. . . .

The majority is wrong to trivialize the continuing impact of government acceptance or use of private institutions or structures once wrought by discrimination. When government channels all its contracting funds to a white-dominated community of established contractors whose racial homogeneity is the product of private discrimination, it does more than place its imprimatur on the practices which forged and which continue to define that community. It also provides a measurable boost to those economic entities that have thrived within it, while denying important economic benefits to those entities which, but for prior discrimination, might well be better qualified to receive valuable government contracts. In my view, the interest in ensuring that the government does not reflect and reinforce prior private discrimination in dispensing public contracts is every bit as strong as the interest in eliminating private discrimination—an interest which this Court has repeatedly deemed compelling. . . . The more government bestows its rewards on those persons or businesses that were positioned to thrive during a period of private racial discrimination, the tighter the dead-hand grip of prior discrimination becomes on the present and future. Cities like Richmond may not be constitutionally required to adopt set-aside plans. . . . But there can be no doubt that when Richmond acted affirmatively to stem the perpetuation of patterns of discrimination through its own decisionmaking, it served an interest of the highest order. . . .

III.

I would ordinarily end my analysis at this point and conclude that Richmond's ordinance satisfies both the governmental interest and substantial relationship prongs of our Equal Protection Clause analysis. However, I am compelled to add more, for the majority has gone beyond the facts of this case to announce a set of principles which unnecessarily restricts the power of governmental entities to take race-conscious measures to redress the effects of prior discrimination.

A.

Today, for the first time, a majority of this Court has adopted strict scrutiny as its standard of Equal Protection Clause review of race-conscious remedial measures. This is an unwelcome development. A profound difference separates governmental actions that themselves are racist, and governmental actions that seek to remedy the effects of prior racism or to prevent neutral governmental activity from perpetuating the effects of such racism. . . .

Racial classifications "drawn on the presumption that one race is inferior to another or because they put the weight of government behind racial hatred and separatism" warrant the strictest judicial scrutiny because of the very irrelevance of these rationales. By contrast, racial classifications drawn for the purpose of remedying the effects of discrimination that itself was race based have a highly pertinent basis: the tragic and indelible fact that discrimination against blacks and other racial minorities in this Nation has pervaded our Nation's history and continues to scar our society. As I stated in Fullilove: "Because the consideration of race is relevant to remedying the continuing effects of past racial discrimination, and because governmental programs employing racial classifications for remedial purposes can be crafted to avoid stigmatization, . . . such programs should not be subjected to conventional 'strict scrutiny'—scrutiny that is strict in theory, but fatal in fact." Fullilove.

In concluding that remedial classifications warrant no different standard of review under the Constitution than the most brutal and repugnant forms of state-sponsored racism, a majority of this Court signals that it regards racial discrimination as largely a phenomenon of the past, and that government bodies need no longer preoccupy themselves with rectifying racial injustice. I, however, do not believe this Nation is anywhere close to eradicating racial discrimination or its vestiges. In constitutionalizing its wishful thinking, the majority today does a grave disservice not only to those victims of past and present racial discrimination in this Nation whom government has sought to assist, but also to this Court's long tradition of approaching issues of race with the utmost sensitivity. . . .

C.

Today's decision, finally, is particularly noteworthy for the daunting standard it imposes upon States and localities contemplating the use of race-conscious measures to eradicate the present effects of prior discrimination and prevent its perpetuation. The majority restricts the use of such measures to situations in which a State or locality can put forth "a prima facie case of a constitutional or statutory violation." In so doing, the majority calls into question the validity of the business set-asides which dozens of municipalities across this Nation have adopted on the authority of Fullilove.

Nothing in the Constitution or in the prior decisions of this Court supports limiting state authority to confront the effects of past discrimination to those situations in which a prima facie case of a constitutional or statutory violation can be made out. By its very terms, the majority's standard effectively cedes control of a large component of the content of that constitutional provision to Congress and to state legislatures. If an antecedent Virginia or Richmond law had defined as unlawful the award to nonminorities of an overwhelming share of a city's contracting dollars, for example, Richmond's subsequent set-aside initiative would then satisfy the majority's standard. But without such a law, the initiative might not withstand constitutional scrutiny. The meaning of "equal protection of the laws" thus turns on the happenstance of whether a state or local body has previously defined illegal discrimination. Indeed, given that racially discriminatory cities may be the ones least likely to have tough antidiscrimination laws on their books, the majority's constitutional incorporation of state and local statutes has the perverse effect of inhibiting those States or localities with the worst records of official racism from taking remedial action.

Similar flaws would inhere in the majority's standard even if it incorporated only federal anti-discrimination statutes. If Congress tomorrow dramatically expanded Title VII of the Civil Rights Act of 1964—or alternatively, if it repealed that legislation altogether— the meaning of equal protection would change precipitously along with it. Whatever the Framers of the Fourteenth Amendment had in mind in 1868, it certainly was not that the content of their Amendment would turn on the amendments to or the evolving interpretations of a federal statute passed nearly a century later.

To the degree that this parsimonious standard is grounded on a view that either § 1 or § 5 of the Fourteenth Amendment substantially disempowered States and localities from remedying past racial discrimination, the majority is seriously mistaken. With respect, first, to § 5, our precedents have never suggested that this provision—or, for that matter, its companion federal-empowerment provisions in the Thirteenth and Fifteenth Amendments—was meant to pre-empt or limit state police power to undertake race-conscious remedial measures. To the contrary, in Katzenbach v. Morgan (1966), we held that § 5 "is a *positive* grant of legislative power authorizing Congress to exercise its discretion in determining whether and what legislation is needed to secure the guarantees of the Fourteenth Amendment." (emphasis added) . . . . Indeed, we have held that Congress has this authority even where no constitutional violation has been found. See Katzenbach (upholding Voting Rights Act provision nullifying state English literacy requirement we had previously upheld against Equal Protection Clause challenge). . . .

As for § 1, it is too late in the day to assert seriously that the Equal Protection Clause prohibits States—or for that matter, the Federal Government, to whom the equal protection guarantee has largely been applied, see Bolling v. Sharpe (1954)—from enacting race-conscious remedies. Our cases in the areas of school desegregation, voting rights, and affirmative action have demonstrated time and again that race is constitutionally germane, precisely because race remains dismayingly relevant in American life. . . .

The fact is that Congress' concern in passing the Reconstruction Amendments, and particularly their congressional authorization provisions, was that States would *not* adequately respond to racial violence or discrimination against newly freed slaves. To interpret any aspect of these Amendments as proscribing state remedial responses to these very problems turns the Amendments on their heads. As four Justices, of whom I was one, stated in University of California Regents v. Bakke: "[There is] no reason to conclude that the States cannot voluntarily accomplish under § 1 of the Fourteenth Amendment what Congress under § 5 of the Fourteenth Amendment validly may authorize or compel either the

States or private persons to do. A contrary position would conflict with the traditional understanding recognizing the competence of the States to initiate measures consistent with federal policy in the absence of congressional pre-emption of the subject matter. *Nothing whatever in the legislative history of either the Fourteenth Amendment or the Civil Rights Acts even remotely suggests that the States are foreclosed from furthering the fundamental purpose of equal opportunity to which the Amendment and those Acts are addressed.* Indeed, voluntary initiatives by the States to achieve the national goal of equal opportunity have been recognized to be essential to its attainment. . . .

Justice **Blackmun**, with whom Justice **Brennan** joins, dissenting.

I join Justice Marshall's perceptive and incisive opinion revealing great sensitivity toward those who have suffered the pains of economic discrimination in the construction trades for so long.

I never thought that I would live to see the day when the city of Richmond, Virginia, the cradle of the Old Confederacy, sought on its own, within a narrow confine, to lessen the stark impact of persistent discrimination. But Richmond, to its great credit, acted. Yet this Court, the supposed bastion of equality, strikes down Richmond's efforts as though discrimination had never existed or was not demonstrated in this particular litigation. Justice Marshall convincingly discloses the fallacy and the shallowness of that approach. History is irrefutable, even though one might sympathize with those who—though possibly innocent in themselves—benefit from the wrongs of past decades.

So the Court today regresses. I am confident, however, that, given time, it one day again will do its best to fulfill the great promises of the Constitution's Preamble and of the guarantees embodied in the Bill of Rights—a fulfillment that would make this Nation very special.

B. Tests for Equality

GOESAERT v. CLEARY

335 U. S. 464; 93 L. Ed. 163; 69 S. Ct. 198 (1948)

At the time the Fourteenth Amendment was being considered, it was obvious that the Southern states, left to their own devices, would subject newly freed blacks to numerous and drastic discriminatory laws and regulations designed to prevent them from achieving anything like a status of legal equality with the white citizens of the Southern states. Accordingly the Fourteenth Amendment contains the explicit statement that no state shall "deny to any person within its jurisdiction the equal protection of the law," a clause much clearer in its meaning than its companion clauses in the amendment relating to "due process of law" and "the privileges and immunities of citizens of the United States." The equal protection clause does not mention race, but when it first came before the Supreme Court for interpretation in the Slaughter-House Cases, in 1873, Justice Miller, with contemporary history and conditions in mind, observed: "We doubt very much whether any action of a state not directed by way of discrimination against the negroes as a class, or on account of their race, will ever be held to come within the purview of this provision." Justice Miller's appraisal of current history may have been correct, but not his prophecy. Over the years equal protection of the law has come to afford broad and general relief against all forms of arbitrary classification and discrimination, regardless of the persons affected or the character of the rights involved. In fact, blacks would probably constitute a minority of those who have invoked the equal protection clause against discriminatory treatment.

The equal protection clause does not, of course, forbid all legal classification. Classification in the law is not only constitutional but desirable and necessary; it is almost impossible to conceive of a law which does not in some way employ it. But however necessary such classification and grouping is, it is a function which lends itself to abuse; and it is this abuse which the equal protection clause seeks to prevent.

When does classification become discrimination? How equal is equal? Over the years the Court's approach to these questions has evolved from a laissez-faire attitude that upheld almost all legislative classifications into a more searching review that barred almost all use of certain classifications. But like the natural evolution of any organism, the evolution of the equal protection clause has been a gradual one. Just as in nature where the older systems survive alongside more recent adaptations, so in equal protection the first test used by the Court to determine the legitimacy of legislative classification still exists to judge certain classifications while newer tests have evolved to judge others.

The first, or traditional test, is often referred to as the "rational basis" test. It requires that the government have a rational basis for treating people or activities differently and that that basis must be related to a constitutionally permissible objective. Thus it is rational to demand of automobile drivers that they be able to meet certain standards of vision, and the highway safety it promotes is a constitutional goal. On the other hand, if the government were seeking to oppress blacks it would be perfectly rational to forbid them to go to school. But the oppression of people is not a constitutionally permissible goal and the government's action would not survive even the traditional test. Nevertheless, "mere rationality," as the Court sometimes calls it, is an easy standard to meet because governments can usually find a plausible constitutional objective to put forth no matter how constitutionally questionable the real objective may be.

The first appearance of the rational basis test in F. S. Royster Guano Co. v. Virginia (1920) suggested a good deal more rigorous requirement of equality than in fact developed. "The classification must be reasonable, not arbitrary, and must rest upon some ground of difference having a fair and substantial relation to the object of the legislation, so that all persons similarly circumstanced shall be treated alike." The words "fair and substantial" defining the relationship between the classification and the government's objective suggest that the Court would examine the fit between means and ends with considerable care. This did not happen, and today when the Court invokes the rational basis test it first asks whether the government's objective is constitutional. If it is, it then asks merely if there is *some* connection between that objective and the classification that divides people or things into categories for differential treatment. The Court does not concern itself with how tight a fit exists between the means and the end; the merits of the classification, or whether there ought to be any classification at all, are simply not considered. The right to treat people differently is simply assumed.

The words "fair and substantial" and the ideas they suggest were dropped long ago from the formula. For example, in McGowan v. Maryland (1961), the Court stated that under this test the equal protection clause is "offended only if the classification rests on grounds wholly irrelevant to the achievement of the State's objective," and in Dandridge v. Williams (1970) the Court said that "a State does not violate the Equal Protection Clause merely because the classifications are imperfect. If the classification has some 'reasonable basis,' it does not offend the Constitution simply because the classification 'is not made with mathematical nicety or because in practice it results in some inequality.' " Thus, where the law undertakes to classify on a numerical basis, as with regard to money earned, hours worked, workmen employed, etc., the choice by the legislature of a maximum or minimum number will not be considered arbitrary merely because those who are just over the line do not differ much from those who are not. To apply the original Social Security Act solely to those who employed eight or more persons was held not to discriminate invalidly despite the fact that those employing seven persons were not significantly different.

In addition, the Court has repeatedly held that in enacting remedial legislation the state is under no constitutional obligation to cure all evils merely because it undertakes to cure some of them. Thus a law forbidding the sale of obscene pictures is not invalid because it does not also apply to obscene phonograph records. As Justice Holmes expressed it in Keokee Consolidated Coke Co. v. Taylor (1914), "it is established by repeated decisions that a statute aimed at what is deemed an evil, and hitting it presumably where experience shows it to be most felt, is not to be upset by thinking up and enumerating other instances to which it might have been applied equally well, so far as the Court can see."

The rational basis test assumes that the legislature had a valid, nondiscriminatory reason for passing the law and anyone challenging its validity bears the burden of proving the legislature's irrationality. This has proved to be a most difficult burden to meet. Currently the rational basis test is most often used in challenges to laws regulating economic activities, but whenever it is invoked the result is more than likely to be a holding that the law is constitutional. In the past the rational basis test was used to uphold many laws that would be struck down today because a more demanding test would be used. This is particularly true of laws that discriminate on the basis of sex, such as the law at issue in the case below. See Mississippi University for Women v. Hogan (1983).

In Goesaert v. Cleary a Michigan law prohibited women from working as bartenders, with an exception for women who were married to or the daughters of men who owned bars. The law was challenged as unconstitutional under the equal protection clause. Note the difference in the Court's justification of Michigan's right to prohibit all women to tend bar and its right to draw the distinction used here.

Mr. Justice **Frankfurter** delivered the opinion of the court:

. . . Beguiling as the subject is, it need not detain us long. To ask whether or not the Equal Protection of the Laws Clause of the Fourteenth Amendment barred Michigan from making the classification the State has made between wives and daughters of owners of liquor places and wives and daughters of non-owners, is one of those rare instances where to state the question is in effect to answer it.

We are, to be sure, dealing with a historic calling. We meet the ale-wife sprightly and ribald, in Shakespeare, but centuries before him she played a role in the social life of

England. . . . The Fourteenth Amendment did not tear history up by the roots, and the regulation of the liquor traffic is one of the oldest and most untrammeled of legislative powers. Michigan could, beyond question, forbid all women from working behind a bar. This is so despite the vast changes in the social and legal position of women. The fact that women may now have achieved the virtues that men have long claimed as their prerogatives and now indulge in vices that men have long practiced, does not preclude the States from drawing a sharp line between the sexes, certainly in such matters as the regulation of the liquor traffic. . . . The Constitution does not require legislatures to reflect sociological insight, or shifting social standards, any more than it requires them to keep abreast of the latest scientific standards.

While Michigan may deny to all women opportunities for bartending, Michigan cannot play favorites among women without rhyme or reason. The Constitution in enjoining the equal protection of the laws upon States precludes irrational discrimination as between persons or groups of persons in the incidence of a law. But the Constitution does not require situations ''which are different in fact or opinion to be treated in law as though they were the same.'' . . . Since bartending by women may, in the allowable legislative judgment, give rise to moral and social problems against which it may devise preventive measures, the legislature need not go to the full length of prohibition if it believes that as to a defined group of females other factors are operating which either eliminate or reduce the moral and social problems otherwise calling for prohibition. Michigan evidently believes that the oversight assured through ownership of a bar by a barmaid's husband or father minimizes hazards that may confront a barmaid without such protecting oversight. This Court is certainly not in a position to gainsay such a belief by the Michigan legislature. If it is entertainable, as we think it is, Michigan has not violated its duty to afford equal protection of its laws. We cannot cross-examine either actually or argumentatively the mind of Michigan legislators nor question their motives. Since the line they have drawn is not without a basis in reason, we cannot give ear to the suggestion that the real impulse behind this legislation was an unchivalrous desire of male bartenders to try to monopolize the calling. . . .

Nor is it unconstitutional for Michigan to withdraw from women the occupation of bartending because it allows women to serve as waitresses where liquor is dispensed. The District Court has sufficiently indicated the reasons that may have influenced the legislature in allowing women to be waitresses in a liquor establishment over which a man's ownership provides control. Nothing need be added to what was said below as to the other grounds on which the Michigan law was assailed.

Judgment affirmed.

Mr. Justice **Rutledge,** with whom Mr. Justice **Douglas** and Mr. Justice **Murphy** join, dissenting.

While the equal protection clause does not require a legislature to achieve ''abstract symmetry'' or to classify with ''mathematical nicety,'' that clause does require lawmakers to refrain from invidious distinctions of the sort drawn by the statute challenged in this case.

The statute arbitrarily discriminates between male and female owners of liquor establishments. A male owner, although he himself is always absent from his bar, may employ his wife and daughter as barmaids. A female owner may neither work as a barmaid herself nor employ her daughter in that position, even if a man is always present in the establishment to keep order. This inevitable result of the classification belies the assumption that the statute was motivated by a legislative solicitude for the moral well-being of women who, but for the law, would be employed as barmaids. Since there could be no other conceivable justification for such discrimination against women owners of liquor establishments, the statute should be held invalid as a denial of equal protection.

KOREMATSU v. UNITED STATES

323 U. S. 214; 89 L. Ed. 194; 65 S. Ct. 193 (1944)

While the Fourteenth Amendment does not mention race, the Court has always recognized that racial discrimination against blacks was the primary concern of its framers and has therefore examined racial classifications with particular care. In 1880 in Strauder v. West Virginia the Court held that a black man had a right to be tried by a jury on which blacks had been eligible to sit. Laws that discriminate against other racial minorities were similarly treated. In Yick Wo v. Hopkins (1886) the Court struck down a San Francisco ordinance that prohibited anyone from operating a laundry in a wooden building without a permit issued by the Board of Supervisors. The Court found that the law as administered discriminated against Chinese applicants; non-Chinese applicants were routinely granted permits while almost all Chinese applications were denied.

As a greater variety of laws began to be challenged under the equal protection clause and the rational basis test began to take on its present form, it became clear that that test was an insufficient guard against racial discrimination. Allowing a state to discriminate on the basis of race any time it could show a rational relationship to a legitimate governmental purpose would provide too little protection for racial minorities. There was little question that states were being held to a higher standard when they attempted to treat people differently based on their race; decisions as early as Yick Wo in 1886 demonstrated that. The higher standard was, however, not spelled out until the decision in the present case in which the Court identifies race as a "suspect" classification for the first time. Justice Black, writing for the majority, states that because it is a suspect classification it must be subjected to the "most rigid scrutiny." Herein lies the genesis of what is usually called the "strict scrutiny" test.

Unlike the rational basis test, the strict scrutiny test assumes that the law is unconstitutional when it includes a suspect classification. Those defending the law bear the burden of proving that the government's objectives are not only legitimate but are compelling. Even more difficult, the law's defenders must show that the suspect classification is necessary to accomplish the government's purpose—that it cannot be accomplished in any other way. The fit between the suspect classification and the compelling government objective must be nearly perfect.

The strict scrutiny test is used whenever a law employs a suspect classification. In addition to race, the prime examples of this are religion and national origin. A classification is more apt to be treated as suspect if its characteristics are immutable, so that a person born into it can never escape it. Generally, a suspect classification is also one that has been used historically to oppress a particular group, and one that discriminates against a "discrete and insular" minority—a phrase taken from Justice Stone's now famous footnote 4 in United States v. Carolene Products Co. (1938) in which he suggested that prejudice against such groups might tend "seriously to curtail the operation of those political processes ordinarily to be relied upon to protect minorities, and which may call for a correspondingly more searching judicial inquiry."

The strict scrutiny test developed to deal with suspect classifications has been applied to another category of cases brought under the equal protection clause. This second category includes cases challenging laws that affect "fundamental rights or interests." There are at least two different concepts underlying the fundamental interest branch of strict scrutiny. The first involves rights, such as the right to appeal a conviction, that are so basic that even though there is no absolute right to them, once a state chooses to grant them it must allocate them equally—unless the state can show a compelling state interest for doing otherwise. Administrative convenience or added expense to the state do not rank as "compelling" in this context.

The second concept is that there are some fundamental rights implicit in the Constitution, such as the right to travel interstate, the exercise of which cannot be made the basis of differential treatment without a compelling government interest that cannot be satisfied in some other way. While this latter concept has been attacked on the ground that it should not require an equal protection clause to protect a right already guaranteed in the Constitution, it is apparent that equal protection does serve to prevent actions which may *discourage* the exercise of a such a right but which do not rise to the level of a violation of the right itself. Thus, while it is clear a state could not directly forbid a person to travel interstate, only the equal protection clause might prevent laws against limiting access to welfare benefits or jobs which would have a discouraging effect on such travel. Criticism of the use of the strict scrutiny test in this area as judicial law-making has perhaps been influential in keeping the list a short one: voting, access to the judicial process and interstate travel.

The rational basis test and the strict scrutiny test are functional opposites: Laws usually pass the rational basis test while they almost always fail the strict scrutiny test. It is therefore ironic that the strict scrutiny test was first articulated in one of the only cases to uphold the use of a racial classification.

The present case involved perhaps the most alarming use of executive military authority in our nation's history. Following the bombing of Pearl Harbor in December 1941, the anti-Japanese sentiment on the West Coast brought the residents of that area to a state of near hysteria; and in February 1942, President Roosevelt issued an executive order authorizing the creation of military areas from which any or all persons might be excluded as the military authorities might decide. On March 2, the entire West Coast to a depth of about 40 miles was designated by the commanding general as Military Area No. 1, and he thereupon proclaimed a curfew in that area for all persons of Japanese ancestry. Later he ordered the compulsory evacuation from the area of all persons of Japanese ancestry, and by the middle of the summer most of these people had been moved inland to "war relocation centers," the American equivalent of concentration camps. Congress subsequently made it a crime to violate these military orders. Of the 112,000 persons of Japanese ancestry involved, about 70,000 were native-born American citizens, none of whom had been specifically accused of disloyalty. Three cases were brought to the Supreme Court challenging the right of the government to override in this manner the customary civil rights of these citizens. In

Hirabayashi v. United States (1943) the Court upheld the curfew regulations as a valid military measure to prevent espionage and sabotage. "Whatever views we may entertain regarding the loyalty to this country of the citizens of Japanese ancestry, we cannot reject as unfounded the judgment of the military authorities and of Congress that there were disloyal members of that population, whose number and strength could not be precisely and quickly ascertained. We cannot say that the war-making branches of the Government did not have ground for believing that in a critical hour such persons could not readily be isolated and separately dealt with, and constituted a menace to the national defense and safety...." While emphasizing that distinctions based on ancestry were "by their very nature odious to a free people" the Court nonetheless felt "that in time of war residents having ethnic affiliations with an invading enemy may be a greater source of danger than those of a different ancestry."

While the Court, in the present case, held valid the discriminatory mass evacuation of all persons of Japanese descent, it also held in Ex parte Endo (1944), that an American citizen of Japanese ancestry whose loyalty to this country had been established could not constitutionally be held in a war relocation center but must be unconditionally released. The government had allowed persons to leave the relocation centers under conditions and restrictions which aimed to guarantee that there should not be "a dangerously disorderly migration of unwanted people to unprepared communities." Permission to leave was granted only if the applicant had the assurance of a job and a place to live, and wanted to go to a place "approved" by the War Relocation Authority. The Court held that the sole purpose of the evacuation and detention program was to protect the war effort against sabotage and espionage. "A person who is concededly loyal presents no problem of espionage or sabotage.... He who is loyal is by definition not a spy or a saboteur." It therefore follows that the authority to detain a citizen of Japanese ancestry ends when his loyalty is established. To hold otherwise would be to justify his detention not on grounds of military necessity but purely on grounds of race.

Although no case reached the Court squarely challenging the right of the government to incarcerate citizens of Japanese ancestry pending a determination of their loyalty, the tenor of the opinions leaves little doubt that such action would have been sustained. The present case involved only the right of the military to evacuate such persons from the West Coast.

In the years following World War II evidence accumulated suggesting that the demand for the evacuation was either the result of racism, encouraged by the local press, or the result of the deliberate efforts of persons who stood to gain financially if the Japanese had to abandon their property on short notice. A congressional commission set up in 1980 reported after a two-year study that the only responsible intelligence report, made by Naval Intelligence, rejected outright the justifications for incarceration advanced by the military. The existence of these reports was deliberately withheld by the Justice Department when it argued both Hirabayashi and Korematsu. See Hohri v. United States, 782 F. 2d 227 (1986). While Congress in the Civil Liberties Act of 1980 required restitution to each living Japanese-American who was held in a relocation center, a number of damage suits were later filed. The government, while admitting in oral argument withholding evidence in the cases, argued that the statute of limitations against further suits should have started running with the decision in Korematsu. See United States v. Hohri (1987).

An unusual tourist attraction is a bronze plaque, installed by the government of the state on the main entry gate of the Manzanar camp located in the desert near Bishop, California. The text is as follows:

* MANZANAR *

ɪn the early part of World War II 110,000 persons of Japanese ancestry were interned in relocation centers by Executive Order No. 9066, issued on February 19, 1942.

Manzanar, the first of ten such concentration camps, was bounded by barbed wire and guard towers, confining 10,000 persons, the majority being American citizens.

May the injustice and humiliation suffered here as a result of hysteria, racism and economic exploitation never emerge again.

CALIFORNIA REGISTERED HISTORICAL LANDMARK NO. 850

In an emotion-laden ceremony on October 9, 1990, Attorney General Dick Thornburgh apologized on behalf of the United States and handed to 107-year-old Mamoru Eto the first $20,000 reparation check to go to 65,000 internees or their heirs. In a note accompanying the check President Bush conceded "we can never fully right the wrongs of the past . . . but we can take a clear stand for justice and recognize that serious injustices were done to Japanese-Americans during World War II."

Mr. Justice **Black** delivered the opinion of the Court, saying in part:

The petitioner, an American citizen of Japanese descent, was convicted in a federal district court for remaining in San Leandro, California, a "Military Area," contrary to Civilian Exclusion Order No. 34 of the Commanding General of the Western Command, U. S. Army, which directed that after May 9, 1942, all persons of Japanese ancestry should be excluded from that area. No question was raised as to petitioner's loyalty to the United States. The Circuit Court of Appeals affirmed, and the importance of the constitutional question involved caused us to grant certiorari.

It should be noted, to begin with, that all legal restrictions which curtail the civil rights of a single racial group are immediately suspect. That is not to say that all such restrictions are unconstitutional. It is to say that courts must subject them to the most rigid scrutiny. Pressing public necessity may sometimes justify the existence of such restrictions; racial antagonism never can.

In the instant case prosecution of the petitioner was begun by information charging violation of an Act of Congress, of March 21, 1942, which provides that ". . . whoever shall enter, remain in, leave, or commit any act in any military area or military zone prescribed, under the authority of an Executive order of the President, by the Secretary of War, or by any military commander designated by the Secretary of War, contrary to the restrictions applicable to any such area or zone or contrary to the order of the Secretary of War or any such military commander, shall, if it appears that he knew or should have known of the existence and extent of the restrictions or order and that his act was in violation thereof, be guilty of a misdemeanor and upon conviction shall be liable to a fine of not to exceed $5,000 or to imprisonment for not more than one year, or both, for each offense.''

Exclusion Order No. 34, which the petitioner knowingly and admittedly violated, was one of a number of military orders and proclamations, all of which were substantially based upon Executive Order No. 9066. That order, issued after we were at war with Japan, declared that ''the successful prosecution of the war requires every possible protection against espionage and against sabotage to national-defense material, national-defense premises, and national-defense utilities. . . .''

One of the series of orders and proclamations, a curfew order, which like the exclusion order here was promulgated pursuant to Executive Order 9066, subjected all persons of Japanese ancestry in prescribed West Coast military areas to remain in their residences from 8 p.m. to 6 a.m. As is the case with the exclusion order here, that prior curfew order was designed as a ''protection against espionage and against sabotage.'' In Kiyoshi Hirabayashi v. United States [1943], we sustained a conviction obtained for violation of the curfew order. The Hirabayashi conviction and this one thus rest on the same 1942 Congressional Act and the same basic executive and military orders, all of which orders were aimed at the twin dangers of espionage and sabotage.

The 1942 Act was attacked in the Hirabayashi case as an unconstitutional delegation of power; it was contended that the curfew order and other orders on which it rested were beyond the war powers of the Congress, the military authorities and of the President, as Commander in Chief of the Army; and finally that to apply the order against none but citizens of Japanese ancestry amounted to a constitutionally prohibited discrimination solely on account of race. To these questions, we gave the serious consideration which their importance justified. We upheld the curfew order as an exercise of the power of the government to take steps necessary to prevent espionage and sabotage in an area threatened by Japanese attack.

In the light of the principles we announced in the Hirabayashi case, we are unable to conclude that it was beyond the war power of Congress and the Executive to exclude those of Japanese ancestry from the West Coast war area at the time they did. True, exclusion from the area in which one's home is located is a far greater deprivation than constant confinement to the home from 8 p.m. to 6 a.m. Nothing short of apprehension by the proper military authorities of the gravest imminent danger to the public safety can constitutionally justify either. But exclusion from a threatened area, no less than curfew, has a definite and close relationship to the prevention of espionage and sabotage. The military authorities, charged with the primary responsibility of defending our shores, concluded that curfew provided inadequate protection and ordered exclusion. They did so, as pointed out in our Hirabayashi opinion, in accordance with Congressional authority to the military to say who should, and who should not, remain in the threatened areas.

In this case the petitioner challenges the assumptions upon which we rested our conclusions in the Hirabayashi case. He also urges that by May 1942, when Order No. 34 was promulgated, all danger of Japanese invasion of the West Coast had disappeared. After careful consideration of these contentions we are compelled to reject them.

Here, as in the Hirabayashi case, ''. . . we cannot reject as unfounded the judgment of the military authorities and of Congress that there were disloyal members of that population, whose number and strength could not be precisely and quickly ascertained. We cannot say that the war-making branches of the Government did not have ground for believing that in a critical hour such persons could not readily be isolated and separately dealt with, and constituted a menace to the national defense and safety, which demanded that prompt and adequate measures be taken to guard against it.''

Like curfew, exclusion of those of Japanese origin was deemed necessary because of the presence of an unascertained number of disloyal members of the group, most of whom we have no doubt were loyal to this country. It was because we could not reject the finding of the military authorities that it was impossible to bring about an immediate segregation of the disloyal from the loyal that we sustained the validity of the curfew order as applying to the whole group. In the instant case, temporary exclusion of the entire group was rested by the military on the same ground. The judgment that exclusion of the whole group was for the same reason a military imperative answers the contention that the exclusion was in the nature of group punishment based on antagonism to those of Japanese origin. That there were members of the group who retained loyalties to Japan has been confirmed by investigations made subsequent to the exclusion. Approximately five thousand American citizens of Japanese ancestry refused to swear unqualified allegiance to the United States and to renounce allegiance to the Japanese Emperor, and several thousand evacuees requested repatriation to Japan.

We uphold the exclusion order as of the time it was made and when the petitioner violated it. . . . In doing so, we are not unmindful of the hardships imposed by it upon a large group of American citizens. . . . But hardships are part of war, and war is an aggregation of hardships. All citizens alike, both in and out of uniform, feel the impact of war in greater or lesser measure. Citizenship has its responsibilities as well as its privileges, and in time of war the burden is always heavier. Compulsory exclusion of large groups of citizens from their homes, except under circumstances of direst emergency and peril, is inconsistent with our basic governmental institution. But when under conditions of modern warfare our shores are threatened by hostile forces, the power to protect must be commensurate with the threatened danger. . . .

[The Court dealt at some length with a technical complication which arose in the case. On May 30, the date on which Korematsu was charged with remaining unlawfully in the prohibited area, there were two conflicting military orders outstanding, one forbidding him to remain in the area, the other forbidding him to leave but ordering him to report to an assembly center. Thus, he alleged, he was punished for doing what it was made a crime to fail to do. The Court held the orders not to be contradictory, since the requirement to report to the assembly center was merely a step in an orderly program of compulsory evacuation from the area.]

It is said that we are dealing here with the case of imprisonment of a citizen in a concentration camp solely because of his ancestry, without evidence or inquiry concerning his loyalty and good disposition towards the United States. Our task would be simple, our duty clear, were this a case involving the imprisonment of a loyal citizen in a concentration camp because of racial prejudice. Regardless of the true nature of the assembly and relocation centers—and we deem it unjustifiable to call them concentration camps with all the ugly connotations that term implies—we are dealing specifically with nothing but an exclusion order. To cast this case into outlines of racial prejudice, without reference to the real military dangers which were presented, merely confuses the issue. Korematsu was not excluded from the Military Area because of hostility to him or his race. He was excluded because we are at war with the Japanese Empire, because the properly constituted military authorities feared an invasion of our West Coast and felt constrained to take proper security measures, because they decided that the military urgency of the situation demanded that all citizens of Japanese ancestry be segregated from the West Coast temporarily, and, finally, because Congress, reposing its confidence in this time of war in our military leaders—as inevitably it must—determined that they should have the power to do just this. There was evidence of disloyalty on the part of some, the military authorities considered that the need for action was great, and time was short. We cannot—by availing ourselves of the calm perspective of hindsight—now say that at that time these actions were unjustified.

Affirmed.

Mr. Justice **Frankfurter** wrote a concurring opinion.

Mr. Justice **Roberts,** dissenting, said in part:

I dissent, because I think the indisputable facts exhibit a clear violation of Constitutional rights.

This is not a case of keeping people off the streets at night as was Hirabayashi v. United States (1943), nor a case of temporary exclusion of a citizen from an area for his own safety or that of the community, nor a case of offering him an opportunity to go temporarily out of an area where his presence might cause danger to himself or to his fellows. On the contrary, it is the case of convicting a citizen as a punishment for not submitting to imprisonment in a concentration camp, based on his ancestry, and solely because of his ancestry, without evidence or inquiry concerning his loyalty and good disposition towards the United States. If this be a correct statement of the facts disclosed by this record, and facts of which we take judicial notice, I need hardly labor the conclusion that constitutional rights have been violated.

Mr. Justice **Murphy,** dissenting, said in part:

This exclusion of ''all persons of Japanese ancestry, both alien and non-alien,'' from the Pacific Coast area on a plea of military necessity in the absence of martial law ought not to be approved. Such exclusion goes over ''the very brink of constitutional power'' and falls into the ugly abyss of racism.

In dealing with matters relating to the prosecution and progress of a war, we must accord great respect and consideration to the judgments of the military authorities who are on the scene and who have full knowledge of the military facts. The scope of their discretion must, as a matter of necessity and common sense, be wide. And their judgments ought not to be overruled lightly by those whose training and duties ill-equip them to deal intelligently with matters so vital to the physical security of the nation.

At the same time, however, it is essential that there be definite limits to military discretion especially where martial law has not been declared. Individuals must not be left impoverished of their constitutional rights on a plea of military necessity that has neither substance nor support. Thus, like other claims conflicting with the asserted constitutional rights of the individual, the military claim must subject itself to the judicial process of having its reasonableness determined and its conflicts with other interests reconciled. . . .

. . . Being an obvious racial discrimination, the order deprives all those within its scope of the equal protection of the laws as guaranteed by the Fifth Amendment. It further deprives these individuals of their constitutional rights to live and work where they will, to establish a home where they choose and to move about freely. In excommunicating them without benefit of hearings, this order also deprives them of all their constitutional rights to procedural due process. Yet no reasonable relation to an "immediate, imminent, and impending" public danger is evident to support this racial restriction which is one of the most sweeping and complete deprivations of constitutional rights in the history of this nation in the absence of martial law.

It must be conceded that the military and naval situation in the spring of 1942 was such as to generate a very real fear of invasion of the Pacific Coast, accompanied by fears of sabotage and espionage in that area. The military command was therefore justified in adopting all reasonable means necessary to combat these dangers. In adjudging the military action taken in light of the then apparent dangers, we must not erect too high or too meticulous standards; it is necessary only that the action have some reasonable relation to the removal of the dangers of invasion, sabotage and espionage. But the exclusion, either temporarily or permanently, of all persons with Japanese blood in their veins has no such reasonable relation. And that relation is lacking because the exclusion order necessarily must rely for its reasonableness upon the assumption that *all* persons of Japanese ancestry may have a dangerous tendency to commit sabotage and espionage and to aid our Japanese enemy in other ways. It is difficult to believe that reason, logic or experience could be marshalled in support of such an assumption.

That this forced exclusion was the result in good measure of this erroneous assumption of racial guilt rather than bona fide military necessity is evidenced by the Commanding General's Final Report on the evacuation from the Pacific Coast area. In it he refers to all individuals of Japanese descent as "subversive," as belonging to "an enemy race" whose "racial strains are undiluted," and as constituting "over 112,000 potential enemies . . . at large today" along the Pacific Coast. In support of this blanket condemnation of all persons of Japanese descent, however, no reliable evidence is cited to show that such individuals were generally disloyal, or had generally so conducted themselves in this area as to constitute a special menace to defense installations or war industries, or had otherwise by their behavior furnished reasonable ground for their exclusion as a group.

Justification for the exclusion is sought, instead, mainly upon questionable racial and sociological grounds not ordinarily within the realm of expert military judgment. . . . [Justice Murphy here reviews and refutes the sociological evidence.]

The main reasons relied upon by those responsible for the forced evacuation, therefore, do not prove a reasonable relation between the group characteristics of Japanese Americans and the dangers of invasion, sabotage and espionage. The reasons appear, instead, to be largely an accumulation of much of the misinformation, half-truths and insinuations that for years have been directed against Japanese Americans by people with racial and economic prejudices—the same people who have been among the foremost advocates of the evacuation. A military judgment based upon such racial and sociological considerations is not entitled to the great weight ordinarily given the judgments based upon strictly military considerations. Especially is this so when every charge relative to race, religion, culture, geographical location, and legal and economic status has been substantially discredited by independent studies made by experts in these matters.

The military necessity which is essential to the validity of the evacuation order thus resolves itself into a few intimations that certain individuals actively aided the enemy, from which it is inferred that the entire group of Japanese Americans could not be trusted to be or remain loyal to the United States. No one denies, of course, that there were some disloyal persons of Japanese descent on the Pacific Coast who did all in their power to aid their ancestral land. Similar disloyal activities have been engaged in by many persons of German, Italian and even more pioneer stock in our country. But to infer that examples of individual disloyalty prove group disloyalty and justify discriminatory action against the entire group is to deny that under our system of law individual guilt is the sole basis for deprivation of rights. Moreover, this inference, which is at the very heart of the evacuation orders, has been used in support of the abhorrent and despicable treatment of minority groups by the dictatorial tyrannies which this nation is now pledged to destroy. To give constitutional sanction to that inference in this case, however well-intentioned may have been the military command on the Pacific Coast, is to adopt one of the cruelest of the rationales used by our enemies to destroy the dignity of the individual and to encourage and open the door to discriminatory actions against other minority groups in the passions of tomorrow.

No adequate reason is given for the failure to treat these Japanese Americans on an individual basis by holding investigations and hearings to separate the loyal from the disloyal, as was done in the case of persons of German and Italian ancestry. . . . It is asserted merely that the loyalties of this group ''were unknown and time was of the essence.'' Yet nearly four months elapsed after Pearl Harbor before the first exclusion order was issued; nearly eight months went by until the last order was issued; and the last of these ''subversive'' persons was not actually removed until almost eleven months had elapsed. Leisure and deliberation seem to have been more of the essence than speed. And the fact that conditions were not such as to warrant a declaration of martial law adds strength to the belief that the factors of time and military necessity were not as urgent as they have been represented to be.

Mr. Justice **Jackson,** dissenting, said in part:

It would be impracticable and dangerous idealism to expect or insist that each specific military command in an area of probable operations will conform to conventional tests of constitutionality. When an area is so beset that it must be put under military control at all, the paramount consideration is that its measures be successful, rather than legal. The armed services must protect a society, not merely its Constitution. . . ,

But if we cannot confine military expedients by the Constitution, neither would I distort the Constitution to approve all that the military may deem expedient. That is what the Court appears to be doing, whether consciously or not. I cannot say, from any evidence before me, that the orders of General DeWitt were not reasonably expedient military precautions, nor could I say that they were. But even if they were permissible military procedures,

I deny that it follows that they are constitutional. If, as the Court holds, it does follow, then we may as well say that any military order will be constitutional and have done with it. . . .

Much is said of the danger to liberty from the Army program for deporting and detaining these citizens of Japanese extraction. But a judicial construction of the due process clause that will sustain this order is a far more subtle blow to liberty than the promulgation of the order itself. A military order, however unconstitutional, is not apt to last longer than the military emergency. Even during that period a succeeding commander may revoke it all. But once a judicial opinion rationalizes such an order to show that it conforms to the Constitution, or rather rationalizes the Constitution to show that the Constitution sanctions such an order, the Court for all time has validated the principle of racial discrimination in criminal procedure and of transplanting American citizens. The principle then lies about like a loaded weapon ready for the hand of any authority that can bring forward a plausible claim of an urgent need. . . .

My duties as a justice as I see them do not require me to make a military judgment as to whether General DeWitt's evacuation and detention program was a reasonable military necessity. I do not suggest that the courts should have attempted to interfere with the Army in carrying out its task. But I do not think they may be asked to execute a military expedient that has no place in law under the Constitution. I would reverse the judgment and discharge the prisoner.

MISSISSIPPI UNIVERSITY FOR WOMEN v. HOGAN

458 U. S. 718; 73 L.Ed. 2d 1090; 102 S. Ct. 3331 (1982)

With two tests for judging cases brought under the equal protection clause, the Court entered the 1970's and found itself facing an increasing number of equal protection claims. The proliferation of government benefits (collectively referred to as the welfare state) and the growing awareness of the disadvantages of the poor and of women generated new and complex equality questions for which the two tests seemed inadequate. Nevertheless, as the Court took up each of these new questions it recited the formula for one of its two tests and proceeded to decide accordingly. It ultimately became apparent even to the Court, however, that the two-tiered approach was straining at the seams.

In San Antonio v. Rodriguez (1973) the Court faced the question of whether the equal protection clause requires the state to equalize the amounts spent on education throughout the districts of the state. The importance of the question to public education would be difficult to overestimate.

The city of San Antonio, Texas, financed its schools with a combination of state aid and local property taxes, the latter being divided between an amount which a district is required to raise and which is roughly proportional to its taxing power, and an additional amount which it may raise if it wishes to do so. Two districts were contrasted in this litigation. The first, which was 96 percent Mexican-American and black, with an average property value of $5,960 (the lowest in the metropolitan area) and a tax rate of $1.05 per $100 (the highest in the metropolitan area), contributed $26 per pupil above its legal requirements. In contrast, the second district was 81 percent white, its assessed value was $49,000 per pupil, and with a local tax rate of $.85 per $100 it raised $333 per pupil above the required minimum.

The Court applied the two-tier formula and decided the disparities between the money raised in the two districts did not deny the students educated in the poorer district the equal protection of the laws. In the first place, the "poor" could not be identified in customary equal protection terms and hence were not a "suspect classification." There was no evidence that people living in the poor school districts were actually poor, and there was no absolute deprivation of rights that could be attributed to an inability to pay as in the case of a person who could not afford to post bail. "The Equal Protection Clause does not require absolute equality of precisely equal advantages." In the second place, education, while important to both the individual and the state, was not a "fundamental right" the deprivation of which would invoke the strict scrutiny test. "It is not the province of this Court to create substantive constitutional rights in the name of guaranteeing equal protection of the laws." The Court's role "lies in assessing whether there is a right to education explicitly or implicitly guaranteed by the Constitution." It found that it was not.

In his dissent in Rodriguez, Justice Marshall argued that two tests for equal protection cases were not enough. The tests had become not tests, but answers: under the strict scrutiny test, the law is struck down; under the rational basis test the law is upheld. He urged the Court to give up the pretense of two tests and concede that in fact it was applying neither.

What the Court was really doing, Marshall said, was asking two questions. First, how important is the interest that is being adversely affected by the alleged discrimination. Second, how invidious is the classification that is being used. The answer to these questions determines the level of scrutiny to be applied.

The difference between this approach and the two-tiered approach is demonstrated by Rodriguez where the Court used the two-tiered approach: education is not a fundamental right, and wealth is not a suspect classification; strict scrutiny cannot therefore be applied; thus the rational basis test must be used. Justice Marshall's approach would be that education, even if not fundamental, is important; wealth, even if not a suspect classification, is questionable. Strict scrutiny does not apply, but neither is the rational basis test appropriate here: an intermediate test should be applied.

Such an intermediate test, sometimes called the "substantial interest test," first made its appearance in cases involving sex discrimination and brought with it the requirement of a fair and substantial relationship between the classification and the objective—a requirement that had been dropped from the rational basis test so long ago; see the note to Goesaert v. Cleary. In Craig v. Boren (1976) the Court held void a law that set a higher legal drinking age for men than for women. The test used to determine whether this law violated the equal protection test involved the considerations mentioned above and was described by the Court in Craig as a midlevel test. Craig was one of the first explicit instances of the Court's use of this intermediate test and is often cited by the Court as precedent for its use.

Probably no group in the country is subject to a more pervasive, firmly established and staunchly defended system of discrimination than are women. Relying on such varied arguments as biblical authority, the woman's lack of muscular strength, her child-bearing function with its attendant incapacities, and the natural capacity for motherhood, male members of society have undertaken to "protect their women" from having to compete against men by assuring them, insofar as possible, a role of their own in society. States have, at one time or another, forbidden women to work at certain jobs, to engage publicly in certain sports, to work while pregnant or to collect unemployment benefits when on maternity leave. Until 1968, a Connecticut statute provided that a woman could be sentenced to three years at the "State Farm" for a crime for which a man could be sentenced to only eighteen months in jail, and until 1982 a state could still establish a one-sex school, while one-*race* schools were held to deny equal protection of the laws.

Even greater is the private discrimination against women. As with blacks, some employers simply refuse to hire women, hire them only for secretarial or clerical jobs, or pay them only about 60 percent of what they would pay a man for comparable work. Section 703(a) of the Civil Rights Act of 1964 provided the first nationwide prohibition against discriminatory hiring practices affecting women. This statute has been the basis for most of the Court's decisions on sexual discrimination since its adoption. For example, in Phillips v. Marietta Corp. (1971) the Supreme Court held that the act forbade the corporation to refuse to hire a woman with pre-school-age children when it hired men with such children; and in Hishon v. King & Spalding (1984) the Court held that this act forbids a law firm from making partnership decisions on the basis of the sex of the law firm associate involved.

For the first 100 years after the passage of the Fourteenth Amendment the Court did not discuss its application to women on many occasions, and when the Court did deal with the rights of women under the equal protection clause, it treated sex as a legitimate basis of classification. As early as 1904 it held, in Cronin v. Adams, that a state could by law not only prevent women from working in saloons, but could even prevent their entering as customers. See the note to Goesaert v. Cleary. Nor was there any constitutional objection to treating men and women differently in regard to jury service. In Strauder v. West Virginia (1880) the Court suggested that a state could "confine the selection to males," and in Hoyt v. Florida (1961) it refused to review the "continuing validity of this dictum . . . which has gone unquestioned for more than eighty years in the decisions of this Court." The Court upheld a state law exempting women from jury service, noting that "despite the enlightened emancipation of women from the restrictions and protections of bygone years, and their entry into many parts of community life formerly considered to be reserved to men, woman is still regarded as the center of home and family life."

As the Equal Rights Amendment (ERA) gathered votes for ratification, the attitude of the Supreme Court began to reflect the changed status of women in society. When, in Taylor v. Louisiana (1975), it effectively overruled the Hoyt case, it acknowledged that "if at one time it could be held that Sixth Amendment juries must be drawn from a fair cross section of the community but that this requirement permitted the almost total exclusion of women, this is not the case today. Communities differ at different times and places. What is a fair cross section at one time or place is not necessarily a fair cross section at another time or a different place." The Court noted that 53 percent of the community were women, and added that the fact that 54 percent of all women between 18 and 64 were part of the labor force "certainly put to rest the suggestion that all women should be exempt from jury service based solely on their sex and the presumed role in the home."

But while the Court seemed prepared to accept the new role of women and viewed state laws treating them differently from men more critically than equal protection standards traditionally required, it was apparently not so convinced of the equality of women as to consider sex, like race, a "suspect" or "invidious" classification that could be used by the state only to achieve some compelling state interest which it could not achieve in any other way.

In deciding Reed v. Reed in 1971, the first case ever to hold void a state classification based on sex, the Court held that women were as entitled as men to serve as administrators of estates. While it conceded that "the objective of reducing the work load on probate courts by eliminating one class of contests is not without some legitimacy," it found that preferring one sex over another "merely to accomplish the elimination of hearings on the merits, is to make the very kind of arbitrary legislative choice forbidden by the Equal Protection Clause."

Although Reed was unanimous, it gave no clear sign as to the philosophy of the justices, and it was not until 1973 with the decision in Frontiero v. Richardson that their attitudes began to emerge. A divided Court held that a female member of the armed forces could claim her spouse as a dependent in the same way a male member could claim his, without having to prove actual dependency. In a plurality opinion, Justices Brennan, Douglas, White, and Marshall reasoned that "classifications based on sex, like classifications based upon race, alienage, or national origin, are inherently suspect, and must therefore be subjected to strict judicial scrutiny." Applying these standards, the four justices, quoting from Reed, found that "any statutory scheme which draws a sharp line between the sexes, *solely* for the purpose of achieving administrative convenience, necessarily commands 'dissimilar treatment for men and women who are . . . similarly situated,' and therefore involves the 'very kind of arbitrary legislative choice forbidden by the [Constitution].' " While Justice Rehnquist dissented and Justice Stewart concurred on the basis of Reed, Justices Powell, Burger, and Blackmun expressly rejected the idea "that all classifications based upon sex" are inherently suspect.

In Geduldig v. Aiello (1974), on the other hand, the Court appeared to retrogress toward the rational basis test. California had set up a medical insurance plan for its employees; the only disabilities not covered were those resulting from pregnancy. The Court stressed that "particularly with respect to social welfare programs, so long as the line drawn by the State is rationally supportable, the courts will not interpose their judgment," and concluded that the state had a legitimate interest in keeping the cost of the system low and the distribution of payments adequate for those disabilities that were covered.

In General Electric v. Gilbert (1976) the Court extended the reasoning of Geduldig to cases arising under Title VII of the Civil Rights Act of 1964 forbidding sex discrimination by private employers. Noting the similarity of language used in the act with that appearing in equal protection decisions, the Court concluded that its decision in Geduldig was "quite relevant in determining whether or not the pregnancy exclusion did discriminate on the basis of sex." Justice Brennan's dissent pointed out that G. E. had a long history of discrimination against women and that its medical coverage included voluntary male-only disabilities such as prostatectomies, vasectomies, and circumcisions. "Pregnancy affords the only disability, sex-specific or otherwise, that is excluded from coverage." In 1978 Congress passed the Pregnancy Discrimination Act to nullify this interpretation.

In a number of cases the Court has been able to view a law favoring women as an affirmative action program to offset the economic disadvantages to which women are or have been subjected. In such cases, despite its division on other aspects of the equality problem, it has found there was no denial of equal protection or due process of law. Thus, in 1974 in Kahn v. Shevin, the Court upheld a Florida property tax exemption for widows but not widowers on the ground that "the financial difficulties confronting the lone woman in Florida or in another State exceed those facing the man. Whether from overt discrimination or from the socialization process or a male-dominated culture, the job market is inhospitable to the woman seeking any but the lowest paid jobs." Noting that this was a tax statute, Justice Douglas for a six-man majority applied the traditional rules regarding classification. "A state tax law is not arbitrary although it 'discriminates in favor of a certain class . . . if the discrimination is founded upon a reasonable distinction, or difference in state policy,' not in conflict with the Federal Constitution." And in Schlesinger v. Ballard (1975) the Court held that a regulation allowing women to stay 13 years in the Navy although twice passed over for promotion did not discriminate against men who could only stay nine years because the opportunity for promotion among men was greater than among women.

In contrast, in Weinberger v. Wiesenfeld (1975) the Court struck down a provision of the Social Security Act providing that a widow with minor children was entitled to benefit from the earnings of her husband, while a widower with minor children was not entitled to benefit from the earnings of his wife. The government argued that, like Kahn v. Shevin, the scheme was designed to "offset the adverse economic situation of women," but the Court found the legislative purpose was to enable the surviving parent to stay home with the child and, as in Reed, this was not a purpose which justified discrimination on the basis of sex.

While a majority of the Court refused to hold that classifications based on sex were "invidious" in the same way as those based on race, it was clearly tightening the reins on the "rational basis" test where the challenged classification was sex. In Stanton v. Stanton (1975) it held void a Utah law setting different ages at which males and females became legal adults, and in Craig v. Boren (1976) it struck down an Oklahoma law setting the age for drinking 3.2 beer at 18 for females and 21 for males. In neither case was the Court willing to accept the state's argument that a legitimate state interest was being advanced, and in the latter case it rejected as unpersuasive the state's statistical evidence purporting to justify the law.

While the failure of the Equal Rights Amendment (ERA) to achieve ratification was a blow to its supporters there are perhaps a number of lessons to be learned from the struggle itself. In the first place, the very fact of the struggle publicized the legitimate and long overlooked claims of women to a status of legal and professional equality. Never again will it be easy to get laws passed denying a wife the right to own property or to enter the business or professional world. In the second place, it became apparent that some women identified with the role they were used to playing, and they both resented and were made to feel insecure by what they viewed as a threat to this role. They saw no reason for shame if they wanted to be a housewife and mother and felt threatened by a movement that seemed to make it hard for them to pursue that role with pride. Third, and this is the point that is most often overlooked, if the ERA had passed there is little assurance that much if any change would have accompanied it. The amending power is touted as the way to make the Constitution say what the people want it to say, but in the long run it is the Supreme Court that decides what the amendments themselves actually mean. One need only view the complete destruction of the "privileges and immunities" clause of the Fourteenth Amendment at the hands of the Court in the Slaughter-House Cases (1873), or the limitations on the right of Congress to tax following the adoption of the Income Tax Amendment to realize that the ERA would have granted women only those rights which the Court was prepared to see them have.

The difficulties of defining an "intermediate" test and knowing when to apply it are illustrated in Michael M. v. Sonoma County (1981). Five members of the Court upheld a state statutory rape law against the challenge that it punished the male participant to a consensual sex act (in this case a minor) but not his minor female partner. The Court gave "great deference" to California's assertion that the purpose of the law was to prevent teenage pregnancies and agreed that this was certainly a legitimate state purpose. Moreover, punishing just the male was sufficiently related to the purpose of the law because the female was already sufficiently deterred from the act by the fear of pregnancy, and were she to become pregnant and have to deal with the consequences she would be further punished while the male would not.

Justices Brennan, White and Marshall dissented, arguing that while ostensibly applying the same test, the majority had failed to carry the burden of showing that a sex-neutral law punishing both parties to the act would not be as effective a deterrent in preventing pregnancy as one punishing only the male. Justice Stevens dissented separately, pointing out that it was "totally irrational" to exempt from punishment the one most likely to be injured by the dangerous act. In contrast to the Michael M. case, the Court in Kirchberg v. Feenstra (1981) found no important governmental interest was served by a Louisiana law allowing a husband to mortgage without his wife's consent their jointly owned home.

The Military Selective Service Act (MSSA) authorizes the President, by proclamation, to require the registration of "every male citizen" and male resident alien between the ages of 18 and 26. The purpose of the act, of course, is to provide a manpower pool should conscription become necessary, although Congress by statute in 1973 forbade any actual conscription under the act. At the time of the Soviet invasion of Afghanistan President Carter invoked the provisions of the act and asked Congress to allocate the necessary funds and to amend the MSSA to permit the registration of women. After prolonged debate Congress declined to amend the act and allocated only sufficient funds to register males.

In Rostker v. Goldberg (1981) the Supreme Court upheld the registration of males against the claim that by failing to register both sexes the act denied a male registrant the equal protection of the laws. Applying the test of Craig v. Boren (1976), the Court agreed that raising and supporting armies was "an important governmental interest," and that this was an area in which judicial deference to the congressional judgment was at its highest. It noted the extensive debates on the issue and found that Congress, in reaching its decision, had not acted "unthinkingly" or "reflexively and not for any considered reason," which might have suggested a mere response to prejudices about women in the armed forces. "The fact that Congress and the Executive have decided that women should not serve in combat fully justifies Congress in not authorizing their registration, since the purpose of registration is to develop a pool of potential combat troops. . . . The Constitution requires that Congress treat similarly situated persons similarly, not that it engage in gestures of superficial equality."

At the same time that the Court was struggling with an increased number of sex discrimination cases, the existence of the welfare state raised a number of other recurring equal protection problems. Specifically, the Court found itself confronted with equal protection claims alleging discrimination against the poor and discrimination affecting access to education. Some argued that the poor, like blacks, were historically the subjects of the most invidious discrimination and that wealth, therefore, should be treated as a suspect classification. While it is true that the poor have been subjected to some of the cruelest discrimination, wealth, unlike race, is not an immutable characteristic and more important, a capitalist society is one that assumes differential treatment based on wealth as a reward for ability and an incentive to greater productivity. The Court is not on the verge of restructuring the economic basis of the nation.

Nevertheless, when discrimination against the poor, or another group not treated as a suspect class such as aliens, is combined with an adverse effect on an important, although not fundamental, right such as education, the Court has apparently abandoned the casual scrutiny of the rational basis test and opted instead for the intermediate test used in the case below. The Court, in other words, often acts as if it has accepted Justice Marshall's analysis in his dissent in Rodriguez, while rejecting this analysis in the actual opinions it issues.

Plyler v. Doe (1982) challenged a provision of the Texas Education Code that denied free public education to illegal alien children and the Supreme Court found the law invalid. It reviewed both the rational basis test and the strict scrutiny test, then noted that "in addition, we have recognized that certain forms of legislative classification, while not facially invidious, nonetheless give rise to recurring constitutional difficulties; in those limited circumstances we have sought the assurance that the classification reflects a reasoned judgment consistent with the ideal of equal protection by inquiring whether it may fairly be viewed as furthering a substantial interest of the State." After carefully weighing the state's arguments and the effect of the law on the children involved, the Court found it "difficult to understand precisely what the State hopes to achieve by promoting the creation and perpetuation of a subclass of illiterates within our boundaries, surely adding to the problems and costs of unemployment, welfare, and crime. . . . If the State is to deny a discrete group of innocent children the free public education that it offers to other children residing within its borders, that denial must be justified by a showing that it furthers some substantial state interest. No such showing was made here."

One year after the decision in Plyler the Court considered a challenge to another provision of the Texas education law in Martinez v. Bynum (1983). The provision challenged in Martinez denied free public education to any minor, living apart from his natural parents or legal guardian, who resided in the school district for the primary purpose of attending school. While the Court conceded that the law was intended to, and did, discriminate against children of Mexican heritage, many of whom were native born American citizens, it held the law valid as a bona fide residence requirement designed to further the "substantial state interest in assuring that services provided for its residents are enjoyed only by residents." While the Court did not discuss the standard it was applying, the use of the word "substantial" suggests that the intermediate test was used just as it had been in Plyler—although with a different result.

Justice **O'Connor** delivered the opinion of the Court, saying in part:

This case presents the narrow issue of whether a state statute that excludes males from enrolling in a state-supported professional nursing school violates the Equal Protection Clause of the Fourteenth Amendment.

I.

The facts are not in dispute. In 1884, the Mississippi legislature created the Mississippi Industrial Institute and College for the Education of White Girls of the State of Mississippi, now the oldest state-supported all-female college in the United States. The school, known today as Mississippi University (MUW), has from its inception limited its enrollment to women.

In 1971, MUW established a School of Nursing, initially offering a two-year associate degree. Three years later, the school instituted a four-year baccalaureate program in nursing and today also offers a graduate program. The School of Nursing has its own faculty and administers it own criteria for admission.

Respondent, Joe Hogan, is a registered nurse but does not hold a baccalaureate degree in nursing. Since 1974, he has worked as a nursing supervisor in a medical center in Columbus, the city in which MUW is located. In 1979, Hogan applied for admission to the MUW School of Nursing's baccalaureate program. Although he was otherwise qualified, he was denied admission solely because of his sex. School officials informed him that he could audit the courses in which he was interested, but could not enroll for credit. . . .

II.

We begin our analysis aided by several firmly-established principles. Because the challenged policy expressly discriminates among applicants on the basis of gender, it is subject to scrutiny under the Equal Protection Clause. . . . That this statute discriminates against males rather than against females does not exempt it from scrutiny or reduce the standard of review,* . . . Our decisions also establish that the party seeking to uphold a statute that classifies individuals on the basis of their gender must carry the burden of showing an "exceedingly persuasive justification" for the classification. Kirchberg v. Feenstra (1981). . . . The burden is met only by showing at least that the classification serves "important governmental objectives and that the discriminatory means employed" are "substantially related to the achievement of those objectives." . . .**

Although the test for determining the validity of a gender-based classification is straightforward, it must be applied free of fixed notions concerning the roles and abilities of males and females. Care must be taken in ascertaining whether the statutory objective itself reflects archaic and stereotypic notions. Thus, if the statutory objective is to exclude or "protect" members of one gender because they are presumed to suffer from an inherent handicap or to be innately inferior, the objective itself is illegitimate. See Frontiero v. Richardson (1973) (plurality opinion). †

If the State's objective is legitimate and important, we next determine whether the requisite direct, substantial relationship between objective and means is present. The purpose of requiring that close relationship is to assure that the validity of a classification is determined through reasoned analysis rather than through the mechanical application of traditional, often inaccurate, assumptions about the proper roles of men and women. The need for the

---

*Without question, MUW's admission policy worked to Hogan's disadvantage. Although Hogan could have attended classes and received credit in one of Mississippi's state-supported coeducational nursing programs, none of which was located in Columbus, he could attend only by driving a considerable distance from his home. A similarly situated female would not have been required to choose between foregoing credit and bearing that inconvenience. Moreover, since many students enrolled in the School of Nursing hold full-time jobs, Hogan's female colleagues had available an opportunity, not open to Hogan, to obtain credit for additional training. The policy of denying males the right to obtain credit toward a baccalaureate degree thus imposed upon Hogan "a burden he would not bear were he female." Orr v. Orr (1979).

**. . . Our past decisions establish, however, that when a classification expressly discriminates on the basis of gender, the analysis and level of scrutiny applied to determine the validity of the classification do not vary simply because the objective appears acceptable to individual members of the Court. While the validity and importance of the objective may affect the outcome of the analysis, the analysis itself does not change.

Thus, we apply the test previously relied upon by the Court to measure the constitutionality of gender-based discrimination. Because we conclude that the challenged statutory classification is not substantially related to an important objective, we need not decide whether classifications based upon gender are inherently suspect. . . .

†History provides numerous examples of legislative attempts to exclude women from particular areas simply because legislators believed women were less able than men to perform a particular function. In 1872, this Court remained unmoved by Myra Bradwell's argument that the Fourteenth Amendment prohibited a State from classifying her as unfit to practice law simply because she was female. Bradwell v. Illinois (1872). In his concurring opinion, Justice Brady described the reasons underlying the State's decision to determine which positions only men could fill: "It is the prerogative of the legislator to prescribe regulations founded on nature, reason, and experience for the due admission of qualified persons to professions and callings demanding special skill and confidence. This fairly belongs to the police power of the State; and, in my opinion, in view of the peculiar characteristics, destiny, and mission of woman, it is within the province of the legislature to ordain what offices, positions, and callings shall be filled and discharged by men, and shall receive the benefit of those energies and responsibilities, and that decision and firmness which are presumed to predominate in the sterner sex." . . .

requirement is amply revealed by reference to the broad range of statutes already invalidated by this Court, statutes that relied upon the simplistic, outdated assumption that gender could be used as a "proxy for other, more germane bases of classification," Craig v. Boren (1976), to establish a link between objective and classification.

Applying this framework, we now analyze the arguments advanced by the State to justify its refusal to allow males to enroll for credit in MUW's School of Nursing.

III.

A.

The State's primary justification for maintaining the single-sex admissions policy of MUW's School of Nursing is that it compensates for discrimination against women and, therefore, constitutes educational affirmative action. As applied to the School of Nursing, we find the State's argument unpersuasive.

It is readily apparent that a State can evoke a compensatory purpose to justify an otherwise discriminatory classification only if members of the gender benefited by the classification actually suffer a disadvantage related to the classification. . . .

. . . Mississippi has made no showing that women lacked opportunities to obtain training in the field of nursing or to attain positions of leadership in that field when the MUW School of Nursing opened its doors or that women currently are deprived of such opportunities. In fact, in 1970, the year before the School of Nursing's first class enrolled, women earned 94 percent of the nursing baccalaureate degrees conferred in Mississippi and 98.6 percent of the degrees earned nationwide. . . . That year was not an aberration; one decade earlier, women had earned all the nursing degrees conferred in Mississippi and 98.9 percent of the degrees earned nationwide. . . .

Rather than compensate for discriminatory barriers faced by women, MUW's policy of excluding males from admission to the School of Nursing tends to perpetuate the stereotyped view of nursing as an exclusively woman's job. By assuring that Mississippi allots more openings in its state-supported nursing schools to women than it does to men, MUW's admissions policy lends credibility to the old view that women, not men, should become nurses, and makes the assumption that nursing is a field for women a self-fulfilling prophecy. . . .

The policy is invalid also because it fails the second part of the equal protection test, for the State has made no showing that the gender-based classification is substantially and directly related to its proposed compensatory objective. To the contrary, MUW's policy of permitting men to attend classes as auditors fatally undermines its claim that women, at least those in the School of Nursing, are adversely affected by the presence of men.

. The uncontroverted record reveals that admitting men to nursing classes does not affect teaching style, that the presence of men in the classroom would not affect the performance of the female nursing students, and that men in coeducational nursing schools do not dominate the classroom. In sum, the record in this case is flatly inconsistent with the claim that excluding men from the School of Nursing is necessary to reach any of MUW's educational goals.

Thus, considering both the asserted interest and the relationship between the interest and the methods used by the State, we conclude that the State has fallen far short of establishing the "exceedingly persuasive justification" needed to sustain the gender-based classification. Accordingly, we hold that MUW's policy of denying males the right to enroll for credit in its School of Nursing violates the Equal Protection Clause of the Fourteenth Amendment.*

B.

In an additional attempt to justify its exclusion of men from MUW's School of Nursing, the State contends that MUW is the direct beneficiary "of specific congressional legislation which, on its face, permits the institution to exist as it has in the past." The argument is based upon the language of § 901(a) in Title IX of the Education Amendments of 1972, 20 USC § 1681(a) [20 USCS § 1681(a)]. Although § 901(a) prohibits gender discrimination in education programs that receive federal financial assistance, subsection 5 exempts the admissions policies of undergraduate institutions "that traditionally and continually from [their] establishment [have] had a policy of admitting only students of one sex" from the general prohibition. Arguing that Congress enacted Title IX in furtherance of its power to enforce the Fourteenth Amendment, a power granted by § 5 of that Amendment, the State would have us conclude that § 1681(a)(5) is but "a congressional limitation upon the broad prohibitions of the Equal Protection Clause of the Fourteenth Amendment."

The argument requires little comment. Initially, it is far from clear that Congress intended, through § 1681(a)(5), to exempt MUW from any constitutional obligation. Rather, Congress apparently intended, at most, to exempt MUW from the requirements of Title IX.

Even if Congress envisioned a constitutional exemption, the State's argument would fail. Section 5 of the Fourteenth Amendment gives Congress broad power indeed to enforce the command of the Amendment and "to secure to all persons the enjoyment of perfect equality of civil rights and the equal protection of the laws against State denial or invasion. . . ." Ex parte Virginia (1879). Congress' power under § 5 grants Congress no power to restrict, abrogate, or dilute these guarantees." Katzenbach v. Morgan (1966). Although we give deference to congressional decisions and classifications, neither Congress nor a State can validate a law that denies the rights guaranteed by the Fourteenth Amendment. . . .

Chief Justice **Burger,** dissenting.

I agree generally with Justice Powell's dissenting opinion. I write separately, however, to emphasize that the Court's holding today is limited to the context of a professional nursing

---

*Justice Powell's dissent suggests that a second objective is served by the gender-based classification in that Mississippi has elected to provide women a choice of educational environments. Since any gender-based classification provides one class a benefit or choice not available to the other class, however, that argument begs the question. The issue is not whether the benefited class profits from the classification, but whether the State's decision to confer a benefit only upon one class by means of a discriminatory classification is substantially related to achieving a legitimate and substantial goal.

school. Since the Court's opinion relies heavily on its finding that women have traditionally dominated the nursing profession, it suggests that a State might well be justified in maintaining, for example, the option of an all-women's business school or liberal arts program.

Justice **Blackmun** wrote a short dissenting opinion.

Justice **Powell,** with whom Justice **Rehnquist** joins, dissenting, said in part:

The Court's opinion bows deeply to conformity. Left without honor—indeed, held unconstitutional—is an element of diversity that has characterized much of American education and enriched much of American life. The Court in effect holds today that no State now may provide even a single institution of higher learning open only to women students. It gives no heed to the efforts of the State of Mississippi to provide abundant opportunities for young men and young women to attend coeducational institutions, and none to the preferences of the more than 40,000 young women who over the years have evidenced their approval of an all-women's college by choosing Mississippi University for Women (MUW) over seven coeducational universities within the State. The Court decides today that the Equal Protection Clause makes it unlawful for the State to provide women with a traditionally popular and respected choice of educational environment. It does so in a case instituted by one man, who represents no class, and whose primary concern is personal convenience.

. . . His constitutional complaint is based upon a single asserted harm: that he must *travel* to attend the state-supported nursing schools that concededly are available to him. The Court characterizes this injury as one of "inconvenience." This description is fair and accurate, though somewhat embarrassed by the fact that there is, of course, no constitutional right to attend a state-supported university in one's home town. . . .

I.

Coeducation, historically, is a novel educational theory. From grade school through high school, college, and graduate and professional training, much of the nation's population during much of our history has been educated in sexually segregated classrooms. At the college level, for instance, until recently some of the most prestigious colleges and universities—including most of the Ivy League—had long histories of single-sex education. As Harvard, Yale, and Princeton remained all-male colleges well into the second half of this century, the "Seven Sister" institutions established a parallel standard of excellence for women's colleges. Of the Seven Sisters, Mount Holyoke opened as a female seminary in 1837 and was chartered as a college in 1888. Vassar was founded in 1865, Smith and Wellesley in 1875, Radcliffe in 1879, Bryn Mawr in 1885, and Barnard in 1889. Mount Holyoke, Smith, and Wellesley recently have made considered decisions to remain essentially single-sex institutions. . . .

The sexual segregation of students has been a reflection of, rather than an imposition upon, the preference of those subject to the policy. It cannot be disputed, for example, that the highly qualified women attending the leading women's colleges could have earned admission to virtually any college of their choice. Women attending such colleges have chosen to be there, usually expressing a preference for the special benefits of single-sex institutions. Similar decisions were made by the colleges that elected to remain open to women only.

The arguable benefits of single-sex colleges also continue to be recognized by students of higher education. The Carnegie Commission on Higher Education has reported that it "favor[s] the continuation of colleges for women. They provide an element of diversity . . . and [an environment in which women] generally . . . speak up more in their classes, . . . hold more positions of leadership on campus, . . . and have more role models and mentors among women teachers and administrators."* . . .

Despite the continuing expressions that single-sex institutions may offer singular advantages to their students, there is no doubt that coeducational institutions are far more numerous. But their numerical predominance does not establish—in any sense properly cognizable by a court—that individual preferences for single-sex education are misguided or illegitimate, or that a State may not provide its citizens with a choice.

II.

The issue in this case is whether a State transgresses the Constitution when—within the context of a public system that offers a diverse range of campuses, curricula, and educational alternatives—it seeks to accommodate the legitimate personal preferences of those desiring the advantages of an all-women's college. In my view, the Court errs seriously by assuming—without argument or discussion—that the equal protection standard generally applicable to sex discrimination is appropriate here. That standard was designed to free women from "archaic and overbroad generalizations. . . ." Schlesinger v. Ballard, (1975). In no previous case have we applied it to invalidate state efforts to *expand* women's choices. Nor are there prior sex discrimination decisions by this Court in which a male plaintiff, as in this case, had the choice of an equal benefit.

The cases cited by the Court therefore do not control the issue now before us. In most of them women were given no opportunity for the same benefit as men. Cases involving male plaintiffs are equally inapplicable. In Craig v. Boren, (1976), a male under 21 was not permitted to buy beer anywhere in the State, and women were afforded no choice as to whether they would accept the "statistically measured but loose-fitting generalities concerning the drinking tendencies of aggregate groups." . . .

By applying heightened equal protection analysis to this case, the Court frustrates the

---

* In this Court the benefits of single-sex education have been asserted by the students and alumnae of MUW. One would expect the Court to regard their views as directly relevant to this case: "[I]n the aspect of life known as courtship or mate-pairing, the American female remains in the old role of the pursued sex, expected to adorn and groom herself to attract the male. Without comment on the equities of this social arrangement, it remains a sociological fact." An institution of collegiate higher learning maintained exclusively for women is uniquely able to provide the education atmosphere in which some, but not all, women can best attain maximum learning potential. It can serve to overcome the historic repression of the past and can orient a woman to function and achieve in the still male-dominated economy. It can free its students of the burden of playing the mating game while attending classes, thus giving academic rather than sexual emphasis. Consequently, many such institutions flourish and their graduates make significant contributions to the arts, professions and business." Brief for Mississippi University for Women Alumnae Assn. as Amicus Curiae.

liberating spirit of the Equal Protection Clause. It forbids the States from providing women with an opportunity to choose the type of university they prefer. And yet it is these women whom the Court regards as the *victims* of an illegal, stereotyped perception of the role of women in our society. The Court reasons this way in a case in which no woman has complained, and the only complainant is a man who advances no claims on behalf of anyone else. His claim, it should be recalled, is not that he is being denied a substantive educational opportunity, or even the right to attend an all-male or a coeducational college. It is *only* that the colleges open to him are located at inconvenient distances.

III.

The Court views this case as presenting a serious equal protection claim of sex discrimination. I do not and I would sustain Mississippi's right to continue MUW on a rational basis analysis. But I need not apply this "lowest tier" of scrutiny. I can accept for present purposes the standard applied by the Court: that there is a gender-based distinction that must serve an important governmental objective by means that are substantially related to its achievement. E.g., Wengler v. Druggists Mutual Ins. Co. (1980). The record in this case reflects that MUW has a historic position in the State's educational system dating back to 1884. More than 2,000 women presently evidence their preference for MUW by having enrolled there. The choice is one that discriminates invidiously against no one. And the State's purpose in preserving that choice is legitimate and substantial. Generations of our finest minds, both among educators and students, have believed that single-sex college-level institutions afford distinctive benefits. There are many persons, of course, who have different views. But simply because there are these differences is no reason— certainly none of constitutional dimension—to conclude that no substantial state interest is served when such a choice is made available.

In arguing to the contrary, the Court suggests that the MUW is so operated as to "perpetuate the stereotyped view of nursing as an exclusively women's job." But as the Court itself acknowledges, MUW's School of Nursing was not created until 1971—about 90 years after the single-sex campus itself was founded. This hardly supports a link between nursing as a woman's profession and MUW's single-sex admission policy. Indeed, MUW's School of Nursing was not instituted until more than a decade *after* a separate School of Nursing was established at the coeducational University of Mississippi at Jackson. The School of Nursing makes up only one part—a relatively small part—of MUW's diverse modern university campus and curriculum. The other departments on the MUW campus offer a typical range of degrees and a typical range of subjects. There is no indication that women suffer fewer opportunities at other Mississippi state campuses because of MUW's admission policy.

In sum, the practice of voluntarily chosen single-sex education is an honored tradition in our country, even if it now rarely exists in state colleges and universities. Mississippi's accommodation of such student choices is legitimate because it is completely consensual and is important because it permits students to decide for themselves the type of college education they think will benefit them most. Finally, Mississippi's policy is substantially related to its long-respected objective. . . .

Appendix

Constitution
of the United States

WE THE PEOPLE of the United States, in order to form a more perfect union, establish justice, insure domestic tranquillity, provide for the common defense, promote the general welfare, and secure the blessings of liberty to ourselves and our posterity, do ordain and establish this Constitution for the United States of America.

ARTICLE I

SECTION 1. All legislative powers herein granted shall be vested in a Congress of the United States, which shall consist of a Senate and House of Representatives.

SECTION 2. (1) The House of Representatives shall be composed of members chosen every second year by the people of the several States, and the electors in each State shall have the qualifications requisite for electors of the most numerous branch of the State legislature.

(2) No person shall be a Representative who shall not have attained to the age of twenty-five years, and been seven years a citizen of the United States, and who shall not, when elected, be an inhabitant of that State in which he shall be chosen.

(3) Representatives and direct taxes¹ shall be apportioned among the several States which may be included within this Union, according to their respective numbers, which shall be determined by adding to the whole number of free persons, including those bound to service for a term of years, and excluding Indians not taxed, three fifths of all other persons.² The actual enumeration shall be made within three years after the first meeting of the Congress of the United States, and within every subsequent term of ten years, in such manner as they shall by law direct. The number of Representatives shall not exceed one for every thirty thousand, but each State shall have at least one Representative; and until such enumeration shall be made, the State of New Hampshire shall be entitled to choose three, Massachusetts eight, Rhode Island and Providence Plantations one, Connecticut five, New York six, New Jersey four, Pennsylvania eight, Delaware one, Maryland six, Virginia ten, North Carolina five, South Carolina five, and Georgia three.

(4) When vacancies happen in the representation from any State, the executive authority thereof shall issue writs of election to fill such vacancies.

(5) The House of Representatives shall choose their Speaker and other officers; and shall have the sole power of impeachment.

SECTION 3. (1) The Senate of the United States shall be composed of two Senators from each State, chosen by the Legislature thereof,³ for six years; and each Senator shall have one vote.

---

¹Modified as to income taxes by the 16th Amendment.
²Replaced by the 14th Amendment.
³Modified by the 17th Amendment.

414

(2) Immediately after they shall be assembled in consequence of the first election, they shall be divided as equally as may be into three classes. The seats of the Senators of the first class shall be vacated at the expiration of the second year, of the second class at the expiration of the fourth year, and of the third class at the expiration of the sixth year, so that one third may be chosen every second year; and if vacancies happen by resignation, or otherwise, during the recess of the legislature of any State, the executive thereof may make temporary appointments until the next meeting of the legislature, which[3] shall then fill such vacancies.

(3) No person shall be a Senator who shall not have attained to the age of thirty years, and been nine years a citizen of the United States, and who shall not, when elected, be an inhabitant of that State for which he shall be chosen.

(4) The Vice President of the United States shall be president of the Senate, but shall have no vote, unless they be equally divided.

(5) The Senate shall choose their other officers, and also a president pro tempore, in the absence of the Vice President, or when he shall exercise the office of President of the United States.

(6) The Senate shall have the sole power to try all impeachments. When sitting for that purpose, they shall be on oath or affirmation. When the President of the United States is tried, the Chief Justice shall preside: and no person shall be convicted without the concurrence of two-thirds of the members present.

(7) Judgment in cases of impeachment shall not extend further than to removal from office, and disqualification to hold and enjoy any office of honor, trust or profit under the United States: but the party convicted shall nevertheless be liable and subject to indictment, trial, judgment and punishment, according to law.

SECTION 4. (1) The times, places and manner of holding elections for Senators and Representatives, shall be prescribed in each State by the legislature thereof; but the Congress may at any time by law make or alter such regulations, except as to the places of choosing Senators.

(2) The Congress shall assemble at least once in every year, and such meeting shall be on the first Monday in December, unless they shall by law appoint a different day.

SECTION 5. (1) Each House shall be the judge of the elections, returns and qualifications of its own members, and a majority of each shall constitute a quorum to do business; but a smaller number may adjourn from day to day, and may be authorized to compel the attendance of absent members, in such manner, and under such penalties as each House may provide.

(2) Each House may determine the rules of its proceedings, punish its members for disorderly behavior, and, with the concurrence of two thirds, expel a member.

(3) Each House shall keep a journal of its proceedings, and from time to time publish the same, excepting such parts as may in their judgement require secrecy; and the yeas and nays of the members of either House on any question shall, at the desire of one fifth of those present, be entered on the journal.

(4) Neither House, during the session of Congress, shall, without the consent of the other, adjourn for more than three days, nor to any other place than that in which the two Houses shall be sitting.

SECTION 6. (1) The Senators and Representatives shall receive a compensation for their services, to be ascertained by law, and paid out of the Treasury of the United States. They shall in all cases, except treason, felony and breach of the peace, be privileged from arrest during their attendance at the session of their respective Houses, and in going to and returning from the same; and for any speech or debate in either House, they shall not be questioned in any other place.

(2) No Senator or Representative shall, during the time for which he was elected, be appointed to any civil office under the authority of the United States, which shall have been created, or the emoluments whereof shall have been increased during such time; and no person holding any office under the United States, shall be a member of either House during his continuance in office.

SECTION 7. (1) All bills for raising revenue shall originate in the House of Representatives; but the Senate may propose or concur with amendments as on other bills.

(2) Every bill which shall have passed the House of Representatives and the Senate, shall, before it become a law, be presented to the President of the United States; if he approve he shall sign it, but if not he shall return it, with his objections to that House in which it shall have originated, who shall enter the objections at large on their journal, and proceed to reconsider it. If after such reconsideration two thirds of that House shall agree to pass the bill, it shall be sent, together with the objections, to the other House, by which it shall likewise be reconsidered, and if approved by two thirds of that House, it shall become a law. But in all such cases the votes of both Houses shall be determined by yeas and nays, and the names of the persons voting for and against the bill shall be entered on the journal of each House respectively. If any bill shall not be returned by the President within ten days (Sundays excepted) after it shall have been presented to him, the same shall be a law, in like manner as if he had signed it, unless the Congress by their adjournment prevent its return, in which case it shall not be a law.

(3) Every order, resolution, or vote to which the concurrence of the Senate and House of Representatives may be necessary (except on a question of adjournment) shall be presented to the President of the United States; and before the same shall take effect, shall be approved by him, or being disapproved by him, shall be repassed by two thirds of the Senate and House of Representatives, according to the rules and limitations prescribed in the case of a bill.

SECTION 8. (1) The Congress shall have power to lay and collect taxes, duties, imposts and excises, to pay the debts and provide for the common defense and general welfare of the United States; but all duties, imposts and excises shall be uniform throughout the United States;

(2) To borrow money on the credit of the United States.

(3) To regulate commerce with foreign nations, and among the several States, and with the Indian tribes;

(4) To establish an uniform rule of naturalization, and uniform laws on the subject of bankruptcies throughout the United States;

(5) To coin money, regulate the value thereof, and of foreign coin, and fix the standard of weights and measures;

(6) To provide for the punishment of counterfeiting the securities and current coin of the United States;

(7) To establish post offices and post roads;

(8) To promote the progress of science and useful arts, by securing for limited times to authors and inventors the exclusive right to their respective writings and discoveries;

(9) To constitute tribunals inferior to the Supreme Court;

(10) To define and punish piracies and felonies committed on the high seas, and offenses against the law of nations;

(11) To declare war, grant letters of marque and reprisal, and make rules concerning captures on land and water;

(12) To raise and support armies, but no appropriation of money to that use shall be for a longer term than two years;

(13) To provide and maintain a navy;

(14) To make rules for the government and regulation of the land and naval forces;

(15) To provide for calling forth the militia to execute the laws of the Union, suppress insurrections and repel invasions;

(16) To provide for organizing, arming, and disciplining the militia, and for governing such part of them as may be employed in the service of the United States,

reserving to the States respectively, the appointment of the officers, and the authority of training the militia according to the discipline prescribed by Congress;

(17) To exercise exclusive legislation in all cases whatsoever, over such district (not exceeding ten miles square) as may, by cession of particular States, and the acceptance of Congress, become the seat of the government of the United States,[4] and to exercise like authority over all places purchased by the consent of the legislature of the State in which the same shall be, for the erection of forts, magazines, arsenals, dockyards, and other needful buildings; and

(18) To make all laws which shall be necessary and proper for carrying into execution the foregoing powers, and all other powers vested by this Constitution in the government of the United States, or in any department or officer thereof.

SECTION 9. (1) The migration or importation of such persons as any of the States now existing shall think proper to admit, shall not be prohibited by the Congress prior to the year one thousand eight hundred and eight, but a tax or duty may be imposed on such importation, not exceeding ten dollars for each person.

(2) The privilege of the writ of habeas corpus shall not be suspended, unless when in cases of rebellion or invasion the public safety may require it.

(3) No bill of attainder or ex post facto law shall be passed.

(4) No capitation, or other direct, tax shall be laid, unless in proportion to the census or enumeration herein before directed to be taken.[5]

(5) No tax or duty shall be laid on articles exported from any State.

(6) No preference shall be given by any regulation of commerce or revenue to the ports of one State over those of another: nor shall vessels bound to, or from, one State, be obliged to enter, clear, or pay duties in another.

(7) No money shall be drawn from the Treasury, but in consequence of appropriations made by law; and a regular statement and account of the receipts and expenditures of all public money shall be published from time to time.

(8) No title of nobility shall be granted by the United States: and no person holding any office of profit or trust under them, shall, without the consent of the Congress, accept of any present, emolument, office, or title, of any kind whatever, from any king, prince, or foreign State.

---

[4]Modified by the 23rd Amendment.

[5]Modified by the 16th Amendment.

SECTION 10. (1) No State shall enter into any treaty, alliance, or confederation; grant letters of marque and reprisal; coin money; emit bills of credit; make anything but gold and silver coin a tender in payment of debts; pass any bill of attainder, ex post facto law, or law impairing the obligation of contracts, or grant any title of nobility.

(2) No State shall, without the consent of the Congress, lay any imposts or duties on imports or exports, except what may be absolutely necessary for executing its inspection laws; and the net produce of all duties and imposts, laid by any State on imports or exports, shall be for the use of the Treasury of the United States; and all such laws shall be subject to the revision and control of the Congress.

(3) No State shall, without the consent of Congress, lay any duty of tonnage, keep troops, or ships of war in time of peace, enter into any agreement or compact with another State, or with a foreign power, or engage in war, unless actually invaded, or in such imminent danger as will not admit of delay.

ARTICLE II

SECTION 1. (1) The executive power shall be vested in a President of the United States of America. He shall hold his office during the term of four years,[6] and, together with the Vice President, chosen for the same term, be elected, as follows:

(2) Each State shall appoint, in such manner as the legislature thereof may direct, a number of electors, equal to the whole number of Senators and Representatives to which the State may be entitled in the Congress: but no Senator or Representative, or person holding an office of trust or profit under the United States, shall be appointed an elector.

The electors[7] shall meet in their respective States, and vote by ballot for two persons, of whom one at least shall not be an inhabitant of the same State with themselves. And they shall make a list of all the persons voted for, and of the number of votes for each; which list they shall sign and certify, and transmit sealed to the seat of the government of the United States, directed to the president of the Senate. The president of the Senate shall, in the presence of the Senate and House of Representatives, open all the certificates, and the votes shall then be counted. The person having the greatest number of votes shall be the President, if such number be a majority of the whole number of electors appointed; and if there be more than one who have such majority, and have an equal number of votes, then the House of Representatives shall immediately choose by ballot one of them for President; and if no person have a majority, then from the five highest on the list the said House

shall in like manner choose the President. But in choosing the President, the votes shall be taken by States, the representation from each State having one vote; a quorum for this purpose shall consist of a member or members from two thirds of the States, and a majority of all the States shall be necessary to a choice. In every case, after the choice of the President, the person having the greatest number of votes of the electors shall be the Vice President. But if there should remain two or more who have equal votes, the Senate shall choose from them by ballot the Vice President.

(3) The Congress may determine the time of choosing the electors, and the day on which they shall give their votes; which day shall be the same throughout the United States.

(4) No person except a natural born citizen, or a citizen of the United States, at the time of the adoption of this Constitution, shall be eligible to the office of President; neither shall any person be eligible to that office who shall not have attained to the age of thirty five years, and been fourteen years a resident within the United States.

(5) In the case of the removal of the President from office, or of his death, resignation, or inability to discharge the powers and duties of the said office, the same shall devolve on the Vice President, and the Congress may by law provide for the case of removal, death, resignation, or inability, both of the President and Vice President, declaring what officer shall then act as President, and such officer shall act accordingly, until the disability be removed, or a President shall be elected.[8]

(6) The President shall, at stated times, receive for his services, a compensation, which shall neither be increased nor diminished during the period for which he shall have been elected, and he shall not receive within that period any other emolument from the United States, or any of them.

(7) Before he enter on the execution of his office, he shall take the following oath or affirmation:—"I do solemnly swear (or affirm) that I will faithfully execute the office of President of the United States, and will to the best of my ability, preserve, protect and defend the Constitution of the United States."

SECTION 2. (1) The President shall be commander in chief of the army and navy of the United States, and of the militia of the several States, when called into the actual service of the United States; he may require the opinion, in writing, of the principal officer in each of the executive departments, upon any subject relating to the duties of their respective offices, and he shall have power to grant reprieves and pardons for offenses against the United States, except in cases of impeachment.

---

[6]Modified by the 22nd Amendment.

[7]Replaced in 1804 by the 12th Amendment.

---

[8]Replaced by the 25th Amendment.

(2) He shall have power, by and with the advice and consent of the Senate, to make treaties, provided two thirds of the Senators present concur; and he shall nominate, and by and with the advice and consent of the Senate, shall appoint ambassadors, other public ministers and consuls, judges of the Supreme Court, and all other officers of the United States, whose appointments are not herein otherwise provided for, and which shall be established by law: but the Congress may by law vest the appointment of such inferior officers, as they think proper, in the President alone, in the courts of law, or in the heads of departments.

(3) The President shall have power to fill up all vacancies that may happen during the recess of the Senate, by granting commissions which shall expire at the end of their next session.

SECTION 3. He shall from time to time give to the Congress information of the state of the Union, and recommend to their consideration such measures as he shall judge necessary and expedient; he may, on extraordinary occasions, convene both Houses, or either of them, and in case of disagreement between them, with respect to the time of adjournment, he may adjourn them to such time as he shall think proper; he shall receive ambassadors and other public ministers; he shall take care that the laws be faithfully executed, and shall commission all the officers of the United States.

SECTION 4. The President, Vice President and all civil officers of the United States, shall be removed from office on impeachment for, and conviction of, treason, bribery, or other high crimes and misdemeanors

ARTICLE III

SECTION 1. The judicial power of the United States, shall be vested in one Supreme Court, and in such inferior courts as the Congress may from time to time ordain and establish. The judges, both of the Supreme and inferior courts, shall hold their offices during good behavior, and shall, at stated times, receive for their services, a compensation, which shall not be diminished during their continuance in office.

SECTION 2. (1) The judicial power shall extend to all cases, in law and equity, arising under this Constitution, the laws of the United States, and treaties made, or which shall be made, under their authority;—to all cases affecting ambassadors, other public ministers and consuls;—to all cases of admiralty and maritime jurisdiction;—to controversies to which the United States shall be a party;—to controversies between two or more States;—between a State and citizens of another State;[2]—between citizens of different States;—between citizens of the same State

---

[2]Restricted by the 11th Amendment.

claiming lands under grants of different States, and between a State, or the citizens thereof, and foreign States, citizens or subjects.

(2) In all cases affecting ambassadors, other public ministers and consuls, and those in which a State shall be party, the Supreme Court shall have original jurisdiction. In all the other cases before mentioned, the Supreme Court shall have appellate jurisdiction, both as to law and fact, with such exceptions, and under such regulations as the Congress shall make.

(3) The trial of all crimes, except in cases of impeachment, shall be by jury; and such trial shall be held in the State where the said crimes shall have been committed; but when not committed within any State, the trial shall be at such place or places as the Congress may by law have directed.

SECTION 3. (1) Treason against the United States, shall consist only in levying war against them, or in adhering to their enemies, giving them aid and comfort. No person shall be convicted of treason unless on the testimony of two witnesses to the same overt act, or on confession in open court.

(2) The Congress shall have power to declare the punishment of treason, but no attainder of treason shall work corruption of blood, or forfeiture except during the life of the person attainted.

ARTICLE IV

SECTION 1. Full faith and credit shall be given in each State to the public acts, records, and judicial proceedings of every other State. And the Congress may by general laws prescribe the manner in which such acts, records and proceedings shall be proved, and the effect thereof.

SECTION 2. (1) The citizens of each State shall be entitled to all privileges and immunities of citizens in the several States.

(2) A person charged in any State with treason, felony, or other crime, who shall flee from justice, and be found in another State, shall on demand of the executive authority of the State from which he fled, be delivered up, to be removed to the State having jurisdiction of the crime.

(3) No person held to service or labor in one State, under the laws thereof, escaping into another, shall, in consequence of any law or regulation therein, be discharged from such service or labor, but shall be delivered up on claim of the party to whom such service or labor may be due.

SECTION 3. (1) New States may be admitted by the Congress into this Union; but no new State shall be formed or erected within the jurisdiction of any other State; nor any State be formed by the junction of two or more States, or parts of States, without the consent of the legislatures of the States concerned as well as of the Congress.

(2) The Congress shall have power to dispose of and make all needful rules and regulations respecting the territory or other property belonging to the United States; and nothing in this Constitution shall be so construed as to prejudice any claims of the United States, or of any particular State.

SECTION 4. The United States shall guarantee to every State in this Union a republican form of government, and shall protect each of them against invasion; and on application of the legislature, or of the executive (when the legislature cannot be convened) against domestic violence.

ARTICLE V

The Congress, whenever two thirds of both Houses shall deem it necessary, shall propose amendments to this Constitution, or, on the application of the legislatures of two thirds of the several States, shall call a convention for proposing amendments, which, in either case, shall be valid to all intents and purposes, as part of this Constitution, when ratified by the legislatures of three fourths of the several States, or by conventions in three fourths thereof, as the one or the other mode of ratification may be proposed by the Congress; Provided that no amendment which may be made prior to the year one thousand eight hundred and eight shall in any manner affect the first and fourth clauses in the ninth section of the first article; and that no State, without its consent, shall be deprived of its equal suffrage in the Senate.

ARTICLE VI

SECTION 1. All debts contracted and engagements entered into, before the adoption of this Constitution, shall be as valid against the United States under this Constitution, as under the Confederation.

SECTION 2. This Constitution, and the laws of the United States which shall be made in pursuance thereof; and all treaties made, or which shall be made, under the authority of the United States, shall be the supreme law of the land; and the judges in every State shall be bound thereby, anything in the constitution or laws of any State to the contrary notwithstanding.

SECTION 3. The Senators and Representatives before mentioned, and the members of the several State legislatures, and all executive and judicial officers, both of the United States and of the several States, shall be bound by oath or affirmation to support this Constitution; but no religious test shall ever be required as a qualification to any office or public trust under the United States.

ARTICLE VII

The ratification of the conventions of nine States, shall be sufficient for the establishment of this Constitution between the States so ratifying the same.

done in Convention by the unanimous consent of the States present the seventeenth day of September in the year of our Lord one thousand seven hundred and eighty-seven, and of the independence of the United States of America the twelfth. In witness whereof we have hereunto subscribed our names.
Go Washington—
Presidt. and Deputy from Virginia

Articles in addition to and amendment of the Constitution of the United States of America, proposed by Congress, and ratified by the legislatures of the several States, pursuant to the fifth article of the original Constitution.

ARTICLE I[10]

Congress shall make no law respecting an establishment of religion, or prohibiting the free exercise thereof; or abridging the freedom of speech, or of the press; or the right of the people peaceably to assemble, and to petition the government for a redress of grievances.

ARTICLE II

A well regulated militia, being necessary to the security of a free State, the right of the people to keep and bear arms, shall not be infringed.

ARTICLE III

No soldier shall, in time of peace be quartered in any house, without the consent of the owner, nor in time of war, but in a manner to be prescribed by law.

ARTICLE IV

The right of the people to be secure in their persons, houses, papers, and effects, against unreasonable searches and seizures, shall not be violated, and no warrants shall issue, but upon probable cause, supported by oath or affirmation, and particularly describing the place to be searched, and the persons or things to be seized.

ARTICLE V

No person shall be held to answer for a capital, or otherwise infamous crime, unless on a presentment or indictment of a grand jury, except in cases arising in the land or naval forces, or in the militia, when in actual service in time of war or public danger; nor shall any person be subject for the same offense to be twice put in jeopardy of life or limb; nor shall be compelled in any criminal case to be a witness against himself, nor be deprived of life, liberty, or property, without due process of law; nor shall private property be taken for public use, without just compensation.

---

[10]The first ten Amendments were adopted in 1791.

ARTICLE VI

In all criminal prosecutions the accused shall enjoy the right to a speedy and public trial, by an impartial jury of the State and district wherein the crime shall have been committed, which district shall have been previously ascertained by law, and to be informed of the nature and cause of the accusation; to be confronted with the witnesses against him; to have compulsory process for obtaining witnesses in his favor, and to have the assistance of counsel for his defense.

ARTICLE VII

In suits at common law, where the value in controversy shall exceed twenty dollars, the right of trial by jury shall be preserved, and no fact tried by a jury shall be otherwise reexamined in any court of the United States, than according to the rules of the common law.

ARTICLE VIII

Excessive bail shall not be required, nor excessive fines imposed, nor cruel and unusual punishments inflicted.

ARTICLE IX

The enumeration in the Constitution, of certain rights, shall not be construed to deny or disparage others retained by the people.

ARTICLE X

The powers not delegated to the United States by the Constitution, nor prohibited by it to the States, are reserved to the States respectively, or to the people.

ARTICLE XI[11]

The judicial power of the United States shall not be construed to extend to any suit in law or equity, commenced or prosecuted against one of the United States by citizens of another State, or by citizens or subjects of any foreign State.

ARTICLE XII[12]

The electors shall meet in their respective States and vote by ballot for President and Vice-President, one of whom, at least, shall not be an inhabitant of the same State with themselves; they shall name in their ballots the person voted for as President, and in distinct ballots the person voted for as Vice-President, and they shall make distinct lists of all persons voted for as President, and of all persons voted for as Vice-President, and of the number of votes for each, which lists they shall sign and certify,

and transmit sealed to the seat of the government of the United States, directed to the president of the Senate;—The president of the Senate shall, in the presence of the Senate and House of Representatives, open all the certificates and the votes shall then be counted;—The person having the greatest number of votes for President, shall be the President, if such number be a majority of the whole number of electors appointed; and if no person have such majority, then from the persons having the highest numbers not exceeding three on the list of those voted for as President, the House of Representatives shall choose immediately, by ballot, the President. But in choosing the President, the votes shall be taken by States, the representation from each State having one vote; a quorum for this purpose shall consist of a member or members from two thirds of the States, and a majority of all the States shall be necessary to a choice. And if the House of Representatives shall not choose a President whenever the right of choice shall devolve upon them, before the fourth day of March next following, then the Vice-President shall act as President, as in the case of the death or other constitutional disability of the President.—The person having the greatest number of votes as Vice-President, shall be the Vice-President, if such number be a majority of the whole number of electors appointed, and if no person have a majority, then from the two highest numbers on the list, the Senate shall choose the Vice-President; a quorum for the purpose shall consist of two thirds of the whole number of Senators, and a majority of the whole number shall be necessary to a choice. But no person constitutionally ineligible to the office of President shall be eligible to that of Vice-President of the United States.

ARTICLE XIII[13]

SECTION 1. Neither slavery nor involuntary servitude, except as a punishment for crime whereof the party shall have been duly convicted, shall exist within the United States, or any place subject to their jurisdiction.

SECTION 2. Congress shall have power to enforce this article by appropriate legislation.

ARTICLE XIV[14]

SECTION 1. All persons born or naturalized in the United States, and subject to the jurisdiction thereof, are citizens of the United States and of the State wherein they reside. No State shall make or enforce any law which shall abridge the privileges or immunities of citizens of the United States; nor shall any State deprive any person of life, liberty, or prop-

[11]Ratified in 1795; proclaimed in 1798.

[12]Adopted in 1804.

[13]Adopted in 1865.

[14]Adopted in 1868.

erty, without due process of law; nor deny to any person within its jurisdiction the equal protection of the laws.

SECTION 2. Representatives shall be apportioned among the several States according to their respective numbers, counting the whole number of persons in each State, excluding Indians not taxed. But when the right to vote at any election for the choice of electors for President and Vice President of the United States, Representatives in Congress, the executive and judicial offices of a State, or the members of the legislature thereof, is denied to any of the male inhabitants of such State, being twentyone years of age, and citizens of the United States, or in any way abridged, except for participation in rebellion, or other crime, the basis of representation therein shall be reduced in the proportion which the number of such male citizens shall bear to the whole number of male citizens twentyone years of age in such State.

SECTION 3. No person shall be a Senator or Representative in Congress, or elector of President and Vice President, or hold any office, civil or military, under the United States, or under any State, who, having previously taken an oath, as a member of Congress, or as an officer of the United States, or as a member of any State legislature, or as an executive or judicial officer of any State, to support the Constitution of the United States, shall have engaged in insurrection or rebellion against the same, or given aid or comfort to the enemies thereof. But Congress may by a vote of two thirds of each House, remove such disability.

SECTION 4. The validity of the public debt of the United States, authorized by law, including debts incurred for payment of pensions and bounties for services in suppressing insurrection or rebellion, shall not be questioned. But neither the United States nor any State shall assume or pay any debt or obligation incurred in aid of insurrection or rebellion against the United States, or any claim for the loss or emancipation of any slave; but all such debts, obligations and claims shall be held illegal and void.

SECTION 5. The Congress shall have power to enforce, by appropriate legislation, the provisions of this article.

ARTICLE XV[15]

SECTION 1. The right of citizens of the United States to vote shall not be denied or abridged by the United States or by any State on account of race, color, or previous condition of servitude.

SECTION 2. The Congress shall have power to enforce this article by appropriate legislation.

ARTICLE XVI[16]

The Congress shall have power to lay and collect taxes on incomes, from whatever source derived,

without apportionment among the several States, and without regard to census or enumeration.

ARTICLE XVII

The Senate of the United States shall be composed of two Senators from each State, elected by the people thereof, for six years; and each Senator shall have one vote. The electors in each State shall have the qualifications requisite for electors of the most numerous branch of the State legislatures.

When vacancies happen in the representation of any State in the Senate, the executive authority of such State shall issue writs of election to fill such vacancies: *Provided,* That the legislature of any State may empower the executive thereof to make temporary appointments until the people fill the vacancies by election as the legislature may direct.

This amendment shall not be so construed as to affect the election or term of any Senator chosen before it becomes valid as part of the Constitution.

ARTICLE XVIII[17]

SECTION 1. After one year from the ratification of this article the manufacture, sale, or transportation of intoxicating liquors within, the importation thereof into, or the exportation thereof from the United States and all territory subject to the jurisdiction thereof for beverage purposes is hereby prohibited.

SECTION 2. The Congress and the several States shall have concurrent power to enforce this article by appropriate legislation.

SECTION 3. This article shall be inoperative unless it shall have been ratified as an amendment to the Constitution by the legislatures of the several States, as provided in the Constitution, within seven years from the date of the submission hereof to the States by the Congress.

ARTICLE XIX[18]

The right of citizens of the United States to vote shall not be denied or abridged by the United States or by any State on account of sex.

The Congress shall have power to enforce this article by appropriate legislation.

ARTICLE XX[19]

SECTION 1. The terms of the President and Vice President shall end at noon on the 20th day of Janu-

---

[15]Adopted in 1870.

[16]Adopted in 1913.

[17]Adopted in 1919. Repealed by Article XXI.

[18]Adopted in 1920.

[19]Adopted in 1933.

ary, and the terms of Senators and Representatives at noon on the 3rd day of January, of the years in which such terms would have ended if this article had not been ratified; and the terms of their successors shall then begin.

SECTION 2. The Congress shall assemble at least once in every year, and such meeting shall begin at noon on the 3rd day of January, unless they shall by law appoint a different day.

SECTION 3. If, at the time fixed for the beginning of the term of the President, the President elect shall have died, the Vice President elect shall become President. If a President shall not have been chosen before the time fixed for the beginning of his term, or if the President elect shall have failed to qualify, then the Vice President elect shall act as President until a President shall have qualified; and the Congress may by law provide for the case wherein neither a President elect nor a Vice President elect shall have qualified, declaring who shall then act as President, or the manner in which one who is to act shall be selected, and such person shall act accordingly until a President or Vice President shall have qualified.

SECTION 4. The Congress may by law provide for the case of the death of any of the persons from whom the House of Representatives may choose a President whenever the right of choice shall have devolved upon them, and for the case of the death of any of the persons from whom the Senate may choose a Vice President whenever the right of choice shall have devolved upon them.

SECTION 5. Sections 1 and 2 shall take effect on the 15th day of October following the ratification of this article.

SECTION 6. This article shall be inoperative unless it shall have been ratified as an amendment to the Constitution by the legislatures of three-fourths of the several States within seven years from the date of its submission.

ARTICLE XXI[20]

SECTION 1. The eighteenth article of amendment to the Constitution of the United States is hereby repealed.

SECTION 2. The transportation or importation into any State, Territory or Possession of the United States for delivery or use therein of intoxicating liquors in violation of the laws thereof is hereby prohibited.

SECTION 3. This article shall be inoperative unless it shall have been ratified as an amendment to the Constitution by conventions in the several States, as provided in the Constitution, within seven years from the date of submission hereof to the States by the Congress.

ARTICLE XXII[21]

SECTION 1. No person shall be elected to the office of the President more than twice, and no person who has held the office of President, or acted as President for more than two years of a term to which some other person was elected President shall be elected to the office of the President more than once. But this Article shall not apply to any person holding the office of President when this Article was proposed by the Congress, and shall not prevent any person who may be holding the office of President, or acting as President, during the term within which this Article becomes operative from holding the office of President or acting as President during the remainder of such term.

SECTION 2. This Article shall be inoperative unless it shall have been ratified as an amendment to the Constitution by the legislatures of three-fourths of the several States within seven years from the date of its submission to the States by the Congress.

ARTICLE XXIII[22]

SECTION 1. The District constituting the seat of Government of the United States shall appoint in such manner as the Congress may direct:

A number of electors of President and Vice-President equal to the whole number of Senators and Representatives in Congress to which the District would be entitled if it were a State, but in no event more than the least populous state; they shall be in addition to those appointed by the states, but they shall be considered, for the purposes of the election of President and Vice-President, to be electors appointed by a state; and they shall meet in the District and perform such duties as provided by the twelfth article of amendment.

SECTION 2. The Congress shall have power to enforce this article by appropriate legislation.

ARTICLE XXIV[23]

SECTION 1. The right of citizens of the United States to vote in any primary or other election for President or Vice-President, for electors for President or Vice-President, or for Senator or Representative in Congress, shall not be denied or abridged by the United States or any state by reason of failure to pay any poll tax or other tax.

SECTION 2. The Congress shall have power to enforce this article by appropriate legislation.

---

[20]Adopted in 1933.
[21]Adopted in 1951.
[22]Adopted in 1961.
[23]Adopted in 1964.

ARTICLE XXV[24]

SECTION 1. In case of the removal of the President from office or his death or resignation, the Vice President shall become President.

SECTION 2. Whenever there is a vacancy in the office of the Vice President, the President shall nominate a Vice President who shall take the office upon confirmation by a majority vote of both houses of Congress.

SECTION 3. Whenever the President transmits to the President pro tempore of the Senate and the Speaker of the House of Representatives his written declaration that he is unable to discharge the powers and duties of his office, and until he transmits to them a written declaration to the contrary, such powers and duties shall be discharged by the Vice President as Acting President.

SECTION 4. Whenever the Vice President and a majority of either the principal officers of the executive departments, or of such other body as Congress may by law provide, transmit to the President pro tempore of the Senate and the Speaker of the House of Representatives their written declaration that the President is unable to discharge the powers and duties of his office, the Vice President shall immediately assume the powers and duties of the office as Acting President.

Thereafter, when the President transmits to the President pro tempore of the Senate and the Speaker of the House of Representatives his written declaration that no inability exists, he shall resume the powers and duties of his office unless the Vice President and a majority of either the principal officers of the executive department, or of such other body as Congress may by law provide, transmit within four days to the President pro tempore of the Senate and the Speaker of the House of Representatives their written declaration that the President is unable to discharge the powers and duties of his office. Thereupon Congress shall decide the issue, assembling within 48 hours for that purpose if not in session. If the Congress, within 21 days after receipt of the latter written declaration, or, if Congress is not in session, within 21 days after Congress is required to assemble, determines by two-thirds vote of both houses that the President is unable to discharge the powers and duties of his office, the Vice President shall continue to discharge the same as Acting President; otherwise, the President shall resume the powers and duties of his office.

ARTICLE XXVI[25]

SECTION 1. The right of citizens of the United States, who are eighteen years of age, or older, to vote shall not be denied or abridged by the United States or by any state on account of age.

SECTION 2. The Congress shall have the power to enforce this article by appropriate legislation.

[24]Adopted in 1967.

[25]Adopted in 1971.

Table of Cases

Entries in boldface (with boldface page numbers) indicate the cases reprinted in this volume; italics indicate cases commented on in the editor's notes; ordinary type indicates cases quoted or discussed in the opinions. For convenience, all cases in which the United States is plaintiff are also indexed under the name of the defendant.